Another section is devoted to the printed rather than the spoken word, and includes Mr. Brown's delightful extended study of Charles and Mary Lamb. This book is a feast for the theatre-lover, a necessity for the student of drama and the historian of the passing scene, and a joy for any devotee of fine writing and witty observation.

JOHN MASON BROWN, in his long career as drama critic, was successively associate editor of *Theatre Arts Monthly* and drama critic first of the *New York Post* for twelve years, and then of the *New York World Telegram*. During World War II he served in the United States Navy on the staff of Admiral Kirk at the invasions of Sicily and Normandy. In 1944 he began his column of play reviews and general comment, under the rubric "Seeing Things," which ran weekly until 1955 in the *Saturday Review,* of which he is still an editor-at-large. He is the author of seventeen books, including *Through These Men, Daniel Boone: The Opening of the Wilderness, As They Appear, Still Seeing Things,* and *Morning Faces;* he has edited *The Portable Charles Lamb, The American Theatre as Seen by Its Critics,* and *The Ladies' Home Journal Treasury,* and has written the introductions to a number of books including *The Portable Woollcott.* Since 1955, though no longer writing play reviews, Mr. Brown has continued his active attention to the theatre by serving as a member of the Pulitzer Prize Drama Jury. He is also one of the judges of the Book-of-the-Month Club, and is widely known as a lecturer and for his television appearances. He is now at work on a *magnum opus,* a biography of Robert Sherwood.

DRAMATIS PERSONAE

BY JOHN MASON BROWN

EDITED BY JOHN MASON BROWN

Dramatis Personae

A RETROSPECTIVE SHOW

By John Mason Brown

NEW YORK : THE VIKING PRESS

ACKNOWLEDGMENTS

My grateful acknowledgment to Norman Cousins and *The Saturday Review* for permission to reprint such pieces as have appeared in *The Saturday Review* since 1942.—J.M.B.

"The Theatre of the Twenties" first appeared in *Esquire* in December 1951.

Published in 1963 by The Viking Press, Inc.
625 Madison Avenue, New York 22, N.Y.

Published simultaneously in Canada by
The Macmillan Company of Canada Limited

Library of Congress catalog card number: 63-12359

Printed in the U.S.A. by The Colonial Press Inc. [MBG]

TO

ROBERT EMMET SHERWOOD

WHO FOR ME AND MANY OTHERS

IS VERY MUCH ALIVE

Contents

vii

4. Headmaster to the Universe—G.B.S.

5. London Pride

6. Star Bright

7. On a Larger Stage

8. The Reach of Words

9. Off Stage, and On

10. Backgrounds

INTRODUCTION

NOT THAT it altered history, but I was born in 1900. I mention the date only because, though a twin of the century may misplace his changing selves as the decades advance, the calendar does not permit him to forget his age. As I write the introduction to this collection of my pieces, the year is '62 and, inescapably, so am I. This places me in time and also the theatre covered in this book, since I became a dramatic critic in 1925. That was thirty-seven years and a good many "me's" ago.

Four years later one of these "me's" (I find it hard to recognize him now) wrote *The Modern Theatre in Revolt,* reprinted here in its brief entirety. It is a historical survey of the conflicts in theory and practice which, during the hundred years prior to the twenties, prepared the way for the theatre the twenties produced. That theatre and the theatre of the violently changing decades which have followed are the chief concern of these pages. Other pieces relating to the stage or about subjects which have drama in them are also included. But this is mainly a volume about the theatre in performance and people who, since the twenties, have contributed to it in various ways.

I have my Harvard classmate, Marshall Best of the Viking Press, to thank for bringing me together. Only a brave man and a true friend would have had the hardihood to plow through a shelf of my books in order to come up with these selections. I marvel at his patience and am grateful for his skill.

Going over what he has chosen has been an odd experience for me. I don't know how other writers feel when they reread what they have written years before. I find that what I once thought I would always remember has long since slipped my mind. Writing and rereading are done in different climates. Writing is equatorial, rereading polar. What was written hotly has become cold, immediate response to still insistent details has faded into blurred recollections, and what was mine has left me to be lost in what I once was. The old words become new again by having been forgotten and so disembodied that I do not remember their being mine at all. I do remember, however, what summoned them and am thankful for that.

Let me go back to the altering "me's" in these pages. My approaches to the theatre have varied inevitably over the lengthening years. This is not only because doing a monthly summary for Edith J. R. Isaacs' *Theatre Arts* was very different from meeting nightly deadlines on the New York *Evening Post* and *World-Telegram,* or having the privilege, because of Norman Cousins, of contributing for a decade to the *Saturday Review* a weekly column called "Seeing Things," unrushed by the pressures of news, and on any subject of my choosing. The changes in my approach have also been due to my own shifts and extensions in interest and to the changes brought about in me by the challenges of changing times.

I have been stagestruck ever since, when eight, I was taken to Macauley's Theatre in Louisville, Kentucky, to see Robert B. Mantell play King Lear, one of the few parts, I realize now, that he was still young enough to act. I was stage-struck when, in spite of coming from a Yale family, I went to Harvard to work with George Pierce Baker and later came to *Theatre Arts Monthly* after a year of studying the theatre up and down Europe. I was stagestruck and wholly satisfied with the theatre's make-believe until the Second World War, when I was introduced to the realities of a larger world by serving in the Navy. I am stagestruck now, though not as I once was. Since the war the theatre has no longer interested me merely as theatre. I have hoped for openings that opened on something more.

Once I likened dramatic criticism to an attempt to tattoo soap bubbles. My contention was that such an attempt was at once the glory and the challenge of the job. My ardent hope is that some of the iridescence of those soap bubbles is caught, however imperfectly, in this passing record of years now past in which I have sought to feel my thoughts and think my feelings.

New York, N.Y.   JOHN MASON BROWN
December 1962

1. The Changing Scene

Some memories which refuse to fade of our theatre during the twenties when it came of age, throbbed with an activity since unknown, and of "the good old days" which for once were really good.

[1951]

THE THEATRE OF THE TWENTIES

ITS TITLE I have long since, and mercifully, forgotten. But what Alexander Woollcott said about it as a drama critic in those far-off days of the twenties I still recall. In the first act of the dreary little flop in question he noted that the hero had been presented as a boy of thirteen, a mere child in his interests and activities. Yet in the second act, laid as I recollect a year later, this same innocent had been shown as the anguished father of an unblessed event. Quite rightly a protest was registered by Mr. Woollcott, who was as unprepared for this turn of affairs as everyone else in the audience. The play's major development, he complained, had taken place offstage. Or, as he expressed it in a phrase unmistakably Woollcottian, during the intermission the hero had "achieved puberty with a bang."

It was not puberty but maturity that the American theatre achieved, and achieved with a bang, during the years which followed World War I and preceded the Depression. Things really hummed then, and hummed as they had never hummed before and will never hum again in the playhouses of Manhattan. To say this is not to indulge in old-fogey talk. It is to state a fact. The twenties *were* good days in the American theatre. They were good theatrically, regardless of how dubious or shameful they were politically. They were good theatrically notwithstanding how cheap was their sensationalism elsewhere, how menacing was their tub-brewed gin, and how juvenile, when not conscienceless or downright crazy, was the general level of behavior.

Some of our younger novelists, poets, and critics may have enjoyed thinking of themselves as members of a "lost generation."

3

But not the figures who emerged in our theatre during that dazzling decade. Certainly not the amazing number of writers suddenly drawn to the stage. Or the young actors and actresses, designers and directors, who were to make their names in the postwar years. Or the groups of valiant experimenters, gifted or merely arty, freakish or fine, who banded together in Greenwich Village, on far-off Grand Street, and on the outskirts of Times Square to defy commercial Broadway. Instead of being "lost," these men and women "found" themselves and in the process created an extraordinary theatre.

Remember, there was no television then. Radio was in the beginning of its prolonged infancy. The talkies did not raise their voices until 1927. In other words, the stage was flourishing on Manhattan, regardless of how the movies were already threatening its road empire up and down the country. Even cold statistics indicate the heat of that theatre's activity. Just before the crash there were some seventy playhouses in New York compared to the thirty at present. Furthermore, where 1950 yielded only ninety productions, the ten years from 1920 to 1930 averaged 225, with 278 in the peak year of 1927-1928. In the rush weeks of each season it was not uncommon to have three, or occasionally four, openings on a single night.

Today's cupboard may seem frighteningly bare because of the shrinkage in numbers of productions and of new writing talents, but the theatrical larder in the twenties was bulging. There was plenty of room then for the in-between offerings that are no longer possible in our current theatre in which, for various economic reasons, everything is either a hit or a flop. If costs were lower (they have risen approximately 166 per cent), admissions were lower, too. They were lowest at the long-vanished Gray's Drug Store, which did a thriving business in the catacombs of Times Square as a sort of Macy's basement where tickets could be had at bargain prices at the last moment for plays which had not sold out.

The proof of the theatre's vitality in the twenties lies in the memories which are its monument. When I speak of memories, I am thinking of such recollections as inhabit the mind unprompted by history books or files. I mean those images of and from the past which insist upon abiding in the present with Technicolor brightness. That they take the form of single scenes or individual portraits rather than entire evenings is no more surprising than that they refuse to be corseted by chronology. I can speak only for myself. From the crazy-quilt of my own recollections the following patches are the ones which stand out most vividly. They are a mixed lot. Some of them have their origins in evenings of high significance; others in sheer trivia. Some speak for unforgotten tragic tensions; others for relaxation at its most skillful and captivating best.

Let me start with musical comedies and revues. Only bogus highbrows would deny that these can be among the glories of the American stage. Heaven knows how many of them I have sat through and forgotten. Some of the highly popular sentimental operettas, such as *The Vagabond King* and *The New Moon,* I have no wish to recall. Allergic as I am to their kind, they seem to me so much molasses set to music. But fortunately (to name but a few, and stifle many recollections screaming for inclusion) the Wooden Soldiers are still on parade for me in *Chauve-Souris.* So is Balieff as, more round-faced than a full moon, he introduced them and the other acts of the engaging revue in his own Russian form of resolutely fractured English. Bobby Lee continues, derby in hand, to strut superbly in *Shuffle Along,* singing "I'm Just Wild about Harry" which then was not cursed with political overtones. Fortunately, too, I can still see Fred and Adele Astaire capering their way through *Lady, Be Good,* exuding youth, a perfect and irreplaceable team.

Then there is *Show Boat.* For me, as for many another, it just keeps rolling along like Ol' Man River himself, with Jerome Kern's melodies and Oscar Hammerstein's lyrics ringing in my ears; with Edna May Oliver's Parthy as drolly shrewish as ever; with Charles Winninger's " 'Appy New Year!" booming with the good cheer of a Dickens Christmas story; and with Helen Morgan, handkerchief in hand and sob in throat, still moaning her fondness for the indifferent man who was just her Bill.

Two other memories of straight musicals I cherish with particular affection. One of these is the Gilbert and Sullivan revivals done with the impeccable taste synonymous with the name of Winthrop Ames. No wonder that, after seeing one of these, the previously mentioned Mr. Woollcott tossed his hat even higher than usual and in the public prints nominated Mr. Ames for the Presidency. The other musical I cannot exile from my mind is *Sally*, in which Marilyn Miller appeared with Leon Errol of the unreliable patella. For me Miss Miller has never stopped dancing. She haunts me as a vision of spangles and sunshine, beautiful of body, empty of face, and supreme in grace, eternally pirouetting as Broadway's Pavlova.

The twenties, regrettably clownish as they were in other respects, were theatrically notable as a period of great clowns. The zanies who then stalked the stage were titans. The roster was an incredible one. The Marx Brothers (really meaning Harpo and Groucho), who by their monkeyshines in *Animal Crackers* made the kind of Marxists of us all that would have won Senator McCarthy's approval. Ed Wynn of the lisp, the tattered shoes, the countless hats, and the comic inventions. Bobby Clark of the glistening eyes, the painted spectacles, the retrieving cane, the bent knees, and his shaggy-coated stooge McCullough. Jimmy Durante, of Clayton, Jackson, and Durante fame, as he nosed his way through endless nonsense, a tornado of energy. Victor Moore, the baby-faced grandfather, hesitant, plaintive, and shy. Joe Cook, the juggler who repealed the law of gravity, whose patter about the four Hawaiians is an untarnishable bit of fooling. Willie Howard of the mournful mug, the intruding eyes, and the hilarious results. Charles Butterworth, the deadpan king, with the milk-of-magnesia complexion, making the after-dinner speech to end after-dinner speeches. They are all of them old soldiers in the good cause of laughter who refuse to fade away.

Many of them appeared in such chromiumed revues as the *George White Scandals,* the *Little Shows,* the *Music Box Revues,* or the *Passing Shows.* The revue of revues, the epitome of the kind, however, was the *Ziegfeld Follies* when Ziegfeld himself produced them. To my shame I confess that I can no longer tell one *Follies* from another. They have merged in my mind like installments in a serial. But what a serial they were! They were the works of a man who had never heard of thrift. Their taste was genuine; their Cartier costliness unmistakable. Ziegfeld's show girls were towering beauties who strutted around with the hauteur of peacocks. Every edition of the *Follies* came closest to the *Folies-*

Bergère in those lavish Ben-Ali Haggin tableaux during which bug-eyed descendants of the Puritans were permitted a snatched glance at damsels posed as Lady Godiva or some other historical female in a deciduous mood.

Ziegfeld's undisputed claim was that he glorified the American girl. No less certainly he glorified the American comedian. The mere mention of the *Follies* is enough to raise images of Gallagher and Shean singing their famous "Mister" song. Of Bert Williams, of "Hambone Tree" fame, shuffling his way through "You Can't Make Your Shimmy Shake on Tea." Of Ray Dooley, whose impersonation of an unhousebroken baby, the brat of brats, was sufficiently sinister to make the Katzenjammer Kids seem saints. Of Eddie Cantor, a dynamo in blackface, prancing all over the place, his knuckles meeting in frenzied pats and his black eyes establishing a model for flying saucers. Of Fanny Brice, unfailingly funny when she turned her mouth up at the corners like a slice of watermelon and permitted her knees to head for opposite poles, who rose abruptly to a kind of tragic grandeur as she dunked her voice in the melancholy of "My Man." Of W. C. Fields, that prince of comedians, with his croaking voice, his bored manner and lordly airs, who was already a Mr. Micawber misplaced in time but entrenched in everyone's affections. Yes, and finally of Will Rogers, gum in mouth, forelock spilling over his eyes, lasso in hand, stepping before the curtain to deliver, full of cracker-barrel wisdom, the sagest and most deflating political commentaries to have been heard in our time.

Three other revues from the twenties continue to live for me. One of these is the *Garrick Gaieties,* blessed not only with youth but with intelligence, which introduced Rodgers and Hart to Broadway. Another is the *Grand Street Follies,* in which for a few summers dramatic criticism became creative in its parodies of plays and the impersonations of Dorothy Sands, Albert Carroll, Paula Trueman, et al. Lastly, there is *Charlot's Revue,* so economical by Ziegfeld standards in everything except gaiety and wit, which made history by introducing Beatrice Lillie and Gertrude Lawrence to an America which has adored them ever since. It was in *Charlot's Revue* that the pint-sized Miss Lillie circled the stage as Britannia in "March with Me"; that Miss Lawrence sang "Limehouse

Blues"; and that the two of them, different and delightful, so captured New York that no one could disagree with the ditty that currently insisted:

Lillie and Lawrence,
Lawrence and Lillie,
If you haven't seen them,
You are perfectly silly.

Naturally the Jazz Age found its release in jazz. In retrospect, however, what is surprising about our theatre in the twenties is that its most memorable moments were serious ones. The period which produced Daddy Browning, John Held's collegians, Texas Guinan's suckers, and Jimmy Walker was the same period that produced John Barrymore's *Hamlet*, the Theatre Guild, *What Price Glory?*, *The Green Pastures*, and Eugene O'Neill. It was as hospitable to Art with a capital A as it was to entertainment with a low I.Q. Though it satisfied the Tired Business Man (not to forget the Butter-and-Egg Man), it dared to appeal to the intelligentsia. It had at its disposal a twenty-year backlog of noteworthy European plays which the older of Broadway's commercial managers had been afraid to tackle. Moreover, it could tap the overflowing reservoir of scripts by a talented new generation of such native dramatists as Sidney Howard, Philip Barry, George Kelly, S. N. Behrman, Robert E. Sherwood, George S. Kaufman, Marc Connelly, Maxwell Anderson, and Laurence Stallings. It was a theatre throbbing with protests—not the social protests which were to come in the tin-cupping days of the thirties, but aesthetic revolt. The "New Movement," as it was called, was to many a cause if not a crusade. It stressed the importance of the director as an interpreter and the significance of the visual contributions of scene painters, now identified as scenic artists. Luckily, however, in this teeming atmosphere of change and growth, of repudiation and experiment, actors were not forgotten. They and their performances were among the glories of the decade.

John Barrymore, for example. He was his own Dr. Jekyll and Mr. Hyde, a fellow who at his best (and the first five years of the twenties were his best years) was on a diamond, not a gold, standard. Although I have sat before many Hamlets, some better read and more solidly conceived, John Barrymore, with his slim, proud figure, the lean Russian wolfhound aquilinity of his profile, and the princely beauty of his full face, continues for me to be the ideal embodiment of the Dane. His Hamlet had a withering wit. It had scorn at its command; passion, too. Though undisciplined, it crackled with the lightning of personality. Toward the end of his career Barrymore may have delighted in mocking his former greatness in such a cheap farce as *My Dear Children*. But, beyond dispute, that greatness had been his in *The Jest*, in *Richard III*, and finally in *Hamlet*. No actor I have seen was so exciting as he was before he deserted both Broadway and himself for Hollywood.

Of all the Shakespearean revivals the decade saw, none did more than Basil Sydney's *Hamlet* in modern dress to blow the dust off the Bard and bring him close to contemporary audiences. The same sense of nearness and rediscovery was delectably present in Mr. Sydney's and Mary Ellis's subsequent *The Taming of the Shrew*, also costumed in what was then modern dress. It was no less present in the lovely lyricism of the Juliet Jane Cowl played opposite Rollo Peters. This was a production traditional in its trappings but uncommon in its beguilements.

The final curtain has refused to fall for me on many other performances I saw during the twenties. Jeanne Eagels in *Rain*, with her plumed hat, cheap finery, parasol, high buttoned shoes, raucous voice, and ready oaths, still wages, as Sadie Thompson, her own kind of war in the Pacific. Her Sadie was a high point, really a peak, in modern acting. . . . Certainly no one who listened to the hunted fear in Pauline Lord's voice or watched her as her hands fluttered about her mouth like wounded doves can fail to recall Miss Lord as the faithless bride in *They Knew What They Wanted*. Or, more particularly, when she burst into the waterfront saloon in *Anna Christie*, supposedly a figure of country innocence but plainly a member of the world's most venerable sisterhood, to demand a shot of whisky.

Then there was Clare Eames, as regal of appearance as the Tudor Bess, playing to perfection the decadent aristocrat married to the tough night-club proprietor in *Lucky Sam McCarver*, that fascinating character study by Sidney Howard which failed for reasons I have never understood. . . . And Alla Nazimova, always a foreigner in her accent but never foreign to any emotion, who was sphinxlike in her quality of mystery. Although sometimes she pushed exoticism to laughable extremes, in Eva Le Gallienne's production of *The Cherry Orchard* down at the Civic Repertory she was the best Madame Ranevsky to have been seen in an American production. . . . Alice Brady, too, who was to come into her own in the thirties with Nazimova in *Mourning Becomes Electra*. But already she, who was to die far too young, had proved her rare skill as a comedienne and indicated in *Lady Alone* the smoldering tragic power which was also hers.

It is as easy to cite outstanding single instances from the theatre of the twenties as it is to treasure them. Frank Craven, the plain-faced, benevolent man, the average-citizen type, as he suffered in the convulsing but agonizing dinner scene in *The First Year* during which everything went wrong that can go wrong at a young hostess's initial party. . . . Gilda Varesi conquering the town with her display of a diva's temperament in *Enter Madame*. . . . Florence Reed as Mother Goddam, the Chinese madame in *The Shanghai Gesture*, with her masklike make-up, her sinister calm, and the grating cruelty of her nasal speech, stands out like the big lettering on a billboard. . . . So does Mae West who, as Diamond Lil, had already added to America's folklore by her *Police Gazette* curves, her barroom flamboyance, her hip-waving, and the muttered insinuation of her "Come up and see me sometime."

Other images are no less enduring. Blanche Bates, Henry Miller, and Margalo Gillmore in *The Famous Mrs. Fair*, shooting the works emotionally (and, what is more, hitting the target) as they showed the sorrows which can overtake a family when the mother has forgotten her home for public life. Noel Coward, a whole switchboard of nerves, as he upbraided his erring mother in his play *The Vortex* and captured New York by the intensity of his performance. Leslie Howard, that master of understatement, demonstrating as the hunted prisoner in *Escape* his strength as a serious actor; and later, in *Berkeley Square*, as the spirit of a modern man carried back in time to eighteenth-century England, showing once again the dry, quietly romantic, and shyly smiling comedic talent by means of which he had won and deserved his fame. Laura Hope Crews in *The Silver Cord* when, as that appalling example of Momism at its worst, she opened the door to her married son's bedroom to coo, "It's only Mother." Chrystal Herne, ice-cold and iron-strong, when in *Craig's Wife* she played the archetype of that terrible woman whose only passion is the neatness of her house. And Louis John Bartels in *The Show-Off,* an early George Kelly play, as that pest of pests and bromide king, Aubrey Piper, laughing like a hyena, slapping people on the back, and crying "Sign on the dotted line!"

Even more vivid are the following recollections. Charles Gilpin, and later Paul Robeson, as they circled, lost, through the West Indian forest in *The Emperor Jones,* with the faraway tom-toms quickening to match the accelerated pounding of their hearts as their fear mounted. . . . *Liliom,* as first presented here by the Theatre Guild. The beauty of Lee Simonson's setting for the railroad viaduct scene and the humor of his police-court Hereafter. The strident voice of Helen Westley as the gaudy owner of a carrousel. Dudley Digges' dust-bowl of a bum, croaking "Look out, here come the damn police!" And, above all, the rambunctious swagger of Joseph Schildkraut's Liliom and the pathos of Eva Le Gallienne's chalk-faced Julie who loved him so much that his blows could not hurt her. . . . This same Miss Le Gallienne, a vision of loveliness, the personification of what every princess should look like, as, wearing a tiara and dressed in glittering white, she moved with marvelous grace through the last act of *The Swan,* another play by Molnar, though this time a comedy.

The twenties knew the welcome sound of laughter. They knew it in the wisecracks and the nonsense, the mild-voiced castigation and fully realized spoofing of such Kaufman and Connelly scripts as *Dulcy, To the Ladies, Merton of the Movies,* and *Beggar on Horseback* (including the Dresden shepherdess charm of its ballet, "A Kiss in Xanadu"). They knew it in the exuberant banter, yet the tenderness, of such of Philip Barry's comedies about well-subsidized worldlings as *Paris Bound* and *Holiday.* They knew it in the shimmering dialogue of S. N. Behrman's *The Second Man.* They knew it, too, in Robert Sherwood's *The Road to Rome,* that antique romp in modern terms in which Philip Merrivale was a most romantic Hannibal and Jane Cowl delightful as the Roman lady who conquered him for a night.

Actors contributed to the winning of this laughter with a skill equal to that of the dramatists, and just as irresistible. Holbrook Blinn, for instance, playing with great cunning and authority the swashbuckling but beloved Mexican bandit in *The Bad Man*. He could proclaim without fear of dispute that he was "the best damn caballero in all Mexico." . . . Or Ethel Barrymore, of the fluttering eyes, the throaty voice, and the imperious beauty, lending her special alchemy to Somerset Maugham's *The Constant Wife*. . . . Or Ina Claire, assuredly one of the most dazzling of comediennes, when, playing an international adventuress opposite Roland Young in *The Last of Mrs. Cheyney*, she stood out with the impudence of an exclamation point and sparkled with the brilliance of cut glass in the noonday sun. . . . And, most especially, Alfred Lunt and Lynn Fontanne (he having made his name in *Clarence* and she as the scatter-brain in *Dulcy*) as they swept through the audacities of *The Guardsman*. They were already in full possession of that style, gusto, and perfection which in countless plays, serious or smiling, have long since established them as the foremost acting couple in the English-speaking world.

The winning of such new reputations was a natural source of excitement. A young woman, old only in experience, named Helen Hayes was proving by her Maggie Shand in *What Every Woman Knows* and her seduced Southern Belle in *Coquette* that she was to become one of the great ladies of our stage. Putting flapperdom behind her, she was already making unmistakably clear the intelligence, all-conquering sincerity, and deep sense of tenderness which have made her one of the most loved and respected of our stars.

Another young woman, seen at the outset of the twenties in *Nice People* with Francine Larrimore and Tallulah Bankhead, and a few months thereafter in *A Bill of Divorcement*, was even then making the name of Katharine Cornell famous. Hers was a haunting beauty, summoning and mysterious. No wonder Shaw wrote her, on first seeing her photograph, "If you look like that it doesn't matter a rap whether you can act or not. Can you?" She could. Her Candida was the warmest and most satisfying our stage has known in my time. It was followed by her Iris March in *The Green Hat*, who turned out to be one of the most typical heroines of those Michael Arlen days. The play may have been trash, but because of Miss Cornell (and Leslie Howard and Margalo Gillmore) theatregoers did not care. They got more than their groat's worth of emotional turmoil and glamour.

It was the group theatres, the Neighborhood, the Civic Repertory, and, more especially, the Provincetown and the Theatre Guild that provided the decade with many of its most important plays and stimulating evenings. Perhaps the finest achievement of the Neighborhood, interested as it was in actors who could dance and dancers who could act, was its English version of *The Dybbuk*, the Yiddish classic. This was a miracle of ensemble and mood, of swirling beggars and chanting elders; the kind of production more commonly encountered in Europe's art theatres than in America. The Civic Repertory, which opened in 1926 down on 14th Street, was Eva Le Gallienne's idea, and for it she abandoned Broadway and commercial stardom. At a top price of a dollar-and-a-half she made playgoing possible for a large audience unable to afford uptown prices. Moreover, with *Romeo and Juliet, Peter Pan, Cradle Song, Alice in Wonderland,* and her revivals of Ibsen and Chekhov, she had her critical no less than her popular successes.

The Provincetown, with its auxiliary playhouse, the Greenwich Village, is rightly remembered and revered as the theatre that established Eugene O'Neill. It is difficult just now to recapture the expectation with which one went down to Macdougal Street or Sheridan Square to see such of the early O'Neill dramas as *The Emperor Jones, Diff'rent, The Hairy Ape, All God's Chillun Got Wings, Desire under the Elms,* and *The Great God Brown.* Good or bad as these plays may have been, no one could fail to realize that the man who wrote them was a figure apart, sizable and significant. He was the big one; the dramatist with the truest sensing of the tragic that the modern stage has disclosed. He wrote what he wanted, not what he thought others wanted. Each of his opening nights was an event. Although poetry may have eluded him, passion and an undeniable grandeur were his.

O'Neill was already world famous when, near the decade's end, the Theatre Guild produced his *Marco Millions* and *Strange Interlude.* The Guild by then was itself famous, and justly so. It too had its courage. And it too made history, first at the Garrick Theatre, and later at the playhouse it built on 52nd Street. It won its huge subscription audiences by treating them to the grimness of St. John Irvine's tragedies, *John Ferguson* and *Jane Clegg*. It dared to produce Andreyev's *He Who Gets Slapped*, Kaiser's *From Morn to Midnight*, Capek's *R.U.R.*, Toller's *Man and the Masses*, Werfel's *Goat Song*, and Pirandello's *Right You Are If You Think You Are*. In those years made the livelier because Shaw was very much alive and at the top of his form, the Guild was as hospitable to G.B.S. as to O'Neill. *Heartbreak House* (Shaw's idea of being Chekhovian) and *Saint Joan* (one of the glories of English dramatic literature) were among the new Shavian scripts presented by the Guild, which also produced *Back to Methuselah* in spite of its length and Herculean problems in staging. Elmer Rice's *The Adding Machine*, John Howard Lawson's *Processional*, Behrman's *The Second Man*, the Heywards' *Porgy*, and Sidney Howard's *They Knew What They Wanted, Ned Mc-Cobb's Daughter*, and *The Silver Cord* were among the new American plays the Guild was then offering. Futhermore, with Lee Simonson as its most regular designer and Philip Moeller as its most constant director, it had in Ernest Cossart, Helen Westley, Frank Reicher, June Walker, Winifred Lenihan, Henry Travers, Edward G. Robinson, Dudley Digges, Clare Eames, and, above all, the Lunts (playing singly or jointly) the nucleus of a permanent company extraordinary in its ability.

The groups were not alone in showing daring and skill during the twenties. Those, after all, were the years when Brock Pemberton staged *Six Characters in Search of an Author*; when William A. Brady captured the heat, smell, and tragedy of a New York tenement in his production of Elmer Rice's *Street Scene*; when Winthrop Ames, in addition to his Gilbert and Sullivan revivals, was presenting George Arliss in *The Green Goddess* and *Old English*, and Leslie Howard in *Escape*. Those were the years when Arthur Hopkins made of the Plymouth Theatre a shrine of raised and usually realized hopes by directing John Barrymore, by working— usually with Robert Edmond Jones as his designer, and by presenting such plays as *Anna Christie, What Price Glory?, Machinal, Burlesque,* and *Holiday*. Those were the years, too, when Jed Harris was deservedly known as the American theatre's Napoleon. They were the years when, with that fabulous skill that can be his, Mr. Harris presented in unbelievably quick succession such shattering hits as *Broadway* (the perfect saga of the Prohibition era), *The Front Page* (a superior melodrama of Chicago's newspaperdom with that irreplaceable actor, the late Osgood Perkins), and *The Royal Family* (in which such a theatrical clan as the Barrymores were lovingly shown with all their eccentricities and virtues).

The twenties, perhaps because they offered less menace in each day's news, produced melodramas which, in the phrase dear to reviewers, really did unhinge the vertebrae. These spine-twisters at the decade's start were sheer thriller-dillers, full of shocks and shivers, such as *The Bat* and *The Cat and the Canary*. As the years passed, however, they grew in subtlety and ambition, achieving not only the adult terror of *Subway Express*, *The Last Mile*, and *The Criminal Code*, but producing in *Rope's End* a work of ghoulishness and grue so literate and fiendish that to this day it remains a model of the macabre. The writing of such melodramas appears to have taken its place, alas, among the lost arts.

Two of the notable plays of these same years had their origins in World War I, and no scripts dealing with World War II have been their equals. The first of these, coming almost six years after the Armistice, was Maxwell Anderson's and Laurence Stallings' *What Price Glory?* with its pre–James Jones soldier talk, its Marine energy, its superb drinking bout, and its tag line, "Hey, Flagg, wait for baby." It remains the play all American writers of war plays are condemned to living up to and to living down. The other drama was as English as *What Price Glory?* was American. It was R. C. Sherriff's *Journey's End*, produced by Gilbert Miller. Although George Jean Nathan dismissed it in a capsule criticism as "The staff of *Vanity Fair* goes to war," it struck deep into the hearts of most people who sobbed before it. It was very, very British in its chin-up attitude, in its talk in the trenches of gardens at home, and its quotations from *Alice in Wonderland* before going over the top. But this to most of us was an essential part of its power and its truth.

Another memory from the twenties which, because it is *The Green Pastures*, is one of the most cherished. Brooks Atkinson hailed it as "the divine comedy of the modern theatre." This is precisely what it was—and remains. In this simple version of

Bible stories as retold to some Negro children in a Louisiana Sunday School class, reverence and humor were wonderfully blended. The play of Marc Connelly's adaptation and direction glowed with exaltation. It was a religious no less than a theatrical experience. Certainly few actors have given so commanding a performance as did Richard B. Harrison without seeming to act at all as de Lawd who walked the earth as a natchel man.

I should, of course, also mention such Ibsen revivals as the productions by the Actors' Theatre of *Hedda Gabler* with Emily Stevens and *The Wild Duck* with Blanche Yurka, Tom Powers, and Helen Chandler. I should include, too, Max Reinhardt's spectacular staging of *The Miracle* at the Century Theatre, which Norman Bel Geddes had transformed into a cathedral. Yes, and the coming of Reinhardt's own troupe in *Danton's Tod* and the silver-voiced Moissi in *Jedermann*. And most assuredly I should dwell at length upon the visits of the Moscow Art Theatre, which had such profound effects on our own stage by teaching our directors the merits of the Stanislavski system. And suggest the ebullience of Sean O'Casey's *Juno and the Paycock* and *The Plough and the Stars* as done faultlessly by Sara Allgood, Arthur Sinclair, and the Irish Players.

I could go on and on. . . . *Young Woodley, Chicago, Outward Bound,* Lillian Gish in *Uncle Vanya,* Laurette Taylor in *The Furies,* George M. Cohan in *The Tavern,* Otis Skinner in *The Honor of the Family,* Walter Hampden in *Cyrano.* . . . A hundred other recollections fight to be set down which I hate to omit. But the point is that in the theatre things hummed in the twenties.

This is not to claim that every production made then was a masterpiece or that each season was not guilty of its hoard of little stinkers. Nor is it to say the theatre is dying today and does not know its people, plays, and productions every bit as good and exciting as those that gave color and distinction to that distant decade. No theatre is dead which is able to produce, as ours has done within the past few seasons, *Death of a Salesman, A Streetcar Named Desire, Mister Roberts, Billy Budd, Darkness at Noon, South Pacific, Kiss Me, Kate,* and *The King and I.* There is a difference, however, between then and now. Our theatre is sadly shrunken. What is perhaps most alarming about it is the extent to which it depends even now for its life upon those who made it so tinglingly alive in the twenties.

*How the stock-market crash, a disrupted economy, tight-
ened belts, and the Forgotten Man abruptly remembered
caused the theatre to change its tune, and sing an angry
song of social significance in the thirties.*

[1 9 3 8]

THESE FULL LEAN YEARS

ALTHOUGH NONE of us realized it at the time, the two most important events known to the American theatre in our day did not take place on Broadway. They were not openings in the usual stiff-shirt sense. They were closings of an extraordinary kind. The scene of one of them was Wall Street, October 29, 1929, when the stock market crashed with so Gargantuan a thud that its echoes still thunder in our ears. The other occurred some four and a half years later in those marble halls where we had dreamed security dwelt, and was identified, with an optimism uniquely American, as the "Bank Holiday."

Closings these events may have been. Yet, with all that they symbolized and all that was to come after them, they set free America's conscience and pried open the American mind to new vistas of thought, no less surely than they left locked and bolted forever the doors leading to our old ways of life and our old habits of thinking.

The boom days were gone; their assumptions discredited. Question marks were written large after the most venerable and hitherto unassailable of our national axioms. A search—selfish, uncontrolled, and mad—for overnight profits had proved worse than disturbing. It had proved unprofitable. America, rich and

poor, tightened its belt and opened its mind. The breadlines, which
fed the stomachs of the poor, nourished doubts in the consciences
of rich and poor alike. Starvation in the midst of plenty was food
for thought.

Young America, like the rest of the world, was sick; sick from
old abuses, sick with the disillusionment of a war fought seemingly in vain, sick from a peace treaty which had made the world
safe for dictators, sick from a host of diseases which had suddenly
become manifest in its own social and economic system. Discontent was in the air. Locusts covered the countryside. Injustices,
long tolerated or overlooked, were dragged into the light. The
"haves" became increasingly aware of the "have nots," as strike
followed strike in the front-page news and then entered one distant home after another in terms of passed dividends. Labor was
on the move. Unrest was all around us. Agitators of every kind
were plentiful; so were the causes for agitation. Fanatical groups
screamed their dogmas shrilly. Termites seemed to be eating into
the foundations of our national structure. The "good society" did
not appear to be so good. But the public good became everyone's
concern. So did politics and economics. The underprivileged suddenly enjoyed the privilege of having the nation's attention. Beliefs for which only small and "radical" minorities would have protested—and then in vain—a few years back, became the common-
places of our national life, as our legislation, our taxation, and our
government agencies indicated. The Forgotten Man was remembered, even if the Remembered Man was forgotten.

A new voice was coming from Washington, and its Groton-
Harvard accent fell on new ears. The many who refused to be
included among the President's fireside "friends," could not, as his
countrymen, escape the problems with which he had newly dealt.
Above everything debatable in this policy or that short-lived
panacea, above everything reprehensible or alarming in such-and-
such a sample of political chicanery, above the hatreds and disagreements of party strife, above everything confusing in the
confusion of shifting means and constant contradiction, that voice,
and the administration for which it spoke, and the conditions
which had swept it into office, made one thing clear. They had
given America a liberal education such as all the schools in the
land had hitherto failed to give it. Whether it liked it or not,

whether it admired the President or detested his policies, had nothing to do with the fact that the American conscience had been jolted into activity. In the days of prosperity, it had refused to look for work. In the days following the Depression, it could no longer be counted among the unemployed.

Long before the government had placed the theatre on relief, the theatre in this country had given relief to playwrights who in the post-Depression years were burning with indignation and anxious to have their say on economic and political subjects. They may have been men appalled by what had happened to justice, as was I. J. Golden when, in *Precedent*, he made eloquent use of the testimony in Tom Mooney's fight for freedom; or as John Wexley was when, in *They Shall Not Die*, he worked the ugly facts of the Scottsboro case into a stirring melodrama. They may have exposed municipal corruption with the bitter mockery Albert Maltz and George Sklar brought to *Merry-Go-Round*, or condemned the Nazi's persecution of the Jews as did such scripts as *Kultur* and *Birthright*. They may have written such a play about strikers as Mr. Wexley wrote in *Steel*. They may have dashed off one bruising melodrama after another showing the horrors of lynching in the deep South. They may have run through a whole catalogue of national abuses as did Elmer Rice in *We, the People*. They may have banded themselves into such a militant Leftist group as the Theatre Union represented when it acquired Miss Le Gallienne's abandoned Civic Repertory down on Fourteenth Street and devoted itself quite frankly to operating as a playhouse of the barricades. They may have brought to the stage, as Mr. Odets has brought, a talent equaled only by their resentment of the "System." Many of these propagandist scripts may have been childishly unfair. More of them may have been crude. Most of them have been feeble. But all of them have given a new vitality to our theatre. Their significance cannot be overstressed. They have not only widened the limited horizons of our stage. They have burst upon it, bringing to it new subjects, new performers, new aims, new interests, new techniques, and, above all, new audiences.

That propagandist scripts were known to America before the Depression, everyone realizes. Each season had produced them, for propaganda in the theatre is as old as the Greeks and as new as today's cause which can win a champion. That we had seen dramas filled with fresh impulses and written from a fresh point no one can forget who sat before John Howard Lawson's *Processional,* Mr. Rice's *The Adding Machine,* or Toller's *Man and the Masses* at the Guild, and John Dos Passos's *The Moon Is a Gong.* Or who saw (perhaps for the first time) a Sunday-morning fashion parade on Fifth Avenue through the eyes of Mr. O'Neill's stoker in *The Hairy Ape.* There was even a playhouse down in Greenwich Village where, as endowed by Otto Kahn of all people, those dramatists who used to be referred to laughingly as the "Revolting Playwrights" produced their bitter indictments of Capitalism and Big Business. Few people took them seriously.

Since the crash and the "Bank Holiday," however, and right down to the Federal Theatre's *Living Newspapers,* or such productions as *The Cradle Will Rock* at the Mercury and *Pins and Needles* at the Labor Stage, there has been a marked difference not only in our propagandist writing but in our theatre. The "Yellow Book" days of the twenties now seem very remote. The ivory towers have crumbled. The protest is no longer of a purely aesthetic kind. Karl Marx, not Gordon Craig or Adolphe Appia, is the storm center of the new insurgents. Ideology has replaced aesthetics. The American scene seems somehow to have become more important than American scenery.

Troubled times, hunger, and old abuses do not make for moderation. It is men with grievances who become agitators. Their hope is to make their own agitation contagious. They are not apt to understate, or to weigh both sides. To the unfairnesses they attack, they are willing to add their own unfairness. From their point of view this seems more than justifiable. If they hit hard it is because their beliefs are militant. That they have not often talked as liberals is not surprising. If one excepts Shakespeare's Brutus as subdued by Orson Welles, the liberal has had a hard time holding his own of recent seasons as a stage character. With his eagerness to weigh the evidence and to grant the opposition its right to state its case, he has had difficulty making himself heard. Speaking with affection for what he hopes the new America will preserve of the old, his voice has been drowned out by the strident cries of those dogmatists who have had anger in their hearts and Red Russia in their minds. Dogmas are noisier than doubts; intolerance can yell down tolerance any day.

But there is more to these propagandist scripts than this. Judged as plays most of them may have been mediocre or inept. Judged as propagandist scripts they may be said to have failed if their authors have persuaded only those who already shared their convictions before they took their seats. For the test of a play of propaganda is not the yes-men who come to it conquered, but the no-men who leave it forced to say "yes." It takes a superior play to accomplish this, which is quite another thing from a previously shared conviction. Yet good, bad, or worse than indifferent as these propagandist scripts may have been, they have proven as socially significant as they may yet prove theatrically important.

All these many years we have been hearing about the theatre's being the most democratic of the arts, forgetting that the only democrats it included were those who could afford to go either to its box offices or to Tyson's. To them, and to them only, has it had any possible appeal, and for them, and for them only, has it attempted to speak. It has stated their viewpoint, echoed or affronted their prejudices, reflected their living, considered their pleasures, and confined itself to catering to their interests. Its admission fees have soared and its old galleries disappeared. Little by little it has closed its doors on all but purse-proud democrats.

If the Federal Theatre had done nothing else, it should have made clear to commercial managers that there are thousands upon thousands of people anxious to come back to the theatre as audiences, if only the ticket rates are within their means. The Federal Theatre has not been alone in teaching this lesson. It has done so along with numerous other groups who have devoted themselves to speaking for the millions of men and women forgotten on Broadway. That these men and women are entitled to consideration, no one can deny. The pursuit of happiness follows life and liberty on their bill of rights.

Of recent years a new department of our theatre has appeared, addressing itself to this new, huge, long-overlooked audience. That it has done so is one of the most encouraging developments to have taken place on our stage during the past decade. The groups who have effected this change have exiled themselves deliberately from Broadway's standards and interests. Their first objective has not been entertainment. They have turned their backs on escape. They have sought to have the theatre function as a place of re-

minder rather than a palace of forgetfulness. They have been
sponsored by or concerned with those very same proud members
of a craft who served Tom Dekker as his heroes in *The Shoemak-
er's Holiday*, even if these craftsmen often appear to have lost their
gentleness. They have devoted themselves to the interests and
the worries, the grudges and the simplicities, the grievances and
the hopes of this new public.

As producers and dramatists some of them may have been as
untrained as their audiences were unaccustomed to playgoing.
They have had scant knowledge of the "Art" of the theatre, and
cared even less for it. They may have made the fatal mistake of
offering their American spectators little or no humor. Their subscribers may have soon wearied of the ever-repeated devices of
their earlier, crasser melodramas. Still, these labor groups have invaded the theatre with such vigor that the so-called "carriage
trade" must at times wonder if it does not really belong back in
the days of the horse and buggy. Whether these proletarian theatres have produced good plays or bad, one thing is certain. They
have not left our consciences alone. They were provocative when
they were angry. They became important when they learned to
laugh.

When Hazlitt reprinted his dramatic reviews in book form, he
insisted in his preface that his opinion of Edmund Kean had not
changed since first he saw him. "Why should it?" he asked. "I had
the same eyes to see with, the same ears to hear with, and the same
understanding to judge with." Unfortunately, I am not William
Hazlitt. Rereading my reviews, I am not persuaded I would have
seen the plays they cover through the same eyes, or heard them
with the same ears, or judged them with the same understanding.
With my statement of their merits or demerits purely as plays I
would in all probability agree. Yet I trust—in fact, I know—that
many of the prejudices through which I saw them have been dis-
lodged. So, too, have the easy assumptions which they and these
troubled years have challenged—and slowly routed. For doing
this, for extending my horizons by having widened the theatre's,
and for having opened my eyes and quickened my conscience, I
feel grateful to the hatred and the violence, and the bad art of
even the sorriest and most sullen specimens in the lot, the over-
stated opinions of which I still disagree with and abhor.

*The strange yet noble pleasures of high tragedy, and some
of the ways in which its nature has been altered by the
contemporary world and modern man.*

[1949]

AMERICAN TRAGEDY

IT WAS the year of the Depression, though that had nothing to
do with the depression which engulfed Joseph Wood Krutch when
he was writing *The Modern Temper*. Mr. Krutch, one of the most
penetrating and far-ranging of our critics—indeed, one of the few
genuine critics we have in the big, proud sense of the word—is
more cheerful now. His book *The Twelve Seasons* proves this on
its every thoughtful page. It is a delectable account of country
living, so all-embracing in its philosophy that even city slickers feel
a part of nature. But Mr. Krutch's mood was different when, at
the close of the twenties, he contemplated Man, Love, Life, and
Death. He was woeful then; woeful to such an extent that there
were those who, in spite of their admiration, were forced to wonder if the apter title for his volume might not have been "The
Modern Distemper."

On no subject was Mr. Krutch more despairing than on the
tragic fate which, as he saw it, had overtaken contemporary tragic
writing *because* it had overtaken modern man. Mr. Krutch held
tragedy, real tragedy, to be among the many good things which
had vanished from the earth. He felt it to be an expression of the
great ages, the Greek and Elizabethan. For this very reason he
would grant it no connection with our own. He saw the world in
which he found himself a shrunken place. It had lost touch with
the heroic. Its vision of life was not of that ample and passionate
kind which had animated Shakespeare or Sophocles. According
to Mr. Krutch, God and man and nature had somehow dwindled
during the centuries since these dramatists had had their say.
Mr. Krutch took as the measure of our littleness not the realistic
creed of modern art which had led our writers to seek out mean

people, but the meanness of the vision of life which had made such a credo acceptable. "A tragic dramatist," he observed, "does not have to believe in God, but he must believe in Man." One gathered that Mr. Krutch, like the modern dramatists he lamented, had misplaced his faith in both.

Mr. Krutch's lament, as I say, was uttered in 1929. Although it made its melancholy points brilliantly, it was guilty of a strange omission. Eugene O'Neill was not even mentioned. Had a historian of the New Deal or the war years written of them without referring to Roosevelt, the omission could not have been stranger. For O'Neill was already full-stream in his career as a tragic dramatist. Ten years had passed since the writing of *Beyond the Horizon*; eight since *The Emperor Jones, Diff'rent,* and *The Straw*; seven since *Anna Christie* and *The Hairy Ape*; five since *Desire under the Elms*; four since *The Great God Brown*; two since *Strange Interlude,* and one since *Dynamo.*

No matter what our opinion may have been of this or that of O'Neill's dramas; no matter how small the biggest of them may have proved compared to the masterpieces of Shakespeare and the Greeks; no matter how tarnished most of them have become by 1949, it was excitingly clear twenty-five years ago when *Desire under the Elms* was produced that in America, of all surprised and surprising places, a dramatist had emerged who was tormented and inspired by the truest sensing of the tragic which the modern world has known.

Few dramatists of his importance have written more unevenly than O'Neill. Few capable of rising as near to the heights as he has soared have sunk into the mire of more pretentious or deplorable mediocrity. Yet even the poorest of his dramas have been enriched by the courage of the man and by that fierce willingness to grapple with the imponderables which has made his best works memorable. What has enlarged the most unsatisfactory of his scripts, and made his career at once heartening and unique, has been the largeness of his concerns. No one, may I quickly add, has attested to this fact with greater warmth or discernment than did Mr. Krutch himself when, in a more cheerful mood, a short four years after his requiem for tragedy, he wrote a preface to a collection of O'Neill's plays welcoming their author to the select company of tragic dramatists.

Whatever the crimes into which their passions may have led them, O'Neill's central characters have cared passionately about the forces controlling their being and their undoing. Not only that, these forces have not been indifferent to them. This high concern in play after play, regardless of its individual merits, has given to the body of O'Neill's work a significance at once solitary and touched with grandeur. Most dramatists in America and elsewhere during this past quarter of a century have at their moments of greatest seriousness gone no further than to oppose their characters to their neighbors or the social systems under which they have lived. Not so Mr. O'Neill. The barricades his people have assailed have been of a kind unfound in city streets. The altitude of his reach has been the measure of his magnitude and more outstanding than any of his plays. It has set him apart, granted him a deserved pre-eminence, left him lonely but a rallying point.

To achieve the tragic view, O'Neill was compelled to outgrow the surrenders to irony, crude melodrama, bathos, and pain for pain's sake which cursed his fledgling efforts. Before he could write with the high intensity attained in *Desire under the Elms*, and even more especially in the first two parts of *Mourning Becomes Electra*, he also has to realize that outward naturalism—in other words, those details devoted to documenting the physical life of the body—has little to do with, and could only serve as an impediment to, the interior and spiritual stuffs out of which true tragedy is wrought.

As early as 1922, two years before he wrote *Desire under the Elms*, O'Neill made for a Philadelphia paper an immensely revealing statement of his awareness of high tragedy as the Greeks and Elizabethans had written it and of his attitude toward life and his own works. "Sure I'll write about happiness," said he, "if I can happen to meet up with that luxury, and find it sufficiently dramatic and in harmony with any deep rhythm in life. But happiness is a word. What does it mean? Exaltation; an intensified feeling of the significant worth of man's being and becoming? Well, if it means that—and not a mere smirking contentment with one's lot—I know there is more of it in one real tragedy than in all the happy-ending plays ever written. It's mere present-day judgment to think of tragedy as unhappy! The Greeks and the Elizabethans knew better. They felt the tremendous lift to it. It roused them spiritually to a deeper understanding of life. . . . They saw their lives ennobled by it. A work of art is always happy; all else is unhappy. . . . I don't love life because it's pretty. Prettiness is only clothes-deep. I am a truer lover than that. I love it naked. There is beauty to me even in its ugliness."

I have a reason for quoting this mention of the Greeks and the Elizabethans, and the ennobling lift, the exaltation, the odd but incontestable happiness created by true tragedy. My reason? Because this statement appeared nine years before O'Neill, at the apex of his powers, was to write *Mourning Becomes Electra*. In it he chose not only to retell a Greek story in terms of Civil War New England but to house his Mannons in a great, chaste, Greek-Revival home, columned as if it were a temple. In spite of his barroom, farmhouse, waterfront, or tenement backgrounds; in spite of his prostitutes, his stokers, outcasts, misfits, alcoholics, or sanatorium inmates, and the pungent Americanism of his dialogue, O'Neill did not have to wait for that setting in *Mourning Becomes Electra* to demonstrate that his best plays were Greek Revival in their spiritual architecture. The worthiest of them, and even some of the less successful such as *The Straw*, followed what in the great periods of the past has been the tragic blueprint.

Religions may change. God may pass under as many names as O'Neill has selected to identify the agents controlling his characters. Yet tragedy in the classic sense has always been, and remains, a kind of religion in its own right. It has sought to impose a pattern upon the patternless; to create an independent logic by relating cause and effect where actual living is most frequently illogical; and to wring ecstasy from misdeeds and tribulations.

Assuredly, tragedy is one of the strangest as well as the noblest of man's gropings for expression. Its subject is anguish, and anguish is the source of the pleasure it gives. No one can explain precisely what Aristotle meant by "through pity and fear effecting the proper purgation of these emotions." But everyone in the presence of an exalted tragedy has an intuitive comprehension of that elusive definition. For true tragedy, regardless of its subject matter, includes those who are adult enough to realize that all men, however happy, are doomed to die and that even a tranquil life, if survived long enough, is bound to be a shorn one.

Even so, tragedy is not concerned with the span of the years.

In the vigorous or the old, it is concerned only with the intensity of the testing moments. It holds dying cheap and the death of its heroes and heroines a release for those who have achieved a certain tranquillity, a certain sublime and transfiguring peace, not merely from but because of the agonies they have endured. None of us would be cruel enough to stay their deaths or to deny them their final ecstasies and self-realization. We know that Death, when he at last appears to collect them, will have to be worthy of his conquests. In tragedy the body is almost an irrelevance; the spirit everything. This is why the wounds of the dying spill no blood.

O'Neill's own tragedy, and ours, has been that though he possesses the tragic vision he cannot claim the tragic tongue. "The spirit of inquiry meets the spirit of poetry and tragedy is born," W. Macneile Dixon pointed out in as fine a book as has been written on the subject of tragedy. O'Neill's spirit has always been inquiring and protesting, but neither his inquiry nor his protest has led him to poetry. The result is that, in spite of the attempts of his tragedies to soar, they fly with one clipped wing even when they are not earth-bound. For O'Neill, like all of us, is a victim of an age of prose, and prose confronts the tragic writer with an almost insuperable obstacle.

Maxwell Anderson has been acutely aware of this. He, too, is mindful of the tragic blueprint, the example of the past, and the need for poetry. Indeed, poetry has found no more stalwart champion in the modern theatre than Anderson. He has despised its deliberate inarticulateness and those climaxes in which the only eloquence has been a gesture or a moment of meaningful silence. Again and again, and unfortunately as if by rote, he has tried to escape from the strait jacket of contemporary realism. If his practice has not lived up to his theorizing, at least he has been haunted by the quickening dream.

Too often for his own good and the theatre's, he has turned to the past in his verse plays, succumbing romantically to kings, queens, and costumes, especially Tudor. When he wrote *Winterset,* however, fourteen years ago, he tried to establish a new convention by seeking to do what "the great masters themselves" never attempted. This was "to make tragic poetry out of the stuff of their own times."

It was in *Winterset* that he came nearest to achieving the hopes and aims so eloquently stated in his prefaces. His contributions as a dramatic poet may be indifferent, but no one can deny that in theory the religion which is tragedy finds him among the faithful. This explains why he is so fond of likening the theatre to a cathedral. To him as a thoughtful, sometimes despairing man, science is not enough. "It may answer a few necessary questions . . . but in the end science itself is obliged to say that the fact is created by the spirit, not the spirit by the fact." Anderson's faith, not a very positive or heroic one, is that man must have a faith. Perhaps his old rabbi in *Winterset* stated this belief for him most singingly when, just before the final curtain, he said:

> *On this star,*
> *in this hard star-adventure, knowing not*
> *what the fires mean to right and left, nor whether*
> *a meaning was intended or presumed,*
> *man can stand up, and look out blind, and say:*
> *in all these turning lights I find no clue,*
> *only a masterless night, and in my blood*
> *no certain answer, yet is my mind my own,*
> *yet is my heart a cry toward something dim*
> *in distance, which is higher than I am*
> *and makes me emperor of the endless dark*
> *even in seeking!*

If tragic times were alone required for the incubation of great tragedies, the years of the Depression, the war, and this unpacific peace would have yielded many of them. But, instead of aiding in the writing of tragedy in the older sense and on the older pattern, these tragic times have, if anything, added to the difficulties.

A period of realism and an age of prose are not the only hindrances. The lost or dwindling religious faith of many people; the encroachments of such a materialistic and earth-bound theology as Marxism; an increasing uncertainty as to accepted or acceptable standards; our living with the threat of possible mass annihilation; great changes in the stresses and basic concepts of our economic and social life; the emergence of the "little man" as the new hero for hero worship; the shrinkage of the individual's importance under the pressures of superstates or ever-growing bureaucracies; indeed, not only the notion but the realization that the century belongs to the common rather than the exceptional man—all these are factors, widening or limiting, which have altered tragedy along with everything else. Because of them, one wonders if the tragic blueprint, cherished for so long as an ideal, has not, at least in part, become a glorious anachronism.

Not that tragedy is dead or will ever die. Or that man has lost his touch with the heroic. No one who has watched men, women, and children rise to the terrible trials of the war years can maintain that man has become mean. The bigness of the so-called "little man" in the face of such trials and of daily living is one of the most hopeful facts of recent history. It is simply that the heroic has become different in scale and kind, and for this very reason tragedy needs to be rediscovered for our own times and in our own terms.

We have come a long way since "gorgeous Tragedy in sceptred pall" came sweeping by. Thebes, Pelops' line, or the tale of Troy divine, and even the kings and courtiers of Shakespeare are not as close to all of us as they once were. But tragedy in the tenement rather than the palace, tragedy different as it may be in speech, action, and outlook, retains some of its old characteristics. It refuses to become merely a play with an unhappy ending. As Arthur Miller pointed out in some prefatory notes he prepared for *Death of a Salesman,* "Tragedy implies more optimism in its author than does comedy. . . . Its final result ought to be the reinforcement of the onlooker's brightest opinions of the human animal."

This is why, much as we admire and are engrossed by such a play as Tennessee Williams' *A Streetcar Named Desire,* we deny it the name of tragedy. It is violent, powerful, and touching; written without mercy and without illusions. No study in disintegration to have come out of our theatre has been more skillful or unflinching. But its people, though fascinating, are too small-spirited to be tragic. They do not grow by suffering; they merely decline. There is no exaltation in them.

There is, however, exaltation in *Death of a Salesman.* At first seeing, it may be obscured by the bruising impact of this story of a "little man" who is sentenced to discover his smallness rather than a big man undone by his greatness. Yet the exaltation is there nonetheless, as the second or third seeing makes clear. It is not strong; it is not meant to be. The play, however, is far from being

as negative as some have mistaken it to be. A positive belief in
man underwrites its compassion and lies behind its sorrows.

What Mr. Miller's future will be, no one can say. We can only
hope. But it is encouraging to have him divorce the pathetic from
the tragic, in those same prefatory notes I have already mentioned,
and to have him state his belief that "the common man is as apt a
subject for tragedy in its highest sense as kings were." Our need
for tragedies, written from and of our times, is great today. For,
surely, never before have we so needed to be reminded of the dignity and worth of man the individual.

*An attempt to explain those exaltations which, in the midst
of pain, soar above the sufferings of the body and are a part
of the tragic pattern.*

[1940]

THE TRAGIC BLUEPRINT

IN NO way are the differences between what is patternless in our
living and the pattern which the drama can superimpose upon life
made clearer than in those differences which exist between death,
as most of us are bound to face it, and death as it is encountered by
the heroes and heroines of so-called high or formal tragedy.

The finest statement of what is enduring in high tragedy's timeless blueprint is to be found not in the *Poetics* but in the Book of
Job. Although Aristotle was on the threshold of truth when
he spoke of tragedy's being an imitation of an action, serious, complete, and of a certain magnitude, and insisted, however errone-
ously, upon its effecting through pity and fear the proper purgation of these emotions, the sage of Stagira halted at truth's portal as
Eliphaz, the Temanite, did not when he was exhorting that prince
of suffering known as Job.

"Man is born unto trouble," said the Temanite, "as the sparks fly upward. I would seek unto God, and unto God would I commit my cause: Which doeth great things and unsearchable; marvelous things without number. . . . Behold, happy *is* the man whom God correcteth: therefore despise not thou the chastening of the Almighty: For he maketh sore, and bindeth up: he woundeth, and his hands make whole."

In all tragedies concerned with the unsearchable, hence high because of the altitude of their search no less than because of the elevation of their agony, the sparks fly upward as men and women, born unto trouble, are made whole by their suffering. By these sparks, which are great words struck from the anvil of great sorrow, are we kept warm in the presence of the pain endured by those wounded men and women who are tragedy's favorite sons and daughters, and illumined in what would otherwise be the darkness of their dying.

That we are able to attend their deaths without tears; that the yield of their anguish is in us a pleasant ecstasy greater than is our sympathy with their distress; that we experience no desire to save them from their fates and would, indeed, feel cheated were they to be robbed of the self-realization which, on the brink of oblivion, is so often theirs—should warn us of how far the Stagirite was from truth when he spoke of tragedy as an imitation of life. One thing is certain. Regardless of the extent to which they may pretend to imitate life as their heroes and heroines are hastened to their deaths, high tragedies discard all pretense of such imitation when death, not life, becomes their high concern. If they extend life while dealing with the living, they transcend it when death is their subject. Then it is most markedly that their feigned reality, however slight, surrenders to the "beneficent illusion" and the arbitrary pattern is consolingly superimposed upon the patternless. The lies they tell at such supreme moments are among the most resplendent and sustaining truths they have to offer.

Whatever our deathbed fates may be, this much we know. Our dying will not be similar to the dying of the heroes and the heroines of high tragedy. When they die, these men and women are apt to be possessors of a talent for verbalization such as we can never aspire to even in our hardiest moments of health. By a convention, born of beauty and of our need, they are fated to leave this earth spiritually cross-ventilated. Furthermore, they die without benefit of hospitalization. Always they go as victims of a design, with a toll to be paid either for a defect unmistakably established or a misdeed meriting punishment.

Our bodies, not our characters, are to blame if we have weak lungs or weak hearts. Thrombosis can switch off our consciousness at any moment without giving us time to light up spiritually or signifying divine disapproval. The arteries of saints no less than sinners can harden with old age. In everyday life longevity is the result neither of moral grandeur nor of Sunday-school applause. The good are asked to suffer with the bad, usually more often and to a greater extent. Cause and effect do not need to be on speaking terms to have any one of us snuffed out. Infantile paralysis is not an affliction which the innocent at five or eleven or at any age can be said to have earned. Death rides through life, not as a moral logician, inexorable in his demands, but as a hit-and-run driver. We who live in cities are aware that, while crossing the street—any street, at any hour, and even with the lights in our favor—to do the best good deed of which we are capable, we run the risk of being struck down by a truck, the driver of which will never have had anything against us except his truck at an unfortunate moment of impact. We say these haphazard misfortunes are beyond our understanding.

So they are, even as they are beyond the possibilities of high tragedy. Melodramas, when hard pushed, may enjoy dalliance with such disasters; never high tragedies. Although their concern is often the inexplicable, they take pains to state their gropings in understandable terms. They take few chances with chance. Where we, as actual men and women, may be confused by the injustice of our lot, the heroes and the heroines of high tragedy live lives and die deaths clearly motivated. They are not ruled by coincidence in our fashion. They are deliberate parts of a visible design, even when, in our manner, their search is to comprehend their place in a larger design, infinite as it is inscrutable.

For them the tree of life is always cut with a single purpose— to make a cross. If they shape their crosses for themselves, it is because they belong to a race apart, these men and women who, by their suffering, give high tragedy its grandeur. In spite of what the church basements may have told us, there would have been no such thing as high tragedy had the world been peopled exclusively by Boy Scouts and Girl Scouts. More often than not the record of high tragedy is the record of splendid sinners who, always *after* sinning—if to no other extent than shirking their manifest duties, or surrendering to their defects—redeem themselves spiritually just before the moment of their taking off. This is but a part of the pattern of high tragedy, and of its moral obligation, too.

We, in our living, are aware every time we pass a hospital, magnificent and indispensable as it may be, that we are in the presence of a brick-and-stone reminder of the frailties of the human body. The body, and all its sickroom failings, figures to an humiliating extent in our more leisurely deaths. In high tragedy what matters is always the flame and never the lamp; never the body and always the spirit.

This lifts high tragedy beyond tears even as it lifts it beyond pain. Run over the long list of the heroes and heroines of high tragedy and you will find that though these men and women have died from multifarious causes—have stabbed themselves or been stabbed, been poisoned, fallen like Romans on their swords, or died from snakebite, more classically known as aspbite—not one of them, at the moment of intense pain and imminent death, has ever surrendered to the mortal luxury of an "ouch." This is why even in an age of realism, no attempt wisely is ever made to deal realistically with their wounds. Their spirits spill the only blood that matters; and it is life-giving even when life is being taken.

Sinners or not, the heroes and heroines of high tragedy belong (as Edith Hamilton has pointed out) to the only genuine aristocracy known to this world—the aristocracy of truly passionate souls. In spite of economists or the most hopeful of Utopians, there is one respect in which men and women are doomed forever to be unequally endowed. This lies in their capacity to suffer. If this capacity is among the most ineradicable of mortal inequalities, it is among the most notable gifts of high tragedy's heroes and heroines. Their genius is to suffer greatly, and in their sufferings to wring music from the very dissonances of life.

By convention they not only feel acutely and speak greatly for their authors and all the rest of us while speaking for themselves, but always have what we shall never have when our lungs are exhausted on hospital cots, and that is the last word. A poet's endowment enables them to sing their way into heaven. They trumpet themselves into paradise, releasing such verbal splendors that we forget their agonies and are sustained by the music with which they orchestrate death.

Pathos is everywhere one of the most common of emotional commodities. In no country is it held in higher esteem than here where we have Sealpack handkerchiefs to keep up with it and Hollywood to see to it that what might be our sympathetic dust bowls are in no danger of not being moist. Although it is as widespread as are the mishaps briefly reported in every daily newspaper, the pathetic is never the tragic. It is only the tragedy of the small-souled, the average, the commonplace. Its dividend is at the least sighs, at the most tears, and never ecstasy because it is no more than unhappy and can claim no fortune in misfortune.

The theatre knows a host of pathetic plays. It knows its tragedies, too—welcome enough, often dissolving, sometimes provocative, occasionally exquisite in their poignancy—which seek to deal with nothing more than the worries of men and women as they hurt, or are hurt by, one another or their neighbors. But high tragedies are more than earth-bound. They are translunary as opposed to terrestrial, if for no other reason than that their heroes and heroines are bent upon facing imponderables. They extend their interest beyond their neighbors to the forces controlling their destinies. There are more things in the heaven and earth of these turbulent worldlings than are dreamed of in the philosophies of the tamer Horatios of this planet, however good or kind. If as characters these heroes and heroines take on spiritually the dimensions of their interests, their interest is not unrequited. The gods, the stars, and nature itself may direct their misadventures, but they care for these people as these people care for them. Cries Hecuba:

> *O thou who doth uphold the world,*
> *Whose throne is high above the world,*
> *Thou, past our seeking hard to find, who art thou?*
> *God, or Necessity of what must be,*
> *Or reason of our reason,*
> *Whate'er thou art, I pray to thee,*
> *Seeing the silent road by which*
> *All mortal things are led by thee to justice.**

---

* Edith Hamilton's translation.

And her cry, in one form or another, addressed to Jove, to God, to Destiny, to Heaven, or the godhead in one's self, is apt, sooner or later, to be the cry of all the men and women whose authors have sought to follow the tragic blueprint. Part of the greatness of these characters is that with their eyes they at least dare to look for the unseeable, and with their ears they hear harmonies to which most of us are deaf.

When they die, self-realized by their suffering, they do not relinquish life but are at last released from it. They fall as mortals so complete that they have lost both their desire and excuse for living. Death for them is not a cessation of life. It is a fulfillment of self. Their living on, when the book is closed, would only mean for them and us the letdown of a sequel. Hence they and we can be happy in their dying. Macbeth is the only one of Shakespeare's major tragic characters who dies unworthily, self-despising and despised. The others feel to varying degrees, in language appropriate to their natures, the exaltation of Mark Antony's

> *I will be*
> *A bridegroom in my death, and run into't*
> *As to a lover's bed.*

Or they die as monarchs of their own spirits in Cleopatra's fashion, when she utters the superb speech beginning

> *Give me my robe, put on my crown; I have*
> *Immortal longings in me. . . .*
> *Husband, I come.*
> *Now to that name my courage prove my title!*
> *I am fire and air; my other elements*
> *I give to baser life.*

No wonder, in the presence of such a spirit, one feels that Death himself has struggled for its surrender. Or that Charmian, when the asp has done its tragic duty, can say as she surveys the body of the dead queen:

> *So fare thee well.*
> *Now boast thee, death, in thy possession lies*
> *A lass unparallel'd.*

If those words form the finest caption for the "beneficent illusion" of high tragedy known to our language, there are plenty of others scarcely less noble or sustaining. When Kent salutes the body of the dead Lear with

> *Vex not his ghost: O, let him pass! he hates him much*
> *That would upon the rack of this tough world*
> *Stretch him out longer*

he is speaking one of these, and following the pattern of death, made painless by its verbal and spiritual splendors, in high tragedy. Although many have tried and only a handful have succeeded, all dramatists, before and after Shakespeare, seeking to write high tragedy have worked, however variously, from the same blueprint. Recently, for example, in *Murder in the Cathedral,* a play which managed to become a play in spite of T. S. Eliot, Mr. Eliot had his Thomas à Becket sing, and sing beautifully, tragedy's timeless song. When his Becket knew his murderers to be at the gates of Canterbury, Mr. Eliot had him send away his protecting priests with these magical words:

> *I have had a tremor of bliss, a wink of heaven, a whisper,*
> *And I would no longer be denied; all things*
> *Proceed to a joyful consummation.*

In our living we know only too well that, New Deal or no New Deal, few things ever proceed to a joyful consummation. The moral pleasure, and one of the aesthetic delights, of high tragedy is to persuade us that all things might so proceed, if only we were or could be better than our clay.

2. Pelops' Line

*A study of the younger and evolving O'Neill as he outgrew
the crude ironies and melodrama of his earliest one-act
plays to reach for the more exalted embroilments of tragedy.*

[1930]

O'NEILL AND GOD'S ANGRY EYE

IT WAS, some said, a beer bottle thrown through a window in the
home of President Wilson that removed Eugene O'Neill from
the list of Princeton's undergraduates. Be that as it may, it was with
a larger and more typical gesture of defiance, aimed at larger and
less accessible gods, that, a short seven years later, this same
O'Neill introduced himself in print to a theatre that would have
none of him. For it was in 1914—a year that will always be
remembered for other things even if it is never remembered for
this—that Richard Badger issued in Boston a slim volume of
one-acts for the publication of which James O'Neill, the author's
actor-father, probably paid from wherever *The Count of Monte
Cristo* happened to be playing, if indeed there was at that time an
unvisited tank town in the country in which this good old melodrama still could play.

The volume, which consisted of five resolutely terrible and im-
mature guignols that are bad enough to bring encouragement to
the most discouraged of beginners, was called *Thirst and Other
One-Act Plays*. And, though its author has since managed to
keep it out of the collected editions of his works, it has an interest
in connection with his maturer writing which cannot be denied.
For in its own way this volume that is no longer published is a
baby picture of the attitude toward man and God and life which
was later to be O'Neill's. And, being his baby picture, it is a photograph that finds him frowning.

One has only to turn to the title playlet in the collection to feel
an authentic impact with that persevering frown of his; to become
aware, too, of other budding qualities which were soon to

39

distinguish him from all his contemporaries. Because in this hectic
sample of juvenilia, in which three very thirsty but equally voluble
unfortunates are discovered shipwrecked on a raft in the middle of
a glassy sea, the O'Neill whose fondness for symbolism has always
been marked was crying in his cradle. Already he was feeling that
the tropic sun which parched his people, more than being just a
tropic sun, was also "a great angry eye of God." And having brought
an angry God into his drama he was even then pitting an angry
man against Him in a conflict that was bound to be unequal. His
statement of that larger antagonism was as crudely melodramatic
as only his life at sea and his reading of Jack London could have
made it. But, when he raised the fists of one of his characters
against that God and forced him to scream, "God! God! What a
joke to play on us!" he was already trying, in his guileless way, to
warble the notes of that song which all the tragic dramatists have
sung.

The second playlet, called *The Web,* is no less determined in its
attempt to connect the misfortunes of its puppets with forces larger
than themselves over which they have no control. If anything, it is
even more dogged in its resolve to see life grimly and to state its
grimness in the grimiest of grim terms. Not only does it laugh
hoarsely at man's injustice to man by delighting in a sordid tale of
murder in which the innocent person is arrested as the guilty one,
but it piles up its horrors so unsparingly that in no time they become the perfect parody of their own conscientious unpleasantness.
Its very setting is heavy with these fallacies—both pathetic and
dramatic—by means of which only a sad young playwright, whose
sadness was wholesale, could hope to fingerprint the miseries of
life. Its squalor is relentless and excessive. For not only is the scene
a hall bedroom on the top floor of a rooming house, but it is a hall
bedroom in which everything rejoices in decay. The wall paper
is torn and dirty and the plaster shows beneath. The mirror over
the washstand is cracked. The table and the chairs are rickety.
And one look through the window which opens on a fire escape
is enough to inform you that it is raining outside.

The owner of so many tragic luxuries is, as Mr. O'Neill describes
her with a considerable dependence upon the perception of his
audience, a young woman of twenty-two who looks thirty. In her

appearance, her dress, and her complaints, she is a creature that the eye of God has looked upon with anger, or has failed to look upon at all. Her hat is a gaudy and cheap affair with a scraggy imitation plume. Her jewelry is false. And her cigarettes are of the cheapest Virginia sort. An empty beer bottle and a dirty glass are on the table at her side. The deathly pallor of her face, and the hollows under her wild and feverish eyes, ought to make it plain that she is suffering from consumption. But if these are not enough, other clues to her malady are not lacking. "From time to time, she coughs—a harsh, hacking cough that shakes her whole body. After these spells, she raises her handkerchief to her lips—then glances at it fearfully."

When she had listened to the monotonous sounds of the rain falling on the flags of the court below and thrown her cigarette wearily on the table, she finally speaks, saying the one thing she could say, "Gawd! What a night! What a chance I got!" If so far she seems merely a somewhat ridiculous creation of a young playwright who is determined to enjoy "the pain of it," she soon emerges as a not unimportant signpost to the later O'Neill. Because, when she has been unjustly accused of killing the man she loves and the realization of "the futility of all protest, the maddening hopelessness of it all" has come stealing over her in a stage direction, Mr. O'Neill has her become conscious of the thing of which he is more acutely conscious than are any of our dramatists. Like him, "she seems to be aware of something in the room which none of the others can see." And that most significant something is nothing less than "the personification of the ironic life force that has crushed her"; that self-same force which has played so large a part in Mr. O'Neill's writings from the time of such of his early sea plays as *The Moon of the Caribbees* and *The Long Voyage Home* to the day of such of his most recent experiments as *Strange Interlude* and *Lazarus Laughed*.

In attempting to deal with this force at all, Mr. O'Neill steers a solitary course in our theatre. He alone among our dramatists looks beyond his people to the agents that control them. His men and women are torn by worries which they do not—cannot—give each other, even as they are scarred by bruises which their strong arms are not strong enough to have inflicted on one another. They stray into no Utopia which is above the moral law. Nor do they lead those guarded, vicarious lives that make for the pleasant artifice from which high comedy is spun. They are not prattling shadows, strutting for the sake of recreation in a playroom of their own fashioning, but unprotected men and women, set down sternly in a world that is not man-made, who face its rawest issues with an awesome directness. Their curiosity extends beyond their neighbors' well-being, just as their woes are greater than their rent-day worries, because, instead of assuming their place among men, they search for their place in the scheme of things. Like Yank in *The Hairy Ape* they want to "belong," to be a part of the life force and an expression of it, to feel the solace of an unavoidable submission to powers which are beyond their control, or the affirmation that comes from identifying themselves with the larger agencies that engulf them. They are the visible cogs in the invisible machinery of the universe, violent with its violence even as they are broken by it. They grapple with these mysteries as Jacob wrestled with his God.

They do not ignore nature any more than nature ignores them. They are near enough to it to have gained something of its strength, to have turned hickory in the way of Ephraim Cabot in *Desire under the Elms,* to have felt his contempt for the soft ones who follow an easy God, to revel as he does in a hard one, and to feel the pride that he feels in matching his strength with the God of stones. "When ye kin make corn sprout out o' stones, God's living in yew!" cries Ephraim. "God's hard, not easy! God's in the stones! Build my church on a rock—out o' stones an' I'll be in them! That's what He meant t' Peter! Stones. I picked 'em up an' piled 'em into walls. Ye kin read the years o' my life in them walls, every day a hefted stone, climbin' over the hills up and down, fencin' in fields that was mine, whar I'd made thin's grow out o' nothin' —like the will o' God, like the servant o' his hand. It wa'n't easy. It was hard an' He made me hard fur it."

The forces with which Mr. O'Neill's people contend may be cruel but they are never indifferent. Unwilling to brood over his characters from afar, they enter in their daily lives as the silent, mocking witnesses of their doom, or the grimly active participants in their undoing. They are personal, finite gods whose interference is so immediate and undeviating that they lose no time in trusting oracles or priests to relay their intentions. They do not hide in the shadows of the heath but palpably abide in the great hall of Dunsinane. It is because they speak directly, and because Mr. O'Neill seeks to have his audiences feel the impact of these greater forces as personally as both he and his characters feel them, that he has no other choice than to work as a symbolist. It is his only possible way of expressing inexpressible things. As a symbolist who is both a mystic and a romantic, his plays abound in tangible manifestations of divine concern, of the interest of the larger forces of the world in the small affairs of men, and of the close relationship that he believes to exist between man and nature.

His men and women belong to a fierce but a caring world. The eye of God may be angry but it is never closed. In *Anna Christie,* for example, the sea is so real and near an enemy that Chris, the old barge-captain father, never tires of shaking his fists at it. It is the sea which has separated Anna from her father, the sea which has ruined her life inland, and the sea which reclaims her and purifies her for Mat Burke. It is that same "ole davil sea" that gave the conclusion of *Anna Christie* a conviction for Mr. O'Neill that it has never carried for his audiences. To them it seemed a happy ending and a false one. To him, with his anthropomorphic vision of things, it was an unhappy ending and a right one because, though Anna and Mat had patched up their lover's quarrel, Mat and Chris were shipping on the same boat and all three of them were once more at the mercy of the sea. "It's queer," says Chris. "Yes—you and me shipping on the same boat dat vay. It ain't right. Ay don't know—it's dat funny vay ole davil sea do her vorst dirty trick, yes. It's so."

As close to the doings of the Cabots as the sea is to the fate of Chris, Anna, and Mat, are the two enormous elms that stand at either side of the farmhouse in *Desire under the Elms.* As Mr. O'Neill sees them they are not ordinary trees, but agents of destiny. "They bend their trailing branches down on the roof. They appear to protect and at the same time to subdue. There is a sinister maternity in their aspect, a crushing, jealous absorption. They have developed from their intimate contact with the life of man in the house an appalling humaneness. They brood oppressively over the house. They are like exhausted women resting their sagging breasts and hands and hair on its roof, and when it rains their tears trickle down monotonously and rot on the shingles."

The symbols Mr. O'Neill employs in his plays are many and various: the fog that lifts in *Bound East for Cardiff* when Yank's face has twitched and his body writhed in its final spasm of agony; the grotesque expression of the Congo mask that asserts a diabolical dominance over the flat of Jim Harris and Ella Downey, his white wife, in *All God's Chillun Got Wings*; the line of hills which stands for promise and for dreams, and beyond which all the wonders of the world seem to happen for Robert in *Beyond the Horizon*; the oil that is the expression of Captain Keeney's pride and that keeps him from turning his whaling ship homeward even at the expense of his wife's sanity in *Ile*; the gold that is the maddening obsession, and the illusion, of Captain Bartlett in both *Where the Cross Is Made* and *Gold*; the door that opens inward on the couple whose marital relations are so closely analyzed in *Welded*; the procession of gaudy marionettes that parades on Fifth Avenue in *The Hairy Ape* "with something of the relentless horror of Frankensteins in their detached, mechanical unawareness," and that represents the upper world of indolence and wealth as it appears to Yank, the stoker; the fountain of youth that beckons Ponce de Leon onward in *The Fountain*; the complicated meaning of the masks in *The Great God Brown* and the very names of such of its characters as Dion Anthony (Dionysus and St. Anthony) and Cybele, the prostitute, who embodies the Earth Mother; the prostitute in *Marco Millions*; Nina who is the "Erdgeist" of *Strange Interlude*; and the silvery laugh of Lazarus that rings out its melodious defiance of death in *Lazarus Laughed*—these are but a small fraction of the symbols within symbols which he uses to connect his men and women with the elemental forces that surround them, and to vitalize the outward facts of their lives in the terms of their spiritual meanings.

Whether he employs symbols or not, and he almost invariably does, the life forces dominate his plays, as surely as in *Strange Interlude* Nina Leeds is haunted by the thought of God the Mother, or as in *Dynamo* Reuben fights the battle between faith and science by denying the psalm-singing Fundamentalism of his father and dedicating himself to the worship of Mother Dynamo. Of recent years in particular, Mr. O'Neill's is a world that suffers because it is ruled by a male god, when it should have been ruled by a god reared in the maternal image of those elms that droop above the Cabot farmhouse in *Desire*. It is a world of a jargon that is increasingly Freudian and pseudo-scientific, in which, as Nina phrases it, "our lives are merely strange, dark interludes in the electrical display of God the Father. The mistake began," says Nina, "when God was created in the male image. Of course, women would see Him that way, but men should have been gentlemen enough, remembering their mothers, to make God a woman! But the God of Gods—the Boss—has always been a man. That makes life so perverted, and death so unnatural. We should have imagined life as created in the birth-pain of God the Mother. Then we would have understood why we, Her children, have inherited pain, for we would know that our life's rhythm beats from Her great heart, torn with the agony of love and birth. And we would feel that death meant reunion with Her, a passing back into Her substance, blood of Her blood again, peace of Her peace!"

The same theology, that search for God the Mother, finds statement in another form in *Dynamo* in a speech, incidentally, which makes clearer than anything else could the dangers, the pretensions, even the absurdities which can overtake a spirit of inquiry that is as ambitious as Mr. O'Neill's. It makes painfully apparent the manner in which the dramatist of his earlier and middle periods has been temporarily replaced by the foggy-minded coiner of cosmic beatitudes. "You're like her—Dynamo—the Great Mother—big and warm—" cries Reuben to Mrs. Fife. Then he breaks away from her, to exclaim, "But I've got to finish telling you all I've come to know about her—how all things end up in her! Did I tell you that our blood plasm is the same right now as the sea was when life came out of it? We've got the sea in our blood still! It's what makes our hearts live! And it's the sea rising up in clouds, falling on the earth in rain, made that river that drives the turbines that drive Dynamo! The sea makes her heart beat, too!—but the sea is only hydrogen and oxygen and minerals, and they're only atoms, and atoms are only protons and electrons—even our blood and the sea are only electricity in the end! And think of the stars! Driving through space, round and round, just like the electrons in the atom! But there must be a center round which all this moves, mustn't there? There is in everything else! And that center must be the Great Mother of Eternal Life, Electricity, and Dynamo is her Divine Image on earth! Her power houses are the new churches!" And so on through many other exclamatory discoveries on the part of Mr. O'Neill of the secrets of a life force that is new to him and that, as he writes of it, still smacks too much of the homework he has devoted to its mastery.

The connection that exists between these larger agencies and the men and women of Mr. O'Neill's plays is more frequently ironic than tragic. Indeed, in many respects it is the acuteness of his sensing of the life force as ironic that has stood in the way of his development as a tragic dramatist. His irony is bitter, melancholy, and unflinching. But as irony it does not rise above pain or exult in the manner of tragedy. It asks us to smile in a sad way at the savage joke that the gods can play on men far more often than it invites us to share the divinity that suffering can bring to man. Too often he leads his people downward rather than letting them rise again from hell, because his preoccupation is so frequently the trick—the dirty trick—that fate has up its sleeve, rather than the ennobling protest that the tragic dramatists have put into the hearts of men.

The undoing of many of his people is so certain that the interest shifts—as it does not in true tragedy—from the men and women who are tested and broken to the destructive agents that test and break them. The inevitability of their outward doom becomes of more importance than the inevitability of their inward undoing. Because instead of tearing the heart by the picture that he paints of the martyr's anguish in the arena, he permits the attention to fasten itself with a grim fascination upon the prowess of the lion that is bound to devour him. It is Mr. O'Neill's awareness of the sad humor in events that causes him in *The Emperor Jones* to send his terror-stricken emperor circling through the protecting forest until he stumbles out of it and into the hands of his pursuers at the very point at which he entered. It is that same obsession of Mr. O'Neill's with the perversities of fortune that causes him to have the emperor slain by one of the silver bullets that the natives have molded in order to break the spell of the silver bullet which he has told them was his life's charm.

It is the same ironic view of circumstance which induces Mr. O'Neill—and Anna—to laugh at the end of *Anna Christie,* when Mat and Chris and Anna find themselves once more at the mercy of that "ole davil sea"; that robs Olson of his dream of returning to his mother and his farm in *The Long Voyage Home* by having him drugged and robbed in a low London dive and shanghaied onto another vessel when Sweden lies just ahead; and that leads the murderous menfolk in *The Rope* off the scent of the old man's hoardings even as it causes the little child to discover them and to toss the bright twenty-dollar gold pieces into the sea as if they were so many toys. It is the identical sense of the God-played trick that one feels in *Gold* when Captain Bartlett has lost his mind and ruined his home in the worship of an illusionary treasure that turns out to be brass; that finds the wife of the scientist pregnant in *The First Man* at the very time that she and her husband were to have set out on their most important expedition; and that causes the Princess Kukachin in *Marco Millions* to waste her pure young love on such a callow and grasping Babbitt in ancient dress as Marco.

Ironic though Mr. O'Neill may be in the majority of cases, he does occasionally write with the fine fervor of tragedy. In the last scene of *Beyond the Horizon,* Mr. O'Neill extends his ironic chronicle of the misfortunes of two brothers who take each other's places in life beyond its sordid externals to give a hint of tragic exaltation. His poet, Robert, who has been such a misfit on the farm that his life has been a painful ruin, dies happily in the knowledge that it is by death alone that he can travel beyond the horizons of which he has dreamed. His death is the beginning, not the end. "You mustn't feel sorry for me," he says in a voice suddenly ringing with the happiness of hope. "Don't you see I'm happy at last —free—free!—freed from the farm—free to wander on and on— eternally!" That same feeling of exaltation lifts the pathetic romance of the two consumptives in *The Straw* above the sanatorium details of the earlier acts, to a final scene of agonizing beauty, which flames with a love that death cannot kill and that pain cannot conquer, because it has been born in pain at the moment of death. Equally fervid is the transfiguring frenzy of the concluding scene of *All God's Chillun Got Wings,* Mr. O'Neill's study of miscegenation, in which the white girl asks her black hus-

band if God will forgive her, and he replies, "Maybe He can forgive what you've done to me; and maybe He can forgive what I've
done to you; but I don't see how He's going to forgive—Himself." It is in *Desire under the Elms* that Mr. O'Neill has
most nearly approached the conception of tragedy that was dear
to the Greeks. For in *Desire* he is not mastered by his details but is
the master of them, even as he is the master of a noble stylization
that is as telling as it is finely austere. For once he advances his
tragedy in the terms of people who are vibrant with the capacity
for great suffering. And by doing so he elevates a tale of wasteful murder, of mean deception, of hideous lust for possession and
of gross carnal love far above its sordid trappings and fills a drab
New England farmhouse with something of the glory of a Theban
palace.

The tragic and ironic forces with which Mr. O'Neill deals he
handles with a power that is uniquely his own. It is a power born
of the grim forces which are his subject matter. Like them his writing surges onward because it must; because it shares with them
their quality of inevitability. It has no time for the subduings of a
blue pencil skillfully wielded or for the niceties that are so dear
to the lesser men and that would do so much to conserve its
strength, because it is as wasteful of itself as nature is and seems
to be equally casual in its editing. Its force is most resilient when
Mr. O'Neill's concern is not the sciences that man must master
with his mind but the crude elements of nature that he must battle
with his arms, because it is as an emotionalist, and not a thinker,
that Mr. O'Neill excels. His strength is of that great, raw, shaggy
kind that Whitman's was. It is soberer, starker, and infinitely more
grim. But it is no less torrential, savage as it is, with the
same energy, heavy with the same profusion and cumulative in
the same headlong way.

Mr. O'Neill's are vigorous words unloosed in vigorous cadences.
Listen to Paddy and to Yank as they compare the virtues of the
sea that was to the merits of the sea that is, in the fireman's fore-
castle of *The Hairy Ape,* and you hear the singing strength
of which his speech is possible when it is at its best. "Oh, to be back
in the fine days of my youth, ochone!" keens Paddy. "Oh, there
was beautiful ships them days—clippers wid tall masts touching

the sky—fine strong men in them—men that was sons of the sea as if 'twas the mother that bore them. Oh, the clean skins of them, and the clear eyes, the straight backs and the full chests of them! Brave men they was, and bold men surely! We'd be sailing, out bound down round the Horn maybe. We'd be making sail in the dawn, with a fair breeze, singing a chanty song wid no care to it. And astern the land would be sinking low and dying out, but we'd give it no heed but a laugh, and never a look behind. For the day that was, was enough, for we was free men—and I'm thinking 'tis only slaves do be giving heed to the day that's gone or the day to come—until they're old like me."

To which Yank replies, "Aw, yuh crazy Mick! (He springs to his feet and advances on Paddy threateningly—then stops, fighting some queer struggle within himself—lets his hands fall to his sides —contemptuously) Aw, take it easy. Yuh're aw right, at dat. Yuh're bugs, dat's all—nutty as a cuckoo. All dat tripe yuh been pullin'— Aw, dat's all right. On'y it's dead, get me? Yuh don't belong no more, see. Yuh don't get de stuff. Yuh're too old. (Disgustedly) But aw say, come up for air onct in a while, can't yuh? See what's happened since yuh croaked. (He suddenly bursts forth vehemently, growing more and more excited.) Say! Sure! Sure! I meant it! What de hell— Say, lemme talk! Hey! Hey, you old Harp! Hey, youse guys! Say, listen to me—wait a moment—I gotter talk, see. I belong and he don't. He's dead but I'm living. Listen to me! Sure I'm part of de engines! Why de hell not! Dey move, don't dey? Dey're speed, ain't dey! Dey smash trou, don't dey? Twenty-five knots a hour! Dat's goin' some! Dat's new stuff! Dat belongs! But him, he's too old. He gets dizzy. Say, listen. All dat crazy tripe about nights and days; all dat crazy tripe about stars and moons; all dat crazy tripe about suns and winds, fresh air and de rest of it— Aw, hell, dat's all a dope dream! Hittin' de pipe of de past, dat's what he's doing. He's old, and don't belong no more. But me, I'm young! I'm in de pink! I move wit it! It, get me! I mean de ting dat's de guts of all dis. It ploughs trou all de tripe he's been sayin'. It blows dat up! It knocks dat dead! It slams dat offen de face of de oith! It, get me! De engines and de coal and de smoke and all de rest of it! He can't breathe and swallow coal dust, but I kin, see? Dat's fresh air for me!"

Set against the speeches of Paddy and Yank, such a speech as
Reuben's psalm to Mother Dynamo, or such a chant as the one in
The Fountain which aims at making a lyric comment on the theme
of the play in such meager words as:

> *Love is a flower*
> *Forever blooming,*
> *Beauty a fountain*
> *Forever flowing*
> *Upward into the source of sunshine,*
> *Upward into the azure heaven;*
> *One with God but*
> *Ever returning*
> *To kiss the earth that the flower may live,*

and you see the difference between the O'Neill whose words throb
with the beat of forces that have possessed him, and the O'Neill
who attempts to work consciously as a poet.

Of recent years, as Mr. O'Neill has grown as an artist and grown
away from immediate contact with his early material, and as his
field of exploration has ceased to be the world of fact and become
the world of modern psychology and mysticism, an increasing self-
consciousness has manifested itself in his work. His thought has
often been impeded in its statement because of the "mystical patterns" and "overtones" that, as he himself has described it, lie
"dimly behind and beyond the words and actions of the characters." An acute illustration of that confusion and of the involutions of his own mind which he expects an audience to follow in
the terms of an elaborate symbolism, is *The Great God Brown,*
where, as Mr. O'Neill explains it, "Dion's mask of Pan which he
puts on as a boy is not only a defense against the world for the
super-sensitive painter-poet underneath it, but also an integral part
of his character as the artist. The world is not only blind to the
man beneath, but it also sneers at and condemns the Pan-mask it
sees. After that Dion's inner self retrogresses along the line of Christian resignation until it partakes of the nature of the Saint while at
the same time the outer Pan is slowly transformed by his struggle
with reality into Mephistopheles. It is as Mephistopheles he falls

stricken at Brown's feet after having condemned Brown to destruction by willing him his mask, but, this mask falling off as he dies,
it is the Saint who kisses Brown's feet in abject contrition and
pleads as a little boy to a big brother to tell him a prayer."

When *Dynamo* was playing at the Guild Theatre the program
carried further indications of Mr. O'Neill's growing self-consciousness as an artist. One bit of evidence was a quotation from one of
his letters to the Board of Managers in which he referred to the
dialogue of the play as "Interludism"; another was a reprint from
an article by Kenneth Macgowan in which Mr. Macgowan mentioned "the Big Grand Opus" Mr. O'Neill was planning, which, in
Mr. O'Neill's words, was to be neither a novel nor a play because
"there will be many plays in it and it will have a greater scope than
any novel I know of. Its form will be altogether its own—a lineal
descendant of *Strange Interlude* but beside it *Interlude* will seem
like a shallow episode." The third bit of evidence was a letter to
George Jean Nathan in which Mr. O'Neill described *Dynamo* as
"a symbolical and factual biography of what is happening in a large
section of the American (and not only American) soul right now.
It is really the first play of a trilogy that will dig at the roots of the
sickness of today as I feel it—the death of an old God and the
failure of science and materialism to give any satisfying new one
for the surviving primitive religious instinct to find a meaning for
life in, and to comfort its fears of death with. It seems to me that
anyone trying to do big work nowadays must have this big subject
behind all the little subjects of his plays or novels, or he is simply
scribbling around on the surface of things and has no more real
status than a parlor entertainer."

Of the fact that Mr. O'Neill has not contented himself with
"scribbling around on the surface of things," there can be no question. He, more than any contemporary dramatist, has risen above
the status of a parlor entertainer. Finding his way into the theatre
by such a hospitable side door as the directors of the Provincetown
Playhouse offered, he less than any of our playwrights has made
concessions to the theatre as the commercial managers have believed the public wanted it to be. It is that very integrity of his—
that unswerving and uncompromising loyalty to what he has believed to be the best that was in him—which, coupled with the

fierce strength of his talents, has made him the most spirited path-finder among present-day dramatists.

From the time of his early sea plays, through the period of his first realistic long plays and such expressionistic dramas as *The Emperor Jones* and *The Hairy Ape,* to such of his more recent breaks with tradition as *Strange Interlude* and *Lazarus Laughed,* he has shown himself to be a fearless experimenter. Daring to state the grim truth, as he has seen it, in the Cinderelladom of our theatre, he has also dared to state it in any form that he may have desired. With a courage that is his alone he has made the theatre adapt itself to him and refused to adapt himself to it. Creating the form to fit his needs, instead of fitting his needs into an accepted form, he has defied all the cut-and-dried conventions of the show shop—discarding realism, employing any number of scenes, using symbols, requiring constructivist settings, relying on a complicated system of masks, offending against the traditional time limit of performances, and using such forbidden fruits of the pre-realistic theatre as the aside and the soliloquy to bring "the stream of consciousness" into the theatre. He has broken rules, not for the pleasure of breaking them, but because he has bowed to no other dictates than his own desire, and his thirst for freedom of expression.

If in spite of his exceptional courage and his no less exceptional power, Mr. O'Neill seems an unsatisfactory genius, it is because he comes so frequently within the range of greatness without achieving it completely. His plays are peaked with greatness rather than sustained by it. They are marred by blemishes from which his taste has not spared them, moments, or whole scenes, that one wishes were other than what they are, because he has not yet learned how to harness his own strength or to be the absolute master of the raw power that is his. But whether he fails or whether he succeeds, the merit of his having tried shines through all that he writes. And it is both the strength and the daring of his attempts which elevate him above all his American contemporaries, making him seem as Smithers said of the Emperor Jones, " 'E's a better man than the lot o' you put together." Like his own emperor, however, Mr. O'Neill has reason to be afraid of silver. Not of bullets, to be sure, but of the silvery thoughts and phrases for which he has

shown a growing fondness of late and which may yet be the cause
of his undoing.

*A first-night report written under the spell of the strength
and grandeur of O'Neill's retelling of the Electra story.*

[1931]

MOURNING BECOMES ELECTRA

FOR EXCITING proof that the theatre is still very much alive, that
it still has grandeur and ecstasy to offer to its patrons, that fine acting has not disappeared from behind the footlights' glare, that productions which thrill with memorability are still being made, that
scenic design and stage direction can belong among the fine arts,
and that the Theatre Guild, in spite of any causes for discourage-
ment it may have given in the past, is still the most accomplished as
well as the most intrepid producing organization in America, you
have only to journey to the Guild Theatre these nights and days,
and sit before Eugene O'Neill's new trilogy, *Mourning Becomes
Electra.** It is a play which towers above the scrubby output of
our present-day theatre as the Empire State Building soars above
the skyline of Manhattan. Most of its fourteen acts, and particularly its earlier and middle sections, are possessed of a strength
and majesty equal to its scale. It boasts, too, the kind of radiant
austerity which was part of the glory that was Greece.

It is one of the most distinguished achievements of Mr. O'Neill's
career. It is—as the dull word has it—uneven, but so—as the no
less dull retort phrases it—are the Himalayas. It has blemishes
which are obvious, especially as it reaches its third section. But it

---

* *Mourning Becomes Electra,* by Eugene O'Neill. Directed by Philip
Moeller. Settings and costumes by Robert Edmond Jones. Presented by the
Theatre Guild. With a cast including Alla Nazimova, Alice Brady, Lee
Barker, Earle Larimore, and Thomas Chalmers. At the Guild Theatre.
Opened October 26, 1931.

remains to the end a *magnum opus* beside which *Strange Interlude* and most of the earlier, simpler plays sink into unimportance. For it is an experiment in sheer, shuddering, straightforward storytelling which widens the theatre's limited horizons at the same time it is exalting and horrifying its patrons.

It retells, as everyone knows, a story of revenge; a saga of the way in which fate calls upon Electra and her brother Orestes to avenge the murder of their father, Agamemnon, by slaying their wicked mother, Clytemnestra, and her no less wicked lover, Aegisthus. It is a myth all three of the great tragic dramatists of Greece have told in their own way, taking their own liberties with its details, distributing the emphasis according to their own sensing of its moral and dramatic values, and managing to make it decidedly their own in each of their independent versions. Mr. O'Neill, needless to say, has taken even greater liberties with this classic myth than any of his ancient predecessors dared to do. By taking them, he has made the story very much his own, without robbing its terrible sequence of catastrophes of either their force or their essential outlines.

The play finds Mr. O'Neill forgetting the pseudo-scientific jargon of Mother Dynamo and the mystic laugh of Lazarus, dispensing with such special technical devices as masks and asides, and writing without any hindrances of form as an emotionalist. As an emotionalist, who knows how to dramatize the curdling rancors of hate, the surgings of thwarted passion, and the taut demands of murder, he has no equal in the contemporary theatre. As his title makes very clear, Mr. O'Neill's concern is with one of the grandest, most spine-twisting tales of murder the theatre's history knows. It is, in short, the Electra story he is retelling in more or less modern terms, substituting the white pillars of a country house in Civil War New England for the Doric columns of ancient Argos.

Mr. O'Neill's play is a testing of his strength with that fable of the luckless house of Atreus which Aeschylus first treated in the *Oresteia*, which Sophocles and Euripides both dealt with in their respective *Electras,* and which such a modern as the late Hugo von Hofmannsthal vulgarized into a Reinhardtian thriller of lights and leers and snakelike gestures. Unlike Sophocles and Euripides, who contented themselves with the writing of a single play about the "recognition" of the long-separated Electra and Orestes, and the murder of Clytemnestra and Aegisthus, Mr. O'Neill has turned to Aeschylus for the model of *Mourning Becomes Electra*. Like this earliest of the Greek tragic writers, Mr. O'Neill has chosen to give the story in full, to prepare for its coming, to catch it at the height of its action, and to follow his avengers (he follows both Electra and Orestes) past the awful deed fate has demanded of them to the time when the Erinyes (or Furies) are pursuing them. Accordingly, just as Aeschylus divided his *Oresteia* into the *Agamemnon, The Choëphori,* or *Libation Bearers,* and *The Eumenides,* so Mr. O'Neill has divided his *Mourning Becomes Electra* into three parts bearing such Bulwer-Lytton titles as *Homecoming, The Hunted,* and *The Haunted.* Contrary to the example of Aeschylus, and much more according to the practice of Sophocles and Euripides, Mr. O'Neill gives his trilogy to Electra. It is she who dominates its action and fuses it, even as Orestes fused the Aeschylean original into one long play—with pauses—rather than three separate dramas.

Mr. O'Neill's Agamemnon (Lee Barker) is Ezra Mannon, a hard, unbending New Englander, who has been off to the Mexican War in his youth, who has studied law, been a skipper, achieved great success in business, and served as mayor of the small town in which his family is outstanding. His Clytemnestra (Alla Nazimova) is Christine, a foreigner who has long been out of love with her husband and who has now come to hate him. Their children, Lavinia (Alice Brady) and Orin (Earle Larimore), are, of course, the Electra and the Orestes of Mr. O'Neill's piece. While old Ezra Mannon had been away from home, winning the praise of General Grant for the military abilities he has shown as a brigadier general in the Civil War, his wife has had an affair with a Captain Adam Brant (Thomas Chalmers), the Aegisthus of *Mourning Becomes Electra,* who in this case is the illegitimate son of a wayward Mannon who has brought shame on his family.

Lavinia, who has also been in love with Captain Brant, follows her mother to New York, learns of her infidelity to her father, and resolves to break up the affair. She confronts her mother, makes her promise to see no more of Brant, and prepares to welcome her father and brother home from the war. Meanwhile Christine has already confided in Brant that their one way to happiness lies in the death of Ezra, who stands between them. She is prepared to murder him, and murder him she does by taking advantage of the heart trouble from which he suffers. Not only does she bring on one of his attacks by naming her lover to him but she offers him as a medicine the poison Brant has sent her. Lavinia comes into her father's room just before he dies, hears him accuse her mother, sees the powder she has administered, and resolves to take justice into her own hands in avenging his death.

Both Lavinia and her mother fight for the love of Orin, but he, like the spineless Orestes of Sophocles and Euripides, soon falls under the domination of Lavinia. She proves her point to him by leading him to the clipper ship Brant commands and there shows him their mother in Brant's arms. Thereupon Orin kills Brant when his mother has left him; she commits suicide when she learns of her lover's death (thus sparing us the mother-murder of the Greeks); the ghosts of the dead who refuse to die haunt Orin and Lavinia; Orin shoots himself; and Lavinia forswears the happiness her impending marriage might have brought her, has the shutters nailed down on the Mannon house, and locks herself inside it to atone during the rest of her life for the sins of her family.

As Mr. O'Neill rehandles this venerable story it preserves its awesome fascination. It emerges, as it has always emerged, as one of the most gripping melodramatic plots in the world. It also comes through its present restatement as a tragic melodrama of heroic proportions. The poetic beauty the Greeks gave it is lacking in Mr. O'Neill's prose modernization. But the dilemma remains, and so does much of the agony and exaltation that belong to it. Mr. O'Neill's treatment of it is vigorous with the kind of vigor our theatre rarely sees. It is stark, unadorned and strong. It has dignity and majesty. Nearly the whole of it is possessed of such an all-commanding interest that one is totally unconscious of the hours its performance freely consumes.

That it is longer than it need be seems fairly obvious, as does the fact that, like so many of O'Neill's plays, it stands in need of editing. It is at its best in its first two sections, and most particularly in its fine middle portion. But its last part seems overlong and lacks the interest of its predecessors. It marks the same falling off from what has preceded it as the *Eumenides* does from the *Choëphori*. Deprived of plotting which sweeps forward to a climax, and dealing with the conscience-stricken course of its avengers, it goes a tamer, more uncertain way. Nor is it helped by the incest motive Mr. O'Neill has added. It rises in the last act, however, to a final curtain that is Greek in its whole feeling and flavor. Alla Nazimova's Christine is superbly sinister, possessed of an insidious and electric malevolence, and brilliant with an incandescent fire. As Lavinia Miss Brady gives the kind of performance her admirers have long been waiting to see her give. It is controlled. It has the force of the true Electra. And it is sustained throughout as long and severe an actor's test as any player has been called upon to meet. The moments when she stands dressed in black before the black depths of Mr. Jones' doorways are moments no one can forget who has felt their thrill. Mr. Larimore's Orin is a vivid picture of frenzy and weakness. All in all, *Mourning Becomes Electra* is an achievement which restores the theatre to its high estate.

O'Neill, in The Iceman Cometh, *revisits a certain saloon and in the process misplaces his watch but not his talents.*

[1946]

MOANING AT THE BAR

EUGENE O'NEILL was talking. He was speaking to a reporter from *The New York Times,* a paper which is rightly and resolutely preoccupied with news. The year was 1924, the month December. Since his *Desire under the Elms* had recently been produced, Mr. O'Neill was then "news," even as he remains "news" today when the Theatre Guild has just staged *The Iceman Cometh,* * his first play to be produced in twelve long seasons.

* *The Iceman Cometh,* by Eugene O'Neill. Directed by Eddie Dowling. Settings by Robert Edmond Jones. Presented by the Theatre Guild. With a cast including Dudley Digges, E. G. Marshall, John Marriott, Frank Tweddell, Nicholas Joy, Russell Collins, Leo Chalzel, Carl Benton Reid, Tom Pedi, Ruth Gilbert, Jeanne Cagney, Marcella Markham, James Barton, Michael Wyler, and Charles Hart. At the Martin Beck Theatre. Opened October 9, 1946.

"In New York," said Mr. O'Neill, thinking back to 1910 and the rough-and-tumble of his seagoing days when his throat was swabbed with stronger stuff than Coca-Cola, "I lived at Jimmy-the-Priest's, a waterfront dive, with a back room where you could sleep with your head on the table if you bought a schooner of beer. . . .

"It was so named because Jimmy, the proprietor . . . seemed to be more suited for a cassock than the bartender's apron he wore. . . . Jimmy-the-Priest's certainly was a hell hole. . . . I was absolutely down, financially, those days. . . . You can get an idea of the kind of room I had when I tell you that the rent was three dollars a month. One roommate of mine jumped out of the window."

In *The Iceman Cometh*, Mr. O'Neill pays Jimmy-the-Priest's another and far longer visit. This time, the saloon-hotel has changed ownership. It now belongs to Harry Hope, a major toper though a minor ex-Tammanyite. Although it remains much the same joint (even to the derelict who jumped to his death) that lodged Mr. O'Neill, and that playgoers came to know as Johnny-the-Priest's in *Anna Christie,* there is a difference. A major difference. This exists in Mr. O'Neill's approach to the place no less than in the dramatic uses he now makes of it.

Mr. O'Neill was twenty-two when, as George Jean Nathan would have it, he slept next to the bunghole of a whisky barrel at Jimmy-the-Priest's, and when Jimmy, the proprietor, coming to work the next morning found the barrel one-eighth emptied. He was thirty-four when the hitherto unseen Anna Christie, who was pictured by her father and the audience as a demure virgin from Minnesota, pushed her way in through the family entrance as palpably a member of the world's oldest profession and turned to the waiter to say as her first words, "Gimme a whisky—ginger ale on the side. And don't be stingy, baby."

Mr. O'Neill is now fifty-eight—prosperous, a model of decorum, a man after Carry Nation's heart, a recluse, a semi-invalid, and a world figure. Honors have been heaped upon him. He has won the Pulitzer award three times, and deserved it more often. Bernard DeVoto notwithstanding, the Nobel Prize has also come his way. In schools and colleges he is studied along with Ibsen as if he were an unassailable figure of the past. Wherever people care about the drama (which means in regions far beyond the reach of theatres), his name is known and respected. Indeed, no other living playwright, with the exception of Shaw, enjoys his preeminence.

If Mr. O'Neill remains "news"—definitely "news"—the reasons are almost intrusive. Whatever his shortcomings may be (and they have been fairly manifest), he occupies a position as proud as it is solitary. He has written some terrible plays, some of the most effective dramas of our time, and a few of the finest. Yet always, the man's courage has been unmistakable. He has always gone his own austere, fierce, usually frowning way, ignoring the cheap whims of our show-shops and making the theatre do what he wanted rather than doing what its timid souls thought would be popular.

No dramatist has ever been a more dauntless experimenter or a more fearless innovator. He has dared in play after play to change his pattern, even when successful, and reach for what for him (and usually for the stage) was the untried. With varying degrees of success, ranging from the pretentious and the preposterous to the very threshold of greatness, he has worked as a naturalist, a realist, an expressionist, a Freudian, a mystic, a symbolist, or as a poet whose poetry was deader than the feeblest prose even when his prose as spoken has burned with the fires of poetry.

What has set him most squarely apart, and granted him a fine loneliness among the dramatic talents of our time, has been the subject which he has made his most constant concern. Whether he has stated this in terms of cheap and juvenile irony (as he most certainly did in the melodramatic excesses of those earliest "My-Gawd-what-a-chanct-I-got" one-acts), or expressed it with the white heat of tragedy (as in the first two parts of *Mourning Becomes Electra,* before the play became mired in Freud), his characters have almost always dared to look beyond their relations with their neighbors and sought to find their place in the universe. Like Yank in *The Hairy Ape,* they have wanted to "belong." However beaten they may have been by life, Mr. O'Neill has endeavored to relate them not merely to men but also to outside forces of a cruel, though caring, nature which are the ultimate agents that control them.

For these agents Mr. O'Neill has had many names, ranging from "the ironic life force," "the great angry eye of God," and "that ole davil sea" to Mother Dynamo and Christ the Crucified. In attempt-

ing to deal with them dramatically, he has—at his best—
manifested an instinct for the theatre so irresistible that even his
father, James O'Neill, would have had to salute it.

Except when he has written as a realist, Mr. O'Neill's language
has been his major drawback. He has functioned as a prose writer
tormented by a poet's vision. That is an unhappy fate. He has been
denied the final power of lyric utterance which would make some
of his biggest scenes soar into those ultimate regions where vibrant
theatre becomes great literature. Yet this must be said to his eternal credit. He has never been unwilling or afraid to try.

Among Mr. O'Neill's many defiances of theatrical conventions
has been his disregard of the time which stage performances normally last so that businessmen (even in these days) can go about
their business and commuters catch the last train home. Someone
really ought to buy him a watch. Or, failing that, at least remind
him of how helpful it is locally, in moments of doubt, to dial
MEridian 7-1212. The Joshua habit is becoming chronic with
him; the Oberammergau example has conquered him.

However contrived the theatre may have to be, it is at least this
true to life. What matters in it is not the time expended but what
is done with that time. The justification of the four hours required
to play it is the first test *The Iceman Cometh* must pass, and one
which, in my judgment at any rate, it flunks disastrously. That the
play has its undeniable virtues I cannot deny, and indeed do not
want to. But that these would be twice as marked as they now are
if only Mr. O'Neill's script were one-half as long as it is at present
seems to me to be no less undeniable.

Speaking of time, it is impossible not to realize how wise Mr.
O'Neill has been in placing his play at the Jimmy-the-Priest's he
himself knew in 1912. This grants his dialogue an immediate immunity from a kind of criticism to which it otherwise might be
subject. It protects it from the needs of being contemporary in its
idioms. It grants an unchallengeable freedom to a man whose fame
and illness have forced him to live, for many years now, an ab-
normally protected life that has thus cut him off from the experiences upon which his first plays were based.

In *The Iceman Cometh* Mr. O'Neill may continue to work as a
symbolist. But instead of seeking to relate men to the unseen agents

of their destiny, he occupies himself with what they must live by within themselves. His conclusion turns out to be nothing more startling than their illusions, though it takes him an unconscionable time to get this stated.

Into his barroom setting, where a whole stageful of penniless Lost Weekenders are assembled, Mr. O'Neill sends a drummer. He is the Mr. Fixit of the piece; the Luka of *The Lower Depths*, the Joe of *The Time of Your Life*. Unlike Yank in *The Hairy Ape*, whose contempt was fierce for those who "hit the pipe of the past," Mr. O'Neill's drummer attacks those whose pipe dreams are centered on the future.

The bums, the barflies, the down-and-outers, the broken men in Harry's flophouse will, he insists, find happiness only if, in his manner, they lay off the booze which nourishes their illusions and face themselves as they are. Several of them are persuaded to try the experiment. One by one, however, they soon slink back to their bottles to dream those alcoholic dreams without which their wretched, frustrated lives would be insupportable.

What the drummer in Mr. O'Neill's drama symbolizes—whether he means death by robbing men of their life-sustaining dreams, or whether he (and the whole play) represents Mr. O'Neill's subconscious protest against those who have chaperoned and tidied up his own recent living—is a matter for individual conjecture. One thing is certain. Mr. O'Neill has turned on the meddlesome idealists as fiercely as ever Ibsen did when in *The Wild Duck* he made it clear that Gregors Werle was always thirteenth at table.

No play that I can think of gets off to a more becalmed start than does *The Iceman Cometh* in that interminable first act which precedes the dinner bell. Compared to it, Prospero's telling to Miranda the story of her life in *The Tempest* can claim an almost honky-tonk sprightliness. I, at least, kept wondering for an hour and a half when the play was going to begin. Meanwhile I felt as if I had started a long serial story one issue late, and hence was being forced to catch up with it in terms of a moribund synopsis. The more ardent champions of Mr. O'Neill's new drama insist that its initial slowness is unavoidable because the first act is meant only as a prologue. To me this seems the most legless of apologies.

From then on the play does pick up. Even when it is doing

nothing more than take one step forward and one step back, it commands the attention. Its garrulity cannot obscure its power. The old O'Neill magic is upon it in scene after scene. There are fine examples of his compassion, his insight, his blazing intensity, and his theatrical skill. Yet considering how little he has to say that is new or enriching on the subject of prostitutes, drunks, or even illusions, there is no excuse for his having said at least twice everything that could have been better stated by being suggested.

Although *The Iceman Cometh* is far worthier than most of our theatre's offerings, it is not without its genuine disappointments and its Gargantuan faults. Not only is it the kind of play that Mr. O'Neill alone could have written, but it is also the kind of play which only he could have got produced. Any manager in his right senses would have begged another dramatist to cut it to its proper length. One trembles to imagine what people would think of *The Iceman Cometh* if it did not bear Mr. O'Neill's mesmerizing name.

However large the doubts created by Mr. O'Neill's script, there can be none—or almost none—on the subject of the production the Theatre Guild has given it. It is one of the most satisfying and masterly presentations our stage has yielded. Eddie Dowling, who has directed it, has faced a problem of staggering proportions, and somehow managed to solve it.

Mr. O'Neill frequently has from thirteen to seventeen of his derelicts dozing in the back room at one time. Much of his dialogue is devoted to quarrelsome duets, when the other characters, if not sleeping, are forced to remain quiet. Mr. Dowling contrives to endow these mass silences with more than conviction. His groupings are fluid; his modulations of pace admirable; and his eye for the pictorial unflagging. He never fails to heighten and interpret the meannesses of life so that they cease to be photography and emerge as art. His stage, particularly as set and lighted by Robert Edmond Jones, breathes, moves, and lives even while seeming to have been caught on canvas by an exceptional painter.

How long it took Mr. O'Neill to compose *The Iceman Cometh*, I do not pretend to know. But of this I am sure. Had he spent half as much time cutting it as he did writing it, his would have been not only a more acceptable script but a vastly better play.

*A backward glance at a figure, solitary and towering, whose
contribution to our theatre was unique, and whose life was
in many ways as tragic as any tragedy that he wrote.*

[1953]

O'NEILL IN RETROSPECT

SINCLAIR LEWIS was speaking, and his speech was heard round
the literary world. He was in Stockholm that December in 1930,
addressing the Swedish Academy as the recipient of the Nobel
Prize for Literature. American authors were very much on his
mind, and, if what he had to say about them enraged some, it
delighted more. His statements were heated with strong convictions; the sulphur of sarcasm was in his words. He was doing two
jobs at once. At the same time that he was gleefully burying some
of our more venerable and genteel writers who were guilty of the
common error of thinking they were living merely because they
were alive, he was championing those Americans whose vital merits he thought entitled them to the award he had won. Among
these was Eugene O'Neill.

Said he, "And had you chosen Mr. Eugene O'Neill, who has done
nothing much in American drama save to transform it utterly, in
ten or twelve years, from a false world of neat and competent trick-
ery to a world of splendor and fear and greatness, you would have
been reminded that he has done something far worse than scoff-
ing—he has seen life as not to be neatly arranged in the study of a
scholar but as a terrifying, magnificent, and often quite horrible
thing akin to the tornado, the earthquake, the devastating fire."

There were those at the time, though not many, who jeered at
such an estimate of O'Neill. Three years later there were those
whose jeers were louder when the Swedish Academy did choose
to honor him with the Nobel Prize. But today there are few with
any real knowledge of the theatre or of O'Neill's work who would
question the essence of Sinclair Lewis's evaluation or the rightness of the Swedish Academy's choice.

As a dramatist the position he occupied was unique, and so was his contribution. He stood alone—magnificently alone—having neither rivals nor equals. This is why his dying is like having a towering volcanic island slip overnight into the swallowing sea.

To be sure, he did not transform our stage "utterly" into a world of splendor or drive out all of its tricksters or save it from its falsities. No theatre in any age or country has ever been without its frauds, its hacks, and cheap artificers, and no individual, including Shakespeare, has ever completely silenced them. But O'Neill when at his best, and always by his example even when at his worst, did endow the American stage with a dignity, an honesty, an importance, and a glory which it had not possessed before.

He saw his job as a big one, and attacked it in a big way, having only contempt for those playwrights who, because they were "simply scribbling around on the surface of things," had "no more real status than a parlor entertainer." The large themes, the great and beckoning themes, no matter how somber, how difficult, or how monumentally treated, became more and more his concern. O'Neill may not have handled them satisfactorily in this play or that, but it was for them that he reached again and again with a dauntlessness unmatched by any other dramatist of his time. Passion did not frighten him nor violence appall him, and he dealt with the upheavals in the lives of his characters in the tumultuous terms described by Sinclair Lewis.

Surely no finer definition can be found of a serious writer's function than that given unwittingly by King Lear when, in one of the most beautiful of all Shakespearean speeches, he says to Cordelia after they have been captured, "We'll . . . take upon's the mystery of things as if we were God's spies." It was the mystery of things that O'Neill dared to take upon himself as a dramatist, and it was as one of God's spies that he was bold enough to observe the anguishes of his characters and pry into their darkest secrets.

The blind are not limited to those who cannot see. There are people blessed with sight who might just as well be blind since they see so little. There are others who make liars of their eyes by permitting them to see only what they want seen. The pleasant, the comforting, the pretty, the surface things, the world reduced to postcard hues, all bright, shiny, and shadowless—these and these only will they face. The depths and the shadows they avoid. Their fear of what they might see, if they had the courage to look, forces them to close their eyes on the mysteries of life.

Fortunately, O'Neill was made of sterner stuff and his faith was greater. He did not shrink from looking upon the Medusa's head and was not turned to stone because of having done so. He had the vision of the tragic dramatist, and hence knew the beauty ugliness can yield and the spiritual splendors which are the fruits of great pain greatly suffered.

It was odd that the leading tragic dramatist of our times should have been an American. To have Melpomene find shelter in Pollyanna's home was strange indeed, because we are not a people whose view of life is tragic. Laughter is supposed to be our affair and optimism a proof of our youth and our resilience. Yet the fact remains that no modern playwright in any country has been so tormented and inspired by such a true and persistent sense of the tragic as was O'Neill. He had to outgrow the tawdry irony of his first one-acts, put bathos behind him, and learn to control the melodramatist within him, who always imperiled his work, before he could write with the high intensity he achieved in *Desire under the Elms* and even more especially in the first two parts of *Mourning Becomes Electra.*

Few dramatists of O'Neill's importance wrote more unevenly than he. Few capable of soaring so high sank more often into the mires of the pretentious or the mediocre. This does not mean that he did not contribute greatly to the theatre of his time. He did. No one was a more fearless innovator than he. No one cared less for success. No one stretched the medium farther, tried so many forms, or was so bold in forcing the theatre to do what he wanted it to do. Among recent playwrights only Shaw enjoyed and deserved such pre-eminence.

If O'Neill wrote tragedies, he lived them, too. His own life was in many ways more tragic than the most tragic of his plays. The suicide of a son, his reported estrangement from his daughter when she married Chaplin, the hard struggle of his early days, his gradual withdrawal from the world, his long torture with Parkinson's disease, the loneliness of his last years, and his ultimate inability to write at all—these would have crushed less hardy spirits. But

O'Neill had something of the titan in him. It was this titan's spirit which gave such drive and strength to the mightiest of his plays and which was unmistakable in the weakest of them. It was the quality which most distinguished his work and because of which he so distinguished our theatre, endowing it with an excitement, a significance, and a splendor it had not known before and is not apt to know soon again.

3. American Borrowers of the Night

A young American playwright demonstrates his fierce, jabbing power in an angry one-act play about a New York taxi strike, and even more markedly in a warm and tender study of a Jewish family living in the Bronx.

[1935]

CLIFFORD ODETS

WAITING FOR LEFTY

YOU MAY disagree violently with Mr. Odets' ultimate solutions. You may regret the simplicity of his Communist panaceas and look askance at his willful stacking of the cards. You may say the results he achieves are easier than he has any right to be proud of. You may quibble about this or that lack which, if you are following his work closely, you are bound to find in it. You may point to scenes which he leaves as raw and as undeveloped as if he were dashing off a hurried first draft at midnight. You may even resent the constant angry jabs at the pit of your social stomach which he does not hesitate to administer during the course of an entire evening.

But you cannot fail to realize, in the presence of such of his one-acts as *Till the Day I Die* and *Waiting for Lefty,** that Mr. Odets is doing more than holding your attention. He is commanding it. As an emotionalist he has a sweeping, vigorous power which is as welcome as it is thundersome when encountered in our theatre.

In the writing of these two short plays Mr. Odets seems to have employed a machine gun rather than a pen. His one-acts are an-

---

* *Waiting for Lefty,* by Clifford Odets. Staged by Sanford Meisner and Mr. Odets. Setting by Alexander Chertoff. Produced by The Group Theatre, Inc. With a cast including Russell Collins, Lewis Leverett, Ruth Nelson, Herbert Ratner, Bob Lewis, Elia Kazan, Abner Biberman, Dorothy Patten, William Challee, Roman Bohnen, Clifford Odets, and George Heller. At the Longacre Theatre. Opened March 26, 1935.

gry dramas, almost fanatical in their single-trackedness, their force, and their militancy. They may be uncouth and gangling. They may leave you with a mind full of ready objections. They may appear to suggest what they really never succeed in doing—at least in terms of any abiding validity. Yet they have the rare virtue of so occupying your attention at the moment they are being played that, at that time, they—and they alone—seem to exist.

Mr. Odets has an extraordinary instinct for the theatre. He shows this in his peppery action and also in his clipped, human dialogue. He hits hard, and below the belt if need be. But at least he hits. The wallop he commands is a considerable one. He does not care whether he is employing an old Reinhardt trick—as he is when he uses "plants" in his audience to heighten the effect of his taxi-strike mass meeting in *Waiting for Lefty*—or whether he is borrowing the tactics of the Grand Guignol to intensify a scene in *Till the Day I Die* by having his hero's wrist smashed by the butt end of a revolver carried by one of his Nazi villains. The simple fact is that his blows rain hard and effectively. The Party ought to find this virtue enough, even if Mr. Odets, as a playwright of genuine promise, is certain to be dissatisfied with it if he continues to develop as a dramatist.

Of his two long one-acts on the Group Theatre's new bill, it is unquestionably *Waiting for Lefty* which is the better play. It bears re-seeing and remains in its present performance as effective as it first was when it was given at special matinees. *Till the Day I Die* has more tension than any of the anti-Nazi scripts yet produced in our theatre. Some of the seven scenes—in which it traces the hideous torture of a Communist who, after his capture by the Storm Troopers, is so abused that he finally has to commit suicide to square himself with the Party—are unforgettable in their bludgeoning strength. But it remains a play "suggested by a letter from Germany printed in *The New Masses*" rather than a play written from life.

It is well enough acted by the Group and has the vigor of its hatred. But it does not disclose Mr. Odets at his best, for the simple reason that it fails to find him writing out of his own experience, from any firsthand observation of character by means of which he can strengthen his melodramatic scenario or prevent it from seeming at times like a parody of itself. One thing is certain. Clifford Odets is a playwright of unusual potentialities, and the Group is to be congratulated upon having discovered him.

AWAKE AND SING!

Although the Group Theatre has produced several interesting plays in its time, and done some of them very well, it has never presented a more fluent production of so living a script as when it brought Clifford Odets' *Awake and Sing!** to the stage of the Belasco. Mr. Odets' one-act revolutionary drama about last year's taxi strike, known as *Waiting for Lefty*, did more than introduce Mr. Odets as an agitator of vigor. It indicated his uncommon ability to heighten the idioms of daily speech into dialogue as seemingly true to life as it was theatrically effective. Hence one looked forward to his first long play with an interest the writing of *Awake and Sing!* has more than justified.

Awake and Sing! finds Mr. Odets deserting the soapbox he so frankly mounted in *Waiting for Lefty* to write a well-balanced, meticulously observed, always interesting and ultimately quite moving drama about the problems of a Jewish family living in the Bronx. If, as is obviously the case, Mr. Odets has drunk deep of the Chekhovian springs before dealing with the Bergers, the simple fact remains that of all the American playwrights who have attempted to employ Chekhov's method none has used it to such advantage as Mr. Odets has in *Awake and Sing!*

Although his text and title are derived from the verse in Isaiah reading, "Awake and sing, ye that dwell in the dust," it is comforting to find Mr. Odets has not written one of those naïve scripts in which the right is always on one side. His Bergers represent many points of view. In fact, the main struggle his drama unfolds is not the battle for the Marxist cause in which the old grandfather believes, but the unheroic fight which the boy and the girl in the

---

* *Awake and Sing!* by Clifford Odets. Directed by Harold Clurman. Setting by Boris Aronson. Produced by The Group Theatre, Inc. With Art Smith, Stella Adler, Morris Carnovsky, Phoebe Brand, Jules Garfield, Roman Bohnen, Luther Adler, J. E. Bromberg, and Sanford Meisner. At the Belasco Theatre. Opened February 19, 1935.

Berger family have to put up in order to free themselves from all that is grubby and enslaving in their sacrificing parents' lives, and to go their own ways in the world.

The weakest thing about Mr. Odets' drama is his plotting. It is somewhat over-elaborate in its details and decidedly familiar in its outlines. There are moments in it—such a moment, for example, as the one in which the Jewish matriarch discovers that her unmarried daughter is to have a baby—which remind you not only of the Spewacks' unfortunate *Spring Song* but also of any number of other plays of Jewish tenement life.

What matters, however, in *Awake and Sing!* is not the story Mr. Odets is telling, but the rich, flavorsome way in which he has told it. If his method is Chekhovian in its pauses, its sudden and meaningful usage of what appear to be irrelevances, its autobiographical outbursts, its seeming indirection, its amplitude, its pathos, and its shrewd eye for the smallest characterizing details —all one can say in fairness is that, when it is re-used as well as Mr. Odets has re-used it, the Chekhovian method continues to be a rich and engrossing one.

What Mr. Odets adds to the technique he has borrowed from his master is an exuberant sense of humor, and an ear for the rhythms of highly colloquial speech which is very much his own. He is no *Potash and Perlmutter* recorder of Jewish family life. His Jewish idiom is no traditional comic banter interrupted arbitrarily with moments of stage pathos. He makes it plain that he knows whereof his characters speak. They command a vital flow of idioms which are as colorful as they are personal and as vigorous as they are effective.

An unfavorable first reaction, stated unfairly and dogmatically, to Mr. Anderson's verse drama about injustice and a shift in opinion brought about by a second seeing.

[1935]

MAXWELL ANDERSON'S *WINTERSET*

MAXWELL ANDERSON is a dramatist to be respected even if he is not always one who can be enjoyed or understood. He has courage, a mind of his own and—rarest of all—he has ears which he likes to bathe in sound. The petty cadences of daily speech and the dull uses to which even the best of words are put by most playwrights do not mark the limits of his interests. He is poet, not a dictaphone. As such he has a proper love for language and dares to take his chances with it even in a theatre where little or no respect for its singing beauties is shown.

He was at his most ambitious and, if I may say so, his least successful last night, when Guthrie McClintic gave a visually stunning but for the most part sadly muffled production to *Winterset*,* that new play of Mr. Anderson's which finds him attempting for the first time to array a contemporary theme in the poetic diction he employed successfully in *Elizabeth, the Queen* and *Mary of Scotland*.

It is not the modernity of his subject which bothers Mr. Anderson and his audiences in *Winterset*. It is his muddled treatment of a story often as cheaply plotted as it is confused in its thinking. Then, too, trouble lurks in the distressing fact that Mr. Anderson's melodramatic action and his frequently beautiful poetic outbursts do not live a single life. They are not—as the headlines in small-town newspapers used to say when announcing an elopement— "two hearts that beat as one." Married they may be, but it is Reno

---

* *Winterset,* by Maxwell Anderson. Directed by Guthrie McClintic. Setting by Jo Mielziner. With a cast including Eduardo Ciannelli, Harold Johnsrud, Margo, Theodore Hecht, Ruth Hammond, Richard Bennett, Burgess Meredith, and Abner Biberman. At the Martin Beck Theatre. Opened September 25, 1935.

rather than posterity which is considerably nearer for them than just around the corner. Each of them—the action and the poetry—requires its own individual thinking. Each of them insists upon going its own way and upon making separate demands on the attention.

By so doing, by failing to achieve that happy fusion which is necessary to all dramatic poetry, by dividing what is to be followed for its storytelling interest from what is to be listened to for the sheer joy of its music, they make it difficult to respond to whatever emotional force may be lurking in either the sound or the sense. At least, they make this response difficult at the Martin Beck, partly because of the poor diction of many of Mr. McClintic's actors but mainly, I feel confident, because of those qualities in Mr. Anderson's script which condemn it to being the kind of literary effort which always reads better than it plays.

In *Winterset* Mr. Anderson has not only turned his back on the tragedies of the Tudors but given vent in poetic form to some of that resentment which the Sacco-Vanzetti case left smoldering in his heart and which he stated in prose some years back with Harold Hickerson's aid in *Gods of the Lightning*. Under the high tower of one of New York's bridges, with its magical span in full view, Mr. Anderson has assembled a group of derelicts. His mob is a cross-section of the waterfront: Communists, sailors, beggars, and lovesick chippies who live at odds with the police and resent the simple pleasures they are denied by the mayor's ban on hurdy-gurdies. His main characters are part of that mob. They belong to the army of the Down-and-Outers who served as a chorus in *Within the Gates* and who peopled the whole of *Night's Lodging*.

Fifteen years have passed since the father of the tortured boy, who is Mr. Anderson's hero, has been "burned" for a crime he did not commit. During all these years the boy has sought to clear his father's memory. He has now come to New York in search of evidence. There he finds under the bridge—owing only to Mr. Anderson's reliance on poetic license—the now insane judge who presided at his father's trial, the gangster who really staged the holdup, and a Jewish boy who, since he was present on the fatal night and knows the identity of the real murderer, lives in constant fear of the gangster. The dead man's son falls in love with the Jewish boy's sister; upbraids the addled judge for his handling of the case; learns of his father's innocence from one of the gangster's enemies, and because of this knowledge is shot down, with his sweetheart, by the gangster's henchmen in a death scene which is so overlong that it likewise kills whatever interest in the play the first act may have aroused.

Although Mr. Anderson's verse is sonorous, alive with modern idioms, often beautiful, and welcome as an experiment, it proves strangely inactive in the theatre. It is more contemplative than dramatic, and more difficult to follow than is either good for the story or suitable to it. It has its purple moments of sheer pretentiousness when it guards the meaning of its lines as carefully as if they were so many state secrets. Mr. Anderson also dresses up some very indifferent generalities in some extremely gaudy plumage. But somehow one does not lose one's respect for his high intentions.

In his visualization of the bridge, Mr. Mielziner has provided *Winterset* with one of the finest backgrounds our contemporary theatre has seen. It is a setting of great majesty and beauty, full of strength, and alive with a poetry of its own. It is as simple, direct and impressive as one wishes the play were.

WINTERSET REVISITED

Ever since it opened, and was severely dealt with by me, Maxwell Anderson's *Winterset* has been more or less on my mind and conscience. Although not yet driven into the streets, as was the remorseful judge in Mr. Anderson's play, I have found myself disturbed by the finality with which I condemned a play that, whether or not it succeeds entirely in doing what it set out to do, is most certainly the kind of play our theatre is fortunate to have written and produced.

A second seeing has made me realize I was wrong about many things. The faults of the first-night performance kept me from surrendering to the excitement the production now engenders in those who see it. This excitement—which is the result partly of the music of Mr. Anderson's lines, partly of the shuddering tension of his melodramatic plotting, partly of the resentment against injustice which the two of these create, partly of Jo Mielziner's magnificent

settings, and partly of the proud way in which most of Mr. Mc-
Clintic's actors now speak their lines—is no common excitement.
It is born of that warming sense, radiated by the play, that the theatre is doing something worth the doing; that its aims are still high;
that its reach can still be heroic; that the mere melody of language,
which has some regard for sound and imagery and rhythm, continues to stir emotions in a way no prose, however eloquent, can
hope to do; and that playwriting can still function as the distilla-
tion of proud man's spirit.

A second seeing has not changed my mind entirely about Mr.
Anderson's verse. I feel now, as I did after the first night, that,
though it has moments of real beauty, it also includes moments of
windy pretentiousness. I still feel it has its many pedestrian
stretches; that the attention its music demands and the interest its
plot creates do not always coincide; that its "Shakespearean" comments are neither as frequent nor as probing as they might be,
and that it does not by any means offer a final or always happy solution to the metrical problems presented by a modern theme. I
still feel Mr. Anderson's play is confused and fuzzy; that something is wrong with either its language or its action which keeps it
from doing completely what it sets out to do. Once again I left the
theatre wishing the writing and the thinking were surer, stronger,
and more pointed than they are.

But these reservations and these doubts no longer blind me, as
they once did, to the positive and compelling virtues of *Winterset*.
I happily confess I can no longer deny—or resist—the strange and
fascinating spell Mr. Anderson's drama is able to cast over those
who sit before it, in spite of its obvious shortcomings. Whether
or not it does what it sets out to do remains a matter of individual
response. As far as I am concerned, it still fails when its last act
comes, and still leaves me unsatisfied. But I have now come to see
that, in the case of *Winterset*, what Mr. Anderson has tried to do
matters much more than what he may or may not have succeeded
in doing. His is the kind of play, although by no means the actual
play, upon which the hope and glory of the future theatre rest.

Some guesses at the many meanings Robert E. Sherwood may have had in mind when he wrote a melodrama about gangsterdom which is also a comedy and could symbolize the fossilization of our society.

[1935]

ALLEGORY AND MR. SHERWOOD

ONE OF the many pleasant features of Robert Sherwood's *The Petrified Forest** is that—in the best Pauline manner—it has been made to mean all things to all men. It is perfectly possible to enjoy it as the fantastic and very exciting and amusing melodrama it is, and to take, at its own story-telling worth, the tale it so adroitly unfolds about a literary panhandler who in the course of his wanderings falls in love with the waitress in the lunchroom of an Arizona gasoline station and is suddenly involved with a famous killer and his gang.

Or it is just as possible to share one's admiration for the melodrama—as a melodrama—with the very real admiration one at all times feels for the uncommonly skillful manner in which it has been directed by Arthur Hopkins and in which it is acted by such capable players as Humphrey Bogart, Charles Dow Clark, Peggy Conklin, and above all (as goes without saying) Leslie Howard.

Yet to those who want to look deeper there is more to find in *The Petrified Forest* than either an enjoyable melodrama or an excellent performance—even if the search for it is sometimes a challenging job. Unless I miss my guess, Mr. Sherwood has put his heart into the writing of a tantalizing allegory which, underneath its romantic and ingratiating trimmings, is as grimly stoical as one could imagine, and which is shot through with interesting implications.

---

* *The Petrified Forest*, by Robert Emmet Sherwood. Directed by Arthur Hopkins. Setting by Raymond Sovey. With a cast including Humphrey Bogart, Leslie Howard, Peggy Conklin, Charles Dow Clark, Blanche Sweet, Walter Vonnegut, Robert Porterfield, Robert Hudson, and John Alexander. At the Broadhurst Theatre. Opened January 7, 1935.

The petrified forest of his tale is no mere natural curiosity in far-off Arizona. It is the whole of our American civilization, which Mr. Sherwood believes to be fossilized. Some talk of Communism in the form of a mild argument is the first thing we hear in his desert lunchroom. Then his more prominent characters stray one by one into his drama. Little by little we begin to get some hints at what it is Mr. Sherwood is saying obliquely and in highly acceptable theatrical terms.

I may be entirely wrong, but I suspect he is telling us that the pioneer (as represented by the waitress's grandfather), who has no new country to explore and who can only look back wistfully to the days of Billy the Kid, is an obsolete figure deserving to die; that the football player (who works at the filling station and is also in love with the waitress) is an example of fatuous but physically courageous "third generation" youth whose only glorious hours were his college years; that the play's American Legionnaires are men who have ceased to be the men they once were in the particular emergency which created them; and that the hard-boiled killer and the disillusioned panhandler (or, if you will, the writer who has failed to do what he set out to do) are the last "rugged individualists" left in our established order as Mr. Sherwood has painted it. The waitress, who is a frustrated artist and who may yet become a great painter, is the hope of the future. For her sake the panhandler gladly persuades the killer to shoot him (without her knowing of his request) so that she can escape from her bondage in the stagnant present and so that the dream which has died in him may become an actuality in her.

I may misread Mr. Sherwood's meaning. His symbolism (which is written so that each spectator can make it his own) may prove somewhat mystifying on occasion. But his play is an engrossing one. It is as entertaining as it is stimulating, as exciting as it is provocative. In its quiet, indirect way it is the most ambitious of Mr. Sherwood's dramas. It has genuine felicity of thought as well as of phrasing. Throughout it protects its fantasy by a sense of humor which is as irresistible in its high spirits as it is neat in its statement. I have already hinted at the skill not only with which Mr. Hopkins has directed the production but with which it is acted. But I cannot resist adding that as good as Blanche Sweet (of movie fame) is as

the rebellious wife of a rich man, and commendable as are the performances of both Charles Dow Clark and Peggy Conklin as the
garrulous grandfather and the sensitive though profane waitress,
Mr. Bogart and Mr. Howard are even better. Mr. Bogart, who
since *Cradle Snatchers* has suffered a good deal from the drawbacks of type-casting, cuts loose from the suave young worldlings
he has played with varying success, to act the killer in an excellent
and quietly dominating "tough guy" way. Mr. Howard is to be
seen at his most charming, casual, and effective best as the literary panhandler. He brings a rich imagination to his playing. He
manages to combine something of the indescribable pathos of
Charlie Chaplin with the attractiveness of a matinee idol. He continues to be the completely ingratiating master he has always been
of pointed and humorous understatement.

*A radiant play by Thornton Wilder which, with the most
engulfing simplicity, presents the growing up and the growing down that is everyone's life and, though laid in a New
Hampshire village, has the human heart as its real setting.*

[1938]

WILDER'S *OUR TOWN*

*No scenery is required for this play. Perhaps a few dusty flats
may be seen leaning against the brick wall at the back of the stage.
. . . The Stage Manager not only moves forward and withdraws
the few properties that are required, but he reads from a typescript
the lines of all the minor characters. He reads them clearly, but with
little attempt at characterization, scarcely troubling himself to alter
his voice, even when he responds in the person of a child or a*

woman. As the curtain rises the Stage Manager is leaning lazily
against the proscenium pillar at the audience's left. He is smoking.

THE CHANCES are that if, during the course of one of those
parlor games which offer to hostesses and guests alike an ideal retreat from bridge and conversation, some playgoers were asked to
identify the play for which these stage directions were intended,
they would not guess *Julius Caesar* at the Mercury. Yet they might
be sufficiently foolhardy, in this season of sceneryless scripts, to
pick upon Mr. Blitzstein's *The Cradle Will Rock* or Mr. Wilder's
Our Town.* If they choose *Our Town*, because the demand for a
Stage Manager, leaning against the proscenium and smoking a
pipe, brought the genial Frank Craven to their minds, they would
at least be "getting warm," as the gamesters have it. Still they
would be very far from being "hot." Although Mr. Wilder is the
author of these stage directions, *Our Town* is not the play for
which they were intended. They were written for a charming one-
act of his called *The Happy Journey to Trenton and Camden*
which was copyrighted in 1931 and which can be found not only
in a volume of his short plays called *The Long Christmas Dinner*
but also in Professor Alexander Woollcott's first *Reader*.

I go back to Mr. Wilder's earlier usage of this frankly presentational form only because some theatregoers have been tempted to
talk and write about *Our Town* as if it were a production which
found Mr. Wilder and Mr. Harris trying to climb upon the Mercury's band wagon. It is important to note that when Mr. Wilder
sent the script of *The Happy Journey* to Washington seven years
ago, all he was attempting to copyright was the use to which he
put this particular form in this particular script, and not the form
itself. What really matters in all art is this very thing. Forms and
subjects are comparatively few. Yet they can be made as various
as are the talents of the many artists who have repossessed them.

Playgoers with short memories have found Benrimo's popu-
larization of the conventions of the Chinese stage in *The Yellow*

---

* *Our Town*, by Thornton Wilder. Produced by Jed Harris. With a cast in-
cluding Frank Craven, Jay Fassett, Raymond Roe, Tom Fadden, Evelyn
Varden, Helen Carew, John Craven, Marilyn Erskine, Charles Wiley, Jr.,
Martha Scott, Arthur Allen, Thomas W. Ross, Carrie Weller, Walter O. Hill,
Aline McDermott, Philip Coolidge, and Doro Merande. At the Henry Miller
Theatre. Opened February 4, 1938.

Jacket a convenient means of pigeonholing the outward form of *Our Town*. They might just as readily have recalled Quince, drawing up a bill of properties for *Pyramus and Thisbe*, "such as our play wants." Or the Chorus in *Henry V* asking the audience to let their "imaginary forces work." Or Mei Lan-fang. Or Ruth Draper and Cornelia Otis Skinner. Or the *Lutterworth Christmas Play*. Or the *Quem Quaeritis* trope. The form Mr. Wilder has used is as old as the theatre's ageless game of "let's pretend" and as new as the last time it has been employed effectively. The cooperation it asks an audience to contribute is at heart the very same cooperation which the most realistic and heavily documented productions invite playgoers to grant. The major difference is one of degree. Both types of production depend in the last analysis upon their audiences to supply that final belief which is the mandate under which all theatrical illusion operates. The form Mr. Wilder uses is franker, that is all. It does not attempt to hide the fact that it is make-believe. Instead it asks its audiences to do some of the work, to enter openly and gladly into the imaginative conspiracy known as the successful staging of a play.

What such a drama as Mr. Wilder's does, of course, is to strip theatrical illusion down to its essentials. Mr. Wilder has the best of good reasons for so doing. What he has done in *Our Town* is to strip life down to its essentials, too. There is nothing of the "stunt" about the old-new form he has employed. His form is the inevitable one his content demands. Indeed, so inevitable is it, and hence so right, that I, for one, must confess I lost all awareness of it merely as a form a few minutes after Mr. Craven had begun to set the stage by putting a few chairs in place. There have been those who have been bothered because the pantomime was not consistent, because real umbrellas were carried and no visible lawnmower was pushed, because naturalistic offstage sounds serve as echoes to the actions indicated on stage. I was not one of the bothered. I found myself surrendering, especially during the first two acts, to the spell of the beautiful and infinitely tender play Mr. Wilder has written.

John Anderson has likened *Our Town* to India's rope trick. He has pointed out it is the kind of play at which you either see the boy and the rope, or you don't. Although I refuse to admit there is anything of the fakir's touch in *Our Town*, I think I understand what Mr. Anderson means. Mr. Wilder's is, from the audience point of view, an exceptionally personal play. More than most plays, since by its sweet simplicity it seeks to get in contact with the inmost nerves of our living, it is the kind of drama which depends upon what we bring to it.

Mr. Wilder's play is concerned with the universal importance of those unimportant details which figure in the lives of men and women everywhere. His Grover's Corners is a New Hampshire town inhabited by decent New England people. The very averageness of these quiet, patient people in the point at which our lives and all living become a part of their experience. Yet Mr. Wilder's play involves more than a New England township. It burrows into the essence of the growing-up, the marrying, the living, and the dying of all of us who sit before it and are included by it. The task to which Mr. Wilder has set himself is one which Hardy had in mind in a far less human, more grandiose way, when he had the Chorus in *The Dynasts* say:

> *We'll close up Time, as a bird its van,*
> *We'll traverse Space, as Spirits can,*
> *Link pulses severed by leagues and years,*
> *Bring cradles into touch with biers.*

Mr. Wilder succeeds admirably in doing this. He shows us the simple pattern behind all simple living. He permits us to share in the inevitable anguishes and joys, the hopes and cruel separations to which men have been heir since the smoke puffed up the chimneys in Greece.

To my surprise I have encountered the complaint that Mr. Wilder's Grover's Corners is not like Middletown, U.S.A. It lacks brothels, race riots, huge factories, front-page scandals, social workers, union problems, lynchings, agitators, and strikes. The ears of its citizens are more familiar with the song of the robin than they are with the sirens of hurrying police cars. Its young people are stimulated to courtship by moonlight rather than by moonshine. They drink soda water instead of gin. Their rendezvous are held in drug stores rather than in night clubs. Their parents are hard-working people. They are quiet, self-respecting, God-fearing Yankees who get up early to do their day's work and meet their responsibilities and their losses without whining. The church organist may tipple, and thereby cause some gossip. But he is a neighbor, and the only good-neighbor policy they care about begins at home.

They do not murder or steal, borrow or beg, blackmail or oppress. Furthermore, they face the rushing years without complaints as comparatively happy mortals. Therefore to certain realists they seem unreal. "No historian," one critic has written "has ever claimed that a town like Mr. Wilder's was ever so idyllic as to be free from intolerance and injustice." Mr. Wilder does not make this claim himself. His small-town editor admits Grover's Corners is "little better behaved than most towns." Neither is Mr. Wilder working as the ordinary historian works. His interests are totally different interests.

He is not concerned with social trends, with economic conditions, with pivotal events, or glittering personalities. He sings not of arms and the man, but of those small events which loom so large in the daily lives of each of us, and which are usually unsung. His interest is the unexceptional, the average, the personal. His preoccupation is what lies beneath the surface and the routine of our lives, and is common to all our hearts and all our experience. It is not so much of the streets of a New England Town he writes as of the clean white spire which rises above them.

There are hundreds of fat books written each year on complicated subjects by authors who are not writers at all. But the ageless achievement of the true writers has always been to bring a new illumination to the simplest facts of life. That illumination has ever been a precious talent given only to a few. It is because Mr. Wilder brings this illumination to his picture of Grover's Corners that I admire *Our Town*. New Hampshire is the state which can claim Mr. Wilder's village, but his vision of it has been large enough to include all of us, no matter where we may come from, among its inhabitants. Personally, I should as soon think of condemning the Twenty-third Psalm because it lacks the factual observation of Sinclair Lewis and the social point of view of Granville Hicks as I would of accusing *Our Town* of being too unrealistically observed.

Anyone who hears only the milk bottles clink when early morning has come once again to Grover's Corners has not heard what

Mr. Wilder wants them to hear. These milk bottles are merely the spokesmen of time, symbols for the bigness of little things. In terms of the Gibbses and the Webbs, Mr. Wilder gives the pattern of repetition of each small day's planning, each small life's fruition and decline. He makes us feel the swift passage of the years, our blindness in meeting their race, the sense that our lives go rushing past so quickly that we have scarcely time in which to hold our breaths.

Only once does he fail us seriously. This is in his scene in the bleak graveyard on the hill. Although he seeks there to create the image of the dead who have lost their interest in life, he has not been able to capture the true greatness of vision which finds them at last unfettered from the minutiae of existence. Both his phrasing and his thinking are inadequate here. He chills the living by removing his dead even from compassion.

Nonetheless Mr. Wilder's is a remarkable play, one of the sagest, warmest, and most deeply human scripts to have come out of our theatre. It is the kind of play which suspends us in time, making us weep for our own vanished youth at the same time we are sobbing for the short-lived pleasures and sufferings which we know await our children. Geographically *Our Town* can be found at an imaginary place known as "Grover's Corners, Sultan County, New Hampshire, United States of America, Continent of North America, Western Hemisphere, the Earth, the Solar System, the Universe, the Mind of God." Mr. Wilder's play is laid in no imaginary place. It becomes a reality in the human heart.

When a religious experience, profound and glowing, and an adventure in theatregoing happen to be one and the same thing.

[1951]

THE EVER GREEN PASTURES

"GANGWAY! GANGWAY for de Lawd God Jehovah!" The modern theatre has produced no entrance cue better known or more affectionately remembered. These are words which even when read make the heart stand still. Heard again in the theatre, heard in the world as it now is, their impact is, if anything, greater than when they were spoken twenty-one years ago in that other simpler and comparatively civilized world in which *The Green Pastures** was first produced.

When Marc Connelly finished his script, he had written a far, far larger play than perhaps he realized. He had been reading Roark Bradford's *Ol' Man Adam an' His Chillun*, that delectable series of Bible stories as retold in the language of devout but untutored Louisiana Negroes. He decided to dramatize these Old Testament tales "about the time when the Lord walked the earth like a natural man."

To do this, Mr. Connelly invented the device of a Sunday-school class and in its preacher, Mr. Deshee, he found a narrator whose human habit it was to visualize the wonders of the Good Book in terms of the everyday experiences he and his people had had. Mr. Connelly went further. Although in some of his scenes he relied on Mr. Bradford's enchanting episodes and phrases, he contributed

---

* *The Green Pastures*, a fable by Marc Connelly, suggested by Roark Bradford's Southern sketches, *Ol' Man Adam an' His Chillun*. Directed by Mr. Connelly. Production designed by Robert Edmond Jones. Choir under the direction of Hall Johnson. Presented by The Wigreen Company in association with Harry Fromkes. With a cast including William Marshall, Ossie Davis, John Marriott, William Dillard, William Veasey, Rodger Alford, Alma L. Hubbard, Alonzo Bosan, Vinie Burrows, Avon Long, Milroy Ingram, and John Bouie. At the Broadway Theatre. Opened March 15, 1951.

not only new material but a new dimension to Mr. Bradford's sketches. Without losing their humor, a humor born of faith at its most innocent, he added a religious feeling as touching, as heart-sprung and all-conquering as that glorifying the spirituals which are an essential part of the production.

The resulting play may have been set in a Louisiana parish, but it shone with qualities which persuaded a whole nation to enroll among its parishioners. Delightful though it was as a work of art, it was more than an adventure in theatregoing. It was a religious experience of a profound and radiant sort. It still is. The years have not diminished its appeal.

No sermon has ever made goodness more contagious. Or so dispensed with preaching and the pulpit manner in illustrating what lies at the core of faith. Without irreverence it smiles in God's presence, worshipful but unterrified, and filled with the kind of happiness that in itself is an expression of love. If its virtuous mortals such as Noah, Moses, Hezdrel, and the rest are as unabashed when facing their Creator as are Gabriel, the cherubs, and the angels at the heavenly fish fry it is because all of them, heaven- or earth-born, are at ease with Him.

And why not? De Lawd in *The Green Pastures* may describe himself to Noah as "a god of wrath and vengeance" but surely wrath never took so gentle a form. Although from time to time he has to punish erring mankind, he seems more saddened than outraged by the need to do so. Sin is something he "jest can't stan'." Yet an eye for an eye or a tooth for a tooth is not among his demands. In spite of having thunderbolts at his disposal, he does not throw his weight about. Instead, he is the kindliest of administrators, tolerant and benign.

The tremendous burden he carries casts its shadow on his spirit even if it leaves his back unbent. He is well aware that "bein' de Lawd ain't no bed of roses," but he never loses his patience, his serenity, or his dignity. He looks and talks like a mortal. Plainly, however, he is more than that. When Noah, who has not recognized him, confesses, "I should have known you. I should have seen de glory," he is telling the truth, for the glory is there. It is there in homespun, uncanonical terms, and never more so than in the beautiful last scene in which the Crucifixion is hinted at and de Lawd realizes that God, too, must learn mercy through suffering.

Quite rightly *The Green Pastures* has long since been saluted and accepted as a folk play. This in itself raises its convention-destroying points. For folk art is supposed to be the product of simple people. It is thought of as being country-bred, hence blessed with that innocence which a dubious tradition is fond of believing rural. It is held to be the expression of peasants, mountaineers, or naïve artisans safely uncontaminated by any contact with cities or sophistication.

Although the Algonquin's Round Table, where the wags wagged and the "Vicious Circle" met, created its own lore, its members were scarcely of that jerkin, buckskin, or calico variety from which folklore springs. Mr. Bradford, a resident of New Orleans, did not belong to this group of latter-day Mermaid Taverners, but Mr. Connelly did. He is one of the wittiest of city slickers and easily distinguishable from Johnny Appleseed. The fleshpots are not foreign to him. Yet these two very knowing men did manage to "r'ar back" and pass that miracle of folk art which *The Green Pastures* is.

No murals in a Dalecarlian home personalizing a Bible story in native dress could be less self-conscious and more honest. Nor could any miracle play in old Coventry have had a more compelling and unstudied purity. When the Custard Maker offers de Lawd a ten-cent seegar, he is following precisely the same impulse which prompted the adoring shepherds in *The Pageant of the Shearmen and Tailors* to present the Christ Child with mittens, a pipe, and a hat.

No one who saw Richard B. Harrison during the five years that he appeared as de Lawd can have forgotten him. His was one of the modern theatre's most memorable performances, if, indeed, acting so seemingly free of calculation and so manifestly dependent upon the shining virtue of a man's own character can be described as a performance. Mr. Harrison's Jehovah added considerably "mo' firmament" to the lives of countless thousands of playgoers. His Lawd was elderly without being patriarchal; the perfect shepherd of a flock often lost and floundering; as human as the most mortal of his worshipers and yet possessed of some heaven-born goodness and authority.

The new Lawd of William Marshall is younger, a fact which in a world as overcrowded with problems as the present one is not without its consolations. His youthfulness (more accurately, his agelessness) of face endows him with an unwearied quality and speaks as comfortingly for his strength as does his giant size. Mr. Marshall does more, however, than tower physically above his angels and his earthlings. His dignity is no mere matter of physique. Human and lovable as he is, he too radiates "de glory," and radiates it abundantly.

Robert Edmond Jones' settings remain wonderful examples of the eloquence of simplicity. They have about them the same feeling of the morning of the world that so distinguishes the writing, the singing of the spirituals, and the production as a whole. Mr. Connelly's direction is once again inspired in the way in which it creates a lovely glowing reverence without ever being sanctimonious and manages to employ humor as a tender expression of devotion. Ossie Davis is an enchanting Gabriel; Alonzo Bosan a perfect Noah, impish but trusting; and John Marriott a profoundly moving Moses.

Let's face it with proper gratitude. *The Green Pastures* is a masterpiece. I came to recognize this early during its initial run and only wish I had had the sense to do so on the night of its opening. But then, to my shame, I missed the boat, which was quite a boat to miss considering it was the Ark. Though back in 1930 I saluted *The Green Pastures* as being brave and meritorious, I felt that, in spite of its charms and delights, it somehow fell short of its ultimate goal.

Perhaps my trouble was that when I first saw the play I had just finished reading Mr. Bradford's sketches and hence resented that grudging credit line which even now perplexes me by saying "suggested by" rather than "adapted from" or "based upon" *Ol' Man Adam an' His Chillun*. Or perhaps, being younger and far more academic, I was theatre-blinded and therefore guilty of judging a work of the spirit in dry technical terms.

Whatever my reasons may have been, this much I know: I was wrong. Not so wrong as that Bishop of the African Methodist Episcopal Church who, closing his eyes to the fundamentals of faith and the inherent sweetness of his people, has recently charged *The Green Pastures* with being "irreligious" and perpetuating "outmoded stereotypes" of Negroes. Even so, I was wrong. I was wrong because on that history-making first night I failed to recognize all that *The Green Pastures* represents dramatically, humanly, and spiritually.

A drama, unflinching and unforgettable, about a Southern schoolma'am who gradually loses her mind, having long since lost her amateur standing.

[1947]

SOUTHERN DISCOMFORT:
TENNESSEE WILLIAMS' *STREETCAR*

THE SENSE of being familiar with the new and the strange is no uncommon experience. We have all had it. We have found ourselves in places unvisited by us before, and yet felt unaccountably at home there. We have been confident that we were looking upon a sight already seen, if not in this existence, in another. Time, like geography, has played these tricks upon us. An unconscious past has been overlaid upon a conscious present. Although this intrusion has been brought about by no willful effort of our own, the result is an unsteady double vision. It is a vision which comes by flashes, and is made the more mysterious since it is the product of our feeling rather than our seeing.

It is precisely this mirage of familiarity which *A Streetcar Named Desire** is bound to raise in the minds of those who saw *The Glass Menagerie.* Tennessee Williams' new play *is* new. No

---

* *A Streetcar Named Desire,* by Tennessee Williams. Directed by Elia Kazan. Setting and lighting by Jo Mielziner. Costumes by Lucinda Ballard. Presented by Irene M. Selznick. With a cast including Jessica Tandy, Marlon Brando, Kim Hunter, Karl Malden, and Gee Gee James. At the Ethel Barrymore Theatre. Opened December 3, 1947.

one can question that. In story, setting, incident, and some of the details of its characterizations, it is a work quite different from its predecessor. It is better, deeper, richer than was that earlier drama in which the late Laurette Taylor gave a deathless performance as a faded, frumpy, Southern belle. Yet new as it is, it is scarcely novel. Even the surprises, many and startling, which it holds resemble more closely misfortunes engulfing old friends than misadventures overtaking new people.

The reasons for this are obvious. The mood of *Streetcar* is the same as that of *The Glass Menagerie*—only more so. Once again Mr. Williams is writing of the decay of Southern gentility. Once again he is a dramatist of despair, though this time frustration has been replaced by disintegration. Once again the world into which he leads us is full of shadows. It is a place of gauzes and transparencies in which the reality is suggested rather than reproduced. Although now set in New Orleans' French Quarter instead of in one of St. Louis's poor districts, the scene continues to be a slum. Its physical grubbiness remains a match for the emotional dilapidation of some of the characters it houses.

Mr. Williams' recurrent concern is with the misfits and the broken; with poor, self-deluded mortals who, in Emerson's phrase, are pendants to events, "only half attached, and that awkwardly," to the world they live in. They are victims of the same negation as the characters in *The Glass Menagerie*, and sustain themselves by identical illusions. If they lie to others, their major lie is to themselves. In this way only can they hope to make their intolerable lives tolerable. Such beauty as they know exists in their dreams. The surroundings in which they find themselves are once again as sordid as is their own living.

Blanche Du Bois, the central figure in Mr. Williams' new play, is a schoolteacher turned whore, whose mind ultimately collapses. Though younger and far more relentlessly explored as a character, she is a kissing-cousin of the dowdy Amanda who, in *The Glass Menagerie*, sustained herself by her unreliable prattle of a white-columned past. The man who falls in love with Blanche is the same Gentleman Caller with whom, in Mr. Williams' earlier script, Amanda's crippled daughter fell in love. His ingenuousness is unchanged; the childlike quality in a hulking male is no less constant.

He is as surely a victim of his mother as Amanda's sailor son, in Mr. Williams' previous work, was the victim of Amanda.

Yet, in spite of these seeming duplications, *A Streetcar Named Desire* is no replica of *The Glass Menagerie*. If it repeats certain patterns, it does so only to extend them. It is a maturer play; in fact, in some respects the most probing script to have been written by an American since Clifford Odets wrote *Awake and Sing!*

Mr. Williams, let me quickly add, is a dramatist who has little in common with Mr. Odets except for his eye for small details and the vitality with which he can project character in the round. The proletarian protest; the flaming indignation; the awareness of how good people are thwarted and wasted; the over-easy blaming of the "System" for this; the sense of writing with a pen held in a clenched fist; the pungent, sometimes too florid, phrases; and the positive hope for the better world that might come—all these Odetsian traits are missing. Yet both writers, different as they are, are plainly men who have read Chekhov with profit and affection.

In general, Mr. Williams has more in common with William Saroyan, another good Chekhovian, than with Mr. Odets. He has something of the same enchantment, of the same lyricism, of the same reliance upon music, and of the same ability to evoke mood and transcend realism. But Mr. Saroyan's innocence; his glistening, youthful belief in man's goodness; his flagrant, unashamed sentimentality; the bluebird's song he keeps singing in the presence of pain or in the midst of misery; and his eruptive, though dangerous, talent for what amounts to written improvisation are characteristics conspicuous by their absence in Mr. Williams.

Mr. Williams is a more meticulous craftsman. His is a manifestly slower, less impromptu manner of writing. His attitude toward his people is as merciless as Mr. Saroyan's is naïve. He is without illusions. His men and women are not large-spirited and noble, nor basically good. They are small and mean; above all, frustrated. He sees them as he believes they are, not as they would like to be or as he would like to have them. They have no secrets from him or from us when he is through with them. They may have little sweetness, but they are all lighted.

Mr. Williams' approach to them is as tough-minded as James M. Cain's would be. This is the more surprising, considering how

Chekhovian or Saroyanesque are his moods. Indeed, there are scenes in *A Streetcar Named Desire* which suggest the most unlikely of collaborations. They sound as if Mr. Cain and Mr. Saroyan had written them jointly. For the magic that one associates with Mr. Saroyan at his best is there. It is there in spite of the brutality of the action, the spiritual squalor of the heroine, the utter negation of the mood, and the sordidness of the episodes. Mr. Williams' new-old play is at once absorbing and appalling; poignant and amoral; drab and magical. Although a smear in a biological laboratory rather than "a slice of life," it has its haunting, moonlit aspects.

I doubt if any woman in any American play has been drawn more unsparingly than is Blanche Du Bois, the schoolteacher whose gradual descent into madness is followed in *A Streetcar Named Desire*. Strindberg could not have been more ruthless in dealing with her selfishness. He, however, would have hated her, where Mr. Williams, without pleading for her, understands—and would have us understand—what has brought about her decline. He passes no moral judgment. He does not condemn her. He allows her to destroy herself and invites us to watch her in the process.

Mr. Williams names an outside cause for the first unhinging of her mind—the fact that Blanche's husband, whom she loved dearly, had turned out to be a homosexual. Upon her discovery of his secret he had blown out his brains. Although this outward tragedy may have damaged her reason, Mr. Williams presents it as being by no means the only tragedy of Blanche Du Bois's life. Her abiding tragedy comes neither from her family's dwindling fortunes nor from her widow's grief. It is sprung from her own nature. From her uncontrollable duplicity. From her pathetic pretensions to gentility, even when she is known as a prostitute in the little town in which she was brought up. From her love of the refined when her life is devoted to coarseness. From the fastidiousness of her tastes and the wantonness of her desires. From her incapacity to live up to her dreams. Most particularly, from her selfishness and her vanity, which are insatiable.

Those who have read Mr. Williams' script (as I have not) assure me that, though scene after scene possesses merit, the real job of pulling it together and transforming it into a play has been done by Elia Kazan rather than by Mr. Williams. It is easy to believe this. Mr. Kazan's direction throughout is brilliantly creative. His imagination is at all times equal to Mr. Williams'. He succeeds in combining stylization with realism. He is able to capture to the full the inner no less than the outer action of the text. He knows when to jab a climax home, when to rely on mood, when to focus the attention pitilessly on the principals, or when to establish, in Reginald Marsh terms, the tenement atmosphere.

Jo Mielziner's share in the evening is as contributive as Mr. Kazan's. His setting is one of the most distinguished he has designed in his distinguished career. It consists of two dreary rooms on the first floor of a dilapidated building in New Orleans. These are flanked on one side by the bathroom in which Blanche takes incessant warm tubs, and on the other by iron stairs leading up to other flats housing other families whose lives, one gathers, are no less wretched and tumultuous. The walls of Mr. Mielziner's tenement are transparent. Through them the French Quarter can be seen. And in them a symbol exists for Mr. Williams' inward and outward approach to his people.

A proof of the virtues of Mr. Williams' new play is that everyone working upon it has been stimulated to do his best. As Blanche Du Bois, Jessica Tandy gives a memorable performance. She does not spare herself any more than Mr. Williams has spared his heroine. She dodges none of the exposures of the text by playing for sympathy. She is what Mr. Williams describes her as being. Her lies, her pathetic ardors, her drinking, her selfishness, and the encroachments of her madness are all clearly and unforgettably established. She has her school-ma'am moments and her interludes of pretended gentility, both of which are interrupted by sudden glimpses into the woman she truly is.

As the victim of momism Blanche almost lures into marriage, Karl Malden suggests movingly all that is trusting, naïve, good, and slow-witted in the character. Kim Hunter plays Blanche's self-effacing sister with warmth and tenderness. As her Polack husband, Marlon Brando is excellent. It is almost impossible to realize that this is the same Mr. Brando who, not long ago, was giving so ineffectual a performance as Marchbanks in Miss Cornell's *Candida*. Where he then seemed weak and plainly inadequate, he is now all force and fire, a Rodin model, a young Louis Wolheim with Luther Adler's explosiveness.

Although no one is apt to describe Mr. Williams' new play as pleasant, its power is incontestable. It could stand cutting, and certain of its scenes, such as its final one, might be bettered by rewriting. Yet both as written and as staged, one thing is certain. *A Streetcar Named Desire* is more than a work of promise. It is an achievement of unusual and exciting distinction.

Arthur Miller's deeply moving tragedy of the ebb-tide years of a little man who lives by the wrong dream and is fated to discover his own smallness.

[1949]

DEATH OF A SALESMAN

GEORGE JEAN NATHAN once described a certain actress's Camille as being the first Camille he had ever seen who had died of catarrh. This reduction in scale of a major disease to an unpleasant annoyance is symptomatic of more than the acting practice of the contemporary stage. Even our dramatists, at least most of them, tend in their writing, so to speak, to turn t.b. into a sniffle. They seem ashamed of the big things, embarrassed by the raw emotions, afraid of the naked passions, and unaware of life's brutalities and tolls.

Of understatement they make a fetish. They have all the reticences and timidities of the overcivilized and undemonstrative. They pride themselves upon writing around a scene rather than from or to it; upon what they hold back instead of upon what they release. They paint with pastels, not oils, and dodge the primary anguishes as they would the primary colors.

Their characters belong to an anemic brood. Lacking blood, they lack not only violence but humanity. They are the puppets of contrivance, not the victims of circumstance or themselves. They are apt to be shadows without substance, surfaces without depths. They can be found in the *dramatis personae* but not in the telephone book. If they have hearts, their murmurings are seldom audible. They neither hear nor allow us to hear those inner whisperings of hope, fear, despair, or joy, which are the true accompaniment to spoken words. Life may hurt them, but they do not suffer from the wounds it gives them so that we, watching them, are wounded ourselves and suffer with them.

This willingness, this ability, to strike unflinchingly upon the anvil of human sorrow is one of the reasons for O'Neill's preeminence and for the respect in which we hold the best work of Clifford Odets and Tennessee Williams. It is also the source of Arthur Miller's unique strength and explains why his fine new play, *Death of a Salesman,** is an experience at once pulverizing and welcome.

Mr. Miller is, of course, remembered as the author of *Focus,* a vigorous and terrifying novel about anti-Semitism, and best known for *All My Sons,* which won the New York Critics Award two seasons back. Although that earlier play lacked the simplicity, hence the muscularity, of Mr. Miller's novel, it was notable for its force. Overelaborate as it may have been, it introduced a new and unmistakable talent. If as a young man's script it took advantage of its right to betray influences, these at least were of the best. They were Ibsen and Chekhov. The doctor who wandered in from next door might have been extradited from *The Three Sisters.* The symbolical use to which the apple tree was put was pure Ibsen. So, too, was the manner in which the action was maneuvered from the present back into the past in order to rush forward. Even so, Mr. Miller's own voice could be heard in *All My Sons,* rising strong and clear above those other voices. It was a voice that deserved the attention and admiration it won. It was not afraid of being raised. It spoke with heat, fervor, and compassion. Moreover, it had something to say.

---

* *Death of a Salesman,* by Arthur Miller. Directed by Elia Kazan. Setting and lighting by Jo Mielziner. Costumes by Julia Sze. Incidental music by Alex North. Presented by Kermit Bloomgarden and Walter Fried. With Lee J. Cobb, Arthur Kennedy, Mildred Dunnock, Howard Smith, Thomas Chalmers, Cameron Mitchell, Alan Hewitt, Don Keefer, Winnifred Cushing, Ann Driscoll, Tom Pedi, Constance Ford, and Hope Cameron. At the Morosco. Opened February 10, 1949.

In *Death of a Salesman* this same voice can be heard again. It has deepened in tone, developed wonderfully in modulation, and gained in carrying power. Its authority has become full-grown. Relying on no borrowed accents, it now speaks in terms of complete accomplishment rather than exciting promise. Indeed, it is released in a play which provides one of the modern theatre's most overpowering evenings.

How good the writing of this or that of Mr. Miller's individual scenes may be, I do not know. Nor do I really care. When hit in the face, you do not bother to count the knuckles which strike you. All that matters, all you remember, is the staggering impact of the blow. Mr. Miller's is a terrific wallop, as furious in its onslaught on the heart as on the head. His play is the most poignant statement of man as he must face himself to have come out of our theatre. It finds the stuffs of life so mixed with the stuffs of the stage that they become one and indivisible.

If the proper study of mankind is man, man's inescapable problem is himself—what he would like to be, what he is, what he is not, and yet what he must live and die with. These are the moving, everyday, all-inclusive subjects with which Mr. Miller deals in *Death of a Salesman*. He handles them unflinchingly, with enormous sympathy, with genuine imagination, and in a mood which neither the prose of his dialogue nor the reality of his probing can rob of its poetry. Moreover, he has the wisdom and the insight not to blame the "system," in Mr. Odets' fashion, for what are the inner frailties and shortcomings of the individual. His rightful concern is with the dilemmas which are timeless in the drama because they are timeless in life.

Mr. Miller's play is a tragedy modern and personal, not classic and heroic. Its central figure is a little man sentenced to discover his smallness rather than a big man undone by his greatness. Although he happens to be a salesman tested and found wanting by his own very special crises, all of us sitting out front are bound to be shaken, long before the evening is over, by finding something of ourselves in him.

Mr. Miller's Willy Loman is a family man, father of two sons. He is sixty-three and has grubbed hard all his life. He has never possessed either the daring or the gold-winning luck of his prospector brother, who wanders through the play as a somewhat shadowy symbol of success but a necessary contrast. Stupid, limited, and confused as Willy Loman may have been, however, no one could have questioned his industry or his loyalty to his family and his firm. He has loved his sons and, when they were growing up, been rewarded by the warmth of their returned love. He loves his wife, too, and has been unfaithful to her only because of his acute, aching loneliness when on the road.

He has lived on his smile and on his hopes; survived from sale to sale; been sustained by the illusion that he has countless friends in his territory, that everything will be all right, that he is a success, and that his boys will be successes also. His misfortune is that he has gone through life as an eternal adolescent, as someone who has not dared to take stock, as someone who never knew who he was. His personality has been his profession; his energy, his protection. His major ambition has been not only to be liked, but well liked. His ideal for himself and for his sons has stopped with an easy, back-slapping, sports-loving, locker-room popularity. More than ruining his sons so that one has become a woman chaser and the other a thief, his standards have turned both boys against their father.

When Mr. Miller's play begins, Willy Loman has reached the ebb-tide years. He is too old and worn out to continue traveling. His back aches when he stoops to lift the heavy sample cases that were once his pride. His tired, wandering mind makes it unsafe for him to drive the car which has carried him from one town and sale to the next. His sons see through him and despise him. His wife sees through him and defends him, knowing him to be better than most and, at any rate, well intentioned. What is far worse, when he is fired from his job he begins to see through himself. He realizes he is, and has been, a failure. Hence his deliberate smashup in his car in order to bring in some money for his family and make the final payment on his home when there is almost no one left who wants to live in it.

Although *Death of a Salesman* is set in the present, it finds time and space to include the past. It plays the agonies of the moment of collapse against the pleasures and sorrows of recollected episodes. Mr. Miller is interested in more than the life and fate of his central character. His scene seems to be Willy Loman's mind and heart no less than his home. What we see might just as well be what Willy Loman thinks, feels, fears, or remembers as what we see him doing. This gives the play a double and successful exposure in time. It makes possible the constant fusion of what has been and what is. It also enables it to achieve a greater reality by having been freed from the fetters of realism.

Once again Mr. Miller shows how fearless and perceptive an emotionalist he is. He writes boldly and brilliantly about the way in which we disappoint those we love by having disappointed ourselves. He knows the torment of family tensions, the compensations of friendship, and the heartbreak that goes with broken pride and lost confidence. He is aware of the loyalties, not blind but open-eyed, which are needed to support mortals in their loneliness. The anatomy of failure, the pathos of age, and the tragedy of those years when a life begins to slip down the hill it has labored to climb are subjects at which he excels.

The quality and intensity of his writing can perhaps best be suggested by letting Mr. Miller speak for himself, or rather by allowing his characters to speak for him, in a single scene, in fact, in the concluding one. It is then that Willy's wife, his two sons, and his old friend move away from Jo Mielziner's brilliantly simple and imaginative multiple setting, and advance to the footlights. It is then that Mr. Miller's words supply a scenery of their own. Willy Loman, the failure and suicide, has supposedly just been buried, and all of us are at his grave, including his wife who wants to cry but cannot and who keeps thinking that it is just as if he were off on another trip.

"You don't understand," says Willy's friend, defending Willy from one of his sons. "Willy was a salesman. And for a salesman, there is no rock bottom to the life. He don't put a bolt to a nut, he don't tell you the law or give you medicine. He's a man way out there in the blue, ridin' on a smile and a shoeshine. And when they start not smilin' back—that's an earthquake. And then you get yourself a couple spots on your hat, and you're finished. Nobody dast blame this man. A salesman is got to dream, boy. It comes with the territory."

The production of *Death of a Salesman* is as sensitive, human, and powerful as the writing. Elia Kazan has solved, and solved superbly, what must have been a difficult and challenging problem. He captures to the full the mood and heartbreak of the script.

He does this without ever surrendering to sentimentality. He manages to mingle the present and the past, the moment and the memory, so that their intertwining raises no questions and causes no confusions. His direction, so glorious in its vigor, is no less considerate of those small details which can be both mountainous and momentous in daily living.

It would be hard to name a play more fortunate in its casting than *Death of a Salesman*. All its actors—especially Arthur Kennedy and Cameron Mitchell as the two sons, and Howard Smith as the friend—act with such skill and conviction that the line of demarcation between being and pretending seems abolished. The script's humanity has taken possession of their playing and is an integral part of their performances.

Special mention must be made of Lee J. Cobb and Mildred Dunnock as the salesman, Willy Loman, and his wife, Linda. Miss Dunnock is all heart, devotion, simplicity. She is unfooled but unfailing. She is the smiling, mothering, hard-worked, good wife, the victim of her husband's budget. She is the nourisher of his dreams, even when she knows they are only dreams; the feeder of his self-esteem. If she is beyond whining or nagging, she is above self-pity. She is the marriage vow—"for better for worse, for richer for poorer, in sickness and in health"—made flesh, slight of body but strong of faith.

Mr. Cobb's Willy Loman is irresistibly touching and wonderfully unsparing. He is a great shaggy bison of a man seen at that moment of defeat when he is deserted by the herd and can no longer run with it. Mr. Cobb makes clear the pathetic extent to which the herd has been Willy's life. He also communicates the fatigue of Willy's mind and body and that boyish hope and buoyancy which his heart still retains. Age, however, is his enemy. He is condemned by it. He can no more escape from it than he can from himself. The confusions, the weakness, the goodness, the stupidity, and the self-sustaining illusions which are Willy—all these are established by Mr. Cobb. Seldom has an average man at the moment of his breaking been characterized with such exceptional skill.

Did Willy Loman, so happy with a batch of cement when puttering around the house, or when acquaintances on the road smiled back at him, fail to find out who he was? Did this man, who worked so hard and meant so well, dream the wrong dream? At least he was willing to die by that dream, even when it had collapsed for him. He was a breadwinner almost to the end, and a breadwinner even in his death. Did the world walk out on him, and his sons see through him? At any rate he could boast one friend who believed in him and thought his had been a good dream, "the only dream you can have." Who knows? Who can say? One thing is certain. No one could have raised the question more movingly or compassionately than Arthur Miller.

4. Headmaster
to the Universe—G.B.S.

The life story of a man who, by his own admission, abandoned a regular job to become a professional man of genius, and encountered no difficulties at this unusual task.

[1942]

SATAN, SAINT, AND SUPERMAN

H ESKETH PEARSON must take his place among the welcome
deliverers. Had he, in his *G.B.S.: A Full Length Portrait,** done nothing except save Mr. Shaw from Archibald Henderson, he would have done enough to win the world's gratitude. Until Mr. Pearson's book appeared, Professor Henderson was the official biographer. Twice, in 1911 and in 1932, he had played chronicler to the Sage of Ayot St. Lawrence. His were the "authorized" testaments. All other versions of the Shavian saga were aprocrypha.

A photograph of Mr. Henderson sent to Mr. Shaw at Mr. Shaw's request had caused G.B.S., in the best tradition of a matrimonial bureau, to put his life in Mr. Henderson's hands. "You look like the man who can do the job," scribbled Mr. Shaw on a fateful postcard. And the misalliance took place.

No one who has suffered through the eight hundred pages of Mr. Henderson's *Bernard Shaw: Playboy and Prophet* can ever again subscribe to the popular fallacy which insists the camera does not lie. Mr. Henderson's is an indispensable book—at least it was until Mr. Pearson's appeared. Its being so only made it the more infuriating even as it makes Mr. Pearson's biography the more welcome.

Mr. Henderson's work had its virtues. It was based on solid research, crowded with excellent illustrations, and filled with statistics elsewhere inaccessible. It was enlivened by countless quotations from Mr. Shaw and written with great affection. The trouble was that Mr. Henderson's love for Mr. Shaw was outdistanced only by Mr. Henderson's love for himself. Mr. Henderson could not keep himself out of the narrative. On page after page

---

* New York: Harper & Brothers, 1942.

the static of his thunderous ego drowned out a fascinating program. What was supposed to be Mr. Shaw's life managed to become Mr. Henderson's scrapbook. The result was a volume, at once invaluable and nauseating, which at many embarrassing moments sounded like the kind of biography of Voltaire that Lou Tellegen might have written.

Mr. Pearson's *G.B.S.* has the high virtue of letting Mr. Shaw speak for himself. The Elderly Gentleman—more accurately The Grand Old Boy—now testifies without a midget sitting on his lap. And what magnificent testimony in behalf of truth and sanity, wit and buffoonery, wisdom and originality, paradox and courage, literary brilliance and the Life Force, Mr. Shaw's own words provide in his behalf!

Although occasionally Mr. Pearson runs the risk of crossing swords with Mr. Shaw, his volume is not a critical study of Mr. Shaw's works. Mr. Pearson knows the market bulges with such tomes. Wisely enough, he does not add to the bulk of these by-products, however deadly and hence un-Shavian, or sprightly and therefore Shavian. Shaw the man, or rather the superman, is his concern; the G.B.S. who as a figure, a personality, and a hydra-headed genius is more fascinating than the finest of his works. "Shaw," says Mr. Pearson, "is the greatest 'character' of his age and his biography should be as Boswellian as the wit of man can make it. I have done my best to Boswellize him."

It is as unnecessary as it would be ungrateful to point out that Mr. Pearson's best is not Boswell's or anything approaching it. It is, however, a very capable best. The book it has produced is not only the best life of Shaw that has been or is likely to be written, but a biography of genuine distinction. In Mr. Shaw, Mr. Pearson has the most colorful of the many literary figures—Hazlitt, Henry Labouchere, Tom Paine, W. S. Gilbert, yes, and even William Shakespeare—that he has so far dealt with. Indeed, he has a personage no less formidable, and certainly far more ingratiating, than the great Dr. Johnson himself.

The man who writes Mr. Shaw's life faces an assignment at once back-breaking and easy. The difficulties spring from the fact that during these long, long decades of ceaseless activity, Mr. Shaw has lived more lives than the average regiment can lose. Moreover, he has lived them simultaneously. He has taken all betterment rather than all learning for his province. It is not his fault, or mankind's entire loss, if the universe is not built in his image. The empire of Mr. Shaw's thought has been as far-flung as that of the England of his incomplete adoption. As an Ibsenite, a Wagnerian, a Fabian, a Communist, a Fascist; as a critic of painting, music, and the theatre; as an authority on prize-fighting, Karl Marx, and religions; as a defender of the rights of the little man and yet a subscriber to the hero myth; as a vestryman, a committeeman, a preface-writer, and a dramatist; as an industrious novelist however bad and a brilliant speaker however industrious; as a mystic, a super-journalist, a vegetarian, a Puritan, an anti-vivisectionist, and a prophet, he has played court jester and merciless corrector to an ailing world.

The biographer who would keep up with Mr. Shaw must be strong of wind and stronger of mind. His task would be a hopeless one had not Mr. Shaw in numberless letters, prefaces, articles, and plays thrown out to his biographers his own life line. On the topic of G.B.S., Mr. Shaw has never been either reticent or dull. All his writing, regardless of its subject matter, has been autobiographical. Unlike the other authors, however, who love to dot their capital I's, Mr. Shaw has always written about more than himself, even when G.B.S. has been his theme.

With scissors, paste, a sharp pencil, some stubborn prejudices (such as an expressed willingness to die rather than read Karl Marx), and yet a discerning mind, Mr. Pearson has pored over Mr. Shaw's works and letters to assemble his full-length portrait. He plays m.c. not to a guest star but to a man who in himself is a whole major network, and who was the best of broadcasters long before the radio was thought of. Mr. Pearson's copy is on the whole excellently expository—clear, helpful, vigorous.

The sources from which it is drawn are, as they would have to be, too numerous for Mr. Pearson to catalogue in full. Of course, they include the superb autobiographical preface to *Immaturity*. And such a dazzling and little known collection of Shavian essays as *Pen Portraits and Reviews*. And *What I Really Wrote about the War*. And the tracts, the prefaces, the plays, the criticisms, and the untiring correspondence of that Mr. Shaw who writes as easily as most people breathe and almost always with a noontime brilliance. Mention is even made of Mr. Henderson's tome, and of Frank Harris's mendacious recollections, the post-humous publication of which under Mr. Shaw's editing, with the facts corrected and the unfavorable verdicts left unchanged, was a typical act of Mr. Shaw's large spirit.

Mr. Pearson's final source, however, has been Mr. Shaw himself, the Mr. Shaw he has long known. On every doubtful point he has consulted that He-Ancient who is one of the youngest men alive, and who as an octogenarian lives in a world that has not yet caught up with him. He has prodded Mr. Shaw with questions skillfully designed to provoke him into response; baited him, badgered him, disagreed with him, challenged him. The revelations thus garnered in letters from, and conversations with, the world's best Shavian are among the most fascinating features of a fascinating volume.

All the many Bernard Shaws emerge here, one chapter at a time. First there is the Shaw born not an upstart but a "downstart," as he described it, in Dublin four years before our Civil War began. This was the young Shaw, raised in shabby gentility, who knew such poverty as can only be known to the second son of a second son of a second son; the Shaw whose family with pride traced its ancestry back to "the third son of that immortalized yet unborn Thane of Fife who, invulnerable to normally accouched swordsmen, laid on and slew Macbeth."

This was the Shaw who inherited his imagination and his intimate knowledge of music from his mother, and from his drunken father "a humorous sense of anti-climax" which he says he used to great effect when he became a writer of comedy. It was from seeing his father drunk—merrily, unashamedly drunk again and again—that he learned to make "trifles of tragedies" instead of "tragedies of trifles."

Thereafter in the most uproarious of Mr. Shaw's own exuberant words on the subject of himself, the multifarious Shaws appear—the child who uttered his warm prayers in sonata form in bed; the boy who resisted the contaminations of orthodox schooling; the youngster who abandoned clerkdom because to his horror he was succeeding at it; and the man who in 1876 fled with his mother to London, there to live unblushingly for nine years off her limited resources as an "incorrigible unemployable."

These years of maternal dependency were all-important and

fruitful ones. They were the years during which the young Shaw dared to fill his mind when most young men feel duty-bound to think only about filling their pockets. These were the years when, marble-pale of face and with scraggly hints of that red beard which was to become world-famous, Mr. Shaw was visiting daily his university, the British Museum, and was seen there by William Archer with the score of *Tristan und Isolde* spread out typically enough side by side on a table with *Das Kapital*. This was the Shaw whose life was changed by hearing Henry George, who had joined the Zetetical Society, turned Fabian, and met William Morris. It was the Shaw whose mind was already "strongly individualistic, atheistic, Malthusian, evolutionary, Ingersollian, Darwinian, Herbert Spencerian, etc." It was the Shaw who was teaching himself to speak without notes on all kinds of subjects, and, in general, relishing "poverty, potatoes, and politics" and busily writing those five novels, the best of which—*Cashel Byron's Profession*—caused Stevenson to groan, "My God, what women!" Although Shaw may have been an unemployable, he was never unemployed. He had already learned to work the way his father drank. He was filling that Shavian reservoir of thought, opinion, facts, and paradoxes; that reservoir which was to break across the world as inexhaustibly as an ocean driven by a hurricane.

Thereafter the other Shaws follow. Shaw the art critic, the music critic, the champion of Wagner and Ibsen, the arch-foe of Henry Irving, the dramatic critic who could boast after four years' service that he had changed Shakespeare from "a divinity and a bore" into "a fellow creature," and who was bold enough to take the theatre seriously "as a factory of thought, a prompter of conscience, an elucidator of social conduct, an armory against despair and dullness, and a temple of the Ascent of Man"—these are dealt with in turn. So are all those other Shaws—Shaw the lover, in a chapter that is brutally frank and not designed for Southern Colonels of the old school; Shaw, so cold of body and so warm of phrase, who was always dashing off notes to women, even after his marriage to the wealthy Charlotte Payne-Townshend, and who in those conspiratorial and enchanting letters to Ellen Terry confessed he was "a writing machine" unendowed with "the small-change of love"; Shaw the dramatist who, by being able to put his critical theories into practice, reoriented and liberated the

English-speaking stage, and who little by little became a world figure. Yes, and the Shaw whose unpopularity sank to new lows and whose courage rose to new heights during the first war because of his insistence upon stating the cold truth as he saw it even in the heat of battle; the dramatist whose career reached its zenith with *Saint Joan*; and finally the white-bearded Mephistopheles whose speech at the Metropolitan Opera House did him no good in this country, who has had kind words to say of Mussolini, who visited Russia with Lady Astor, and who has kept on writing, writing, writing, even when his later plays, with the exception of *In Good King Charles's Golden Days,* have proven Mr. Shaw's mortality by showing a steady falling off—all of these G.B.S.'s are sprightly pigments in Mr. Pearson's full-length portrait.

In other words, in Mr. Pearson's biography Mr. Shaw is assembled, with Mr. Shaw's constant and invaluable aid, in the full, baffling, and magnificent range of his extraordinary talents as both a man and a writer. Almost any devoted Shavian could point to anecdotes, letters, prefatory confessions, and other source materials which here and there Mr. Pearson has chosen to omit or for lack of space has had to abbreviate. Almost any student would have to regret that, in the back of his indispensable and lively book, Mr. Pearson has not indicated, by page and title, the Shavian works from which he is quoting, if for no other reason than that the samples he has given tempt one to read further. Even so, Mr. Pearson has done glowing justice to his subject. This is the highest of high praise because no literary biographer has ever had a more intriguing, brilliant, entertaining, versatile, or provocative subject than Mr. Shaw.

Almost thirty years ago Max Beerbohm drew a caricature in which a very comfortable G.B.S. was pictured standing on his head in the presence of a stranger. The caption read, "Mild surprise of one who, revisiting England after a long absence, finds that the dear fellow has not moved." To many people, especially to those who have not read him or who, worse still, have misread him, Mr. Shaw has been no more than that perverse upside-down fellow in Beerbohm's caricature. They have been scandalized by his irreverence, shocked by his immodesty, outraged by his iconoclasm, maddened by his brilliance, horrified by his impersonality, terrified by his economics, irritated by his sanity, and infuriated by his good humor. Yet the truth is that, while pretending to stand on his head, Mr. Shaw has held his head high and turned the Victorian world of his youth upside down. A good many dullards cannot forgive him for having made them uncomfortable or for having dared to deal gaily with serious subjects.

Disagreement has been more than Mr. Shaw's stock-in-trade; it has been his prophetic duty no less surely than gleeful overstatement has served him as one of the most provocative of his virtuoso talents. "It is an instinct with me," he once confessed, "to attack every idea which has been full grown for ten years, especially if it claims to be the foundation of all human society." The strategy of that attack was perhaps best revealed by Mr. Shaw in one of his blasts at Shakespeare. "To read *Cymbeline*," he wrote, "and to think of Goethe, of Wagner, of Ibsen, is, for me, to imperil *the habit of studied moderation of statement which years of public responsibility as a journalist have made almost second nature to me.*" In those words which I have italicized, in the mock seriousness with which "studied moderation of statement" and "public responsibility as a journalist" are wedded, and especially in that crowning "almost," is as good a key as can be found to the Shavian method.

Always a propagandist, Mr. Shaw has shortened the life of many of his plays by turning them into battlefields for contemporary ideas. It is because his ideas have won that what was newest in these scripts now seems old-fashioned. They have been dated not so much by Mr. Shaw's concerns as by his victories. *Androcles and the Lion, Caesar and Cleopatra, Saint Joan, Heartbreak House,* and *Candida* may just now seem to be among the Shavian scripts most fated to endure. Yet the least of Mr. Shaw's plays contain proofs of that superior mind, that inexhaustible wit, that dazzling sanity, that wonderful cleanliness of spirit, and that superb command of the language which are his and his alone. Even when the plays fail, there are always the prefaces to fall back on, those prefaces which are among the glories of the language, and which are spread out before the dramas that follow them not as teacups are placed in saucers, but like huge soup tureens set down on doilies. Then there are those amazing letters, written always with the fluency of the writing man to whom writing is a joy, not a labor, who has something to express which must be expressed, and who is one of the few people alive who still writes a letter as if the telephone had never been invented.

Although Mr. Shaw is always linked with Ibsen in any mention of the drama of ideas, no two men could be more dissimilar. What a satyr is to an old grizzly, what Mephistopheles is to Grumpy, what a tarantula is to a bison, what Pan is to Cotton Mather, or what ever-green Ireland is to the frozen fjords, that accretion of paradoxes known to the world as G.B.S. is to Ibsen. It is not because Ibsen frowned where Shaw laughed that the two men are different. Or because Ibsen's characters were drawn by a psychologist who could remember others, where those of G.B.S. have largely been dummies speaking for a ventriloquist who could not forget himself. Or because the blight of bismuth is upon the Master Builder's admirable efforts where Shaw's talents are volcanically eruptive. The truth is that Shaw's is by far the larger mind, and, what is more, by far the larger spirit. Where the one wrote with labor, the other has written because he has had no other choice.

Mr. Shaw is one of the greatest instinctive writers literature has known. He has been an artist in spite of himself; in spite, too, of his hatred of the breed. One feels that silence is the only form of expression to have cost him any pain. His giant intellect, his irrepressible wit, his magnanimous spirit—all these are kept in a constant state of cross-ventilation by his ever-articulate genius. The reticence of an artist he does not know, but the eloquence of the literary artist is always at his command. His prose—now mystical and full of music, now Puckish in its mischief—has always the easy cadences of speech.

One does not merely read Mr. Shaw; one hears him speak. Mrs. Patrick Campbell insisted that Mr. Shaw had a thrush in his throat. Certainly there is music in his prose. "I have never aimed at style in my life," he confessed, though he had to add, "style is a sort of melody that comes into my sentences by itself." Mr. Shaw does not record ideas, he orchestrates them. He annihilates the medium while making one rejoice in it. His clarity is matched only by his energy. Among his chief audacities as an author is the fact that each of his sentences starts with no end in view that can be anticipated and yet concludes, regardless of its length, by falling by chance into patterns that seem inevitably planned. His mind dominates everything, including even his fingers, which can easily keep up with the most acrobatic of his thoughts.

The one predictable thing about Mr. Shaw is now, and always has been, that he will be unpredictable. His chief consistency has to many seemed to be his inconsistency. Yet always he has been readable. He is one of the few authors who has never been guilty of a *cliché*. Garrulous he has been to a fault, and is, but what dulls the reader in Mr. Shaw's writings is Mr. Shaw's unrelieved brilliance rather than any surrender to dullness on his part. In his case, the style is the superman. One has to rejoice in the word to rejoice in Shaw; and if one rejoices sufficiently his opinions lose their irritation, though never their stimulation.

His defects are plain enough. They stand out, however, like spots on the sun. Unfortunately one important segment of his mighty brain appears to have been made from Leon Errol's kneecap. It keeps collapsing just when it needs most to sustain him. Chesterton described Mr. Shaw's incompleteness as a genius by likening him to the Venus de Milo, and insisting that, in his case as in hers, all that there was of him was perfect.

It is not hard to see Chesterton's point. Mr. Shaw has understood everything but the average values of average living. His virtues, like his values, have all been exceptional. This is why he has meant so much to the commonplace world he has set out to correct, provoke, and instruct. Like the gods, he has served from Olympus. Although mankind is his business, and he has mingled with men under all sorts of disguises, Olympus is his home. "Whether it be that I was born mad or a little too sane," wrote Mr. Shaw, "my kingdom was not of this world: I was at home only in the realm of my imagination, and at my ease only with the mighty dead. Therefore I had to become an actor, and create for myself a fantastic personality fit and apt for dealing with men, and adaptable to the various parts I had to play as author, journalist, orator, politician, committee man, man of the world, and so forth."

In the realm of ideas Mr. Shaw has been not only the most amazing receiving set but the most amazing sending set modern literaature has known. Although he has borrowed freely from others, he seems always to have influenced his influences. If you look in his work for Ibsen, for Butler, for Wagner, for Henry George, for Marx, for Nietzsche, or for Chekhov, you will look in vain; at least if your hope is to find them in their original states. Mr. Shaw transforms them all. He does not borrow. He appropriates and possesses. He turns his influences into Shavians, just as he damages so many of his plays by turning most of his characters into Shavians, too.

As an author Mr. Shaw represents a host of apparently irreconcilable characteristics. To approximate his qualities you must imagine the impossible. You must try to conceive, if you can, Charles Dickens and John Bunyan being one man. You must think of Chesterton and Nietzsche inhabiting the same head. You must picture W. S. Gilbert and Oliver Cromwell as occupants of the identical body. You must suppose Sidney Webb and Harpo Marx as having been miraculously combined. You must imagine Ibsen and P. G. Wodehouse, Synge and Henry George, or Isaiah and Fielding as being one. Or convince yourself that *The Trojan Women* is an inseparable part of *The Frogs*. Also you must think of a fighter who, though he dotes on battle, never fights a man but always an idea. This is why the astonishing Mr. Shaw is more remarkable than the most remarkable of his works.

A journey to Ayot St. Lawrence made two months before the Normandy invasion in the vain hope of gaining from one of the best of minds some clarification of the problems of a war-torn world.

[1944]

BACK TO METHUSELAH

IT WAS in the nature of a pilgrimage. The April sky was cloudless over Hertfordshire, and the English countryside all greens and blossoms and smiling proofs of life which mocked the approaching days of death.

Ayot St. Lawrence was our destination.

Does the name mean nothing to you? Does it ring no bells; no liberty bells such as Ferney would have rung anywhere for troubled people in the eighteenth century indebted to the dauntless independence of Voltaire's mind? Then you are no Shavian and have not guessed the excitement and the curiosity in our hearts.

Surely as a reader you must have stumbled upon Ayot St. Lawrence. Although it is only an hour from London, reaching it in print can take a longer time. In the theatre you by-pass it. But in the library (certainly you remember it now), it has written "Finis" to the Grand Tour through many a Shavian preface.

Even nowadays readers—or rereaders—are apt to come upon it breathless. Even nowadays they are apt to reach it with their prejudices more jostled than the veiled hats of early motorists. They arrive blinking from the relentless sanity of a mind admitting no hour except noon. After the jolts to which they have been subjected on the way, they tend to feel as if they had been reading the Book of Revelation on a roller coaster.

Behind us now were the terrifying night noises of the Baby Blitz, the bleak ink-filled hours of the black-outs, and a bruised London. The sunshine and fresh air we greeted as no more than proper symbols. Because on a free afternoon (another symbol), the three of us—Lieutenant Bundy* and an Irrepressible Virginian† and I—were heading for a place which we could never imagine as having known a black-out, inasmuch as Mr. Shaw was its First Citizen.

In wartime it is not only threatened cities which seek the security of a black-out. The human mind, in its play of reason, at least most reasons save the major one, goes into eclipse. It has to. It has no other choice. The need for military objectives eliminates the luxury of objectivity. When the hurricane is howling through your house, any treatise on air currents is bound to seem an irrelevance, if not an impertinence. The passions of war number dispassion among the enemy.

Certain questions, simple enough in peacetime, cannot be asked

---

* Lieutenant, later Captain, McGeorge Bundy, USA, Admiral Alan G. Kirk's military aide, now Presidential aide.
† Lady Astor.

even of oneself, and, if asked, expect no answers. The color scale
of thought dwindles into black and white. Indeed, the only easy
feature of this long, difficult, and bloody struggle is that for most
of us never has white been whiter or black blacker.

But what about Mr. Shaw? What about the Elderly Gentleman
who has always seen red when the world sees black and to whom
nothing is either white or black? Would the supporting orthodoxies
of our thinking be safe with him? To his high credit no orthodoxies ever have been. What could one of the globe's few professional Wise Men say about a world forced hourly to demonstrate
its lack of wisdom by destruction?

As intermixed meadows and suburbs slipped by, and the talk
skimmed hummingbird-wise over many subjects, I could not help
thinking back to the wars Mr. Shaw's mind has survived, and the
warfare furiously waged by, and against, him during the first war.

God knows, thought I, his old eyes have looked out often enough
upon a world which has expressed its sickness in battle. When he
spoke at the Metropolitan Opera House in 1933, he confessed that
our Civil War was his first memory. He was four when it began,
and eight when he heard of Lincoln's assassination. He and wars
have never got along. They could scarcely be expected to do so.

He was already red-bearded and well known when the Boer
War taxed British arms and patience. He was celebrated when he
scandalized "right thinkers" by suggesting in *Arms and the Man*
that chocolate is more necessary to the soldier than the gun he carries. He was world-famous and gray when during the last conflict
he infuriated the English by dashing off his *Common Sense about
the War*.

To most men, including those incapable of it, pure reason is a
peacetime privilege, eyed with suspicion even then. In wartime
the moths fly away in horror from its flame. Who knows but that
by so doing they prove themselves wiser than the wisest Wise Men?
When desperate mortals, prepared to die for an idea, however
hazily understood, demand for that idea's safety that no neutrals
exist among their neighbors, the impartial truth is more than most
can tolerate, especially when it is as paradoxically and humorously
stated as if no tragic crisis existed.

The man who persists in thinking his own thoughts runs the
sniper's risks when conventional patriots have surrendered theirs.

"The Nag Sedition was your mother, and Perversity begot you; Mischief was your midwife and Misrule your nurse, and Unreason brought you up at her feet—no other ancestry and rearing had you —[you] freakish homunculus germinated outside of lawful pro-creation." Thus Mr. Shaw's old friend, Henry Arthur Jones, had fulminated against him during the first war. In his anger and his outrage Mr. Jones was not alone.

H.G. Wells had dubbed Shaw's behavior that of "an idiot child laughing in a hospital." Mr. Shaw's fellow playwrights had de-manded his resignation from the Dramatists' Club. W. J. Locke had refused to stay in the same room with him. Even actors had de-clined to be photographed with him. Once-doting readers clamored for his beard if not his blood.

What had Mr. Shaw said? Very little for which he was not for-given when peace found him resaying it in *Heartbreak House.* Very little for which he was not praised when the years of dis-illusionment had settled upon the world. The daring independence of *What I Really Wrote about the War* was as applauded in 1932 as it was condemned and despised during the war years.

In peacetime the iconoclasts and the court jesters come back into their own. In wartime they are fated to exist at their own and everyone else's peril. What the conventional have always found doubly hard to forgive in Mr. Shaw is his habit of saying serious things gaily. They read him, unable to determine whether he is a philosopher or a buffoon, and are appalled by the suspicion that he may be both.

During a war, soldiers, sailors, and marines are both expected and demanded to show physical courage. But in wartime, when salvation lies in the mass movements of massed men, the moral courage of a mind insisting upon its singularity naturally goes unappreciated. Mr. Shaw's intellect has always remained as un-drafted as his body. The only certainty about him has always been that he will be different.

"You may demand moral courage from me to any extent," he had once said, "but when you start shooting and knocking one another about, I claim the coward's privilege and take refuge under the bed. My life is too valuable to be machine-gunned." Al-though this may be a statement Falstaffian in its realism, and be-traying more courage than most medal-wearers could muster, it could hardly be expected to be understood by the expendables who, by being machine-gunned, make it safe for the contrary-minded to think their contrary thoughts. Mr. Shaw had realized his courage. Being Mr. Shaw he had of course appreciated it. "I have been giving exhibitions of moral courage far surpassing anything achieved in the field," said he, "but so far I have not received the V.C.; in fact sarcastic suggestions that I should receive the iron one have not been lacking."

I could not help thinking of these Shavian skirmishes, well known to all readers of Shaw or Hesketh Pearson, as in the midst of an even more awful and ruthless war we sped toward Ayot St. Lawrence.

Almost before I knew it, it came into sight. The country thereabouts is lovely and rolling; great trees and gentle risings in the fields. It could be days distant from London. Suburbia has somehow by-passed it. A little village with a charming inn, clean and, for a wonder, freshly painted. A Norman church in ruins. Another, and a later church. Some gates to large estates. Roads closely lined by hedges. Then a sudden turning, and an entrance leading to a brick house far back from the road and surrounded by undulant lawns. A stop because of the gate which has to be swung back by hand as if it had been encountered on a farm in Virginia or Kentucky. Thereafter the house.

As the three of us drove up, a maid could be seen inside, becapped and deep in a newspaper. In a moment she was at the door, telling us in a whisper that Mr. Shaw had not yet finished his nap.

We were shown into the garden at the back of the house where the Irrepressible Virginian, as an old friend of Mr. Shaw's, proceeded uninvited to pick at random a generous armful of his flowers. The gardener, clipping his way from behind a hedge, surveyed the ravaged beds with proper bourgeois amazement.

"Don't worry," drawled the Virginian, with a gesture toward the house, "he's always writing communistic stuff. It's high time someone practiced what he preaches."

The words were freshly uttered when the Elderly Gentleman, who is seldom caught napping, emerged and started walking toward us across the lawn. At first glance he looked as pale as his beard and leaner than a soda straw. His neck was as erect as ever; his back, too, even though he swayed a bit uncertainly as he approached.

He was wearing gray knickers, gray woolen socks (especially woven for the left and right foot, according to the Virginian), a gray short coat, and a bulbous cap. When near enough for introductions, I could see how much he had aged since I had met him twelve years before.

His beard was thinned, though even now gloriously prophetic and whiter than typewriter paper before being sullied by an author. Close up, his skin looked much as if the pink and blue periods of Picasso had been jointly transferred to alabaster. His eyes were at moments frosted by age. They could, however, clear cloudlessly into the most animated nursery blue. His voice remained an instrument, in register and as used, to which he would have had to give his full approval in the distant days when he was a music critic. The resonance of his speech was as extraordinary as the glory of his English—an English in which the Irish long ago became neutral. No one could create anywhere a finer figure of a prophet than time and G.B.S. have made of Mr. Shaw.

He led us around the garden, showing us the wood he saws. The cuts were feeble, as he freely confessed, pointing out that one soon grows tired of that sort of thing. Then he took us to his doll's house of a study down at the lawn's edge; that prefabricated one-room house, which he turns by a crank so that the sun is always full upon him. It was jammed with papers, books, and a typewriter—telltale because uncovered.

"I've been writing an article," he confessed.

"But why," asked the Virginian, "when you should be resting?"

"Because"—and at this a grin from ear to ear which lifted the beard—"because I'm being paid twenty-five pounds for it."

He admitted he had just finished a book on *Everybody's Political What's What,* and (I dreaded to have him say it) was about to begin a new play.

By the time we had followed him back to the house, he had already lunged into sex, marriage, primogeniture, cattle, the English clergy, Norman architecture, and Victorian bad taste.

"Sit down, sit down," he exclaimed when we had come into the living room, which was all windows and sunlight and shadowless, and highly polished furniture and books. "No special chairs here."

Then tea was served to us—delicious tea, beautifully served—while he took a glass of hot milk. The talk continued, wobbling from subject to subject much as he had swayed in his walking. As he talked he pinkened, gathering strength with his thoughts.

His talk?

"The Navy's a strange life," he said for no apparent reason, except that I was wearing blues. "Men go into the Navy—at least, they do in this country—thinking they will enjoy it. They do enjoy it for a year. At least the stupid ones do, riding back and forth quite dully on ships. The bright ones learn they don't like it in a half year. But there's always the thought of that pension, if only they stay in. So they do stay in. They stay in and are promoted as a matter of time, if not of course.

"Gradually they become crazy. Crazier and crazier. Only the Navy has no way of distinguishing between the sane and the insane. I know this because a friend of mine once took a ship across the Bay of Biscay. Even his crew knew he was mad when he crossed and recrossed the Bay five times without ever putting in. Then they threw him in the brig. Only about five per cent of the men in the Royal Navy have the sea in their veins. These are the ones who become captains. Thereafter they are segregated on their bridges. If they are not mad before this, they go mad then. And the maddest of these become admirals. Tell your Admiral this."

With the speed, and often with the brilliance with which he hedgehops from subject to subject in the subdivisions of his prefaces, the Elderly Gentleman held forth. On Lunacharsky. On Mrs. Shaw's will. On his disappointment in the man known to the world as Uncle Joe. On his visits to the front in the last war. On General Haig. On Mrs. Patrick Campbell. On Hesketh Pearson. On Mr. Shaw—"the historic Shaw, the man of my middle years, the Shaw the world will remember," as he put it. On the movie of *Caesar and Cleopatra*. And as casually as you mention a friend seen last week, on Stanley, the Stanley of "Dr. Livingstone, I presume." "I remember Stanley telling me that only five per cent of the men under him were ever equipped to take over his command, if he had to delegate authority. That's how rare real leadership always is."

"My actuarial expectancy," said the Elderly Gentleman, sipping his hot milk, and smiling as wholeheartedly as at the best of jokes, "is three days. As a matter of fact, I may die while you are sitting here. Death has no terrors for me."

But what about the war which for the tranquil moment in the midst of such good, civilized talk was as lulled as if by an armistice? What about this war, in reality so near, and the next one, God willing, so far away?

"If they are not careful at the peace conference," the Sage of Ayot St. Lawrence was saying, "there will be another war in ten or twenty years. The best guarantee of future peace is that war is no longer anything but economically ruinous. Once upon a time it used to pay. This made men unable to resist it.

"You would conquer a town, and having conquered it, you had it to take as plunder. A Wallenstein or a Marlborough would enter with his army, granting his soldiers two days' leave for rape and pillage. Even then, when order was re-established, there was the town itself as a plum for the conqueror. But nowadays what happens? We conquer not to take but to destroy. All this bombing of Berlin would justify itself, if after it we still had a Berlin to take, as it deserves to be taken. But we don't. Instead we destroy what we might have used. And have to destroy it in order to survive."

"But is there no way in the future . . . ?"

"There would be no wars if only men read my books. And took them to heart." Then he smiled again, as gaily as if he were discussing the possible nearness of his own death. "That's silly of me, really silly. I ought to know better. They wouldn't understand."

By the visit's end, the Elderly Gentleman, so frail and mortal behind his prophet's beard, seemed tired. Slowly and unsteadily, though erect as an exclamation point, he preceded us to the gate. As he stood there in the road while we drove off, with the breeze ballooning his cap, with the sun hallowing his beard, and an arm upraised, the saintly old Satan or, more accurately, the satanic old saint looked more alone than any man I have ever seen. He was as alone as only old age and such a mind as his can make a man.

In the preface to *Heartbreak House* he had written, "Only those who have lived through a first-rate war, not in the field, but at home, and kept their heads can possibly understand the bitterness of Shakespeare and Swift, who both went through this experience."

We left him standing there by the green hedges of an England once again at war. We left him standing there, once again surrounded by a world of death and destruction. It was a world which must have made him feel as if all these decades during which he has preached, his millions of words have been heard only by the deaf. It was a world beset with more ills than any single mind— even his with its all-embracing inconsistencies—could hope to suggest remedies for. It was a tragic world, which tragically for him and us had passed beyond him.

In the lengthening distance he looked as if he were a revivalist about to address a meeting.

"I must preach and preach and preach," had said the character in *Too True to Be Good,* "no matter how late the hour and how short the day, no matter whether I have nothing to say."

Although there was only sunlight in the fields, one suspected that in such a world Mr. Shaw must have felt himself enveloped by a fog; the same kind of fog that enveloped the preacher in *Too True to Be Good.*

"There is left only fog," runs the stage direction there; *"impenetrable fog, but the incorrigible preacher will not be denied his peroration, which, could we only hear it distinctly, would probably run—*

"I must preach and preach and preach—no matter whether I have nothing to say or whether in some pentecostal flame of revelation the Spirit will descend upon me and inspire me with a message, the sound of which shall go out unto all lands and realize for us at last the Kingdom and the Power and the Glory for ever and ever. Amen."

Like everyone else, we were too far away. We could not hear him.

*An iconoclast who has himself become something of an
icon is discussed along with Shakespeare, dramatic critics,
and the schizophrenic contemporary world.*

[1947]

PROGRESS AND THE SUPERMAN

"ENOUGH, THEN, of this goose-cackle about Progress: Man, as
he is, never will nor can add a cubit to his stature by any of its
quackeries, political, scientific, educational, religious, or artistic."
Thus Mr. Shaw, alias John Tanner, in "The Revolutionist's Handbook" which serves *Man and Superman** as an appendix.

Though then in his middle years, Mr. Shaw was still sufficiently
redbearded to be saluted by an unawed street urchin as "Ginger
Whiskers." He was pleading for a more planned parenthood than
is nowadays fought for. The Life Force rather than the individual
alcove was his concern, the omnipresent Yahoo (meaning you and
me) his enemy.

As a Nietzschean who had turned the dead, hence defenseless, Nietzsche into a Shavian, Shaw was championing the Superman. In him he saw our only hope. The Superman would belong
to a new type, a new race. He would not, therefore, be condemned to repeat in each generation the errors and cruelties of his
forefathers. Our chances of survival depended upon creating a
world where the unaverage mortals would be the average ones.
Man as we have known him, insisted Shaw, has proved himself
incapable of net progress. Accordingly, he must be replaced by
the Superman, a figure achievable only by the socialization of selective breeding.

---

* *Man and Superman,* by George Bernard Shaw. Staged by Maurice Evans.
Associate director, George Schaefer. Setting by Frederick Stover. Costumes
by David Ffolkes. Presented by Mr. Evans. With Maurice Evans, Frances
Rowe, Chester Stratton, Carmen Mathews, Jack Manning, Tony Bickley,
Victor Sutherland, and Malcolm Keen. At the Alvin Theatre. Opened
October 8, 1947.

Although Shaw admitted that during recorded history Man had added to his outward conveniences, his contention was that morally Man had not moved forward one iota. Shaw refused to believe that the chauffeur who drove a motorcar from Paris to Berlin was a more highly evolved creature than the charioteer of Achilles. Or that the modern prime minister was a more enlightened ruler than Caesar because he rode a tricycle, wrote his dispatches by electric light, and instructed his stockbroker through the telephone. Our notion of Progress, thundered Mr. Shaw, was only an illusion. It was civilization's most disastrous conceit.

Instead of actually happening, the forty-four years which have slipped by since *Man and Superman* was written must seem in many respects to have been invented by Mr. Shaw for the sole purpose of proving his argument. Anyone who in the contemporary world would serve Progress as its defense attorney faces a dismaying task. Although our doctors have learned to prolong individual life, the facts of peace no less than of war encourage many to ask why. For what kind of persons morally, for what sort of world internationally, has this private longevity been achieved?

Assuredly, we have outdone the Red Queen in racing forward in order to stand still. There are those who from personal experience may question whether we have succeeded even in doing this. We have followed a tragic dual course, heading simultaneously for the North Pole and the South. We have gone forward so as to go back, and added in order to subtract. A negative springs to mind to offset every positive one can name.

We have endured the bloodiest wars in history. We have seen once civilized countries overrun by governments brutal in their means, ruthless in their denials of freedom, and proud of their lack of conscience. We have been witnesses of minority persecutions of a scale and savagery fortunately undreamed of in the past. We have been confronted with more wreckage, mortal and moral no less than architectural, than any of our forebears knew. We have had to accustom ourselves to living with mass catastrophes. We have moved in a world made hideous by more disease, death, hunger, homelessness, despair, and cruelty than history has hitherto equaled.

When John Tanner, speaking for Shaw, mentioned war, he had the Boer War in mind. That was child's play. No cynical denier of Progress could contend that, in the intervening years, in warfare we have not grown more adult. The tank has replaced the cavalry. The airplane has become the new battleship. The flame-thrower and the V-bomb have multiplied the victims of the rifle and the cannon. Yet surely such advances are only proofs of a retrogressive progress. Not even Pollyanna could congratulate Man glibly upon having moved forward while war remains necessary, when city after city has been left in ruins, when victory vanquishes the rightful victors, when famine stalks a supposedly pacific world, when distrust is a major delegate at the peace tables, and the threat of wholesale obliteration is part of each individual's consciousness.

Yet the ledger is not all in red ink. We would find life purposeless, hence insupportable, if it were. The entries in black are many and written in a bold hand. They may add to the confusion of the picture but, more than being an essential feature of a tragically schizophrenic universe, they provide us with the only hope we have. In literacy, in popular legislation, in the recognition of the rights of the common man, in the forward march of labor, in our lost complacencies, in our heightened awareness of abuses and injustices, in all the sciences that make for health and comfort, and at least in our dreams of world government, we have moved ahead.

The world as it is is our problem, and a problem sizable and complex enough to depress us and overtax our talents. Certainly we have not the time to wait for the appearance of the Superman. Such dictators as have mistaken themselves for him have been unpersuasive salesmen of the idea. Nor has the notion of socialized breeding increased in its appeal. Natural selection retains its popularity in and away from the marriage-license bureaus. Sex has proved harder to nationalize than the coal mines. Nowhere are there signs that people are anxious to abandon what in some countries is their most genuine freedom of expression.

To console ourselves in the gales of a melancholy universe, we may be tempted to reach for straws. That is better than reaching for nothing. One of these straws is offered by *Man and Superman* itself. Our reception of it in its current revival demonstrates that some progress, however minuscular, has been made during this catastrophic half-century.

When Shaw noted that Napoleon had supplied Talma with a

pit of kings, with an effect on Talma's acting that is not recorded, he added, "As for me, what I have always wanted is a pit of philosophers." To his way of thinking, *Man and Superman* was a play for such a pit. Even in the interests of hope we cannot pretend to have provided him with such an audience today. Yet, undeniably, the world has caught up a little with its favorite Superman. Shaw's audacities, though delectable, no longer seem as audacious as they once did.

The Elderly Gentleman has not lived and thought and written and laughed entirely in vain. He remains far ahead of us all in sanity, brilliance, intellect, eloquence, wit, goodness, knowledge, and conscience. Yet there is some consolation to be had from the fact that a world shaken by Shaw's impact does not think (however it may act) as the globe did in its pre-Shavian days. The distance which separates *Man and Superman* from its audiences today is less great than it was at the century's turn.

The eternal iconoclast has become something of an icon himself. His plays are confronted with the awful fate of being received as classics. Classics usually are works accepted without protest because they are admired without thought. Shaw himself was conscious of this altered attitude and the hazards it presented when *Man and Superman* was first produced. "They used to laugh when I was serious," he wrote Forbes-Robertson, "but now the fashion has changed: they take their hats off when I joke, which is still more trying."

Another faint instance of progress comes from a surprising source—believe it or not, from today's dramatic critics. You may say that my being compelled to fall back on them is a measure of how desperate are the times. Nevertheless, the changed attitude toward what constitutes a good play, as shown in the recent reviews of *Man and Superman*, indicates that in some respects we have inched forward a little even in a troubled world. This advance is not limited to the reviewers alone. It includes the audiences for whom they speak.

There were real giants on the aisles of London's theatres when Mr. Shaw's comedy was new. Yet, distinguished as William Archer, A. B. Walkley, and Max Beerbohm were as critics, theirs was a far more dogmatic, therefore narrower, notion of playwriting than is nowadays prevalent.

They had not learned the wisdom of Coleridge's "You cannot pass an act of uniformity against the poets." Although they had few poets to deal with, these truly able men were prisoners of a special image of dramatic correctness. They were the victims of Sardou and "Sardoodledum," of Pinero and "Pinerotic" craftsmanship. Their enthusiasms were corseted by definitions. They were worshipers of the "well-made play"; slaves of such Archerian technical points as "exposition," "foreshadowing," "the obligatory scene," "the peripety," held scenes, big climaxes, carry-over curtain lines, and what not.

Although they said their ideal was plays that were true to life, what they meant by this was plays which remain faithful to the stage—as it then was. Their passion for construction was such that they wanted dramatists to be engineers no less than architects. They could admire a playwright who, in the interest of thought, of freedom, or imagination, extended the stage's limited scope. If, however, he proved larger in spirit, mind, or practice than the form they prized, they refused to recognize him as a playwright. What all this amounted to was saying that a swimmer who had swum the Atlantic was no swimmer at all unless he wore a regulation bathing suit.

Beerbohm, for example, who was truly "incomparable," found *Man and Superman* "infinitely better, to my peculiar taste, than any play I have ever read or seen enacted." Yet even he was quick to add, "But a play it is not." In his confusion he was driven to compare it with Lucian and Landor; above all, with Plato. Although he admired it as a Platonic dialogue, Shaw's dramaturgy was too different from Pinero's for him to accept it as a play. Beerbohm was stubborn in his insistence that Shaw was "a critic, and not a creator at all."

The suave and charming Walkley was no less adamant. It is he, of course, in whose debt we stand for *Man and Superman*, since it was he who challenged Shaw to write a play on the Don Juan theme, even as Archer had once dared him, with *The Doctor's Dilemma* as the result, to write a play about death. In a coruscating review Walkley admitted he had been "immensely amused" (as who wouldn't be by Shaw's comedy?). Nonetheless, he was firm in his contention that its author was "no dramatist at all."

Whatever the lacks of contemporary playgoers or critics may

be, we are freer now. We have at least shed those fetters of that earlier day. Mr. Shaw has been one of the major forces in the modern theatre to rid us of them. He has won his conspiracy against the stage of Sir Henry Irving. He is now universally revered, not only as a prophet, a preface writer, the world's foremost critic at large, a wit, and a Fabian, but also as a playwright. We find him funnier than Plato and thank God he is not Pinero.

By and large, the worship of the *pièce bien faite* is deader than Queen Alexandra. Today we smile at tight definitions because we distrust them. We are glad when a new work so goes beyond them that it demonstrates their futility. We rejoice when the stencil is broken, the form extended, the theatre enlarged. The stage irks us when it stands still. Our wan hope is that, instead of following us, it will invite us to follow it.

If we must have indefinable terms defined for us, we are willing to settle for Professor Baker's "A good play is an accurately conveyed emotion." Yet, having welcomed so all-inclusive a definition, we are delighted to find that *Man and Superman*, by being an accurately conveyed *lack* of emotion, fails to hold either water or Shaw.

We do not give a tinker's beldam at present whether Mr. Shaw's text has been built in the image of Pinero or Jones, Dumas or Augier, Ibsen or Hellman. We are happy because palpably it is Shaw's property and no one else's. We know only—and care only —that, as revived by Maurice Evans, *Man and Superman* is beyond question the gayest, the brightest, the most original and delectable comedy to be seen in New York just now.

A New York manager, when Robert Loraine was trying to get the play produced in 1905, may have been horrified by its plot idea of a woman chasing a man. He may have rejected the script because he feared its theme was "indullicate." No one finds it so today. To us Shaw's theme is at the core of his text's pleasure. In itself this may be a proof of progress—in the collapse of the romantic dream, the awakening to reality, or the spread of sad disillusionment.

My "old sobersides" approach to so diverting an entertainment may strike you as odd, if not utterly misplaced. I have my reasons. What we see and relish in the theatre ("that last sanctuary of unreality," as Shaw dubbed it) is no more the whole of *Man and Superman* than what glitters above the ocean's surface is the whole of an iceberg. Mr. Evans cannot be blamed for this. Not even people who would submit to being repeaters at *The Passion Play* or theatregoers accustomed to O'Neill's "mastodonic" dramas (courtesy of Richard Watts, Jr.) could be expected to absorb all of *Man and Superman* at a single sitting. For *Man and Superman* does not consist only of the three sprightly acts which Mr. Evans, like his predecessors, has found practical to play. Taken by themselves, these acts are self-reliant and vastly entertaining. Yet, above and beyond them, and an integral part of the thesis Shaw is advancing with his glorious garrulity, there is, first of all and not unsurprisingly, the preface. This is a dazzling affair which, in the midst of its intellectual acrobatics on the subject of sex, marriage, woman in general, style, the purpose of life, its author's contempt for the pure artist, and Shaw only knows what else, explains what Shaw is doing with the Don Juan theme.

Then, there is the necessarily omitted third act. Beginning with the bandit Mendoza, and the mountain-pass meeting of the League of the Sierra, it reaches its climax in the famous "hell scene." This is long enough to make an evening in itself, and is one of the most eloquent and witty of all Shaw's dialectics. Finally, there comes, both as appendix and summation, "The Revolutionist's Handbook," which all too often is ignored. In it John Tanner sets down Shaw's philosophy unimpeded by plot; denies Progress; pleads for the Superman; and offers some maxims, some of which are brilliant but many of which find Shaw a nodding La Rochefoucauld.

Don't misunderstand me. None of this homework must be done in order to enjoy Mr. Evans' production of *Man and Superman*. But all of it must be done (and the doing of it is as painless an operation as this world knows) to have a full understanding of what Shaw is up to. As usual he had more on his mind than he could squeeze into dramatic form. As usual, too, though he seemed to be laughing and makes us laugh, he was in deadly earnest.

When Tolstoi was confronted with a copy of *Man and Superman*, he complained at the gaiety with which Shaw dealt with a serious subject. "Why should humor and laughter be excommunicated?" replied Shaw. "Suppose the world were only one of God's jokes, would you work any the less to make it a good joke instead of a bad one?"

Being a Shavian jest, the comedy covers, even in its abbreviated form, a dizzying amount of territory. Art for art's sake it most decidedly is not. But talk for talk's sake it most certainly is. And what wonderful talk! A plot, which soon becomes the scenario for an extravaganza, leaves Shaw free to ventilate his unpredictable views on predatory and mendacious females, the inanities of respectability, the Life Force, the chauffeur as the prototype of the New Man, the American man's idealization of woman, and any number of other topics, all of which as treated betray the incredible agility of Shaw's mind.

Mr. Evans has set the comedy before us in terms which are, on the whole, irresistible. Quite rightly he and his better players act it, plumage, style, and all, as if it were a period piece. They treat it much as if it were a comedy by a more intellectual Oscar Wilde. Part of the evening's fun, however, comes from seeing not how much but how little of Shaw's thinking refuses to be dated.

In his make-up as Tanner Mr. Evans does not attempt to resemble Shaw as Granville-Barker is said to have done. No character in a Wilde comedy could look more debonair than he does. Yet there are undeniable traces of Hamlet in Mr. Evans' gay and engaging performance. There are moments, for example, when you could swear he was on the verge of addressing the players, seeing his father's ghost, mocking Rosencrantz and Guildenstern, sending Ophelia trotting, or apostrophizing Yorick's skull. Always, however, Mr. Evans catches himself in time, remembering his present whereabouts.

My suspicion is that these hints of Hamlet would please Shaw. The linking of Shakespeare and Shaw would come as no surprise to G.B.S. He long ago anticipated it. Shaw would, no doubt, consider it his just desert to have his lines read as if they were at least as good as Shakespeare's.

Although he may have pretended to hate Shakespeare's mind, Shaw has always doted on his music. Why not? As a word-musician, the author of *Man and Superman* is also capable of infinite magic. He, too, can strum the dictionary and fiddle the language. No one in the English-speaking theatre since the Bard's time has written speeches livelier in their melodies or lovelier in their cadences than has Shaw at his most eloquent. His great tirades, though in prose and filled with humor, have about them the aria quality of Shakespearean soliloquies.

When he was a dramatic critic, Shaw stated his contempt in no uncertain terms for actors who prided themselves on muffling the music in Shakespeare's lines by speaking them as if they were prose. We should be equally resentful of any players who, instead of luxuriating in Shaw's prose rhythms, seek to over-colloquialize them. The performer who would do justice to Shaw must keep up not only with Shaw's music but with his mind. Mr. Evans does both—admirably.

We may sneer today at Shaw's notion of the Nietzschean Superman. No one, however, can deny in these imperiled times the urgency of Shaw's plea that for the sake of his survival Man must become better and wiser than he is. We have progressed, indeed rushed forward, to this tragic and decisive point.

A heavenly evening with Don Juan in a Hell where ideas are the plot, wit is the lighting, eloquence the scenery, and four fine actors do justice to a memorable script.

[1951]

THE ARTS OF LIFE AND DEATH

WHAT—SHAW again? Yes, because he makes it inescapable. Yes, because his deathless voice has once again brought our so-called living theatre to life. Yes, because for the second time in a season up to now cursed and largely overrun by the efforts of pygmies he has stood out like a colossus, an intellect among the thoughtless, a genius among hacks, and a seer among the blind.

It is the *Don Juan in Hell* * scene from *Man and Superman,* as read by Charles Laughton, Charles Boyer, Cedric Hardwicke, and Agnes Moorehead, which leaves me with no other inclination or choice than to write about Shaw once more. For some time now audiences in city after city up and down the United States (and England, too) have had the opportunity to enjoy this seldom performed interlude that Shaw wrote fifty years ago. Now, at last, an underprivileged New York has been permitted to respond to its excitements.

Nothing Broadway has had to offer since Laurence Olivier's *Oedipus* has been more absorbing than this theatrically unorthodox presentation of a play which is not a play in the ordinary sense. The performance is in the nature of a reading. Only a shallow forestage is used, and it is backed by a black curtain. In front of this curtain are microphones and stools, and music stands to hold the bound copies of the text carried in by the actors. The three men are dressed in dinner jackets and Miss Moorehead wears an evening gown. Mr. Laughton briefly and charmingly tells the essentials of the Don Juan story and announces the cast. Thereafter he leads us into the script by letting us hear Shaw's stage direction. As far as the trappings of production go, that is all. But what an all and what an evening it proves to be!

If any members of Local 829 managed to squeeze into Carnegie Hall, they—and they alone—in a huge and rapt audience must have felt a certain discomfort. They may even have had a clearer understanding of Othello's feelings when he complained his occupation was gone. For Local 829 is the United Scenic Artists. And here was Shaw proving, as Shakespeare demonstrated long ago, how unnecessary scenery is when great language sets the stage.

Anyone can cite examples of the way in which Shakespeare relied on his pen to do the brushwork most contemporary playwrights assume will be done for them by scene designers with the aid of dependable electricians. In *Macbeth* the First Murderer's "The west yet glimmers with some streaks of day"; Horatio's

---

* *Don Juan in Hell,* by Bernard Shaw. Directed by Charles Laughton. The First Drama Quartet presented by Paul Gregory. With Mr. Laughton, Charles Boyer, Cedric Hardwicke, and Agnes Moorehead. At Carnegie Hall, October 22, 1951.

"But look, the morn, in russet mantle clad,/ Walks o'er the dew of yon high eastward hill . . ."; and Lorenzo's "The moon shines bright. In such a night as this,/ When the sweet wind did gently kiss the trees/ And they did make no noise . . ." are familiar instances of the kind of verbal scenery Shakespeare supplied in play after play.

Shaw's employment of the language proves no less self-sufficient in this uncostumed and unset "reading" of *Don Juan in Hell*. Yet there is a striking difference. Shaw has no interest in conjuring images to evoke a physical setting. He makes fun of Dante for having described hell as a place of mud, frost, filth, fire, and venomous serpents. He is equally contemptuous of Milton for having introduced cannon and gunpowder as a means of expelling the Devil from heaven. Shaw's hell is visually nonexistent. In his own words "there is nothing; omnipresent nothing. No sky, no peaks, no light, no sound, no time nor space, utter void." There is only somewhere the faint throbbing buzz of a Mozartian strain and a pallor which "reveals a man in the void, an incorporeal but visible man, seated, absurdly enough, on nothing."

In the course of *Don Juan* Shaw pays tribute to the wonders of that slowly evolved bodily organ, the eye, which has permitted the living organism to "see where it was going and what was coming to help or threaten it." Even so, his concern is with neither the eye nor the visible world. Instead, it is with the evolving mind's eye and its higher plane of vision which should enable us to see "the purpose of Life." He makes his hell a void so that he can fill it with ideas. His intellect sets the stage; his fervor and his wit light it. What absorbs his attention and ours is not a place but the plight of Man. It is Man's foolishness and his potentialities—what he has been, what he is, and what he must become if he is either to justify his existence or safeguard his survival.

There are those beyond counting who expect a play to have a plot. They want it at least to tell how Jack gets Jill or Jill Jack. The story of Ann Whitefield's pursuit and conquest of John Tanner is the narrative basis of *Man and Superman*, into the third act of which *Don Juan in Hell* is tucked as a detachable dream sequence. Being spirits, the characters in this interlude are no longer plotbound.

Having already lived their personal histories, the Devil, the

Commander, Doña Ana, and Don Juan are free in hell to concentrate on a far larger, more universal story—the story of Mankind. This is the subject of their dialogue. To be more accurate, it is the theme of their "great debate." Although they do nothing except talk, such talk is in itself an exciting activity. The very thrust and fascination of their arguments create drama. Because of the mind at work, this battle of ideas is far more dramatic in its action than a thousand trumped-up plots.

Shaw's hell has nothing in common with the hell that fires the imagination of those who hit the sawdust trail. It is not even the satanic realm with which milder ministers are fond of threatening sinners. Instead, it is as unconventional an inferno as only Shaw could make it. He establishes it as a delightful retreat for seekers after happiness who intellectually and spiritually have not outgrown its pleasures. Its pleasures are such that it is visited frequently by those who are bored with heaven.

Shaw's heaven is no less exceptional. It is open only to those who have become the masters of reality. This sets it very much apart from earth, where mortals are reality's slaves. In this Shavian paradise what is done cannot be undone by repentance and spoken words cannot be unspoken by withdrawing them, any more than the truth can be annihilated by a general agreement to give it the lie.

One of Shaw's most typical and engaging paradoxes is that such a heaven attracts, of all people, Don Juan the libertine. Juan has tired of the license which won him earthly fame and come to see the emptiness of the diversions offered him in hell. His belief in Man is greater than the Devil's disbelief. The Devil may argue against heaven and Man with all the skill at Shaw's command, but it is to this heavenly refuge of realists that Don Juan is determined to go. And go he finally does, as the champion of the Life-Force, Creative Evolution, and the Superman.

Most readers and playgoers remember lines from Shaw's memorable preface to *Man and Superman*, from the play and the interlude, or from "The Revolutionist's Handbook," which concludes the volume. None of Shaw's works bulges with more passages which refuse to be forgotten and cry to be quoted. His mind never had freer play than in *Don Juan in Hell*. His prowess as a debater was never more irrefutably established than in the discussion where the voices of Shaw and Anti-Shaw are heard, and each is given the benefit of all Shaw's eloquence, wit, and moral passion. Following such an argument may make hard demands on those unable to concentrate and antagonistic to thought. But in spite of G.B.S.'s confessed wordiness, listening, to anyone with half a mind, has seldom been easier or more rewarding.

One of the incredible aspects of *Don Juan in Hell* is that it remains utterly and urgently contemporary. The half-century which has passed since it was written has left it undated. Take, for example, the Devil's speech in the first part of the evening when he appears to have the better of the debate. Don Juan has claimed that Man's hope lies in his brain. "And is Man any the less destroying himself for all this boasted brain of his?" asks the Devil. "Have you walked up and down upon the earth lately? I have; and I have examined Man's wonderful inventions. And I tell you that in the arts of life man invents nothing; but in the arts of death he outdoes Nature herself, and produces by chemistry and machinery all the slaughter of plague, pestilence, and famine. The peasant I tempt today eats and drinks what was eaten and drunk by the peasants of ten thousand years ago; and the house he lives in has not altered as much in a thousand centuries as the fashion of a lady's bonnet in a score of weeks. But when he goes out to slay, he carries a marvel of mechanism that lets loose at the touch of his finger all the hidden molecular energies, and leaves the javelin, the arrow, the blowpipe of his fathers far behind. In the arts of peace Man is a bungler."

Toward the end of the present "reading," divided as it is into two parts so as to ease the strain of taut listening, Don Juan speaks not only for himself but for Shaw. "I tell you," he insists, "that as long as I can conceive something better than myself I cannot be easy unless I am striving to bring it into existence or clearing the way for it. That is the law of my life. That is the working within me of Life's incessant aspiration to higher organization, wider, deeper, intenser self-consciousness, and clearer self-understanding. It was the supremacy of this purpose that reduced love for me to the mere pleasure of a moment, art for me to the mere schooling of my faculties, religion for me to a mere excuse for laziness, since it had set up a God who looked at the world and saw that it was good, against the instinct in me that looked through my eyes at the world and saw that it could be improved. I tell you that in the pursuit of my own pleasure, my own health, my own fortune, I have never known happiness."

Thus the Don Juan–Shaw—entirely uncynical. Thus Shaw, the philosophic man, with all his energies in revolt against the wrong or the merely adequate, and mobilized in a campaign for improvement. Thus Shaw, the militant reformer, the wrecker who destroys to rebuild, the firm believer in the "continual ascent of Man on the stepping stones of his dead selves to higher things." Thus Shaw with his conviction that Man's need and hope lie in evolving into a being better than he now is. Thus Shaw with his extension of the theory of the Superman which he derived from Nietzsche, who, though named in the original text, is for some strange reason left unmentioned in the present version.

The Performance *Don Juan* is given is far more than a reading and in every respect worthy of Shaw's writing. Although it has an irresistible informality, it can claim a splendid dignity. Among its igniting qualities count the fact that it puts the imagination to stimulating work at the same time that it keeps the mind racing with delight. The members of the quartette read from memory rather than from their texts. This is what makes "reading" so inadequate a word as a description of the presentation.

Charles Laughton has directed his associates so that they play beautifully and generously together. Perhaps it would be more accurate to say he has conducted the performance, treating the script as both the intellectual and vocal score it is. He and his actors have given their whole minds to Shaw's words, and by having done so they make it the easier for us to give our whole minds too.

Long and triumphant experience as a public reader has made Mr. Laughton a virtuoso of platform appearances. He is entirely at home in an enterprise of this kind. His moon-round face is quick to register and project every needed nuance of expression. His voice is equally flexible. It is a fine, rich, varied instrument, fortified by the most precise diction. His Satan is a doubly dangerous fellow for being so ingratiating in the ingenuity, the perversity, and the persuasiveness with which he states his diabolical arguments.

Charles Boyer is no less fine. Charming as he is, he turns his back resolutely on the kind of Boyer charm that in movie after movie transformed dowagers into bobby soxers. From the moment he first speaks his Don Juan is a man no longer interested in his earthly pursuits. He is tired of the frivolities of the hell in which he finds himself, and inspired with a purpose. He is high-spirited, yet behind his smile and his gift for gaiety there is a glowing zeal which is the foundation of his faith. His French accent may occasionally create some difficulties, but these are few and unimportant. Well as he reads throughout (using "reads" in the ordinary theatrical sense of understanding and communicating an author's meaning), he rises to stirring heights of prophetic eloquence when he releases and illumines the magnificent speeches in which the Shavian credo of affirmation is ultimately stated.

Though Cedric Hardwicke, as the Commander, and Agnes Moorehead, as Doña Ana, have the lesser parts, they contribute richly to the evening. Mr. Hardwicke suggests to the full the arrogance of the military type and speaks, as always, with his mind in full command of his tongue. Miss Moorehead is highly pictorial, possessing visually something of the quality of Sargent's Madame X. She makes the most of the text's least interesting part. May I add, however, that the writing which is least interesting in *Don Juan in Hell* is a hundred times more interesting than that to be found in most recent plays.

Surely, no dramatic critic has performed for the theatre a finer service than A. B. Walkley's when he urged Shaw to write a drama about Don Juan. No less surely, few contemporary actors have performed a greater service to Shaw, the theatre, and all of us than this quartet of excellent actors by letting us see and hear *Don Juan in Hell*.

Shaw proves his wisdom by rushing in where Shakespeare
dared to tread, with the result that the applecarts of both
history and historical drama are upset in a manner brilliantly
Shavian.

[1949]

HAIL, CAESAR—AND CLEOPATRA

SHAKESPEARE GOT there first with his *Julius Caesar* and his *Antony and Cleopatra*. But did this intimidate Shaw? It did not. Most fortunately, it did not. Instead, it served him as a come-on. The Bard has always enjoyed a priority among G.B.S.'s irreverences. He took to the challenge like a cat to catnip. He was no more dismayed by his late arrival on the scene than Napoleon was by Alexander's having reached the Nile before him.

When in 1898 Shaw decided to invade Egypt, to come to grips with the mighty Julius, and as a vegetable-fed Puritan to run the risks of Cleopatra, he had something very much his own to say, which, as usual, he managed to get said in his own way. He was the first to admit the value of what he had written. The fact that Walkley and the critics who originally reviewed *Caesar and Cleopatra** had described it as *opéra bouffe* did not depress Shaw. To him prophecy is routine employment. "In 1920 *Caesar* will be a masterpiece," he wrote in 1908. Readers have long since agreed with him. It was not, however, until the current and brilliant revival of his play that American theatregoers, too young to have seen Forbes-Robertson in it, have realized how right Shaw was.

Certainly Gabriel Pascal's screen version with Vivien Leigh

* *Caesar and Cleopatra*, by Bernard Shaw. Directed by Cedric Hardwicke. Settings and costumes by Rolf Gerard. Presented by Richard Aldrich and Richard Myers in association with Julius Fleischmann. With a cast including Cedric Hardwicke, Lilli Palmer, Ralph Forbes, Arthur Treacher, John Buckmaster, Nicholas Joy, Bertha Belmore, Ivan Simpson, and Henry Irvine. At the National Theatre. Opened December 21, 1949.

and Claude Rains did no justice to Shaw's work. The film, though well meant, was a colossal bore. It misplaced the play in the pageant, allowed the Shavian wit to evaporate in limitless expanses of Technicolor sky, and reduced G.B.S. himself to the equivalent of a scenarist for Cecil B. De Mille. The Theatre Guild's production of *Caesar and Cleopatra* in 1925 failed, even with Helen Hayes and Lionel Atwill, to project the text's real qualities. It was a stuttering, static affair, the inadequacies of which become all the clearer in retrospect when compared to the excellences of the present performance. The exciting truth is that, as staged with an admirable cast headed by Lilli Palmer and Sir Cedric Hardwicke, Shaw's play, written more than fifty years ago, seems as fresh as if it had been written today. At last behind local footlights, its humor is released, its wisdom communicated, and its stature preserved.

Shaw, being Shaw, did not hesitate to offer *Caesar and Cleopatra* to the public as an improvement on Shakespeare. "Better than Shakespeare" was the title he chose for his preface. By this, he pointed out with surprising modesty, he did not mean that he professed to write better plays than Shakespeare. He did, however, claim the right to criticize Shakespeare, to discard and discredit his romantic notions of passion and history, and to substitute new ideas and a new approach born of a new age.

The first change, an inevitable one in Shaw's case, was that where Shakespeare had written a tragedy Shaw wrote a comedy. The side of Shaw which is John Bunyan pretended to be shocked by Shakespeare's Cleopatra. He dismissed her as a Circe who, instead of turning heroes into hogs, turned hogs into heroes. He would have nothing to do with the mature woman, a tawdry wanton as he saw her, whose lustfulness had transformed a world leader into a strumpet's fool. For that matter, he would have nothing to do with the youthful Cleopatra who, according to history, had a child by Caesar. In her place he preferred to draw, and drew delectably, the portrait of a kittenish girl who under Caesar's tutelage flowered into a queen. His Cleopatra's youth was more than a puritanic evasion. It was a Shavian device by means of which superstitions could be mocked and Caesar, the conqueror, humanized by being seen through the irreverent eyes of a child. In other words, it was Shaw's characteristic way of taking the starch out of the stuffed-shirt approach to history.

As for Shakespeare's Caesar, Shaw had only contempt for him. His contention was that Shakespeare, who knew human weakness so well, never knew human strength of the Caesarian type. Just why Shaw, also a man of words, felt that he had a greater claim to understanding the inner workings of a man of action, is something he did not bother to explain. But that he succeeded with his Caesar where Shakespeare failed with his, few would deny.

In his preface to *Caesar and Cleopatra* G.B.S. described himself as a crow who has followed many plows. Surely none of these has led him down stranger furrows than his flirtations with the dictator principle. The champion of the Superman, who was fascinated by Napoleon and who has had kind words to say about Stalin and even Mussolini, was bound sooner or later to be drawn to Caesar.

The major source for his Julius was not Plutarch. As he confessed, it was Mommsen, the nineteenth-century German historian. He liked Mommsen's account of the Egyptian visit and agreed with his estimate of Caesar. Shaw also admitted his debt to Carlyle for his concept of the historical hero capable of bearing "the weight of life" realistically rather than suffering from a passion to die gallantly.

The Caesar Shaw drew would not have been recognized by Suetonius or Plutarch, neither of whom liked him. But the man who wrote *The Gallic Wars* would have recognized this Shavian Julius—with gratitude and relief. The clemency and statesmanship, the largeness of mind and spirit, which for the sake of the record he had been careful to establish as his, are qualities that shine in Shaw's Caesar. Caesar's self-love could not have been greater than Shaw's almost romantic infatuation with the benevolent despot he depicted.

But there was a difference—an immeasurable difference. Where Plutarch was dignified, Suetonius scurrilous, Caesar determinedly official, and Shakespeare rhetorically athletic, Shaw was Shavian. This in itself represented a complete abandonment of the orthodox ways of writing not only history but historical plays. It meant that, more than upsetting an applecart, Shaw had brought about a one-man revolution in the theatre and in literature.

He approached the past unawed, anxious to see it in contemporary terms, eager for a laugh, and with a wit which, though impudent, was wonderfully humanizing. The effects of his innovations are still with us, though in lesser hands they have never achieved the same dimensions and have sometimes been downright sophomoric. Quite rightly, it has been pointed out that what is widely thought of as Lytton Strachey's method was something for which Shaw prepared the way. But what is often overlooked is that G.B.S., regardless of his impertinences, was never a debunker. His spirit was always too positive for that, his intellect too superior.

Caesar and Cleopatra is a proof of this. However flippant or hilarious its means may be, its concerns are serious and sizable. For Shaw's real interest, so gaily presented in a very funny play, is nothing less than a study of the anatomy of earthly power and greatness. Although his Caesar may laugh and be laughed at, he is palpably a great man misunderstood by those around him and even by the Cleopatra he has instructed in queenship. If in delineating this greatness Shaw deliberately substitutes colloquial prose for what he had once condemned as the melodious fustian and mechanical lilt of Shakespeare's blank verse, he is nonetheless able in speech after speech to rise to a glorious eloquence of his own.

Caesar's apostrophe to the Sphinx is a sample. It is with this, and neither of the alternate prologues, that the present production opens. Other samples are the wisdom of Caesar's "He who has never hoped can never despair" and his "One year of Rome is like another, except that I grow older whilst the crowd in the Appian Way is always the same age." Or the beauty of his leave-taking of Cleopatra, when he describes Mark Antony to her in these words, "Come, Cleopatra: forgive me and bid me farewell; and I will send you a man, Roman from head to heel and Roman of the noblest; not old and ripe for the knife; not lean in the arms and cold in the heart; not hiding a bald head under his conqueror's laurels; not stooped with the weight of the world on his shoulders; but brisk and fresh, strong and young, hoping in the morning, fighting in the day, and reveling in the evening." In almost every instance the organ plays full and strong, only to be interrupted by a jest. Even so, the sense of greatness is not lost. Moreover, it is part and parcel of the current revival.

Sir Cedric Hardwicke is no plaster-bust Caesar. He is the perfect embodiment of the Shavian conqueror: patrician, accustomed to command, and no less used to meeting the harder challenges of thought. Although his majesty is genuine, his simplicity is equally real. If he can make a joke, he can also take one. His manner is quiet. His eyes twinkle with amusement at the foibles of those lacking his qualities. His humor is kindly, not condescending. It is born of his patience, even as that patience is backed by an iron will. One believes in him not only as a general but as a thinker. More than acting with his body, he acts with his mind. Instead of speaking Shaw's lines as if he had memorized them, he speaks them as if he had thought them. The wit of Shaw's Caesar is his. So is the eloquence; so is the wisdom.

Surely, Lilli Palmer is the most eye-filling and eye-haunting Cleopatra the stage has known in our time. After seeing her one is bound to feel a new sympathy for Mark Antony. She is blessed with all the physical attributes that one likes to associate with Egypt's queen, but her endowments do not stop there. Hers is a truly exciting personality. What is more, she acts Cleopatra as perfectly as she looks her, changing with great skill from the kittenish girl of the earlier scenes to the violent and imperious monarch of the later ones.

The happy truth is that this revival of *Caesar and Cleopatra* succeeds in living up to Shaw's comedy. It makes the past provocative, history human, and greatness gay.

*A lady who was for burning, and for sainthood too, as Shaw
points out the meaning of her martyrdom in* Saint Joan.

[1936, 1951]

THE PROPHET AND THE MAID

CORNELL'S JOAN

OF ALL Shaw's plays, *Saint Joan* seems to have upon it the most
enduring marks of greatness. In it he stumbled upon a subject
larger than himself and by surrendering to it succeeded in making
it as large as any noble statement of it needs must be. His play is
final proof of Joan's sorcery. It shows that the simple Maid of Orleans, who was accused of witchcraft in her day, was still able to
cast her spell on Mr. Shaw even when she had been so long dead
she could with safety be admitted to the company of saints.

Her conquest of Mr. Shaw must be counted among her major
victories. She can be credited with having changed his spirit as
a dramatist just as surely as once upon a time her prayers were
credited with having changed the wind upon the Loire. Certainly
the Mr. Shaw of *Saint Joan* is not the ordinary Mr. Shaw. In it
he has listened not only to her voice but to the bell-like voices of
the saints she claimed to have heard. She turned him into a poet
who does not have to write in verse to achieve poetry. Most of
all she brought him a discipline as a playwright he has never
shown before or since.

In *Saint Joan* his subject comes first and Mr. Shaw afterward. He
steps aside to give Joan the stage. He illustrates the quickening
qualities of her miracles and her faith. He makes clear the problems which she, like anyone with advanced ideas, presented to her
age. He shows how in word and deed she incurred the quite understandable disfavor of the Church and her secular contemporaries.
He characterizes the men who followed her into battle, who deserted her when her prison doors stayed closed, or who gave her a

far fairer trial than the melodramatists are willing to admit. And he points the final irony of her canonization in a world not yet ready to receive its saints which would doubtless burn her all over again were she ever to revisit it. In setting forth these things Mr. Shaw keeps himself out of the picture. He does not turn monologist or go off on tangents, regardless of how tempting or diverting they may prove. He gets off his occasional gibes at the English, but he refuses to cut capers for their own sakes, or to turn clown. Neither does he grow pompous in the manner of so many historical dramatists when they attempt to recreate the language of another day. His speech is easy, effortless, colloquial, witty, and very much alive. Yet at all times it is relevant, even when it becomes more copious than may be comfortable or necessary. Again and again it rises to passages unforgettable in their eloquence.

In *Saint Joan* Mr. Shaw shows himself to be a dramatist who has abandoned his slouchy Norfolk jacket and donned the same kind of shining armor the Maid of Orleans was wont to wear. The result is a play above which hovers a light similar to the one Joan saw dancing above Robert de Baudricourt's head. It is the most stirring expression the modern theatre has produced of the hungry rationalities of the spirit which transcend the limited rationalities of the mind. If, by Mr. Shaw's definition, a miracle is an act which creates faith, *Saint Joan* is indeed a dramatic miracle of good humor and fairness, of tension and eloquence, of fervor and reason which confirms one's faith in the theatre. Even its epilogue, which was widely condemned when the Theatre Guild first produced the play back in 1923, now seems to be a further demonstration of Shaw's wisdom. In spite of its talkiness and the abrupt change in mood it represents after the glories of the Inquisition scene, it succeeds, as Shaw meant it should, in granting a sad point and a great glory to this story of the Maid.

The production Katharine Cornell has given *Saint Joan** is a memorable one. It has been beautifully set and costumed by Jo

---

* *Saint Joan,* by George Bernard Shaw. Directed by Guthrie McClintic. Settings and costumes by Jo Mielziner. Produced by Katharine Cornell. With a cast including Miss Cornell, Maurice Evans, Charles Waldron, Brian Aherne, Kent Smith, Tyrone Power, Jr., Arthur Byron, George Coulouris, John Cromwell, and Eduardo Ciannelli. At the Martin Beck Theatre. Opened March 9, 1936.

Mielziner in a series of quickly changing backgrounds enclosed in three Gothic arches. The brilliant colors of the costumes stand out dramatically from the darkly suggested depths of Rheims Cathedral, the threatening shadows of the Inquisition Court, the gray-browns of the scene by the Loire and the tapestry-like qualities of the interiors. Only when Cauchon and Warwick are crowded together at the front of the stage for their first meeting does Mr. Mielziner's scenic scheme fail to be highly helpful and imaginative. Guthrie McClintic's direction is fluid, sensitive, and evocative. It is possessed of the same kind of energy and the same kind of pictorial qualities which characterized his *Romeo and Juliet*. It is not his fault if Mr. Shaw is not given to using the blue pencil as much as he should.

Miss Cornell's Joan glows with all the radiant qualities of the text. To the Maid she brings the same shimmering sense of innocence and youth she brought to her Juliet. Only this time it is a peasant girl, ruddy and healthy, she creates; a peasant girl whose ears, one is willing to believe, hear divine voices and whose eyes see beyond the stars. There is a definite growth in Miss Cornell's Joan from the moment of her first entrance as a smiling rustic to the final plea which she speaks in a suit of golden armor for a world that will be ready for its saints. At first sight she belongs so naturally to the soil that one can understand all the more poignantly the paean to the freedom of the countryside with which she turns relapsed heretic at the trial. Yet even at the outset there is an illumination about her which must belong to the saints. It is a quality born of the spirit which almost shines through the flesh.

Miss Cornell's Joan is neither bumptious nor sanctimonious. She is the mixture of modesty and assurance Mr. Shaw describes. Her modesty is her own; her assurance heaven-sent. Miss Cornell takes as readily to armor as the real Joan did. She looks extremely well in her boyish costumes, handles her slim body gracefully, and completely creates the difficult illusion of the warrior Maid. At times she pitches her voice a little higher than she might. At other times, as when she comes to the dithyramb to the countryside, she plunges somewhat breathlessly into speeches that would benefit by a more lyric treatment. But her Joan comes as a triumph for her not only as a manager but also as an actress. It is one of the finest things she has done.

ANOTHER INCARNATION

Statements beyond challenge are as rare as virtue untested. In spite of this, it would seem safe to say that *Saint Joan* is not only Shaw's greatest play but one of the greatest plays to have come out of the modern theatre. Yet as I write these words I realize their rashness. I recall how even *Hamlet*, a tragedy the world has been dull enough to accept as a masterpiece, was once dismissed by T. S. Eliot as being "most certainly an artistic failure."

It is this same Olympian Mr. Eliot, however, who at this moment gives me courage. In his recent *Poetry and Drama* he has admitted that his *Murder in the Cathedral* may have been written "slightly under the influence of *Saint Joan.*" Such a statement from such a source, though not expressed in the ordinary terms of praise, is no doubt meant to be taken as praise from Sir Hubert. I know it makes me feel the safer from attack when I assert that most people (notice I say "most") have a special and rightful admiration for Shaw's drama about the Maid who heard voices.

Saint Joan may not have been Shaw's own favorite among his works. In her *Thirty Years with G.B.S.* Blanche Patch reports it was not. She reveals that in Frank Harris's copy of *Heartbreak House* Shaw wrote, "Rightly spotted by the infallible eye of Frank Harris as My Best Play." Nonetheless, to the majority of Shavians, regardless of how high is their esteem for other plays by him, *Saint Joan* is his masterpiece.

Shaw was sixty-seven when he finished it in 1923, and Joan had been made a saint only three years before. Her posthumous fate had not been without its ironies. As Shaw reminds us, she had been burned for heresy, witchcraft, and sorcery in 1431; rehabilitated after a fashion in 1456; designated venerable in 1904; declared Blessed in 1908; and finally canonized in 1920.

There was everything about Joan as a subject to interest Shaw, and everything about her to release his mightiest gifts once his interest had been won. Yet apparently he resisted Joan as a theme and would have continued to do so had not Charlotte Shaw employed strategy to get her husband started on a play she wanted him to write. Being a good wife, in other words a woman blessed with Maggie Shand's knowledge, she did not argue with Shaw or let him feel that she was influencing him. Instead, she left books about the Maid and her trial around the house in places where he was certain to see them, pick them up, and read them in his moments of idleness. He fell for the bait and, once having fallen, became absorbed in Joan.

When *Saint Joan* first appeared there were many even among the most stalwart of Shaw's followers who were surprised by the reverence of the play which the notoriously irreverent G.B.S. had written. They had long since admitted his brilliance. They had recognized his audacity. They had prized his originality and laughed at his jokes. But they had grown so accustomed to identifying him as a professional iconoclast and jester that they had lost sight of his seriousness. Remembering his wit, they had forgotten his eloquence. They had closed their eyes to the fact that his spirit was as sizable as his mind. Above all, they had failed to recall, or, worse still, misunderstood, *Androcles and the Lion* and the noble simplicity of the scene in which the Roman soldier asks the Christian woman who is about to face martyrdom in the arena, "What is God?" and she answers, "When we know that, Captain, we shall be gods ourselves."

A man who in Shaw's manner could refuse his government's offer of the Order of Merit by saying he had already conferred it upon himself was bound to be suspected by the humorless of immodesty. When it came to *Saint Joan*, however, he was far more modest than he had any right or cause to be. Hesketh Pearson reports that Shaw said to Sybil Thorndike, the first actress to play the part in England, "I have told the story exactly as it happened. It is the easiest play I have ever had to write. All I've done is to put down the facts, to arrange Joan for the stage. The trial scene is merely a report of the actual trial. I have used Joan's very words: thus she spoke, thus she behaved."

Count this among the least reliable of Shavian utterances. In *Saint Joan* Shaw matters at every turn and with the turn of almost every phrase. What makes the play magnificent is not that he retells the familiar story but that this story comes to life in a new and memorable way as the issues involved and the problems raised by Joan provoke his eloquence, appeal to his mysticism, stir his imagination, and ignite his thinking.

Though a Protestant himself, Shaw refuses to use Joan's trial and burning as a means of attacking the Catholic Church. With all the fairness of his incredibly fair mind he insists she was given a very careful and conscientious trial by men who were anxious to save her.

To understand her fate, he points out, one must understand not only her character and claims but the mind and beliefs of the Middle Ages. Joan's paradox, he maintains, was that though a professed and most pious Catholic she was in fact one of the first Protestant martyrs. In a feudal period when nobles were jealous of their prerogatives, she imperiled these prerogatives by being an early exponent of nationalism and championing the powers of her king. That a country girl in her teens presumed to tell military leaders what they should do was bound to antagonize the Brass Hats to whom she gave orders. Moreover, she was an individualist who invited religious disfavor by claiming that she could speak directly to God through her visions and voices without the intercession of the Church.

Beyond and above these causes for Joan's unpopularity with her contemporaries there were, as Shaw demonstrates, other and more disconcerting reasons for her undoing. Because she was exceptional her contemporaries could not tolerate her, and because she was their moral superior they burned her. Indeed, the point of Shaw's play is summarized by two ageless questions asked in the Epilogue. The first is Cauchon's "Must then a Christ perish in torment in every age to save those that have no imagination?" The second is Joan's "O God that madest this beautiful earth, when will it be ready to receive Thy saints? How long, O Lord, how long?"

The dimensions of the tragedy (the poetry of its prose, the unfettering simplicity of its construction, its tenderness, its intellectual power, indeed its grandeur) are unmistakable throughout. No scene in the modern theatre is more touching as an affirmation of faith than the one by the banks of the Loire when the wind changes. None is more charged with the electricity of ideas than the discussion by Cauchon, Warwick, and De Stogumber of the religious and political problems raised by the Maid. No on-stage trial is more stirring than Joan's and no single speech mightier in its language than the one addressed to the court by the Inquisitor. As for the Epilogue, it is hard to see why it was subject to furious attacks when the play was originally produced. It is the needed summary of what has gone before and is essential to our understanding both of Shaw's meaning and of Joan's posthumous fate and ultimate canonization.

Although Uta Hagen* has on many occasions demonstrated how fine a performer she is, Joan eludes her. She has her good scenes, reads intelligently, and is properly earthy and unsentimental. At her best, however, she is no more than competent, and at her worst plainly inadequate. The final requisite for Joan is that inner radiance which is in the text and which flamed in Katharine Cornell's performance. This is missing, and the absence of this simple, shimmering spirituality is a major loss.

Several actresses have played Joan, and many more will. But the Joan of all Joans I should like to have heard—and seen— was the one Margaret Webster once told me was the best she ever saw. It was Bernard Shaw himself; Shaw when he read the part to Sybil Thorndike's company in which Miss Webster was an understudy. Apparently as one listened to his marvelously flexible and musical voice, his beard and age, his sex and dress were all forgotten, and the spirit of the real Joan, his Joan, came magically to life.

Doubtless Shaw read his Joan as well as he had written her because both he and she, by his own insistence, were geniuses. A genius, says he in his superb preface to the play, "is a person who, seeing farther and probing deeper than other people, has a different set of ethical values from theirs, and has energy enough to give effect to this extra vision and its valuations in whatever manner best suits his or her specific talents." No wonder, therefore, the old Prophet understood the young Maid so well, or that from

* *Saint Joan,* by Bernard Shaw. Directed by Margaret Webster. Settings by Richard Harrison Senie. Costumes by Elinor Robbins. Music by Lehman Engel. Produced by the Theatre Guild under the supervision of Theresa Helburn and Lawrence Langner. With a cast including Uta Hagen, John Buckmaster, Alexander Scourby, Frederic Worlock, and Frederic Warriner. At the Cort Theatre. Opened October 4, 1951.

his understanding he was able to write a play the greatness of which cannot be obscured even in a production that fails to do justice to its splendors.

An incredible Elderly Gentleman and why, on the basis of his mind, spirit, personality, and works, the world has had to agree with his own high estimate of himself.

[1950]

PROFESSIONAL MAN OF GENIUS

OF COURSE, *Pygmalion* had a preface—even on the screen. Otherwise it would not have been Shaw's. There was the Old Gentleman himself, reading it as only the world's best actor could. There he was, looking like that most unlikely of mortals, a prophet with a sense of humor. There he was, exuding the charm which is held to be Irish and was known to be his. As usual, he was smiling his way through immodesties and overstatements calculated to win attention and laughter. No less characteristically, he was distributing insults as if they were cookies, and persuading people to gobble them up as such.

And what was he saying in his role of self-appointed headmaster to the universe? "You will have to make up your mind that you will lose me presently, and then heaven only knows what will become of America. I have to educate all the nations. I have to educate England. Several Continental nations require a little educating, but America most of all. And I shall die before I have educated America properly, but I am making a beginning."

All this was in 1938, when Shaw was a mere stripling of eighty-two. Now we have lost him, and for many of us there is a kind of emptiness in the world. How the citizens of Rhodes felt when an earthquake toppled over the Colossus in their harbor, we do not know. We do know, however, the incredulity with which we face a universe without Shaw. In spite of increasing signs of his fatigue and warnings that he, too, must die, we had come to take his being here for granted. He was so palpably a natural phenomenon that we are bound to feel just now as if Niagara had dried up or Old Faithful had ceased to erupt.

When Mr. Roosevelt died, there were American teen-agers who, never having known any other President, could not imagine one. There are plenty of grandparents the globe over who, since their teens, have no memory of the literary scene when Shaw was not among the most towering of its landmarks. Longevity was one of his preachings which he practiced. He practiced it not only by keeping dazzlingly alive himself but by making this planet a far livelier—and different—place during those sixty years in which he functioned superbly as the challenger of every orthodoxy and the embodiment of his own Superman.

No one under seventy can pretend to have experienced the full detonating impact of Shaw when first he released the armory of his audacities against Victorianism in its every form. Those septuagenarians find it difficult even now to describe the heady delight and happy amazement with which they read him in their youth. They followed him gladly, not quite understanding or daring to understand, but with the joy of the emancipated. Although we, their children, got there later, there were plenty of wonders left and countless surprises.

We, too, knew the excitement of having him snatch the bandages from our eyes and lead us out of the shadows into a realm of sunlight. He pricked our consciences, routed our smugness, jostled us into thoughts undreamed of. He gave us a new boldness, and an unbelievable illusion of freedom, all the while that he was providing us with pleasures fresh and to this day unequaled.

Since nothing is deader than an idea or a cause which no longer needs to be fought for, younger people encountering Shaw at present are bound to find some of his audacities tame and some of his arguments superfluous. They cannot be expected to know how much of what they assume has become accepted only because his fighting helped to make it so. Take the "New Woman" he so ardently championed. Certainly she has lost her youth and grown into a very, very old lady. But they fool themselves, these young people (in the manner of their elders), if they think they have caught up with Shaw. To the end he remained almost as far ahead of them as he was of their grandparents. The likelihood is that their great-great-grandchildren will follow his circuitous trail, panting and out-distanced.

In *Sixteen Self Sketches* Shaw's explanation of why he had never written a complete autobiography was that "things have not happened to me: on the contrary it is I who have happened to them." This was a statement, however unshrinking, of a truth from which no one can shrink. Shaw was not only a genius; he was an event. Someone likened him to a centipede with a foot in every cause. The range of his curiosities was so prodigious that the sun never set on his interests. From economics to religion, from government to painting, from history to music, drama to medicine, vivisection to literature, phonetics to Communism, the causes of war to the difficulties of peace, or yesterday's news to creative evolution, his mind leaped untiringly and with an athlete's prowess.

It was an extraordinary mind put to extraordinary uses. No one can read a page of Shaw's prefaces, his journalism, his letters, or his better plays without feeling its lunge, its force, magnificence, sparkle, and originality. It was an intellect giant-sized yet agile. In the field of letters only Voltaire's has been comparable with it in its mixture of lightness and vigor. It worked overtime and hummed like a dynamo.

It was an ebullient mind as sudden in its contradictions as it was constant in its brilliance. If it borrowed freely and unashamedly the coinage of other men's thinking, it nonetheless managed to melt down what it had appropriated and remint it into a currency glitteringly golden and unmistakably Shavian. Its lacks were plain enough, but its virtues were plainer still. It spoke for a man who had the courage to say what he felt instead of what he ought to have felt, and who possessed to a supreme degree a genius for illumination, stimulation, revelation, and provocation.

No subject daunted Shaw, and few were touched upon by him without at least having been made the more interesting. Was his Caesar in his apostrophe to the Sphinx convinced, without ever giving her a chance to speak, that he had read her riddle? Shaw himself was always ventriloquizing for the Sphinx, expecting her

PROFESSIONAL MAN OF GENIUS 151

to be as quiet as a dream-wife while he spewed forth answers to all the problems known to men and gods. The fact that he was childless no more deterred him from pontificating (hilariously and quite sensibly) as the final authority on parenthood than the fact that he was a Socialist prevented him from marrying a millionairess and emitting angry cries of outrage when, as a millionaire himself, his taxes were mercilessly increased by a Labor government.

Any Shavian can point out the inconsistencies in Shaw, and a lot of dullards as well as bright people have. But the Ph.D.'s in economics or government who will haunt his ghost in the years to come, sniffing and tracking down his deviations from himself, will always present the sorry picture of Lilliputians trying to take the measurements of a Brobdingnagian. Although they may, as the Bardolaters do, buy Bendixes at the expense of the man who is involuntarily their prey, they will only prove their own stature by trying to reduce his.

Even a literate student in a School of Education must be aware that Shaw is as apt to disagree with himself as he is to disagree with everyone else. Everyone who is not a citizen of Dogpatch must also know that Shaw, throughout his many teetotaling years, swerved like a drunken driver in his allegiances.

He was an Irishman who preferred England. He was a Fabian who became a capitalist. He was a defender of the people, indeed a soapbox orator, whose questionable gods at one time were Napoleon and Caesar. He was a champion of the downtrodden who flirted, briefly and dangerously, with the dictator-principle in terms of Mussolini, Hitler, and Stalin.

As Bartlett will remind those who have never read his essay on "Self Reliance," Emerson held a foolish consistency to be the hobgoblin of little minds, adored by little statesmen and philosophers and divines. Not even the fools who parade this world as wise men have accused Shaw of having a little mind. The dimensions of his mind can in a way be measured by its inconsistencies and perversities.

His opinions were subject to change without notice and beyond anticipation. His variability was a part of his irreplaceable value. His surprises were unceasing. What mattered most in Shaw was not what he thought but that he made others think.

In the essay already referred to, Emerson, who included among his gifts a talent for freshening the wilted lettuce of bromides, observed that to be great is to be misunderstood. No great man has, I will wager, embarked upon such a far-flung, deliberate, and successful conspiracy to be misunderstood as Shaw. To most of the pygmies (meaning you and me) who are not only well-mannered enough but sufficiently realistic to realize how pint-sized are whatever talents they may possess, Shaw has seemed a titanic egotist.

Take, for example, his assertion, "I should have been a clerk still if I had not broken loose in defiance of all prudence and become a professional man of genius—a resource not open to every clerk." Or his famous explosion, "With the exception of Homer, there is no eminent writer, not even Sir Walter Scott, whom I can despise so entirely as I despise Shakespeare when I measure my mind against his." Or his claim, "I know a great deal more about economics and politics than Jesus did and can do things he could not do."

These were utterances of which no finishing-school graduate would have been guilty. Although they were shockers, planned with gleeful care, they were not meant to be blasphemous or even self-doting. On the subject of Jesus, about whom he has written beautifully, Shaw's only purpose was to point out the facts of economic and political change over the centuries.

So far as Shakespeare was concerned, he was (from his deep love and profound understanding of Shakespeare's merits) merely trying to make "a fellow creature" out of the Bard who had been "a divinity" and "a bore." He was doing this even while waging his usual warfare against Henry Irving and for "the drama of ideas" Ibsen had inaugurated. When it comes to Shaw's reference to himself as "a professional man of genius," he would have been a liar had he described himself in any other terms.

By temperament and habit Shaw was an honest man. The truth as he saw it, which was the truth as very few others had seen it or could bear to face or state it, always mattered more to him than such manners as the world expected. If, as he put it, he could not respond to the "demand for mock-modesty," neither was he ever guilty of mock-conceit. No one capable of writing and thinking as

Shaw did could have failed to realize that when he wrote he was outwriting and outthinking other men.

Said he in 1944, "When I contemplate what I know and have done (not that I ever do) I have a high opinion of myself. When I contemplate what I don't know and cannot do (which I am often forced to do) I feel as a worm might if it knew how big the world is." He was equally candid when, in a passage dashed off nearly a half-century earlier, he wrote, "I am ashamed neither of my work nor of the way it is done. I like explaining its merits to the huge majority who don't know good work from bad. It does them good; and it does me good, curing me of nervousness, laziness, and snobbishness. . . . I leave the delicacies of retirement to those who are gentlemen first and literary workmen afterwards. The cart and trumpet for me."

Shaw never ceased being one of G.B.S.'s favorite subjects, and he made him a favorite subject throughout the world. No one has ever written about him so well as he has, and no one ever will. He was his own advance man to his own circus, his Dexter Fellowes to what beyond question was the Greatest Show on Earth.

As he phrased it, "Half my time is spent in telling people what a clever man I am. It is no use merely doing clever things in England. The English do not know what to think until they are coached, laboriously and insistently for years, in the proper and becoming opinion. For ten years past, with an unprecedented pertinacity and obstination, I have been dinning into the public head that I am an extraordinarily witty, brilliant, and clever man. That is now part of the public opinion of England and no power in heaven or on earth will ever change it. I may dodder and dote; I may potboil and platitudinize; I may become the butt and chopping block of all the bright, original spirits of the rising generation; but my reputation shall not suffer: it is built up fast and solid, like Shakespeare's, on an impregnable basis of dogmatic reiteration." This was way back in 1898 and must be hailed as one of Shaw's more accurate prophecies.

Plato got along very nicely by contenting himself with being Plato. But Shaw was a modern Plato who could not resist also being Puck and Pantaloon. When it comes to clowning, Grock and the Fratellinis were amateurs compared with him. He could be downright silly. The gags he got off for the benefit of the wire services were often feeble, sometimes in questionable taste, and never dignified. If Shaw dispensed with dignity, however, it was not only because it was alien to his nature but because he did not need it. He had something far rarer and finer to offer. He had grandeur.

His wit delighted the public but misled it. Conventional people were confused by a man who said grave things gaily. Their belief was that men who are to be taken seriously must be dreary sobersides incapable of smiling. They found it easier to pigeonhole him as a humorist when he pleased them and as a buffoon when he shocked them. Shaw was well aware of the dangers he invited by laughing. "I have got the tragedian and I have got the clown in me," he once confessed, "and the clown trips me up in the most dreadful way." He explained this by saying that, like his father before him, he was in the grip of a humorous sense of anticlimax.

As a prophet, an economist, propagandist, and social reformer, Shaw realized that his inconsistencies no less than his wit blurred the effects he had hoped to achieve. The world had been guilty of the sorry, if understandable, error of mistaking the paradoxes of G.B.S. for his purpose. Far more important than the polemicist, however, was the artist. The specific causes for which he fought have been or may be forgotten, but the artist will always be remembered and treasured. Eric Bentley once contended that the final paradox of Shaw's paradoxical career was that "by not saving the world [he] saved his dramas as art and, therefore, as teaching."

Like Molière's doctor, Shaw was an artist in spite of himself. He was the best, the sprightliest critic ever to review plays. He was no less lively on the subjects of painting and music. As *Pen Portraits and Reviews* makes blindingly clear, he was a journalist with Promethean powers of firing a reader's interest. Perhaps the final proofs of an instinctive writer's gifts are his letters. Shaw's letters and postcards are miracles of invention, perception, gaiety, and fluency. We already have many samples of his superiority as a correspondent. We shall have more. Indeed, one of the greatest and most fascinating literary adventures the future will know is bound to be those many, many volumes of Shaw's letters which will some day be published, even as the Walpole and the Boswell papers are now being issued.

Certainly *The Intelligent Woman's Guide to Socialism and Capitalism,* printed when Shaw was seventy-two, is one of the finest examples of expository writing on the subject of politics and economics known to any library. Then, of course, there are the plays—and the prefaces. Some of the plays are trifles. Others are dated. No one can say with any certainty which ones will speak most directly to unborn generations. But I, at least, would have only pity for a world which could not be touched by *Candida,* melted by *Androcles and the Lion,* amused by *Man and Superman* (including its scintillating interlude in hell), quickened by *Caesar and Cleopatra,* and stirred by *Saint Joan.* Better than Shakespeare Shaw may not have been. Different he palpably was. Yet that his was the most fecund genius to have turned to the theatre since Shakespeare's time seems safe from challenge.

Shaw explained that he wrote prefaces, as Dryden did, "because I *can.*" I do not mean to subtract from the enrichment Dryden made to English prose when he was in a prefatory mood. I must insist, however, that Shaw's prefaces are in a class of their own. They are sizable additions to the gaiety of nations and the joys of reading. Prolix they may be. If they tire, however, it is only because in them Shaw gives us no rest from his own untiring brilliance.

"Effectiveness of assertion," he contended, "is the alpha and omega of style. He who has nothing to assert has no style and can have none." Shaw never lacked something to say and always said it with incredible vitality and apparently without effort. His sentences, as Winston Churchill (himself no mean stylist) observed, are colored with "a debating tinge."

The two vital qualities Shaw demanded of literature were "light and heat." Both of these his writing possessed to an unmatched degree. He did not believe, as many now seem to, that a great writer uses his skill to conceal his meaning. Although he did not object to writing for profit, he seldom wrote without a purpose. He had only contempt for "art for art's sake." However gay his words or bold his overstatements, Shaw's intentions were apt to be serious. He may have been the born mountebank he described himself as being, but he was also a Puritan.

He was an author who, as a boy, had been brought up in a musical household. This training was not wasted on him. His prose has the dancing lightness and the shining precision of Mozart. It is also capable of deeper Wagnerian sonorities. Hazlitt described wit as "the eloquence of indifference." Shaw, however, was witty not because he did not care but because he did. He could also rise to passages of great melodic beauty. His plays are studded with speeches quivering with a prophet's fervor and with sentences which literally sing themselves. Although not written in verse, they make most contemporary dramatic speeches written as poetry seem like the most meager and muffled of prose.

In spite of the multiplicity of his interests and his talents, the often ignored source of Shaw's greatness lay in the dimensions of his spirit. As surely as there was nothing little about his thinking, there was nothing little about his feeling. He never waged war on individuals. He waged war on the ideas for which they stood. His gift for forgiveness was even greater than his need at times to be forgiven. He was essentially good, kindly, clean, and gentle. His spiritual largeness explains why he, the supposed clown and acknowledged wit, was able to understand the dilemmas of such a man of action as Caesar, and to write in *Androcles and the Lion* and *Saint Joan* the two most beautiful religious plays to have come out of the modern theatre.

Although Shaw, the iconoclast, saw through men and institutions, he never lost his hope for what men might become if only they resolved to live up to their potentialities and outgrow their present limitations. The Life-Force, about which he wrote, was a potent factor in his own living. His plea was for progress. He loathed the shirkers, the loafers, the talent-squanderers, and time-wasters who deny themselves "the true joy in life" by not being used for a purpose they recognize "as a mighty one." The demands he made on himself were as unrelenting as those he made on others. Yes, and on God, too.

It is something to have lived on this planet as the contemporary of such a titan as George Bernard Shaw. Although he was mortal enough to die, we have not lost him. Of him it can be truly said, as he said of William Morris, "You can lose a man like that by your own death, but not by his."

5. London Pride

In which it is imagined that Mr. Sheridan sends an admiring letter that is truly ghostwritten to Mr. Coward, comparing the problems they have faced because of their multiple talents and discussing comedy as each of them has written it.

[1935]

RICHARD BRINSLEY SHERIDAN
TO NOEL COWARD

My dear Sir:

I hope this unsolicited communication will not lead you to the alarming conclusion that an M.P. with Irish blood in his veins cannot be silenced even by Death. But in my lifetime I died so early as the playwright you remember, and yet managed to live on for so many years as the orator of whose brilliance you may be dimly aware, that the habit of speaking after death is, I fear me, one which comes as naturally to me as does the dolorous habit of speaking after dinner to those who are addicted to it.

Though I survived my demise in one career to achieve a no less startling distinction in another, I loved life far too well and lived it much too recklessly to be comfortable in the presence of any reality as implacable as Death. Like Justice Credulous in my *St. Patrick's Day,* I found no consolation in the thought that "there is nothing in it: a moment, and it is over," because with him I was inclined to answer, "Ay, but it leaves a numbness behind that lasts a plaguy long time."

For more years than I care to contemplate I have been the victim of this numbness in the safe security of Poets' Corner at Westminster. Doubtless I, whom you may have pictured as lying snug in the Abbey, would not have been empowered to overcome its paralysing quiet even now were it not that Death—having robbed me of my pleasures as well as my worries—has forced more time for reverie upon me than I was wont to enjoy in my impromptu life, and that your own bright and varied successes, won in the theatre at an early age, have recalled to me my own extra-ordinary beginnings there. These have given urgent rise to some observations which I beg you to accept in good faith.

As you know, the dusty society in which I find myself in the Abbey is distinguished, to say the least. I am not friendless in the midst of the great and near-great who pave the floor and brick the walls of this much-coveted alcove, for among them are giants who flourished before my day, but whose printed works I have conned with admiration, as well as those whom I was proud to know in life. Opposite me is my good friend and companion, Dr. Goldsmith, who won much applause with his merry farce-comedy, *She Stoops to Conquer,* two years before I wrote *The Rivals.* And as my near neighbours I have Dr. Johnson, that saviour of our language, who urged my admission to his famous Literary Club when I was only twenty-six, and the incomparable Garrick, whom I succeeded at Drury Lane.

But though other men (among whom you no doubt have the wisdom to count yourself) would be entirely happy to be dis-covered by Time and tourists as an equal in such a group as this, candour compels me to admit it has taken me many fretful dec-ades to derive any satisfaction from my placing.

I had neither your pride in authorship nor your love of the thea-tre. Like Congreve before me, I wanted to be known as a gentle-man rather than a man of letters, and as a gentleman I hoped I would be honoured for the notable part I had played in public affairs rather than because of any contributions which (as it pleased me to phrase it) absolute indigence had driven me to make to the stage. The happiest moment of my life was not that triumphant May evening in 1777 when the screen fell for the first time to re-veal Lady Teazle in *The School for Scandal*—and old Drury paid proper tribute to my craftsmanship by rocking with such tumultu-ous laughter and applause that Frederick Reynolds, who happened to be passing the theatre at the time, ran for his life, convinced that the playhouse had collapsed—but the night two years later when, after I had heard the returns from Stafford and learned of my election to the House, I stole away by myself at the end of din-ner to speculate upon those prospects of distinguishing myself which had just been opened to me.

In other words, as I confided to Lord Thanet and will confess to you, Poets' Corner was my aversion. I wanted to be placed near my friend Charles Fox among the Statesmen—with Pitt and Burke and the other men who on the larger stage of politics had helped to shape England's destiny. For thirty-two years I, who had made my mark as a dramatist in a short five seasons, had laboured in their company, amazing them by my eloquence, delighting them with my charm (which they found so persuasive as to be dangerous), and entertaining them by the readiness of my wit (which they of course distrusted). I had toiled with them to meet the emergencies presented by such far-flung events as the American and French Revolutions and the subsequent threat of Bonaparte's rise in France, and had never failed to infuriate them by the bland manner in which I chose to put personal principles above party allegiances. More than the mightiest of them, I had distinguished myself in such a great display of oratory as the trial of Warren Hastings. And with the stoutest of them I had fought the ticklish battles of two Regency crises, not only championing in the face of their opposition the pretty Mrs. Fitzherbert's secret marriage to the Prince of Wales, but having long enjoyed, for this and other reasons, the confidence and friendship of the Prince himself.

I might in my lifetime have taken more pride in my writings and in the major role I played as manager of Drury Lane if the stage had offered me the full release for my talents that it has afforded you. But it was not large enough to house my genius or to encompass my dreams. It was a mere urchin compared to the giant of my ambition. It catapulted me into fame, but the fame it gave me was not the fame I sought. If the wit which distinguished my dramas was Irish in its origins, so was the relish for politics which led me to seek a more personal outlet for my gifts than playwriting made possible. As Coleridge had to admit—even when in the careless fashion that was typical of me I had lost the manuscript of the tragedy he had submitted to me as a manager—my mind was possessed of a wildly various power. But, as I was to learn from sad experience, my multiple endowments were nearly always at odds with one another.

If old Tom, my father, had been an actor who had gained my complete respect either as a man or a performer, and if, when he brought me over as a boy from Ireland, he had not packed me off for my education among the young gentlemen at Harrow, where the stage was held in scant esteem, I might—I say I might if my temperament had been different and my aspirations far less worldly—have found the enduring satisfaction in the theatre that you appear to have found there. But even this is doubtful; aye, more than that. Although I was by nature as much an actor as you have shown yourself to be, I am afraid that I could never have tethered my histrionism to the footlights as you have done. The floor of Parliament was the stage upon which I wanted to appear, and England's history, rather than any comedy of my own or another's writing, was the script in which I sought to play a leading role. The truth is, I desired the applause, not of an audience, but of the nation, and the approval, not of critics, but of kings.

As a youth at Harrow and afterwards at Bath, where my father had abandoned the stage for lecturing and was endeavouring to open an oratorical academy, I had come too close to the world of fashion not to want to become a part of it. Like the figures in Plato's cave who sat happily in the darkness with their backs to the entrance until the shadows they saw cast upon the wall before them destroyed their tranquillity by making them aware of a new world of light of which they had not previously dreamed, I, too, had surveyed the tantalizing shadows cast by a world to which I did not belong. The more my charm and genius brought me as young man into the realm of fashion, the more discontented I became with the stage.

I won my triumphs in the theatre too easily to have the theatre win and hold my admiration for long. From the outset I used it, not as the end that you have found it, but as a means, and the goal towards which it brought me in even less time than it has taken you to gain your enormous and very varied successes was the world of politics and society. I was willing to fly in the face of prudence to give myself the airs and notions of a gentleman, and was happy to honour the code of fashion when I did not command the resources.

Though I was practically penniless when at twenty-two I gained the hand of lovely Elizabeth Linley, and she was a concert singer whose beauty and voice had made her the toast of all England, I absolutely refused to allow her to continue her profitable career. You, with your greater respect for your calling and your professional's knowledge of the satisfaction which other professionals can derive from their labours, would not, I venture to say, have acted in my rash manner had marriage offered you a similar temptation. Even if you had been confronted with the dilemma that I faced, and had made my choice, I question if the London of your day would have given you such dogmatic approval as Dr. Johnson gave me, when, after commending the wisdom and nobility of my resolution and asking, "Would not a gentleman be disgraced by having his wife singing publicly for hire?" he abruptly settled the whole question with a "No, Sir, there can be no doubt here."

My decision was not without its bravery, for I was then at an even more unsettled period in my career than you were when, at twenty-one, as a boy actor who had grown up and a young author whose first play, *I'll Leave It to You,* had been indifferently received in London, you obeyed the *Wanderlust* which has always been strong in you and quitted England for America, only to find yourself ignored, for the short time that you stayed there, by the New York you were later to conquer. My romantic ardour—which had led Elizabeth and me into a sensational elopement and a secret marriage in France, not to forget the two much-talked-of duels I had fought on Elizabeth's account at Bath with a rascal known as Captain Mathews—was, I fear me, the most tangible asset I had to offer my wife at this time; that is, of course, if I except my firm ambition to play the gentleman and my as yet untrained aptitude for writing.

With a friend gained at Harrow, I had issued an unprofitable translation of *The Love Epistles of Aristænetus,* projected a magazine which was never published, written a farce which both Foote and Garrick were quick to refuse (though it foreshadowed *The Critic*), and on my own had been admitted to the Middle Temple. But while I was struggling—even as you once had to struggle —to gain a foothold, Elizabeth was at the top of her profession. Young though she was, this daughter of the composer who was afterwards to forgive us our marriage and write the music for my comic opera, *The Duenna,* had, by appearing on the same programme with my father, attracted greater crowds to his lectures than he could ever have collected without her. Britain was plainly in love with her, and in London, as in the provinces, there were those who gladly admitted every other diversion was forsaken in her favour.

At Drury Lane's Lenten Oratorio she had met with the kind of admiration and applause which had formerly been only Garrick's portion. And at the same performance even George III himself, in the years of his sanity, had—as Horace Walpole described it— ogled her as much as he dared do in so holy a place as an oratorio and at so devout a service as *Alexander's Feast*. When I tell you this, and add that (though our income was but forty shillings a week at the time of our marriage) I did not hesitate to cut short Elizabeth's career and refused offers of £3000 and upwards rather than let her appear again in public as a professional entertainer after she had once become known as my wife, I do so only to inform you of how strong was my determination to cut a figure in London's great world as a very proper gentleman.

But the butcher (who was always the problem to me that he has long since ceased to be to you) had to be paid if the mutton were not to continue stationary on his counters. So I, who was still feeling my way and had no real desire to turn Cupid into a turnspit wheel, set myself to writing as a means of gaining a livelihood, addressing to Queen Charlotte a scheme for the education of the daughters of impoverished noblemen, attacking "Novus" in the columns of the *Public Advertizer*, and launching upon a commentary of Lord Chesterfield's *Letters*. Since my father was the play-actor to whom I have already referred, and since my mother—after she had enjoyed much success by producing *Memoirs of Miss Sydney Biddulph,* a novel which had caused Dr. Johnson to remark, "I know not, Madam, that you have the right to make your readers suffer so"—had amused herself by writing several plays, among which *The Discovery* was one that took the town by storm and provided Garrick with a favourite part, and *A Trip to Bath* was another, which, though unfinished, contained a character that afterwards suggested Mrs. Malaprop to me; it was but natural, I suppose, that my pen should have been drawn to the stage.

I had not lived the theatre as you had lived it when playwriting first commanded your attention. Since the time when you were ten and your mother had wisely permitted you to leave Teddington for London and make your début as Prince Mussel in a children's fairy play known as *The Goldfish*, the world of the theatre had been the world in which you had moved almost without interruption. In a long list of plays, ranging from *The Great Name* to *Peter Pan*, you had appeared in London in smaller parts. With the Repertory Theatre in Liverpool you had acted in *Hannele*. And you had even headed a company up and down the countryside in that stout old farce, *Charley's Aunt*. You had in other words matured as an actor before you undertook to become a dramatist, and were therefore equipped from the outset to bring to your playwriting that actor's knowledge of your craft which is apparent in so much of your dramaturgy. I did not have the advantage of this first-hand experience when I began to write. Indeed I was by no means conversant with plays in general either in reading or upon the stage. Yet I had a knowledge of stagecraft which was even more instinctive than is your own. Much as I might resent it when I came to see the handicap such origins presented me in a snobbish age, the theatre was in my blood, and I could no more resist its call than I could afterwards abide the easy taunts which my success in it offered ready-made to such of my opponents in Parliament as Pitt and Courtenay.

Accordingly, while Sir Joshua Reynolds was painting Elizabeth as St. Cecilia, and when Elizabeth and I had moved with high hopes into a town house in Portman Square that was well beyond our means, and smart London was beginning to feel about us as Fanny Burney did when she dubbed us a "too aspiring and enchanting couple," and invitations were flooding in upon us from such great gentlemen as Lord Coventry, and we were becoming the rage, and winning not only the patronage but the close friendship of such exalted ladies as Georgiana, Duchess of Devonshire, Lady Duncannon, her sister, and Mrs. Crewe, I sat myself down out of sheer need in the summer of 1774, and in six or eight weeks (for the life of me I can't remember exactly just now) wrote that comedy which you and a great many others, both since my day and in it, have admired as *The Rivals*.

To you, who are now but thirty-five and who enjoyed your first taste of fame in the joint capacities of actor and author when at twenty-four you appeared in your own play, *The Vortex*, the very mention of youth must be somewhat tedious. During the past decade you have been hailed so often as an infant prodigy and a bright young man that I would not blame you if you were wearied with all references to your precocity. But at the risk of boring you, I must recall to you the early age at which I also triumphed, if for no other reason than to show you how sudden was my demise as the dramatist who now rests in the Abbey, and to lead me into those very observations which have called this letter into being.

I was twenty-three when I wrote *The Rivals* and *St. Patrick's Day*; twenty-four when I achieved the kind of success with my romantic operetta, *The Duenna*, which *Bitter Sweet* has brought to you; no older when I had the honour to succeed David Garrick at Drury Lane and become the manager of a company which already included such famous performers as Mrs. Yates and Mrs. Abington and which was soon to be strengthened by the addition of Mrs. Siddons and her brother, John Philip Kemble; twenty-five when to satisfy the more modest tastes of my period I refashioned Vanbrugh's *The Relapse* into *A Trip to Scarborough* and wrote *The School for Scandal*; and twenty-eight when, after composing that hilarious lampoon of the theatre known as *The Critic*, I died an abrupt death as a dramatist. Thereafter I liked no allusions to my playwriting and went so far as to pretend I thought *The Rivals* the worst play in the language and to wish that I had never written it. Yet twenty years after *The Critic* had been produced, and though my time, which was then somewhat spent upon the details and worries of management, was largely consumed by affairs of state, I did put in my appearance once more as a playwright.

Taking intentional advantage of the patriotic feelings the Napoleonic wars had created in England, even as your *Cavalcade* (without your meaning it to do so) had given expression to the popular emotions felt at the time of a Conservative victory in a general election, I made from Kotzebue's *The Spaniards in Peru, or The Death of Rolla*, that adaptation entitled *Pizarro* which filled the coffers of Drury Lane as it was acted there by Kemble, Mrs. Siddons, and Mrs. Jordan, and which was crammed with such resolute fustian that it long remained an actor's favourite in English-speaking countries. But the real Sheridan who was willing to sign his name to the bombast of *Pizarro* was not the Sheridan who had written either *The School for Scandal* or *The Rivals*. That other Sheridan had already been dead for two decades, and in his place had come a humourless dramatist who was willing to indulge in all the excesses of false tragedy which the true Sheridan would have hated and which he had once ridiculed to perfection in *The Critic*.

It is as the author who died so young, and whose passing I have come to regret, that I now address you. In my lifetime I did not fancy him, and after my death I used to blame my political enemies for being so unkind as to place Sheridan the dramatist, rather than Sheridan the politician, among the immortals in the Abbey. But I am at present persuaded that, by acting as they did, my enemies were better friends to me than were my own desires.

Though once I boasted, while the flames were destroying Drury Lane and hence my fortune, that I, who had suffered many things, had never suffered the pangs of self-reproach, yet will I now confess to you I do reproach myself for not having taken the proper pride in my playwriting which you have taken in yours, and for not having husbanded my genius for the theatre as wisely as you have made use of your many theatrical talents. Time, however, has brought me a contentment with my placing in Poets' Corner which I did not experience when Death claimed me as the politician who had survived the dramatist, and which no doubt I would not feel today were I to find myself again among the living. Such was the conflict in my nature that were I out of the Abbey and moving once more in the world of men, the artist in me would unquestionably be swallowed up for the second time by the statesman, even as the playwright would again give way to the manager. But it is as the dramatist, who I now realize has outlasted the orator in the affections of mankind and whom Death has spared from the ambitions which tormented his other self, that I now choose to write you.

When Walpole wondered by what witchcraft such a fellow as myself, who had no diamonds to bestow, could fascinate the world; when Wraxall admitted no individual of my time stood less in Fortune's debt or owed more to Nature for his vast reputation and success than I did; and when Mrs. Siddons set me down as the greatest phenomenon that Nature had produced in centuries, these good people might with equal justice have been your own contemporaries letting off the steam of their enthusiasm for you. Without intending to turn practitioner in the art of panegyric, or without meaning to assault your senses with what I once made fun of as the puff direct, the puff preliminary, the puff collateral, the puff collusive, the puff oblique, or the puff by implication, I salute you as the most versatile talent that in the long history of England's theatre has been an ornament to her stage. Other men, among whom I must count myself, have been possessed of minds of far more range and depth than yours can claim, and have likewise been endowed with different and much greater gifts which no playhouse could hope to hold. But no other theatre man in the chronicle of Britain's drama has brought to her stage so surprising an assortment of theatrical talents as you have done. You have shown yourself to be, not a man of the theatre, but (if one makes the single exception of your as yet unattempted adventures in the art of scenic design) a complete theatre in yourself.

As a performer, your equipment is such that you can add as much gaiety to a madcap turn in a revue as neurotic tension to a tragedy of post-war nerves, or high polish to a sophisticated comedy. As a writer, your pen has proven itself as hospitable to romance as it is to cynicism, to tragedy as it is to nonsense, to patter as to prose, to farce as to melodrama, to plays as to revues, to operettas as to comedies, to rough-and-tumble burlesques as to sentimental lyrics, and to the patriotism of such a stirring pageant of Empire as *Cavalcade* as it is to the pacifism that not only vents its hatred of war but that condemns the futility of sacrifice in the bitter pages of *Post-Mortem*. You can sing and dance acceptably, play the piano with ease, write charming melodies for the scores of your own musical comedies, invent dance steps for the chorus numbers you may want to use, and direct your own productions with the virtuoso's touch you brought to the staging of *Cavalcade*. I am not surprised, therefore, to find that those lackeys of literature—the critics—for whom you have no more respect than I had, have been compelled in their bewilderment to describe you as the modern theatre's "wonder boy." Truly you are that, and so amazing is the number, if not always the quality, of your endowments, that there is no period in the drama's past in which your gifts would prove any less phenomenal than they now do.

Yet it is the quality of your efforts rather than their multiplicity that I would discuss with you. Such marked versatility as you and I have possessed in our different ways is not an unmixed blessing, as I came to learn in my later years and as you may have sensed at times in your own extraordinary career. Quite naturally it is the cause for immediate wonder in those who contemplate it. But it can spread thin the talents of those who have it; reducing them as a fortune of uncommon size can be reduced by being divided among too many heirs. It is apt to be a freakish endowment rather than an important one. As such it merits the rapt attention it is bound to get. Yet it is well for those who in our fashion have been granted a superfluity of gifts to remember that, though it is the five-legged calf, and not the two-legged man, that attracts the greater crowd to the side-show, it is the two-legged man, and not the five-legged calf, who finds it easier to scramble up to the mountain-top. We must—if you will forgive me for being so moral among friends—aim more at excelling than we do at amazing if it is our ambition to outlast the moment of our triumph. Recognizing the obligations which our gifts put upon us, we must face the fact that it is not the number of one's talents but the excellence of one's works which wins enduring admiration. And the enduring admiration that three of my plays have enjoyed is a distinction merited by their qualities which I, with my high opinion of your capacities, would like to feel with more confidence than I do that your dramas will procure for you.

I was a young man when Dr. Johnson commended me for writing the two best comedies of the age, and an old and broken one when Lord Byron, who was the friend and champion of my sunset years, delivered himself of his famous encomium upon me. A cruel winter had set in on the brilliant but irresponsible youth who for a few enchanted seasons had found life to be the unending spring that Lady Teazle wished it might be. My marriage to Elizabeth Linley had not continued to make either of us happy, and, after she had died, I had married again only to bring as much unhappiness to the flighty girl who was my second wife. I had lost the friendship of Fox several years before his death, and the favour of the Regent for whom that friendship had been sacrificed. I had gained the dislike of my party; had been ejected from the management of the theatre in which for so many years I had shown myself to be "The Grand Master of Delays"; and, after failing to be re-elected to Parliament and hence losing my cherished immunity from the duns who had long pursued me, I had suffered the final humiliation of having to sell my household properties and of being carried off by the bailiffs to be placed for a while in a sponging house. The carefree comic dramatist you think of, who had once conquered London as easily as a bird masters song, had become the hero of an ugly tragedy written by his own temperament. Yet in these dark days it moved me as much as it consoled me when I learned that behind my back (where opinions really matter) young Byron had said of me, "Whatever Sheridan has done or has chosen to do has been, *par excellence,* always the best of its kind," and credited me with having written the best comedy, *The School for Scandal;* the best opera, *The Duenna;* the best farce, *The Critic;* the best address, *The Monody on Garrick;* and "to crown all, delivered the best oration, the famous Begum speech, ever conceived or heard in this country."

It is not from immodesty, or because I subscribe to such over-generous praise as this, that I quote you Byron's well-known tribute, but because I am anxious to have you, who have been so abundantly rewarded with the renown and applause your unprecedented versatility has earned you, set your mind upon deserving the kind of praise which can only be expressed in superlatives. As the talk of your playwright in *Design for Living* has made clear, you are already beginning to discover how empty is the cup of success even when it is full. I was older when I learned how bitter its dregs can be. But both of us I trust have reached the point when we have come to see it is ourselves, and not the world, that we must satisfy if we would really satisfy the world, or derive any lasting pleasure from our works when the world has turned against us.

Both of us have been blessed with more talents than as dramatists we have felt the need of. And both of us, for these and other reasons, have threatened our own lives as artists. Where I allowed my procrastination, my snobbery, and my political ambitions to stifle my dramatic genius, and was for ever permitting my desire for managing things to cut into the time I might more profitably have been devoting to the writing of my plays, you have allowed the facility which crowns your talents to rob your compositions of that final polish and perfection of which they stand in need. Where I leaned heavily upon my personal charm to gain my conquests in society and politics, or to make creditors forget my debts, or to coax Mrs. Siddons into acting when her salary was long overdue, you

have relied more often than is good for you upon the same dangerous asset in yourself, or upon your skill in casting or direction, to
cover up those defects in your scripts which are easily discovered
in the cooler tribunal of the study when Coward, the man of the
theatre, is no longer at hand to come to the aid of Coward, the
author.

Admiring your writing talents as I do, I find this lack in your
plays disturbing. It does not prevent me from enjoying many of
them vastly, or from prizing the shrewdness with which you have
contrived this scene or that, or from holding in high esteem the
skill with which much of the dialogue is written, or from delighting
in the smartness of the mind which is responsible for it, or from
valuing several of your farce-comedies for the undoubted virtues
they possess as entertainment. Nor does it lessen in any way my
amazement at the number of your gifts. But it does cause me to
come away from your dramas still looking for something in them
that is not there—indeed, for the very quality of sustained excellence which they so often promise but which they so rarely achieve.

I do not mean to say that as a playwright, working in many
more forms than I would have thought of attempting or could ever
have employed with success, you have not written extremely well.
The command of farce-comedy you have shown in such a delightful trifle as *Hay Fever,* your charming libretto for *Bitter Sweet,* certain of your emotional scenes in *Post-Mortem* and *The Vortex,* the
suave exuberance that has found expression in such sophisticated
romps as *Private Lives* and *Design for Living,* and the adroit phrasing and planning of all your "above-stairs" scenes in *Cavalcade*
(particularly in such poignant episodes as the funeral of Queen
Victoria and the incident on the *Titanic*), are tantalizing proofs of
your dexterity as a craftsman and your genius as a dramatist. But
while they amply demonstrate the uncommon range of your powers and the skill with which you can make use of them, they also
indicate, if I may say so, certain limitations born of your mind and
temperament which run deeper than the mere excess of facility
that is at once your special blessing and your curse, and which for
that very reason have stood in the way of your development as
both a comic and a tragic playwright.

It is when you turn your attention to the writing, not of comedies or farces or burlesque skits or sentimental romances, but of

plays which are supposed to be strongly emotional, that you force me to become most aware of these limitations. Though *The Vortex* and *Post-Mortem* are the best of your serious works (if one excepts *Cavalcade*, as one must, for reasons I shall subsequently reach), these scripts compel me to conclude, as surely as do such of your less fortunate excursions into the same field as *The Rat Trap, Sirocco,* and *Easy Virtue,* that you are not yet equal to the task of delving deeply into human passions or of composing earnest dramas which are possessed of more than a passing interest.

I do not object to your emotional plays on the ground that they have very little to say that is generally applicable, for I was never one to confuse the pulpit with the stage. Nor am I more upset than you would expect me to be by their so-called "decadence," though I must admit they have a tone to them which I neither understand nor like. But I do find them disappointing because in them you have so often bestowed your pity (where in a comedy it would be only just to have you bestow your contempt) upon a special coterie of sophisticates who abuse Nature rather than upon those whom Nature abuses. Your emotional plays have a shallowness to them which, though it may facilitate the gaiety of a manuscript whose only aim is laughter, prevents a serious one from being taken as seriously as it might like to be taken. They are cynical and bitter and worldly, but they have neither compassion nor exaltation in them. Their protest is petulant and shrill, instead of being angry or profound. And more often than I like, they seem to me to be written from your nerves rather than from your heart, and reveal you when you are committing the fatal error of mistaking hysteria for tragedy.

If you will forgive me for saying so, these serious plays of yours show that you are still too much interested in your own generation, your own special group, and above all in yourself, to be capable of the larger sympathies from which true tragedy is sprung. More than that, they indicate with greater clarity than does the most ingenious of your comedies, that you are a boy actor who has grown up into a dramatist.

Not for an instant would I bring against you the charge of plagiary which those who were jealous of my success so often brought against me, for nothing could be farther from the truth. But I do mean to say that such emotional dramas as *The Vortex* and *Easy Virtue* are haunted by memories of the stage tricks to which you must have been exposed since your childhood. They are actor's plays which you appear to have written with greasepaint rather than with ink, and smell as strongly of the glue and paint and canvas of the theatre as do the back-stages of any of the playhouses in which they have been acted. Though they are as modern in their language and their point of view as you are yourself, they remind me of new buildings reared on old foundations. For in their plotting they are near relations to those creaky fables Oscar Wilde was wont to make brilliant with his epigrams before you appeared upon the scene at Teddington. That the "big scenes" of these emotional dramas of yours happen to coincide admirably with your own wants as a performer, or with your intuitive knowledge of the desires of other performers, only adds (as add it must) to their immediate effectiveness behind the footlights. But it does not increase their importance or bring them any nearer to the truth as men know it when the final curtain has fallen on any play and life has once again engulfed them.

I suspect it indicates that as a serious dramatist you are more theatre-wise than is good for you. Not only theatre-wise, but facile. For you have so many quick releases for your moods that your thinking, like your feeling, lacks the cumulative strength which it might have if the statement of it cost you more anguish, and if as a technician it were not so easy for you to drain your mind and heart of whatever it may be that has concerned them.

Your *Post-Mortem*, which has its fine moments, is a case in point. Where you might have fashioned a notable play from this fable of a dead soldier's return to the disillusioning and forgetful London for which his life has been sacrificed, you have written one which is of little more significance than was the passing mood of hysteria which occasioned its composition. By your own confession, in the interesting preface you contributed to that one-volume collection of your favourite works known as *Play Parade*, this drama that might have been a memorable indictment of war is "sadly confused and unbalanced" and has only "certain moments of genuine passion in it which redeem it from bathos." It was, you say, written primarily as a gesture to yourself. But, as you must be fully aware, great plays of this kind and on such a subject, are born of great emotions, not of mere gestures.

It is for this very reason that *Cavalcade* stands out to me as the exception among your serious works to which I have previously referred. You may admit, as you have done, that it was written by chance, and point out that it was only a picture of a troop-ship leaving for the Boer War you happened to see in an illustrated journal, which kept you from inventing in its place a pageant of the French Revolution or the Second Empire. Your chief interest in undertaking it may have been the long-cherished ambition, to which you confess, of trying your hand at a "big play on a big scale" for production at the London Coliseum. And when you were unable to secure this playhouse, and old Drury was chosen as its substitute, your natural preoccupation as an experienced man of the theatre may have been, as of course it was, the building of a play that would accommodate itself to the special mechanical conditions of the stage on which it was to be performed. But when you contend—almost as if you were fearful lest England's response to this work might imperil your standing among sophisticates—that in its writing you "had not one moment to waste on patriotic fervour," you force me to conclude it is your whim to indulge in humour rather than in candour.

As Drury Lane's manager I sponsored the production of far too many meretricious spectacles, such as *Cymon* and *The Castle Spectre*, not to know the difference between a script which is backed by an honest emotion and one which aims merely at doing its duty by the pit. Moreover, I am not blind to the fact that, whether you liked it or not, "patriotic fervour" was bound to be your chief objective as a technician when once you had glanced at that picture of the troop-ship and, having thus stumbled upon the idea for *Cavalcade*, you had begun to study the back-stage of the theatre in which it was to be played. That you achieved this fervour you cannot deny, any more than I can deny that many of the words you wrote for your panoramic drama fell like a grenadier's march upon my heart. I prize your spectacle the more, not only because in it you gave such dignified expression to British patriotism and because you wrote some excellent scenes for it and staged them with remarkable skill, but also because in *Cavalcade* you managed for once to surrender, consciously or unconsciously, to an idea that was bigger than yourself and chose to speak for England rather than for Mayfair.

While I do not admire the majority of your serious plays as much as I do your comedies, I do understand the emotional need which has prompted you to write them. You are not a happy man, Sir, and neither was I. Yet such is the paradox of our fates that to the world (which seldom comprehends the shrewd distinction the Frenchman drew between those who laugh and those who make us laugh) both of us are known as gay and smiling creatures who have epitomized sophistication for our times, who are blessed with wit, and who have always been ready to release our exuberance in quick sallies of a mirth-provoking sort.

You may not remember it—and certainly my comedies and farces will not tell you—but in more ways than in the mounting pressure of his debts I was like my own Charles Surface, whose distresses were so many that he could not afford to part with his spirits. My contemporaries could hail me as the new Congreve. London was kept amused by repetitions of my latest sayings or stories about my practical jokes. My comedies were the delight of the period. My speeches had such sudden and unexpected turns of humour to them that they could cause the grave members of the House of Commons to rock with laughter. And I, who had always been esteemed as the most agreeable of dining companions, could be so persuasively gay and charming, even in my old age, that Lord Byron was forced to conclude there had been nothing like me since Orpheus. But when left to myself I was a different man. Where I was brave and cheerful in public, I was often despondent and afraid in private. I had a morbid hatred of darkness and needed a profusion of candles about me to light me on my way to happiness. I lived a slave to the dread of what I once described as Death's dart; was painfully conscious of my own shortcomings, although I was unable to overcome them; and was tortured by the conflicting elements in my nature which, as the years went by, waged an increasingly successful warfare against my peace of mind.

I surmise we are not unlike in having the gaiety with which we are both associated backed with a disquieting melancholy. It is with much interest that I have noted the sadness which lurks beneath the surface of so many of your writings; the bitterness which is born of your disbelief; the agonizing lack you feel of convictions in which you can find stability or comfort; and the cynicism which, though it may be no more profound than is fashionable, eats its way like an acid into your contentment. In its thinking it may run no deeper than does the disillusionment of a smart young sophisticate who has found his champagne flat. In its philosophy it may be as shop-worn as was the *motif* you once restated in one of your more popular revue numbers as "Dance, Little Lady." But this unhappiness; this successful young man's sense of "the emptiness of things"; this nervous negation which is so marked in those who, like yourself, have chosen to be the spokesmen of your post-war generation, is almost always with you.

In even the glibbest passages of your comic dialogue, there is a tension to your fooling which is more taut than lasting happiness can hope to be, and which informs me not only of how frayed your nerves are but of how uncertain is your faith in the future. Though I heartily enjoy these over-energetic outbursts of your high spirits, they nonetheless make me slightly uncomfortable. There is something hysterical about their laughter which causes me to feel you are trying desperately to defy the future by crowding more pleasure and excitement into the present than it can well accommodate.

If your writings had not told me of your unhappiness, your face, when as an actor you are required to laugh, would have served me as an eloquent informant. Your smile is the smile of a comedian. It is as gaily debonair as one could wish, and as sunlit as your happiest dialogue. It is free of care, charmingly alert, good-natured in its suggestion of mockery, and creates the atmosphere of easeful pleasure in which high comedy is most at home. But when it broadens into a grin, when whole-hearted gaiety is supposed to have possessed you and convulsing joy is your acknowledged master, your face ceases for me to have any relation to comedy. It becomes as distorted as a tragic mask; lacks the health which demands its release in laughter. It wrinkles itself away from all connexion with the Court of Momus; cracks into an expression which is as sinister as a Chinese demon's; bespeaks the raucous dissonance of your spirit; and lays bare the anguish which I believe besets you.

One of the more disturbing sources of conflict in your nature is, I suspect, the fact that sophistication does not rule your mind alone. It dwells there, even as it dwelt in mine, in perpetual conflict with so uncongenial a consort as sentimentality. And by so doing it not only disturbs the harmony of your temper but creates a confusion in your writings which often mars the purity of form that might otherwise be theirs either as high comedies and sheer romances, or as serious dramas in which complete statement is given to a genuine emotion.

I know whereof I speak when I say this, for I, like you, was a man whose spirits were bewildered by the contradictory edicts of such jealous sovereigns as wit and sentimentality. I know how ill-paired, though how common, are these attributes and what dissension they can occasion by their joint occupancy of so small a kingdom as a single mind. I know with what distrust they are bound to survey one another, realizing as they do that each of them has it in its power to undermine the other's strength and snatch away its reputation. I know how painful to sentimentality's inevitable softness is the hardness of wit's necessary malice; and how mortifying to the rational intricacies of a supposedly sophisticated head are all those simple promptings of the sentimental heart which, since they have no relation to doubt or reason or to the smart world's claims to knowledge, are despised for their very simplicity. But from my own experience as a dramatist I also know that men in whose natures these warring elements continue to abide as they do in ours must determine to listen to the Sirens' song of only one of them at one time, if to the melody of either of them we would do proper justice in a single play.

It was with difficulty that I brought myself to do this. Yet bring myself I did, as the differences in mood and approach which distinguish *The School for Scandal* from *The Rivals* will make clear to you. I was a romantic young fellow with an unbounded sense of gaiety when I wrote *The Rivals*. My humour was rough-and-tumble, my wit farcical in its breadth, and my sentimental inclinations so strong that I could not resist the temptation of lugging into this otherwise laughing tale those tedious lovers—Julia and Faulkland —whom I, along with the rest of the world, have come to regret. That in *The Rivals* I happen to have composed a farce-comedy which, in spite of its first-night failure, is so genuine in its merriment and so artful in its distribution of acting honours that in its rewritten version it continues to be the delight of audiences and has taken its place among the classics of the stage, does not blind me to the fact that I was not then the master of high comedy I was later to become.

I had neither the final self-control which high comedy demands, nor was I able to steel myself sufficiently against the contradictions in my temperament to make a complete surrender to one—and only one—mood, and to place the need for sustaining that mood above the dictates of my volatility. Even in this happy period of my youth I was somewhat disturbed as an author by the very same conflict in my nature which as the years went by was to cost me increasing vexation as a man, and which (since I believe it to be still more fundamental in your nature than it was in mine) appears to have troubled you constantly both as man and author. Yet heavy as was the toll demanded of my happiness by this conflict in the years that lay ahead, I did so manage to overcome it in the better of my subsequent writings that I was able, for example, to prevent my worldliness from intruding too rudely upon the romantic fooling of *The Duenna* and had the wisdom (and the restraining self-knowledge) to remove from the earlier drafts of *The School for Scandal* the sentimental passages which, though dear to me, would have imperilled it as a comedy by tarnishing its brilliance and destroying its tone.

Although my plays are my witnesses that I was never a purist in the strictest sense of the word, I wish I could persuade you of how much you would improve your wide variety of efforts if only you were to convince Coward, the author, of his need for exerting a more unrelenting authority over Coward, the man. I wish I could prevail upon you to see of how much greater importance is the integrity of any single work of yours than is the continued fidelity to all that is antithetical in your nature which your works proclaim. I wish I could make you realize that as an author you have gone too far, and are possessed of too many astonishing potentialities, to continue making each of your dramas as autobiographical as if you were a beginner to whom the opportunity had at last come for ventilating his springtime ego in his first play or his first novel.

For then you would not force me to be so constantly aware of your own personality as you now do. My interest would be permitted to centre upon your works rather than upon yourself, and from them I could derive the satisfaction of listening to what you might be saying that is universally applicable to mankind instead of having to focus my attention upon what it is you may have chosen to reveal about yourself.

My concern could be what is common to the ego of all men rather than what is peculiar to (and generally delightful in) your own. I would not have to strain my eyes as frequently as I now do to detect other characters besides yourself included in your scripts. I would not be disturbed as repeatedly as I am at present by discovering that the sophisticate in you is attempting to excuse by his blushing mockery what the sentimentalist has just done in all sincerity; or that the sentimentalist in you is vitiating your wit by taking undue pains to dilute the acid of the sophisticate. I would not find such a song as "We All Wore a Green Carnation" destroying momentarily the nostalgic tenderness which gives *Bitter Sweet* its charm; or be harshly reminded of your cynicism in such a romantic melodrama as *The Queen Was in the Parlour*; or feel as if I were eavesdropping on one of your private conversations when, in the course of such a bitter, though essentially sentimental, attempt at a serious drama as *The Vortex,* you allow your post-war hero to state your own dilemma by saying he thinks it wiser to be "ridiculous" than to be "blurred by sentiment."

These personal comedies of yours are skillful beyond all conscience. As you have written them, and as they are apparelled in your modern theatre, and even more particularly as they are played by you and Miss Lawrence, or by you and such exuberant but polished comedians as Alfred Lunt and Lynn Fontanne, they personify suavity itself. They are mirthful Tsars that banish dullness to the Siberia in which it belongs. They are gladdened by a spontaneity which annihilates time as cheerfully as boys kill flies. And the delight which you and your fellow performers take in what you are doing is at once so manifest and so ingratiating that it spreads like a pleasant contagion among the spectators who sit before you.

But if, in spite of their many captivating attributes, your excursions into the field of comedy still seem disappointing to me; if they remain delectable promises of what it is you might do as a comic dramatist rather than stable proofs of what you have done, I fear me the reason is that in both *Private Lives* and *Design for Living* you have shown yourself to be the master of a hundred and one

adroit and highly deceptive substitutes for high comedy rather
than of high comedy itself.

In place of the smiling insight into the ageless foibles of mankind which the true lords of laughter have always had at their
command, you put your expert sense of situation, which keeps
these comedies galloping so furiously on their way that the mere
act of laughing becomes as much the preoccupation of your audiences as does the mere act of breathing to the rider of a runaway
horse, and your playgoers are granted no more leisure in which
to analyse the causes of their laughter than the rider of the runaway horse is given time in which to contemplate the merits of the
landscape that is rushing past him. Your comedies are frolics
which, instead of being addressed to the reason of mankind, make
their appeal to all that is sportive and forgetful in man's nature.
Their concern is the larks of people who are gay exceptions rather
than the frailties of individuals who are large enough to serve as
types. They do not use their heads to exercise that jeering sanity
which endows Comedy with its corrective powers, but raise their
rapiers in a cause which by your own intention is jubilantly deranged. Their raillery does not sound the curfew upon that which
is excessive—and hence ridiculous—in the human race: it rings a
recess bell that summons spectators to a playground on which the
freakish ones (who are your heroes and your heroines) lord it like
bullies over all the normal beings who are the children of convention.

These comedies do not invite common sense to don cap and
bells. They merely stick a paper hat upon the forehead of frivol-
ity. They are glib hiatuses in life rather than mirthful connectives
in its sequence. Their wit travels a brightly lighted road which
leads no farther than yourself. The abundant pleasure they provide has its origins not in the incisiveness of their comments but
in the nervous exuberance of their spirits. They reveal a knowledge of the theatre which is more profound than is their knowledge of men and women, since in them this last-named attribute
is more clearly indicated by the manner in which these plays satisfy the wants of audiences than by the finality with which any of
their characters are drawn. You will search them in vain for mortals who are individualized in the sense that Millamant and Mira-
bell live a life that is independent of all performers in Congreve's

pages; or for types, stemming as so many of mine did from the old English tradition of "humour" comedy, which are compounded of the familiar human traits that have gone into the making, as well as the naming, of a Lady Sneerwell and a Mr. Candour.

Although the skirmishes between your quarrelsome lovers in both *Private Lives* and *Design for Living* have a brilliance to them which occasionally reminds me of my Lady Teazle's encounters with Sir Peter, you do not—if you will permit me to say so—appear to place a proper valuation on your wit. Being well aware that you have a score of agreeable makeshifts for it, as well as for the other stuffs from which a comedy is fashioned, you do not lean upon it as if it were a crutch for your support as a comic dramatist, but flourish it as casually as if it were a walking stick you carried merely for decorative purposes. You show your doubt in its sustaining powers by interrupting it at will to sing a handful of your sentimental songs, or by making your lovers forget that as comic characters their tongues are the weapons with which they should duel and forcing them into the most violent sort of fisticuffs which, though laughable in their way, do not—you must admit—add to the intellectual content of your comedies, however much such farcical devices may cause the galleries to roar. Not only do you endanger the very texture of artificial comedy by thus permitting your creatures to romp and tumble as if they were the children of Nature rather than of society, but also in your comedies you are tempted more frequently than I wish you were to squander on irrelevancies the precious time for comment which is at your disposal.

When, as in *Design for Living,* you hint at the disillusionment success can bring to a man who has succeeded as amazingly as you have done, I recognize with joy that your mind and wit and spirit are grappling with a subject that is worthy of Comedy's highest reach. But when you parade the travel diaries of your trips around the world, as if the mere mention of the ports that you have visited had any relation to comedy, you compel me to feel that as a comic dramatist you are marking time.

Your frequent reliance upon nonsense as a means of delighting an audience also disturbs me—indeed it disturbs me almost as much as it delights me. I would not have you think I do not prize your fooling to the full. It affords your modern playgoers with as joyful a release from all that is mundane in life as they can find anywhere. But the laughter you evoke by having a stupid maid (who is as unaccustomed to the telephone as I would be) bungle the messages which are meant for her master and mistress, and the games of "Let's pretend" in which your characters, while dancing with each other, adopt the grand manner of society, and admire dear old Lady Bundle for blowing all those shrimps through her ear trumpet or casually inquire if that is the Grand Duchess Olga lying under the piano, are escapes from Comedy rather than true manifestations of the Comic Spirit. Hilarious as they unquestionably are, their very point and value is their lack of sense. And arrant nonsense, as you must admit, is no blood relation of High Comedy, which is logical beyond all things, or of wit, which is the laughing child of reason. My own suspicion is that nonsense is the only neutral ground on which the sophisticate and the sentimentalist can meet in safety, protected as they are there by the white flags of amity which nonsense always flies.

I raise these objections to your work, Sir, in no carping mood of meanness but in the friendliest of friendly spirits. And in such a spirit I beg you to receive them. You may think that I have overstepped the mark, and accuse me of failing to be what Mrs. Malaprop, my Queen of the Dictionary, would describe as the very pineapple of politeness. But I assure you, the admiration I feel for your many high talents runs deeper than politeness.

I have unbounded faith in your future. And this faith is based not only upon the conspicuous merits of your past performances, and the courage with which you have faced bitter failures, and the independence you have evinced in going your own way to new and different triumphs, and the increasing mastery over negligence and haste that is apparent in your growth as a stylist, but also upon the fine manner in which you have stood—as I was unable to— the cruel test of success.

If then I ask even more of you than this; if I would have you conquer the conflicts in your nature which, as I see it, mar your writings; and wish you to achieve a mastery of form you have not yet attained; it is not I that you must blame for this but the potentialities for true importance which I discover in your works. No doubt the Abbey must likewise come in for its share of blame, since one of the drawbacks of resting where I do is that this quiet

Corner takes one's mind off the pleasures of the world and centres it, quite dully, not upon thoughts divine, but upon the merits from which temporal immortality is born.

Believe me, Sir, to be one of the most genuine, hopeful, and sympathetic of your plentiful admirers,

From Burke's Peerage to Bohemia, or English society as its changes have been clearly recorded by three such unintentional historians as Wilde, Maugham, and Noel Coward.

[1946]

ENGLISH LAUGHTER— PAST AND PRESENT

PAINFUL AS it may sound for a playgoer to have his attention "riveted," he is in infinitely greater pain when it is left "unriveted." I utter this lament knowledgeably. It was as one of the "unriveted" that I sat before *Present Laughter,** watching Clifton Webb struggle with a part written of Noel Coward, by Noel Coward, and for Noel Coward.

Had Mr. Coward been present, snapping at the Coward con-

---

* *Present Laughter,* by Noel Coward. Directed by John C. Wilson. Setting by Donald Oenslager. Presented by Mr. Wilson. With a cast including Clifton Webb, Evelyn Varden, Doris Dalton, Marta Linden, Jan Sterling, Grace Mills, and Cris Alexander. At the Plymouth Theatre. Opened October 29, 1946.

sonants as precisely as he alone can do, I might have been deceived into finding this Mayfair version of a Palais Royal farce enjoyable entertainment. I know I missed Mr. Coward, not in scene after scene but in syllable after syllable. I missed him as much as all of us would miss the Lunts had we, with properly high hopes, gone to see them in *O Mistress Mine* and been confronted with a pair of understudies.

I could hear Mr. Coward polishing, by his mere delivery, lines which, as spoken by Clifton Webb, were clearly left unwritten. I could see him, too, as, spruce, brittle and self-assured, he granted a redeeming authority to this nonsensical moment or that. Indeed, I was made constantly aware of how Mr. Coward could have served the cider we were getting so that we might have mistaken it for champagne.

However, with Mr. Webb on hand or under foot, functioning as Mr. Coward's supposed stand-in, and with the performances in general (save for those of Evelyn Varden and Grace Mills) of a competence encountered as a rule in summer theatres, I found my attention gypsying. Nay, more than wandering by cart through foreign fields, I discovered it was journeying without benefit of rockets almost to the environs of the moon. Accordingly, I sought to while away the long evening by such diversionary tactics as thinking of other things. The technique can claim no novelty. Every theatregoer has employed it in the manly art of self-defense at one time or another.

Although my body was a prisoner in C-101, my mind was free. Perhaps not without reason, since I was in the presence of a Noel Coward play which I was not enjoying and had a few weeks earlier seen a revival of *Lady Windermere's Fan* which I did enjoy, I began to ruminate upon the course followed by modern English comedy in general, and upon the contributions of Oscar Wilde, Somerset Maugham, and Mr. Coward in particular. At any rate, I did this except when interrupted by the intermissions.

These three men, said I to myself said I, have without question been the outstanding representatives the Comic Muse has known in Albion during the last fifty years. Different as each is from the other, all of them have been uncommonly gifted. As may go without saying, their versatility is not the only feature they share in common. The three of them have been runners in the relay race of sophisticated laughter. Each has started where the other left off, running a different course over the same track. If their courses have been different, it is because the three of them have been faithful not only to themselves but, without meaning to be so, to the manners and assumptions of the different periods for which they have spoken.

Suddenly two lines from *A Woman of No Importance* popped into my itinerant mind. I mean the ones when Lord Illingworth says to Mrs. Allonby, "The Book of Life begins with a man and woman in a garden," and Wilde has her reply, "It ends with Revelations." It is a terrible sin to take light things seriously—a sin if for no other reason than that killing pleasure is a form of murder which, alas, usually goes unpunished. Had I found pleasure in *Present Laughter,* perhaps I would not now be guilty of this crime.

The revelations made by Wilde, Maugham, and Coward in their flimsiest concoctions began all at once to interest me. Playdreaming as I was, I indulged in the kind of fantasy encouraged by this atomic age. Why this age? Because unconsciously the starting point of my thoughts was mass destruction.

Suppose all the other records of English society (in the Mayfair sense) during the past half century were destroyed, I wondered. What sort of portrait of British manners would be painted by the plays of these three men? Could not a surprisingly accurate notion of what had happened in a very special world in those fifty years be obtained merely from the evidence supplied by their comedies? Certainly, not one of these men meant to function as a grave social historian. Yet, in spite of themselves, each has had his fascinating disclosures to make in the midst of (perhaps because of) his gilded nonsense.

As comic dramatists, Wilde, Maugham, and Coward are, of course, as different as the three societies of which they wrote. The first storm warning of these differences would be recognizable in their photographs, were these to be included in their excavated works.

In Wilde a future student would see a man resembling a bloated Greek statue; an overfed Alcibiades carved not in marble but in library paste. Even the dullest archaeologist, looking at Wilde's picture, would spot him as a complete hedonist—soft, heavy-lidded, comfortable, and conceited, with his nerves insulated by too much flesh.

Were ocean liners still in use when my imaginary student retrieved a photograph of Mr. Maugham, he might conclude, here is a fellow who could have been a ship's doctor—the kind of ship's doctor who never leaves the smoking room for the air and the sun of the decks outside. The costume has changed since Wilde's day. The velvet coat has given way to the sack suit. The poseur has gone; the arrogance vanished. This is a businessman of letters. His is a wise face; cynical, tight-lipped, far more nervous than Wilde's, with eyes that are piercingly alert. It is a sad and disenchanted face. Plainly it belongs to someone who has dared to look upon the Medusa's head of human misbehavior without blinking and with a clinical interest.

The same archivist coming upon a snapshot of Mr. Coward would again be bound to note a difference. As he studied Coward's picture, he would see the wizened head of an Eton boy set on a body made of chopsticks. Perhaps he would wonder where the Buster Brown collar was. He would notice at once that Coward had fed on a more meager diet than Wilde. He would sense a personality dapper, debonair, and patent-leather bright; a man who was a dynamo of nerves rather than a bundle of them. He could not help observing that Coward's face was at the same time haggard and ageless, merry and sad, scornful and eager; in fact, so volatile that it would have to belong to an actor.

These three photographs would, of course, be mere prologues to the disclosures provided by the texts themselves. The changes —more precisely, the steady and bloodless revolution—which England has undergone during the past fifty years would be reflected in the most light-hearted works of the three men. Their every smiling irrelevance, when so scrutinized, would take on an unsuspected relevance. All their plays, as is the way with comedies supposedly genteel, would be found to have dealt with the overprivileged. Yet each dramatist would present a very different image of privilege.

Wilde was the spokesman for that late Victorian England which was already Edwardian; Maugham for Georgian England, the England which preceded the First World War; Coward for the

Britain of Windsor and the international set and the years before this last conflict (which, no doubt, explains why much in *Present Laughter* seems dated).

A fairly complete chronicle of the decline of the old aristocracy and the emergence of the new is to be found in the comedies of the three men. What starts as Burke's Peerage in Wilde ends up in Coward as straight Bohemia. The *haut monde* gradually gives way to the demi-monde; the castle to the café; the peerage to the professional. The stately homes in England little by little lose their stateliness and dwindle into flats or studios. The characters belong less and less to the so-called "Great World" and more and more to the general public. Inevitably, their attitudes toward government, education, women, sex, and society undergo drastic alterations.

Wilde wrote as a gentleman born a snob; Maugham as a dispassionate observer; Coward not only as an actor accepted by society but a career man who, because of his gifts, created a society of his own. Wilde's Lord Darlington would feel as out of place with Mr. Coward's Gilda in *Design for Living* or the playwright in *Present Laughter* as Coward's characters would be bored by the oppressive good breeding of Wilde's aristocracy. Maugham's men and women, however, could—and did—shuttle back and forth quite comfortably between the two extremes.

Wilde's ladies and gentlemen were born rich, though not necessarily richly endowed save as conversationalists. Maugham's, whether commoners or nobility, were often adventurers and adventuresses forced to live by their wits. Coward's characters, on the other hand, have for the most part won their place because of their talents, unabetted by their morals.

As realism, Wilde's plays can no more be taken seriously than the entrance of the Peers in *Iolanthe* which, at many moments, they closely resemble. Unintentionally, however, Wilde, like his laughing successors, was as much a social historian as Galsworthy. When Wilde wrote, the House of Lords, in spite of all his jests at its expense, was a dominant body in English politics. Although protests against it were already familiar, it still spoke for the then sovereign power of the British aristocracy.

Very few commoners presumed to stray into Wilde's best-known dramas. Even such fallen women as gained admittance to them were apt to be related by marriage to the peerage. His were mainly titled people who felt they were entitled to everything. They lived a life as undisturbed (except by the plot) as only the ruling class of a mighty empire could enjoy after a fabulously prosperous century and before its self-assurance was shaken by the Boer War. In Maugham this overweening assumption of the prerogatives of privilege has almost ceased to exist. By Coward's time it has disappeared entirely, save where the egotism of artists has replaced the arrogance of aristocrats. What was once as tranquil as it seemed secure has turned into a nervous uncertainty, frequently bordering on hysteria and rejoicing in a sense of the "lost generation."

The talents Wilde admits in women are few. Of course, he endows them with his own mastery of the epigram. He also recognizes their biological usefulness in bearing little baronets before the first curtain has risen. Thereafter he limits their unpredatory activities either to painting china or writing bad novels (as does the governess in *The Importance of Being Earnest*) which are fortunately lost.

Maugham's more colorful women are hardheaded, practical schemers. Even his shadiest females have to excel as hostesses if they are to succeed. Like Wilde's, many of his men are in politics. The difference is that they are apt to do their talking in the House no less than out of it.

Coward's people are quite different. They are in the main artists, actresses, playwrights, journalists, and musicians. If they have no other gifts, they possess a high talent for domestic quarrels and a genius for separation, though frequently they are less endowed so far as marriage is concerned. They are transients in domesticity and strangers to propriety.

In no way are the figures in the plays of Wilde, Maugham, and Coward more sharply contrasted than they are in their attitudes toward newspapers. Wilde's characters may buy the *Times* (and read the *Morning Post*), but they dread to read about themselves in a newspaper. Theirs is what in Washington was recently known as a passion for anonymity. It is one of their few passions.

Maugham's men and women are already newspaper-conscious. The old taboos of Edwardian gentility are disappearing. In *Our*

Betters we are told that "at Lady Grayston's you are in the very hub of society. I don't mean the stuffy, old-fashioned society that goes about in barouches and bores itself stiff, but the society that counts, the society that figures in the newspapers." In Coward's comedies the professionals who inhabit them have no other choice, as dramatists or actresses, than to desire to see their names in print. Publicity is their need. They feed upon it and are fed by it. Hence they wait for their reviews to appear, however much they may scoff while reading them.

No change is perhaps more revealing in the plays of the three men than the varying esteem in which America is held. To Wilde the United States was an uncouth, savage, overlarge country. On the subject he was nothing if not patronizing. Americans offered him one of the most reliable of his jokes. Maugham's respect for us was greater. His Londoners may still have wanted us to be the fantastic people they liked to imagine. But his American heiresses had already gone in for that Mayfair–Fifth Avenue forerunner of Lend-Lease whereby they offered their fortunes in exchange for British titles. Coward's professionals are as at home in America as they are in Britain. The Atlantic has shrunk, and the old colonial attitude (still insufferably present in *Middle East Diary*) has gone underground.

All comedies of manners are games played against nature in a drawing room or its equivalent. The real point of their joke, as John Palmer once noted, is that man is pretending to be civilized. "The elaborate ritual of society is a mask through which the natural man is comically seen to look." From Wilde's time to Coward's this joke, like everything else, has altered. It has altered if for no other reason than that so many of Coward's characters make no pretense of being civilized, in the Wildean sense. They are hilarious rebels from society's elaborate ritual. That is one of the sources of the pleasure they usually give. They remain comic characters, but they have misplaced their manners. Oddly enough, though their gifts have increased, their minds seem less sharp. Perhaps one of the surest manifestations of their "nerves" is that they substitute nonsense—delectable as it can be—for the wit of Wilde and the glittering precision of Maugham's mind.

At their best, however inferior that best may be to Wilde's and

Maugham's, the comedies of Coward can be taken seriously as social histories. My complaint against *Present Laughter* is that, though it makes every panting effort to be gay, I found it difficult not to be serious in its presence.

The confusions of the modern world as T. S. Eliot adds to them in two verse plays which everyone seems to understand until asked to explain them.

[1950, 1954]

TWO PLAYS BY T. S. ELIOT

THE COCKTAIL PARTY

THEY WERE there, the faithful and the devout, for the opening of *The Cocktail Party.** They were there, carrying their reverence with them much as pilgrims might carry candles in a procession. They were there, filled with a sense of the night's eventfulness; confident, because Mr. Eliot, *their* Mr. Eliot, was the dramatist, that before final curtain time they would enjoy, as he once put it, "a tremor of bliss, a wink of heaven." That they were rewarded with both the tremor and the wink, I am in no position to deny. Even those to whom T. S. Eliot is a man and not a religion could not fail to be grateful for certain of the evening's qualities.

Beyond dispute actors of extraordinary excellence were being seen. What is more, they were being heard. With the exception of Irene Worth, they were English. They were such gifted English actors as Alec Guinness, Cathleen Nesbitt, Robert Flemyng,

---

* *The Cocktail Party,* by T. S. Eliot. Directed by E. Martin Browne. Settings supervised by Raymond Sovey. Presented by Gilbert Miller by arrangement with Sherek Players, Ltd. With Alec Guinness, Cathleen Nesbitt, Robert Flemyng, Eileen Peel, Ernest Clark, Grey Blake, and Irene Worth. At Henry Miller's Theatre. Opened January 21, 1950.

Eileen Peel, and Ernest Clark. Moreover, all of them (including Miss Worth, an American who has become as British as the rest) were playing with that finish and authority and that genius for handling the language at which the English are unrivaled.

Beyond dispute, too, there were proofs that the mind responsible for the dialogue these actors were speaking so well was no ordinary mind. It was subtler, lonelier, colder, stouter, more questing than that lying behind most playwriting. Yet I could not help wondering, as I watched the absorption of the devout in what I doubt they at all times understood more clearly than I did, what their reactions would have been if, instead of being hallowed by T. S. Eliot's name, this play in verse had been written by some unknown dramatist.

"You don't expect me to know what to say about a play when I don't know who the author is, do you?" asks Bannal, one of the critics, in the Epilogue to *Fanny's First Play*. It helps a lot, of course, to know that T. S. Eliot is the author of *The Cocktail Party*. No living writer is more revered or has been written about more extensively than he. One has only to turn to *T. S. Eliot: A Selected Critique* and read such worthies as Conrad Aiken, Richard Aldington, E. M. Forster, Mark Van Doren, Paul Elmer More, Malcolm Cowley, John Crowe Ransom, Stephen Spender, William Butler Yeats, or Allen Tate to learn what one should—and should not—say about Mr. Eliot. The dicta and dogma of these gentlemen have taken their place among the flora and fauna of the present's higher-browed criticism.

A relative of Mr. Eliot may once have described him to me as being "the best British poet ever to have been born in St. Louis," but no one else would dream of being so lacking in piety. Mr. Eliot is a Nobel Prize winner. His scholarship is enormous. His critical contributions are vastly respected. His poetry is widely acclaimed by thousands whether they comprehend it or not. Campuses ring with his name. Intellectuals, young and old, here and abroad grow bright-eyed when he is mentioned. *The Waste Land* is usually cited as being an event no less than a poem. Indeed, such is his pre-eminence that few statements made by any literary figure in our time have provoked more consternation or applause than his declaration that he was "an Anglo-Catholic in religion . . . a classicist in literature and a royalist in politics."

Though he has excelled at poetry and the essay, he has not limited himself to them. As a close student of Euripides, Seneca, the Elizabethans, the Jacobeans, Dryden, and the theory of poetic drama, the theatre has also attracted him. His *Murder in the Cathedral,* a play about Becket's martyrdom, relied heavily upon its choral interludes. Slow in starting as it was, it rose to moments of high beauty, became dramatic almost in spite of itself, and brought poetry back to a prosaic stage.

Since then, Mr. Eliot has written two other plays in verse, *The Family Reunion* and *The Cocktail Party.* In the first of these he made some use of a chorus; in the second he has dispensed with a chorus entirely. In both of them he chose to place his action in modern settings. If he has turned his back on dramas laid in the past, it is because, as he has confessed, he now wishes to write only plays about contemporary life. His conviction is that "if poetic drama is to establish itself again, after three hundred years, it has got to show that it can deal with what appears to be the most re-fractory material." It must concern itself with such "men and women as we know, in the usual clothes that they wear today, in the same perplexities, conflicts, and misunderstandings that we and our acquaintances get involved in, and uttering no lines that are not relevant to the situation, the mood, and the dramatic action."

Mr. Eliot has admitted that he is working as an experimental-ist. To him the iambic pentameter is an anachronism. He rightly refuses to don Elizabethan tights in order to deal with his own times. In the anarchy of the present, when there is no one accepted verse form for poetic drama, he is seeking to find the right con-temporary form for himself, even as he believes all other poets drawn to the theatre must nowadays endeavor to do. Mr. Eliot is not of the trombone-and-oboe school. He does not want his verse to call attention to itself. He is willing to have an audience mis-take it for prose when the action is not intense. He wishes by the rhythms in his casual speeches, rhythms perhaps unnoticed by playgoers, to prepare for those crises when his characters have been lifted into poetry by the intensity of their feelings. A first-rate drama, he thinks, should make us believe that there are moments in life when poetry is the natural form of expression of ordinary men and women.

So much for Mr. Eliot's theory as stated by him in a very frank and disarming address delivered in London to the Poets' Theatre Guild. The theory, as theory, makes sound sense and is easy to follow. But, as *The Cocktail Party* once again proves, practice and theory are not always brothers, much less twins. In spite of its intervals of communicated tension; in spite, too, of the fine felicity and beauty of its occasional phrases, the sharpness or wit of scattered lines, and the dazzling brilliance of its performance, it is obscure, not clear.

Mr. Eliot's new play starts as trivially as if he were writing a flat sequel to the highly successful "Yatata, Yatata" scene in *Allegro*, and ends in a pea-soup fog of mysticism. Its poetry is a secret almost too well kept. It is optical rather than auditory. Although on the printed page it looks like poetry, when spoken it seldom explains why it has been set as verse. This is as true of most of its intense climaxes as it is of its calmer stretches.

I approach Mr. Eliot's verse with proper caution. When, in the same address referred to above, Mr. Eliot noted the need of training professional critics of poetic drama and added that very few dramatic critics are especially equipped at present for this task, he was not pointing at me but he might have been. I have my other reasons for being shy about discussing Mr. Eliot's text in detail. He is a great one for playing solemn jokes upon his public —to the delight of his academic devotees. It amuses him to interlard his own creations with lines borrowed here and there from the works of others, as a test of his readers' scholarship. Edmund Wilson, for example, pointed out that in *The Waste Land*, a poem of only 433 lines (to which are added seven pages of notes), Mr. Eliot managed to include "quotations from, allusions to, or imitations of at least thirty-five different writers (some of them, such as Shakespeare and Dante, laid under contribution several times) —as well as several popular songs; and to introduce passages in six foreign languages, including Sanskrit."

I remember the late Theodore Spencer smiling happily when he told me that a speech which I had admired of one of the knights in *Murder in the Cathedral* had been snipped as a merry jest from A. Conan Doyle's *The White Company*. Whether or not Mr. Eliot has been indulging in any such playful appropriations in *The Cocktail Party*, I do not know. I only remember Shaw's warning

to critics when, for fun, he rewrote his novel *Cashel Byron's Pro-*
fession as a play in blank verse called *The Admirable Bashville*.
Shaw confessed he had purposely stolen or paraphrased lines from
Marlowe and Shakespeare (not to mention Henry Carey) so that,
if any man dared to quote him derisively, he should do so in peril
of inadvertently alighting on a purple passage from *Hamlet* or
Faustus.

In the instance of *The Cocktail Party*, therefore, I do not presume to say whether Mr. Eliot is writing *solo* or *ex libris*. Speaking
only as a member of the theatregoing laity, I must nevertheless
observe that in my opinion the drama is a medium which seems
to resist his advances. Notwithstanding his aroused interest, his
honorable intentions, and his vast erudition in the field of dramatic
literature, he and the professional stage (at least as most of us
know and enjoy it) do not make a congenial couple.

In *The Cocktail Party* Mr. Eliot, if I understand him clearly,
and I am not at all certain that I do, is writing about a group of
Mayfair sophisticates as interslept as if they were the interchangeable sixsome in Benn Levy's *Clutterbuck*. Mr. Eliot's approach,
however, proves ultimately as portentous as Mr. Levy's is farcical
throughout.

In the most high-minded way, he is interested in the emotionally
maladjusted. His pivotal character is a psychoanalyst who serves
not only as a doctor but as a priest to those of little faith. Among
these count the husband and wife and the husband's mistress, who
turn for help to this psychoanalyst. The love of which these three
people are capable exists on planes as different as are their spiritual potentialities. The husband and wife are earth-bound. They
represent the unloving and the unloved. Bringing them together
again is merely a matter of psychiatric readjustment. But the mistress is made of finer stuffs. She has a sense of sin and is worthy
of a saintly atonement. Sent to what she thinks is the doctor's sani-
tarium, she is dispatched as a nurse to the Far East, where she
finds redemption by dying, crucified by natives near a colony of
ants.

Mr. Eliot's play begins and ends with a cocktail party. It is
against the background of such trivia that his characters, nervous
products of a nervous age, are explored. In revealing their problems and their natures, Mr. Eliot is at his most effective in

the scenes dominated by the psychoanalyst, and at his least witty and most tedious when trying to write the brittle chitchat of the drawing room. The vigor of his mind and his precise command of language are the most strongly felt when his touch is both sardonic and serious. Even so, the difference between dialogue and talk (and far too much talk at that) is something that he does not appear to have mastered any more than he has managed to endow deliberately conversational verse with the lift or song of dramatic poetry.

The actors in *The Cocktail Party* are a joy to watch and listen to. The most spectacular performance may be Alec Guinness's wonderfully trenchant and dynamic playing of the psychoanalyst. But Robert Flemyng as the husband, Eileen Peel as the wife, Irene Worth as the mistress, and Cathleen Nesbitt as the older woman are all admirable. They rise triumphantly to meet the challenges of a difficult script. They do their best—and a shining best it is— to protect it from its obvious and sometimes irritating shortcomings. But, exciting as is their contribution and extraordinary as is their skill, they cannot hide the fact that Mr. Eliot in *The Cocktail Party* has not yet found a plot, a poetic idiom, or a dramatic method which realizes his dreams or our hopes.

THE CONFIDENTIAL CLERK

If everybody did not know that T. S. Eliot was its author, it would be instructive to see what people would say about *The Confidential Clerk*.* But everybody does know and, because of knowing, comes to the theatre in a special mood. The stalwarts to whom Mr. Eliot is a religion approach his latest work as pilgrims, with heads bowed and hallelujahs already formed in their throats. Even the less devout, who suspect he may be mortal, are intimidated by his name.

And why not? Few literary figures in our time have had so pro-

---

* *The Confidential Clerk,* a comedy by T. S. Eliot. Directed by E. Martin Browne. Settings by Paul Morrison. Presented by Henry Sherek and The Producers' Theatre (Roger L. Stevens, Robert Whitehead, Robert W. Dowling). With Ina Claire, Claude Rains, Joan Greenwood, Aline MacMahon, Newton Blick, Richard Newton, and Douglas Watson. At the Morosco Theatre. Opened February 11, 1954.

found an influence as this tall, haggard Englishman from St. Louis, who in looks is so much closer to John Foster Dulles than Byron. Both as poet and critic his work has been of that kind which, instead of merely winning admirers, creates idolators. Among the latter, in Mr. Goldwyn's phrase, include me out. I know of no writer I respect, and respect profoundly, who can irritate me more than Mr. Eliot. His pedantry, his love of the obscure, his frequent unwillingness to say simple things simply, his ability to make the obvious seem difficult, and his reluctance to have dramatic poetry sound like poetry—all these I find annoying. Yet I trust I recognize Mr. Eliot's exceptional merits. Having recently reread his *Complete Poems and Plays* and dipped again into his *Selected Essays*, I am all the more aware of the firmness of his critical mind, the sinewy and conquering power of his serious poetry at its best, and the beguiling, though often overlooked, gaiety of his humor as it shows itself in his light verse.

Mr. Eliot cannot be blamed for the foolishness of his more worshipful followers. The history of literature is filled with important writers who have been the victims of their disciples. Mr. Eliot is one of these. Had he been only a poet willing to sing songs the meaning and music of which were always clear, he would not have been so embarrassed as he must be by some of his votaries. But he is also a scholar, at home with the recondite and given to playing grave academic games in his verse. His immense erudition has made him, though a creator, the pet of those who are only scholars. In him the double-domes have found a stately pleasure dome; in his poems and plays, a sacred river which runs through caverns measureless to man, down to a sunless sea. The more "swaddled with darkness" his meaning, the greater their delight.

My hope had been that in *The Confidential Clerk* Mr. Eliot would disappoint his esoteric devotees. The word from England was that simple people could sit before it without discomfort. Advance reports from the Boston-Cambridge area, where Eliotites are as plentiful as elms used to be, were reassuring. I was told by some of the elite of learning that, though they of course understood Mr. Eliot's newest work, I would have a good time at it even if I could not understand it. It was a farce, they said, and all I would have to do would be to relax and enjoy it.

But then, as often happens, bad news came from Washington.

From *The New York Times* I gathered that Mr. Eliot had once again refused to make his intentions clear. "Old Possum," in other words, was up to his familiar tricks and his impractical cats, the meaning-hunters, were having their biggest field day since *The Cocktail Party*. To my dismay I read in the *Times* that scholars had found an obvious Trinitarian significance in Mr. Eliot's new work. According to them, Act I is the Father, Act II the Son, Act III the Holy Ghost. Others delighted themselves by wondering if Colby (one of the illegitimate children in the play) is meant to be a latter-day Christ; if Sir Claude (the possible father of two of these children) is a slightly disillusioned Divinity; and Lucasta (another of the illegitimates) a Soho Mary Magdalene.

Please, I beg of you, do not expect me to give any answers to these questions, which failed to agitate me. Instead, permit me, with what clarity I can muster, to state what I assume (assume, mind you) are the plot essentials of Mr. Eliot's latest joke with himself and on his public. Let us begin before the beginning. Apparently the scholarly Mr. Eliot finds comfort, when starting a modern play, in knowing that the Greeks had a plot for it. Just as *The Cocktail Party* is alleged to have been derived from Euripides' *Alcestis,* so *The Confidential Clerk* has its very remote origins in his *Ion*. Gilbert would seem more relevant to me, or the Wilde of *Earnest,* Miss Prism, and the Brighton Line.

Roughly, very roughly, Sir Claude Mulhammer (Claude Rains) and his wife, Lady Elizabeth (Ina Claire), have had no children *since* their marriage. Before that, however, out of wedlock Lady Elizabeth had a boy (Richard Newton) and Sir Claude a girl (Joan Greenwood), and he thinks he is the father of Colby (Douglas Watson), his new confidential clerk. The trouble is that Lady Elizabeth is convinced and hopes that Colby is her son. It turns out that, instead of being the child of either of the titled Mulhammers, he is the offspring of a Mrs. Guzzard (Aline MacMahon), a poor woman who, in order to secure for Colby advantages he would not otherwise have had, has pretended all these years that she was his aunt and that Colby was the son of Sir Claude by her sister who had died in having him.

If you follow me, which I find myself dizzied by trying to do, you must admit that such a complicated saga of baby swapping and illegitimacy points to a laughing treatment. But Mr. Eliot has no Mayfair "Pinafore" or 3-D version of *The Importance of Being Earnest* in mind. He is in a grave mood. What happened to the farce benevolent Bostonians promised remains a mystery like Mr. Eliot's real meaning. Although he inserts jokes here and there, they are as infrequent as the plums in the pudding at an orphanage. Perhaps the best line of the evening is the flighty Lady Elizabeth's "I don't believe in facts." Typical of some of the others is such an interchange as, "She has lapses of memory?"—"I don't mean that. No, she hasn't very much memory to lose." The more fervid of Mr. Eliot's followers were loyal enough to laugh heartily at this point. Some of the rest of us, however, who were no less anxious to have a good time, found that most of Mr. Eliot's jests ended not with a bang but a whimper.

There are those who believe that in *The Confidential Clerk* Mr. Eliot has made an advance in his mastery of stagecraft. I wish I could agree with them, for it is important to have the theatre served by such a talent as his. Perhaps there is a little more facility in spreading the plot through three acts. Nonetheless, his new play seems hopelessly wordy to me, lacking in its many serious stretches the intensity and interest which gave such compulsion to the second act of *The Cocktail Party.*

Printed as verse, his dialogue is deliberately stripped of poetry and has the quality of clean, though colorless, prose. It is surprising and disappointing to have Mr. Eliot, a master of language, suggest loneliness by such an image (wilted even before Frances Hodgson Burnett used it) as "You have your secret garden to which you can retire/ And lock the gate behind you." Yet this is characteristic of much of the writing.

Far be it from me to say with certainty what Mr. Eliot is up to or to read religious symbols into his text. My guess would be, however, that he is writing about frustrations and the cost of choices— the frustration of a man of affairs who would rather have been a potter; of a young musician who has been forced into business because he knows he will always be a second-rate organist; and of a husband and wife who have never understood each other and have been denied the love of children.

From an audience's point of view the delight of the evening is Ina Claire as Lady Elizabeth. All the farcical joy, all the glitter of high comedy, that Mr. Eliot meant to supply in his script, she supplies in her person. She is a chic Lady Bracknell, a delectable worldling, an irresistible scatterbrain, writing comedy that is unwritten for her by the sparkle of her eyes, the laughter in her voice, and the implications of her expressions. More than being a superb comedienne, Miss Claire is the Comic Spirit incarnate. She proves her range when, suddenly, she changes her mood:

> . . . Of course, there's something in us,
> In all of us, which isn't just heredity,
> But something unique. Something we have been
> From eternity. Something . . . straight from God.
> That means that we are nearer to God than to anyone.

As she speaks these words that "something" seems very near indeed.

The pity is that in *The Confidential Clerk* Mr. Eliot never seems to have made up his mind what kind of play he was writing, and that in both its serious and farcical moods so much of it is a waste land in which only the most avid meaning-hunters among his devotees will find the pleasure we all hope for.

6. Star Bright

*The exciting development of a player who is a match for
kings and a king among actors, and his unforgettable performances in* Henry V *and* Oedipus.

[1946]

OLIVIER COMES INTO HIS OWN

UNTIL I SAW him in *Oedipus,* I was not certain. His Henry V
had almost convinced me. Yet, in spite of its magnificence,
it was a single performance. Moreover, it was seen on the screen.
And screen performances are hard to judge, at least with accuracy,
if for no other reason than in them it is impossible to tell where
the editing leaves off and the acting begins.

His virtues had been made clear enough. Exceptional virtues
they were, too. Certainly no one who had watched the Old Vic's
repertory, as unfolded in New York, could doubt that, with Ralph
Richardson, he was one of this British company's most compelling
attractions. Nor could anyone question either his skill as a comedian or his versatility.

That insouciance of his which was to find its fullest release in
The Critic, when Sheridan's japery was staged as an after-piece to
Oedipus, had already manifested itself in his Shallow in the second part of *Henry IV* and his Doctor in *Uncle Vanya.* It had
quickened his Hotspur, too.

In each new part he had proved he was possessed of those
chameleon qualities which actors are supposed to have but which
precious few of them can claim. So completely had he taken on the
colors of these various, and very different, characters that it had
become increasingly difficult to spot the real Laurence Olivier.
Yet—and this is what had begun to persuade me even before I
was convinced by *Oedipus*—each of Mr. Olivier's new interpretations had been colored by an excellence which I commenced to
realize was Mr. Olivier's own. Each was informed by the same
acting intelligence, showed the same detailed thoroughness, the

203

same energy in attack, and an almost equal mastery both of the script and of himself.

I realized, along with everyone out front at the Old Vic, that Mr. Olivier was an excellent actor; adroit, personable, and far more than reliable. His past performances in this country, on the stage in *The Green Bay Tree* and on the screen in *Rebecca* and *Wuthering Heights,* had prepared me for this, though I sensed— as who could help doing?—that he had ripened wonderfully. Indeed, remembering how unfortunate was his Romeo of six seasons back, I was conscious that he had developed more than any actor I had ever watched over a like period.

I had seen him first (and forgotten him) in 1929 when he had appeared as the young playwright in a soporific melodrama by Frank Vosper, called *Murder on the Second Floor.* Again in *Private Lives,* when he did nicely enough in a supplementary part Mr. Coward had forgotten to write. And next, after his sensitive performance in *The Green Bay Tree,* when he proved too light to play opposite Miss Cornell in *No Time for Comedy.*

But I was not prepared for the change in him disclosed by the Old Vic. Where once Mr. Olivier had been a wavy-haired juvenile, however skillful, he had grown into a character actor. He had, moreover, taken the next and most important step. Exceptional as he was as a character actor, his endowments did not stop there. They were not of what, as a rule, proves to be so secondary a nature. He was a straight actor who could lose himself in a character. Or, better still, lose the character in himself. His personality was that all-inclusive.

His Justice Shallow, for example, was wizened to the point of transparency. He was a dried seedpod of a man; a cobweb walking; an ancient cricket chirping. The only heroic thing about him was that in him a Shakespearean low comic managed to remain comic even to modern audiences. In itself this was no picayune achievement. In contrast to his Shallow, Mr. Olivier's Hotspur was sprung from so different a race that one could have sworn a different actor must have created him. He was splendid in his fire and recklessness; such a stalwart and headstrong figure as would have plucked bright honor from the moon. Yet he was no abstraction. His skillfully suggested stammer, his braggart's walk, and his mocking laugh—all these no less than his strawberry wig kept him individualized.

The Astrov Mr. Olivier revealed to us was again a new creation. Unlike Mr. Richardson's Uncle Vanya, which was a continuation, or rather a diminution, of his Falstaff, Mr. Olivier's Russian doctor had no connection—physically, vocally, or spiritually—with either his Hotspur or his Shallow. His Astrov was a melancholy, intelligent, yet smiling modern. More than any of his fellow actors, Mr. Olivier appeared to have caught the flavor—the sad, autumnal flavor—of the frustrated Russia of pre-revolutionary days. His Doctor bore in spirit no less than in appearance a marked similarity to Chekhov himself. Although perhaps slighter as a characterization than the text invites, his Astrov had the virtue of having been approached and understood from within.

As for Puff in *The Critic,* Mr. Olivier was to turn him—a short fifteen minutes after having played Oedipus—into a fellow all energy and unction, laughter and lightness, who scampered and skittered around the stage, blowing the dust off Sheridan's old parody. Like his previous creations, the Puff of Mr. Olivier was not merely a product of a new costume, a new wig, a new make-up, or a nose reshaped by putty until, in this instance, its tip was given the coarseness of an Hogarthian caricature. The difference was deeper. Its origins were interior.

Before *Oedipus* each of Mr. Olivier's single performances with the Old Vic had been admirable. When considered not one by one but as a whole, and in relation to each other, they were more than that. They were astonishing. Yet, by their very nature, they were limited to being proofs of high dexterity.

The *Henry V* movie had, as I say, almost persuaded me Mr. Olivier's talents were of a more sizable and substantial kind. His Henry stood out with the bright, bold colors of the English standard. He combined heat with dignity. He had humor, too, and was of those large dimensions appropriate to the hero-myths. Mr. Olivier removed from Henry the priggishness invited by the very excess of his royal virtues. Of a prince he made a man, even as of a man he made a prince who was an ideal of embattled kingship—an ideal, in this case, brilliantly humanized. In speech, appearance, posture, thought, and feeling, his Henry was a performance of superlative merit. He shone with spiritual splendor, a quality as rare in actors as it is in other human beings.

As I have hinted, such were the excellences of his Henry that I was driven against my will, but not against my judgment, to reach for that adjective which every critic hates to employ, and apply it to Mr. Olivier as an actor. I have in mind that precious, dangerous, final adjective—"great."

No word spills more infrequently or reluctantly than it does from any critical pen. For everyone's sake, for the well-being of the art involved, in the interests of criticism, out of respect for the language, and in defense of standards, "great" is an adjective which ought to be kept buried in the deep freeze. It cannot, it should not, it must not, be squandered lightly unless criticism, which is all too profligate in its enthusiasms, is to become as debased, inflated, and meaningless as the vocabularies of Hollywood's press agents.

But Mr. Olivier's Oedipus, considered along with his Henry and judged in the light of his earlier contributions to the Old Vic, has left me no other choice. I may be right. I may be wrong. I do not know. I can remember only William Hazlitt's sustaining line. "I am not one of those," wrote he in his theatregoing days, "who, when they see the sun breaking from behind a cloud, stop to ask others if it be the moon."

This line gives me the courage to overcome that cowardice— that fear of commitment and that embarrassment in the presence of emotion—which is as much the curse of criticism as are its thoughtless, churlish misappropriations of the dictionary's fund. I can only say that in *Henry V* and *Oedipus* I have seen the sun rise. And I refuse to mistake it for the moon, or salute it as such, when for me it is the sun.

Mr. Olivier's Oedipus is one of those performances in which blood and electricity are somehow mixed. It pulls lightning down from the sky. It is as awesome, dwarfing, and appalling as one of nature's angriest displays. Though thrilling, it never loses its majesty.

His Theban king is godlike in appearance. Although he has Henry's authority, the extrovert has disappeared. The proud figure from the tapestries, the warrior monarch, the dashing symbol of those days when all the youth of England was on fire and silken dalliance in the wardrobe lay, has become a Greco-Roman statue brought to life; sullen, willful, august, and imperious. There is something of the young Napoleon in him too, but he is a Napoleon pursued by the Furies rather than following the Eagle.

At the outset his is the arrogance of a man who feels himself secure. He can judge others rapidly, because he believes he is himself above judgment. He speaks slowly, with a frightening casualness at first, when addressing the suppliants. His decisions are as swift as his speech is deliberate. He dares to take pauses of uncommon length. Yet the passion of his nature makes itself felt at once; the passion and the violence.

He prepares us completely for the man who, in his maturity, has been condemned by his youthful hotheadedness. Mr. Olivier's Oedipus is, as it should be, the victim of his character. His character is his own evil destiny. His instantaneous surrender to torrid impulses, which we have demonstrated for us in his conversations with Creon and the Old Shepherd, is what has doomed him. It is this selfsame instability which has embroiled him, in an even fiercer form, in that fight at the crossroads long ago during which, without meaning to, he had killed his father, King Laius.

Oedipus's gradual comprehension of his guilt, which is scored so inexorably in Sophocles' text, is given its fullest theatrical expression in Mr. Olivier's performance. The evening's suspense is draining and almost unendurable. When the fearful realization at last inundates him, and his Theban king knows beyond doubt that he has murdered his father, married his mother, and had children by her, Mr. Olivier releases two cries which no one who has heard them can hope to forget.

They are the dreadful, hoarse groans of a wounded animal. They well up out of a body that has been clubbed by fate. They are sounds which speak, as no words could, for a soul torn by horror, for a mind numbed by what it has been forced to comprehend. Yet fearful as these groans are in their brute savagery, they serve only to magnify the stature of Oedipus's kingly woe. The subsequent moments when Oedipus appears, self-blinded with the blood trickling down his face, are almost more terrible than audiences can bear. But even these final scenes are redeemed from gruesomeness by their grandeur. The question is one of spiritual scale rather than physical detail.

The William Butler Yeats translation is a vast improvement over the Gilbert Murray version. It is freed from the Swinburnian flourishes and the Albert Memorial fussiness. It is stark, direct; strong and pure of line; and full of power. From curtain rise to curtain fall the Old Vic's *Oedipus* rivets the attention. I have never known an audience to be so silent as during the enactment of this tragedy. All my life I have read about a stillness great enough to be heard. This is precisely what the audience's silence is in the presence of this *Oedipus*. That is, until the play is over and the auditorium thunders with cheers and bravos. These bravos are deserved, however, because here is the theatre at its mighty best, and Sophocles in all the glory of his power, building so surely and inextricably that, beside his austere structure, the most dramatic edifice of such a modern contriver as Ibsen seems prefabricated.

What Mr. Olivier will prove to be in the future, I cannot pretend to know. The aisle seat, not the Delphic tripod, is the critic's place. But this I do know: as both Henry V and Oedipus he has shown us what great acting can be, and given us excitements, pleasures, and memories which, as playgoers, we are bound to treasure, since they come so seldom in the most questing lifetime.

The blood-soaked tale of a princess who had a talent for murder, and Miss Anderson's technically brilliant playing of her.

[1947]

JUDITH ANDERSON'S MEDEA

THE MAN and the moment—these were the essentials in Matthew Arnold's recipe for greatness. The two had to be in happy conjunction. In the theatre the player and the part can also coincide so that the result is greatness. If not greatness, a brilliance, an excitement, a rightness, perhaps more accurately an inevitability, any one of which (the opportunity being of sufficient splendor) can prove a cousin of greatness, capable of creating its illusion.

Judith Anderson and *Medea** are a case in point. Robinson Jeffers has dedicated his free adaptation of the Euripidean tragedy "To Judith Anderson, for whom this was written." No one can be surprised by such a confession; certainly no one who has seen the production or followed Miss Anderson's career. So right is she for Medea, so right is Medea for her, that it almost seems as if Euripides, not Mr. Jeffers, must have had Miss Anderson in mind.

Miss Anderson has been acting in America since 1918. And nearly always with distinction. No performer on our stage is a more consummate technician than she. Her acting intelligence is limitless. Beauty she may not have, but interest she does possess; interest ample enough to rank as fascination.

As the mother of Jesus in *Family Portrait*, she was all motherhood, without sentimentality though the embodiment of compassion. Yet admirable as was her Mary, virtue is not Miss Anderson's specialty. She excels in parts that are on speaking terms with evil.

The worthless rich woman in *Behold the Bridegroom;* Nina in *Strange Interlude;* the Unknown One in *As You Desire Me;* Lavinia in *Mourning Becomes Electra;* the strong sister in *The Old Maid;* Gertrude in Mr. Gielgud's *Hamlet;* Lady Macbeth opposite Mr. Evans; and, on the screen, Mrs. Danvers in *Rebecca*—such characters as these are the ones we associate with Miss Anderson. They either have or should have coincided with her talents and released her fine gifts. I say *should have released* rather than in every case actually did release her talents because her Gertrude seemed to me a failure, and her Lady Macbeth more brilliant in spots than it was throughout, in spite of the fact that, by temperament and endowment and with creative direction, Miss Anderson could be the perfect Lady Macbeth of this generation.

Outstanding though she has been in her best parts in the past, one thing is now clear. Her triumphs like her failures at present

---

* *Medea*, freely adapted from the *Medea* of Euripides by Robinson Jeffers. Staged by John Gielgud. Setting by Ben Edwards. Costumes by Castillo. Original music by Tibor Serly. Presented by Robert Whitehead and Oliver Rea. With a cast including Judith Anderson, John Gielgud, Florence Reed, Kathryn Grill, Leone Wilson, Albert Hecht, and Hugh Franklin. At the National Theatre. Opened October 20, 1947.

appear to have been no more than homework for her Medea. Her Colchian princess summarizes and consolidates her previous efforts. It is the crowning achievement of her career. Being accurate as a characterization, her Medea is also a pyrotechnical display, quivering, eruptive, and spectacular. Moreover it is a performance of a scale, freedom, and kind that Miss Anderson alone among our present-day actresses could supply.

E. H. Sothern once insisted that most contemporary players use their hands as if they had been trained as department-store clerks. By this he meant that in their gesturing they were as constricted as if they had counters eternally in front of them; that they never moved their elbows away from their ribs or straightened out their arms or dared to strike heroic attitudes. Had he lived to see Miss Anderson, Mr. Sothern could have proved his rule by naming her as an exception to it. She is not afraid of acting. She takes to it the way Xenophon's Greeks welcomed the sea. She refuses to be held down by the diminuendoes of a dull realism.

Miss Anderson is a virtuoso unashamed of her virtuosity. Her courage in demonstrating her mastery of her craft is uncommon. Most modern actors are forced by the demands of our tea-sipping, telephone-dialing, pistol-packing, cocktail-raising, ash-flicking stage to hide their ability to act. If they can act, they mask this terrifying fact as discreetly as most Americans who wish to be asked out again, and not dropped as poseurs or highbrows, keep their true culture dark.

Actors cannot be blamed for this. They have no other choice than to bow to the will of a public which likes to fancy itself as being tough and literal in a realistic age. To remain employed in a naturalistic theatre, players inevitably limit themselves to being natural and no more. Their pattern of on-stage behavior is not what the kings and queens of tragedy might do in a kingdom of imagination but what the average man or woman would do on a settee, in an office, or over a Bendix in daily life, if certain they were unobserved. Our current actors are trained to dread the grandiose and to fear the expressed emotion almost as much as the emptied one. They tremble before the threat of being called "hams."

Not so Miss Anderson. She approaches antique tragedy unafraid. Playing Medea and playing her to the last drop of cruelty, frenzy, and revenge that is in her, Miss Anderson cannot be expected to do what Hazlitt praised Mrs. Siddons for having done. "She raised Tragedy to the skies, or brought it down from thence," wrote Hazlitt of the great Sarah. "It was something above nature. We can conceive of nothing grander. . . . She was not less than a goddess, or than a prophetess inspired by the gods. Power was seated on her brow, passion emanated from her breast as from a shrine. She was Tragedy personified. She was the stateliest ornament of the public mind."

Being true to Medea, Miss Anderson does not raise tragedy "to the skies" or bring it down from there. She rightly refuses even to leave it as a part of this earth. Instead, at the dictation of the text, she burrows with it into the heat of hades, flinching from none of the horrors to be found there.

Medea is a special kind of tragic heroine. Although Jason may have sinned against her by deserting her for Creon's daughter, her own sins are multitudinous. She is as accomplished at murder as she is at sorcery. She is not, and could not be, Tragedy personified in the more exalted sense. She is no goddess but an animal in agony. She is a ruin rather than an ornament; a wretch whose heart has cracked and whose sole obsession is revenge. Hers is the fury of hell no less than of a woman scorned. She is hate incarnate; misery broken out of all control; loathing unleashed until, hurricane-wise, it sweeps everything and everyone before it.

When the Greeks sat before *Medea*, they enjoyed their advantages over us. They knew the fable in advance. Hence they realized that the love which preceded the action of the play was as great as is the hatred which alone fuels this action. We, as moderns, stumble upon the last act of a tragedy, the terrible ecstasy of which has already occurred. We see an ignoble, not a noble, mind overthrown, and encounter it only after its collapse.

Medea, on our meeting with her in her last days in Corinth, does not spill blood for the first time when she sends her rival and her rival's father to their agonizing deaths, and murders her two little boys. She is blood-soaked at the curtain's rise and has been ever since Jason's arrival in Colchis on his quest for the Golden Fleece. A murderous Medea merely wades the deeper into a sea of horrors. The tragedy deals with her final crimes. If we do not realize that the love which has gone before is as great as the hate we are asked to contemplate, we find ourselves confronted with a monster whose one claim to greatness is the intensity of her hatred.

Mr. Jeffers has not attempted the impossible task of prettifying the Medea story. He has employed his poet's skill to streamline the text, to bring it closer to the contemporary stage, to rid its speeches of those stylistic villainies of which E. P. Coleridge was guilty in his translation. Mr. Jeffers' language, though not always satisfactory, has about it—at its best—a driving, iron quality that Gilbert Murray's more liquid version cannot claim. What it loses as poetry it gains as theatre. Its tension is undeniable, and is immediately communicated by Miss Anderson.

No dynamo could surpass her in energy. As she moves up and down the steps of the cheerless palace Ben Edwards has designed for her, her body is always at the command of her emotions. She uses gestures that are large, bold, and varied. Her arms speak a language of their own. Her voice, which is uncommon both in its range and timbre, can wheedle, plead, accuse, or mock. At one moment it crackles like a roaring fire from passion's heat. At the next it hisses like a pit full of snakes.

Some of my confreres, I note, have contended that, excellent as Miss Anderson is as Medea, she starts her first act at so high a pitch that she cannot hope to top it in her second. This may have been true on the first night. I know only that, when I saw her later in the run, Miss Anderson's command of her performance was so undeviating that there was no hint of anticlimax in the awful horror of her final scenes.

From what I had read I had been prepared to find Mr. Gielgud's Jason disappointing. The part is certainly a thankless one. Yet to me, Mr. Gielgud, who always reads intelligently, seemed as effective as any man could hope to be in Medea's presence. Helmeted and hidden behind a borrowed beard as he was, I must confess I would never have recognized him had I not known that he was playing Jason. No doubt this is some kind of compliment in itself.

What bothered me about Mr. Gielgud was his direction, not his acting. It seemed stodgy. It lacked the qualities of ultimate ignition. It had the repertory touch of adequacy without inspiration. I was especially unhappy about his casting and handling of the three women who formed the Chorus. The Chorus is always a problem in a Greek play. These particular crones of Corinth remained, for me at least, an unsolved problem. I could not help thinking in their presence, with Medea bursting to confide in them all her innermost secrets, how easy the life of a gossip columnist would have been in ancient Greece.

The evening, however, is, as it was bound to be, Miss Anderson's. Magnificent as she is, I cannot pretend for a split second that either she or the production to which she lends distinction possessed for me the excitement of Laurence Olivier's *Oedipus*. I discovered that I kept on admiring (as anyone would have to admire) so superlative a technical performance. Yet somehow, even when I wanted to applaud, I remained unmoved. Due, no doubt, to the very nature of the text, mine was that strange, cheated feeling one would have if left cold when standing before a blazing fire.

Shakespeare's tragedy, modern uniforms replacing its togas, is moved forward in time to make its thrilling comment on a world threatened by Fascists and Nazis.

[1937]

CAESAR AND ORSON WELLES

THIS IS no funeral oration. I come to praise *Caesar** at the Mercury Theatre, not to bury it. Of all the many new plays and productions the season has so far revealed, this modern-dress version of the mob mischief and demaguery which can follow the

---

* *Julius Caesar,* by William Shakespeare. Staged by Orson Welles. Setting by Samuel Leve. Incidental music by Marc Blitzstein. Revived by Mr. Welles and John Houseman. With a cast including Orson Welles, Joseph Cotten, George Coulouris, Joseph Holland, Martin Gabel, Hiram Sherman, John Hoysradt, Ted Reid, Norman Lloyd, and Evelyn Allen. At the Mercury Theatre. Opened November 11, 1937.

assassination of a dictator is by all odds the most exciting, the most imaginative, the most topical, the most awesome, and the most absorbing. The touch of genius is upon it. It liberates Shakespeare from the strait jacket of tradition. Gone are the togas and all the schoolroom recollections of a plaster Julius. Blown away is the dust of antiquity. Banished are the costumed Equity members, so ill at ease in a painted forum, spouting speeches which have tortured the memory of each member of the audience.

Because of Orson Welles' inspiration and the sheer brilliance of his staging, Shakespeare ceases at the Mercury to be the darling of the College Board Examiners. Unfettered and with all the vigor that was his when he spoke to the groundlings of his own day, he becomes the contemporary of us who are Undergroundlings. What he wrote with Plutarch in his mind, we sit before with today's headlines screaming in our eyes.

New York has already enjoyed its successful Shakespearean revivals in modern dress. There was *Hamlet*. There was *The Taming of the Shrew*. Then, under this same Mr. Welles' direction, Harlem flirted with a tantalizing, if unrealized, idea in its voodoo *Macbeth*. But these productions, vivifying as they have proven, have at their best been no more than quickening experiences *in* the theatre. The astonishing, all-impressive virtue of Mr. Welles' *Julius Caesar* is that, magnificent as it is as theatre, it is far larger than its medium. Something deathless and dangerous in the world sweeps past you down the darkened aisles at the Mercury and takes possession of the proud, gaunt stage. It is something fearful and turbulent which distends the drama to include the life of nations as well as of men. It is an ageless warning, made in such arresting terms that it not only gives a new vitality to an ancient story but unrolls in your mind's eye a map of the modern world splotched increasingly, as we know it to be, with sickening colors.

Mr. Welles does not dress his conspirators and his Storm Troopers in Black Shirts or in Brown. He does not have to. The antique Rome, which we had thought was securely Roman in Shakespeare's tragedy, he shows us to be a dateless state of mind. Of all the conspirators at work in the text, Mr. Welles is the most artful. He is not content to leave Shakespeare a great dramatist. He also turns him into a great anticipator. At his disposal Mr. Welles places a Time Machine which carries him away from the past at which he had aimed and down through the centuries to the present. To an extent no other director in our day and country has equaled, Mr. Welles proves in his production that Shakespeare was indeed not of an age but for all time. After this surly modern Caesar, dressed in a green uniform and scowling behind the mask-like face of a contemporary dictator, has fallen at the Mercury and new mischief is afoot, we cannot but shudder before the prophet's wisdom of those lines which read:

> *How many ages hence*
> *Shall this our lofty scene be acted over*
> *In states unborn and accents yet unknown!*

To fit the play into modern dress and give it its fullest implication, Mr. Welles has not hesitated to take his liberties with the script. Unlike Professor Strunk, however, who attempted to improve upon *Antony and Cleopatra,* he has not stabbed it through the heart. He has only chopped away at its body. You may miss a few fingers, even an arm and leg in the *Julius Caesar* you thought you knew. But the heart of the drama beats more vigorously in this production than it has in years. If the play ceases to be Shakespeare's tragedy, it does manage to become ours. That is the whole point and glory of Mr. Welles' unorthodox, but welcome, restatement of it.

He places it upon a bare stage, the brick walls of which are crimson and naked. A few steps and a platform and an abyss beyond, from which the actors can emerge, are the setting. A few steps— and the miracle of spotlights that stab the darkness with as sinister an effect as the daggers of the assassins which penetrate Caesar's body. That is all. And it is all that is needed. In its streamlined simplicity this setting achieves the glorious, unimpeded freedom of an Elizabethan stage. Yet no backgrounds of the winter have been as eloquent or contributive as is this frankly presentational set. It is a setting spacious enough for both the winds and victims of demagoguery to sweep across it like a hurricane. And sweep across they do, in precisely this fashion.

Mr. Welles' direction is as heightening as is his use of an almost empty stage. His groupings are of that fluid, stressful, virtuoso sort one usually has to journey to Russia to see. He proves himself a brilliant innovator in his deployment of his principals and his movement of his crowds. His direction, which is constantly creative, is never more so than in its first revelation of Caesar hearing the warning of the soothsayer, or in the fine scene in which Cinna, the poet, is engulfed by a sinister crowd of ruffians. Even when one misses Shakespeare's lines, Mr. Welles keeps drumming the meaning of his play into our minds by the scuffling of his mobs when they prowl in the shadows, or the herdlike thunder of their feet when they run as one threatening body. It is a memorable device. Like the setting in which it is used, it is pure theatre; vibrant, unashamed, and enormously effective.

The theatrical virtues of this modern dress *Julius Caesar* do not stop with its excitements as a stunt in showmanship. They extend to the performances. As Brutus Mr. Welles shows once again how uncommon is his gift for speaking great words simply. His tones are conversational. His manner is quiet; far too quiet to meet the traditional needs of the part. But it is a quiet with a reason. The deliberation of Mr. Welles' speech is the mark of the honesty which flames within him. His reticent Brutus is at once a foil to the staginess of the production as a whole and to the oratory of Caesar and Antony. He is a perplexed liberal, this Brutus; an idealist who is swept by bad events into actions which have no less dangerous consequences for the state. Like many another contemporary liberal he is a Caspar Milquetoast, so filled with the virtues of Sir Roger de Coverley that he can do nothing.

George Coulouris is an admirable Antony. So fresh is his characterization, so intelligent his performance, that even "Friends, Romans, Countrymen" sounds on his tongue as if it were a rabble-rousing harangue he is uttering for the first time. If only he began it with "*My* friends, Romans, countrymen," you could swear last night's radio had brought it to you freshly heated from a famous fireside. Joseph Holland's Caesar is an imperious dictator who could be found frowning at you in this week's newsreels. He is excellently conceived and excellently projected. Some mention, however inadequate, must also be made of Martin Gabel's capable Cassius, of John Hoysradt's Decius Brutus, of the conspirators whose black hats are pluck'd about their ears, and Norman Lloyd's humorous yet deeply affecting Cinna.

It would be easy to find faults here and there; to wonder about the wisdom of some of the textual changes even in terms of the present production's aims; to complain that the whole tragedy does not fit with equal ease into its modern treatment; and to wish this or that scene had been played a little differently. But such fault-findings strike me in the case of this *Julius Caesar* as being as pic-ayune as they are ungrateful. What Mr. Welles and his associates at the Mercury have achieved is a triumph that is exceptional from almost every point of view.

The lovely lyricism and grace by means of which Katharine Cornell conveys the ardor and youth of the star-crossed Capulet.

[1934]

THE JULIET OF MISS CORNELL

THE WELL-KNOWN tragedy of most actresses who are sufficiently experienced to do justice to Juliet is that for five long acts they are haunted by a merciless text which insists the total number of their years is no more than fourteen. Fortunately for all of us, including Shakespeare, Miss Cornell* does not convince us against our wills that it must be Lady Capulet rather than her moonstruck daughter who is answering to the call of Cupid. She is not one of those Juliets who carry their own balconies.

Obviously Miss Cornell is more than fourteen. Yet just as ob-viously she manages to be youth incarnate. The script and her performance are not in conflict. Without being the age of Shake-

---

* *Romeo and Juliet,* by William Shakespeare. Directed by Guthrie McClintic. Settings and costumes by Jo Mielziner. Music by Paul Nordoff. Dance direction by Martha Graham. Produced by Katharine Cornell. With a cast including Miss Cornell, Basil Rathbone, Edith Evans, Brian Aherne, Orson Welles, John Emery, Charles Waldron, Moroni Olsen, Brenda Forbes, and George Macready. At the Martin Beck Theatre. Opened December 20, 1934.

speare's heroine, she suggests the illusion of Juliet's years. To the creation of this illusion she brings not only her own extraordinary personal glamour but all the technical richness her career has yielded her.

Of all the Juliets we have seen, Miss Cornell's is the only one which satisfactorily embodies the descriptions of Juliet's movements as given in the script. Her "fair daughter of rich Capulet" may be adult in form but she is young in motion and in heart. She literally runs, as Richard Lockridge phrased it, with her arms outstretched to love. As she glides, free-limbed and lovely, with enchanting and seemingly unconscious grace, across the stage, one feels instinctively the young girl Shakespeare saw in his poet's mind has come to life.

"O, she is lame!" is Juliet's own complaint when she waits impatiently in the orchard for the tidings from Romeo her old nurse has been sent to fetch.

> . . . love's heralds should be thoughts,
> Which ten times faster glide than the sun's beams,
> Driving back shadows over louring hills:
> Therefore do nimble-pinion'd doves draw love,
> And therefore hath the wind-swift Cupid wings. . . .
>   Yet she is not come.
> Had she affections and warm youthful blood,
> She would be as swift in motion as a ball.

Later, when Juliet enters Friar Laurence's cell for her secret marriage to Romeo, Shakespeare is no less specific in characterizing her actions. "Here comes the lady," says the Friar.

> . . . O, so light a foot
> Will ne'er wear out the everlasting flint.
> A lover may bestride the gossamer
> That idles in the wanton summer air,
> And yet not fall; so light is vanity.

Miss Cornell's Juliet is Shakespeare's Juliet in all these respects. She does seem to move with the rapidity of thought. She is carried on the wings of a "wind-swift Cupid." She is possessed of such affections and of such warm, youthful blood that she is "swift in motion as a ball." She treads the earth with feet that will "ne'er wear out the everlasting flint." She is a lover who could bestride, without falling, "the gossamer that idles in the wanton summer air."

Her actions are not the only virtues of Miss Cornell's performance. Her Juliet is innocent and unawakened yet hotly eager for love. Later she is vibrant with the all-consuming passion which seizes upon her. Girlish as she is, her heart and mind are mature enough to do justice to the poetic beauty and the human anguish Shakespeare wrote into the character of his fourteen-year-old maiden. Miss Cornell's voice, which in her prose parts of the past has always been a haunting instrument, now not only adjusts itself to the entirely different demands of verse but is more than equal to its new-found opportunities.

A Hamlet very different from his predecessors in vigor and drive is brilliantly projected by Maurice Evans, and some of the secondary characters also benefit from fresh interpretations.

[1938]

THE UNCUT *HAMLET*

MAURICE EVANS' Hamlet,* so unconventional in its vigor, so extrovert in its virtues, so contrary to tradition in its very mascu-

---

* *Hamlet*, by William Shakespeare. Directed by Margaret Webster. Settings and costumes by David Ffolkes. Incidental music by Lehman Engel. Produced by Maurice Evans in association with Joseph Verner Reed and Boris Said. With a cast including Mr. Evans, Mady Christians, Katherine Locke, Henry Edwards, George Graham, Donald Randolph, Sydney Smith, Augustin Duncan, Alexander Scourby, Whitford Kane, Wesley Addy, and Rhys Williams. At the St. James Theatre. Opened October 12, 1938.

linity, has burst upon this town as a new and welcome interpretation of a Prince usually played as if he were a fugitive from a psy-
chopathic hospital, a cross between Dr. Caligari and Rodin's
Thinker, and the first male interior decorator.

To maintain that Mr. Evans' is the only interpretation of the
part would be to tell a lie, for one of the proofs of the play's greatness is that it refuses to admit a final Hamlet. Also it would be to
turn one's back churlishly on those actors who, in our time and in
their own ways, have illumined the cut texts in which they have
chosen to appear. Forbes-Robertson's Hamlet was a notable creation, the vocal beauties of which still ring in the ears of those who
saw it. But when seen, as I happened to see it, at the time of the
farewell tour, Forbes-Robertson's Dane was so unmistakably autumnal that, as one listened to him talking about having just come
down from college at Wittenberg, even a playgoer as young as I
was then was forced to wonder if Hamlet were not a sad case of
arrested development. Robert B. Mantell's performance had about
it more of the feeling of a poetic undertaker than of a noble mind
in deep distress. E. H. Sothern, though expert both as Malvolio
and Petruchio, always acted a stolid Prince, a sort of early broker,
in mourning for his losses, who had just voted for Landon.

To claim the aforesaid finality for Mr. Evans' Hamlet would
also be to overlook the excellent and touching tragic figure
Walter Hampden created in his early matinees, before his Dane
had become so scholarly that he substituted a Phi Beta Kappa key
for a rapier. It would be to forget the dynamic splendors of
John Barrymore's realization of the Prince as a hot-tempered neurotic capable of magnificent theatrical effects. It would be to ignore
Basil Sydney's memorable modern dress performance which was
expertly read, especially in the speech to the players, and did much
to rediscover for contemporary audiences the wonders of the play
as a play. It would be to discount, as one cannot, the brilliant
flashes of cerebration by means of which John Gielgud's fiery
weakling cast a new and brilliant light upon many familiar passages.

Yet a major glory of Mr. Evans' Prince is the hitherto unre-
vealed and unsuspected Hamlet he establishes. Between all the
previous Hamlets, good and bad, that I have seen, a certain bond
of orthodoxy has existed. Dissimilar as they may have been be-

cause of the gifts and temperaments of their projectors, most of these Hamlets have either been, or sought to be, brothers in much the same kind of melancholy. They have been solitary fellows, white-faced squatters on Savonarola chairs, black mourners, spotlight searchers, tragic poets in a rough age, or heartbroken soliloquizers. All of them have been men of inaction, condemned by fate to do deeds for which they had no liking and were ill equipped.

They have taken literally Hamlet's description of himself as being "so poor a man a Hamlet is." For them the time has been out of joint, as out of joint it must be no matter how the play is interpreted. Their special tragedy has always been the "cursèd spite" that ever they were born to set it right. On this line they seem to have built their whole characterizations as surely as Peter's church was built upon a rock. Moreover, they have often so superbly justified their morbid Danes on the basis of the cut text that, until Mr. Evans came along justifying his extrovert Hamlet on the authority of the unabridged script, no other Hamlet had seemed quite possible.

Now at least we know the tragedy can yield a Prince totally different from the Prince we had begun to take for granted. We have also come to realize with much joy that not only the part but also the play as a whole gains enormously in freshness and vitality when it is given the benefit of a re-evaluation as exciting as the one which Mr. Evans, Miss Webster, and their actors have given it at the St. James.

Mr. Evans' Hamlet is very much a man. He bounds into Elsinore with the vigor of a Legionnaire. In part, at least, he is the soldier Fortinbras deems worthy, after death, of military honors. His is the "noble heart" Horatio salutes. He is one of the few Hamlets of our time who has waited for his soliloquies before beginning to soliloquize. He is the only Hamlet I have seen who has explained why he should have made friends in college who would have bothered to look him up afterward. If he despises Osric, it is because he makes clear, as many contemporary Hamlets have failed to do, the differences in type and temperament which set him apart from "this water-fly." It is easy to understand his dashing Prince's eagerness to test his skill with Laertes upon hearing of Laertes' prowess with the rapier.

From the first, however, he is unhappy in his heart. Unlike his predecessors, he does not wear his sufferings on his sleeves. Thoughtful as he is, he is not a sandwich man for melancholia. He has wit. He has charm. He is normal, though distressed. With all the beauty of Mr. Evans' voice and the controlled surety of his excellent readings, he does justice to both the poetry and the passion of the text. Mr. Evans' Hamlet is a Prince born of the whole play. He is not a creation made possible by whittling it down until only a stellar part is left.

It is the full-grown Hamlet of the full-grown tragedy Mr. Evans seeks to explain. Just as surely as the secondary characters are permitted to grow on the authority of such a text, so does Hamlet himself take on new dimensions. Mr. Evans is, for example, the only Hamlet of our time who, in addition to his gifts as a thinker and a poet, is a Prince in the executive sense. One feels that, if everything had gone well around the palace, as he might have hoped it would, Mr. Evans' Hamlet could have succeeded his father and become an admirable ruler in his own right. Obviously his spirit has been touched, as an Elizabethan princeling's would have been, by Machiavelli's. Whereas most of the Hamlets of our time, at the moment of their dying, would have been right in reaching for the collected works of Freud, Mr. Evans is the only Hamlet I have seen who died thinking about the state and the Danish equivalents of such political issues as the Third Term and the New Deal. In other words, he is the only Prince whose misadventures I have followed in Elsinore who is statesman enough to make one understand why Hamlet, before crying, "The rest is silence," should be curious about the election news from England, and trouble to give Fortinbras his dying voice.

Then, too, unlike most Hamlets, he does not wait until after Ophelia is safely dead to make known his love for her. No moment in the play gains more by its disregard of stage tradition than does Mr. Evans' scene with Ophelia. By postponing Hamlet's glimpse of the hidden king and Polonius until "Where's your father?" Mr. Evans and Miss Webster change the whole meaning and value of "Get thee to a nunnery." In their hands it ceases to be the usual bitter, almost hysterical cry of rage. It becomes a tender and protective declaration of love. For Mr. Evans speaks the speech in a voice heavy and sweet with affection. His arms are around Ophelia; his head is buried in her bosom. His one pathetic hope seems to be to protect her from the world full of sinners he has been forced into knowing.

You may wonder why so vigorous a Hamlet as Mr. Evans creates can be so slow in revenging his father's murder. Certainly, his Dane is colored with a "native hue of resolution" which is never "sicklied o'er" with a "pale cast of thought." Yet he finds as much justification for his active Hamlet as the pallid, indecisive Hamlets have been able to find.

Although Mr. Evans' Dane is no coward, he has a conscience. It is this conscience which turns awry his enterprises of "great pitch and moment" until they may seem to "lose the name of action." Like every Hamlet, Mr. Evans' healthy young intellectual curses the spite that has doomed him at his birth to the doing of bloody deeds. When he utters this complaint, however, it does not come from the heart of a weakling incapable of action and filled with neuroses. Both his dilemma and his "dull revenge" are fully explained in his "How all occasions do inform against me" soliloquy. It is on this speech, rather than on the more familiar cry against spiteful doom, that he builds his Hamlet, and by means of which he seems to justify it. One believes implicitly in Mr. Evans' Dane when he points out he has the "cause," the "will," the "strength," and the "means" to do what he has been fated to do. The only thing delaying him, as Mr. Evans makes clear, is "some craven scruple of thinking too precisely on the event."

THE LESSER ROLES IN *HAMLET*

Fine though his performance is, Mr. Evans' Dane is not the only untraditional and illuminating feature of the uncut *Hamlet*. Margaret Webster shares with Mr. Evans the honor of being the hero of the occasion. Her direction is an almost constant source of wonder and delight. Freshening as it is, however, its revelations would remain unrealized were it not for the supporting cast with which Mr. Evans has been both wise and generous enough to surround his Prince. The extensions and innovations in the following secondary characters are typical of the new theatrical qualities gained by the play at the St. James. They may serve to explain why some of us have not hesitated to maintain that no one can claim to have seen *Hamlet* who has not sat before the play as Mr. Evans and Miss Webster have presented it in the unabridged version.

The King. Anyone who recalls the Claudiuses in the *Hamlets* of the last twenty years must remember they have been acted as deep-dyed villains. They have tended to wear brass crowns around the palace at all times of the day or night to establish their kingship. Most of them have gone so far as to cover their chins with blood-red beards in order to advertise their divine right to be hated as potential murderers. They have always looked as if they had just stolen the Brooklyn police records. They have been Desperate Desmonds in ancient dress. They have wandered around the castle as if they were looking for some room in which they could fingerprint themselves. Spotting them as the public enemies they have so aggressively been would never have caused J. Edgar Hoover's men any difficulty. The wonder has been that they have ever fooled the Court. Or that Gertrude (innocent or an accomplice) should ever have consented to marry them after having lived with such a nice old fellow as King Hamlet must have been.

Henry Edwards' Claudius is fortunately not sprung from the Krimsky Brothers' line of hissables. Instead of resembling one of the regal Jack-the-Rippers of tradition, he is wise enough to mask the wickedness of his Claudius. His King is spiritually a slyer fellow than the Musica family could boast. He is a suave man who, as all temporarily successful villains must be, is capable of committing a crime and hiding his guilt without arousing the suspicions of everyone except a house detective. He is a courtier and a king. He shows how heavy his crime hangs upon him (in other words, how right the Ghost is) only when he attempts to pray or watches the play. He is a palace intriguer attractive enough to feel safe in gratifying his ambitions. The Comte de Provence and the Comte d'Artois, those Iscariot brothers of Louis XVI, could have exchanged fraternity grips with him.

Furthermore, Mr. Edwards' Claudius is the first I have ever seen who either feels, or is justified in feeling, the physical attraction for his brother's wife about which young Hamlet minces no words. His love for Gertrude is so poignantly established that one is forced to wonder why, at the very moment the Queen is drinking from the poisoned goblet, Miss Webster should have missed one of her few humanizing values by allowing Claudius to cry to the whole Court the aside reading, "It is the poison'd cup; it is too late," without rushing sadly to her side.

The Queen. Most Queens in the cut versions have sauntered through the text as if they were mute sisters of Lady Macbeth who, among the duties of their high office, had been obliged to become honorary president of the Garden Club. Or they have pouted around the palace resembling nothing so much as pigs searching for truffles.

Mady Christians is a brilliant exception. One look at her is almost enough to explain why Claudius wished to get his older brother out of the way. Obviously the Queen Miss Christians creates did not mean to be unfaithful to her first husband when she married her second. Plainly she is the kind of woman who did not bother to distinguish between them, because of her group interest in men. Miss Christians' Gertrude is a forerunner of the female lean-to Chekhov had in mind when he wrote *The Darling*. In the frosty Court of Denmark she burns on the overtime schedule of the midnight sun. She is unaware of the dirty work in the garden which has changed the seating of her breakfast table.

She is attractive, interested, and queenly—at least on state occasions. She is at once a doting mother, a considerate queen, and a more than doting wife. She is a compassionate and seductive Gertrude who is the more ardent because of her age. If she is capable of tragedy in the closet scene, she indulges in coquetry throughout. She is so busy ordering dresses and keeping her "men folk" happy that it is little short of miraculous she does not find time to sing one of *India's Love Lyrics* while reading the *Boston Cook Book* on the throne.

Ophelia. Ophelias have a way, of course, of succeeding either in their earlier episodes of sanity or in their later mad scenes. None to my recollection has ever succeeded in both to the extent that Katherine Locke does. She is the first Ophelia I have ever watched who did not act as if the entire Court had anticipated her lunacy all these many years. She is the first Ophelia who, when her madness has descended upon her, has not rushed to her room upstairs to get down from her closet that sort of public nightgown which can be described only as her little mad dress, and which apparently she has had hanging there for many seasons along with her other clothes for every occasion.

Most Ophelias, of course, when they return to the stage so dressed, have always taken pains to let down their hair. When a woman lets down her hair in the theatre, needless to say, it always means one of two things, and the second of these is insanity. Although Miss Locke may bow to convention by deranging her coiffure, she creates something of a precedent by not forcing one to look forward to her lunacy when she is sane, or to her death when she is mad. In her introductory scenes she appears as a young woman both intelligent and charming. She is intelligent enough to have been to Vassar, and charming enough to win forgiveness for having gone there.

She is the first Ophelia I know of who so fully projects her passionate love for Hamlet that she explains his no less passionate love for her. The country dances she executes with her back turned to the King and the Queen, while singing her mad songs, are welcome escapes from the traditional Raquel Meller "Will-you-buy-my-violets" business and even Miss Gish's effective stocking tuggings.

What is true of the King, the Queen, and Ophelia as they are revitalized at the St. James is no less true of the process of vitalization which quickens the whole of Mr. Evans' *Hamlet*. Small wonder, therefore, when so superb a play is realized in such superb and tingling terms, that Mr. Atkinson should write in his most classical style, "Only the dopes will stay away from this one!"

*Ten years after Tallulah Bankhead barged down the Nile
as Cleopatra—and sank—Katharine Cornell triumphantly
makes the same journey, which is here considered not only
in relation to her and Shakespeare but also to Plutarch and
Shaw.*

[1947]

O EASTERN STAR!

THAT CLEOPATRA triumphed over Antony was not news even to
Plutarch. But that Katharine Cornell has triumphed over Cleopatra is news—and exciting news—to anyone aware of how stubbornly one of the most glorious of Shakespeare's tragedies has
resisted performance behind the footlights.

The difficulties of the play from the theatrical point of view are
as plentiful as its wonders are self-evident to the reader. Its characters are most sovereign creatures. Their legs bestride the ocean.
Kings wear their livery. The ancient world is the tragedy's stage.
It sweeps from Alexandria and Rome to Actium and back again
with the freedom of a poet's unfettered mind. Its range is global.
It moves by land as swiftly as it darts with ships "o'er green Nep-
tune's back." Its images are grandiose. Their scale is heroic. They
envisage men as demi-Atlases and triple pillars of the earth, and
dare to reach skyward to the spheres, the sun, and the visiting
moon.

The themes interwoven by Shakespeare are many and complex.
They are as varied as the moods; as changeable as the inundating
beauties of the verse. Although they include the turncoat's dilemma, the loyalty of a young soldier to his fallen general, the
rivalries of leadership, and pride of Romans who stalked the earth
as toga'd fascists, lust is the tragedy's major concern. This lust is
more than the hot, destroying desire which has driven Antony to
kiss away kingdoms and provinces for Cleopatra. It is also the lust
for power which finds Octavius, Lepidus, Pompey, and Antony
incessantly at war.

The play's politics are part of its passion. The echo raised by the heartbeats of the lovers is the drumbeat of moving armies. The two create a plural melody, providing an emotional counterpoint as continuous as it is essential. The measure of Antony's love is the empire he was willing to lose because of it. His having done much is a vital part of his being undone. Denied his preeminence as a leader, the tragedy of his being misled by a woman would have been no more than a single doom. A moiety of the world would not have been involved.

You will not, you could not, find *Antony and Cleopatra** in a volume called *Three Plays for Puritans*. But you will find *Caesar and Cleopatra* there. That is a difference, and a significant one, not only between the two dramas about Egypt's Queen but between Shaw and Shakespeare.

Never in the long history of dramatic literature have the agonies and ecstasies of sexual infatuation been so gloriously orchestrated as they were by Shakespeare in his study of the mature Cleopatra and her doting Antony. The verses leap like flames from the hearts of this man and woman who are the survivors of many gaudy nights. Their passion is a sickness which destroys them. They are weakened by its fever, helpless against its heat.

To those of us who are not Puritans the magnificence of Shakespeare's drama of desire is beyond challenge. But not to Shaw. Most emphatically, not to him. His point of view is not one which, fortunately, any of us lesser, meat-fed mortals are apt to share. As a Puritan, Shaw was scandalized by *Antony and Cleopatra*. As a vegetarian, he was apparently shocked by its animalism. As an intellectual and a prophet, contemptuous of physical passion and admitting only moral passion, he was left cold by the warmth of Shakespeare's text. He was mortified by the tragedy's flesh. To him it represented no more than "folly gone mad erotically." As a believer in minds sharpened by thinking, he despised Shakespeare's picture of lips quickened by kissing. Accordingly, when Shaw came to write his own play—a fine one—about the young

---

* *Antony and Cleopatra*, by William Shakespeare. Staged by Guthrie McClintic. Settings by Leo Kerz. Women's costumes by Valentina. Men's costumes by John Boyt. Music by Paul Nordoff. Presented by Katharine Cornell. With a cast including Miss Cornell, Godfrey Tearle, Kent Smith, Ralph Clanton, Lenore Ulric, Joseph Holland, Douglas Watson. At the Martin Beck. Opened November 29, 1947.

Cleopatra and a truly mighty Julius, he dismissed Shakespeare's tragedy as "intolerable."

He granted that Shakespeare had painted a faithful portrait of a soldier broken down by debauchery. He admitted that he had been no less successful in creating the typical wanton in whose arms such men perish. But Shaw, the rationalist, could not forgive Shakespeare, the romantic, for having strained "all his huge command of rhetoric and stage pathos to give a theatrical sublimity to the wretched end of the business."

Instead of rejoicing in the wonders of the final speeches, Shaw resented them. He accused Shakespeare of covering our eyes with the undertaker's handkerchief, duly onioned (as he put it) with pathetic phrases. The very same Shaw, who did not object to Shakespeare's having made a tragedy out of ambition in the case of *Macbeth,* jealousy in *Othello,* and indecision in *Hamlet,* was outraged (or at least pretended to be outraged) by Shakespeare's employment of sexual infatuation as a tragic theme. His insistence was that such infatuation could be effective only if approached in the comic spirit.

By advancing such a contention even in jest, Shaw was for the moment not only divorcing himself gaily from the rest of the human race, but was being misled by his Puritanism into one of his most indefensible perversities. A Puritan of Shaw's pretensions does not necessarily have to believe in the stork. Yet he is apt to look upon sex as at best a necessary evil. With reluctance he must grant that it is the only earthly means by which the number of possible Puritans can be increased. Its pleasures, however, win his frowns, not his sympathy. His attempt to laugh off the whole business as a bad joke is a measure of how mortals embarrass him by being mortal rather than Shavian.

It is the superb red-blooded mortality of *Antony and Cleopatra,* made immortal by Shakespeare's transcendent powers as a poet, that has persuaded nearly everyone except Shaw to treasure the play. Had not Shaw been indulging in a paradox, he would have blamed Dryden instead of Shakespeare for seeming to maintain that, since Antony and Cleopatra loved each other as they did, the world for them was "well lost."

Shakespeare plainly did not think it was. The "well lost" phrase was Dryden's subtitle for his Kelvinator rewriting of Shakespeare's classic. Shakespeare neither used it nor believed it. But he was writing a play, not preaching a sermon—and such a play! He was facing without blinking the florid, doleful facts of a tragic romance as they had fired his imagination when he came upon them in North's Plutarch. His trappings may have been Egyptian, his language Elizabethan, but the emotions he felt and phrased are eternal. No one has ever approached him in delineating, at once so fervently and remorselessly, a mature passion, mercurial in its moods, raging in its recriminations, shameless in its self-destruction.

The beauties of the verse must, from the production standpoint, be included among the difficulties of the play, along with the battle scenes and the script's torrential sweep. The score is one requiring not only intelligence but musicianship from the actors. If they must satisfy the mind and eye (in itself no easy assignment in this case), they must also delight the ear. The tragedy is a symphony no less than a story. To muffle its music would be to smother its beauty. The players have no other choice. Their throats must produce these melodies which readers hear in their inner ears without having to create them.

The text proclaims at every turn how amazing and prodigal was Shakespeare as a word-musician. To stand the more in awe of his genius both as poet and dramatist, one has only to track him to his source materials. To read or see *Antony and Cleopatra* and then to dip into Plutarch's *Antonius* in North's translation is not to have genius explained (because genius is a miracle defying explanation), but to eavesdrop on genius at the moment of creation.

The model, the marble, and the sculptor's tools are all there. So is that bridgeless gulf which always divides what the artist uses from the uses to which he puts it. Plutarch's narrative, a gossipy and sprightly one, in many instances is Shakespeare's scenario. Yet, and this is where the wonder lies, in spite of similarities it is no more than the point of departure, the crag from which the eagle soars. On page after page parallels can be found. These, however, turn out to be no more than suggestions or, more truly, provocations. Although a hundred illustrations could be cited, I must content myself with a symptomatic three.

Plutarch's description of the barge is an obvious example of

Shakespeare's capacity to strike imperishable fire from what at best were soggy logs. "[She took] her barge in the river of Cydnus," writes Plutarch, "the poop whereof was of gold, the sails of purple, and the oars of silver, which kept stroke in rowing after the sound of the music of flutes, howboys, citherns, viols, and such other instruments as they played upon in the barge. And now for the person of herself: she was laid under a pavilion of cloth of gold of tissue, apparelled and attired like the goddess Venus commonly drawn in picture."

As everyone knows, this is transformed and elevated into:

> The barge she sat in, like a burnish'd throne,
> Burn'd on the water. The poop was beaten gold;
> Purple the sails, and so perfumèd that
> The winds were lovesick with them; the oars were silver,
> Which to the tune of flutes kept stroke, and made
> The water which they beat to follow faster,
> As amorous of their strokes. For her own person,
> It beggar'd all description. She did lie
> In her pavilion, cloth-of-gold of tissue,
> O'erpicturing that Venus where we see
> The fancy outwork nature.

For another sample of this same alchemy at work, there is Antony's apostrophe to the fallen Eros, who, in spite of his oath, could not bring himself to stab Antony and had, when ordered to do so, stabbed himself. Plutarch supplies Shakespeare with no more than a cue. "O noble Eros," says his Antonius, "I thank thee for this, and it is valiantly done of thee, to show me what I should do to myself, which thou couldst not do for me." On the lips of Shakespeare's Antony this becomes:

> Thrice nobler than myself!
> Thou teachest me, O valiant Eros, what
> I should and thou couldst not. My queen and Eros
> Have by their brave instruction got upon me
> A nobleness in record. But I will be
> A bridegroom in my death, and run into't
> As to a lover's bed. Come then; and, Eros,
> Thy master dies thy scholar. To do thus
> I learn'd of thee.

Among all the lovely speeches Shakespeare wrote for his heroes and heroines at the moment of their dying, none is more exquisite than the one spoken by Cleopatra in her death scene. Plutarch's hint for it is meager. It is no more than what the seed is to the full-blown blossom. "When [Caesar's soldiers] had opened the doors," writes he, "they found Cleopatra stark dead, laid upon a bed of gold, attired and arrayed in her royal robes." The facts are there in prose. As extended by Shakespeare they erupt into song. Cries his Cleopatra:

> *Give me my robe, put on my crown. I have*
> *Immortal longings in me. . . . Husband, I come!*
> *Now to that name my courage prove my title!*
> *I am fire and air; my other elements*
> *I give to baser life.*

The rare, the radiant virtue of *Antony and Cleopatra* as Guthrie McClintic has set it behind the footlights is that it is so acted and so staged that the production, at almost every turn, triumphs over the glorious difficulties of the script. In the speaking, the language loses few of its splendors. The action careens across the ancient world, breathless in its pace. The scale of the emotions is preserved. So is their heat. So, too, is the wonderful complexity of the story itself.

One of the most tiresome of scholarly contentions is that the Elizabethan playhouse enjoyed a physical freedom unknown to our own. That the nature of its make-believe did differ from that to which the proscenium arch has accustomed us is undeniable. The apron of Elizabeth's day did permit actors to be three-dimensional, at least from the groundlings' point of view. But our own stage, due to the prowess of the switchboard and the invention of modern designers, can claim a matching liberty of its own. At any rate it achieves this liberty when its limitations are triumphed over as imaginatively as Mr. McClintic triumphs over them in his direction, and as Leo Kerz has done in his settings.

Antony and Cleopatra contains one of the most tantalizing stage directions in all theatrical history. When its contending forces are hotly embroiled on the plains near Actium, two opposing armies are supposed to pass each other in their march. "After their going in," the direction reads, "is heard the noise of a sea-fight." How Shakespeare solved this problem no one knows, and neither Granville-Barker nor Admiral Nimitz could guess. Mr. McClintic wisely dodges it. He gives us the illusion of battle. He permits the shadow cast by great events to speak for the events themselves. By the use of moving flags and combatants, picked up in the dark by spotlights on the various levels of Mr. Kerz's helpful setting, he suggests the ubiquity which permits an itinerant script to wander.

Visually, a more beautiful production of Shakespeare has not been made in our time than this *Antony and Cleopatra*. It succeeds in evoking Egypt and Rome without losing its way in a museum. It is never guilty of the mistake of trying to be history. It belongs proudly and poetically to a realm of the imagination. The uniforms supplied the men by John Boyt, with their reds for Antony's forces, their greens for Pompey, and their blues for Caesar, have genuine majesty and serve as needed political guides. Valentina's costumes for Cleopatra are brilliantly creative. One may regret, as I do, the black and white battle dress which raises memories of camouflaged ships in the last war. Miss Cornell's other dresses, however, are lovely in their lines and colors. They are statuesque though wearable, and alive with grace.

As for Miss Cornell herself, she has never given a more enchanting performance than she does as Antony's Egyptian dish. No actress playing Cleopatra can hope to realize in every scene the various Cleopatras Shakespeare wrote. To be wanton and witty, lustful and regal, mischievous and sublime, as the part demands that Cleopatra must be, is to ask for the impossible away from the printed page. Yet Miss Cornell succeeds in being all these things to an amazing degree. One has only to remember how Cleopatra suffered in Miss Bankhead's, Miss Cowl's, and Miss Marlowe's hands to realize the extent to which she is released in Miss Cornell's.

Miss Cornell more than achieves an infinite variety. Vocally and in her person, she captures nearly all of the changing moods of this chameleon who happened to be a monarch. She looks her loveliest. She walks with a panther's grace. And she dies magnificently, resplendent in her robe, a woman all fire and air who has risen above her baser life, a queen not only of the Nile but of herself.

There are those who are apt to think of Cleopatra merely as a trollop or a creature of the midway, because she was known to be "riggish," was said to possess a gypsy's lust, was variously referred to as a strumpet and a whore, and was fond of lascivious wassails. But, to my way of thinking, those who see her in such hootchy-kootchy terms miss her entirely. They have Doll Tearsheet rather than Cleopatra in mind. Theirs is a smoking-car error, Minsky-bred. They not only deny Cleopatra the subtlety which was part of her fascination but overlook the fact that she was a very capable queen. Tarts have no monopoly on passion. To be passionate one does not have to be common. Passion is common enough. Shakespeare's own sorceress dreaded the thought that she might live to see some squeaking Cleopatra boy her greatness "i' the posture of a whore."

Godfrey Tearle's Antony is nothing short of superb. He surmounts the final difficulty of the part by persuading us not only that Antony was great but that greatness still flickers in him. He is a conquered conqueror. Although Cleopatra may have overrun his body and his mind, a segment of his captain's heart remains his own. Even when we see him drinking Cleopatra's wine, we believe in him as a warrior once capable of eating the vile foods Caesar describes him as having formerly fed upon. Mr. Tearle's Antony is the Roman patrician, proud, lust-ridden, and brave; a man lost in the quicksand of his pleasures. His charm matches his arrogance; his weakness overcomes his strength. The pathos of his fall is realized to the full. From his first slightly reeling entrance to the cornered and self-loathing agony of his final scenes, he gives us every detail of a merciless study in disintegration.

Equally fine is Kent Smith's Enobarbus. He is, as he should be, the conscience of the play. He is wise, sardonic, disenchanted. Above the clamor of battle and through the incense of love, his voice can be heard, speaking calmly, sagely, wittily. His suicide after he has deserted Antony is movingly played, his heartbreak almost audible. He reads, moreover, the barge speech to perfection, avoiding all the temptations for sheer recitation in which it abounds.

Ralph Clanton's Caesar is manly, imperious, and vigorously

spoken. Among the many other characters, most of whom are competently played, Lenore Ulric's Charmian proves as inexcusable as Douglas Watson's Eros is affecting. The truth is that Miss Cornell and Mr. McClintic, by their courage, their generosity, and their skill, have accomplished the unexpected. They have broken the jinx which over the long years has dogged one of the marvels of dramatic literature. Shakespeare's tragic Alexandrian revels are now ours to revel in as theatregoers.

Why some of us prefer reading As You Like It *to seeing it, even when the Rosalind is Katharine Hepburn, who in her person supplies poetry that is easy to scan.*

[1950]

HEPBURN IN ARDEN

IN HIS reviewing days (and what days they were!) Mr. Shaw insisted that the wrestling scene was for him always the main attraction of a revival of *As You Like It*.* His reason? Simply his conviction that "it is so much easier to find a man who knows how to wrestle than to find one who knows how to act."

Dodging the Gorgeous George aspects of this generality and limiting myself to matters histrionic, I must agree that Charles the wrestler has an easier time of it in Shakespeare's comedy than anyone else in the cast. He is thrown when the first act is but two

---

* *As You Like It,* by William Shakespeare. Directed by Michael Benthall. Settings and costumes by James Bailey. Music by Robert Irving. Presented by the Theatre Guild under the supervision of Theresa Helburn and Lawrence Langner. With a cast including Katharine Hepburn, William Prince, Ernest Thesiger, Aubrey Mather, Cloris Leachman, Judy Parrish, Pat Englund, Whitford Kane, and Ernest Graves. At the Cort Theatre. Opened January 26, 1950.

scenes old and carried off speechless. The others, however, who are as talkative as they are amorous, must quit the wicked Frederick's court and hie themselves to the Forest of Arden. There, amidst plots, subplots, and disguises which could fool only their wearers, they must create the illusion of hunting in a lyric way, of loving no less lyrically, and in general of living a life in which Yale's ever-vocalizing Whiffenpoofs have somehow bobbed up as Robin Hood's Merry Men, carrying *The Oxford Book of English Verse* in their hands instead of cudgels.

The assignment is not an easy one. That there are lovely scenes in *As You Like It,* that there are speeches of pure song and moments of enchantment, no one can deny. But for some of us who were brought up surrendering to the play, the comedy has of late, in *Twelfth Night*'s fashion, lost its magic when encountered in the theatre. Where once its sylvan atmosphere, its picnic laughter, and springtime innocence used to beguile us, these nowadays elude us. We find that they resist embodiment behind the footlights.

They are still there in the library. They are there because as readers our minds are free. Arden is then a forest only of the imagination. Those who dwell in it are not real persons but the products of our fancy. We do not see them except with our mind's eye. Their words have no need to be spoken since they speak for themselves. When we come to what bores us in the text, we can skip, racing ahead to what delights us. We are not bothered, much less irritated, by the silliness—indeed the downright asininities—of the story told. Ours is not a questioning mood because on the printed page our idealizations are unchallenged by flesh-and-blood individuals.

That those of us who feel this way are in the minority is made clear by the success of the current revival of *As You Like It.* It proves that audiences in droves remain as anxious to see the comedy as players without number (for reasons which escape me) have always been anxious to appear in it. Certainly the production which Michael Benthall has directed for the Theatre Guild has been staged unstintingly. In many respects it is as competent a revival of *As You Like It* as our theatre has seen within the last quarter of a century. Its secondary characters are not entrusted, as so frequently happens, to actors who are palpably tertiary.

Whether impersonating courtiers or bumpkins, philosophers or clowns, they speak clearly. They even attempt to make probable the improbable people Shakespeare drew. This is a measure of their industry.

If, as a designer, James Bailey has broken with tradition by introducing us to a wintry Arden before allowing us to see the forest in the full ripeness of its summer foliage, the text supplies him with justifications. It also justifies the kind of settings he has supplied. Quite properly, these have the quality of backgrounds for a toy theatre. They capture what is childlike in the play by being childlike in their own way. Their theatricalism is unashamed. In their more artful and very pleasing fashion they can claim kinship with the kind of make-believe at which Skelt excelled and with which Benjamin Pollock's descendants to this day brighten the luckier of the world's nurseries.

There is one speech which I dread in every revival of *As You Like It*—for the actor's sake no less than for the audience's. This, of course, is "All the world's a stage." Apparently it is the only speech in the comedy that playgoers know. They take to it as they do to the "Toreador Song" in *Carmen*. Once Jaques is launched upon it the house is stilled by a reverent hush of recognition. This is broken only when those out front, whose lips are ostentatiously forming the words, get so carried away by their knowledge that they begin to recite aloud. By the time "sans teeth, sans eyes, sans taste, sans everything" is reached, spectators are sans control. Up go their hands and out comes a thunderous barrage of applause—for Shakespeare, for the actor who knows what they know, and for their own erudition. Ernest Thesiger does not seem to mind the ordeal. He approaches it with patience and grave resignation. But where he finds the courage to clear his throat, assume a properly sententious expression, and plunge into a speech so school-contaminated and worn treadless by repetition I, as a mere aisle-sitter, will never know.

To recall how enraptured we once were even by Rosalinds who in their Ganymede moments looked more like brood mares at pasture than foresters at play is difficult enough. It is still more difficult to fight off the faint nausea with which at present we read the automatic lyricism of some of the bygone critics. Take William

Winter, for example. In his more or less empty *Wallet of Time* on the subject both of *As You Like It* and Rosalind, words spill out of him like flour from a broken barrel.

"As we ramble through those woodland dells," says he of the comedy, "we hear the mingled voices of philosophy, folly, and humor, the flying echo of the hunter's horn, the soft music of the lover's lute, and the tinkle of the shepherd's bell. The sun shines always in the Forest of Arden; the brooks sing as they glide, and the soft, happy laughter of a sweet woman floats gaily on the scented wind."

Much more of this leads Mr. Winter by-and-by to Mary Anderson's Rosalind. Then he is off again. "Care had not laid its leaden hand upon her heart. Grief had not stained the whiteness of her spirit. The galling fetters of convention had not crippled her life. Accumulated burdens of error and folly had not deadened her enthusiasm and embittered her mind. . . . For her the birds of morning were singing in the summer woods, while her footsteps fell not on the faded leaves of loss and sorrow, but on the blown roses of youth and joy. Strong in noble and serene womanhood, untouched by either the evil or the dullness of contiguous lives, not secure through penury of feeling yet not imperiled through reckless drift of emotion, rich equally in mental gifts and physical equipments, she seemed the living fulfillment of the old poetic ideal of gypsy freedom and classic grace that Byron saw in his 'Egeria' and Wordsworth in his 'Phantom of Delight.' " Etc., etc., *ad infinitum.*

I cannot say that I wish Katharine Hepburn had inspired me to write about her in the same vein. Whether or not she hears birds of the morning singing in the summer woods as she strolls through Mr. Bailey's scenery, I am not in a position to state. I do know, however, that her Rosalind's physical equipment is exceptional. No one playing the part since I was old enough to sit up unstrapped in a baby buggy has been lovelier to look at or blessed with a figure which takes so readily to a jerkin and tights. If Miss Hepburn does not fill the bill, she does fill the eye. She does this in spite of being unflatteringly lighted; in spite, too, of wearing make-up and a coiffure that do scant justice to her beauty.

Mr. Shaw, in the dramatic opinion already referred to, pretended the popularity of Rosalind is due to three main causes: (1) she speaks blank verse only for a few minutes, (2) she wears a skirt only for a few minutes, and (3) she makes love to the man instead of waiting for the man to make love to her. Subject to dispute as such reasoning may be, there are two indisputably good reasons why Miss Hepburn's Rosalind deserves its popularity. Both of these at their lower extremities are encased in her slippers. For, regardless of how much prose she may utter, Miss Hepburn's legs are always poetry, and poetry that is easy to scan.

As a fan of Miss Hepburn since *The Warrior's Husband, Morning Glory,* and *Little Women,* I wish I felt she took to Arden as naturally as William Winter took to his thesaurus. I admire her gifts. I enjoy her looks. I like her chiseled cheekbones and find pleasure in her twangy voice. She has grace, breeding, and a sort of matter-of-fact elegance which is not without its own very special glamour. Even so, as Rosalind she does seem to me to be something of a Connecticut Yankee at Duke Frederick's court. Although she has her excellent moments and tries valiantly to give the play its song, I cannot help feeling that she mistakes the Forest of Arden for the Bryn Mawr campus.

When I happened to see the movie *Adam's Rib* just after seeing *As You Like It,* I was the more aware of Miss Hepburn's charms but the less convinced of her talents as a comedian. Though her intelligence is beyond question, the laughs she wins are won by the lines she speaks without the aid of her facial expression or her inner spirit. Her approach to comedy is essentially deadpan. It is as earnest as a Junior Leaguer's molestation of the poor.

If I may fall back once again on Mr. Winter, Miss Hepburn's performance needs more of the soft music of the lover's lute in it; more, too, of Arden's scented wind. In fact, it needs a great deal more of the song and sunshine which are at the comedy's heart. Heresy though it may be to say so, for me the abiding trouble with Rosalind lies with Shakespeare.

Macbeth *as exposed to a "reading" by Dame Edith Sitwell is compared to* The Lady's Not for Burning *as acted by John Gielgud and Pamela Brown.*

[1950]

POETS AND PLAYERS

Macbeth and *The Lady's Not for Burning** would, you might think, be safely beyond coupling. The one is all terror, horror, and decline; the other is all, or almost all, bounce, fooling, and gaiety. At first it might seem that the two of them have no more in common than the fact that Englishmen wrote them and wrote them in verse. In spite of the centuries and endowments separating them, Shakespeare's tragedy and Christopher Fry's comedy share, however, another feature equally obvious and equally important. Both were written for the theatre; both, in other words, were meant to be given the benefit of a production and to be spoken by actors.

What leads me to bracket two plays so dissimilar is that within a few days' time I chanced to sit before them as they were being performed in very different ways under very different circumstances. *Macbeth* was being subjected to a recital or a reading (call it what you will) by Dr. Edith Sitwell at the Museum of Modern Art, and *The Lady's Not for Burning* was being acted in a regular theatre by such superior professionals as John Gielgud and Pamela Brown. The question raised not only by these methods of presentation but by Monroe Wheeler's introduction of Dr. Edith was whether poets or actors can do greater justice to the words of a poetic dramatist.

Mr. Wheeler, the museum's director, told us that Dr. Edith had always dreamed of performing *Macbeth* "in one way or an-

---

* *The Lady's Not for Burning*, by Christopher Fry. Directed by John Gielgud. Setting by Oliver Messel. Presented by Atlantis Productions (The Theatre Guild, Tennent Productions Ltd., John C. Wilson). With John Gielgud, Pamela Brown, Richard Burton, Penelope Munday, Eliot Makeham, and Esme Percy. At the Royale Theatre. Opened November 8, 1950.

other." Her intention was to give a poet's conception of Shakespeare's dramatic verse. That she had had no training as an actress was, one gathered, a mark in her favor since Mr. Wheeler next proceeded to comment on the bad eloquence of actors. With a good deal of relish Mr. Wheeler told the story of how Dr. Johnson had once corrected Garrick's misreading of his lines and had further offended him by insisting "the players, Sir, have got a kind of rant, with which they run on, without any regard either to accent or emphasis." Considering what was to come, such a prelude seemed in the nature of a calculated risk.

The morning dress rehearsal of this *Macbeth*, which I attended, was an experience I shall not soon forget. Although ostensibly given for the working press, the audience was composed mainly of those worshipful followers Dr. Edith and Sir Osbert Sitwell have won for themselves in New York. No incense was burned, yet the scent of it seemed to hang heavy in the air, because those who know the Sitwells love them with a love which is utter adoration.

At a few minutes past eleven Dr. Edith's three assistants trooped down the aisle and took their places at a long table to the left of the stage. These assistants included Glenway Wescott, the novelist, who also enjoyed the assumed advantage of not being a member of Equity, and Bernard Savage and Gertrude Flynn, two professionals who had their courage with them.

Mr. Wescott, the recital's Macbeth, was innocent of the horned helmet, heavy armor, and kilt favored by tradition. He wore a dinner jacket. So did Mr. Savage, who served as a sort of accommodator, capable of changing without batting an eye from Banquo to the Doctor. Miss Flynn, a pretty young woman condemned to sit like Patience on a monument until she appeared as the Gentlewoman in the sleep-walking scene, wore a gray evening dress. These three helpers seated themselves behind microphones and glasses of water. And there they sat, looking for all the world as if they were engaged in a Prohibitionist production of *The Cocktail Party,* until Dr. Edith made her entrance.

The entrance she made was a considerable one. Preceded by Mr. Wheeler, she moved through the darkened auditorium like a priestess approaching a pagan altar. She was tall, turbaned, and impressive, a figure deserving reverence and expecting it. It was only when she appeared under the platform's lights, pale of face, queenly, and acknowledging with upturned, swallow-like flights of her beautiful hands the applause of her devotees, that it was possible to appreciate the splendor of her singularity. It was only then, too, that the rich brocade in which she was tented could be appreciated.

Soon thereafter she sat down to the right of the stage, a personage mysterious and mighty, until with a poet's proper defiance of period details she opened a very modern black handbag, reached for a very modern handkerchief, blew her nose, and covered her fine but small and piercing eyes with some very modern horn-rimmed spectacles. While Mr. Wheeler was providing his challenging overture to the promised music, Dr. Edith occupied herself arranging the voluminous folds of her heavy brocade gown. As she sat there waiting, it was hard to tell, in the irreverent words of a neighbor of mine, whether she was covering a teapot or a telephone.

When Mr. Wheeler left the stage Dr. Edith, whose voice he had described as "the most beautiful in the world," began her recital. This consisted partly of reading scenes from *Macbeth* with the aid of her assistants and partly of Dr. Edith's own analysis of Shakespeare's poetry and meaning. No one who has read *A Poet's Notebook* or the chapters therefrom which first appeared in *The Atlantic* can question Dr. Edith's devotion to Shakespeare, her poet's insight into his technical devices, or the occasional grandeur of her own language when seeking to explain Shakespeare. No temptation to laugh, no awareness of what was pretentious to the point of freakishness in the whole proceedings, however, could quite destroy the illusion in those out front that this extraordinary woman, who has created her own mythology, might very well be on speaking terms with the sibyls.

It seems equally certain that Shakespeare would never have recognized himself in the poet by that name she was dissecting. He might have been interested to learn that some of his words, as his tragedy progressed, were "rusty as though they had lain in the blood that had been spilt." Human vanity being what it is, he would no doubt have been touched by her dedication to him and pleased by the liturgical quality of her praise. But so overintellectualized was Dr. Edith's approach to what Shakespeare did instinctively that in all probability he would have been befuddled by her prating about "schemes of tuneless, dropping dissonances," "a thickened, darkened assonance," and his "placing of double-syllabled and treble-syllabled words and quick-moving, unaccented, one-syllabled words." My own suspicion is that such highfalutin talk would have caused Shakespeare to outlaugh Little Audrey.

Now to Dr. Edith's recital of such scenes and speeches as she had selected. A lecture is one thing, a play another. The two do not mix. No drama can be expected to survive if it is cut up into canapés, and if critical comments are always interrupting the line of its action and destroying its suspense. The supposed justification of this hodgepodge treatment of Shakespeare's tragedy was, as I have hinted, to let us hear his poet's words spoken by a poet. As it turned out, this proved to be a poetic fallacy, if ever there was one. That Dr. Edith has an arresting voice no one can deny. But that she has scant knowledge of how to use it dramatically seems equally incontestable. Reading with an ear for assonance rather than an eye for character, she succeeded chiefly in reducing Lady Macbeth to a lesson in prosody.

Most of us when we sing hymns are apt to adopt an astral quaver, devotional and thin, which has nothing in common with our voices as we release them out of church. Dr. Edith's reading of Shakespeare was done in what I assume is her "poetry voice" —a voice quite different from the one she employed on her own text. It was all boom and incantation, less designed for dialogue than for a Gregorian chant.

Oddly enough, it was lacking in any emphasis except a maintained and indiscriminate overemphasis. Even at the fearful moments of the planning and carrying out of Duncan's murder it refused to subside into a whisper. Throughout the morning Dr. Edith was so anxious to do justice to all the technical subtleties of Shakespeare's verse that she ended by doing dramatic justice to none. She followed vocally the course of the cargo ship in *Mister Roberts,* making trips from Tedium to Monotony and back again.

Mr. Wescott, who has a deep and agreeable voice even if his "r's" are resolutely loyal to Kewaskum, Wis., stood up from time to time to read Macbeth with manifest affection, and no doubt commendably enough by classroom standards. I know, however, I was grateful (and I do not think I was alone) whenever Mr. Savage spoke as only a trained actor can. I know, too, that I could have cheered when at overlong last Miss Flynn was given a chance to speak, and spoke admirably, the lines of the Gentlewoman. I would never have believed that so insignificant a part could become the stellar role in Macbeth. Yet this is precisely what happened during Dr. Edith's "recital," and must be taken as the measure of its failure.

Granting that *The Lady's Not for Burning* is as different from Macbeth as teatime is from midnight, the sheer relief of having actors in the cast to deliver Mr. Fry's verse (in the sense of acting rather than reading it) was supreme. Since the time of Plato's *Ion,* if not before, actors have occupied a dubious position in the hierarchy of artists. Many critics have been unwilling to admit them to the ranks of true creators inasmuch as, since they usually speak lines written by someone else, they are interpreters of an interpreter. This is often held to give them a secondary status.

However, Dr. Edith's recital, in which Shakespeare was murdered along with Duncan and Banquo, persuades me actors are grievously underestimated. Having listened with enchantment to the ease, sparkle, authority, and variety with which Mr. Gielgud and Miss Brown project Mr. Fry's sprightly lines, I know that I for one will turn cottoned ears to all lyre strummers deluded enough to believe that poets are the best readers of poetry and actors mere sounding boards for the sensibilities of others.

Christopher Fry is a Britisher of forty-three who, within the year, has won and deserved international attention. As everyone must know who has seen *The Lady's Not for Burning,* or read it, *A Phoenix Too Frequent,* or *Venus Observed,* his is one of the most exciting talents the postwar theatre has yielded. Under Attlee's prosaic government, in a theatre made brackish by its realism, and during times aggressively unlyrical, he has triumphed as a poetic dramatist.

Mr. Fry has invited straphangers, accustomed to traveling on the subway, to take a ride on Pegasus. More than that, he has made them like it. "What a wonderful thing is a metaphor," cries the hero in *The Lady's Not for Burning.* Plainly Mr. Fry agrees with him. He loves the language. He uses it with a glorious profligacy. He thinks, sees, smells, and tastes in terms of verbal images.

Whether he is writing about a British nobleman's decision to have his son choose a wife for him (*Venus Observed*), dramatizing Petronius's tale of the Ephesian widow who, when preparing to die in her husband's tomb, falls in love with a guard (*A Phoenix Too Frequent*), or telling, as in *The Lady,* the story of a soldier who upsets a village by pretending to want to be hanged in order to save a young girl suspected of witchcraft, metaphors and similes come galloping from his pen so fast that they almost trip over one another. That Mr. Fry overwrites is undeniable. But that he can write with shimmering magic is equally and delectably apparent.

Most people today have been fed for so long upon a thin porridge of prose in the theatre that they have almost lost a taste for listening. Mr. Fry's verse makes its uncompromising demands on the ears. To be fully relished, *The Lady* should perhaps be read before it is seen—and heard. Even then it can at moments prove exhausting. This exhaustion, however, is in itself pleasant inasmuch as it is brought about by the richness rather than the poverty of Mr. Fry's talent.

The Lady is a comedy in which the laughter, in typical Fry fashion, is interrupted from time to time by sudden stabs of disenchantment. Its spirit, nonetheless, is essentially ebullient. It is as full of bravura as if Dick Dudgeon in *The Devil's Disciple* and the braggart Irishman of *The Playboy of the Western World* had been merged into one character.

If Mr. Fry's shimmering lines were exposed to a "poetry voice," his play would die an abrupt and painful death. Mr. Gielgud and Miss Brown are, of course, at once too wise and expert to smother it in this manner. So are such of their associates in an admirable cast as Richard Burton and Eliot Makeham. All these players are masters of their profession. They know how to bring out the song in a poetic speech and give it style at the same time that they keep it conversational. They read precisely, with an unflagging instinct for emphasis and a superb sense of pace and variety. Poets they may not be, but skillful actors they are. For this very reason the poetry they speak gains rather than suffers as it leaves their lips.

Some overlooked differences between Chekhov's Russians and our Southerners which may explain why The Cherry Orchard *cannot be transplanted, and some sage advice from Stanislavski.*

[1950]

LOUISIANA CHEKHOV WITH HELEN HAYES

"ALL BLAME for the existence of *The Wisteria Trees*," * explained Joshua Logan in the *Times* on the Sunday before the New York opening, "I lay at the feet of Miss Helen Hayes. One day two years ago she said to me, 'I'd like to do *The Cherry Orchard.*' I had always thought that Chekhov's play is as much the story of Louisiana's plantation life as it was that of the great Russian estates.

"We agreed that I was to try to transpose the Russian play to my home state. Parallels were obvious. In both countries slavery had been abolished at about the same time. The decline of power in the landed gentry of both countries took place during the same years. The agonies of change are universal, we felt. That's how Helen got me into trouble, but how she got me out of trouble is another story."

It is easy enough to understand why *The Cherry Orchard* in American dress beckoned both Miss Hayes and Mr. Logan. Miss Hayes would not be the fine actress she is were Madame Ranevsky a part which held no fascination for her. Certainly, Chekhov's drama is one of the few unchallengeable masterpieces of the modern theatre. The tragedy of change and decay to which it gives so

---

* *The Wisteria Trees*, a play by Joshua Logan, based upon Chekhov's *The Cherry Orchard*. Directed by Mr. Logan. Setting by Jo Mielziner. Costumes by Lucinda Ballard. Musical arrangements by Lehman Engel. Presented by Leland Hayward and Mr. Logan. With a cast including Helen Hayes, Kent Smith, Walter Abel, Peggy Conklin, G. Albert Smith, Maurice Ellis, Alonzo Bosan, Bethel Leslie, Georgia Burke, Ossie Davis, and Douglas Watson. At the Martin Beck Theatre. Opened March 29, 1950.

magical a statement is a tragedy timeless in its truth and universal in its application, however Slavic in its setting. Moreover, most of us had long been persuaded (at least we had until we saw *The Wisteria Trees*) that the Russian landowners in *The Cherry Orchard* were close enough in mood and spirit to be interchangeable with the fading aristocracy of our own South at the century's turn.

The parallels seemed to run even deeper than those suggested by Mr. Logan. Southerners of a certain kind and class possessed their unmistakable Chekhovian characteristics. Many suffered from the same sadness. They were subject to the same sense of frustration and futility. They were the victims of the same poverty in the midst of proud reminders of gentility. They, too, were aware of being helpless and condemned. Theirs was an identical willingness to live nostalgically in the past without doing anything about the present. They were symbols and expressions of an old order passing and a new one taking over.

No one had stated these parallels more eloquently than the late John Anderson when, as long ago as 1930, he had contributed an article to *Theatre Magazine* called "Look Away, Dixieland." I know that I was one who agreed with Mr. Anderson when he said the analogy is so close "that such plays as *The Cherry Orchard* and *The Sea Gull* could be transplanted with few changes to the remote country houses of Virginia, Georgia, Alabama, or Mississippi and leave the essentials intact." The ex-serfs, he had indicated, would turn color. Old Firs would become "a woolly-headed Uncle Tom." Yet the trueness of the characters would remain undimmed. "Nations apart," he concluded, "these gentle people touch hands."

These resemblances, as I have hinted, had struck some of us as being beyond challenge until Miss Hayes and Mr. Logan, sharing this belief, sought to give *The Cherry Orchard* a Louisiana background. However, there was a factor—the vital one, as we have been taught by *The Wisteria Trees*—which had been lost sight of by those of us who believed the South to be completely Chekhovian. This was an elusive feature. Even now, it is hard to capture and make tangible.

Undeniable as are the similarities between Chekhov's Czarist Russia in its twilight years and the late post-bellum days of the

South, these prove to be more superficial than I, at least, had suspected. What some of us had overlooked is a question involving
inner intensity. It has to do with race, a subject which foolishly
(though out of a wise respect for dangerous generalities) is now
held to be all but unmentionable. That Chekhov's estate owners
and their contemporary Southerners, who were also doomed to
lose their plantations, were equals in inertia, no one can deny.
Nonetheless, as a comparison of *The Cherry Orchard* and *The
Wisteria Trees* demonstrates, the two peoples were inert in very
different ways.

Although Southerners were then, as they are now, capable of
strong emotions, they did not share the Russians' passion for introspection. If they fed their minds on memories and dreams, they
were, I suspect, Anglo-Saxon enough to be reticent about Life
with a capital "L." Climate may have made them languid. Cheap
labor, which had once been slave, may have made them indo-
lent. Living on the bitter diet of defeat may have left them maladjusted and contributed to their melancholy. But, unless present-
day Southerners are a totally different breed, which I doubt, and
unless my memories of the older generation mislead me, the
South's men and women who correspond to Madame Ranevsky
and her intimates did not plunge into metaphysical depths. Wisely,
gaily, or ruefully, they prattled on about the surface of subjects.
They were happier when discussing people, clothes, food, or
events than abstract ideas. Theirs was a fierce family or sectional
pride. It was the conditions of their life, past or present, which interested them more than the exploration of their psyches. Their
troubles were many, but the "soul" in the Russian sense was not
one of them.

Chekhov's people were different. Passive as their outward lethargy may have been, their inward activity was unceasing. A critic
such as Matthew Josephson may, in current fashion, dismiss "the
mysterious Slavic soul" as a form of *blague,* but to Chekhov's
characters this same "soul" was a matter of constant concern.
Their preoccupation with it supplies a special energy to the most
becalmed of Chekhov's speeches.

His plays substitute interior action for outward happenings. Although his people may be trivial, life in its largest sense speaks
through them. Gay as they can be, and gay as they must be to

preserve the comedic richness of Chekhov's sorrowful scripts, at heart (more accurately, in those "Slavic souls" of theirs) his characters are sad. In oversimplified terms, the intensity which distinguishes their sadness from that of their Southern counterparts can perhaps be suggested by comparing the sheer sorrow of "Massa's in de Cold, Cold Ground" (which is accepted as being Southern) with the fateful, almost electric melancholy of "The Volga Boat Song."

The vibrancy which underlies the seeming languor of Chekhov's Russians is missing in *The Wisteria Trees*. Mr. Logan cannot be blamed for this. His Southerners, as I have come to realize, would be Russians if they possessed it. Yet the lack of it is sorely felt. All the fine talents involved in the production cannot compensate for its absence.

Before the curtain has gone up the evening presents another difficulty. The program describes *The Wisteria Trees* as "a new American play written and directed by Joshua Logan." Then, a few lines down in parentheses it adds, "The play is based on Anton Chekhov's *The Cherry Orchard.*" The problem immediately arises how a script can be at once new and old, original and derived, foreign and domestic, transplanted and native, borrowed and created.

Obviously, the only persons equipped to accept *The Wisteria Trees* as a new play are those who have never seen or read *The Cherry Orchard*. But, as Mr. Logan has himself confessed, such playgoers are harder to come by than one might think. For those who have read or seen it and who cherish the faintest recollections of *The Cherry Orchard*, *The Wisteria Trees* is bound to suffer from a cruel disadvantage. Palpably it is *The Cherry Orchard,* yet just as palpably it is not. It is a work haunted by a masterpiece. It not only has to live up to *The Cherry Orchard* but to live it down. In other words, it starts off its supposedly independent life as handicapped as the son of a great father.

In its major essentials the story Mr. Logan tells is the same story Chekhov told. Often his single speeches are Chekhov's speeches, even as his scenes are suggested by Chekhov's scenes and his characters are cut from the general pattern of Chekhov's originals or are adaptations of them. But the alterations forced upon Mr. Logan by a new locale and people belonging to a different race subtract from the old play's greatness without creating a satisfactory new play. Pruned of their "Slavic souls," denied their sudden eruptive outbursts of autobiography, unable of necessity to speak tangentially, and forced to address one another with American directness, Chekhov's characters lose their depth. The story itself shrinks in significance. Where once it managed to speak for a whole condemned generation, indeed to symbolize the anguish of all change, it now seems no more than the chronicle of a very silly woman who deserves to lose her plantation.

Our theatre does not boast individuals more respected and endowed than those who have collaborated on the production of *The Wisteria Trees*. Jo Mielziner's single setting is a room rich in beauty and decay. Its elegance, though tarnished, is unmistakable. As a children's parlor, it is filled with poignant reminders of the days that were. Its great French windows, with their broken shutters, open on a bower of wisterias with which Mr. Logan, in a moment of inspiration, has supplied Mrs. Ransdell as a substitute for Madame Ranevsky's cherry orchard. We see these wisterias, first in full and glorious bloom, then bare and gnarled when their clutching branches seem to reach out to threaten the Ransdell home. In line, form, color, and detail Mr. Mielziner's setting succeeds, as the rest of the production fails, in stating in Southern terms the Chekhovian essence of the play itself.

Miss Hayes gives one of the best performances of her career as Mrs. Ransdell. It is a glowing performance, radiant and moving, which comes from both the heart and the head. The spell it casts is genuine. Yet, in spite of Miss Hayes' excellence, Mrs. Ransdell in her de-Russianized form is no match for Madame Ranevsky. As her impractical brother, Walter Abel not only plays with charming sensitivity and skill but manages to make his listening as telling as his talking. Kent Smith, a good actor who continues to get better and better, is admirable as the poor-white-grown-rich who purchases the plantation. Although there are many other performances of merit, I, for one, wish that Mr. Logan had not pushed some of his capable Negro actors—including Alonzo Bosan, the Firs of the occasion—so perilously close to caricature.

Mr. Logan, as goes without saying, is one of the most adept and brilliant people in our theatre. His skill and ingenuity do not desert him in his writing and directing of *The Wisteria Trees.* Plainly, his is a labor of love which yields its fine single scenes here and there. Even so, it seems to me a labor that is largely lost if for no other reason than that Chekhov's Russians and our Southerners prove to have less in common than most of us had thought.

Throughout the evening I found myself thinking of the advice Stanislavski had given Mr. Logan in 1931. Mr. Logan, as he tells in his introduction to Stanislavski's *Building a Character,* had left Princeton in the middle of his senior year to make a pilgrimage with the late Charles Leatherbee to study at the Moscow Art Theatre. The two young men were starry-eyed in their admiration for Stanislavski. Stanislavski became interested in them the minute they told him about the University Players and their plans to establish with college students a permanent repertory theatre in the United States. His face fell, however, when Mr. Leatherbee confessed their hope was to duplicate the Moscow Art Theatre in America.

"You must not duplicate the Moscow Art Theatre," said Stanislavski. "You must create something of your own. If you try to duplicate, that means that you merely follow tradition. You are not going forward."

"But your System," protested Mr. Logan, "the Stanislavski System! We have read so much about it, talked so much about it. We have traveled so many miles to study it first hand."

Stanislavski's answer was, "Our methods suit us because we are Russian, because we are this particular group of Russians here. We have learned by experiment, by change, by taking any concept of reality that has become worn and substituting something fresh, something always nearer and nearer the truth. You must do the same. But in your own way, not ours. . . . You are here to study, to observe, not to copy. Artists must learn to think and feel for themselves and find new forms. They must never be content with what someone else has done. You are American, you have a different economic system. You work at different times of day. You eat different food and your ears are pleased by different music. You have different rhythms in your speech and in your dancing. And if you want to create a great theatre, all these things must be taken into consideration. They must be used to create your own method, and it can be as true and as great as any method yet discovered."

Mr. Logan's productions of *South Pacific* and *Mister Roberts* prove how right Stanislavski was.

What two of our foremost players owe to their marriage license and what our theatre owes to them.

[1946]

THE LUNTS' REUNION
WITH NEW YORK

THERE WAS the dear old lady, a wearer of black dresses covered with beads, one of those jet-propelled older women, who saw the Lunts for the first time in a comedy a good many seasons back. She was as regular a pew occupant as our churches know. Like everyone else, she had relished the dash, the unblushing intimacy, the unabashed honesty with which they had just romped through a love scene on a sofa. The old lady hated to have this scene come to an end. She sighed regretfully when it was over. She sighed, and turned to her companion, a dowager no less militantly respectable. Then she whispered, with more resonance than she had meant to muster, "It's nice, my dear, to know they are really married, isn't it?"

Her point is not hard to see. It *is* nice to know that Alfred Lunt and Lynn Fontanne are married. It is as comforting to know it when you watch them in *O Mistress Mine** as it was when the antimacassar matron saw them in *Caprice* in 1929. Their mar-

---

* *O Mistress Mine,* by Terence Rattigan. Presented by the Theatre Guild and John C. Wilson. Settings by Robert Davidson. Directed by Mr. Lunt. With a cast including Alfred Lunt, Lynn Fontanne, Dick Van Patten, and Margery Maude. At the Empire Theatre. Opened January 23, 1946.

riage sets the Lunts free. They are liberated by it, and have been all these years. The justification of freedom is not freedom itself but the uses to which it is put.

Millamant dreaded dwindling into matrimony. But then she had never seen the Lunts. If marriage—the mere act of being married —were a guarantee of acquiring their skill as players, then marriage by the self-same minister who united the Lunts should be obligatory for all actors, as surely as Lincoln wished Grant's whisky could be distributed to his generals.

Marriage, however, is not enough. The certificate which goes with it certifies only that a man and woman are legally wed. It does not promise they will be brilliantly endowed. It does not even promise they will be happy.

The Lunts are both. Although I have no way of proving this, I suspect they must have been married near the altar of Dionysus. The theatre with them is their married life no less than their public life. Undoubtedly, had they trooped up the gangplank of the Ark, they would have turned it in no time into a Showboat. The contemporary stage does not know a couple that can hold a spotlight to them when it comes to their skill in playing together. Of dialogue they make the best of duets; of what is left unphrased, but said in terms of glances, of shared laughs, of pattings, gropings, silences, or crossings, they create a closer harmony than any singers know.

On the air we hear a great deal about Bulova watch time. As citizens, we master each spring the intricacies of Daylight Saving Time. As travelers, we learn, however painfully, the differences between Eastern, Central, Mountain, and Pacific Time. The war taught us all kinds of new tricks we could play on the sun with our watches. But the Lunts have a sense of timing which is their own.

A cat could not have more fun with catnip than they do with the lines they speak. They do not hammer them; they play with them. They pounce on them, toss them in the air, pull them earthward, romp with them, and roll on them. They know how to hold a sentence back, and then send it scurrying suddenly to its conclusion. They never miss the meaningful or explosive word, and never overstress it.

They are shrewd judges of what to underscore and what to throw away. They realize that the very act of seeming to throw a phrase or a word away is in itself a form of emphasis. They are no less adroit in altering the tempo of their separate scenes than they are in changing the pace of their single sentences. What is more, their watches are always synchronized.

The Lunts are never uncertain about what they are doing. Their acting is always the result of a shared plan. It is a long game of affectionate give-and-take. It is a model of domesticity only in the generous concern each shows for showing the other off to advantage.

Except for the unflagging courtesy they show their craft by showing each other, the playing of the Lunts is incarnadined with theatricality. It is bold, informed, and exquisitely professional. They give to it their every energy, holding nothing back except what would be excessive. They squeeze whatever they are doing to the final half-drop it may contain of merriment or meaning. Since their skill is the equal of their confidence, we sit before them alert—and yet strangely relaxed. We are happily aware we do not have to worry for them; they have done their worrying for us.

Heaven knows, the Lunts have given notable performances in a large number of ambitious plays. No actors whose names have been associated, singly or jointly, with such productions as *Goat Song, Strange Interlude, Volpone, Juarez and Maximilian, Outward Bound, Marco Millions, The Brothers Karamazov, Arms and the Man, The Doctor's Dilemma, Pygmalion, The Sea Gull,* or *There Shall Be No Night* can be fairly accused of not having made their important contributions to the serious drama.

But there is a kind of comedy at which the Lunts excel, and in which their huge public rejoices to see them. *The Guardsman* set the giddy pattern. *Caprice, The Second Man, Reunion in Vienna,* and *Design for Living* were all cut from the same cloth. *O Mistress Mine* hails from the identical counter, even if from a different bolt. Satin or sateen as these comedies may have been, the Lunts have always granted them a sheen of their own.

Who does not remember the Lunts in the theatre box in *The Guardsman*? Who can forget them patching up their difficulties in *The Second Man*? Squabbling as mistress and lover in *Caprice*? Waltzing toward the bed in *Reunion in Vienna*? Or the moment when Mr. Coward and Mr. Lunt, as Miss Fontanne's past lovers, suddenly bobbed up at her husband's New York penthouse in the hurly-burly of *Design for Living*?

Because of the Lunts all these comedies, right down to Terence Rattigan's *O Mistress Mine*, have been parts of a gleeful serial. They have been different coaches on the same red and gold circus train. The Lunts have swept through them, sweeping everything before them. In each of these comedies the Lunts have played with fire, protected always by the asbestos of their perfect taste. In each of them they have set up joy as the only legal code of the realm they have created and over which they reign as undisputed sovereigns.

In each they have led us into a world glitteringly different from the one we live in. It is a higher-voltage universe than drab mortals know, a land where the sun itself seems to rise not above the horizon but above the footlights. Its air is in truth as exhilarating as the travel ads would persuade us the breezes are at seaside and mountain resorts. In it everything shines, has luster and vivacity. It would seem to belong to the empire of artificial comedy if all that happens in it did not appear to be so natural.

If *O Mistress Mine* is a slight comedy, why not? All things do not have to have weight. A balloon needs only helium to keep it aloft. The fact that helium is not heavy does not mean it is without a value of its own.

Mr. Rattigan is concerned with the troubles faced by a wealthy English cabinet minister and his mistress when her young son, a violent believer in Professor Laski's theories, returns one day from Canada. This boy succeeds in separating his mother from her comforts, and persuades her to live for a while according to his own economic doctrines.

Granting that Mr. Rattigan has cut his light cloth with the Lunts in mind, it seems only right that his skill as a tailor should win its own applause. Some of my colleagues, I note, have dismissed the script of *O Mistress Mine* as if it were nonexistent. They have frowned on it because it is jubilantly unimportant. Mr. Nathan has even spanked the Lunts for appearing in so trivial a comedy. As I see it, however, its unimportance is the point of Mr. Rattigan's play, and one of the sources of its pleasures. I should think it would have to be judged in terms of the opportunities with which it provides the Lunts, and the laughs it supplies the audience, rather than in terms of what it does not pretend to say.

For the past two years the Lunts have done a fine, arduous, and brave job overseas in bombed London, and on the Continent with our troops. If *O Mistress Mine* finds them taking a holiday, it must be said of it that it invites playgoers to go on one, too.

One thing is certain. The Lunts never permit their skill to have a vacation. In a charming curtain speech on the opening night, Mr. Lunt said that Miss Fontanne and he would feel justified if they could contribute any laughter to "an angry and suspicious world." As the responses of their audiences reach them across the footlights at the Empire, they must feel more than justified. So must Mr. Rattigan. They must be as happy as for a few hours at each performance they make others.

The incredible Mae West re-seen in these post-Kinsey days, and some discussion of the undeniable figure she presents as an actress.

[1949]

MAE POURQUOI

ON MY way to *Diamond Lil** I could not help wondering what Time, Kinsey, and John O'Hara might have done to Mae West. Sixteen years ago when last I saw her (this was when the New Deal was new and other much-needed relief agencies were mushrooming), she had already become a national institution.

---

* *Diamond Lil*, by Mae West. Directed by Charles K. Freeman. Settings by William De Forest and Ben Edwards. Costumes by Paul Du Pont. Presented by Albert H. Rosen and Herbert J. Freezer. With a cast including Mae West, Richard Coogan, Charles G. Martin, Walter Petrie, Miriam Goldina, Val Gould, James Courtney, and Billy Van. At the Plymouth Theatre.

Since then, however, the ever-changing world has changed in ways uncountable and with unprecedented swiftness. The Kinsey Report and the atom bomb have both been dropped. We are supposed to be tougher now—war-toughened and peace-toughened, too. We are franker in our discussion of the pleasant blushful subjects. Our approach to the facts of life is nothing if not factual. We call a spayed a spayed, or worse. Grandmothers are not unconversant with, or always ungiven to, the language of GIs. The small talk of the smoking room, more than having become the conversation of the entire car, has invaded the drawing room. Our eyes have grown accustomed to four-letter words which at least simplify the task of typesetting. Even sex, that three-letter word in which Miss West has always had a rather open interest, is being talked, written, and thought about in terms so different from those of sixteen years ago that naturally I approached *Diamond Lil* in an apprehensive mood.

Would—could—La West possibly be and seem the same, thought I. Might not her boldness have become tame, her lustiness anaemic? How could she hope, even granting her superior equipment, to hold her own with the fanciful enlargements of those wind-swept females who are at present plastered across the jackets of historical novels and the covers of cheap reprints? Wouldn't the sand have run out of her hourglass figure? In short, like certain other pounds, weren't hers bound to have undergone a devaluation?

But my worries, though chivalrous, were absurd. They were the sillier because I had forgotten that, in spite of her dedication to what Percy Hammond used to refer to as the "obstinate urge," Miss West has never asked to be taken seriously. Sex itself is for her a cartoon which she delights in animating. If she is a high priestess of desire, she is also its most unabashed and hilarious parodist. When she gets through with the Tenderloin, it is ham— sheer, unadulterated Smithfield.

As an archetype of the predatory female, Miss West is about as sinister as a retrieved copy of *The Police Gazette*. She remains dateless (I mean this, of course, only in the historical sense) because her choice has always been to be an anachronism. For all her contours, and in spite of the dromedary dip with which she walks, the incessant pelvic rotations that punctuate her sentences, and the steaming sultriness of her voice, her chief invitation is now, as it was in the beginning, to laughter. Had she been only a siren, Puritan America could never have been "had" by her. But she is also a *farceur* and a comedienne. And it is these endowments which originally saved her and which continue to endear her.

Sixteen years ago when she was conquering the country as a survival of the most tightly fitted, I tried to point out that she was that rarest of all specimens among contemporary artists. She was a pre-Freudian, than which a Miocene mammal could not be harder to find. Her scarcity value has grown with the years, even as she has. Vocally she is still a hootchy-kootchy artist. Visually she remains as modernistic as a barroom nude. She can still turn the simplest statement into a scorching insinuation. She can still make the most innocent "Hello, boys" sound like a traveling sales-man's idea of *The Decameron*. The course she pursues so grandly is still down the midway. Her lack of subtlety remains the most subtle thing about her.

Only the Statue of Liberty has been carrying a torch for a longer time than Mae West. She, moreover, seems no more fatigued by maintaining her chosen attitude than does the iron lady down the bay with her eternally uplifted hand. Always, and proudly, an armful, Miss West is a bigger girl today than she used to be. But what devotee of the madame could object to there being more of her? She would not have had to come from Tennessee or India to be a grandmother by now. Yet few people could bear a more re-mote resemblance to Whistler's Mother or Grant Wood's D.A.R. than she does.

No one has ever looked quite like Mae West, or ever will. She fills the eye no less surely than she fills the stage. She is several dreams walking; several nightmares, too. She commands more curves than Christy Mathewson thought of doing. What a poster is to Proust she is to Kinsey, and also to O'Hara, in her own flam-boyant person. The dictionary assures us that in mathematics a curve is the locus of a moving point continuously deviating from a straight line. A more accurate description of La West could not be written.

She never deviates into Christendom any more than she wan-ders within the outskirts of reality. To her, sex is more than an obsession. It is a joke with no primal eldest curse upon it but with the most ancient of blessings. Her voice, like her person and her incredible costumes, disturbs the risibilities far more than it inflames the senses. A nest of attacked vipers could not emit hisses more insistent than are all her conscienceless sentences. She is an actress who seldom reacts but who is always being reacted to; a soloist in a duet world. Accordingly, she seems lonely even in her thickly populated plays.

Although she is credited with having written *Diamond Lil,* she can scarcely have bothered to use a pen or pencil. After all these years, it persists in being a dreary charade which still sounds as if it were being improvised. That is, of course, except at those plentiful moments when Lil herself is hard at work, as the professional she magnificently is, rasping and undulating, undulating and rasping. Then the evening becomes the ultimate in calculation, the final word in skilled deliberation.

The truth is that, like *The Constant Sinner* and *Sex* before it, *Diamond Lil* is no play at all. It creates a category of its own which can only be defined as a Mae Western. If it is a drama, then so is it a trip to Chinatown on a sightseeing bus. Without Mae West it would be nothing. With her it is Mae West. And that is decidedly something. Miss West is a lesson in geography as well as in acting. Compared to her terrain, that of Hollywood's young sirens (true or false) is what the Appalachians are to the Rockies.

The world may have changed to a terrifying extent, but when it comes to toughness it has not yet caught up with La West. More than being a person or an institution, she has entered the language and taken her place in the underworld of the present's mythology. She is the Bobby Clark of the boudoir. She does not bother with the flowers when teaching about the bees. She continues to be what every playgoer, young and old and in search of a laugh, ought to know.

The amazing versatility and charm of a woman whose talents were the equal of her energies, and who gave an irreplaceable incandescence to the lights of Broadway.

[1952]

BLITHE SPIRIT—
GERTRUDE LAWRENCE

WITH REASON the lights on New York's and London's theatres were dimmed in memory of Gertrude Lawrence the night after her funeral. They came on again within a minute, seeming to burn as brightly as they had before she died. But this was only an illusion. It fooled no one who had ever seen her.

Miss Lawrence was one of the irreplaceable performers of our times. One of the irreplaceable people, too. Even when she was a scraggly, long-legged girl of thirteen—"one of Pharaoh's lean kine," as her grandmother described her with a loving relative's frankness—there was something about her that was different. A friend of her father had the perception to realize this. "You've got something, Gertie," this older woman said, thereby proving herself to be one of the more reliable of latter-day prophets.

Most assuredly, Miss Lawrence did have something. It was not one thing; it was many things; and in time all of them united to form a sort of grand alliance of endowments which made her resplendently unlike anyone else.

There were dancers who could dance better than she. There were singers whose voices were truer. There were women who were greater beauties. There were actresses who proved their deeper abilities by testing their strength in more important plays. Yet none of them combined in their persons all the gifts and graces which set Miss Lawrence apart.

When she danced—when, for example, she sent her huge hoopskirt dipping and billowing to the rhythm of the polka in *The King and I*—no one bothered to remember other dancers. They recognized only Miss Lawrence. She was the epitome of grace, and did not cease her dancing when the music stopped. Even when she walked across a stage or romped on a sofa, she moved with a dancer's lightness.

Miss Lawrence did not have to sing like an angel to sound like one. No one could capture more completely than she the lilt and nuances of such a ballad as "Jenny" in *Lady in the Dark*. Or be funnier and rowdier in such a parody of a music-hall turn as the sailor bit in "Red Peppers." Or more enslave an audience than she did when she took possession of "Limehouse Blues." No one could be more alluring than when in *Private Lives* she surrendered to the sentiment of "Some Day I'll Find You." Or more captivatingly gay than when in *The King and I* she swung round the stage to "Shall We Dance?" She may sometimes have failed a song, but she never failed to put over a number. Even toward the end when she was very tired and some of the high notes eluded her, her speaking voice was in itself a song, rippling and lovely and glowing with warmth.

When it comes to beauty, Miss Lawrence had long ago, in Noel Coward's phrase, appropriated it to herself. Though by her own admission she was plain as a child, she became one of the most glamorous of women. She was lithe and slim, and had great style. Her face, with its ever-shining eyes, its up-turned nose, and mobile mouth was never in repose. Its animation was so sparkling and incessant that it created the impression of beauty. Certainly, because of its vivacity it possessed an interest and an invitation unknown in women with more perfect features whose becalmed faces are merely beautiful and therefore dull.

Whether Miss Lawrence dreamed about the theatre, no one has disclosed. But during all her waking hours she was an actress, carrying the theatre with her wherever she happened to be. By temperament and training, and because of the supercharge of personality and energy which was hers, her every appearance on stage and off was an entrance. Life for her was an unending show, and she always put on a good one, giving it everything she had.

Miss Lawrence did not bother with the Greeks, Shakespeare, and Ibsen. *Pygmalion* was the only standard work in which she acted, and then with marked success. Hers was not the theatre of the classics. It was of a different kind. It was neither literary nor formidable. It was a place of delight, a palace of unashamed make-believe and beguilement. It offered sanctuary to those whose search was for entertainment and enchantment. Miss Lawrence knew and treasured the importance of pleasure. By giving it she rightly won both importance for herself and an enormous and devoted following.

She was a far brighter and more beckoning star than those shown at the Hayden Planetarium. Her skill was as extraordinary as her versatility. She could do almost anything—and did. She could play seriously, as in *Susan and God*, and by her magic persuade audiences to take seriously even the psychoanalysis offered them in *Lady in the Dark*. But until she achieved the full serenity and control of her Anna, comedy was her forte, the kind of comedy she played to perfection in *Private Lives* and in the laughing sketches in *Tonight at 8:30*.

Miss Lawrence was a musical-comedy performer who, though she grew into an admirable actress, had gifts which the legitimate theatre could not release. For the full freeing of her powers she needed the singing, dancing, color, and direct communication with an audience made possible by the poster-like values of a musical.

She was charming and irresistible when in 1924 she first conquered New York in *Charlot's Revue*. In the following years she remained equally charming and no less hard to resist. Although sometimes her enthusiasm was greater than her discrimination and her exuberance misled her into overplaying, Miss Lawrence was a performer who continued to grow. It was as an actress who had mastered the legitimate stage and her own ebullience that she added to the delights of such a musical as *The King and I* by giving the most glowing and disciplined performance of her career.

Restraint cannot have come easily to her. Her spirit was too buoyant to be harnessed. Her vitality was tremendous. Compared to Miss Lawrence, a windmill in a hurricane seemed lethargic. She was as extravagant with her energies as she was overgenerous with her money. She never spared herself. No entertainer worked harder during the war, first for the British, and then for our own troops. In the midst of long runs and strenuous tours she was forever rushing to the aid of charities and taking on outside tasks. To play Anna, you might think, would have been a full-time job. Not for Miss Lawrence. She was giving a course in acting at

Columbia and had become so excited about it that only illness could keep her away.

Playgoers responded to this warmth of hers. It leaped across the footlights. Even people who had never seen her realized that her heart was as big as her talent. This was one of the reasons she was loved with unique affection, and men and women everywhere felt a sense of personal loss when they heard of her sudden death. They realized that something gay, ornamental, and delectable had gone out of their lives. Something good, too.

Miss Lawrence seemed like the most fortunate of worldlings. The outer gloss of the International Set appeared to be hers. She could sound English, look French, and be the perfect expression of American rhythms and the American tempo. But alluring as she was as the symbol of Mayfair and Park Avenue, she never lost touch with or denied the simplicities of her upbringing in Clapham. This was one of the most winning things about her, and a source of her wide appeal.

She was so vital a part of the gaiety of our past and present and such a guarantee that gaiety would endure that it is hard to lose her. Without Miss Lawrence the theatre is undoubtedly diminished. But this we must say to comfort ourselves. She died at that luckiest of times—when the tide was high. She was too young in spirit and looks ever to be asked to face the humiliations of age.

The incomparable Danny Kaye, past master of patter and superior entertainer, brings vaudeville back to life at the Palace when he makes an hour and a half seem like a minute.

[1953]

OKAYE

TO MAKE a liar out of the clock, to make its unstoppable hands seem paralyzed is at once one of the duties and triumphs of showmanship. During the second portion of the program at the Palace Danny Kaye is on stage for a little more than an hour and a half. That is a long time—for any performer, for any spectator. Theatrically it is a period protracted enough for the building of Rome or, for that matter, its burning.

Try to hold anyone's attention for such a span or dare anyone else to hold yours, and you soon discover how long a time it is. But in Danny Kaye's case everything is blessedly different. Mr. Kaye is as much a master of time as he is of timing. He knows that the only timeless interludes are those during which everyone is having a good time. Accordingly, a hilarious time is what he devotes his incredible energies and skill to giving all those lucky enough to crowd into the Palace to see and hear him. From the moment he hurries into view until he takes a reluctant farewell of an audience even more reluctant to have him stop, all awareness of the ticking seconds comes to an end.

Mr. Kaye's admirers the world over are too numerous to be counted and have a special feeling for him. Consider, for example, what happened in Glasgow when he was making a royal progress through Scotland. The ovation he received at the conclusion of his last performance there would have been—for anyone else—a demonstrative statement of affection. Pleased as he was by it, however, it did not satisfy the hundreds of supposedly reserved Scots who had cheered and applauded him. They followed him back to his hotel. There they massed in the square outside and called for him until he appeared. Then they began singing as one, "Will Ye No Come Back Again?"

Recently at a matinee at the Palace two elderly ladies showed their friendliness for Mr. Kaye in a manner less spectacular though equally untraditional. Playhouses continue to be sanctuaries of individual liberty. Theatregoers are free to leave them at any time without explanation. Halfway through his performance Mr. Kaye noticed that these women were putting on their hats and coats. He was about to kid them for going when, to his amazement, he saw they were leaving their seats in the eighth row and coming down the center aisle toward him. Their admiration had triumphed over whatever embarrassment they may have felt. "Forgive us," one of them said, halting the program and speaking right up in the most neighborly way. "Please forgive us, Mr. Kaye. We hate to go but we are commuters and have just got to catch a train. We hope you will understand. We are coming again."

The reasons for the regard Mr. Kaye creates in those out front are hard to avoid. To the perceptive they have demanded mention ever since his appearance, first, in *The Straw Hat Revue* and, later, in *Lady in the Dark*. When I touch upon Mr. Kaye's unique gifts, I do not happen to have his contribution to *Hans Christian Andersen* in mind. That is a film I have not seen nor does it tempt me. What I have heard and read about it persuades me I am either too young or too old for it. Apparently it is guilty of sentimentalizing and subduing the ebullient and resolutely unmawkish talents of Mr. Kaye.

Along with millions of others, I like Mr. Kaye untamed. In his slightly deranged, hence native, state I can never get enough of him. I like him when his extraordinary gift for nonsense is running wild. I like him when he is exercising his giant-sized satiric gifts in a way which may seem to be merciless but which nonetheless is strangely merciful. I like him when, unencumbered by a plot and uninterrupted by fellow actors, he is free to do whatever he chooses to do. In short, if I may employ a barfly term, I like my Danny Kaye neat. This is why I have never relished him more than I did at the Palace.

It is right to the point of inevitability that Mr. Kaye should make his entrance while the orchestra on stage is blaring forth the introductory measures of "There's No Business Like Show

Business." Most decidedly, there is none when Mr. Kaye is around. If he can be the most energetic of entertainers, he can also be the most relaxed. When he wrinkles up his rubber face to do a parody, when he rattles off a patter song with the rapidity of a machine gun, or when he hurtles himself into a dance, he is not a dynamo—he is a one-man powerhouse. His drive is superhuman. It is of that self-emptying kind which only top-flight performers have and share so unsparingly that their audiences soon feel as if they possess it too.

Midway in his exuberant activities Mr. Kaye gives both his enthusiasts and himself a rest. He comes to the footlights, sits down, and talks as informally to those out front as if he were caught at home on a Sunday afternoon by an old friend who just happened to drop in. Any subject that pops into his mind finds its way to his tongue. His ad-libbing may or may not be spontaneous. But one thing is certain. It is not unfortified by design because he is far too fine a professional ever to trust entirely to chance.

After having bummed a cigarette from some surprised smoker in the front rows, Mr. Kaye returns to the unserious but inspired task of being Danny Kaye, the performer. He does this with precisely the same cunning with which during his talkative siesta he has pretended to be Danny Kaye, the casual conversationalist.

And what an anthology of hilarity, what a grab bag of delight, what a compendium of heaven-sent nonsense his performance proves to be! As surely as it quickens old memories, it creates new ones. Except when he is singing "Just a Wee Deoch-an-Doris" or promoting *Hans Christian Andersen* by doing three numbers from it quite winningly, Mr. Kaye is in a mood which is effulgent in its lack of sentimentality.

His genius for varying accents is no less genuine than his ability to assume different facial expressions or to suggest nationalities or types by the slightest and most subtle changes in posture. Negro spirituals, Spanish dancers, an English ballad-singer giving his fifty-fourth encore, a German soloist relaxing after a program of Wagner, a child at the zoo, a frenetic musical-comedy performer whose physical exertions are supposed to compensate for what he lacks in voice, a draftee being inducted, or a gypsy singing "Dinah"—all these and many more are the subjects, new or old, of Mr. Kaye's benevolent but irresistible spoofing.

Although Mr. Kaye's act may run a little more than an hour and a half, it seems a minute long. It is an amazing exhibition. When at its conclusion the great Danny says he has had more fun than anyone else, he is speaking what at best is no more than a half-truth. That he has had fun is beyond denial. Yet that by having it he has given it is equally self-evident. At the Palace he is offering not only vaudeville as we like to remember it at its best but the comic theatre of today at its best, too.

7. On a Larger Stage

A civil war in Spain which tested men everywhere, a film dealing with it, and the difference between European and American faces.

[1947]

MAN'S HOPE

SPAIN WAS the test case. Anyone can see it now. Everyone does, including thousands of those who failed to see it then. Hindsight always finds the world's vision at its clearest.

Today it is a commonplace to say that what occurred in Spain during her Civil War was only a small-scale rehearsal for what was to sweep around the globe like a prairie fire in World War II. Historians, without so much as puckering their brows, at present recognize that the Spanish agony bore the same relationship to what followed it as the Kansas struggle of the 1850s bore to our own Civil War.

Tom Paine's "These are the times that try men's souls" was not a phrase limited to the American crisis. With or without being aware of it, men are being tested at all times, and not only by the stands they take on happenings close at hand. The Spanish Civil War was one of these events. When it broke out in the midsummer of 1936, it tried the souls of men everywhere, men to whom Barcelona and Madrid were mere names. It was a matter of conviction, not geography; of where the heart and hopes were placed, not the body.

There were those who saw it all clearly, and at once. Their spirits were immediately polarized—at the correct pole. They were never fooled by Franco, and all the talk about law and order and the safety of the Church. Although they had no love for the Communists, the Popular Front and Republican Spain had their sympathy from the outset. Our history knows no heroes braver, certainly none more imaginative, than those young men who, for the sake of faraway freedom, fought in the Lincoln Battalion. They were drafted only by their decencies. Thousands of others, who did not fight, at least knew. No wonder they are proud today, or that they have the envy of those of us who failed ourselves by not seeing that moment clearly.

Although it shames me to admit it, I know I did not. For Richard Watts and Marshall Best, two of my very close friends who did and from the very first day, I have a special respect. Most of us who were wrong—even to the extent of being no more than confused, wavering, or indifferent—feel this way about those who were right. Plenty of people can always be found to climb on the bandwagon. The ones who matter are those who are in their places when the whip cracks and the wheels first turn.

A few months were required before some of the rest of us were so bludgeoned by events that we saw the light. To this day we feel cruelly the sense of guilt at having been unaware of what was at stake for all of us in Spain. We were tried by those times and found wanting. Yet we owe much to the Spanish Civil War. It lifted the blinders, however tardily, from our eyes. It dragged us out of the hermetically sealed rooms of our special interests.

This confession has been wrung from me by a film called *Man's Hope*. It is a picture which has come our way even more tardily than some of us came to realize the extent to which the Spanish Civil War, which is its subject, was a turning point in our thinking and living.

The film's history is a story in itself. Basing it upon his novel known here under the same title, André Malraux produced and directed it in Barcelona in 1938 while the city was still enduring a savage bombardment. When Franco came into power, the picture was smuggled out of Spain to be edited in Paris. It was there that Darius Milhaud wrote his score for it. It was in Paris, too, that French censorship, influenced by a certain pact signed at Munich, forbade its public exhibition. During the German occupation it was hidden, and remained hidden until after the Liberation, when its editing was completed.

Seen now, it makes us all relive yesterday as if it and today were one, and look forward to tomorrow. The fact that Franco still blusters in Madrid, in spite of the protests of the UN and a world war which has blotted out Hitler and Mussolini, does not detract from this story of his people's magnificent fight against him.

It may rob it of the happy ending expected in most revolutionary melodramas. Indeed, it may deny it the conclusion which in this instance is history's hope. Yet it adds to its poignancy.

A cause is never lost if enough people believe in it. In the final sequences of Malraux's film, we are shown shot after shot (really far too many) of a rescue party. This rescue party is bringing back the wounded or dead bodies of some men whose attacked plane has crashed on a mountain while on a successful bombing expedition behind Franco's lines.

A cheap wooden casket sways and bounces on the back of a mule. An aviator whose face has been riddled almost beyond recognition writhes on a litter. The crippled fliers who can still walk hobble down the steep paths or are lifted painfully over the rocks. But the news spreads that these men who have suffered for the people are passing through the countryside. Individually or in little groups, the people come out to greet them. They converge in such numbers that the mountain is dotted with them. What was meant to be a single rescue becomes an expression of mass hope. It may be stated at too great length and in terms which are too camera-conscious. Even so, its eloquence is plain and irresistible. And, one trusts, prophetic.

Man's Hope is an epic of the Popular Front told in terms of the people's struggles and sacrifices for freedom, and with scarcely a glance at their enemies. It is a saga, at once desperate and glorious, of the heartbreaking improvisations with which simple folk —uninformed, unmoneyed, and unorganized—must fight against trained forces properly equipped. It is the story of how humble Republican townsmen and peasants dodge enemy tanks, snipers, and gunners to escape from a guarded city. It is a record of how they communicate with their straggling forces far away; of how, in their fierce need, they collect any containers which will hold dynamite. It is the narrative of how they assemble volunteer motorists just before dawn to illuminate an airport with their headlights. It is the chronicle of how they send up their few planes, bomb a new enemy airfield, and blow up an all-important bridge.

Offhand, such ingredients may seem bound to promise a rehash of *For Whom the Bell Tolls*. There is a difference, however; a major difference. In fact, there are major differences. These do

not stop with M. Malraux's refusal to draft Cupid; to whoop it up
between the sexes; and to rely on Mr. Hemingway's comfy, if incredible, sleeping bag.

What Mr. Hemingway wrote frankly as a novel, and Hollywood
turned into a film often closer to Beverly Hills than to the Spanish
Sierras, M. Malraux has written and directed as a documentary.
Not an actual documentary, any more than *Open City* is one. But
a film which in *Open City*'s way seems to be a documentary and
which, though not quite so cumulative in its action, creates the
same overpowering effects by concerning itself with the facts
rather than the fiction of war.

Sometimes the details of its narrative are a little hard to follow,
especially if we must rely on the English subtitles. Sometimes its
photography seems flat, even amateurish. Yet its crudity is a
strength, not a weakness. The blight of studio contrivance is not
upon it. It creates the illusion of being the real thing, sprung from
an actual, not a rehearsed, despair. Its excitements are not fabri-
cated by scenarists. They are born of history.

There are many sequences filled with that highly charged, unthinking action which in the theatre is called melodrama and in
life heroism. There is, for example, the anguishing moment when
two Republicans, knowing that this means their death, slip quietly
into a stolen car and race through narrow streets, head on into an
enemy battery, in order to silence it. There is also the long sequence of the flight of the bomber before it is shot down behind
Franco's lines. A peasant, flying for the first time, is guiding the
crew to the new enemy airfield near his village. The bomber must
reach its target at just about dawn because enemy fighters will by
then be on its trail. The peasant is addled. The land his hands
know so well, his eyes cannot recognize from the air. That is, until almost the last second.

The climaxes in *Man's Hope* are culled from such incidents
as these. What makes the film notable, however, is its driving,
unadorned authenticity throughout. This, and the sense it communicates utterly of belonging to the people of Spain rather than
to a band of actors. Only three among the hundreds appearing in
it are listed as professionals. They are the men who play the captain, the pilot, and the peasant. The others are either members of
the International Brigade or Spanish peasants. Their faces are in

themselves dramas. In them their autobiographies are written plain. Experience is their make-up man. They do not have to speak lines. The lines furrowing their cheeks and brows, and tightening their mouths and eyes, speak for them.

In few ways is what Europe has endured and we have been spared made clearer than in the faces of average people seen here and there. Every American to have been overseas must have felt this. So must every European who has come this way. It is not merely a question of diet, of a gauntness there and a fullness here. It is a matter of spiritual age, of historic conditioning, of individual hope.

Our very faces proclaim that we hail from the New World just as theirs reveal they were reared in the Old. As a people we manage, when adult, to resist maturity no less surely than Europeans can be born both adult and weary. We may like to fancy that ours are the more abundant lives. Even so, there is no doubting that we possess the emptier countenances. Many Americans have faces which, in spite of the war, look like paper waiting to be written on. In contemporary Europe there is scarcely a countenance upon which the tragic events of these past years have not been scribbled and scrawled and blotted. This is what Edmund Wilson meant when, some fifteen months ago on his return from the Continent, he reported that at first glance our faces here appeared to be lacking in focus, our personalities devoid of flavor.

What World War II wrote on the faces of Europeans by having written it across the map of Europe, the Spanish Civil War wrote on the faces of the men and women in Spain as far back as 1936. This expression is engraved unmistakably and stirringly on the actors in *Man's Hope,* who have also played their gallant parts in history. Suffering is no new experience to these people. Neither is resistance. Theirs has been so hard a struggle for life that they can afford to lose this battle or that in their fight for freedom. And then wait until the next testing of their strength. This is why, though M. Malraux's film is really the record of a gallant defeat, it is also the promise of a future victory.

*The Normandy beaches and the fringe of a liberated France
just after D-day as seen by one assigned by Admiral Alan
G. Kirk to report to the men on the USS Augusta.*

[1944]

THE VARYING SHORE

EVEN BY the morning of D plus two, we had not grown accustomed
to the thought of having France so close at hand. To approach her
in a landing craft; to see her so that the greens on her shore line
became first a swirl of trees, then single trees with individual leaves
shadowed by the sunlight; to see her so that the men on her
beaches who had been insects through our binoculars became not
only men but Americans moving, as the British and Canadians
were moving to the east, on French soil, held by Germans only
two days before, was to be awake in a blissful dream. It was to
confuse the hot dust lifting from the beaches with dark clouds at
last lifting. It was to realize that the landings in Africa, in Sicily,
at Salerno, and Anzio had finally reached their great crescendo—
and explanation—in Normandy.

The nearer we came to the beaches the less we thought about
France, and the more we thought about what was going on ahead
of us; about the Germans, and hence about ourselves. An enemy
shell, lobbed in over the hills, raising a cloud on the land near
by, was a sharp reminder of present business.

The beaches throbbed with activity. They were all bustle and
traffic, pushing and hustle, crisscrossing and shoving, and mainly
life. They hummed with a song of their own. It was an odd music
made up from the backfires of huge trucks, the shout of voices, the
scrape of feet, the grinding of brakes, the giant grunts and groans
of bulldozers breaking their way through the landscape, and the
scrunching wheels of DUKWs as they grabbed on to the gravel
near the shore to lift them from the water. It was broken by gun-
fire, and by the sound of mines being destroyed inland.

Plainly we were newly arrived in this area, and our arrival

had been costly. Debris was strewn across the sand where the German barriers had been destroyed. Debris lapped against the coast line in the water. Broached landing craft or the skeletons of wrecked vessels sprawled against the shore. An LST, scorched as if forgotten in an oven, was near us, with its cargo of tanks burned paintless and blistered, with the brown blankets of its men charred into little chips the size of cornflakes. Its sole survivor was a pair of freshly polished tan shoes, belonging to an officer. They were untouched, placed neatly side by side, waiting patiently to be used.

The sands were littered with stuffs; stuffs being added to by boats newly arrived; stuffs subtracted from by returning trucks; stuffs that just sprawled in the sun and waited. At some points the beaches had the strewn look of circus grounds, when everything is spread out before the Big Tent goes up. Only these beaches were getting ready for more than one circus, however mammoth. They were preparing to hold what in reality was The Biggest Show on Earth.

The beaches were a freight yard in the sand, a freight yard without trains or tracks. On them the backlogs of an expedition were spread out. They housed a frontier city being born all at once; man-cleared and man-made but mechanized, with guns and tanks for its vigilantes, with bulldozers for its axmen, with jeeps for its broncos, with trucks and DUKWs for its covered wagons, with its labor in uniform, with foxholes and slit trenches for its residences, and barbed wire for its fences. The roads of this settlement were being laid by Seabees, and order was being established by beach battalions and the Army even while traffic groaned up the nearby hills and inland.

The harborless beaches were struggling to become a port: a major port, fed by more ships than most ports have ever emptied in their harbors at once. Then there was the traffic, moving laterally across the stretches of sand in front of the hills, grunting up the hills, with one vehicle following another as closely as coaches on a train. At the sides of these improvised and dusty roads marched an endless file of infantry. GIs spilling from the little boats and wading into shore in numbers so prodigally fertile that they made the Trojan horse a barren amateur. GIs resting on the beaches for a tired moment, chewing on their K-rations. GIs in limitless lines moving up the hills, silhouetted against the

sky like the peasant force of Russia in a Soviet movie. GIs and
trucks on their way in, already passing captured Nazis being
marched out. And all this under occasional fire.

Everywhere along the beaches were dumps, resembling Indian
burial mounds, where incoming GIs had shed their life belts. Not
all of their life belts had been abandoned in these piles. Singly or
in heaps, they fringed the roads for miles inland, an American edition of the poplars.

Brown and crumpled, these discarded life belts looked like
faded *leis*. They marked more than the lightening of a GI's load,
whenever he had had the time to think about the weight he was
carrying. They marked his farewell to the Navy. They were mon-
uments to that phase of his adventure. Wherever they were found,
"for those in peril on the sea" had become "for those in peril on
the land." There are no life belts ashore.

After we had waded in from our landing craft and scrambled
halfway up a hill, breathless in the attempt to keep pace with General Bradley, he had turned to us and said, "Gentlemen, I'll be
going back to the *Augusta* at about five this afternoon. Meet me
here at that time. Meanwhile you can come along with me or be
on your own. That's up to you. I'm going to hitchhike."

General Bradley uses the language with exactitude. When he
said hitchhike, hitchhike was what he meant. He is the simplest
of gentlemen. His weapon of command is understatement. He
makes the role of general the more important by underplaying it.
He goes in for none of the tawdrier dramatics with which military
authority can exhibit itself. No flourishings of side arms, no yodel-
ings at those who cannot answer back, no bullying, and no swagger. Just the unchallengeable authority, imperceptibly exerted, of
a good, patient man who is a master at his job and genuinely cares
for his men.

No official car was waiting for him. He stood by the roadside,
a tall, slim figure, with the thumb of his right hand jerking inland,
surveying the unbroken stream of jeeps, DUKWs, and trucks
which passed. In his dark eyes was that look of hope which brightens the eyes of all hitchhikers.

A driver would suddenly notice the three stars on the General's helmet or recognize his face. A jeep would come to a sudden halt, with everyone in it freezing to attention.

"Won't you have my seat, sir?" a private or a sergeant would ask.

"No, son," General Bradley would reply, swinging onto the running board and giving the boy a pat on the shoulder. "No, thank you, son. You're much more tired than I am. I just wanted to see how things are getting along here. Go ahead."

For five minutes or so he would remain, standing on the running board, finding out what he wanted to know before swinging down off the jeep, investigating an outpost, and hitchhiking his way on the next vehicle to come along.

The soldiers liked him for his American approach to authority and to war. They liked him enormously. Once, when he had gone ahead in a jeep and some of us were following him in a reconnaissance car, we got separated from him. Every time we passed an MP, we asked if he had seen General Bradley. Every MP's reply took one of two forms but was the same tribute. Either they would say, smiling proudly, "Yes, he's just passed this way." Or, looking glum, "Not today"; then with a sudden smile, "But we saw him yesterday."

Whether we could keep up with General Bradley or whether we hitchhiked or walked on our own, we saw much on our visits to both American beaches on those three days when he took us ashore.

Early each evening on the *Augusta*, before our sleepless nights began, we would get reports of the British advances around Bayeux or Caen; of our own lines as they deepened on both beaches; of the gradual consolidation of our two beachheads around the estuary; and later of the fierce fighting near Carentan. Our days ashore were ceaseless demonstrations of how different the impersonal battle maps are from the individual men and incidents, their real cartographers.

We saw the big German gun emplacements, sheltered from our Air Force by their ten-foot roofs of cement, where the Navy guns had scored their silencing hits. We saw enemy pillboxes scattered through the hills facing the beaches, pillboxes from which machine guns had taken a heavy toll of our men during the initial landing. We trudged down roads where the fields on either side were lined with stone walls or hedges against which the Germans with only moderate consideration had left signs reading, *"Achtung, Minen!"* We traveled through a countryside, blotched and bruised by war, but still green and lovely, old and meticulously cultivated. The countryside had that outraged look of a wounded neutral, which is always nature's wartime look when it is victimized by the foolishness and brutality of men. The meadows and the vegetation were different from those just across the Channel. The foliage and the agriculture were somehow coarser, rougher. The fields, though combed and rolled for centuries, appeared to have been finished with a fluffy paintbrush rather than with that pencil which Emerson contended had replaced the plow in England.

In our hitchhiking or our walking we talked to countless soldiers —privates, sergeants, corporals, young officers—all of them dusty, sweaty, and in good spirits. They cheerfully admitted they had had a hard time at first; only they told us so in stronger language.

We passed house after house with its walls punctured or destroyed. We saw two gnarled old people, a man and woman, models for Millet, poking in the ruins of what three days before had been their home, seeking to retrieve all that remained of their possessions and carry them off in a baby carriage.

We saw a few blown bridges, small ones, and some tanks abandoned at the roadside. Our Army Engineers had already replaced these old stone bridges with structures of their own. The fact that more bridges were not blown may have indicated the speed of the Germans' retreat. We saw the widespread, glistening wings of some gliders that had been happy in their landings and the wreckage, in fields spiked with posts, of others that most decidedly had not.

We passed meadows with cows grazing in them, the whole scene so idyllic that we questioned the Invasion's reality. On the first Sunday, with our faces coated, our eyes smarting from the dust raised by the never-ending procession of our guns and vehicles, we passed through a village, hardly visible. Yet at the side of the street in this war-created Dust Bowl, we saw a little French girl, her curls as neatly ordered and her pink dress as chic as if on a peaceful Sabbath she were strolling to the Madeleine.

We visited a headquarters near the front in one area where officers, grim, unshaven, and intent, were poring over maps. On a grassy hill nearby we saw the disemboweled body of a young American, his arms spread, his head sunk to one side. His body was kept there as a warning to save others from paying his price for having been so unwise as to walk, in spite of orders, across lands not yet cleared of mines.

We entered the courtyards of old Norman farmhouses, their roofs tattered in places and their resistant stone walls downed here or there. Alongside old wagons we found our jeeps as orderly in their placing as cars serving a headquarters should be; while in front of them geese conducted their undisturbed parades, and all around them the centuries waged a conflict of their own.

We saw stunned peasants standing in little groups on sidewalks rough with rubble and glass. Some of these peasants waved. Many did not. Quite naturally, they were dazed by what had happened to their villages. Their interest was the number of their friends or families killed or wounded; their concern was what was left of those belongings it had taken them lifetimes of hard labor to acquire. Were they apathetic? Were they undemonstrative because in France they represent the temperamental equivalents of our New England farmers? Rot. They had been bludgeoned by war. They were still reeling from its blows. They were confused. Liberators who must destroy in order to liberate are confusing. It must be difficult, even in the interest of nice news stories, to cheer men who in the cause of freedom—your freedom and their own—have just been compelled to flatten your home or kill your brother.

The children waved more than the old people. They asked for gum and often got it. Our soldiers were friendliness itself. They waved and waved. And smiled good-naturedly. And called *"Bonjour"* and *"Vive la France"* in accents new to the Academy. One small boy of about eight, responding to our Army's salutations from the roadside, made clear in a single gesture how confusing these past and present happenings were to all Norman youngsters. For four years, in other words for half his life, this boy had lived under German occupation. Now, overnight, France was free; and so was he. With the best of good intentions, he returned our soldiers' waves with one of the most eloquent, the most revelatory compromises ever achieved in pantomime. First, with great solemnity he raised his right arm skyward in a manner guaranteed to win the Fuehrer's approval. Then, no less earnestly, the small fingers on his right hand spread to form Mr. Churchill's famous V for Victory. Events had moved too swiftly for him.

Along the shoulders of the roads and in the fields we sometimes saw soldiers raking the ground with mine detectors. The crop for which they gardened scientifically was death scientifically planted. They and their harvest were symbols of the double life lived by modern science; expressions of its positive and negative genius; of its coexistent strivings to cure or kill.

We stopped one day by General Joseph L. Collins' temporary headquarters. No setting could have been more Hollywood-French than this one now serving as a center for the grim business of war. A gray plaster building pretending to be a château; a courtyard and a stable, modern though striving to look old; an artificial mill pond; even a huge, flowering horse chestnut. At least the horse chestnut was real, in a background more photogenic than authentic. It was as real as the American soldiers everywhere visible. Like them it cast real shadows, too.

In the midst of destruction, in villages at first glance blasted and empty, it amazed—and reassured—us to see how quickly, how doggedly, life reasserts itself. The life force is as strong in men as it is in ants—which is fortunate, since in wartime men and their villages are held as expendable as ants and their hills.

Timidly men, women, and children would reappear, blinking at what they saw, dazed by what they had undergone. Then they would set about excavating their new lives from the ruins of the old, piecing together bits of the lost pattern, continuing as best they could to do what they had done, and searching for the means to do it. Some of them, impassive and indestructible, continued to live in their own worlds, scarcely noticing the traffic which choked their streets and roads or the new military world which engulfed them.

Seeing them, all I could think of was those peasants I had seen on the rim of the hill facing Cassino the day after the monastery had been bombed. Both the German batteries and our own were blackening the sky with a heavy barrage. Yet I remembered passing in the midst of the battle a partially destroyed Italian farmhouse, behind the remains of which an American gun crew was stooping for protection as it fired. Although the war was in truth in their backyard, the peasant owners of this farmhouse ignored it. Oblivious to its dangers, they went about their business, unhelmeted and unarmed; the old women bending over a nearby brook to do their washing and to gossip, some young children laughing under a tree while milking their goats. In Normandy we encountered many times the same odd themes of life and death, of peace and war, played contrapuntally.

We could not help noticing as we drove through the villages, or passed farmhouses that had been hit, or looked at the toppled steeples of churches where the Germans had placed machine-gun nests, how mortal are the wounds man can inflict on what man has built, and how picayune are the scars left upon the landscape by man's biggest guns or bombs.

Whenever we thumbed a ride in a jeep or a DUKW, as the long lines of our mechanized strength drove through the remnants of a French village—St. Laurent-sur-Mer, Vierville, Isigny, it did not matter which—some of us experienced, however illogically, that uncomfortable feeling, which conquerors must enjoy, of having forced our way into someone else's house.

Although the mere suggestion of the conqueror's role embarrassed us so far as France was concerned, we were genuinely happy whenever we saw German prisoners. The Nazis were the enemy. Their presence in France explained ours. What distressed us was what we had had to do to France and the French in order to rid them of their conquerors. This only increased our dislike of the Nazis.

We saw four groups of Nazi prisoners on our first day ashore. One of these was near the water's edge, just behind the barbed wire, now neatly pierced, which these Nazis had once thought added to their invulnerability. Two other groups of some two hundred each we came across in bull pens further inland. The fourth group consisted of three German hospital corpsmen. They were sitting on the ground, under guard, in a field hospital, watching with no show of interest a young American soldier, with a bandaged, blood-stained head, die on a stretcher. His face was just being covered by his Army blanket when we came up. All around him were other dead or wounded young Americans or Britishers.

We were to see many more German prisoners on our next two

days ashore. We were to see them being marched to the bull pens in great numbers, to see columns of them walking out across the beaches as our own men streamed in. We were to see them sitting sullen or silent behind barbed wire; laughing as they gobbled up K-rations or smoked cigarettes; digging latrines at the field hospitals; carrying their own wounded or ours; digging graves for our dead or theirs. We were to see one captured Lieutenant Colonel, a surgeon, re-equipped by our doctors, working with his own corpsmen and taking excellent care of German casualties.

For the most part, these Nazis were thin, scrubby, and sorry examples of the Super Race. They bore no resemblance to the fine physical specimens we had brought back from Sicily and Africa. They were a mixed lot, too; strange sandwich men for their master's theory of racial purity. They were Czechs, Poles, Yugoslavs, no less than Germans. One group was even Mongolian, claiming to be from Turkestan but at first glance easily mistaken for Japanese.

Many of the Germans were boys of sixteen or seventeen. Invariably, if they could muster any broken English or when spoken to through interpreters, these youngsters were the ones who still championed Hitler, who still could not understand what had happened to them, who still expected a German victory. They made one wonder about the future. No armistice, no peace treaty would set them right. Their minds had been captives since childhood. Being prisoners was to them no new experience. Hitler had seen to that. The older men were different. They had had enough. They were glad the war was over for them.

To come face to face with captured Nazis is an odd experience. Before Tamerlane and ever since, men have doubtless surveyed prisoners through strange eyes. They dislocate the normal vision. They are so many men all at one time. The fact that prisoners are men, like their captors, only complicates the judgment and adds to the disesteem in which they are held.

Men they are, men in deep trouble, men broken and denied the source of their pride and strength; but they are the enemy, too. In the case of these Nazis not only had their guns been pointing in different directions from our own; their minds had been no less opposed. This is what placed them in a category far removed from those who, having taken their final chances in the lottery of

war, just happen to have lost. It was hard to have the normal respect for losers who were lost before they began. The guilt of their
masters was on these men. They could not escape their share in
the horrors they had permitted to occur.

These prisoners were different not because they belonged to a
different race. Race creates no barriers between men whose spirits speak the same language, whose eyes are fastened on the same
goal, whose hearts share the same hopes. These men were different in their approach to life, perhaps even to death. Each one of
them was a small embodiment of the reasons for the world's agony.

We saw them through insurmountable barricades of belief,
through the eyes of their propaganda no less than our own. Which
propaganda was the more damaging it was hard to say. We saw
them remembering not only their past and our present, but considering our future. We saw them with hatred tempered by contempt, and contempt diluted by a kind of side-show curiosity.

We looked at them with wonder that men could be so, could
believe what they must believe. We were aware that they, like us,
were only doing what they felt it was their duty to do. Yet we were
appalled that men could have made a duty of murder, pillage, terror, injustice, race slavery, and darkness. We knew that the army
of which they had been a part had, among professional armies,
been one of the finest. But we were compelled to judge that army
in terms of the state it had been willing to serve. We held these
prisoners both dangerous and despicable for having consented to
function as so much as commas in the living edition of *Mein
Kampf.*

We also knew, however, that these men who were the enemy
were now the enemy stripped of his pretensions. They were the
enemy trapped and taken, removed from the field. Because of this,
each one of them was reassuring. Each one meant that the myth
of supremacy to which he had subscribed was a lie. Each one was
a guarantee that—to his small extent—the horror was abating.
Even so, they were pitiable as men because they were defeated;
left dreamless, helpless, and, we hoped, disillusioned. Enough of
our own men were prisoners in Germany to make us realize how
these men must feel and how we would feel were the situation
reversed.

But to look at them, and to think of the Germany which

Madame de Staël discovered a little more than a century ago for a France suffering then not from being conquered but from a conqueror of her own, was to despise them the more. They had betrayed not only our present but their past.

No one could have remained untouched by the field and evacuation hospitals or by the gallantry shown there by the doctors and corpsmen no less than by the wounded. We visited several of these hospitals, led to them by the red crosses on the tops of their brown tents and the shell-scarred ambulances which kept heading back to them, rolling down those same roads on which young Americans by the thousands were streaming to the front to form that two-way traffic which is war.

Off the main road, a village of tents would emerge above the hedges; a corner of salvation; movable; ready to follow the lines forward, though functioning as if it had been there always and always planned to remain in just this place. Turning into this village, past bushes floured with dust, we would come upon ambulances being unloaded. And upon row after row of litters which, when sorted, had been placed in various sections according to the seriousness of the cases, with our wounded here, the German wounded there, often with wounded civilians being cared for too.

There were civilians—white-haired old women, dressed in black, with faces of ivory; middle-aged men in smocklike coats; and little children. Modern warfare distributes its pains impartially. It makes no distinctions between those in and out of uniform. It tolerates no immunities. Its eagerness to wound is total.

One morning at a field hospital we looked up to see a horse come through the entrance, pulling the kind of cart that was a tumbrel in the bloody days of the Revolution. It was precisely the kind of cart that David saw when he sketched the Widow Capet being taken to the guillotine. A peasant woman, tired, bespectacled, and scared, was driving. She was bringing a strange produce to a strange market. Loaded on sacks at the bottom of the cart were four little girls, their eyes swollen and damaged, their faces bloody and encircled with rags. We were told that they had been playing too near to enemy booby traps or hand grenades.

The hush of city hospitals was on these emergency wards, even under the open sky. Only the mildly wounded talked. With their arms in slings or their heads bandaged, they talked about their home towns; about Brooklyn, dear old Brooklyn and the Dodgers, about 42nd Street at night, about Detroit, Waco, or Champlain.

The paratroopers in particular had stirring tales to tell of tumbling earthward at 1:45 on the morning of D-day, near the town of Beaumont, and landing in the black swamp waters of those pastures which the Germans had flooded behind the beaches in Admiral Moon's area. Some had been shot at by machine guns before they could do the shooting themselves; then mortars had turned on them. Yet many had escaped lightly. These laughed when they thought of their good fortune. It is something to have survived; just to be alive after having come so close to death. They laughed until they remembered Jack or Jim who had not been so lucky. Then the lines of their faces would fall. Then they would do the only thing they could do—shake their heads.

The seriously wounded, and those suffering from lesser wounds, waited in silence under their brown blankets. Either with pained eyes rolled partially back they stared straight above them, or they kept their eyes closed tight and pressed their teeth against their lower lips. And waited. They were waiting their turn for plasma, for fresh dressings, or for the operating tables in the central tents.

Funny things—those central tents, so hot in the sun. When first we entered them, they made us think of the tents used for side shows in small circuses at home. The same smell of parched and trampled grass underfoot; the same scent of sun-drenched canvas. Soon, however, rows of litters became discernible in the darkness. They were long rows, stretching far on either side of the sunlit entrances into a mist of shadows. Before we had left these tents, what originally, in the horror of first impressions, had struck us as a menagerie of pain seemed a miracle of mercy.

These doctors and these corpsmen were working unstintingly, on twenty-four-hour shifts if need be. They were writing down case histories on the labels attached to each patient. They were washing these dusty, bleeding men. They were feeding them, giving them blood transfusions, administering sulfa or penicillin. Or, under the glaring lights in the long operating tents, where two operations were in progress at the same time, they were performing, as spotlessly in white as if they were in any good hospital back home, surgical feats of every variety and difficulty. .

Whatever could be done to undo what had been done a few miles away by the destructive sciences of battle they were doing. Their function was life; the gunners', death. They were positives in a world of negatives. Even in the inferno of war, they must have wondered by what mischance Hippocrates had become confused with Sisyphus. They were matching their skills against the skills of the gunmakers, the shrapnel manufacturers, the grenade producers. More frequently by far than one might have believed possible, they were winning. Their victories were against death itself.

But guns have their labors to perform no less than doctors. They also speak for science, and no doctors can prevent them from doing their wartime duty. At the water's edge and in the countryside back of both beaches, Madame Tussaud had spread her waxen horrors out of doors.

In fields inland or crumpled under dusty bushes at the roadside, we saw many of our young dead; many German dead, too, the latter often with their faces the gray-green of their uniforms. Many of our dead were the victims of snipers. Sometimes the blood had already rusted their pale cheeks. Sometimes on their temples it was still as shiny and bright as wine-red lacquer. Always these boys clutched at the earth, with their yellowed nails black at the tips. Almost always, in spite of mutilations or the frozen agony of their bodies, their faces were so strangely relaxed that one understood afresh why death is spoken of as a release.

To us who passed them each was not only a soldier unknown but an Unknown Soldier. Each stabbed the heart, though never again with quite the same sickening disquiet as did the first one we saw. It is melancholy to realize how quickly in war one grows accustomed to death. Not as a threat to the ill or the old, but as the lot of the healthy and the young. One is never hardened to it. Never entirely prepared to accept it. But ready to expect it as a commonplace; to admit it as what must be, hastened though it is in the coming; to know it will be there like the shadow on the sundial; to try to look upon it as a part of victory; to try to take it on war's own premises.

Of all the ways in which war overrides and ignores what is individual in men none is so hard to accept as the way in which, when it is too late, death re-creates an individual out of someone who has fallen singly from the ranks. In his loneliness by a foreign roadside, this man or that ceases to be Government Issue, a mass commodity produced by a mass response out of a mass need and hope. He once again becomes man's issue, and woman's too. He is one life cut short and scarcely tasted; with something of that life written on the mask which is now his face; with more written there than the form telegram can hope to express which will leave his family disconsolate, with a sorrow beyond remedy, and the world how much the poorer no one will ever know.

Men appear to become smaller in death. Their bodies shrink when denied the spirits they once housed. Their uniforms hang loose, styleless, disheveled, as if suddenly a size too large, as if they had found new owners. When these men were gathered up for burial, when their blankets covered their faces, what remained of their living had likewise dwindled. The little batch of blood-stained letters from home, the wrinkled snapshots, the unfinished package of cigarettes, the chewing gum, the stale half-eaten chocolate bar, the bits of string, the jackknife, and the overseas edition of a book—these were all that now spoke for the hungers they had once known and for lives which had reached out to touch other lives. These possessions were the more poignant because of the resemblance they bore to the ill-assorted but eloquent trophies to be found in any young boy's pockets.

We saw these men when they had fallen singly. We also saw them when some four hundred of them, soldiers and sailors, and about two hundred Germans were stretched on the ground awaiting burial. The cemetery in which prisoners had dug the graves was a meadow, high on a hilltop overlooking the beach on which many of these boys had died. Out to sea our ships darkened the blue water.

In this quiet meadow, where less than a week ago the enemy had felt impregnable, these young men had again surrendered their individuality. They were too numerous, too anonymous, too commonplace to be granted that concentration of affection suffered in the flower-banked funerals of those we love at home. Yet they disturbed the heart. Also the mind.

They were now parts of a force once more; fragments of the Invasion; reminders of how costly so precious a thing as liberty must be. They were covered with canvas which shone white in the sun. Only a clutched hand emerged here or there. Or a tuft of hair, stiff with dust or dandruff.

The smell of death was heavily upon this meadow. We, inhaling it, thought of Ernest Hemingway's description. The smell haunted our nostrils. It was sickly sweet, and over-sweetly sick, as if a gardenia had been dipped in vomit. In spite of the fresh breeze blowing in off the Channel, it made us, out of doors, long to open a window. It too was part of war; very much a part.

But even in war death cannot keep pace with life. At least for long. The beaches below us were teeming with new arrivals; the landing craft and LSTs were pouring in, the transports continuing to empty. When we left the cemetery, the smell of death still with us, and came back to the main road, this road had never before seemed so crowded or alive. Vehicles and men without number were surging up it.

They were far too numerous to be counted as replacements. Trucks, guns, jeeps, supplies, ambulances, and great columns of trudging infantry were overrunning the countryside. In her soda jerkers and mechanics, her clerks and laborers, her teachers and farmers, America had found a harvest of armed men to make ridiculous Jason's military seedlings. The Americans who marched or rode were dusty, young, alert, and strong; the life force in full tide and in khaki.

The men and materials America had moved to Britain across a perilous Atlantic had been moved again, this time to the Continent and in spite of greater dangers. The plans, so long made, so minute in detail, so grandiose in scale, so hazardous in execution, had become history. One trembled to think of what would have happened had they miscarried. The Invasion, however, was now securely launched. Our beachheads were established. We were streaming ashore, even as a few miles to the east of us the Canadians and British were pouring in. The mass migration was once again on the move, this time augmented; indeed, doubled in its size and strength by our Allies.

We knew by our last day ashore that our Invasion was a conquest, our conquest a liberation. It was then that in front of or over numerous buildings we saw the tricolor flying. At the outset, these flags had reappeared slowly. Now in the villages and over farmhouses there were many of them. Among all the spring flowers none was so welcome that year.

From a purely material point of view a flag may be no more than a strip of bunting, discolored by the dyes of a nation's tastes. No material, however, is stout enough or large enough to hold what a flag holds. Its pigmentation is not limited to the obvious reds or whites or blues one sees on it. It is colored by a nation's history and a people's hopes. It is at once a reminder of what has been faced in common and a gesture to advance. To those living under it, which means living by it, a flag expresses what no amount of words can hope to say. In a world scientific and materialistic, and supposedly rational, it still speaks as a symbol, proud, coalescing, mystical.

The tricolor was for us the most reassuring of symbols. It meant more than that a strip of France was now made free, hence French, again. It meant that the whole of France could now be freed, that other flags would in time fly unthreatened where the swastika had flown. This meant that the long, dark agony was approaching its end in Europe, its reason justified, its meaning made the clearer.

We thought much about that peace, whether it could avert the next war. We thought, too, about war as we had this time encountered it. We thought about what it had taught us in democracy and sacrifice, and what it had offered us in comradeship, excitement, and experience. We thought about its waste and cruelty, its barbarisms which were the more barbarous because they were the practice of men pretending to be civilized. We thought about science and how it had had to be perverted into an agent of destruction; about a world which, having waited too long, had been compelled to save itself by pouring its resources into fireworks, and squandering its time, its talents, its energies, and its youth on scientific murder. We thought about the living no less than the dead. About the fatigue which will follow the peace as the enemy's last and most formidable division. About the danger of men expecting or hoping, however naturally, to withdraw again to the kind of living which had made all this necessary. We also thought about the high courage exacted by war.

Courage we had seen everywhere. Men dying gallantly, or facing death cheerfully, for what they felt but could not phrase. Without subtracting one iota from that courage or the admiration due it, we wondered about the emphasis in our thinking which so glorifies the mere act of dying.

Everywhere the patriotic emphasis is on the gallant death for one's country, rather than the gallant life. The worship of the hero's death is a romantic flourish oddly out of place in the credo of an age priding itself on its realism. Men who find the pattern for it in the Crucifixion apparently forget that this death was the last, not the first, of the glories of the life which preceded it. The esteem in which we hold the hero's death, stressing it even more than we do his life, is an odd survival. It is a medievalism which insists that this world is a poor threshold to the next and that we exist here only to live there.

Men stand in proper awe of death because of its finality. Their fear of it is the fear of the unknown. For those willing to embrace it for an idea, they have the respect such high and selfless courage merits. But they forget that the known, which is modern warfare, holds terrors the unknown cannot exceed.

Unquestionably men lose their manhood when they are not willing to die for the belief which is their country. Yet no less unquestionably they also lose that manhood by their dying. They lose their usefulness too. The mere dying, though magnificent, ought not to be enough. The living for one's country should count for more.

Such is our fetish of the gallant death that we forgive the Charleses of this earth because we believe they have redeemed their foolish lives by ten manly minutes on the scaffold. We respect our heroes more for their willingness to die than for their ability to live. Yet if ever there is to be a peace which is not an armistice, men must learn to live at least as well as they now know how to die. Because the mischance of death in action is the price of war, and active living should be the responsibility of peace.

Perhaps in our self-questionings we were asking for too much. Perhaps we should have been satisfied with a mammoth Invasion, brilliantly planned and triumphantly executed, and the hopes of freedom and peace which it had everywhere raised. But it is impossible for rational men to be satisfied with war, thankful as they must be to have the side of freedom win.

If only men could learn to act in time. If only men could realize that the maintenance of a proud peace requires more vigilance than the prosecution of a just war. Yes, and equal courage. And greater character and characters. If only, among all the things this war has taught us, we have gained sufficient wisdom to make another war unnecessary and unthinkable. Because the last people on earth who want a war are the men in their right senses who must fight it.

A look into the courtroom at Nuremberg, and at the Nazis there on trial whose faces could not hope to record the full enormity of their crimes.

[1946]

CENTURY OF PROGRESS— NUREMBERG

"ARE THE father and mother of the defendant in this courtroom?" A youngster of seventeen with brown eyes and black hair, a budding cockney with the look of a grocery boy, stood in the dock at the Old Bailey. His eyes patrolled the floor. Guiltily, miserably. Or stared at the backs of his large, outstretched hands, as they rested on the railing before him. His face was reddened with a blush which rarely left it. He kept biting his lower lip to fight off tears.

Below him was a sizable inkspot of barristers, their gray wigs showing white above their black gowns. Confronting the boy across a well of lawyers and clerks sat the judge. He dominated the scene as a mountain dominates the valley that lies in its shadow. He was higher than the boy, and, like him, alone, but not so lonely. He was a man, costumed as a symbol and trying to think and act like one, though still a man. He was an individual and an abstraction; a modern, yet a figure out of Hogarth. His scarlet robe and pow-

dered wig glowed in the yellow grayness of the courtroom. So did
the fine dispassion of his face. He was awesome in his dignity,
fearsome in his power, and as imperturbable as men learn to be
who dare to ventriloquize for justice.

"No, Your Lordship," came an answer from the far side of the
dock. "The defendant's parents are not here. They are waiting in
the corridor."

"Do you mean to say . . ." His Lordship's voice, so sonorous
and impersonal before, had thunder in it now. "Do you mean to
say that, while room has been made for idle spectators in this court,
no place has been found for the father and mother who have labored to raise this unfortunate boy? Are these luckless parents
supposed to overhear from a chance passerby outside what most
vitally concerns them? Bring them in at once."

They appeared, and in turn took their places in the witness
stand. He was a little storekeeper, the cockney character who
seems overdrawn when he wanders into an English comedy. He
was oily of hair, pink of face, and flashy of dress. He sported
handlebar mustaches, and wore the inevitable thick watch chain
across his ample vest. She was a meek, faded woman in black; a
dressed-up version of the char to whom condescending British
dramatists turn when in need of a reliable laugh. Her upper plate
kept slipping, while tears trickled down her cheeks. Her blue eyes
found their way but once to her son's face. She appeared to see
only the judge.

There was nothing comic about this couple now. It was impossible not to sense how complete their happiness had been with
each other—and with their son—and how utter was their present
wretchedness. They had ceased to be cockney, or English. They
were a father and mother—any father, any mother—bludgeoned
by life, and compelled to say publicly what it cost them anguish to
admit in private.

"Before your son was guilty of this immoral attack on a boy of
fifteen, what was he like—as a son?"

" 'N it please Your Lordship, 'e was always a good boy. Hin-
dustrious, book-lovin', 'elpful around the 'ome 'n shop. I carn't
rightly imagine what it was that got into 'im that night."

The father and the mother, they both said this in their different
ways. He brusquely, embarrassed by having to praise no less than

to defend; she proudly, not bothering to hide that her heart was broken. No one could fail to feel their shame. Or the misery which was theirs. Yes, and the boy's too. Nor could anyone miss the gratitude which lighted the mother's eyes, and lifted her mouth into a brief half-smile when the judge leaned over to her, before passing sentence, to confide, "Madam, you shall have your son back—not now, but very soon."

I could not help thinking back to this boy, this family, and this English court when, a few weeks later, I found myself in the old Bavarian Palace of Justice in Nuremberg. Such samples of naked grief as these Britishers represented, of families with their lives blighted, of individuals with crimes to their discredit, are common sights in the courtrooms of any country. In these cases the faces of the accused can register the misdeeds they have done. If they are guilty, their countenances are part—not the legal but a human part—of the evidence. Moreover, the grief for which they have been responsible is no less visible on the faces of the affected parties. The whole ugly business is within the scale of what features can record.

But as I looked at these twenty-one men in the dock at Nuremberg, I realized that their faces, however evil, could not bear the full imprint of their crimes. What their expressions should have said, what I had half hoped, half expected they would say, they did not, could not, reveal. A Hauptmann, a Judd Gray, a Loeb, a Leopold, a Lonergan, or a Heirens can look his part when brought to justice; look it to the full. Or if not, look it enough so that we can read into his appearance what we feel must be there. But not these men.

No mouths regardless of how cruel; no eyes no matter how brutal or how shifty; no chins in spite of their ferocity; no lines however depraved could record their guilt. Their crimes were too far-flung, too grandiose, for their countenances to hold. They were of a mass scale, hideously beyond any individual register. What their faces could not say, the face of Europe—indeed of the world—says for them. Their guilt was written in Coventry and London; in the charred corpses of Stalingrad and Rotterdam; in the stench of Buchenwald. It was written in the agony of slave labor, in the helplessness of displaced persons, in the rubble of millions of homes, of lives, of hopes. It was written in the hunger of the old and the young, in the heartbreak of families, the despair of nations, the moral degradation of our times, and the ruin—epitomized outside this courtroom by the fate of Nuremberg's old Walled City—of that very Germany these men had led to her destruction.

In the dock they looked mediocre enough. Indeed, at first glance I was forced to wonder if they would have seemed different from any group of felons or scoundrels rounded up by the police over a fortunate week end for a Monday morning line-up. That is, had they not figured in our nightmares, and had their histories been unknown to us. Foreknowledge is the most detailed of painters. It can clothe the barest outlines. Any chance spectator was bound to appraise these men as much by their reputations as their looks. At least, until their faces had been scrutinized long and carefully. Even then they proved inadequate vessels for their villainy. As men, they could claim this much humanity.

In the courtroom they were shadows of themselves. They bore little relation to what they had been. To comprehend their significance, it was necessary to think back to the years of their ruffians' prowess. Even this was not enough. Our memories accommodate themselves too readily to the pressures of the present. If the most recent image does not superimpose itself upon the first impression, it is apt to become blurred with it.

No, to realize the full menace of these men it was necessary to see them as they actually were; to see them in the heyday of their power; as they saw themselves, and as they mesmerized their people into seeing them. Their vanity made this possible. So did their Teuton thoroughness in keeping records. Downstairs in the labyrinth of the courthouse was a projection room. There, under the same roof where these defendants were struggling for their lives, an American sergeant ran off a film. It was a documentary which they had assembled for propaganda purposes as the official chronicle of their glory. It proved an unanswerable witness against them and the threat they had represented to all our living.

It was called *Triumph of the Will*. In it they—and their Fuehrer —shouted and strutted. They harangued and paraded. They raised their arms to "Heil Hitler!" Their faces and bodies were as swollen with power as with beer. All of them were distended with triumph, full blown with fanaticism and fury. On the screen they were puff-adders compared to the black snakes upstairs. Their faces were insolent, their voices screams. They went in for mass hypnosis, moving always in groups and appearing always before crowds. They specialized in ritual on the grand scale, in banners and pageantry, in bands and masses, and the obliteration of the individual man. Their witchcraft included fire worship, and hatred was one of their strongest flames. They were Ku Kluxers and Druids and Prussians all strangely mixed.

Goering, in appearance part ringmaster, part lion, and mainly circus tent, was taking over, too, the functions of a calliope. He made it plain that he enjoyed being the biggest circus—at least in his own person—on the German earth.

Hess with his black eyes burning above the open portcullis of his mouth, and his jowls quivering, was screeching his madman's chant, *Hitler ist Deutschland! Deutschland ist Hitler!*

Von Ribbentrop, in the full, smiling, confident display of his salesman's wares . . . Keitel, haughty of head and carriage, a totem pole for Prussia's militarism . . . Kaltenbrunner, with a face all dangerous cliffs and no shore line . . . Rosenberg, a bully, heliumed to the ascension point with authority . . . Doenitz, dapper enough in his admiral's uniform for one of Germany's provincial companies of *Pinafore* . . . Schirach, a full moon baying at German youth; a Pied Piper meant to charm rats, not mortals . . . Sauckel, his features those of a mortgage collector playing Nero . . . Von Papen, a library lion turning his back on books, his nostrils spread as if pleased to smell them burning . . . Jodl, in appearance a Bavarian with a touch of Ludwig in him . . . Schacht, a purse-proud sharper who could have sold marijuana to schoolchildren on the side.

They were all there, puckered with pride, deafened with cheers, surrounded by crowds. Frank, Frick, Streicher, Raeder, Speer, Fritsche, Seyss-Inquart, Neurath, and all the rest of their pompous crew. They were all there, speeding down lined streets in huge bulletproof cars, or marching through hoarse thousands to mount the podium of Nuremberg's vast Sportspalast. Yes, even Himmler and Ley (who hanged himself in his Nuremberg cell not inappropriately on the toilet), they were all performing their voodoo dances in front of frenzied mobs before the Hitler who was their witch doctor.

But there was more to them than their banners and their speeches, their threats and promises. There was also the record of what they did with their power after they had grabbed it, when Europe was prostrate under their iron heels. This could be sampled in the uncut Buchenwald, Dachau, and other prison pictures which were shown next. To look at these films required a strong stomach. For the triumphant days of the men in the dock called for agonized shrieks no less than approving roars. The applause they won was paid for in such torture as leaves us in this supposedly enlightened twentieth century with at least one foot in the darkest of dark ages. In addition, there were the "exhibits" to be seen—and smelled—in a small room upstairs. As witnesses against the defendants, both the documentaries and the "exhibits" were of a kind to freeze the blood.

In America I had seen the Dachau and Buchenwald pictures, and wished that they could be made compulsory for everyone, especially for those who, in the natural pessimism of these days of the letdown, wonder what the war proved anyway. But in Nuremberg the films I saw were uncut. The gas chambers; the furnaces; the listless, half-crazed eyes of the starved and verminridden prisoners; the feet rendered toeless by gangrene—these I saw again. Then came a stack of decapitated heads upon which experiments had been performed. And the SS troopers and strongarmed women prison attendants as they picked up shrunken and dangling cadavers to toss them into a communal grave. Next, a relentless bulldozer, driven by a man wearing a mask to protect himself against the stench. This bulldozer nudged against a mound of easily jostled bodies, pushing them for sanitation's sake into an open pit, as their arms drooped, their legs sprawled, their leering faces tumbled upside down with no regard for the dignity of death.

I also visited the small room where the "exhibits" were kept. I saw the steel rod, bent from beating captives; the lampshade made from tattooed human skin; a Pole's shrunken head, now black in color, the mouth swollen, the beard and hair reddish, which a proud Nazi had mounted on a tiny pedestal as a trophy for his den. And I lifted, unsuspectingly, the lid of a jar containing a gray, cheeselike substance, to inhale—and be sickened by—the scent of soap made from dead human bodies. I looked through the beautifully bound volume which was the official report to headquarters on the wiping out of Warsaw's ghetto. It was extra-illustrated with photographs, triumphantly captioned, of children and mothers being shot, and a man, his arms raised above his head, plunging to his death from the fourth story of his burning home. "They gave their utmost, their life," read the Nazi tribute to the fifteen SS men who fell on the first day of this extermination, "while performing their duty. . . . We shall never forget them."

Naturally I wondered the more about those men in the dock upstairs. Elsewhere in the courthouse I had seen them not only at the zenith of their power but with all their "crimes broad blown, as flush as May." Perhaps inevitably I halfway expected, when I stared at them again from the visitors' gallery, that they would look their former selves. But in the courtroom they were different. They were fractions of what they had been. Their faces, which were incapable of registering their crimes, had long since ceased to register their triumphs.

A sorrier group of men than those who had found their Valhalla in the Nuremberg dock could scarcely be imagined. The prison pallor—that pallor which can reduce the most florid complexion to a whiteness not unlike a fish's belly—was upon them. They were to what they had been in the films shown downstairs what the shell is to the locust. Their bodies, like their authority, had shriveled. Only the cruelty in their faces remained undwindled. Inescapable as this was, it was insufficient to encompass their mass crimes. They had lean, though not hungry, looks. It was not so much that they had become thin as that they had ceased to be gross. The change in their diet did not end with a different menu. They were nourished by what they had eaten but starved for that which they had once fed on. Adversity had whittled away their persons no less than their powers.

Their meetings in the dock, before the judges entered or left the courtroom, were their major opportunities for conversing among themselves. No matter how they may have felt about one another (and there were those who insisted that not one of them would be left to bring to judgment, were each of these men handed a pistol and turned loose in the prison courtyard), their public encounters were models of German military etiquette. Each morning, as they filed in with MPs sandwiched between them or entered singly, each trailed by a single MP, they clicked their heels, or bowed slightly from the waist, in salutation. Their ceremonious politeness to each other was the more grotesque, considering the millions who would not remember them for their manners.

The clothes they wore in the courtroom they were permitted to wear only there. The minute they returned to their cells, through the boarded passageway connecting the courthouse with the jail, they changed into their prison garments. These were without suspenders or neckties and such trimmings as might aid a man in hanging himself. The Judases of this earth do not all take to a leafy tree, or have one named after them.

In the film recording the glory they had known most of the defendants were costumed for their sadism. They wore uniforms of a flamboyance beyond a state trooper's dreams. Yet only three of the men in the dock suggested by their dress the armed strength of the Germany they had misled.

Doenitz and Raeder were not among these. Clothes may make the man, but the conquering hero can owe as much to the imagination of his tailor as to the lack of it in his foes. Out of uniform these two former grand admirals were worse than commonplace; they were contemptible. They were sunk entirely. Any distinction their uniforms may have given them was scuttled by their loss. Doenitz in particular was a sorry sight. His body was small, his mouth weak, his eyes were shifty. He was a mole caught at last above ground in the daylight. If the Nazi fleet had not produced him, David Low would have invented him. As a counterfeiter he might have been convincing; as a naval figure he was nonexistent.

Keitel, Jodl, and Goering were the three defendants still in uniform. The suits of the others were German in cut. In color they varied from dull browns, blues, and black to Frick's startled gray tweeds. Against their will and in spite of their hopes, these defendants had been reduced to civilians once more. To most of them the process would never have seemed an elevation. Having raised huge armies, they now had to content themselves with the khaki of the two MPs who guarded the door leading to their cells, of the seven MPs who stood rigidly behind them, and the vigilant one who faced them, flanking Goering's right in the front row of the dock. They were trim figures, these young MPs, with their glistening white helmets, their white belts, white gloves, and gaiters. They were ever-present reminders, symbols not to be taken lightly, that the forces once commanded by these leaders were shrunken, that their uniforms had changed color, and that the command had shifted unalterably.

Goering wore the light gray, double-breasted field marshal's uniform of his own designing; Jodl and Keitel the Wehrmacht's olive green. Being stripped of their insignia and decorations, these three uniforms had a clipped, shamed, and mangy look. They were uniforms, yet they were not. They had the bare feeling of a room, otherwise furnished, in which the rugs, curtains, and lamps were missing.

Although a broken man, Keitel remained a proud Prussian in behavior and manner. Frederick would have recognized a quality in him no less surely than he would have been horrified—and embarrassed—by the others. Spiritually, the monocle was still in Keitel's eye. A Tyrolean cap on Jodl's bald head, and a stein in his hand, would have equipped him as a singing waiter in any Bavarian restaurant.

Among all the defendants Goering alone appeared to be enjoying himself—and the show. His was the corner seat in the front row, facing the visitors' gallery, and, far more important, nearest the correspondents' section. No matter how great the stakes, the stage was his, and Goering was ham enough to revel in the realization. He was an extrovert who did not care about the noose which might hang about his neck, or the bullets which might pierce his hide, so long as the eyes of the world were on his person. They were. And he rejoiced in that fact.

His gray tunic dangled as loosely from his shoulders as the wraparound of a delivered mother. But, though vastly reduced, Goering remained a fat man in his manner. He still employed the fat man's gestures; gestures wide enough to be free of the body they had once had to clear. He continued to play a diabolical Falstaff even after the curtain was down and most of his padding had been removed.

He stood out because of his animation. He had his eyes on history no less than on his audience. They were eyes that shone as coldly as the sun on icebergs. The leonine countenance from which they gleamed had power. It caught the attention as much as it played for it. What is more, it held it. Because, in spite of the shocking brutishness of this face, it was capable of a coarse, cruel

joviality which took possession of the withered remnants of
Goering's jowls, and showed in the wide, loose spread of his lips.
His was an alert, intelligent, and commanding face. It was un-
defeated. It registered its ever-changing emotions, and registered
them at once. Moreover, it projected them so that at a distance it
was its own close-up.

Goering may have seemed bisected because of the dehydra-
tion prison life had forced upon him. Yet he appeared healthy.
He did so in spite of the brown army rug in which, because of a
slight sniffle, he would wrap his legs before sitting down, as if he
were tucking himself in a steamer chair. Hess, with his wildly star-
ing black eyes and the simper on his pale face of an animal painted
by Rousseau, was also a blanket-wrapper. But he did not put
on a show equal to Goering's. No one else in the dock did. The
rest, with their lawyers' aid, ran like rats from their records, their
responsibilities, and their Fuehrer. Not Goering. He was at any
rate consistent. He could not bring himself to deny the importance
which had been his by putting the blame on others. He continued
to be true to his false colors. That was something.

Occasionally von Ribbentrop, looking very tired, would smile.
His was a salesman's smile, easy and automatic. It had that neon
quality of lighting up the façade. Yet there was something to it of
the diplomat's dignity. It was not without charm, a charm which
grew in illusion if for no other reason than that the features
it brightened were of a type quite different from those of the other
prisoners. They had less of the thug's thickness to them. They
were both more thoughtful and more sensitive.

Very few of the others smiled at all. Once, when a German
attorney described his client's advent in a conquered land as
"God's blessing," all the prisoners snickered uneasily among themselves. They seemed to be as embarrassed by any mention
of God's name as they were amused by their attorney's audacity.
Rosenberg, to be sure, moved restlessly on the bench. He bit his
nails. Or scratched his neck. Or looked at his hands again and
again as if they belonged to someone else. But most of the other
prisoners sat grimly, stolidly.

They listened with their earphones on, as we did who were
there as transients in the visitors' gallery. As the members of the

press did in the reserved section at the end of the courtroom below us. As the Allied prosecutors or their staffs did at the long tables just in front of us. As did the gowned German defense attorneys at their desks directly in front of the dock. As did the court recorders facing them. And as the eight justices of the Tribunal also did as they sat, huddled over their papers, behind the bench opposite the defendants.

We all listened. We all listened as, over the multilingual speaking apparatus, the interpreters behind glass panels just beyond the dock droned simultaneous translations of the proceedings in Russian, German, French, and English. To hear them, you could manipulate the dial on the armrest beside you to get the language of your choice.

It was undeniably exciting when, at ten in the morning or at two in the afternoon on each of the two days I was there, an American voice called out "Attenshun!" and the judges entered the court. The whole room rose to its feet, including the defendants, to show respect to Justice and the Law. Since both the Law and the Justice were in this case international, the defendants' recognition of it, though immediate at each sitting, must be described as tardy.

The judges took their places on their high-backed chairs. These chairs, being wine-colored as were all the other seats in the courtroom except the bare wooden benches in the dock, stood out against the light green velvet curtains which hid the dark paneling behind them. Against this light green background the bright colors of the flags of Russia, France, the United States, and Great Britain also stood out. These flags were placed so that each of them rested behind and between the two judges who represented each of the four powers conducting the Tribunal.

Above the whole room hung two sets of lights. One was fluorescent. It created an illumination as impersonal as the law, and was used except when a new witness or an attorney spoke. Then the other system suddenly flooded on. Journalism can scarcely be more yellow than it was. And some of the defendants, including Goering of course, often went through the act of whipping out their dark glasses to protect their vision, now grown so sensitive.

The two Russians of the Tribunal were, perhaps not unsurprisingly, in uniform. They were youngish men, serious and silent. The gold of their shoulder boards blazed in the room. The British judges, who sat next to them, did not wear the powdered wigs they might have worn at home. Yet they were as English, especially Lord Justice Geoffrey Lawrence—the Tribunal's President—as the Old Bailey, the Lord High Chancellor, or the legal interludes in Dickens and Galsworthy. Francis Biddle, lean, aristocratic, and almost dapper, was a Philadelphian who might have sat for Sir Thomas Lawrence. He was as different from Judge Parker of our Court of Appeals as the Main Line is from the Tar Heel State. Both, nonetheless, were unmistakably Americans. And Americans of whom we could be proud. As for the French members of the Tribunal, they, with their long starched white cravats cutting the fronts of their black gowns, were straight out of Daumier.

When I was in Nuremberg, it was supposed to be the dull season. The trial had dragged on for nine months beyond the three that some had thought it would take. It had lost its novelty. Its first sensationalism was exhausted. The world was hot on the trail of new murders. It was feeding its tabloid hungers elsewhere, on more local horrors. The prosecution had by then presented its case against the individual offenders, though not against the Nazi organizations. This was to come later. The defendants were silent. One after another I heard their lawyers take the stand, trying to defend the indefensible. In true Teutonic fashion they indulged— at least until challenged dryly by the Tribunal's President—in hazy harangues on "The Renaissance," "The French Revolution," "Subjectivism," "Darwinism," and "The Development of the History of Intellectual Pursuits in Europe." Or, most unmilitarily, they sought to clear their clients by insisting that they could not be held responsible for all the orders they had signed.

No doubt proceedings were becalmed. To me, however, they were anything but dull. They could claim a drama unmatched in the contemporary world, and a significance equaled only by the recent international conferences. Of these they were a vital part. So far as the plans for peace went, they were as yet one of their most helpful flowerings.

Perhaps, quite naturally, my first interest, like everyone else's, was the men in the dock. I found it hard to take my eyes off them.

Why not? They were villains in the most villainous scenario history has known. About them was something much more sinister than even that strange fascination which all criminals at the bar possess. These men were the wicked—and the mighty—fallen. They were disrupters not of single homes but of this planet. If convicted, they had only twenty-one lives with which to pay for the twelve million deaths they were charged with causing, not to forget the universal misery and destruction they had brought about. Regardless of what fate might come their way after a fair trial, they could never make amends.

It was exciting to go through the cell block in which the prisoners were confined, led there, while they were in court, in Chinatown parties by an American colonel. It was exciting to see the barbershop in which they were shaved daily with a safety razor by a trusted prisoner of war. It was exciting, too, to walk into their cells and survey their family photographs and personal effects. And no less exciting to observe the flimsy wooden table in each cell which would collapse if the occupant sought to escape through the single window. It gave one a strange sensation to look at the scant luggage these men had brought with them; to hear the routine of their waking and sleeping hours; and to know that they lived nakedly under constant surveillance of our guards, who watched them through portholes in the cell doors. It was also interesting to be told that von Ribbentrop was the only one of the prisoners who was physically dirty, and punished himself by refusing to cleanse his own washbowl.

Yet such facts, however ghoulish, satisfying, or spine-tingling, were irrelevancies. These defendants might provide the thrills, but they could not supply the truest thrill. As men, they did not really matter. At least not any longer.

There were lawyers who questioned the legality of the whole proceedings. They were slaves to the dangerous principle that what had not been could never be. There were hotheads, too, who wondered, humanly, if it wouldn't have been simpler for our armies just to have lined these bastards up against the walls and shot them down. But, to my way of thinking, both of these factions missed the point.

The men who mattered at Nuremberg were not the defendants in the dock. They were the judges on the Tribunal. They were the governments of the Four Powers who had drawn up the charter and the members of the nineteen other nations who had subscribed to it. They were the Prosecutors. Above all, they were men, such as our own Mr. Justice Robert H. Jackson, who had given the principles of the case their noblest statement.

Justice Jackson may not excel at either the banter or the mongoose tactics of a prosecutor. He is a jurist, not a district attorney. He is a man who has fought for a principle—a great principle— and defended it magnificently. He scored victories, which I trust may yet affect all of our living, when he made his opening address and his more recent summation.

"That four great nations," said he in his opening speech, "flushed with victory and stung with injury, stay the hand of vengeance and voluntarily submit their captive enemies to the judgment of the law is one of the most significant tributes that Power has ever paid to Reason."

Justice Jackson and his associates have battled to see that the law, instead of remaining static, grows to meet world needs. He has sought by legal means to have international aggression take its place among recognized crimes. He has emphasized the absurdity of subjecting petty malefactors to punishment while the great ones go scot-free. He has realized that the mortals he seeks to have punished are broken, miserable men whose individual fate is at present of little consequence. Yet Justice Jackson has been aware, as most people seem anxious to forget, that "these prisoners represent sinister influences that will lurk in the world long after their bodies have returned to dust."

He has felt the shame that we should all have felt because of what has been barbarous in a supposedly civilized age. He has admitted the reality that "in the long perspective of history the present century will not hold an admirable position unless its second half is to redeem its first." If we cannot eliminate the causes and prevent the repetition of the savage events which have branded these past two score years as "the most bloody in all annals," he has insisted, "it is not an irresponsible prophecy to say that this twentieth century may yet succeed in bringing the doom of civilization."

It is to prevent such a doom that the trial has dragged on and on amid the warning ruins of Nuremberg. Although it may have exhausted our patience, it must have raised both our hopes and our self-respect.

> *The "Boys in Blue," meeting as centenarians for the last encampment of the Grand Army of the Republic, give younger veterans food for thought.*

[1949]

OLD GLORY

THEY HAVE long since met and gone home, those wizened reminders of the past who were still able to travel. The youngest of them was a mere stripling of one hundred; the most venerable was eight years his senior. From Portland, Oregon; from Duluth and Pontiac; from Princeton, Kentucky; from Long Beach, California, and Rochester, New York; by plane, train, or automobile these veterans of long marches and decisive battles in the Brothers' War had arrived in Indianapolis, there to be met by trained nurses, by Red Cross station wagons, and wheelchairs.

Ten more of their comrades-in-arms, who had lived through and outlived so much history, were still alive. At least they were still breathing. They, however, were too frail to travel and face the fatigues of this, the GAR's last encampment. The wearied and the aging mind being as relinquishing as it is, perhaps these ten survivors who could not make the trip were too frail even to distinguish between Shiloh and Antietam, Vicksburg and Lookout Mountain, those names which for decades had been at once the milestones and the pivots in their thinking.

The six who did meet must have felt the loneliness which progresses geometrically with the mounting years. They must also have been aware of many other changes, although one hopes not too many. In 1890 the GAR had numbered 400,000. For them that had been a big year, comparable to the kind of bumper year the American Legion was celebrating in Philadelphia at the very moment when these six old men were holding their invalids' bivouac in Indianapolis.

Did President Truman, unable to find the time to lay the cornerstone for the UN's new building, discover his schedule was sufficiently free for him to address the Legionnaires in 1949? President Benjamin Harrison in 1890 had traveled all the way to Boston to speak to the GAR. Numbers count in a democracy. Seventy-five thousand Legionnaires, veterans of two wars, young men and oldish and still able to get to the polls, had marched by the reviewing stand this August in the City of Brotherly Love. In Indianapolis it was different. What had once been an army—the Grand Army of the Republic—had now shrunk to two squads of very tired, very feeble, very old fellows. From these two squads only a half dozen could be mustered who remained able to march—in wheelchairs.

One of these was a Negro. Born a slave one hundred and five years ago, he had run away from his master to fight at Vicksburg. This was his first encampment. Although blind now, he liked it so much he hoped there would be another. Two others, including the commander in chief, were of a different opinion. They felt "the boys should stay home hereafter and take care of themselves." The commander in chief had his own personal and very human reason for feeling this should be their final reunion. Age apparently does not wither vanity. It leaves pride unscathed. The commander in chief wanted the honor of being the last to bear that title. But there were others who had their eyes on the office. The senior vice commander was one of these. He was the next in line of succession. At one hundred and two he coveted the same honor.

On the first day of their three-day session at the Claypool Hotel, the six old men had discussed such questions amiably. They had exchanged views with the aid of amplifiers and a portable microphone, since all of them were deaf. The arguments pro and con had never become heated. The talkers tired too easily for that.

The commander in chief had called for a "yea" or "nay" vote for permanent adjournment. Six quivering voices, broken by age and emotion, were reported to have murmured "Yea." "I close this last meeting of the Grand Army of the Republic," said the commander in chief. And that was that—the closing not only of a meeting but of a great page in history.

Before this vote had been taken, the senior vice commander had asked a very human question. "Commander," he had said, "can I hold the gavel just a little while?" "Sure enough," had been the reply, and for a few minutes the vice commander had fondled it in his wrinkled hands and then, smiling, given it back.

Another veteran had also spoken. The oldest member present, the ex-soldier whose years number one hundred and eight, had bent forward in his dark blue uniform to say a few words. In a quavering voice he had confessed his hope had been that the final encampment of the GAR might be a joint meeting in Washington with the last survivors of the United Confederate Veterans. "It is just a suggestion," he had said. "I know it can never be, but I have lived in the hope that we might see it some day, to prove to the world that we are united states."

Some of the Legionnaires in Philadelphia, between drinks, parades, and business sessions, must have stolen glances at the newspapers stories about the GAR encampment. Some of the vigorous young MPs assigned to pushing these old soldiers in their wheelchairs through the crowds in Indianapolis must have looked at their charges—and wondered. Some of the non-joining veterans of the Spanish-American War, the Mexican Border incident, World War I, and World War II must, in the freedom of their civilian lives, have read their newspapers and smiled at first, as smile we will at age which is abnormal and warriors who have ceased to be warlike. Then suddenly they must have stopped smiling. For those stories and those pictures out of Indianapolis were at once ridiculous and sobering, ironic and pathetic, and frightening if for no other reason than the hints of prophecy they offered.

"You are me forty years from now," cried Anna to Marthy, the frowsy old woman in O'Neill's *Anna Christie*. All of us pass daily, without recognizing them, older people whose presents are forecasts of what our futures will be like, if only we last to their age. We seldom see ourselves in these passersby. We do not want to. We live nourished by the illusion that each of us is somehow different. The repeated pattern, being an uncomfortable idea, is something we reject.

The young men to whom Anzio, Iwo Jima, or Normandy are real, personal, and everlasting names have as hard a time believing as their fathers have in comprehending the nearness and actuality in the reality and closeness of Château-Thierry and Belleau Wood of Gettysburg and Chickamauga to those ancients who assembled in Indianapolis. Remember, the oldest of these gray old men was twenty-four when Grant and Lee met at Appomattox, and the youngest a green sixteen. As they grew up, they must have tired of hearing tall tales of Buena Vista and Chapultepec, and a heavy mist must by then have settled on the battles of Lake Erie and New Orleans. The first person lends life to a story, but history heard or read is never the same as history lived. Other people's adventures are bound to lack for us the vividness of our own. Experience, after all, and tragically, is an untransferable commodity.

In their youth these participants in the Civil War could have talked with palsied centenarians who had fought with Washington. (This is the measure of how young our country is.) If they did happen to do so, they must have found it as impossible to see ragged Continentals in the eroded faces at which they looked as we found it impossible to see "Boys in Blue" in the faces of those six GARs photographed at their final meeting. From the watch fires of a hundred circling camps to wheelchairs and trained nurses in the Claypool Hotel is more than a sea change.

In a famous paragraph, written when Mrs. Siddons had been unwise enough to come out of retirement and act again, Hazlitt wrote: "Players should be immortal, if their own wishes or ours could make them so; but they are not. They not only die like other people, but like other people they cease to be young, they are no longer themselves, even while living. Their health, strength, beauty, voice, fail them; nor can they, without these advantages, perform the same feats, or command the same applause that they did when possessed of them. It is the common lot: players are only not exempt from it."

It is the common lot indeed, and from it veterans also enjoy no exemption. Although they may have volunteered during a war, none of them can escape being drafted by Time. They come home from combat full of youth and impatience with the old, only to grow old themselves. With the passing years they cease to look their words. Their bodies age, sag, soften, fatten, or shrink. They contradict what they have to say and what is said about them.

Where once these men of action were capable of scaling walls, charging up hills, or trudging through miles of mud, they dwindle into men of inaction, no longer able to climb stairs. Their rifles are replaced by canes. Their eyes ultimately fail them; their hearing goes. If only they live long enough, the final Ages of Man overtake them. They may find inner strength and abiding satisfaction in the knowledge that they have had their St. Crispin's day. But should they follow the warlike Harry's counsel and be so foolhardy and so tiresome as to strip their sleeves and show their scars on each anniversary of their big moment, they would discover to their humiliation that their arms are no longer what they were and that their neighbors were running from them.

No one has ever written better about the returned soldiers' fate than Dixon Wecter in his fascinating *When Johnny Comes Marching Home*. From Yorktown to V-J Day, the repeated pattern has certainly been present in all our hours of demobilization. We have no monopoly on it. It must be as old as the history of conflict; as familiar to the troops of Epaminondas as to those of Grant or Eisenhower. The hero soon ceases to be a hero in the public mind and, when the need for him has vanished, little by little he turns into a bore.

When long ago the news of Appomattox reached them, the six old men in Indianapolis must have thought everything was over but the shouting. They could not have guessed how quickly the shouting would be over, too. It always dies down with merciless swiftness. Before all uniforms can be exchanged for civilian clothes, the welcoming debutantes and hostesses at the stations have disappeared and the service clubs have disbanded. *Tommy Atkins*, more than being a complaint written in cockney, is a definitive history of both the soldier and the public everywhere in war and peace.

As Mr. Wecter makes clear, the time comes inevitably when

the job hunter, who once would have been asked for his war record, begins to conceal it. All too soon, instead of winning him a position, such a record loses him one by advertising his age. It dates him. Worse than that, if he is cursed with undue longevity, it stamps him as out of date. If he lives too long, he becomes something of a joke; poignant because helpless, touching as a reminder, gallant as a symbol, but laughable as an anachronism.

This is cruel. This is shocking. This is lamentable. This is the ultimate in ingratitude. Yet it is inescapable. And perhaps not without its signs of health. The inrushes of the present in every period are so insistent and confusing that no people could be expected to live in the past. The veteran who makes a career of being a veteran is not an endearing figure. We say too much about what the country owes us and never enough about what we owe the country. The true Welfare State is that in which citizens, instead of assuming that they will be subsidized, take it for granted that they must do everything in their power for the nation's welfare. It would consist of more givers than takers; be made up of the prideful, not the prideless. It would be a country of self-reliant individuals, not dependent groups; of producers rather than extractors.

At moments of danger, military service is an obligation which, when discharged, should not be converted into a profession. If one tires of the reminders of war, it is because one is anxious to get on with the fulfillments of peace. Time marches forward far faster than the fastest troops advancing into battle. Those ever-ready replacements, who are the young, are forever pushing to the front. In the relay race of history, the torch is passed so quickly from older to younger hands that no one ever sees it being passed.

Even the youngest and least reflective of the Legionnaires who met in Philadelphia, if they followed the story of the GAR's final encampment, must have sensed without pleasure that they too, due to the calendar's inexorability, will someday be condemned to the same kind of shrunken farewell. No doubt, these young Legionnaires were not downed for long by the thought. It is difficult to identify yesterday's sorrows with tomorrow's. Moreover, all things considered, including the urgencies of today's action, it is just as well that people have no inclination to do so.

"Never send to know for whom the bell tolls; it tolls for thee." Life would be insupportable, in fact it would be already death, if we squandered our time cupping our hands to hear that bell. For the GAR it has finished tolling.

England's famous Archer-Shee case as the source material for a play, and an infamous occurrence in a small American town which has made a travesty of both liberty and justice.

[1947]

"LET RIGHT BE DONE"

AMONG THE great cases brought to trial, many and varied, solved and unsolved, but usually having to do with murder, the terrifying plight of Master Archer-Shee holds a fascination of its own. Unlike most courtroom battles of similar notoriety, this one involved no throat cut, no gun fired, no culprit to be hanged.

There was a culprit, however. More accurately, there were two culprits—the Royal Naval Academy at Osborne and the British Admiralty. Though both of these were somewhat outsized for the noose, in this instance they deserved punishment. The crime for which they were responsible was against a small boy. It must, therefore, have seemed like a small crime. At least it must have to many impatient Britishers when first they read in their newspapers that their government, busy with imperial problems, was squandering its time on the guilt or innocence of a mere lad and his alleged theft of a sum too trifling to capture the attention of light-fingered politicians.

No wonder the case caught the interest of the world in those quieter days before the First World War when Martin Archer-Shee, young George's father, was resolved to spend his meager all clearing his innocent son's name. Or that Alexander Woollcott, connoisseur though he was in matters gory, had an especially warm spot in his hospitable heart for this particular trial. Or that

Terence Rattigan has based on this same suit *The Winslow Boy*,* which is beyond dispute the best play he has so far written.

The Archer-Shee case had its undeniable elements of drama. It did not reveal a timid Oliver Twist asking only for more porridge. It disclosed Oliver's parent boldly demanding, with the aid of so pre-eminent an advocate as Sir Edward Carson, full justice for his son. The contest gained in absorption by being uneven. It pitted one man (as "little" and commonplace as you and I) against the Crown. Hence it made that timeless raid on the sympathies which has always sent cheers into the throats of people everywhere when any David has dared to take on any Goliath in single combat.

There are other, and worthier, reasons why this case deserves remembrance. Infinitely more was at stake than a youngster's reputation, a father's proud and stubborn faith, or a forged and stolen five-shilling postal order. To men with a proper passion for freedom the trial abounded in overtones. Although the situation was exceptional, it touched upon the rights of average citizens. The principles for which the barons met at Runnymede were involved in the fate of a Liverpool family. A small boy and the Magna Charta suddenly and somehow found themselves fused.

Mr. Woollcott went straight to the matter's core. In his admirable retelling of the story in *Long, Long Ago* he described the incident as "a microcosm in which was summed up the long history of British liberty." "Here," said he, "in the small visible compass of one boy's fate was the entire issue of the inviolable sovereignty of the individual."

Mr. Rattigan is no less keenly aware of the implications of the case. His sensing of the story's ricochets and the taste with which he suggests rather than emphasizes these are proofs of his skill in *The Winslow Boy*. Since his concern is the case itself, and only the case, he is stalwart enough to forswear any hint of what actually became of young Archer-Shee. This was the final irony of an ironic career. The boy was thirteen when, in the fall of 1908, he

---

* *The Winslow Boy*, by Terence Rattigan. Directed by Glen Byam Shaw. Setting by Michael Weight. Presented by Atlantis Productions (the Theatre Guild, H. M. Tennent Ltd., John C. Wilson). With a cast including Alan Webb, Frank Allenby, Valerie White, and Michael Newell. At the Empire Theatre. Opened October 29, 1947.

was dismissed from Osborne. Two long and costly years passed before his good name was publicly made good again.

You may feel that Fate by then had already been overgenerous in dealing him unlucky cards. She had been. Even so she had an-other card, this time an ace of spades, tucked up her sleeve. She slipped it on the table, face up, when he was nineteen. The August of that year, when the First World War broke out, found (accord-ing to Mr. Woollcott) young Archer-Shee working in New York City for the Wall Street firm of Fisk and Robinson. England was calling up her young men. His love for her was undiminished. He managed to get home. He managed, too, and quite understand-ably, to get into the Army this time rather than the Navy. He also managed to get over to France. Yes, and to get killed at Ypres in the war's first October.

It is the earlier misfortunes of this same ill-starred English youth to which Mr. Rattigan limits himself. He follows the real case closely in all its key incidents and legal aspects. He may move it a little closer on the calendar to the previous war. The Archer-Shees may have become the Winslows. The Winslows may live in Lon-don's Kensington instead of Liverpool. Sir Edward Carson may have been rechristened Sir Robert Morton. The older son may have ceased to be an M.P., a major, and a D.S.O., and dwindled for dramatic contrast into an undergraduate, more devoted to his Victrola than his studies, who must sacrifice his degree at Oxford in order to save money for his father's battle for justice. The family may now include a daughter whose marriage to a prig is called off because of the prospective father-in-law's objections to the publicity the trial is attracting.

Nonetheless, the major incidents in a deeply moving story re-main identical. The curt letter of dismissal from Osborne. The family's despair. The father's mobilized resolve to demand a hear-ing. Sir Edward's pulverizing cross-examination in private of Master Archer-Shee before he would undertake the defense. The intricate maneuvering necessary to secure a public trial by having a Petition of Right reach the King and having the monarch scrawl across it the stirring words, "Let right be done." The family's con-stant temptation to be practical rather than idealistic. The collapse on the witness stand of the postmistress's flimsy testimony. The final triumph in the courtroom, and the crowds cheering on the streets outside, for the courageous father, for Sir Edward, and, more particularly, for justice. The humanizing fact that the boy was young enough to sleep soundly when the case was reaching its crescendo and had slipped off to a theatre when the verdict was turned in. All these true occurrences chart the action of *The Winslow Boy*.

It is to Mr. Rattigan's credit, however, that he has found his own ingenious ways of developing them, motivating them, and illustrating them in dramatic form. The first two of his four scenes are especially effective. If the last two, though still interesting, lose something of the tightness and urgency of their predecessors, it is because Mr. Rattigan is unwilling to follow his story into the courtroom where it belongs. Instead, he continues to place it in the Winslow living room. This means that several of the characters begin to function as Greek messengers. They must not only tell us what is happening at the trial, when we would like to see and hear it for ourselves, but they are forced into improbable explanations of their own absence from it.

Despite this slight falling off, *The Winslow Boy* provides an engrossing evening. It is, if anything, better played here than it was in London. As the unfortunate child, Michael Newell continues to give a poignant performance, unspoiled by any blemishes of the stage brat. His suffragette sister is acted by Valerie White so that she dispels for all time the myth that a young woman cannot be at once causeful and desirable. Alan Webb admirably realizes the wit, the crotchets, the kindness, and the averageness of the father. And, as Sir Robert, Frank Allenby succeeds in projecting a figure formidable of mind and austerely aristocratic in appearance, where Emlyn Williams created a barrister who was fearsome to the point of being monstrous.

In a world where the importance of the individual has dwindled, where it is frankly menaced by bureaucratic encroachments, where the respect for what is expedient has alarmingly outdistanced the regard for what is right, and where in many countries there is not even a pretense to justice as we understand the word, the restatement in *The Winslow Boy* of the Archer-Shee case acquires a special significance.

Though it provides theatregoers with an absorbing evening, it cannot be classified as mere make-believe. It is too near the brave and hopeful truth for that. Its almost factual account of how one English family was willing to sacrifice everything for a principle compels us to look into ourselves and wonder how we, as Americans, would act, collectively and individually, under similar circumstances.

The British love of "fair play," especially within their own borders and certainly in the instance of Englishman *versus* Englishman, is a national characteristic so generally admitted as to have become a cliché. The same esteem in which the French hold logic, which we show for personal independence, the British have for justice. It is a British passion; the passion of a people who pride themselves upon keeping their other passions in check.

Mr. Woollcott was right beyond fear of contradiction by Goebbels' ghost or *The Daily Worker* when he said the Archer-Shee case could not have happened in any totalitarian state. He described its story of a whole nation getting worked up about a little matter of principle, and the foremost men of the land taking up the cudgels against the state because a youngster had been unfairly treated, as being "peculiarly English." I wonder. I hope not.

Recently I was in Des Moines. A friend there was kind enough to show me a story which had appeared three days earlier on the front page of that truly liberal, truly courageous newspaper, the *Des Moines Register*. It was a terrible and disheartening story, so ably written by George Shane, a staff writer, that I trust it will come to the attention of the Pulitzer judges.

As I read it, I could not help thinking back to the Archer-Shee case. In condensing the story here, I lean heavily on Mr. Shane and apologize to him for the damage I shall do to his own telling of it. Had I been able to get a plane, and had my lecture schedule permitted, I would have flown down to the southwest corner of Iowa myself. For there it was in a small town of six hundred people, a town known ironically as Pacific Junction, that the whole distressing incident occurred and that, though our own passion for "fair play" showed itself, American justice was reduced to a farce.

Pacific Junction, I gather, is a sleepy village. It includes some two dozen stores, one of which is just now being remodeled into a gospel hall. Mr. Shane noted a couple of sheep grazing in the yard of one home in the eastern part of the business district. Apparently no one would guess from looking at so tranquil a scene that a favorite boast of the place is that "no nigger can light in Pacific Junction for more than twenty-four hours." Not everyone there is prejudiced. Only eighty per cent, one witness guessed later. But, because of them, the other twenty per cent are afraid to speak out.

Well—an American citizen, unaware of this boast, did venture into this town. He just happened to be a Negro. His error, a simple and natural one, was to mistake the place for an American city. No doubt he believed, certainly he behaved as if, he was a free man in the land of freedom. His name was Alfred Twitty, and he came from Washington, D.C. I name him at once because, though he is the person most concerned, he seems to have dropped out of the picture entirely. By now he has long since moved on to another town. I trust one more hospitable, more American.

Twitty had some money on him. He was neat, clean, well spoken, and, in this land of free enterprise, willing to work. Bill Johnson, a local café owner, could, and did, testify to all this. He had paid and fed Twitty for mopping his restaurant. In the opinion of the woman cook, Twitty "did a good job of cleaning up."

But Twitty made a mistake. As an American citizen, he dared to walk openly down a street. It was there that he ran into the mayor of Pacific Junction, John Lutter. Lutter is a man of fifty-eight who has held his high office for two years. Before then he had served thirty-four and a half years in the Navy, specializing in submarine torpedoes. He was a chief warrant officer when he was honorably discharged on February 1, 1945.

Lutter was looking for the Negro. He was aware, as Twitty was not, of Pacific Junction's boast. "I believe you are mooching for work and are a vagrant," was the mayor's charming substitute for a welcome.

Later, when the case had come to trial before a Justice of the Peace, Lutter caused laughter in the courtroom by mimicking the Negro's answer in "a Deep South voice." What Twitty had replied

was only, "Ah'm willin' to work; Ah'm no vagrant." Nothing more.
Nothing less. Even if his accent was the same as Bilbo's. Funny
that. Funny as hell. This answer did not satisfy the mayor. He
gave the Negro an hour to leave town.

When Lutter saw Twitty on Main Street a half-hour later, he
repeated his warning. This time, however, Twitty was not alone.
This is where the story suddenly brightens.

Six young citizens, five of them veterans, were with the Negro
now, discussing his case. He had not known what to do. He had
appealed to them. One was Victor Hopkinson, twenty-nine, a
millworker; married and the father of three children. Another was
Richard E. Stoney, twenty. He is an electrician now, but he had
been in the Air Force. Then there was Otis Turner, also twenty.
He is a Navy veteran turned cement finisher. And Abe Fisher, Jr.,
age not given, at present a carpenter, who served with the Navy
in the South Pacific. There was also Lawrence Turner, twenty-
eight. Although at present a millhand, he went overseas with the
34th Division. For twenty-nine months Turner had been a prisoner
in a German camp. He admitted later that these months had given
him "quite a bit" of time in which to speculate on man's inhu-
manity to man. As he put it, in notable words, "If some of these
prejudiced people in Pacific Junction went through that for half
that time, they would have a lot better understanding of how to
live and let live."

Finally there was Russell Coppock, thirty-four. He is a college
graduate; is married, and has four sons ranging from three to seven.
For a year he has taught in Pacific Junction. He is also the coach
at the high school. Spiritually, he must be a cousin of the elder
Archer-Shee. He is made of the same stuff and, as you will see,
shares the same passion for right. He comes by this willingness to
protest naturally. It is in his blood. He may spell his name differently, but he is descended from the family which contributed the
Coppoc brothers, Edwin and Barclay, of Springdale, Iowa, to
John Brown for the 1859 raid on the Federal Arsenal at Harpers
Ferry.

These were the six young Americans Mayor Lutter encountered when, after his first warning to the Negro, he again
approached Twitty half an hour later. Warrant officers are not

fond of receiving orders from enlisted men. What these veterans were saying must have sounded uncomfortably like insubordination to Lutter's indignant ears.

The six men were excited. Properly so. They may even have been a little angry. Why not? It would have been disgraceful had they not been. At least one of them shook a raised finger in the mayor's face. When it came to Lutter's right to run the Negro out of town, they had their definite opinions. "God damn it, you can't do that!" they shouted. "Very harshly," the mayor later testified, "as if they were going to show me." As Lawrence Turner put it, "This is the kind of thing we fought a war to do away with."

Hopkinson offered Twitty his shed as a night's lodging. Lawrence Turner was subsequently quoted (again filthy laughter in the courtroom) as saying the Negro could sleep with him. Lutter would have none of this. "By God," cried he, shaking his fist. "I'm running this town."

What happened thereafter is no less shameful than what had already occurred. The mayor did not file a charge against the Negro, but Twitty did leave town. He spent his last night in Pacific Junction sleeping in the depot, waiting for a train to take him to some other refuge in this country founded as a refuge for those in search of freedom.

His defenders, however, faced their difficulties, too. Mayor Lutter swore out warrants the next day against the six of them. The charge was interference with an officer through "violent and tumultuous assembly."

The men are scarcely to be blamed for raising their voices both on the street and later when they were hauled to the home of Mrs. Lola Boquette, Justice of the Peace. I find it heartening that their sense of outrage was so strong that they made it impossible for Mrs. Boquette's husband, a railway engineer, to continue reading his evening paper in the same house.

When the Negro's six defenders were given a one-day trial in nearby Glenwood before a six-man jury of their peers, they were found guilty on the first ballot. The jurors recommended, however, that any fine or sentence be suspended. In passing sentence Justice of the Peace William P. Allbee, who confessed he had "thought all night how to make this agreeable to the public," fined each of the young men $25 plus costs of $31.50 to be divided among the group, or $5.25 each. Since the sentence was suspended, the men did not have to pay the $25 fines. But they did have to pay the costs.

To be sure, on the eve of the trial an offer was made that charges would be dropped if the defendants would "apologize" to the mayor. To their credit, and America's also, all six men declined.

Five of them, upon having paid their $5.25, concluded that they could not fight the case further. They had neither the money nor the time. They would have to drop out of it, even as Twitty had dropped out of sight.

Coppock was different. Of course, there were friends—practical people—who came to him and said he should not have got mixed up in the whole affair. They were quick to remind him he had a wife and children to look after. But he, as I say, had in his veins something of that precious fire which burned in Archer-Shee's. Furthermore, he *was* being practical. He knew that back in Pacific Junction his chances of reappointment as a teacher would be slight under a mayor he had dared to oppose. What will happen in the future, I do not know. I am cheered to find that Coppock is continuing his battle and that the Civil Liberties Union has come to his assistance.*

All of which takes me back to *The Winslow Boy* and Mr. Woollcott's insistence that the case upon which it is based was "peculiarly British." Coppock persuades me that it was not. At least in the willingness of an individual to espouse the cause of right. Yet there is a disgraceful difference between the two trials. That we in America share the British love of justice, white man to white man, no one can deny. When we say justice, however, we apparently do not mean equal justice for all Americans.

Justice is a matter of conviction, not of pigmentation. Until we have advanced to the necessary point where all people living in this country are recognized, in and out of the law courts, as Americans, our usage of the word "justice" is bound to be no more than

---

* It is heartening to learn that on March 25, 1948, Russell Coppock was exonerated, but disheartening to realize that no amends whatsoever have been made to Twitty.

mockery; the kind of mockery it was recently in Glenwood and Pacific Junction.

"Let right be done," indeed.

Some well-meant but misguided and dangerous attempts to achieve tolerance by intolerant means, or the folly of pretending that what was wasn't and what is isn't.

[1949]

WISHFUL BANNING

MR. CHURCHILL'S is the right approach. Explaining in *Their Finest Hour* why epidemics did not sweep London when millions were crowded in air-raid shelters, he says, "Man is a gregarious animal, and apparently the mischievous microbes he exhales fight and neutralize each other. They go out and devour each other, and Man walks off unharmed." Then Mr. Churchill adds, "If this is not scientifically correct, it ought to be."

There are so many things that ought to be, even if they are not. The microbes which assail men's minds are as mischievous as those which attack their bodies. One wishes that they too would fight and neutralize each other, allowing Man to walk off unharmed. Unquestionably they should, but they do not, as is proved by the epidemic of odd and sorry suppressions which has swept the world with increasing fury since V-J Day and the coming of the "cold war" or, more accurately, the hot peace.

Freedom was a big and beckoning word in wartime. There were even the Four Freedoms, the first of which was dedicated to "freedom of speech and expression—everywhere in the world." The fourth—who can have forgotten it?—promised freedom from fear. The source of fear it suggested did not go far enough. It was limited to aggressive warfare. It failed to include those other fears which can destroy freedom of speech. I mean those fears to which minorities and special groups appear to be heir; those fears born of insecurity, false pride, hypersensitivity, or a strange, self-deluding surrender to the notion that safety and esteem can be guaranteed by the placing of a ban or the action of a censor.

Take the now notorious case of *Oliver Twist*. This British film has provoked rioting among displaced Polish Jews in Berlin. Protests against it have been lodged by Jews in Vienna and other Old World cities. So far its public release is not planned in the United States. Indeed, it has been prohibited in New York because of the action taken by the New York Board of Rabbis under the leadership of Rabbi Theodore N. Lewis, who admits he has not seen the film.

Why this rioting, these protests, and this suppression? Of course because of Fagin, because some Jews there and here have objected to the alleged indignity done their people by showing on the screen a Jew who is such a deep-dyed villain. Their fear is that Fagin will arouse anti-Semitism, that movie audiences will forget Fagin is a caricature of an individual and be persuaded that all Jews are Fagins. Precious few of the millions still free to read Dickens' novel have, I will wager, succumbed to such an error. Yet this is the point of view as stated by Rabbi Lewis. The Rabbi, incidentally, is as adamant on the subject of *The Merchant of Venice* as he is on *Oliver Twist*. He is determined to have it kept off the stage and banned from schoolrooms for the same reasons—because in his eyes Shylock and Fagin are equally insulting, unbearable, and dangerous as characterizations of Jews.

I know this is the Rabbi's attitude because I heard him state it when he appeared on the television program *Critic-at-Large* with Morris Ernst, Louis Kronenberger, and myself. In combating the Rabbi's stand, the three of us found ourselves as one. All of us abhorred the idea of such censorship. All of us felt that it was contrary to the American tradition. All of us insisted that the film was entitled to be shown before being condemned and that, if it proved offensive, the case could and should be carried to the courts. All of us expressed our conviction that the Rabbi, with the best of good intentions, was doing his people greater harm than good. All of us believed that more anti-Semitism would result from such a banning by a minority pressure group than would ever be created by Fagin.

Mr. Ernst was the only one of us who had seen the film, a fact which did not subtract from his right to an opinion. Instead of being offended by *Oliver Twist,* he had found it commendable as a transference of a classic to the screen. Mr. Kronenberger's judgment was that literature could not get along without its villains, and that a villain role in *Oliver Twist* on or off the screen just happened to be Fagin's, precisely as it was Bill Sikes's or the Artful Dodger's.

When I asked the Rabbi if, on the basis of his logic, the Danes would not be justified in picketing *Hamlet,* since it shows that a Danish prince can be indecisive, Mr. Kronenberger pointed out that the Danes had an even more valid reason for suppressing the play—i.e., it specifically states that there is something rotten in the state of Denmark.

The Jews who have protested against *Oliver Twist* and sought to have it, *The Merchant of Venice,* and now it seems *Ivanhoe,* banned are not the only persons who have reached for censorship as a weapon with which to combat the horrors of racial or religious discrimination. Some Negro groups appear to be equally touchy, just as humorless, and no less given to trying to change what is past, or pretending that classics, written long ago and still available, can be unwritten and erased from men's minds by the edict of a censor.

There was, for example, the case of *Uncle Tom's Cabin*—of all things. Three years ago in Bridgeport a new musical version of it was temporarily banned because of the protests sent in by CIO Negro groups, the Bridgeport Pastors' Association, and the Communist Party. Their incredible objection was that *Uncle Tom's Cabin* "refreshed memories that tend to portray only the weaknesses of a racial minority," and held up to ridicule "peoples who in the early days of our country were unfortunately subjected to exposures that today would be considered atrocious." In other words, the desire of these protesting Negroes was to forget, and have others forget, that their people had ever been slaves.

What they forgot, however, was that it was the slave owner, not the slave, who came out badly in Mrs. Stowe's pages. They also seemed willing to overlook entirely how much *Uncle Tom's Cabin* had done for their people. Yes, and to deny the encouragement it offers today by making clear how far both the whites and the Negroes in this country have advanced since the novel first needed to be written. Booker T. Washington did not attempt to dodge history when he wrote his autobiography. He called his volume *Up from Slavery*. The significant word in his title is not the "Slavery." It is the "Up."

There are, too, some well-meaning Negroes, working for that true realization of democracy which should be every American's preoccupation, who object even to *The Green Pastures,* I am told, because they find its naïveté offensive and because the young people in Mr. Deshee's Sunday School class have not a sufficiently enlightened conception of the Bible. There are other Negroes, just as well-meaning and just as falsely sensitive, whose hope is said to be to have *Little Black Sambo* suppressed. Their reason, I gather, is that Little Black Sambo, so endearing as a figure of all childhood, has a rather wholesale appetite for pancakes and is afraid of tigers!

The pressures of Catholic groups are no less evident. The suppression of *The Nation* in the public schools of New York City, because it ran a series of articles critical of the Catholic Church, is a case in point. So, of course, are the operations of the Legion of Decency in the realm of filmdom. The Legion does not have to ban to make itself felt. Fear of its disapproval exerts a constant influence upon motion-picture producers. Perhaps it was dread of this disapproval which resulted in the unfrocking of Cardinal Richelieu in the latest filming of *The Three Musketeers.* In the picture the Cardinal, a gifted and not unworldly cleric, though allowed to be as worldly as Dumas and history demand, is denied his robes, apparently in order to give no offense. Such pressures from other religious groups are, no doubt, continuous even if they are not so well organized.

In Chicago recently Jean-Paul Sartre's *The Respectful Prostitute* was banned. A police captain in charge of the Crime Prevention Bureau reported to his superior that the play was likely to provoke interracial troubles. This, in spite of the fact that it had run in New York for many months without having done so. One explanation which I read, and certainly an odd one, was that Sartre's script was "unfair to the Negro." Perhaps the final word about *The Respectful Prostitute* in Chicago came from Mayor Martin Kennelly. His enlightened statement was, "The title alone would ban it."

As further proof of the growing tendency to believe that abuses can be corrected by running away from the facts, let me cite two other examples. The first of these is the campaign which, out of the highest of motives, Walter Winchell conducted some time back against any comedians who dared to tell stories in dialect. As if all of us did not speak with dialects; as if dialects were not part of the truth as well as the vigor of our speech! It is not the dialect —Jewish, Yankee, Southern, Western, Italian, Irish, or Scotch— which is offensive. It is the story told, the uses to which dialect can be put.

For my second illustration I must come a little nearer home. In fact, to the *Saturday Review of Literature* and an editor's note which appeared on the letters page. A well-intentioned reader from Charleston, S.C., had written in to ask when the magazine was going to stop "Jim Crowing" Negro writers. "If you always say a book is by a Negro, etc., you should, to be consistent, say another is by a white, etc.," wrote this correspondent. This was followed by one of those thunderous generalities, seemingly so fine in their liberalism, which unfortunately are apt to be as fuzzy-minded as they are untrue. "Only where literature has no race or religion will it be completely free."

Although I cannot speak for anyone else, I know I was saddened and distressed to read the editor's answer. It said, "After having applauded various publishers for omitting racial identification in their promotion of Negro authors, we are ashamed of ourselves. It won't happen again." Rot!

Certainly I would agree that nothing is gained and only harm done by insisting upon cataloguing a writer as a Negro, if his book has nothing to do with the problems which he himself has faced as a Negro. But I do not see how anyone could make an intelligent or just approach to such volumes, say, as Richard Wright's *Black Boy*, Walter White's *A Man Called White*, William Gardner Smith's *The Last of the Conquerors,* or Ann Petry's *The Street,* without mentioning the fact that the Americans who wrote these books are Negroes. The whole point of their writing and the reason for their having been written as they are is that they reflect the handicaps and humiliations to which Americans who are Negroes are heir. The source of their authority is that their authors are what they are.

As I see it, any citizen of the United States is an American. It is as simple as that. Yet it is absurd to pretend that all Americans, just because they live here, are sprung from the same race, are of the same color and the same religion, have the same accents, enjoy identical opportunities, are equally endowed, and have been exposed to the same agonies or privileges. These differences are facts. To ignore them is to surrender to the silliest and most self-deluding form of ostrichism.

We get nowhere by banning books just because they contain characters which do not flatter us. We get nowhere by pretending that there are not heroes and villains of all creeds and colors. We get nowhere by allowing any minorities to enjoy what John Haynes Holmes has admirably described in the *Saturday Review of Literature* as a "literary immunity from the sins that beset the rest of the human family." Our one hope is to face the facts.

Nowadays we appear to be misled by the best of good intentions. To conquer the horrors of intolerance and racial or religious discrimination, we seem more and more inclined to turn to the book-burning tactics of our enemy in the last war or to the gross suppressions of our opponent in the present peace. Neither literature nor freedom gains anything by such means. Certainly minorities are entitled to the protection of their rights. But in a democracy a majority also has its rights. "Ye shall know the truth, and the truth shall make you free." Apparently there are those today who would reverse this, and have it read: avoid the truth, and such avoidance shall make you free. Thomas Jefferson's "I have sworn on the altar of God eternal hostility to every form of tyranny over the mind of man" is a pledge which nowadays is as important to minorities as it is to majorities. That is, if freedom which is everywhere imperiled is to endure as we have cherished it and enjoyed its benefits.

A play in which an old Communist finds himself the victim of the order he helped create and, though he knows the truth, dies telling the lie that his imprisoned mind makes natural to him.

[1951]

THE IRON TRANSPARENCY

"I SERVED THE Communist Party for seven years—the same length of time as Jacob tended Laban's sheep to win Rachel his daughter. When the time was up, the bride was led into his dark tent; only the next morning did he discover that his ardors had been spent not on the lovely Rachel but on the ugly Leah. I wonder whether he ever recovered from the shock of having slept with an illusion. I wonder whether afterwards he believed that he had ever believed in it."

In this manner, and a vivid manner it is, Arthur Koestler concludes his contribution to *The God That Failed*. Surely most readers interested in following the inner workings of the Communist Party and learning the extent to which it degrades and humiliates artists and thinkers must by now have read this important anthology. In it such writers as Ignazio Silone, Richard Wright, André Gide, Louis Fischer, Stephen Spender, and Mr. Koestler have frankly analyzed the misplaced idealism which in the twenties or thirties persuaded them to become Party members. With the utmost candor they have described their disillusioning experiences and given the reasons which sooner or later compelled them to renounce a faith that had failed them. Although each of these "confessions" is fascinating, in none is the sense of betrayed hope more graphically stated than in Mr. Koestler's allusion to Jacob and Leah.

Painful as Mr. Koestler's misadventures must have been, his "Lost Weekend in Utopia" was by no means wholly lost. Out of those seven years (1931-1938) of strange assignments, mysterious meetings, two imprisonments, journeys to Russia and Spain, and acquaintanceship with stalwart revolutionists who were fated to be executed after trials that were mockeries of justice, came *Darkness at Noon.* And few would dispute, unless as card-carrying Party members they were forced to do so, that this novel, which Sidney Kingsley has dramatized,* is one of the finest to have emerged from our tumultuous times.

A decade has passed since *Darkness at Noon* was published. But the years, which bury books unmercifully, have not been able to rob Mr. Koestler's novel of its life. Although its initial impact was tremendous, its power continues undiminished. As a matter of fact, with each rereading *Darkness at Noon* seems the more remarkable. The muscularity of its thinking, the skill of its planning, the vividness of its characterizations, the adroitness with which it shuttles from past to present, and the sense it creates of inhabiting a tortured mind (indeed, many minds, including the reader's) while it is laying bare the horrors of a governmental dream which has become a nightmare—all these are merits that stand out more unmistakably on the fourth reading than on the first.

Equally notable is the manner in which Mr. Koestler has avoided the usual stencils and the expected physical brutalities a propagandist would have relied on. He was writing from disenchantment, no doubt from sorrow and anger too, about a topical event. He shared the outrage which rocked the world when the so-called Moscow Trials made a gauze transparency of that dividing curtain now spoken of as being iron. His, however, must have been a special fury when, as one of the enraptured, he was forced to realize that the cause upon which he had squandered his ardors was a Leah, not a Rachel. His book was dedicated to the memory of the men he had known personally who were victims of those trials. He had every reason for allowing bitterness to get the better of his skill and scorn to submerge his craftsmanship. But Mr.

---

* *Darkness at Noon,* a dramatization by Sidney Kingsley of the novel by Arthur Koestler. Staged by Mr. Kingsley. Settings and lighting by Frederick Fox. Costumes by Kenn Barr. Associate producer, May Krishner. Presented by the Playwrights' Company. With a cast including Claude Rains, Walter J. Palance, Alexander Scourby, Philip Coolidge, Richard Seff, Allan Rich, Kim Hunter, Herbert Ratner, Norman Roland, Will Kuluva, and Geoffrey Barr. At the Alvin Theatre. Opened January 13, 1951.

Koestler, being the exceptional writer he is, did more than keep himself and his materials under control. He was able to transform what in lesser hands could easily have provided the stuffs of indignant journalism into a work of art.

His story of how Rubashov, an old and famous Communist, is imprisoned and put to death for crimes of which he was innocent, is a masterly piece of work. No book of the many I have read on Soviet Russia or Communism has demonstrated so memorably how the Communist intellect, in or out of prison, is always imprisoned. None has shown in terms more terrifying how in Stalin's Russia the "means" have become the "ends." None has presented more graphically the cleavage which divides the older Party members from the younger generation they have spawned, a generation born (in Rubashov's phrase) without an umbilical cord.

The excellences of Mr. Koestler's novel are many. Among these count the sweep of its narrative, the firm sketching of its vignettes, the expert use it makes of small sensory details such as the smell of Gletkin's revolver belt, the tension of its cross-examinations, its depiction of the miseries and hungers of those who huddle in prison cells, and the brilliance with which it gets at the very essence of ideas. No feature of the book, however, is more admirable than Mr. Koestler's delineation of Rubashov. He is drawn without sentimentality, a figure every bit as ruthless as his opponents. His final tragedy is that though he has come to see the Party's faults he cannot forsake its precepts. He dies a perpetuator of the lie, fully aware of the crimes that are, yet willing to confess to crimes he himself has not committed.

Almost inevitably some of the literary qualities of *Darkness at Noon* have been mislaid in the process of bringing it to the stage. This was bound to be so, considering the very form and nature of the novel. Even so, and to a degree I would have thought impossible, Mr. Kingsley has succeeded in both his production and his dramatization in turning a fine book into an exciting and distinguished evening in the theatre. Mr. Koestler may be a man of genius and Mr. Kingsley a man of ingenuity. In the world behind the footlights, however, Mr. Kingsley's ingenuity is not to be underestimated.

The major performance of the evening is, of course, Claude Rains' Rubashov. Always a good actor, Mr. Rains has sometimes in the past been tempted to be too much of an actor. His Rubashov, however, never gets out of hand. It is beautifully controlled and modulated, underplayed rather than overplayed, and doubly effective for this very reason. The demands of the part are backbreaking. Quite aside from what it represents as a feat of memory, its other requirements for concentration are merciless. Yet Mr. Rains manages to meet all these tests triumphantly. The iron of Rubashov is in him, the knifelike quality of his mind, the habit of command, and the force that is his.

The human being is also there, alive though submerged, but guilty of thinking and feeling at moments in terms of the first person singular. This is a sin according to the Party. It is a bourgeois weakness which Mr. Koestler described as "the grammatical fiction." Nonetheless, the fact that Rubashov is a man no less than a Communist, even though an individual stifled and ultimately self-erasing because of loyalty to the Party, is a source of the strength both of Mr. Rains' playing and Mr. Koestler's and Mr. Kingsley's writing.

I notice that some of my confreres have complained because in his dramatization Mr. Kingsley has named the USSR as the setting of his play whereas Mr. Koestler specified no country in his novel. Surely this is an illogical objection. Mr. Koestler's dedication made clear beyond doubt the scene he had in mind. So, for that matter, did the story he had to tell on each of its haunting pages. It would seem a little late in the day for liberals, no matter how liberal, to pretend to themselves that *Darkness at Noon* is laid in Cuckoo-Borough-on-Clouds. It is, alas, anchored in reality and its truth is part of its power.

The terrible plight of the artist in Soviet Russia, and the stirring speech with which Meyerhold courageously chose to end his career.

[1951]

"PEOPLE'S ARTIST"

AT THE third cross-examination Gletkin had said, "Your testimony at the trial will be the last service you can do the Party." He was speaking to Rubashov, one of the revered makers of the Revolution, who was facing sentence of death on some trumped-up charges of counterrevolutionary activities. As everyone knows who has read Arthur Koestler's *Darkness at Noon* or seen Sidney Kingsley's dramatization of it, Rubashov did go to his death, having performed his final service to the Party by telling the expected lie.

"Citizen Judges," he had said at the travesty of justice which was his trial—"Citizen Judges, covered with shame, trampled in the dust, about to die, I will describe to you the sad progress of a traitor, that it may serve as a lesson and terrifying example to the millions of our country. . . ."

Such words of self-abasement have a familiar ring. They fit into a pattern the contemporary world has come to know all too well. They may still seem incredible to men whose minds are free. They may sicken those who live in countries accustomed to prizing the individual. Even so, every sudden shift in the Kremlin's policy, every purge that such a shift has brought about, and every public trial staged in Moscow have forced us in spite of the stubbornness of our disbelief to expect such a crumbling of will and distortion of truth.

If I come back to Rubashov and *Darkness at Noon*, it is because I have been reading with fascination and a heavy heart *Taming of the Arts.** This is a backstage account of what happened between

---

* By Juri Jelagin. Translated from the Russian by Nicholas Wreden. New York: E. P. Dutton, 1951.

1930 and 1940 to music and the theatre under the Soviet dictator-ship. Its author is Juri Jelagin, a Russian-born violinist, who was intimately acquainted with the artists of Moscow. Formerly he was attached to the Vakhtangov Theatre. He then became a member of the Moscow Conservatory. As a soloist, he gave concerts that carried him on tours even to Siberia. During the war he was captured by the Germans and deported. Since then he has come to this country and is now with the Houston Symphony.

In Mr. Jelagin's pages can be found the words spoken publicly by another famous revolutionary figure when he too had fallen into disfavor. In this instance the speaker was not a fictional character. He was Vsevolod Meyerhold, one of the modern theatre's best-known directors, the first important manager to proclaim himself a Communist in the days of the Revolution, and a leader of the Soviet stage so outstanding that he had long since been made a "People's Artist."

There are hundreds of incidents in *Taming of the Arts* dealing with the strange and unhappy experiences of such artists as Stanislavski, Tairov, Kachalov, Maxim Gorki, Aleksei Tolstoi, Vakhtangov, and Shostakovich, which tempt me to touch upon them. There are stories which I find hard to resist retelling about Stalin, his sudden telephone calls, his likes and dislikes in music and the drama, and the ordeal of an actor who understandably lost his voice when he had to impersonate Uncle Joe with Stalin in the audience. There is the cumulative picture, drawn unforgettably by Mr. Jelagin, of the dizzying privileges, the abrupt reprimands, merciless dismissals, and general uneasiness of Soviet artists that I should like to discuss at length. If I single out Meyerhold's story and concentrate upon it I have my personal reasons for doing so.

I met Meyerhold three or four times in Paris in the distant summer of 1928. He was then at the height of his power, an imperious-looking man to whom command came naturally. His face was thin and decisive. There was no mistaking his force or the fact that he was accustomed to acclaim. He was so highly regarded by his government that his theatre had been chosen to represent the USSR at the International Season which Firmin Gémier was holding at the Odéon. How I met him I cannot remember, but I also met his actress-wife, Zinaida Raikh, a pretty brunette who, as I recall her, resembled a somewhat plump version of Pola Negri. With the aid of a French woman who acted as interpreter we managed to carry on the semblance of conversations.

I was then a recent graduate of the staff of the old *Theatre Arts Monthly* and was very anxious to go to Russia in order to study its stage. I had tried without success in London, Stockholm, Copenhagen, and Berlin to get permission to enter the Soviet Union in those days when we had no diplomatic relations. Had it not been for Meyerhold my request would have been turned down again in Paris. He, however, was kind enough to take my case in hand, and I soon realized how powerful his hand was.

He took me to the Soviet Embassy and put in a long-distance call to Moscow, and within a few days I received my permit. It was as simple as that. Meyerhold's helpfulness did not stop there. He insisted, since he would be in Paris, that my friend and I should stay at his apartment in Moscow during the two weeks we were allowed to remain in Russia. On our arrival his secretary met us with a car at the airport, and everything during our visit was made the easier because of the magic of his name.

All this, as I say, was in 1928. At that time the Soviet theatre, in spite of its wearisome preoccupation with propagandist themes, was extraordinarily stimulating in its production techniques. Its vitality was tremendous. Its importance as a means of mass instruction was recognized by the authorities. Its artists enjoyed exceptional privileges. Its offerings were of many kinds and styles. The battle line had not yet been drawn between "bourgeois formalism" and "socialistic realism," whatever those mystifying terms may mean.

In that throbbing world of the Soviet stage no person was more dominant or more respected than Meyerhold. He was the high priest of the revolutionary theatre, the innovator of innovators, the radical of radicals, the champion of constructivism, and the creator of such renowned experimental productions as his tradition-destroying *The Inspector General* and *Roar China!* He had won the idolatry of the Party's leaders by asking actors to look upon themselves not as stars but as "instruments for social manifestoes," by relegating to the past the "soul junk" and "rickety ego" of bourgeois characters, and insisting that what mattered most behind the footlights was the glorification of the "unindividual."

Meyerhold's apartment, in which I stayed, may have been a

squalid, bug-infested, and dreary dump, but the government was building a beautiful new apartment house for him and his company. It was also planning to reward him by constructing a brand new playhouse, startling in its unorthodoxies. Though the ground was broken for this new theatre in 1934, the building was never to be completed. For soon thereafter Meyerhold himself was to learn how treacherous is the quicksand of official Soviet approval.

Mr. Jelagin reminds us that the atmosphere in Moscow began to change in 1934 when Sergei Kirov, one of Stalin's closest friends, was murdered. Two years later the terror was felt by everyone. Arrests were wholesale. The first of the great public trials had taken place. The one-time head of the NKVD had been arrested and the merciless Nikolai Yezhov had replaced him. Theatre after theatre became suspect. Shostakovich, who later was to recant in words very similar to Rubashov's, was denounced. Meyerhold enjoyed no immunity. He too was castigated. In 1936 he had dared to present his wife in a production of *Camille* which was sensitive and restrained and innocent of all the expected stunts. About the same time for the Leningrad opera he staged Tchaikovsky's *Queen of Spades* in an equally restrained manner.

Instantly *Pravda* turned its guns upon him. His theatre was described as being "foreign." Meyerhold was denounced as "the father of formalism." He was charged with having exercised a pernicious influence on other directors. He was singled out as the spokesman for hostile, anti-national tendencies. He was condemned for his desecrations of the classics. Most terrible of all, it was pointed out that in 1920 he had dedicated one of his productions to Leon Trotsky. Mr. Jelagin tells us that a few days after the appearance of the *Pravda* denunciation the Party took action. Meyerhold's theatre was liquidated by government decree, and the Committee on Arts ordered all the playhouses in the Soviet Union to hold meetings at which actors and directors were to condemn Meyerhold and endorse the government's procedure.

Meyerhold himself was not arrested. Being out of favor, however, meant that he was out of work. The only person in Moscow brave enough to offer him a job was old Stanislavski. Meanwhile the imprisonments and executions of artists multiplied. By 1938 it began to seem, according to Mr. Jelagin, as if the government were prepared to forgive Meyerhold. His name started to reappear in the press uncoupled with such adjectives as "formalistic" or "decadent." In June 1939 he was even asked by the Committee on Arts to be one of the speakers at the First National Convention of Theatrical Directors, soon to be held in Moscow. On the night of the meeting the auditorium was filled to overflowing. Everyone's expectation was that Meyerhold would follow the weasel's course, denounce his own work, praise his persecutors, and promise to reform. But Meyerhold could not bring himself to do what Shostakovich and many others have done. There was no Rubashov blood in him.

After two preliminary addresses the chairman announced, "The next speaker is Vsevolod Meyerhold." The auditorium rocked with applause. When Meyerhold appeared behind the desk, briefcase in hand, a tired, gray-haired man, the ovation continued from artists who had forgotten their differences with him and fully sympathized with his dilemma. Then he began to speak. Mr. Jelagin, who was there, says he started slowly, in a low, deliberate voice. Little by little a light came into his eyes. Before long his strengthening tones had in them the ring of steel.

Although the whole of Meyerhold's speech, as Mr. Jelagin has reported it, merits quoting, excerpts from it are enough to show how memorable it was. It was fierce in its integrity and thrilling in its courage.

Meyerhold began in the expected manner by seeming to admit his mistakes. Yet even when he enumerated them, it was clear that his spirit had not been broken. He spoke as an artist rather than a puppet. His old fire was not extinguished, his independence still flamed. His contempt for the inferior directors who had tried to imitate his style was as great as his pride in the best of his own work. His defiance grew with each bold sentence his conscience compelled him to utter. When he had failed, he said, he had done so only because he had exercised his right and need as a master to experiment.

With audacity he mentioned his "creative individualism." Next he mocked the mumbo-jumbo of such Communist aesthetic terms as "socialistic realism" and "anti-formalism." Then, knowing that his were self-destroying words, he rose magnificently to his peroration.

"I, for one, find the work in our theatres at present pitiful and terrifying. I don't know whether it is anti-formalism, or realism, or naturalism, or some other 'ism,' but I do know that it is uninspired and bad.

"This pitiful and sterile something that aspires to the title of socialistic realism has nothing in common with art. Yet the theatre is art, and without art there can be no theatre. Go to the Moscow theatres and look at the colorless, boring productions which are all alike and which differ only in their degree of worthlessness. No longer can anyone identify the creative signature of the Mali Theatre, of the Vakhtangov Theatre, of the Kamerny Theatre, or of the Moscow Art Theatre. In the very places where only recently creative life was seething, where men of art searched, made mistakes, experimented, and found new ways to create productions some of which were bad and others magnificent, now there is nothing but a depressing, well-meaning, shockingly mediocre, and devastating lack of talent.

"Was this your aim? If so you have committed a horrible deed. You have washed the child down the drain with the dirty water. In your effort to eradicate formalism you have destroyed art!"

What happened next? Meyerhold was arrested the following day and has never been heard from since. A few weeks later his wife was found in her apartment brutally murdered, with seventeen knife wounds in her body. The apartment was sealed by the NKVD and all personal property confiscated. In the autumn of that same 1939 a volume appeared in which a stenographic report was given of all the speeches made at that First Convention of Theatrical Directors. But, says Mr. Jelagin, Meyerhold's speech was missing and his name was not included in the list of those who attended. *Pravda*, to be sure, on June 15, 1939, had referred briefly to his appearance before the convention. This was the last time Meyerhold's name was mentioned in the Soviet press.

8. The Reach of Words

*The murder most foul, strange, and unnatural committed
on* Macbeth *by turning it into a comic book, and some of
the widespread misconceptions represented by such a deed.*

[1950]

KNOCK, KNOCK, KNOCK!

I DO NOT happen to know John W. Griffin, but on the basis of a
form letter he has written as president of Seaboard Publishers,
Inc., I am persuaded he is an utterly sincere man. Seaboard Publishers are manufacturers of comic books, and Mr. Griffin approaches
this sometimes unadmired industry as a realist and a reformer.

The little number he has sent my way as a trial balloon is,
of all things, a comic-book edition of William Shakespeare's *Macbeth.** Like many another so-called comic, this cartoon version
of Shakespeare's tragedy is not meant to be funny. Yet it must be
catalogued as a comic if for no other reason than that it employs
the methods and format of those polychrome publications which
are usually so classified. The result, to put it mildly, is a production of *Macbeth* quite different from any to which the play has
been exposed in its long and varied history.

Before coming to this new *Macbeth* it seems only fair to let
Mr. Griffin explain the service he thought he was performing
by undertaking it. Did I say Mr. Griffin was at once a realist and
a reformer? Let me make both points clear. Mr. Griffin reminds
us that over forty million comic magazines are sold each month
and nearly two hundred titles are regularly published, ranging, as
he puts it, "all the way from the completely harmless to some
which are highly objectionable." Furthermore, he says, and he
ought to know, though it depresses me to share this knowledge,
that such books "are about the only reading matter purchased by
many children and an increasing number of adults."

---

* *Macbeth*, by William Shakespeare. No. 6 in a Treasury of Celebrated
Literature; Stories by Famous Authors Illustrated. Adapted as a Comic Book
by Dana E. Dutch, illustrated by H. C. Kiefer, lettered by H. G. Ferguson.
New York: Seaboard Publishers, Inc. 30 pp. 10¢.

"The comics are here—and here to stay," states he, as if any parent would challenge him. Mr. Griffin's lofty aim, therefore, is to make the best of a bad situation by providing "as fine a 'comic book' as it is possible to produce." The first step toward doing this, he believes, is to derive comics from authors who have "real cultural worth." Hence this *Macbeth*.

In reading this *Macbeth* Mr. Griffin urges us to keep in mind the audience for which it has been written: "First, the adult who has read few, if any, solid, substantial books; and, second, the high-school student who is seeking an auxiliary aid to his high-school work." Mr. Griffin is well aware that his *Macbeth* is not "an effective substitute for the original." His hope is, however, that it will serve as a sufficient indication of "this great drama's . . . breadth and power" to lead perhaps some readers to Shakespeare himself.

A slight but not unwarranted uncertainty seems to have Mr. Griffin in its grip. At one moment he confidently risks the guess that his comic-book *Macbeth* will be recognized "as an interesting experiment in literature." At the next he invites a candid opinion as to whether it "will serve any good purpose" and if other such Shakespearean comics should be released.

My last desire is to be impolite to so well-meaning a fellow as Mr. Griffin. But, since he has asked for candor, candor he shall have. Mr. Griffin, it seems to me, is about as wrong-headed in his pursuit of what is right as it is possible to be. He is not lonely in his errors. Like many another, he appears to have been misguided by his good intentions. He and his benevolent associates at Seaboard have, in my opinion, succumbed in the name of literacy, culture, or what you will, to a list of fallacies based upon misconceptions so widespread that they merit discussion.

In fairness to Mr. Griffin and his firm it must be admitted that they are not the first offenders in a misleading practice. They are merely followers of a false tradition. There have been so-called classic comics for some time—comics masquerading as educational which have sought to turn such defenseless novels as *The Three Musketeers, Ivanhoe, Don Quixote, Moby Dick, The Last of the Mohicans,* or *Huckleberry Finn* into blood brothers of Li'l Abner, the Lone Ranger, Captain Marvel, Gandy and Sourpuss, Flash Gordon, and Mandrake the Magician.

These have been bad enough. That they were designed to do good I am willing to concede, but that they have succeeded in doing good I cannot bring myself to believe. They have had no other choice than to make molehills out of mountains and mud pies out of classics. For the misapprehension underlying them is the same one which lies behind this comic-book *Macbeth*.

In its fashion they have confused one medium with another. They have offered chromos with captions, asking their readers to accept them as masterpieces. They have peddled what is not even a substitute and pretended it was an equivalent. They have become victims of the false notion that those who might just as well be illiterates can be made lovers of literature by reading an aggressively unliterary version of a classic. Moreover, they have deceived American youngsters by inducing them to accept as truth an untruth apparently subscribed to by many of their elders; namely, that to know the story an author tells is not only to know the author and his book but to have shared in the pleasures and distinctions of his writing.

Gross as the vulgarities of these earlier classic comics have been, their offenses somehow seem mild compared to those which this cartoon *Macbeth* is bound to commit. To rob a prose writer of his prose can be, depending upon the writer in question, either petty or grand larceny. But to rob a sublime poet of his poetry and a supreme dramatist of the form at which he excelled is mayhem plus murder in the first degree.

Much as I love them, I have to confess that when Charles and Mary Lamb collaborated on their *Tales from Shakespeare* they set a bad example. Without their realizing it, they were opening wide the sluice-gates for future generations of lesser synopses manufacturers and addicts. Their hope was to earn a needed penny and to help a publisher friend. Elia had no illusions about the results. "I think it will be popular among the little people," wrote he. He was right. It was. Yet I doubt if he foresaw how numerous the "little people" were even then, how their numbers would multiply down the decades, and how abundantly they would, in our times, include alleged grown-ups in their ranks.

What Elia as the Bard's first nursery-popularizer would say of this new Mandrake-the-Magician adaptation of *Macbeth*, I tremble to think. My conviction is that he would be outraged by every picture and every caption on every page of the whole melancholy proceedings. For this very reason he would, no doubt, blush Kremlin-red because of his own share in the "Tales" which, though the work of angels compared to the witches' brew of this present-day *Macbeth,* inadvertently prepared the way for it.

Although I have sat through many revivals of the tragedy, some of which have claimed their scattered excellences but most of which have been inadequate, I never expected to be confronted with a production as wretched as the one these well-meaning publishers have made in the hope of tempting young people of all ages to Shakespeare. The plot is there, faithfully followed yet whittled down to its bare essentials, with all its excitements gone, its tensions lost, its scenes denied the suspense and terror of their building.

Snippets of the original dialogue are here and there to be encountered, running true for a sentence or two, then suddenly being cut, colloquialized, or altered so that the song of the speeches is muted, their sense abandoned, their grandeur destroyed. What once soared no longer has wings to flutter. It is earthbound throughout, a travesty of itself, and by its very solemnity almost a travesty of the ineptitudes of comics, too. Although the tale is murderous and gory, it never rises beyond cheap horror into true tragedy or even superb melodrama.

If the language deflates the drama, so do the drawings. The colors are hideous. The human figures are empty parodies of what the parts demand. The witches are Dogpatch-ugly without being Dogpatch-funny, and the medieval backgrounds are scenery of so outmoded a kind that even Edwin Forrest would have refused to play before them. The mystery of darkness, the supernatural terrors of the heath, the agonies of introspection, the drive and depth of the drama, indeed its greatness which in the theatre or in the library is its excuse and glory—all these are pitifully missing. What is left is not a tragedy. It is trashcan stuff.

Certainly no one can be hurt by knowing the story of *Macbeth.* Yet just as surely no one can pretend to know *Macbeth* who knows only its story and has encountered it in such a form. This is the glaring delusion to which Mr. Griffin and his confreres have surrendered in the interest of what they apparently believe, and would have their readers young and old believe, is "culture."

A final comment on their comic-book *Macbeth* is the note on its garish cover, "Adapted from the Original Text for EASY and ENJOYABLE Reading!" Perhaps one of the reasons so many people in this country have been left uneducated by their educations is that everything is made too easy for them. To be understood and enjoyed, the great works, which are the products of strong feeling or hard thinking, require similar responses. Giving of the best, they demand the best, to be appreciated. They cannot be vulgarized without being violated. Theirs is an integrity no less than a beauty which should summon from us an integrity of our own.

The difference between Shakespeare's *Macbeth* and Seaboard's is too great for comfort and almost great enough for nausea. Give me Li'l Abner and Daisy Mae any day. Please, Mr. Griffin and your high-minded associates, stop trying to create "culture" by deriving comics from authors who, in your unhappy phrase, "have real cultural worth." Let us have comics which are comics, not classics which have ceased to be classics but have dwindled into comics. Leave the masterpieces unraped. Don't fool yourselves and us by pretending that what they are not is what you would have us believe they are. Don't be guilty of trying to make everything easy. Greatness in literature is bound to present its challenges if not its difficulties. This is one of the reasons for its being enjoyable.

A devotee of Donald Duck is confronted for the first time with a tragedy called Hamlet.

[1946]

DISNEY AND THE DANE

OF COURSE, I wanted him to like it. I can't deny this. If I did, I would lie in my paternal teeth. Every parent knows the same hopes, the same fears when *that* afternoon at last comes around.

For both of us, this Saturday matinee was an adventure. For him, because it was the first time he had ever seen *Hamlet*; for me, because I was seeing it with him. And *Hamlet* shared with a boy of nine is *Hamlet* rediscovered.

He had seen other plays. *The Rose and the Ring*, for example, as done, and charmingly done, by the children of King-Coit School. This had been his initiation. In it he had found nothing to doubt, everything to believe, and suspense almost unbearable. But that had been at least five years back, when both he and the world were younger.

Since then he had seen *It Happens on Ice*. He had laughed at the clowns, marveled at the spectacle, and in a voice filled with dread asked at the conclusion of each number, "Is it all over now?" He had also seen *Oklahoma!* He had come to it, Victrola-prepared, knowing all its songs. "Neat" was the word for *Oklahoma!*

But Maurice Evans in the GI *Hamlet*—this was something else. He did not know its song. My fingers were crossed. As I say, I hoped he would like it. You never know; you can never tell.

No form of cruelty is more cruel than exposing the young, when still too young, to books and plays ill-fated enough to have become classics. It is a murderous error; the kind of sulphurous mistake of more than paving-stone size, for which only good intentions can be responsible. The fact that both the living and the dead are equally defenseless against such foul play is the measure of its meanness.

To make a chore out of what should be a pleasure, to put the curse of obligation on what was meant to be absorbing, is to kill in the child the willingness to be pleased, and in the classic the ability to please. Masterpieces are masterpieces not because such grim conspirators as parents or teachers have told us that they are good. They are masterpieces because they tell us so themselves.

Yet they cannot be expected to speak for themselves until we are ready to hear them. Not to coin a phrase, there's the rub. For that happy conjunction of the man and the moment is as necessary for a book and its reader as Matthew Arnold knew it to be for the emergence of greatness in this world. When that moment will tick itself off, no one can foretell. It depends entirely upon the book and the individual.

Fortunately *Hamlet* can be approached on various levels. The difficulties of its language may pass unnoticed. Its inner anguishes may not be comprehended. Still it tells a story—and such a story. To the modern, no less than to the Elizabethan, its action remains the first of its excitements. The Ph.D.s move in only when the playgoers have moved out.

Quite naturally, one would expect a child to be more interested in what happens in the play than in what happens within the Prince's mind. But nowadays a boy comes to *Hamlet*—oh, perish the word!—"conditioned" in ways productive of unforeseeable results.

These war years, for example. They have accustomed him and his friends to every known weapon of mechanized destruction. After frequent newsreel exposures to, and hourly imitations of, the crash of buzz bombs, the drone of airplane motors, the rumble of tanks, the rat-tat-tat of machine guns, the swish of rockets, and the roar of navy guns, would a world seem unbearably tame in which death is brought about by mere poison or the quiet click of foils?

Then the comic books, those appalling polychrome termites which eat their way into every home, no matter how well guarded; into every weekly allowance, no matter how small; and into every budding mind, no matter how eager. They cannot be kept out. No doubt, in fairness they should not be. The young ought not to be exiled from an experience, common to their generation, which will one day prove a group memory. But what chance would Mary Arden's boy have against Blondie, or Superman? Was the Phantom the best homework for Shakespeare? Or Gandy and Sourpuss the proper preparation for Rosencrantz and Guildenstern? I must admit I wondered, more and more as that Saturday approached, with ever-increasing alarm.

And what about Disney, the greatest Walt the world has known since Whitman? In toy form in the nursery. In color in the comics. In books beyond counting. Above all, in the movies. Disney everywhere, Disney delectable because destructive. His creatures asking for no pity; creating pleasure by pain, living only to sock and, having socked or been socked, socking again. Could the Dane hope to compete with Donald Duck, Pluto, Monstro, the Big Bad Wolf, the Three Little Pigs, Dopey, and most particularly the redoubtable Mickey? Again I wondered. And hoped. And had my doubts.

How to unroll the red carpet for *Hamlet* was another question. I meant to prepare his mind for what he was to see without putting upon it the stigma of homework. I mentioned the play at breakfast for a week, naming it with as much excitement as if its title were synonymous with a fishing expedition, or a visit to the Hayden Planetarium, the Museum of Natural History, Schrafft's, or the Fleet.

Like many another apprehensive parent, I even fell back on the Lambs. Not for long—for only two pages, to be exact. I found my own eyes glazed as swiftly as his when I read that interminable first paragraph which begins, "Gertrude, Queen of Denmark, becoming a widow by the sudden death of King Hamlet, in less than two months after his death married his brother Claudius, which was noted by all people at the time for a strange act of indiscretion, or unfeelingness, or worse," etc. and etc.

Before I knew it, Saturday was upon us.

We lunched first. Not at home. At a restaurant. At Giovanni's, in feast-day style worthy of the event. While he sipped a preliminary Coke downstairs and I an old-fashioned, I tried in simpler language than the Lambs' to explain what he would see. It took more explanation than I had thought it would. I noticed that his eyes brightened whenever the Ghost was mentioned. Or whenever, in my narration, a cadaver bit the dust.

"Why don't they use pistols?" he asked while I was outlining the duel scene with its multiple jobs for the court mortician. It was only when I had described the poison foil, the poisoned wine, and the fury of the duel that he appeared to forgive Shakespeare for not having anticipated the age of the machine.

When he demanded, "They won't really be dead, will they?" I knew he was interested. For him, make-believe and reality were still blissfully, terrifyingly one—at least up to an uncertain point.

Traffic held us up so that we were a minute or so late in getting to the theatre. Hence we missed the first scene on the parapet. But a friendly Negro doorman did his bit for Shakespeare that afternoon.

"Yessuh," the doorman said to him, "the Ghost is walkin' now. It's too dark to go in there. You gotta wait. But never you fear— he'll walk again."

While we were waiting for the first scene to be over, I assured him for the tenth time that the Ghost was not real, and tried to tell him how the illusion of his disappearance would be achieved.

The auditorium was dark when, with other stragglers, we pushed our way in. After we reached our seats, I could hardly persuade him to take off his coat and muffler. His eyes were glued on the stage. I was pleased to see how, even for the young, *Hamlet* sweeps forward on its own feet without having to rely on footnotes.

He listened to every word. He was never bored. He sat far back in his seat, relaxed only during soliloquies. Whenever there was a threat of action, he pushed forward. Whenever the Ghost appeared, he stood up. Once, when an offstage cannon sounded in the darkness, he came close to turning a somersault into the lap of the woman who was sitting beyond him.

"Holy smokes, what's that?" he cried.

The intermission almost broke his heart. When I suggested that he go out with me while I had a cigarette, he was at first unwilling to leave. His was that nicest of nice fears. He was afraid they might start without waiting for the audience.

On the sidewalk we encountered the doorman for the second time. "Did you see the Ghost?" He beamed. "Well, you'll see him again. He ain't done walkin'."

On the way back to our seats came, "Is Mr. Maurice Evans married?"

"No," I replied, "I don't think so."

"Why doesn't he marry Ophelia?" he suggested. "She's a mighty pretty girl."

He was standing bolt upright during the whole of the play-within-the-play scene. The death of Polonius grieved him. "He's such a funny, nice old man; he made me laugh." But he started laughing again when Hamlet reached behind the curtains for

Polonius's body, to say, "I'll lug the guts into the neighboring
room."

He jumped as if dynamited at that moment when Laertes and
his followers were storming the castle. And I almost had to hold
him to prevent his crawling over the seat in front of him during
the duel.

After Hamlet's body had been carried by the four captains up
the stairs and the curtain had fallen, he stayed—taped to his
seat—applauding. He applauded, and applauded, and applauded.

"How'd you like it?" I asked in the taxi, homeward bound.

"Gee, it was swell! I liked it better than *Oklahoma!*" Then a
pause. "I liked it better than Donald Duck." Another pause—a
long, reflective one. " 'A little more than kin, and less than kind.'
—Gee! That's pretty, isn't it?"

*Alfred Lunt and Robert Louis Stevenson as proud entre-
preneurs of toy theatres, and a magical, if vanished, world
that could once be purchased for a penny plain, twopence
colored.*

[1947]

CHILDREN OF SKELT

READER, DOES the name Skelt mean nothing to you? Does it leave
your heart unquickened; your eyes unfilled with images, gaudy
but delightful, and delightful because gaudy? And does this beginning of mine, this daring to address you directly as "Reader,"
this tossing of questions at you just as if you could answer back
before another sentence comes your way, strike you as an affectation?

Do you resent this use of "Reader" (there, you see—another question) because it is as out of fashion as gas lights, bustles, or whiskers Dundreary? Its passing is to be regretted. Count it among the lost amenities; as one of time's harmless victims. It is a good and friendly form, as Hazlitt knew and all his admirers realize. "Reader, have you ever seen a fight?" he dared to ask halfway through a magnificent essay in a paragraph which Gene Tunney has by heart. "If not," continued Hazlitt, "you have a pleasure to come, at least if it is a fight like that between the Gas-man and Bill Neate."

If "Reader" as so employed is an archaic form, that is my present reason for returning to it. Blame Skelt for this; Skelt and Webb, Redington and Pollock. If their names are unknown to you, add Alfred Lunt's to the list. His will shed light, especially if you have been lucky enough to see his latest production. No. I don't mean *O Mistress Mine* at the Empire. I mean the no less joyful, though less sophisticated, show Mr. Lunt is staging in three rooms on the third floor of the Museum of the City of New York. Mr. Lunt in a museum—already? Should these preliminaries leave you in the dark even now, think back to Robert Louis Stevenson and the chapter in his *Memories and Portraits* called "A Penny Plain and Twopence Coloured."

Mull over that title. It should lift the fog for you. At least it should cause a faraway bell to tinkle, if not to ring. For a penny plain and twopence colored is what they cost. I am thinking, of course, of those wondrous sheets, those packages of sheer joy and irresistible temptation, those papers bulging with actors, properties, and settings, for the possession of which children in the nineteenth century were separated from their coppers.

Once saved for (a pleasant privation), once selected (a terrible agony), these paradisiacal packets were to be carried home along with the text of the melodrama for the staging of which they were designed. Then, they were to be colored (sheer ecstasy) by those adventurous young owners who were neither so low nor so lazy as to stoop to purchase the twopenny kind which were already more prismatic than the rainbow. Next, they were to be cut out. Then, mounted. Yes, and finally displayed before an audience of dutiful parents, coerced domestics, and envious contemporaries, behind the proscenium arch—complete with musicians and occupied boxes—of a toy theatre.

No wonder Stevenson called these sheets of "Juvenile Drama" for which Skelt and his successors were responsible "bundles of delight." Or that visitors to the three rooms now darkened (but, oh, so full of light) on the top floor of the Museum of the City of New York should surrender to the spell of this collection of nineteenth-century toy theatres which Mr. Lunt has lovingly collected and lovingly displayed. For in the presence of this collection a wonderful and welcome thing can be rediscovered. This is the mislaid innocence of childhood, with its imagination untamed by the dull oppression of facts, with its love for the violent and the incredible still hot, and its dream world happily crowded with barbarous but enchanting visions. Not unnaturally, this lost innocence of childhood turns out to be the theatre's own lost innocence.

Stevenson confesses that, out of all the years of his life, one, and only one, homecoming brought him the delights he knew when he would steal upstairs with one of these nursery dramas under his arm. This other joy came one night when he brought back with him a fat, old, double-columned copy of *The Arabian Nights*. In linking the realm of Skelt and his clan with *The Arabian Nights* Stevenson did more than recall a personal pleasure. He defined the very nature and magic of the exhibition Mr. Lunt has brought together.

Without Skelt and company we might never have had *Treasure Island, Kidnapped,* or *The Master of Ballantrae*. In their beguiling way these novels are only Skeltery housebroken, grown up, turned self-conscious, but raised into art so that the dross is lost and the pure gold glitters. For Stevenson worshiped the very name of Skelt—"so stagey and piratical." As a boy reared in Scotland, he knew Skeltdom long before he visited England. When at last he crossed the border, he says it was only to come home to Skelt.

"What am I? what are life, art, letters, the world, but what my Skelt has made them?" wrote Stevenson. "He stamped himself upon my immaturity. The world was plain before I knew him, a poor penny world; but soon it was all coloured with romance."

As a grown man, if Stevenson went to the theatre to see a good old melodrama, he found that what he saw was only Skelt a little faded. If he visited a bold scene in nature, he knew that Skelt would have been bolder. "Indeed," says he, "out of this cut-and-dry, dull, swaggering, obtrusive and infantile art, I seem to have learned the very spirit of my life's enjoyment." From the rude cuts for these toy theatres, Stevenson admits, he acquired a gallery of scenes and characters with which, in the silent theatre of his brain, he might "enact all novels and romances." From them he derived "an enduring and transforming pleasure."

The transforming pleasure R.L.S. found in Skeltduggery continues to be transforming in Mr. Lunt's fine collection. It remains so even for those of us never privileged in our childhood to invest our savings in these penny-plain and twopence-colored passports to delirium.

Most children have owned toy theatres. Certainly, every adult (in age only) who remains stagestruck when he does grow up *must* in his youth have had a playhouse in the attic. It is part of each theatre worker's legend. It is one of the indispensable items in the autobiography of all those spending their lives near the footlights. What toy soldiers are to a future general; what the Bible was to Lincoln; what a miracle is to a saint, miniature theatres are to those who flutter like moths around the candle of "The Profession."

I do not have in mind the poor, shrunken examples of juvenile stagecraft which at present can be bought at the more expensive toy shops. These do nothing for the imagination—except congeal it. They are intended only for poor little rich boys and girls who are fated to grow up into bankers, Brass Hats, brokers, lawyers, teachers, social workers, and mere practical and useful citizens. Though blessed with a proscenium arch and blood-red curtains, with wood wings and backdrops and non-Equity actors for the production of such pale stuff as *Little Red Riding Hood*, these new-fangled toy theatres have as much relation to the tribe of Skelt or his French counterparts as a Greek bootblack bears to Homer.

Denied Skeltery, the truly stagestruck in this land and century were left to their own juvenile devices. They could not purchase

a fairyland of make-believe and romance. They had to create it
—for themselves and by themselves. In fact, Mr. Lunt did not
assemble his present exhibition until, during the war years, he
found himself playing in a London which Miss Fontanne and he
had conquered. Most American youngsters born since McKinley
have been compelled to make their own attic theatres—in Mr.
Lunt's fashion. Not so well as he did, as his exhibition makes clear.
The settings and costumes he painted at the ripe age of eleven for
Julius Caesar, Twelfth Night, or *The Winter's Tale* clearly mark
him as a child bound to be someone in the theatre. The Messrs.
Skelt, Webb, Redington, and Pollock, however, provided those
born in Britain in the last century with a fairyland that was ready-
made. It is this same fairyland into which Mr. Lunt allows us to
wander at the museum.

Did Emerson call snow "frozen architecture"? Well, here on
that third floor are three rooms of frozen theatre. Not cold, mind
you. Anything except that. Hot to the boiling point. Melodramas
caught at their most purple peaks of climax; big scenes impaled
for all time in the full hocus-pocus tide of their passions; and
"stills," so to speak, of gloriously tawdry moments which refuse
even now to be still.

Here is a world of apotheoses; of wounded duelists quitting
in spirit (with the aid of visible wires) their wounded bodies for
the pearly clouds above; and of a Robinson Crusoe and a Friday
who face, in the wildest wilds God or geology ever fashioned, a
group of friendly Indians dressed in Roman togas and sporting
Roman shields.

It is a nightmare world in which the more frightening the nightmare the more cherished it is as a dream. In it you will find the
serpents, spirits, and peasants of *Der Freischütz.* And Aztec temples for *Pizarro,* all of which Queen Victoria could have designed.
You will discover, too, such notables as Wellington, the Prince of
Orange, General Blücher, and Napoleon fighting a *Battle of Waterloo* which, though bloody as paint can make it, blessedly finds the
discharging guns and cannons more silent than a Christmas mouse.
And Bill Sikes and Nancy in the fearsome shadows of the bridge.
Or a flash-colored windmill for *The Miller and His Men* in the
most terrible state of permanent explosion. Or Eliza dashing with-

out moving across the immobile ice with static bloodhounds in eternal pursuit. And Mazeppa strapped to a mad stallion which races without advancing across a cataract that is wet without being damp.

There are plenty of other exhibits—*Timour or the Tartar, The Silver Palace, The Forty Thieves, The Maid and the Magpie, Robin Hood,* and *Three-Fingered Jack.* Their colors are as violent as the stories they tell. Their outlines, even when nature is their model, are contours which nature has not yet achieved. They belong to an era of make-believe in which we must make believe in order to believe at all. Yet their enchantment is genuine.

Perhaps it is just as well that all their actors are silent. For us, in this different age, the words they ought to be speaking would break the spell. We would recognize these words as balderdash, fit only for the snickers of spoof revivals. Being trained in the theatre of a new period, we would judge what we were hearing as literature and not accept it merely as theatre. Accordingly, our ears would reject those very excesses upon which our eyes feed with such great delight in the visual kingdom of Skelt.

Our theatre is supposedly a playwright's theatre. Ibsen and Shaw and a host of others have sought to intellectualize it. They have turned their backs on the old claptrap. They have endeavored to make it literate, sophisticated, adult. But, though much has been gained, as is the way of things, in the process something has also been lost. It is this something—this frenzied, unthinking, vernal excitement—which can be recaptured in all its vibrant and blessed tawdriness in Mr. Lunt's collection of nineteenth-century juvenilia.

Being good theatre in itself no less than a good theatrical exhibition, Mr. Lunt's show possesses a villain. His name is Charles Kean. At first glance his villainies may seem mild enough. Not inappropriately, the younger Kean is to be found lurking in a corner. It is there that you will find the sketches for *The Winter's Tale* as he produced it at the Princess Theatre in 1856. Although they are agreeable to look at, do not be deceived by their pastoral appearance. For they and Kean were the congenital enemies of Skelt.

Kean had an accurate mind, a commodity with which Skelt was not cursed. William Shakespeare embarrassed Kean. He was horrified to find that chronological contradictions abounded in Shakespeare's text. Being a logical man, Kean was convinced that, "when an attempt is made to combine truth with history, conflicting epochs cannot all be illustrated."

Needless to say, Reader, though no one guessed it then, this was the beginning of the end. At least for Skelt and his tribe. Thereafter, realism was on its way.

Introduction to The Viking Portable Charles Lamb *in which Elia, the man, the critic, and the writer, is placed against the tragic story of his life with his sister Mary.*

[1948]

THE SHORN LAMBS

CHARLES AND MARY

AMONG THE tantalizing "ifs" of literature is what Charles Lamb might have been like as man and writer if, in a fit of madness, his sister Mary had not slain their mother when he was only twenty-one. The "gentle Elia" the world loves was the product of ungentle and terrible events. He was the stepchild of a calamity as bloody as any to be found in the most bloodstained Elizabethan dramas of which Lamb was later to become a champion. To a tragic extent Lamb's life, hence Elia's character, was carved out for him by the case knife which poor, deluded Mary drove straight and deep into their mother's heart.

Surely never in the strange annals of authorship has the world

gained so much in pleasure or an innocent man lost more in freedom than in the instance of the catastrophe which resulted in
Lamb's becoming the most beloved bachelor of letters literature
has produced.

When he quit his desk at the East India House on the afternoon of September 22, 1796, and started to walk home through
the London he loved, Lamb was not without his worries. His sister Mary, ten years his senior, had already shown symptoms of
insanity. Not for the first time, either. As a person who had himself been confined the previous year for six weeks in a madhouse
at Hoxton, these symptoms may have had a special meaning for
him. In any case, Mary's condition was sufficiently disturbing to
have sent Lamb, on his way to work that very morning, in search
of a doctor who was not to be found. Aware though he was of the
gathering clouds, Lamb could not have been prepared for the violence of the storm which had broken out in the house where he
lived with his old father, his invalid mother, his sister, and his
Aunt Hetty.

The sight he beheld when he opened the door was of tabloid
gruesomeness. Above the bustle of Little Queen Street he may
have heard the cries of his father and shrieks of Mary and her
assistant as he approached his home. If he had not, the landlord's
presence was in itself a warning. Certainly his eyes must have
disbelieved the nightmare of reality which confronted them. The
room, in which the table was laid for dinner, was in a turmoil.
Charles's aged aunt was unconscious on the floor, "to all appearance like one dying." His senile father was bleeding from a wound
in his forehead. His mother was dead in a chair, stabbed to the
heart by Mary who was standing over her with the case knife still
in her hand. Lamb arrived only in time to snatch the knife from
her grasp.

What had provoked this scene no one knows. Perhaps, as a professional seamstress, Mary had been overworking, and the stress
of a dependent household had become too great for her. Perhaps
the final straw had been the additional cares which had come her
way because of the leg injury recently suffered by her brother
John, her elder by a year and a half. Perhaps, as moderns have
hinted, an ugly, long-suppressed animosity between her and her

mother had at last erupted. In any event, Mary had had an alter-
cation with the young woman who, in her mantua-making, was
her helper. Mary had reached for the knives and forks on the
table, throwing them at this frightened girl in the hope of driving
her from the house. It was one of the forks thus thrown which had
struck her father. Her mother might have been spared had she
not attempted to intercede in the apprentice's behalf.

"I date from the day of horrors," wrote Lamb to Coleridge
soon after the disaster. Although by this he meant merely to place
in time events described in his letter, he unwittingly summarized
the rest of his adult life. To these sensational occurrences which
cost him dearly, we owe, in part at least, the writer we cherish as
one of the least sensational of authors. For the next thirty-eight
years Lamb lived a gallant and, on the whole, a cheerful prisoner
to the happenings of that fatal afternoon. In no sense of the word
a tragic hero, he emerged as the hero of a tragedy. We pity him
the more because he was without self-pity.

There are people, luckless mortals, who by the injustice of circumstances or because of a certain granite in their characters are
doomed to be caryatids for the suffering of others. Charles Lamb
was one of these. He could have fallen back on the law and allowed his sister to be committed to a public insane asylum. He
could have walked out on Mary. In other words, he could have
done what his older brother John did and wanted him to do.

Yet even when John washed his hands of the whole problem,
Lamb was able to rise, "not without tenderness," to his brother's
defense. He knew John to be "little disposed . . . at any time to
take care of old age and infirmities." Charles went so far as to
persuade himself that John, "with his bad leg, had an exemption
from such duties." He was well aware that John would make
speeches about the money needed to maintain Mary in a private
institution. But Charles and John, though brothers, were made of
very different stuff. Young and poor as he was, Charles faced the
fact without complaining that "the whole weight of the family"
had been thrown upon him. From the outset he was determined,
regardless of the sacrifices, that Mary should not go into a public
asylum.

Nor did she. Instead, he assumed full responsibility for her.

More than that, he devoted his life to her. Because of this utter devotion his own life was altered inescapably. Had it not been for Mary, age would not have fallen so suddenly and engulfingly upon him. Without her, we might be able to imagine Lamb as a young man rather than always picturing him as a smoky and eccentric oldish fellow, settled in both his habits and his singleness, whose youth had come to an abrupt end with his childhood. Without Mary, Charles' dream children might have been real. The "fair Alice W——n," she of the light yellow hair and the pale blue eyes for whom he claimed to have pined away seven of his "goldenest years," might have been the "passionate . . . love-adventure" he once described her as being instead of a reference, true or fanciful, which biographers have been unable to track down. He might not have waited so many years to propose to Fanny Kelly, the actress with the "divine plain face," and Fanny might even have accepted him.

Without his "poor dear dearest" Mary, Charles might have continued longer to try his hand at poetry and not so soon, as he put it (with wonderful inaccuracy, in his case), have "dwindled into prose and criticism." His spirit would have been gayer, his laughs less like sighs. He might not have been so "shy of novelties; new books, new faces, new years." The present, not the past, might have been his delight. He would not have been driven, as driven he was by the events of that appalling afternoon, to find happiness by thinking back to happier days. Retrospection would not have become his refuge. The "boy-man" that he felt himself to be would not have clung with such tenacious affection to his own boyhood. The texture, the range, the very tone and temper of his work would have been different.

From the moment of his mother's murder and the time that he stepped forward to become Mary's legal guardian, Lamb knew that he and Mary were "in a manner *marked*." This was bound to be a portion of their fate. There was no hushing their story. It not only pursued them; it ran ahead of them. Sometimes it even forced them to change their lodgings. No shelter could be found from the nudgings, the whisperings, the stares, and the embarrassments it provoked. Charles' determination to care for Mary involved more than living with her. It also meant his living with the knowledge that everyone around them knew her case and their history. If this increased his shyness, it also brought him and Mary closer together. It was only one more of the many bonds, tender and tragic, which united them.

Fortunately, theirs was a relationship based upon more than the perilous stuffs of gratitude or an embittering sense of obligation. Positive as each of them was as a personality, they were united not only by misfortune but by shared tastes and minds which, in spite of dissimilarities, were complementary. When dedicating a volume of his verse, Charles called Mary his best friend. From the dedication of his life she knew she had no better friend than he. Their devotion to each other was genuine and abiding. It shines through their letters. It is unmistakable in every reference to Mary as Bridget in Charles' essays. They were collaborators in life no less than in literature. No brother and sister in history are more inseparably linked. To Lamb their life as old bachelor and maid was "a sort of double singleness."

The glimpses we have of them together are at once heartwarming and heartbreaking. "You would like to see us," wrote Mary to Sarah Stoddart, "as we often sit, writing on one table (but not on one cushion sitting), like Hermia and Helena in the *Midsummer Night's Dream*; or, rather, like an old literary Darby and Joan: I taking snuff, and he groaning all the while and saying he can make nothing of it, which he always says till he has finished, and then he finds out he has made something of it."

That is a picture of them at their happiest. It belongs with those other pictures we conjure when we imagine them together. Playing cards. Seeing a play. Going to exhibitions. Reading books, she doting on narratives—any narratives; he delighting in the reflective passages of the older authors. Visiting friends. Enjoying the adventure of one of their short summer journeys. Presiding over one of their delectable "evenings" at home (held first on Wednesdays, later on Thursdays), which Hazlitt immortalized with his "How often did we cut into the haunch of letters, while we discussed the haunch of mutton on the table!" Or discussing, in the financial comfort of their later years, the greater pleasures they had known when, in their youth, they had been forced to skimp, save, and plan in order to make a purchase or crowd their way into the pit.

Against these brighter moments must be set the darker ones. These are black indeed. By common agreement Mary, in her right mind, was one of the most amiable and admirable of women. But Mary was not always in her right mind. She was "perpetually on the brink of madness." If this was Mary's tragedy, it was also Lamb's. Their sunniest days together were never cloudless. The threat under which they lived was fearful and incessant. At all times the Furies stalked them. Small wonder this brother and this sister have been likened to a cockney Orestes and Electra.

Mary's was a recurrent illness. There was no telling when it would return. There was only the certainty that return it would, with ever-increasing frequency, with ever-mounting seriousness. Some hints, such as a sudden moroseness or irritability on Mary's part, preceded its coming. For these dreaded signs Charles watched anxiously. Apparently Mary did, too.

"You would laugh, or you would cry, perhaps both," Mary wrote in another letter to Miss Stoddart, "to see us sit together, looking at each other with long and rueful faces, and saying, 'How do you do?' and 'How do *you* do?' and then we fall a-crying and say we will be better on the morrow. Charles says we are like Tooth Ache and his friend Gum Boil, which though a kind of ease is an uneasy kind of ease."

Their ease at its best was the epitome of uneasiness. Surely few scenes could be more touching than the one several of their friends had witnessed. It was the common sequel to each reappearance of Mary's symptoms. When these had shown themselves, Charles would get ready to take her to the private asylum at Hoxton. She would gather together a few clothes, replace with a bonnet the mobcap she wore indoors, and prepare for the street. He would lead her, unresisting, to the door. Then they would start out hand in hand, two figures as somberly dressed as Quakers, walking the whole way, weeping as they walked, and carrying Mary's strait jacket with them.

Even so, Mary, between interruptions, brought Charles a happiness almost as complete as was the unhappiness her madness had brought upon them both. The debt we owe her is at once incalculable and unpayable. If, as readers, we delight in Lamb as he is, we do so because his writing is the product of his life as it

was. He never objected to his lot. He faced it squarely, gaily, without whining, and with inexhaustible courage.

The world that knows him as the "gentle Elia" does Lamb an
injustice. Gentle he always was with Mary and in most of his writings. It was, however, his strength which enabled him to be gentle
and not any softness which forced him into being so. He hated the
phrase "gentle-hearted" when applied to him as much as Sir James
Barrie abhorred the word "whimsical." "For God's sake (I never
was more serious)," wrote Charles to Coleridge, "don't make me
ridiculous any more by terming me gentle-hearted in print, or do
it in better verses. . . . The meaning of gentle is equivocal at
best, and almost always means poor-spirited."

Certainly Lamb was anything but poor-spirited. He had a resilience unknown to noisier men and a toughness unsuspected by
those who have read him sparingly, and then only in his fanciful
or sentimental moods. Did he look like a clerk? He did not act like
one. He was no Timid Soul. He was fiercely independent. His father may have been a servant, but in a snobbish age Lamb was
subservient to no one. He was at all times ready to stammer
out his opinions without fear. Everyone who described him noted
the sadness of his brown eyes, the thoughtfulness of his expansive
brow, the sweetness of his expression, and the smallness of his
body. Lamb knew that physically he was "less than the least of
the Apostles." A friend thought he looked so fragile that "a
breath would overthrow him." But there was iron in his "im-
material legs." His slight body contradicted the largeness of his
spirit.

Although Charles knew great sorrow, he was not discontented.
If he could refer to Mary and himself, playfully though correctly,
as "shorn Lambs," his belief in the tempering wind was nonetheless strong. Living with sorrow was as much a habit with him as
climbing up on his high stool each morning to work as a clerk at
the East India House. The prospect of any change so staggered
him that he convinced himself he would no more reverse the un-
toward accidents and events of his life than he would alter the
incidents of some well-contrived novel. Such was his love of life
that he even loved his own. He meant what he said when he confessed, "I am in love with this green earth; the face of town and

country; the unspeakable rural solitudes, and the sweet security of streets."

THE MAN WHO WAS LAMB

The portion of the earth that Charles Lamb loved best was not green. He preferred cobblestones to grass any day. He was a city man if ever there was one, a cockney in every inch of his small person. The nightingale never released a song so sweet to his ears as the sound of Bow Bells. Had he been compelled to choose between Skiddaw and Soho, Wordsworth's mountain would have had no chance. The pleasure William found in a daffodil, Charles derived from a chimney sweep.

He did not object to nature—for others. But human nature and the hum of city streets were his delight. Although, with Mary, he liked to venture into the countryside, for a while and as a break, even in the country he was a cockney on vacation. He dared to write to Wordsworth, of all people, "Separate from the pleasure of your company, I don't much care if I never see a mountain in my life." Nature to him was "dead"; London, living. The sun and the moon of the Lake District did not shine for him as brightly as the lamps of London. It was not the beauties of the outdoors which he found "ever fresh and green and warm," but all the inventions and assemblies of men in the congested boroughs by the Thames.

Few writers have described a city more affectionately than Charles his London. Few have outdone him in making strangers, both by the calendar and geography, feel like citizens of vanished times and places. There were scarcely any aspects of the metropolis he did not cherish. He, to whom much of life was denied, often shed tears of joy on his night walks about London at encountering so much life.

He never tired of the lighted shops of the Strand and Fleet Street; of the innumerable trades, tradesmen, customers, coaches, crowds, wagons, and playhouses; of "all the bustle and wickedness round about Covent Garden, the very women of the Town, the Watchmen, drunken scenes, rattles"; of the city's pungent smells and the very dirt and mud; of the sun shining upon houses and pavements; or of the print shops, the old bookstalls, and the coffeehouses. He rejoiced in the sense they gave him of London being a pantomime and a masquerade where life itself was at last awake. The city for him was at once a stimulant and an escape. Urbanwise, he lived on it no less than in it. He measured his fortune, good or ill, by his distance from the Strand. He was jubilant when, after one of their frequent changes of address, he found that the house in which he and Mary were then stopping was "forty-two inches nearer town."

The city he lived in, though a metropolis, was not for him a capital. Its government was an irrelevance, its politics nonexistent. An historian, hoping to find in Lamb's essays or letters some reflection of the great events of turbulent years, would be hard put to determine whether history had by-passed Lamb or he history. He lived through England's wars as if Europe were at peace. So far as he was concerned, they were undeclared and unwaged. He came to admire Nelson, admitted Wellington's existence, had no love for the early Hanovers, in a mild way championed Queen Caroline's cause, and was curious about Napoleon's height. But the French Revolution left no visible mark upon him, and, though he must have heard of Trafalgar, Austerlitz, and Waterloo, we never hear of them through him.

Did the younger Pitt die in 1806? For Lamb he never seems to have lived. Did "Boney" threaten England with invasion? Did the Peterloo Massacre spill blood in Manchester? Were trade unions allowed for the first time? Did the Prince Regent's marriage to Mrs. Fitzherbert rock society? Were both the Roman Catholic Emancipation and the First Reform Bill passed? Contemporaneous as he was with all of these occurrences, Lamb was apparently the contemporary of none of them.

Unlike such of his intimates as Coleridge, Hazlitt, Leigh Hunt, and Wordsworth, he had no interest in public affairs. Society for him was always a circle of friends and never the collective well-being of a community. "Public affairs—except as they touch upon me, and so turn into private," Lamb wrote to Thomas Manning, "I cannot whip up my mind to feel any interest in." By his own admission, he was deaf to the noises which kept Europe awake, and could not make present times present to him.

He was as insulated against political events as he was susceptible to human, literary, and gastronomic values. In his scheme of things "important people" were unimportant, and for him the "Great World" possessed no fascination. The bearers of titles, more than leaving him unimpressed, left him unamused no less surely than official leaders left him unled. A benevolent eccentric himself, he delighted in the benevolent eccentricities of others. The heads he prized were not those highly placed but those "with some diverting twist in them"; heads lightened by "out of the way humors and opinions."

His absorptions were personal, not public, and small-scaled rather than outsized. Covent Garden was his Buckingham Palace; the art galleries were his House of Commons; the bookstall, his House of Lords. Londoner, utter and complete, though he was, Lamb never felt, thought, or wrote as a citizen but always as an individual. He took the same pleasure in the "delicious juices of meats and fishes, and society, and the cheerful glass, and candlelight and fireside conversations, and innocent vanities and jests, and irony itself" that he did in the passages, sublime or melancholy, of his favorite old authors. If the oddities of authorship were dear to him, so were the oddities of people and places, and it was these which enchanted him in London.

The London through which Lamb trudged was apt to be two cities—the one he saw as a man, and the other he remembered from his youth. Accordingly, even when solitary, he seldom walked the streets alone. For the author whose attachment to the past was so great that he could exclaim, "Hang the age; I'll write for Antiquity!" London's past was superimposed upon its present. On his strolls he was attended by the shades of the boys and teachers he had known as a student at Christ's Hospital; by the ghosts of departed players or of journalists with whom he had worked; or by the figures of Old Benchers, long since dead, whom he had watched in his boyhood in the Inner Temple. These rose constantly before his eyes. So double was Lamb's sense of time, so eager his search for reminders of his "joyful" days, that, in spite of his best known poem, the "old familiar faces" were for him never "all, all . . . gone."

London offered Lamb a source of vicarious life. The city which touched and diverted him by doing so provided him with a release

from both his "cold bed of celibacy" and his long years of confinement at the East India House. During most of his writing life,
Lamb was a full-time clerk, a part-time author. He contended
that his real "works"—"more MSS. in folio than ever Aquinas
left, and full as useful"—were the great ledgers he had filled day
after day for the thirty-three years of his clerkdom, and not the
printed volumes to be found at booksellers. There was little of
the free-lancer in his nature. There could not be. His being married, as he put it, to Mary's fortunes meant that he was unable to
run risks with his own. Instead of writing to live, he clerked in
order to be free to write. Generous as he was in his gifts and loans
to others, he could not afford to be without steady employment
himself.

He was horrified when Bernard Barton confided he was thinking of giving up his job in a Quaker bank to live by his pen. "Keep
to your Bank," he urged Barton, "and the Bank will keep you.
. . . What, is there not from six to eleven p.m. 6 days in the week,
and is there not all Sunday?" For Lamb this was writing time
enough. It spared him the insecurities of being a "slave to Booksellers" and "the miseries of subsisting by authorship." It meant
that, when at last he was at liberty to write, his pen felt its "promotion." His writing was thus kept an escape from drudgery, and so
avoided being drudgery itself.

He was, of course, fond of seeing himself as a prisoner at the
India House; of claiming that he sat there like Philomel all day
(but not singing) with his "heart against this thorn of a desk."
But he liked his job better than he guessed, and was lost when he
retired from it. The routine of working at India House from ten
to four at once supported and soothed him. It comforted him in
his loneliness and appealed to what was essentially gregarious in
his nature. He missed the friendly eminence of the high stool upon
which he had sat for so many years. He missed not hanging his hat
each day on the same peg. He missed the amiable ease of an office where, though he labored faithfully, he could still find time to
write some of his best letters. He missed the companionship of his
"old desk fellows"—his "co-brethren of the quill." He missed "the
hot huddle of rational creatures." He missed, too, being able to
excuse his habitual tardiness by such an explanation as "I m-make
up for that by g-going away early."

The truth is he missed his chains. Like many another, he came to realize they had become a necessary part of his apparel. Nothing in his story is more poignant than the sadness which inundated him when, at fifty, his dream of liberty became a reality and he was freed from what he had thought was bondage. During the next nine years, until his death in 1834, he sensed that freedom in itself could be a bondage. He had lived so long "*to* other people" that he could not happily fill his own emancipated hours. Time stood still for him and was empty in its idleness. He lost the "Wednesday feelings" and the "Saturday night sensations" he had once known. To his despair he discovered he walked about, not to and from. Having all holidays, it was as though he had none. No Babbitt and no Dodsworth could have been more rudderless upon retirement than was this man, part Yorick, part Jaques, when he was at last freed by a generous pension.

His Yorick side is known to every reader whose knowledge of him does not stop with the *Tales from Shakespeare*, "The Dissertation on Roast Pig," or "Dream Children." Lamb turning suddenly to Martin Burney at cards to comment, "Martin, if dirt were t-trumps, what a hand you would hold!"; Lamb crying out, "Wordsworth says he could have written *H-Hamlet* if he'd had the m-mind!"; or Lamb answering Coleridge's question as to whether or not Charles had ever heard him preach in the days of his Unitarian ministry with, "I never heard you do anything else" —all these are instances of his "punch-light" humor which, though familiar, have not become tired.

As a conversationalist, his stammer was part of his comic equipment. He relied upon it the way acrobats rely upon a net. He was a fellow whose jests were infinite, instantaneous, impudent, and deflating. He had the virtues, and the wisdom, of not being a continuous conversationalist. His stutter, like his discretion, made that impossible. His hatred for the "long and much talkers" was as lusty as theirs for him. He knew the value of silences, broken suddenly and unexpectedly, and, one gathers, of dead-panning his way to a joke. Pomposity he despised, dullness he abhorred, and seers he loathed when they were "seering."

To be at his best he had to be among people he knew and liked. To strangers and incompatibles he was an enigma, if not an irritant. Carlyle, with his genius for fermentation, was never sourer than on the subject of Lamb. "A more pitiful, ricketty, gasping, staggering, stammering Tomfool I do not know," fumed he. "He is witty by denying truisms and abjuring good manners." Yet to Hazlitt, as to many another, this same Lamb was "the most delightful, the most provoking, the most witty and sensible of men. . . . No one ever stammered out such fine, piquant, deep, eloquent things in half a dozen half-sentences as he does. His jests scald like tears: and he probes a question with a play upon words."

Among his friends, on the kind of drinking, talking, smoking evening which he cherished, his relaxation was to enliven the passing moment as certainly as, when alone, his consolation was to dream of the moments that had been. He had a reply—and an unanswerable one—for those who complained he was always aiming at wit. He said that to do so was at least as good as aiming at dullness.

Macready was shocked to hear Lamb confess at Talfourd's one night that "the last breath he drew in he wished might be through a pipe and exhaled in a pun." Lamb's fondness for puns was notorious. He loved them as much as all people dislike them who cannot make them. There is no such thing as stooping to a pun. There is only the challenge of being able to rise to a good one. Few cadavers could be deader or more emaciated than those occasional puns which, in his letters, Lamb quotes approvingly, pointer in hand, with the subtlety of a window demonstrator. Lamb, however, knew a pun must be heard, not read, and heard at the moment of its birth if it were to live completely or to be fully enjoyed. "A pun," wrote he, "hath a hearty kind of present ear-kissing smack in it; you can no more transmit it in its pristine flavor than you can send a kiss."

That Lamb laughed and could make others laugh, everyone knows. But the nature of his laughter, the keen and enjoying manner in which he detected frailty, the amused details which underwrite his fantasy and are the basis of his reveries, along with the man who could be as realistic in his observation of men as he was in facing the unpleasant realities of his own life—these are what the sentimentalists forget who have made him as sentimental as themselves.

Many authors suffer at the hands of their detractors; just as many (and no less cruelly) at the hands of their admirers. Lamb belongs to this well-nigh smothered brotherhood. He has almost been killed, not so much by his own kindness, which was true and very human, as by the bogus, treacly kindness which others have palmed off as being his. Thornton Wilder once described a modern playwright, addicted to cute and elfin phrases and marshmallow thoughts, as writing in the manner associated with Lamb by people who have not read him. This false notion of Lamb, with its attendant misunderstandings and proper revulsions, is a ghost which, worse than haunting the real Lamb, has all too often obscured him.

In his eagerness to canonize Lamb's palpable and radiant virtues, Thackeray may have dubbed him "Saint Charles." Charles, however, was the more of a saint because he was so much of a man. Although there are those who choose to bury him in lavender, to cushion him on sachets, and to confuse him with old lace, they do Lamb a genuine injustice.

Lamb could be sweet beyond comfortable endurance. He could be whimsical to a disqieting extent. He could dip his pen far too deep in sirup and produce copy, on occasions, which to modern eyes reads like literate valentines from yesteryear. These, however, were the excesses into which his tenderness led him. They were the expressions of his frustration, his regrets, his loneliness, and, in a way, of his period. Though full of sentiment, Lamb was no sentimentalist as a man, and only as an author when he nodded, which he was mortal enough to do at moments. That he was kind and that he was witty, everyone knows. But that he was both kind and witty at one and the same time has so surprised his admirers that some of them have overlooked entirely the sharpness of his mind and tongue.

In his letters, as in his talk, a spade was a spade. It was only in his essays that it became a shovel, a gardener's utensil, or something like Triptolemus's tool. When he informed Manning that Coleridge's wife was expecting a baby, did he do so by referring to "a little one" or "an addition to the family"? He did not. As directly as if he were a GI in the Army he wrote, "Coleridge is settled with his wife (with a child in her guts)."

No one has written about childhood more tenderly than he. Even so, his was not the bachelor's idealization of all children. He knew that the young, like their elders, were either amiable or unamiable. He saw no reason "to love a whole family, perhaps eight, nine, or ten, indiscriminately—to love all the pretty dears because children are so engaging." His phrase, when a sick child had at last been removed from his home, after robbing Lamb of his rest, was, quite simply, "The little bastard is gone."

He pulled no punches with his friends, and was much too good a friend to do so. His candor was as great as his charm. "Cultivate simplicity, Coleridge," wrote he, "or rather, I should say, banish elaborateness. . . . I allow no hotbeds in the gardens of Parnassus." No one ever derived more amusement from a friend's faults than Lamb did from those of poor, foolish, bumbling George Dyer. His letters about Dyer, like his references to him in his essays, are as full of mocking laughter as they are of love. Few people have played more knowledgeably, or with greater relish, upon human frailty than Lamb did when, by "beslabbering" a book Joseph Cottle had written, he so appealed to its author's vanity that Cottle forgot all about his dead brother in the next room.

Although by his own confession he could not hate anyone he knew, Lamb was terrifyingly aware of people's defects. Shelley's voice was to him "the most obnoxious squeak I ever was tormented with, ten thousand times worse than the Laureat's, whose voice is the worst part about him except his Laureatcy." Lamb's aversion to Byron's character was "thorough" and his admiration for his genius "very moderate." "He is great in so little a way" was Lamb's summary of his Lordship.

Once at Godwin's, Holcroft and Coleridge were fiercely disputing which was better, *man as he was* or *man as he is to be.* "Give me," said Lamb, "man as he is *not* to be." If, in general, he was willing to take all people as they were, he was taken in by no one. His eye for human absurdity was as keen as his enjoyment of human oddity. Was it a poor relation remembering a birthday so as to drop in just in time for dinner? Was it a liar spinning fabulous yarns on a boat to Margate, or a fact-loving bore on the top of a stagecoach? Lamb saw their failings plain. His gentleness did not prevent his feelings from being strong. "Now, of all God's creatures," wrote he, "I detest letters-affecting, authors-hunting ladies." His loathing for booksellers was equally strong. So was his disrelish for the Scots. Lamb was as "essentially anti-Caledonian" as ever Dr. Johnson was.

The fact—the fine, the beckoning, the all-conquering fact— about Lamb is that he could look "with no indifferent eye upon things or persons." "Whatever is" was to him "a matter of taste or distaste." He knew, as some of his admirers have forgotten, that he was "a bundle of prejudices—made up of likings and dislikings— the veriest thrall to sympathies, apathies, and antipathies." Without these prejudices Lamb would not be Lamb. Nor would he be Lamb had he not felt and phrased them in a way so unmistakably and beguilingly his own that, though it has won him countless friends, it has removed him from the reach of imitators.

ELIA VERSUS LAMB

An affectionate rather than a passionate man, Charles Lamb nourished prejudices as substitutes for passion. It was in them that he lived, and because of them, in part, that he lives for us. They were the proofs of his awareness, his sensibility, his discernment, his humanity. Characteristically enough, he chose to refer to these prejudices as "imperfect sympathies" no less than as prejudices.

One of the major paradoxes of his paradoxical mind was that, as a rule, he could be sympathetic even when he was being witty. His wit was the expression of his love, not his contempt, for men. People who would have irritated others amused him. His knowledge of life was too complete for him to be surprised by human frailty. If he never failed to observe it, he seldom failed to enjoy it. Since he expected it, he was tolerant of it.

His was the laughter of acceptance not protest, of recognition instead of revulsion. His gaiety was as divorced from scorn or cynicism as it was wedded to melancholy. It smiles without being insulting. Unchilled by the arrogance which is the curse of professional wits, it is as warm and human as the "rather smoky, and sometimes rather drinky" little man from whom it emanated. It sprang from a superior mind, unconscious of its superiority; a mind which is the more endearing because its modesty remains unlost in the midst of its most dazzling exhibitions of prowess.

Lamb's mind was the antithesis of neat and office-like. It resembled an antique shop or an old bookstore where, in spite of the clutter, the dust, and the overlay of accumulation, the proprietor can at a moment's notice bring to light whatever treasure is desired. It never judged "systemwise" but always by "fastening on particulars." It was proudly unmethodized, desultory, tangential. If it worked obliquely in ways beyond prediction, it was because it fed upon the tantalizing obliquities of life no less than of literature. Its knowledge was a matter of informed tastes rather than of pursued facts.

Lamb had no desire to keep up with the Joneses. He had a hard enough time keeping up with the whims of his own interest. The topical left him uncoerced; the popular, unpersuaded. When a new book came out, he read an old one. He would have been both amused and amazed by the manuals, digests, and sugar-coated textbooks in which those who mistake facts for learning nowadays stalk culture as if it were a butterfly to be pinioned in a net. Although the most bookish of bookish men, he was no chaser after information for information's sake. Instead, he was a savorer, content to taste and retaste what was best or most flavorsome in the volumes he cherished. If his devotion to what was special, limited, and wayward in his preoccupations was one of his limitations, this did not bother him. Lamb was comfortable in his ignorance of what he did not choose to know.

On all matters relating to science, Elia could boast he was "a whole Encyclopaedia behind the rest of the world." He was equally, and just as proudly, unknowledgeable about geography, modern languages, the shapes and textures of the commonest trees, herbs, or flowers, and tools, engines, or mechanical processes. In spite of his attachment to the past, history as a mere sequence of events had so little interest for him that he could brag he had never deliberately sat down to read a chronicle even of his own country. As for astronomy, it did not exist in the orbit of his shining concerns. "If the sun," wrote he, "on some portentous morn were to make his first appearance in the west, I verily believe that, while all the world were gasping in apprehension about me, I alone should stand unterrified, from sheer incuriosity and want of observation."

One of the reasons for Elia's dislike of the Scots was that no excursions could be taken with them, since they always insisted upon keeping to the path. Lamb's thinking, though it could lead to the summits, was nothing if not excursive. The straight highroads dear to historians were not the routes he either elected or was equipped to travel. When he did not spurn the obvious views and inevitable sights, he preferred to reach them by a back door or secret passage. He gave both his mind and heart (the combination, in his case, meaning his attention) to the ignored vistas and overlooked curiosities. Even these he approached by those unblazed trails which, to the personal essayist, are the royal road.

If these footpaths were roads which led to himself, the reason was his modesty, not his egotism. Lamb was one of the most autobiographical of authors. To read him on virtually any subject is to read about him. It is to know him with a sense of daily intimacy with which few writers are known. In his copy Lamb could no more escape from himself than in his living he could leave Mary. Yet self-centered in the ordinary sense he was not. The world, for the conceited man, starts and ends with himself. For Elia, Charles Lamb was merely the point of departure to the world around him. Although with him the first person singular was a favorite pronoun, as he used it, it somehow managed to seem printed with a small "i."

Lamb was too unpretentious to pretend to be omniscient. He was poignantly aware that few people are able to speak for themselves, much less for others. Speaking of and through himself was his way of speaking for all. He knew his own voice contained the echoes of other voices. In this way he chose to write, intertwining with his identity griefs and affections which were not his own, "making himself many, or reducing many unto himself."

Since truth to Lamb was as personal as everything else, facts enjoyed no immunity from his prankishness. It diverted him to distort them when, as Elia, he wrote of his friends, his family, or himself. His love of mystification was one of the abidingly boyish aspects of his character. It pleased him in his essays to mislead his readers by false scents; to write Oxford when he meant Cambridge; to make Bridget his cousin, not his sister; to merge Coleridge's boyhood with his own; or to paint himself as a hopeless drunkard when, as a matter of fact, he was a man who, though he loved to down a drink, was seldom downed by drinking. By deliberate, sometimes mischievous, design his familiar essays were but the "shadows of fact." They were "verisimilitudes, not verities." Yet Lamb was present, quintessentially if not factually, in their every phrase and sentence. At least an important part of him was present, though not by any means the whole man.

Closely related as Elia is to Charles Lamb, they were not—they are not—in any sense of the word identical. When it came to authorship, there were two Charles Lambs. If not that, there was, at any rate, one Lamb who wrote in two styles so different that he could be suspected of employing his left hand for the one, his right hand for the other. As in the case of countless others, ink-stained or ink-free, Lamb had a public and a private manner. He did not write to his friends as he wrote for the magazines. Although in either case a natural-born essayist, and a matchless critic of books and men, his style, which was always intimate, altered according to whether his pen or a printer was to be the transmitter of his words.

Hazlitt's portrait of him as a nobleman of another day caught the spirit, not of Lamb the private letter writer, but of Lamb the public essayist. Certainly, the Lamb who contributed to periodicals was not the Renaissance figure Hazlitt envisaged. Yet Hazlitt was right beyond dispute in dressing this Lamb in the clothes of an age other than his own. When he wrote for publication, Lamb did go into costume as surely as, when he dashed off notes to his friends, he donned a dress so modern that after the passage of more than a century it seems as contemporary to us as it did to them.

The highly, at moments even dangerously, self-conscious artist we cherish as Elia emerged late in Lamb's life as the flowering of his varied career as a professional writer. By that time Lamb had long since mislaid, except for album purposes, the poet of slight endowment he had started out by being. Years before, too, he had discarded the novelist whose all but nonexistent talent for narrative stamped *Rosamund Gray* and his contributions to *Mrs. Leicester's*

School as no more than apprentice work. He had also buried the dramatist with "no head for playwriting" whose blank verse tragedy *John Woodvil* was but the feeblest of Elizabethan echoes, and whose little farce *Mr. H . . .* was so disastrous a failure that its author had joined in the hissing.

In the same way Lamb had outgrown those un-Lamblike *Tales from Shakespeare* upon which he had collaborated with Mary. Although he had predicted such a potboiler would be popular "among the little people," he had never guessed how enduring its popularity would prove among those grownups of little courage who, apparently, are grateful for anything which spares them Shakespeare in the original.

The first volume of the *Elia* essays was published when Lamb was forty-eight; the second, and last, ten years later. In print, and in such memorable papers as his "On the Genius and Character of Hogarth" and "On the Tragedies of Shakespeare," Lamb had already established not only his brilliance as a critic but his unique public manner as an essayist. Yet during all these formative years, in fact from his first preserved letters to Coleridge before and after Mary's murder of her mother, right down to the last note scribbled off to Mrs. Dyer (about a book, appropriately enough) five days before his death thirty-eight years later, Lamb was the possessor of an epistolary style quite at odds with the style we know as Elia's.

More than being the best introduction to Lamb, Lamb's are among the world's best letters. In them we almost hear him talk. To be sure, his stutter is gone, and an incredible fluency has replaced it. But, as in all good letters, the illusion of direct communication is maintained. Both the moment and the mood are captured in all the heat of their passing sorrow or amusement. The small details, the great agonies, the first impressions, the play of mind and the play on words, the reflections by means of which a particular instance is lifted into a generality, the tastes of food, the smells of London, the look of friends, the résumé of last night's party, the book just read, the anecdote just heard, this day's sadness, the next day's gaiety—they are all there, caught hot, caught frankly, and transferred without effort by a pen scratching swiftly against stolen time at the office.

Perhaps the speed of their composition was the guarantee of their simplicity. In any case, again and again Charles' letters deny their datelines by remaining undated. They are not so much the products of an age as they are models for all time. Whether they are "thank you" notes for a visit paid or a roast pig sent; apologies for having to be carried home from an overconvivial evening; his proposal of marriage to Fanny Kelly; the gossip of London dispatched across the oceans to Manning in China; religious musings; discussions of death; the account to Coleridge, magnificent in its dignity, of his mother's murder; appraisals of Defoe, Cervantes, Godwin's *Chaucer*, or the second edition of the *Lyrical Ballads,* they are perfect of their kind.

They show the warmth, the originality, the humor, or the grandeur of the astonishing little man who wrote them. They are the spontaneous distillations of a writer, instinctive and superior. They make us companions not only in Lamb's daily living but in his adult life. Their every episodic entry fits into a sequence. Without meaning to do so, they form an autobiography from which Lamb's biographers must quote and to which everyone who would know him must turn. They give us Lamb unadorned; Lamb, the writer, without self-consciousness, hence often at his finest; Lamb, so to speak, at his slippered ease, relaxed, using short sentences, hitting directly; Lamb employing the most vivid and abrupt of colloquialisms, thus avoiding the calculated, beautiful, and antique cadences so dear to Elia.

The difference between the letter writer who signed himself C.L. and the essayist known as Elia is the difference between a candid-camera close-up and a full-length portrait in oil, appareled for effect and so posed that its very casualness is studied. It is the difference between jewels unset and a necklace painstakingly matched. It is, in short, the everlasting difference between the impromptu and the planned.

When Thackeray's "Saint Charles" wrote for the public prints, he heard voices, Joan-wise. The sonorities of such favorite prose writers as Sir Thomas Browne, Burton, Marvell, and Fuller haunted his ears. "I gather myself up into the old things," wrote Lamb. More accurately, he gathered the old authors up into himself. Their outmoded language was an expression of what was backward-glancing in his spirit. It pleased him by being out of date. It orchestrated his melancholy. Not only that. When appropriated for his casual personal essays, its very gravity served as a foil to his humor.

Lamb loved the stately rhythms and obsolete words of these older writers. While playing chameleon to their style, he could achieve a style of his own. He imitated in order to create what is inimitable. The borrowed pencil Hazlitt accused him of employing as an essayist was put by Lamb to his own uses. He was aware that, as Elia, his writings were "villainously pranked in an affected arrangement of antique modes and phrases." But he knew these writings would not have been his, had this not been so. "Better it is," said he, "that a writer should be natural in a self-pleasing quaintness, than to affect a naturalness (so called) that should be strange to him."

Quaint Elia was, and is, and in a manner pleasing not only to himself but to readers everywhere once they have become Elians. This is no hard thing to do, if only in a more hurried age, when prose is thinner and the language employed more often than it is enjoyed, readers are willing to give Elia and themselves a chance. His essays never were *in date,* except for what is dateless in their insight. Stylistically, they were intentional anachronisms when they were published. Their antique flavor was, and remains, a source of their charm.

To modern eyes, accustomed as they are to sentences being the shortest distance between a subject and a predicate (if, indeed, they extend that far), the long, leisurely, and intricate constructions of Lamb the essayist may at first glance appear forbidding. Yet forbidding is the very last word anyone in his right senses, and with the slightest acquaintance with Lamb, would dream of using for those gloriously warm and intimate essays which Lamb wrote as a critic of life, or of art, the theatre, and books. If, at the outset, their subtle and sustained sentences seem difficult, with their "me-thinks," their "thees" and "thous," their "arts," "werts," "readers," and other pressed flowers from another day, or their addiction to such words as "agnise," "additaments," and "dulcifying," these difficulties soon turn into delights. However truffled, archaic, or self-conscious was Lamb's formal style, it is rich in its rewards. Costume prose it may be, but costume jewelry it never was because its gems are genuine.

More than taking knowing, Elia survives it. His better essays belong in that class of literature he described as being "perpetually self-reproductive." They bear reading and rereading, and then can be read and reread again. They are habit-forming rather than time-passing. If the style in their case is not the whole man, it is at any rate the essayist. Elia cannot be separated from it. Nor would anyone who has once cultivated a taste for that style be denied its enjoyment. Although, as a word man, Lamb was deaf to music and could complain about its "measured malice," Elia was able with words to release an incomparable music of his own.

He was the opposite of those writers he dismissed as being "economists only in delight." His prodigality with the pleasures he provides is limitless. The joy he creates from small things is large. The conceits in his phrasing are redeemed by the sincerity of his feeling. If he seldom wrote a bromide, it was because he seldom thought one. The commonest reaction became uncommon in his statement of it. His vocabulary was as much his own as his mind, and both were unpredictable.

As is true of all good essayists, not too much of Elia is to be read at one sitting. He fatigues, not by the ardor of his emotions, but by the incessant probing of his perceptions, by the sudden quiet dartings of his mind and the abundance of his allusions. To be enjoyed fully, he must be lingered over, read with the same disregard for the present that he showed, savored as he savored the subjects of his choice. He is a writer who does not raise his voice. He avoids emphasis. His finest phrases spill from his pen without warning. They are tucked away, not paraded. They come jostling, one so close upon the other that they are apt to be overlooked. To miss them is to miss the true satisfactions of Elia, because in his phrases he gives the pleasures other authors give in their paragraphs.

His mood is ruminative, his mind associational. For all the amusement to be had from the felicities of his observations, his was an essentially tragic nature. He was a tragedian who smiled instead of crying. This not only deepens his humor, it insures its humanity.

On the subject of his family, his youth, his London, the places he had visited, or the "characters" he had known, his vision was as detailed and unblinking as it was in his criticism. Yet, uncanny as was his accuracy as a reporter, Lamb was never a journalist.

What he wrote as journalism somewhow managed to be literature. "In eternity," pointed out Sir Thomas Browne, "there is no distinction of Tenses." This line in the *Religio Medici* was one which, as both a familiar essayist and a magazine critic, Lamb must have hugged to his heart. For him datelines did not exist. He had no interest in news and less sense of it. News, as he saw it, was whatever happened to interest him, however personal or remote. The measure of his ability is that he made it interesting to his contemporaries, and even now makes us feel contemporaneous with it.

As a critic no less than as a man, Lamb lived in a world where watches had stopped. Yet he creates the illusion that they are still ticking. What he was fond of reviewing was not last night's or last week's play but his memories of twenty or thirty years ago. Although this was all a part of his being unable to make present times present to him, it has never prevented him from making times past present to us.

LAMB AS A CRITIC

If Charles Lamb does not belong in the company of the greatest critics, neither do they belong in his. It is not so much that they stride ahead of him as that he elects to amble to one side of them, well off the main thoroughfares. Even in criticism, he is a lonely figure who goes his own way. That the paths of his choice happen to be bypaths is part of the enticement and originality of his approach. He is one of the most satisfying and least pretentious of critics; major in a minor way, though major nonetheless.

Greatness, among other things, is bound to involve scale. Size, spiritual or actual, is part of it. Breadth, width, depth are among its common dimensional attributes. These qualities, in the ordinary heroic sense, were not Lamb's. Perfection, however, is not a matter of size. Although a Borglum may reach the peaks by mutilating them, that he produces bigger works than a Cellini does not mean he is the better artist. It was on the Cellini scale that Lamb worked. In criticism, as in his essays, he was a jeweler, a goblet-fashioner, an unrivaled craftsman in gold and silver. The fact that he was not a titan does not condemn him to being a midget. As a critic, he was an extraordinary artist. His genius as an artist is the reason for his greatness as a critic.

Dryden, Dr. Johnson, Coleridge, Hazlitt, or Shaw, for example, rejoice in a muscularity, a lunge, an intensity, a bigness, or a purpose Lamb does not possess. Yet he possesses charms they cannot claim, perceptions they do not have, and merits which are not theirs. They delve into fundamentals which for him have no interest. They risk complete estimates of a man, a work, or a period which he avoids. They come to their subjects head-on, excelling at large-scale frontal attacks where he excels at minor skirmishes and sudden, fruitful forays at the flanks or behind the lines. Or, convinced that the truth as they have seen it is the whole truth, they can fight lusty battles for causes which leave him unmobilized.

Critically, they and their kind are warriors; male, aggressive, and so magnificent in their energies that they are forces. Lamb is no force. He is only a phenomenon, and a joy. To the embattled realm of opinions he brings his vagaries rather than his convictions, his paradoxes instead of principles. He does not destroy; he re-creates. His critical weapon is a gold miner's sieve, not a battle-ax. He rises to appreciation with the same happy subtle discernment most critics muster for depreciation. He writes less to persuade others than to state for himself what, for the moment, he has been persuaded of. Even his deliberate half-truths are so engagingly advanced by him that, in the reading, they seem preferable to the full truths advanced by others. If Lamb proves little, he almost always proves delightful. In his case, that is enough. Having sought pleasure, he gives it. "It is not in my method," said he, "to inflict pain. I leave that to heaven."

"Criticism," noted Dr. Johnson, "is a study by which men grow important and formidable at very small expense." Lamb had no desire to be either. He disliked "being treated like a grave or respectable character." His sympathy with professional critics was nonexistent. He abhorred all the airs they take on, without the graces, and the way they pride themselves upon being unable to share in the joys of others.

Lamb's attitude toward the theatre was typical of his attitude toward books and paintings. Theatrically he remained in spirit, as in his fondest recollections, a gallery god long after financial ease and his own prominence assured him the best of seats. He could neither understand nor tolerate the "frigid indifference" and "impenetrability" of those who sat in the boxes. Even in the pit he deplored the beginnings of "that accursed critical faculty, which, making a man the judge of his own pleasures, too often constitutes him the executioner of his own and others!"

To Lamb such standoffishness, worse than being incompatible, was downright "vile." Professional critics and reviewers, in his eyes, were "animals." Fastidious, special, and searching as were his tastes, he preferred to identify himself with the *genuine spectators*. By these he had in mind such simple people as a "shop-keeper and his family, whose honest titillations of mirth" could not wait "to take the cue from the sour judging faces about them." In spite of his own inquiring and scholarly spirit, Lamb gave his love to the "uninquiring gratitude" of such spectators. Although with them he mistakenly identified himself, he wrote delectably from an unmistakable capacity for enjoyment which they might well have envied.

Lamb's shortcomings as a critic are self-evident. He does not soar as one of the eagles in a profession more often than not wing-less. He hovers like a bee, avid for the taste of honey. Moreover, beelike, he is quick to find it, to linger over it, and to transfer it. He neither intends to be reliable nor pretends to be impartial. He must be read with a caution which comes from understanding him, and from being both able and willing to enter into the game he can play. Since he is truer to his whims than his subject, he is not to be taken literally. He does not bother about being infallible. He writes quite frankly and disarmingly from his prejudices.

He is apt to be fanciful when he seems most dogmatic, or only half in earnest when he appears to be most serious. This aspect of Lamb not only eluded Macaulay but exasperated him. Yet it is the point and pleasure of Elia's defense of that "Utopia of Gallantry" which, as he saw it, was the true setting of Restoration comedy and hence lifted it beyond moral judgment "out of Christendom into the land of cuckoldry." It is no less clear in the famous contention of Lamb, the most ardent of theatre-lovers, that Shakespeare is the playwright whose works are "less calculated for performance on a stage than those of almost any other dramatist whatever."

George Saintsbury, a devoted and discerning "Agnist" if ever there was one, had to admit that, notwithstanding his excellence as a critic, Lamb could be guilty of *capriccio* (a word which Elia, no doubt, would have praised every bit as much as did the professor). This is why Saintsbury insisted that Lamb, rather than Leigh Hunt, deserves to be known as the "Ariel of Criticism." Beyond dispute, that is better than being the Caliban.

When he described such critics as belonging to the "Occult School," Hazlitt had Lamb in mind. "They discern no beauties but what are concealed from superficial eyes," wrote he, "and overlook all that are obvious to the vulgar part of mankind. . . . If an author is utterly unreadable, they can read him for ever; his intricacies are their delight, his mysteries are their study. . . . They will no more share a book than a mistress with a friend." The charge of occultism, in Lamb's case, is not unfair. It is just in spite of Lamb's affection for the gallery gods. It is part and parcel of his addiction to oddity. Yet, like the affectations of his public style, it is the natural expression of himself.

Lamb's blind spots were many, his tastes more eccentric than catholic. If he rejoiced in his lack of orthodoxy, so should his readers. Any mediocrity can be orthodox. (Most of them are.) Lamb, however, was nothing if not exceptional. Even the historical persons whom he once startled a company by naming as the people he would most like to meet were unaverage choices. Heading his lists were Pontius Pilate, Sir Thomas Browne, and Dr. Faustus.

In matters literary or artistic he was no less individual. He could discover no merit in *Candide* or *Gil Blas*. As an ardent admirer of Smollett, he was persuaded by Hazlitt, and then only with difficulty, to concede Fielding's superiority. When current authors were being discussed, he talked endlessly of John Donne and Sir Philip Sidney; when others were devouring the Waverley Novels, like as not he was poring over George Wither. If he was allergic to Scott, Byron, and Shelley, he was among the first to recognize Coleridge, Burns, and Wordsworth. His pioneering did not end there. As a critic of painting, his major concern may have been, unfashionably enough by our contemporary standards, the story told. Even so, he was the first to show a proper appreciation for Hogarth and Blake. Moreover, when he writes of their paintings he so succeeds in using his pen as a brush that he turns painter himself.

Coleridge did not lecture on the early English dramatists, except for Shakespeare, until 1818. Hazlitt's courses were not given until three years later. Yet it was in 1808 that Lamb published his *Specimens of English Dramatic Poets Who Lived about the Time of Shakespeare.* In them, in spite of the spadework already done by specialists, Lamb can be said to have made well-read, though unscholarly, Britishers feel for the first time that Marston, Heywood, Webster, Beaumont and Fletcher, Massinger and Ford were writers they *ought* to know. His notes, fragmentary and informal as they are, are among the most personal and revealing of his critical writings. Shaw, being Shaw, could lament Lamb's fondness for these figures as a "literary aberration." He could say he forgave this addiction of Lamb's "as we forgive him his addiction to gin." But most people, including Shavians, would not deny their debt to Lamb because of the way in which he salvaged the beauties of a body of literature which had come to be almost ignored.

No one has written about the theatre with greater warmth or perception than did Lamb about vanished players or the playhouses of his youth. By common consent, owing to common experience, few things are apt to be deader than the review of a forgotten play or a tribute to an actor the reader has neither heard about nor seen. Writing about the stage is usually doomed to be as evanescent as the pleasure or pain which prompted it. Those of us who attempt it professionally know this to our sorrow and chagrin. Nonetheless, there are uncommon, blessed instances when journalism takes on the stature of criticism and criticism that of literature. This happens when the copy read, having lost its immediate or practical usefulness to the reader, somehow survives in time without relying upon news interest, not as a guide to pleasure but as itself a pleasure, self-sustaining and self-contained. It happens when yesterday endures as today and tomorrow.

Lamb joins the proud company of the elect who have been able to pass this test, and to pass it triumphantly. He could put reviewing to his own uses as when, for example, he proposed to Fanny

Kelly (with negative results) in a notice of *Rachel*. "What a lass that were to go a gypseying through the world with!" sighed he in the public prints, pretending to quote a mythical neighbor. But, more than putting criticism to his own uses, he could put it to ours.

Bensley, Powel, Munden, Liston, Dodd, and Elliston are truly forgotten men. Except to a stage archivist, their names could not mean less had they been stumbled upon on broken tombstones in an abandoned graveyard. Yet Lamb's writing about them is so lively that not only do they live for us as if we had seen them but we know we are the luckier for having seen them through his eyes. To choose where choice is difficult, Bensley who seizes upon the moment of passion with greatest truth "like a faithful clock never striking before the time—never anticipating, or leading you to anticipate"; Bensley looking, speaking, and moving through the part of Malvolio as an old Castilian nobleman; Bensley keeping back "his intellect as some have had the power to retard their pulsation"; or Bensley allowing "a gleam of understanding" to "appear in a corner of his eye and for lack of fuel go out again" is more than a player described. He is a lesson in comic acting.

The same extension of an assignment, the same complete realization of an opportunity, is shown by Lamb in his notable essays "On the Artificial Comedy of the Last Century" or "On the Tragedies of Shakespeare." In both cases he writes mimetically as a critic should, taking the hint and color from his subject matter. Wycherley or Congreve did not produce prose wittier, more belaced, or of greater sparkle as verbal marquetry than he did when, in playful earnestness, he rose to the defense of their amoralities.

In "Barbara S——" Lamb could tell sentimentally, with skillful, hot, forced tears, the one backstage story that has come down to us which Woollcott might have written. To read Lamb, however, on the reasons why Shakespeare's greatest tragedies, in the fullness of their tragic statement, were beyond the posturing, grimacing, and gesturing of actors is to realize the extents to which he could carry theatrical writing. As many have pointed out, Lamb, with his admiration for actors, could of course have taken the other side of the argument with equal felicity. But even Lamb the theatre-lover stood no chance against Lamb the bookman or Lamb the intellectual. As a profound man who doted on the stage, and was more entitled than most to the escapes it offered him, he was too well aware of the theatre's limitations to be limited by them. In a style worthy of his subject he could so enter into Lear's mind that Lear ceased to be a character and became a mortal in agony.

The same Lamb who had abandoned poetry early in his career wrote as a poet when he was at his best as a critic or a correspondent. The stuttering, jesting, smoking, drinking little fellow, valiantly linked to Mary, was little in an abidingly big way. He was big of heart, large of mind, and unique in his endowments. Victim of life though he was, he was never victimized by it. He lived an interior life externally. It was his mind and the abilities out of which he fashioned his style which made his living, on the whole uneventful, eventful for the world no less than for him. Perhaps Pater, another stylist, wrote the best summary of Lamb in these words, "Unoccupied, as he might seem, with great matters, he is in immediate contact with what is real, especially in its caressing littleness, that littleness in which there is much of the whole woeful heart of things, and meets it more than half-way with a perfect understanding of it."

9. Off Stage, and On

The four Georges—the classroom lecturer, the conductor of a famous class in playwriting, the able director, and the frustrated actor—who combined to turn Mr. Baker into an outstanding teacher and active force in the theatre.

[1935]

GEORGE PIERCE BAKER AT WORK

HAD THERE been only one George Pierce Baker, and had he been the arbitrary teacher of playwriting that some of his critics have imagined he must be because he dared to give courses in the writing of plays, his influence would not have extended beyond his classrooms, if indeed it would have stretched that far. But there were at least four Bakers functioning simultaneously in the two great universities which claimed him. And at Yale, as at Harvard, all four of them were significant.

First, there was the Baker most widely known to undergraduates at Harvard, at Radcliffe, and at Yale; the formal classroom Baker whose business it was to teach the history of the drama to anyone who might care to learn it. He chose his materials so wisely (they were new when he first presented them) and showed such a happy instinct for limiting his attention only to what was theatrically most significant in each man or period he dealt with, that hundreds of those who have sat under him, and then turned teacher, have been compelled to follow in his footsteps down the straight trail he blazed through history. This classroom Baker, seated behind a broad desk, with a sheaf of faded notes before him, and a black brief case stuffed with dusty books beside him, was the most professorial of the four Bakers, and, for that very reason, of later years the least important of the lot.

For some years he was a slightly bored and tired man. Even in his last terms at Harvard, his lectures on the essentials of a play, the four tellings of the Electra story (this was before O'Neill had raised the number to five), Aristophanes, *The Cid,* Victor Hugo, or what have you, showed the long-run system can be as dangerous for teachers as it is for actors. When he spoke of Lope de Vega or Tom Robertson he did so in tones as mechanical as Joseph Jefferson's must have been when, after countless seasons of playing Rip, he called for his dog Schneider.

There was much good stuff in these outline courses. Whether the subject was the English drama from its beginnings to the closing of the playhouses in 1642, or from the Restoration to modern times, or a general survey of the world's drama, the facts were all there, earnestly investigated, and set forth with the precision of the man who had edited the *Belles Lettres* series, who had published an interesting batch of Garrick letters, performed the same service for the Charles Dickens–Maria Beadnell correspondence, written in *The Development of Shakespeare as Dramatist* a penetrating, if outmoded, study of Shakespeare's technique, and helpfully set forth the common-sense essentials of playwriting in his *Dramatic Technique.*

Yellow as his notes may have been, and slightly bored as he may himself have seemed in the classroom, these lectures of Mr. Baker's had the decided advantage of being delivered by a man whose primary interest was the theatre. He never abused dramatic literature by treating it as if it had no connection with the stage. He kept it smudged with grease paint. Even in his weariness, he managed to give the impression that the desk behind which he was lecturing was surrounded by footlights.

Witty as many of his comments were, clarifying as his perceptions proved, and amusing as he used to be when he would roll out long sentences and make a classroom roar at their intentional involutions, the moments one remembers best were those in which he forgot all about facts and tendencies, and abandoning his professorial calm, began to make his points as an actor. He had his favorite characters by means of which he would expose the virtues or the follies of a type of playwriting.

Sir Fopling Flutter in *The Man of Mode* was one of these. When he came to him, Professor Baker's blue-gray eyes would deepen behind his pince-nez, his face would beam with pleasure, his portly body rock with mirth. Still seated at his desk, with his coat, usually dark gray, tightly buttoned, he would begin to assume the airs and graces of a Restoration fop. His voice would change and take on the mincing tones of Etherege's hero. His hands, which he always used swiftly, would begin to race in circles. Artificial gallantries would be slightly indicated in a way which seemed so courtly and was so deliciously right that one could have sworn his sleeves were fringed with lace.

Professor Baker was no less happy when, during his talks on Henry Arthur Jones and Arthur Wing Pinero, those transitional dramatists who were his friends, he could show the strides they had made as playwrights by quoting from their earlier works. In Mr. Jones' *Saints and Sinners* he used to give as admirable a performance as he did in *The Man of Mode*. By doing so he pointed out all that was absurd in the older melodramas. Standing up, with his left hand pushed far into the pocket of his coat and still holding a copy of the play in his right, he would act the scene in which Fanshawe, the extremely wicked villain of the piece, confesses in a soliloquy that his intentions toward the parson's daughter are not honorable. A terrific scowl would spread across Mr. Baker's face and seem to take possession of his vocal cords. As he leaned against the blackboard, imitating Fanshawe who was supposed to be resting against a tree, flicked ashes off an imaginary cigarette, and indulged in chuckles far more diabolical than any Jones had dreamed of, the classroom turned into a theatre. On that academic stage, a melodrama of not-so-long ago was spoofed far more entertainingly than have been many of the older melodramas which have recently been revived.

To those who took his historical courses at the same time they were working with him in other capacities, the reason for his coldness in the lecture hall was clear enough. He was a teacher who had tired of teaching in the ordinary way. His notes were left yellow and unadded to because his heart was no longer in them. They held as little interest for him as a train does for the person who has left it after it has carried him safely to his destination. From the fall of 1903, when he was first allowed to experiment at Radcliffe with a course in playwriting, he must have realized with an ever-increasing clarity that the drama's present, and not its past, was his goal. Undoubtedly he felt indebted to these historical courses he continued to give, because it was by means of them he had been directed to his new field of interest. Perhaps he also hoped they would perform the same service for those who took them that they had performed for him. From an intimate knowledge of the theatre's past might come a desire to contribute to its present-day practice. Be that as it may, the Baker who "walked through" these courses, year after year, was much too much of a New Englander and far too well trained as a professor to succeed in faking what he did not feel. In this respect his acting talents, even his theatrical instinct, failed him.

The man who met his incipient playwrights in an upper room in Harvard's Widener Library did not have to act. He was doing what he liked, and his liking for what he had to do was plain from the moment he hurried in, deposited his black actor-y hat on a nearby bookcase, took off his dark coat, pulled some blue-covered manuscripts out of his bulging brief case, and seated himself at the circular oak table around which the students were grouped informally. This second of the four Bakers was beholden to no notes. The job ahead of him required patience, but for some miraculous reason he did not look upon it as a chore. The forbidding, un-get-at-able Puritan who put the underclassmen off was beginning to thaw. The chalky mask of professordom was being laid aside. A new man was emerging.

This Professor Baker who dared to teach such an unteachable subject as playwriting was the least dogmatic of men. He had no Golden Rules of Dramaturgy. He did not pretend to be able to turn out playwrights in ten easy lessons. He did not claim to be able to turn them out at all. He was among the first to admit dramatists are born, not made. But he did hope to be able to shorten the playwright's period of apprenticeship by granting him the same instruction in the essentials of his craft that the architect, the painter, the sculptor, and the musician enjoyed in theirs.

There was nothing oracular about his methods in these seminars. He did not lecture. He dodged the absolute. He issued no proclamations and passed no laws as to what dialogue or plotting or characterization should be. His distinctions between the materials available to the novelist and the dramatist were given in his book. So, too, were his common-sense pleas for clarity, for the scenarios he felt it advisable for playwrights to draft before beginning their actual scripts, and his endless illustrations of what was good and bad in dramatic practice and why.

But what was inelastically stated in *Dramatic Technique,* with that finality which can attach itself to words set down in black and white, was flexible and free when spoken by Mr. Baker and applied to a case in point. His verbal comments had another advantage over his written ones, inasmuch as they could keep pace with tastes of changing years. Where the date 1919 on the title page of his book was bound eventually to seem printed on many of the pages which followed it, Mr. Baker's point of view remained undated. Born a contemporary of Jones and Pinero, he managed to continue as the contemporary of each class that came to him.

When he had hurried into that upper room at Widener and seated himself at the table, with the window behind him and the light pouring down on the manuscript he held in his hands, it was obvious that his belief in "the play's the thing" was stronger than any Hamlet's has ever been. He spoke briefly, except at the early meetings of the class when he was making his initial assignments and waiting for his playwrights to turn in their first scripts. His custom was to let the plays speak for themselves.

His program for his beginners was as similar each year as the results were different. Invariably the course would start off with a one-act dramatization of a short story. Three short stories, culled from anywhere, could be selected by each of the tyros for Professor Baker's approval (or his demon assistant's). Always the one presenting the most insurmountable technical problems was the one chosen. Next came an original one-act play, and, finally, by spring, a long play. As many others as the students happened to write and wanted comment upon were gladly received.

A sure test of the merits of a play was Mr. Baker's reading of it. He was an exceptional reader, and he made a point, whenever possible, of reading a manuscript at sight, without revealing the author's name. Naturally enough, he got scripts of all kinds and was forced to be as ready as an old-fashioned stock actor with quick-study characterizations and every conceivable dialect. He was compelled to vary French with Irish, Irish with Italian, Italian with English, English with American. Even as an American he was called upon to suggest tough guys of the toughest sort undergraduates could imagine, prostitutes who made Mae West seem virginal, Indians who grunted about Manitou on the mesa, Negroes who put Mrs. Stowe to shame, and Southern colonels who were more Southern than the Confederacy. He had to rip out oaths that only occasionally pinkened his cheeks or caused him to hasten madly through a speech, which was his other way of blushing. He had to read love scenes that must have disturbed everything New England in him. The number of pleas he was forced to make to imaginary juries would undoubtedly have captured Max Steuer's envy.

The wonder was he never succumbed to the temptation of making fun of the stuff he was reading. He could spoof the classics, real and pseudo, in his history courses, yet he never made sport of his young playwrights' work. He was on their side. He was fully aware that their fellow students would tear them limb from limb when the time for comment came. Accordingly he acted as their defender. He would plunge into the first manuscript on the pile before him (neatly typed in black and red, of course, in order to distinguish the dialogue from the stage directions) and read it through in the dialects required. Or, if none were needed, he would give it the benefit of that deep Boston voice of his which had a surprising way of going Brooklyn in its pronunciations every now and then. Perhaps it should be added that everyone thought Professor Baker was a good reader except the person whose play he happened to be reading. It was not hard to identify the dramatist in question. Author's vanity and a poker face are not compatible.

When the last page was finished and the final curtain read, the class had its merciless but helpful say. Mr. Baker merely presided over these discussions, throwing a word in here and there and waiting for his private conference with the playwright to give his own opinion or to make suggestions. Come to think of it, there was not any teaching, as teaching is ordinarily understood, in English 47. The course was as free from pedagogy as is the MacDowell Colony. There were only twelve or fifteen people who shared a common interest, who knew as they sat informally around that table that they were aiming at the same goal, and who were aided in their writing, first of all, by the simple knowledge that they had to get their stuff in on a certain date, and, secondly, by the reassuring thought that Mr. Baker somehow believed in them, for reasons which were not always clear. There was, of course, more to it than this. All-important was that indefinable evocative gift of Professor

Baker's which made him a great teacher even when he did not seem to be teaching at all.

The third of the four Bakers known to his Cambridge students was the tireless Baker, who, when he had lectured to his history courses at nine in the morning, spent several hours dictating letters in his small cubbyhole of an office, met with two of his four playwriting courses (he gave an elementary and an advanced course both at Harvard and Radcliffe), conferred with his dramatists, worked in the garden of his Brattle Street home, and eaten a hurried dinner, used to come rattling up to Massachusetts Hall in the dusty Dodge which his energy and his driving had aged so prematurely that it had begun to resemble his wrinkled brief case. Once arrived at the Johnson gate, and looking slightly surprised and pleased at having made a safe landing, he would wriggle out from behind the steering wheel, jump to the street, bang the door behind him, rush into the yard as if a host of demons were pursuing him, give a presidential salute to the men and women who were inhaling their last cigarettes and going over their lines beside the unperturbed bust of James Russell Lowell, and scurry through the two-story room which was the Cain's Warehouse of his past productions, prepared to spend the evening rehearsing the better plays his course had yielded.

Outside, Massachusetts Hall was (and still is) one of the truest architectural joys of the Harvard landscape. As one of the oldest structures in the Yard, it could boast that trim grace which early New Englanders were able to give to their buildings. Inside it was, at least in the days when Mr. Baker and his designers worked in it, a fascinating nightmare. Its hollow shell, cluttered with flats and drops which stretched to the ceiling, and smelling strongly of paint and glue, was a defiant contradiction of its chaste exterior. If Bernhardt's heart had beaten in Priscilla's body the effect could not have been more startling than it was to find this topsy-turvy, greasepaint kingdom enclosed by brick walls which had housed troops during the Revolution.

In the center of this confusion was a space cleared for a rehearsal stage. Facing it, with innumerable little paint-specked chairs flanking it on either side, was an equally spattered black table behind which Mr. Baker sat with the author. As he took up his position there night after night, half in the shadows and half-blinded by the light that beat down from above on the script he held in his hands, the Baker who in his youth was supposed to have resembled Edwin Booth came to life once more. His scraggly gray hair was darkened by the shadows. His long, sensitive face had a rapt intentness about it. There was something about his straight, tight lips which gave him an expression startlingly similar to the one that forever repeats itself in Booth's photographs.

At rehearsal, as in his sessions in Widener, Mr. Baker was the most stalwart defender his playwrights could find. His job was a far harder one than anyone realized, even as his work as a director was far more skillful than many people gave him credit for. Not only was he working with scripts which as student offerings had the right to be bad and for the most part took advantage of their right, but he made it his duty to protect these plays from actors who generally were inexperienced amateurs.

His faith in his dramatists was endless. He never forced them to rewrite, even when it was as obvious to him as it was to everyone else (except the playwrights in question) that drastic rewriting was necessary. His hope was that his playwrights would learn by having had a real production in front of a selected audience, every member of which was supposed to turn in a criticism. Those productions of his were, he knew, his surest means of instruction. They could teach more to dramatists possessed of any instinct for the theatre than hours of idle theorizing.

With his actors, as with his playwrights, Mr. Baker's patience knew no bounds. With them, too, though officially it was not supposed to be among his duties, he functioned as a teacher. He was an excellent judge of acting. He was blessed with that alert inner ear all good directors must have. It allowed him to hear a line as it was being read at the same time that it enabled him to hear it as it should be read. He had a sure sense of timing, a shrewd eye for character, and the all-important ability to get results from beginners.

When things got too bad, when his actors failed completely to give him what he wanted, he would push his chair back, dig his hands deep into the pockets of his coat, and rush onto the scene, with short, mincing steps and with one foot put before the other as if he were walking the tightrope, to illustrate how this or that part should be played.

He did not scold. In fact, he hardly ever lost his temper. But when he did, it was an impressive display; horribly dignified, chilly as the banks off Newfoundland; devastating as Cotton Mather's threats of brimstone. Almost always he was equability itself. This man who could straight-arm strangers so effectually, could be warmly intimate with the few to whom he gave his friendship each year. There was nothing of the palaverer in him. He kept his friendships, like his work, on the gold standard. As a scholar he valued the real meaning of words. As a dyed-in-the-wool New Englander he had an honest detestation of those amiable phrases which most people render meaningless by squandering lightly.

He was sparing, almost stingy, with praise. His thanks for something he liked or appreciated was a slight pat on the back, a hastily muttered "That's fine." This was all. Yet it was by means of these few words, as treasured by those who earned them as if they were public testimonials, that he reared the astonishing organization which flourished at Harvard; that he persuaded men and women, who received no pay and little credit for it, to sit up night after night to slave on his stage crews; that he got his actors, in spite of the courses they might be taking and the fact that the 47 Workshop counted for nothing as an undergraduate activity, to feel duty-bound to come promptly to all rehearsals; that he mesmerized designers into competing for the pivilege of setting one of his productions; and that he built up and held together that loyal Cambridge audience (he did the same thing in New Haven) which felt itself honored to be allowed to sit in at the performances of what were usually very bad plays.

This Baker who inspired more active loyalty than any other teacher at Harvard (not excepting the great "Copey" himself) was the fourth of the four Bakers. This man Baker, with his extraordinary personality, was the keystone upon which everything else rested. He may have put people off. His seeming coldness may have terrified some and antagonized others. Yet everyone who actually worked for him, and hence knew him—because he was the kind of man who revealed himself only in his work—felt affectionately toward him. He was not Professor Baker to them. He was "G.P.," but always, significantly enough, he was "G.P." only when he was safely out of earshot.

It is because these four Bakers existed side by side that there was—and can be—only one George Pierce Baker, as Yale has doubtless learned by now, and as Harvard discovered some years ago when Mr. Baker put the Cambridge elms behind him for New Haven and what Harvard was foolish enough to think at the time was "blue obscur-i-tee."

A little-known aspect of a well-known career, with an account of two of Wolfe's plays which were produced when he was a young graduate student at Harvard.

[1938]

THOMAS WOLFE AS A DRAMATIST

WHEN THOMAS WOLFE fell like a giant pine before the ax of a wasteful death, most of the newspapers commented upon his early interest in the theatre. They mentioned his having worked with Professor Frederick H. Koch at the University of North Carolina, and having then continued his studies with Professor George Pierce Baker at Harvard. Quite naturally, it was the novelist who had fathered such sprawling, though exceptional, books as *Look Homeward, Angel* and *Of Time and the River* rather than the young playwright whose scripts were never professionally produced that won their attention.

Still there is something to be said about Thomas Wolfe the dramatist who was and might-have-been. In spite of the fun he made of Mr. Baker's playwriting course in the bitterly sarcastic pages of *Of Time and the River,* the Tom Wolfe I remember at Harvard was one of the most earnest of Mr. Baker's dramatists.

To those of us who were stagestruck undergraduates at the time, Tom loomed large under the Cambridge elms as a man who had grown and grown until he was already as huge as his own legend. He was even taller than his talk. Words poured from that small head of his as red-hot lava flows down the slopes of a volcano whose top is almost hidden in the clouds.

His talk was hesitant at first, but could become brilliant, fevered, and exciting. Where most of his contemporaries were proud of having a thought to state in a single sentence, his ideas rolled out even then in chapters. What added to the color of his conversation was the frenzy which burned in his black eyes, and the vehement intensity with which all he had to say was said. His speech was nervous. It was halting and jerky in its separate cadences, and filled with suddenly asked questions which were thrown out without waiting for answers or expecting them. Yet it achieved smoothness by the very magic of its volume, by beating down upon his astonished listeners like a cloudburst of improvisation. It was made the more impressive because Tom himself called to mind a titanic hillbilly, a Paul Bunyan of the Southern mountains who, in the course of his protracted feuds with an idea, might stoop down above the door at any minute and reach for a shotgun with which to puncture his sentences.

The mountains were very much in Tom's thoughts when he first reached Harvard. He had already written for Professor Koch a lurid one-act tragedy called *The Return of Buck Gavin* for which, at Chapel Hill in 1919, he had pasted on some false whiskers to play his own mountain outlaw. If you doubt me, you have only to turn to the second series of Mr. Koch's *Carolina Folk Plays* and, before reading Mr. Wolfe's early effort, look at a picture of him in make-up. In this photograph you cannot fail to notice in the man the "suggestion of . . . pantherlike power" which Tom asked for in his stage direction. Though some of this power is "veiled" behind his beard, it flames in Tom's tortured eyes.

Tom carried the mountains with him to the Workshop. The first of his plays Mr. Baker produced was an utterly conventional little one-act, known accurately enough as *The Mountains*. Although it might almost have served as a mountain play to end all mountain plays, unfortunately it did not. Its hero, as is the custom in hillbilly scripts, was an unhappy young fellow, anxious to get away from the mountains. As I remember, the curtain had not been up two minutes before he walked to a window and shook his fists vehemently at an inoffensive peak painted on the backdrop, crying "Goddamn you, Baldpate [for that was the mountain's name], yuh hemmin' me in!"

Two years later, in May 1923, Mr. Baker staged the first of Tom's plays to bear signs, however faint, of his genius. It was *Welcome to Our City,* a long, occasionally expressionistic drama in ten scenes. It was not a good play. Although it was as undisciplined as you would have expected a play by Thomas Wolfe to be, it contained some promising writing. It boasted, moreover, one hilarious satiric scene, written in dumb show (amazingly enough). In this episode a phony Carolina governor (played by Leon Pearson) was shown up in all his phoniness by the simple act of permitting the audience to watch him undress. He had retired alone to his hotel bedroom, full of political pomposity. First he surveyed himself in a mirror, making fine oratorical gestures. Then little by little he shed both his clothing and his dignity. First he removed his padded coat. Then his layer-after-layer of vests. Then he took off his toupee. Finally, just as he was getting into bed he slipped his false teeth in a tumbler. Before this scene was over more than the body of this governor was unclothed. His character was naked.

Tom must have been amused as he watched the Cambridge performances of *Welcome to Our City.* His play was deeply concerned, among other things, with the way in which a proud young Southern aristocrat seduces a pretty young mulatto. In choosing his actors Mr. Baker could never have been accused of type-casting. New England was conscripted, much to its surprise. It was Cambridge's Dorothy Sands who assumed a sweet-potato voice to impersonate the wronged mulatto. And it was the elder Senator Henry Cabot Lodge's grandson, John, since turned movie actor (and more recently Congressman, Governor, and Ambassador), who played the rebel seducer.

Welcome to Our City came near to being done professionally in New York. Tom submitted the script to the Neighborhood Playhouse, which was very much interested. As I recall Helen Arthur's telling of the story, she sent Tom a letter expressing her enthusiasm for the play, and saying the Neighborhood would like to do it. As a matter of routine, she suggested some necessary alterations.

But she did not then know her author. Practically by return mail she received an irate letter from him, filled with expletives, demanding the immediate return of the script, and asking who the hell she thought she was anyway to know more about his play than he did.

If Miss Arthur had been a mountain named Baldpate, Mr. Wolfe could not have been angrier at her. Had he gone on with the theatre Tom would always have been shaking his huge fists at it. It would have hemmed him in. Even in his novel-writing he was hemmed in, and fought like the genius he unquestionably was for a complete freedom he never quite found. Of such geniuses, however, the theatre stands permanently in need.

The luminous contributions to our stage of an artist who served as the theatre's high priest of beauty and helped make it a place of wonder.

[1954]

ROBERT EDMOND JONES—1887-1954

THE MAN speaking, though supposedly worldly and endowed with a fine mind and sharp eyes, had no heart. Literally, no heart at all. He had no name, either. But some of the observations he made about our theatre in 1947 to the late Robert Edmond Jones remain as true today as they were then.

"Your theatre," he said in effect, "is filled with uncertainty and is weary in its inner feeling. The insecurity it reflects is not the insecurity of the life that goes on around us, but an insecurity in the body of the theatre itself, an insecurity as to its own nature and its own purposes. There is plenty of ingenuity there, and lots of novelty, and lots of experimentation, of a sort. But the plain truth is that it doesn't deal, either in subject or in form, with matters that truly concern us. I cannot escape the impression that the writers and the producers and the actors and the directors of your theatre have lost their sense of wonder. They prefer the dim view. They ignore our hunger for nobility."

The reason this not unshrewd observer had neither heart nor name was that he never lived except in Bobby Jones' imagination. Bobby had come across a passage in which Walt Whitman, when he was dramatic critic of the *Brooklyn Daily Eagle,* had written, "It would be a curious result—and a profitable one—to take a while to the theatre some man highly educated and knowing the world in other things—but totally fresh to the stage—and let him give his real opinion of the queer sort of doing he would see there." Thinking about this sentence, Bobby, in an essay called "Curious and Profitable," had created the kind of hypothetical visitor Whitman had in mind and taken him as his companion on a tour of our theatres and movies. Inevitably this visitor, while speaking for himself, spoke for Bobby, employing his very special vocabulary and seeing the stage through his exceptional eyes. The lacks he found in our theatre were deficiencies Bobby had long noted and often gloriously made up for in his own work.

Most decidedly, the theatre Bobby Jones believed in and created was a theatre that did not take the dim view and had not lost its sense of wonder. It was an extension of life, not a duplication, a heightening rather than a reproduction. The vision of what the theatre might be, as opposed to what it is, was present in almost every word Bobby ever wrote or spoke. On the printed page, as in his settings, he was our stage's high priest of evocation. No one who heard him could doubt his dedication, no one who saw his work question his genius. He was an unashamed pleader for beauty and, far more important, an unsurpassed creator of it.

"The artist should omit the details, the prose of nature, and give us only the spirit and the splendor," Bobby contended in *The Dramatic Imagination,* and he practiced what he preached. "The spirit and the splendor," plus "an excitement, a high rare mood, and a conception of greatness," were with him life-long dreams which he turned into realities.

The theatre for him was always "an exceptional occasion." That is why Bobby hated it when its dialogue was dictaphonic, its concerns humdrum, or when it fed the eye on the drab, the nonselective, or the undistinguished. At one point in *The Dramatic Imagination* he said in a parenthesis, "it would be hard, perhaps, to make the waterfront saloon setting of *Anna Christie* lustrous." Then he added, "But I am not so sure." In his case he had no reason to be unsure. Just as Midas had the touch of gold, Bobby had the quickening touch of radiance.

The ugliest scenes in real life throbbed with beauty when he had transformed them into scenery. Not an insipid or self-advertising prettiness. Not that at all. Instead, they acquired a tension, a sense of mood, a luminosity, and a quality of drama which made spectators at once aware that reality had been lifted into theatre, and theatre into art. "Lustrous" was precisely what Bobby did make that waterfront saloon in 1921, even as "lustrous" to a greater extent is what he made the backroom and bar of Harry Hope's saloon in *The Iceman Cometh* twenty-five years later. Throughout his career this very attribute of being "lustrous" was an outstanding characteristic of his work, and one that set it apart.

I have to write about Bobby and his career in personal terms. Not to do so would be as false as referring to him as "Mr. Jones" and pretending that I had not known him long and fairly well. Since we were friends in spite of occasional fierce fights and disagreements, he was "Bobby" to me and his career is one that I followed almost from its beginning. As a matter of fact, the first article about the theatre I ever wrote for a newspaper was about him. It appeared in the *Louisville Courier-Journal* in the winter of 1919 under the title of "Craftsmanship of Robert Edmond Jones." I was then a freshman at Harvard who had been introduced the year before to a new world by "Mr. Jones' " unforgettable settings for *Redemption* and *The Jest*.

The first time I ever saw Robert Edmond Jones was when he came to speak at Harvard during my sophomore year. To those of us already stagestruck his coming was the cause of considerable excitement. Art with a capital "A" was very much in the theatrical air and this Jones man was known to us as one of its chief votaries and practitioners. We undergraduates who cared about the stage had not read our Kenneth Macgowan for nothing. We were steeped in Gordon Craig's *On the Art of the Theatre* and *The Theatre Advancing*, in Hiram Moderwell's *The Theatre of Today*, in Sheldon Cheney's *The New Movement in the Theatre* and *The Art*

Theatre, and in the pages of Mrs. Isaacs' *Theatre Arts* (still a quarterly).

Bobby stepped onto the pink and white platform of the Music Building, wearing evening clothes as if they pained his spirit. His face was paler than the moon. He looked young, incredibly young. His hair was full and black, and in addition to the mustache he wore throughout his life he then sported a beard which, more than being "Left Bank," was almost sacrilegious.

He seemed shy, frightened really, and there was something about him of the holy man which he did not try to hide. It seemed to come naturally to him, and we sophomores accepted him on his own terms. His speech, though hesitant, was sonorous. Most of what he said I do not now remember. I can, however, hear the richness of his voice. I also recall surrendering to his gift for conjuring visions with words.

Toward the lecture's end he confessed that he looked forward to the time (he seemed to see it right in front of him, too) when in the theatre the imagination would be set free, and realism abandoned because no longer necessary.

"Some day," said he, as if in a contagious trance, "we will play the duel scene in Macbeth with Macduff standing far off at one side of the stage and Macbeth standing far off at the other. Their swords will never cross and will not have to. Yet we, following the eloquent suggestion of their pantomime, will think their blades have crossed. With our own imaginations we will complete their gestures for them."

Just what all this meant, or what was to be gained by such a stylized laying on, I did not know and do not know now. The point is that Bobby made all of us think we understood. At any rate, he made us realize that the outward fact was not the end-all of art.

It was during that same season that Bobby did his celebrated settings for the Arthur Hopkins production of *Macbeth* in which Lionel Barrymore and Julia Arthur appeared. The revival, though a brave attempt, was a resounding failure. One reason was that the all too solid flesh and realistic performances of Mr. Barrymore and Miss Arthur were constantly at war with the symbolical abstractions of Bobby's scenery. On the Sunday before this *Macbeth* opened, however, Mr. Hopkins contributed an article to the *Times* which, tattered and yellowed, is still pasted in my Temple edition of the play. I continue to cherish it as a statement of courageous intentions and particularly value the opening line which reads, "In our interpretation of *Macbeth* we are seeking to release the radium of Shakespeare from the vessel of tradition." When I came to know Bobby after my graduation and during my years on Mrs. Isaacs' *Theatre Arts Monthly,* I realized more and more that he was always trying to release the radium not of Shakespeare alone but of whatever he touched "from the vessel of tradition."

.There are the cathedral and the Broadway approaches to the theatre. These are the two extremes. Bobby's approach, though he worked brilliantly on Broadway, was unquestionably the former. But it would be both unfair and untrue to suggest that he was a kind of grave St. Cecilia of scenic art. He loved life and he loved laughter, and his own laughter was the merriest of music. If he could be *précieux,* he could be salty and earthy too. He was as ready to welcome the theatre of Valeska Suratt, Eva Tanguay, Olga Petrova, the Fratellinis, Bill Robinson, Florence Mills, or the Marx Brothers, as he was the theatre of Sarah Bernhardt, Duse, Chaliapin, Nijinsky, John Barrymore, or the Lunts. His one desire was that what he saw on a stage, regardless of its level or kind, should be something different from life and more highly voltaged, something that had vitality and style, something that he could recognize and respond to at once as "theatre."

It was when Bobby sought to state his dreams and beliefs in words that he became solemn. In spite of often achieving beauty in his writing, he just as often wrote English of a fancy and florid kind that had a Bunthorne ring to it. Even in it, however, the beauty of his sensibilities and hopes was always clear.

His sketches were as strong in their simplicity as his writing could be elaborate. Jo Mielziner, who once was his assistant, says that Bobby was "the most practical of all dreamers." He assures me that, beautiful as his drawings were, Bobby never sketched for the sake of making beautiful drawings. The lines that he put down were always capable of realization on a stage. The Renaissance glories of his backgrounds for *The Jest*; the ominous outline of the Tower of London which dominated his *Richard III*; the great arch at the top of the long flight of steps in John Barrymore's *Hamlet*; the brooding austerity of his New England farmhouse in *Desire under the Elms*; the background of mirrors, as bright as

Congreve's wit, in *Love for Love*; the lovely Sunday-school inno-
cence of his cut-outs for *The Green Pastures*; the way in which he
connected the portico of the Mannons' Greek-Revival home in
Mourning Becomes Electra with the house of Agamemnon; the
subtle suggestions of decadence in his living room for *The Green
Bay Tree*; the bold bursts of Chinese red in *Lute Song*; or the
George Bellows-like depths and shadows of his barroom for *The
Iceman Cometh*—all these are stunning proofs of how completely
Bobby was able to turn his dreams into realities and produce
settings which lived as characters in the plays for which they were
designed.

His driving hope was to give the theatre glory and dignity and
excitement. This he did again and again in visual terms and as no
one else has done for our stage. It is easy to smile at some of the
language he used in describing his hopes. But, believe me, I, for
one, would suppress those smiles happily now and forever if only
more people at present dared to talk and write as Bobby did because they shared his determination and ability to restore dreams
to our almost dreamless theatre.

*The fabulous range of the language and the various uses to
which writers and lawyers often put it, as touched upon in
a speech delivered in Washington before the American Law
Institute on May 23, 1952.*

[1952]

LANGUAGE, LEGAL AND LITERARY

AT THIS moment I understand more fully than I ever have before
what Percy Hammond meant when, writing about some happily
forgotten play, he said that in its presence he felt as out of place as
an Elk at Oxford. I face you quakingly as a DP, untutored in your

language and addressing you in a tongue which to some of you may seem foreign.

In the past you have demonstrated your wisdom by limiting your speakers to lawyers and jurists. I am honored to follow them, humbled by the remembrance of their distinction, and more frightened than it would be manly to admit. Surely, on the damaging evidence of my presence, the American Law Institute has decided to turn this evening into a kind of "Amateur Night." No less surely, if I may use a word which has been occupying the attention of the Supreme Court and the country, the judgment of your president has for once, and once only, been the victim of a "seizure." For I am here as what Justice Cardozo called an "uninitiated interlocutor."

Although I come from a long line of lawyers, certainly my knowledge of the law is anything but professional. It is, I am afraid, largely derived from Portia, Dickens, Galsworthy, Edmund Pearson, William Roughead, and such melodramas as *On Trial, The Thirteenth Chair,* and *The Trial of Mary Dugan.* There is a reason for this which might as well be confessed at once. By employment I am a critic and a writer. I am, in short, what is sometimes identified as a "word-man." But you are "word-men," too. This is one of the things we have in common, regardless of how much the language as we choose to use it may sound as if it had been taken from different dictionaries.

The mention of word-men leads me to Gertrude Stein. She was a word-girl, and a wise one. Although she could write clearly when she wanted to, she sometimes eluded being understood as successfully as if she had been a lawyer. In a recent critical study Donald Sutherland has given an unforgettable account of Miss Stein's death. He tells us, "Just before she died, she asked, 'What is the answer?' No answer came. She laughed and said, 'In that case, what is the question?' Then she died." I know of no better proof of Miss Stein's wisdom, which was part of her originality.

I will not be able to give the answers this evening. But, at least, I know the questions I am trying to find the answers to. My endeavor will be to touch upon the differences and similarities between the language of the law and the language of literature. Yes, and to discuss the means, the goals, and the obligations of good writing in both fields.

With all my heart I wish what I have to say here were as worth saying and said as well as what Catherine Drinker Bowen said in "The Lawyer and the King's English," that brilliant paper she read in Philadelphia in 1951 before the Brandeis Lawyers Society. Mrs. Bowen pointed out that, though "you and I—the lawyer and the writer—do not, actually, belong to the same species, at least we can be classified under one genus . . . *articulate man*." Lawyers and writers, she added, are "interested in the techniques of utterance, and in what lies behind utterance—*intent:* the motivations of man."

In Mrs. Bowen's fashion I am concerned tonight with the shared articulateness of lawyers and writers, and the different techniques of utterance we so frequently employ. Perhaps Washington, D.C., is not the ideal setting for a discussion of the nuances, the beauties, and the noble possibilities of language. Anyone attempting such a discussion here is bound to resemble a preacher who has strayed into the pulpit of a church of another denomination.

For surely in no free area of the earth are there more men and women crowded together who daily do more damage to language than in the government bureaus of Washington. So far as the beauties of language are concerned, they form a wrecking crew. Their talent for misusing it, for making it drab, ugly, or deliberately incomprehensible can be described only as genius. Yet, in spite of those responsible for the gibberish of Governmentese, some of the truest eloquence this country or the world has known has been produced by those working for the government in high and varied stations in this very city.

Among the troubles with Washington from a literary standpoint is that it is a place where a writer does not have to be dead to be a ghost. The scale and absurdity of Washington as a ghost town was indicated by Yale's president, A. Whitney Griswold, when a few months back he spoke to the National Booksellers Association in New York. Mr. Griswold had learned with proper dismay that in Washington a university was about to open a course for ghostwriters, who "will be taught to write in such a way that orators will understand at all times what they are saying." There are more than one hundred and fifty such writers on the top level in Washington alone, an official of that university declared, and most of them have a hard time adjusting their talents "to fit the mental and oratorical capacities" of the men for whom they are writing.

Speaking words that others have written, having a voice but no style of your own, may be a necessary practice for overworked officials. But one thing it is not—and that is authorship. An author's style is his written voice; his spirit and mind caught in ink. It is as individual, hence unmistakable, as the cadences of Winston Churchill, a government official who, however overworked, has never failed to make himself heard in print. Mr. Churchill must also have had suggestions submitted to him by scores of experts, but what they have suggested he has possessed. And as surely as possession is nine-tenths of the law, possession (in terms of one's own very personal usage of language) is ten-tenths of authorship.

The late Alexander Woollcott was fond of describing himself as an ink-stained wretch. All of us, writers and lawyers alike, are ink-stained in our different ways. "Ink-stained" brings to mind another kind of wretch, one that offers a warning to us all by his ugly, if protective, habits. I am thinking of the squid which releases his homemade ink for the sole purpose of creating obscurity. You, as lawyers and judges, have, of course, never been guilty of such a practice any more than have we, the unbenched and ungowned writers. Clarity is one of our joint aims, at least I assume it often is.

Over a revolving door in the Ritz Hotel in Boston there is a sign printed large which reads, "This door is not an accredited egress." A squid or a bureaucrat could have written that. It is not a sentence which perpetuates the literary tradition of Emerson, Thoreau, or William James. As language, it could be said to represent the deflowering of New England. Unfortunately, there are those who, because they do not like the law and are confused by its terminology, would be willing to mistake such phrasing for standard legal usage.

Let us face the truth. Critics and lawyers have more things in common than their addiction to words. We have detractors, if not enemies; men and women who, oddly enough, do not dote on us and have attacked us with eloquence. Precious little criticism has been as sprightly or vivid as the abuse it has provoked. I could cite a hundred treasured phrases which creative writers have used to castigate reviewers with the understandable scorn that Man o' War would have shown had he, in the long and fruitful years of his retirement from the track, been judged by a jury of geldings. Let me content myself with repeating one of my favorites, Maxwell Anderson's dismissal of New York's drama critics as "the Jukes family of journalism."

You who have crossed the bar also have your belittlers. Some of these feel your gift for obfuscation is such that Prince Hal must have had you, rather than Falstaff, in mind when he said, "How now, my sweet creature of bombast?" Burton in *The Anatomy of Melancholy* was another of your depreciators. "Our wrangling lawyers . . . are so litigious and busy here on earth," said he, "that I think they will plead their clients' causes hereafter—some of them in hell."

I regret to say the picture of the law most securely hung in the minds of many people is scarcely a flattering likeness, if indeed it be a likeness at all. It is—you must remember it—the description in *Bleak House* of Jarndyce and Jarndyce, that "famous scarecrow of a suit," which over the long and dragging years had become so complicated that no living man knew what it meant. What were the symbols Dickens chose for the law and its processes? It pains me to state—fog, and gas, "Fog everywhere, fog up the river . . . fog down the river—gas looming through the fog in divers streets—never can there come fog too thick, never can there come mud and mire too deep" as "some score of members of the High Court of Chancery . . . are mistily engaged in one of the ten thousand stages of an endless cause, tripping one another up on slippery precedents, groping knee-deep in technicalities . . . and making a pretense of equity with serious faces, as players might."

That is the popular conception, or shouldn't I as your guest say misconception, of the law held both by the law's victims and the clients of lawyers, if a distinction from the layman's point of view can be made between the two. Like Shakespeare's reputation and Shaw's, this notion of the law is built, in the phrase GBS used to describe his own fame, "fast and solid . . . on an impregnable basis of dogmatic reiteration"—and, no doubt, some truth.

Dr. Johnson refused to subscribe to such an idea. He came to the defense of your profession. "It is unjust, sir," he rumbled to

Boswell, "to censure lawyers for multiplying words when they argue; it is often necessary for them to multiply words." Authors have been guilty of the same indulgence, especially when paid space rates. Then they have been tempted to set down thousands of words they should have been paid to omit.

At this point we are forced back again without choice to a consideration of words, hence to writers and lawyers as word-men. Words are a strange and tantalizing commodity. The mere twenty-six letters in our alphabet are responsible for the limitless variety and the full, fabulous range of our language, call it English or American. Gathered together in dictionaries, these words are available to everyone. They literally pine for suitors. They are like the suffragette of long ago who wanted something badly, and thought it was the vote. They yearn to be possessed. Yet they are used by each individual as differently as those individuals use life itself. They are either wasted or enjoyed, faced drably or approached with zest, accepted as routine or converted into that high adventure which is literature.

Certainly most of what is written or published has no more relation to literature than ordering meals has to do with conversation. The businessman who dictates "Yours of the 15th inst. received and duly noted" is getting off a letter, but he neither seeks nor pretends to be functioning as a man of letters. Although he is employing words, his only interest in them is to transact business. If his answer were phrased in language such as Horace Walpole, Lamb, Shaw, Ellen Terry, or Thomas Wolfe might have used, he would soon be without a job. And rightly so.

In the same way, signs reading "Exit," "No Parking," and "Keep off the Grass" fulfill their function admirably. They are as eloquent as they are meant to be. Yet, though they warn and inform us, they hardly inspire us. They feed none of the hungers which are among the excuses, the pleasures, and the needs of literature.

All of us sense the distinction between communication on the low level of utility and communication when it is raised to literature. The main Post Office in New York City supplies an illustration of these two extremes. Inside the building are signs for "Stamps," "Letters," "Parcel Post," "Air Mail," etc., and we are grateful for these directions. Outside, however, above the row of columns are curved those great, singing words of Herodotus,

"Neither snow, nor rain, nor heat, nor gloom of night stays these couriers from the swift completion of their appointed rounds." Instantly, instead of leading us to a window, these words open windows for us on the challenges of nature, the concept of duty, and the invincibility of the human spirit.

Most of what we read in newspapers, magazines, or books is mere hack work. Most legal writing is drudgery of the same kind. Assuredly, drawing up a contract or a will is not an act of creative authorship. No one doubts the advisability, indeed the necessity, of both wills and contracts. Even so, preparing them must be as tedious as reading them for pleasure is impossible unless, above the dissonances of their English, can be heard the sweet music of the prospects of money. Those dreary parties, "the party of the first part" and "the party of the second part"; those ugly "whereases" and "aforesaids"; those strung beads of synonyms, such as "give, devise, and bequeath," "rest, residue, and remainder," are not fashioned to delight. Their sole purpose is to make the document water-tight by closing up the chinks.

It is plain libel to assume, as some people do, that lawyers and jurists always employ English as if they were drawing up wills. Lawyers and jurists as writers do face certain dangers unknown to professional authors. They are excused from the necessity of entertaining and interesting their readers, and all too often—let's face the evidence—they take a cruel advantage of this enviable exemption. Nonetheless, some of the best writing that we have has come from the pens of lawyers and especially judges.

Experience itself, if only one has the ability to respond to it and translate it into words, is a better teacher of composition than our colleges know. Those who preside over courtrooms or argue in them cannot escape from life. They may not approach it as novelists, dramatists, journalists, or historians would, but they cannot duck it. This constant confrontation with the actual is what Dr. Johnson had in mind when he said, "Lawyers know life practically. A bookish person should always have them to converse with. Lawyers have what the writer wants."

Although every exposure to living helps, there are professions which, even if followed briefly, seem to make their unique contributions to a writer's training. Painting is one of these. The years were not wasted which William Hazlitt spent as a young man trying to become an artist by painting in the manner of Rembrandt and Titian. When he discovered he could not "engraft Italian art on English nature," he may have flung away his brush and pencil "in disgust and despair," but he never stopped being a painter. He merely exchanged words for colors and used them as if they were pigments. He had learned to see life with a painter's eyes; to develop a sharp awareness of shadows and highlights; above all, to seize upon those details in a man's face, dress, or posture which lay bare his spirit.

Medicine is another profession which can contribute to the writer's growth. Chekhov and Somerset Maugham are proofs of this. "If I am a writer," Chekhov once wrote, "I have to live among people." As a physician, he had done this and in the process learned much from the confessional of pain. Maugham's clinical dispassion can, at least in part, be traced to his years at St. Thomas's Hospital. By his own admission it was there he first became aware that "the normal is what you find but rarely" and that the most amazing contradictions "can all exist in a single person and form a plausible harmony."

Although listening to music with a hearing ear may or may not offer a man professional employment, it too can contribute much to the writer. Shaw, in this respect, is the ideal witness. "Do not suppose for one moment that I learned my art from English men of letters," he boasted. "My masters were the masters of a universal language. They were Haydn, Mozart, Beethoven, and Wagner." Among these, count Mozart the chief influence, as anyone must know who, again with a hearing ear, has listened to Shaw's prose. His claim was that *Don Giovanni* had taught him how to write seriously without being dull. "If it were only for the sense of the value of fine workmanship which I gained from it," Shaw added, "I should still esteem that lesson the most important part of my education."

Count law among the professions which may help the writer whether he lives by it or escapes from it. The law's perils from a literary point of view are many and grave. Its advantages, however, can be no less real. Chief among its dangers is that heavy-footed jargon which so many lawyers are persuaded by the pressure of their duties and their deafness or indifference to language to mistake for English. But arguing a case, preparing a brief, or writing a decision offers a superb and muscular exercise in the ordering of facts, the integration of ideas, and the mastery of logic. Surely, Scott and Stevenson were no more hurt as writers by having studied law than Jefferson and Lincoln were harmed as stylists by having practiced it.

All great writing is the result of more than a great gift. Yet the gift must be there before the man, however large of spirit or mind, can write greatly. As for the gift itself, there is no explaining it. Like health, physical graces, and a talent for life, it is among the inequalities that no "Deal"—Square, New, or Fair—can correct. If all of us in my profession, for example, could write as well as we would like to, the world would be cluttered with masterpieces. You in your profession face the same disparity between hope and ability. Some of the best justices, I am told, have been among the most maladroit of writers. The judges who have contributed to literature as well as justice belong to an overprivileged breed. They are doubly endowed. They happen to be fine writers in addition to being fine jurists. Perhaps George Orwell found the best expression for this inequality when he said, "All men are born equal, but some are more equal than others."

Although the best writing judges and the best authors share more than a command of words, they do not write for the same reasons. Since their minds are preoccupied with different concerns and their purposes have little in common, they are bound to employ the language in different ways. The law is as special in the demands it makes upon those who serve it as the drama, poetry, fiction, history, criticism, or journalism.

What, after all, is the law? At its best, at least as laymen see it, isn't it an attempt to methodize the madness of mankind? Isn't it a high-minded endeavor to create group sanity out of individual surrenders to folly, and to regulate personal impulse so that it becomes social order? Doesn't it seek to superimpose a pattern of reason on a world of passion, and to offer a guarantee of continuity by relating the precedent of the past with the dilemmas of the present?

Coleridge, a colossus among literary critics, was wise enough to recognize that you cannot pass an act of uniformity against the poets. As critics of behavior, judges are obligated to pass acts of uniformity in the interest of society. The great judges are concerned with interpretation, the great writers with revelation. Judges are devoted to protection—the protection of human rights, of property, of men against man, the structure of the state, and that beckoning and majestic concept known as justice. Creative writers do not share this absorption. They apply their gifts to human emotions, problems, frailties, or possibilities seen in terms of persons rather than abstractions. Where the great judges' interest is, so to speak, the spine and bony structure of society, the creative writers' interest is the flesh. Jurists do not see people caught in controversies or misfortunes as particular individuals, but as invitations to establish, reaffirm, or advance principles.

The justice writing an opinion carries a burden unknown to the playwright, the poet, or the novelist. It is a burden of public responsibility so heavy that its weight often makes itself felt in his prose. Wisdom is what we want from a judge, not wit; clarity of phrase, before beauty; decision rather than diversion. No wonder judges' opinions, being the awesome things they are, using language as an instrument of action and capable of changing the history of a nation, are seldom read as literature. No wonder the official judicial style has had throughout history a ponderous, Roman cadence, and has been Corinthian in its ornamentation. No wonder, as Justice Frankfurter has pointed out, the pens of even gifted judges are inevitably constrained. "Caution and reticence in writing," said he, "make for qualifications and circumlocutions that stifle spontaneity, slow the rhythm of speech, check the play of imagination. . . . Law as literature is restricted by its responsibility."

Fortunately, this is not always so. The grave demands of the law have been unable to muffle the writing gifts of such justices as Holmes, Cardozo, Brandeis, or Learned Hand. These men, and there are many others, have functioned as masters of the language no less than of the law. What we admire as the high judicial calm —that calm which comes from thinking on an altitude far above the timberline of the trivial—has been theirs. Yet it has never chilled them or their writings.

Their speeches, their books, even their opinions, though models of rationality, have always been warmed with emotion. Their pages are heated by the strong, undeviating passion they feel for what Holmes called "our mistress, the law," and their proud conviction, again in his phrase, that no other calling plunges one so deep in the stream of life . . . its passions, its battles, its despair, and its triumphs, both as witness and actor.

Deep personal emotion can make men eloquent who are not noted for their eloquence. It did this to Calvin Coolidge when, crushed by the death of his son Calvin, he inscribed a friend's book with these words, "To my friend, in recollection of his son and my son, who, by the grace of God, have the privilege of being boys throughout Eternity."

Moral passion even more than sorrow can fuel the minds and spirits, and hence the language, of those fired by it. It is moral passion of the finest sort which has directed the considerations and ignited the prose of the great judges, including those I have named. Light and heat, Shaw insisted, are the two vital qualities demanded of literature, adding that he who has nothing to assert has no style, and can have none. The great judges have never lacked something to say and, at their best, have said it with light and heat.

They have loved words. They have relished the adventure which the quest for the right ones represents. They have known that there are no such things as wilted words; there are only wilted people who use them. They have hated verbosity and taken pains, when expressing themselves, to clear away the thick underbrush and ugly weeds which obstruct most legal language. They have shared Hazlitt's contempt for the "Occult School" and Joubert's dislike of "words which have not been able to get currency in the world and are only calculated to form a special language." English to them has been a music which they have heard and which, in their writing, they have made us hear. They have had Churchill's veneration for the structure of a sentence. They have known better than to believe, as someone tried to prove a few years ago, that the ideal sentence is seventeen words long. Part of their wisdom is that they have recognized that a good sentence is as long as it needs to be and no longer, and that a long sentence is more than acceptable if only it seems short.

These judges have belonged to what Mrs. Bowen called a race of "poet lawyers." Only a lawyer who was also a poet could write such a sentence as Holmes' "Who of us could endure a world, although cut up into five-acre lots and having no man upon it who was not well fed and well housed, without the divine folly of honor, without the senseless passion for knowledge outreaching the flaming bounds of the possible, without ideals the essence of which is that they never can be achieved?"

To turn to Holmes again—and it is hard to turn away from him —only a poet-lawyer could have written, "I was walking home-ward on Pennsylvania Avenue near the Treasury, and as I looked beyond Sherman's statue to the west the sky was aflame with scar-let and crimson from the setting sun. But, like the note of downfall in Wagner's opera, below the sky line there came from little globes the pallid discord of the electric lights. And I thought to myself the Götterdämmerung will end, and from those globes clustered like evil eggs will come the new masters of the sky. It is like the time in which we live. But then I remembered the faith that I partly have expressed, faith in a universe not measured by our fears, a uni-verse that has thought and more than thought inside of it, and as I gazed, after the sunset and above the electric lights there shone the stars."

May I add that only a poet-lawyer could have told us what lib-erty is in a definition as stirring as Judge Hand's. "What do we mean when we say that first of all we seek liberty? I often wonder whether we do not rest our hopes too much upon constitutions, upon laws and upon courts. These are false hopes; believe me, these are false hopes. Liberty lies in the hearts of men and women; when it dies there, no constitution, no law, no court can save it; no constitution, no law, no court can even do much to help it. While it lies there it needs no constitution, no law, no court to save it."

The great judges, whose business is opinions, dissenting or fa-vorable, have never been opinionated. Being philosophers as well as poets and lawyers, they have searched for truth with open minds. "One learns from time," Holmes observed, "an amiable latitude with regard to beliefs and tastes."

There are some words which Judge Hand has confessed he would like to see written over the portals of every church, every school, every courthouse, and every legislative body in the United States. What are they? They are the words Oliver Cromwell spoke just before the Battle of Dunbar. "I beseech ye in the bowels of Christ think that ye may be mistaken."

Such judges belong, as I have admitted, to an overprivileged breed. "There is more truth in law than in lawyers, more poetry in justice than in judges," David Loth reminds us in his life of John

Marshall. "But once in a while a man mounts the bench with the salt of life, the spice of wisdom, and the sweetness of humor blended in him so subtly yet so successfully that those who are quite unlearned in the law glimpse some of its beauties."

The beauties of the law are not the only ones the great judges have opened up to us. They, like their blood relations the great word-men in literature, have lighted up the world for us by using language as a beacon. The shadows will always be with us. They are a part of the health of our thinking. They mean that we recognize gradations, that we keep even our certainties open to question, and do not sink into the dangerous oversimplification of believing everything is either black or white. Shadows and darkness, however, are not the same thing. Illumination, the kind of illumination which banishes darkness though it leaves shadows, is among the paramount obligations of literary no less than legal writing. It has never been more needed than now when so many are tempted to lose hope and to surrender to despair.

The difference in our judgments of the people we encounter in life and those we see on a stage, and some notes on that strange giant, Demos, who is all of us when we have become part of an audience.

[1936]

OURSELVES WITH OTHERS

THE MEN and women to whom we are introduced in a play may touch our hearts, provoke our laughter, wound our consciences, accelerate our thinking, or widen our horizons. In them we may recognize fragments of ourselves and our acquaintances. Or with them we may even identify ourselves. But always these characters enjoy an advantage over real people we meet for the first time, inasmuch as we know we neither can, nor will ever have to, confront them face to face exactly as they are under precisely the same circumstances.

We are narrowed by the hard necessities of life. They tend to make us hopelessly self-centered in our daily living. Consciously or unconsciously we are apt to appraise the men and women with whom we come in contact on the basis of how we think they will fit into our scheme of things—our prejudices, our interests, our standards, our diversions, or our work—without ever stopping to consider how we may be fitting into theirs. Our desire to know them better depends upon our surmise of how comfortably they will find a place in our lives as we have already organized them and become accustomed to their intellectual and physical routines.

Fortunately we are less egocentric in our appraisals of the characters we meet in plays. A form of charity begins to show itself in us at the theatre of which we seem to be incapable at home. We find it as easy to be bystanders in the lives of these fictional figures as it is impossible for us to be bystanders in our own. We do not forget about life, and what it may have taught us, in forming our estimates of them. But it is as Daniels of a different sort that we come to judgment in a playhouse.

It is not our lives which count; it is theirs. While we may want to know everything worth knowing about these men and women, we may often be comforted by the fact that we do not have to know them. We eavesdrop in their homes, emboldened by the realization we can never ask them to our own. We have paid off our obligations to them at the box office. We need not worry about entertaining them. Our sole concern is whether or not they are entertaining us.

From the protection of the intervening footlights most of us derive a new courage and a new curiosity. We face what they illumine with an eagerness to see life whole such as few of us show, or are able to show, within the petty confines necessity has forced upon us in our own living. Our tolerance grows as our self-interest is temporarily dimmed with the lowering of the houselights. Our egos are suspended with our disbelief. Our individual defenses are down. The sentinels who wear our liveries and ordinarily guard us are off duty. Our imaginations are set free. And in their new-found freedom they promptly put our everyday selves to shame by exceeding them in sympathy no less than valor.

The freedom from self-interest which enlarges both our curiosity and compassion in a playhouse is a boon to dramatists. Because of it we are ready to follow them wherever they may lead us, and anxious to share in the joys or woes of whatever characters they may choose to have us meet. But our increased receptivity is not a boon which exists without its attendant handicaps.

As individuals we may be more tolerant at a play than we are in life. Yet it is not entirely as individuals that we assemble in a theatre. If the production we are seeing is a good one, we sit there as one among many. We are part of a crowd. "Dat ole davil" Demos is all around us. Although we may shake our fists at him, we find ourselves forced to walk in his train, even if we are out of step. To psychologists he has proven a somewhat satanic problem child. To the theatre he has been at once the greatest blessing and the greatest curse that it has known. Without him there would be no theatre. He is its reason for being and support; its patron saint and final arbiter. Yet because of him, and more especially because of what managers and actors and playwrights have thought would capture his fancy, the theatre has suffered abundantly.

He is no monster, this Gargantuan fellow known as Demos. He is you and I and the people around us, upstairs or downstairs, or standing at the back of the house, when we have gathered together in the sight of the drama.

He is not any one of us, but all of us put together. None of us as individuals resembles him when by assembling on any particular night at a particular playhouse we have summoned him once more into being. If we are present in sufficient numbers it does mean, however, that he is there too, and that dramatists who, with the aid of actors, seek to create such adult and fully rounded characters as we may be searching for, or who attempt to project ideas, or win tears and laughter, are faced with the necessity of appealing to two audiences at one and the same time—the audience which consists of each of us as individuals and the audience which all of us combine to form in the person of Demos.

Now Demos is really no devil. It is fairer to liken him to a giant than to Mephistopheles. His horns are by no means always visible. The smell of sulphur is much stronger on his courtiers than it is on him. That he is a tempter no one can deny. Yet in all honesty it must be admitted he inspires people to do their best, even as because of him they are enticed into doing their worst.

It is his size which makes him what he is. He is the victim of his huge proportions. He is slow-moving, ill-co-ordinated, ungainly, and as hard to start as he is to stop. Although his mentality is made up of all of ours, the addition which this process should represent defies the undefiable laws of mathematics inasmuch as it results in an odd sort of subtraction which finds Demos, who is the sum total of our collective minds, less smart than we are as individuals.

Poor fellow, do not be too harsh with him if he seems somewhat backward. He is a little hard of hearing, and his mental processes are at best leisurely. Things have to be made clearer for him than they do for us. He tends to confuse dramatists with the Bellman in *The Hunting of the Snark*, and believes only that is true which they tell him three times.

Slow-witted though he may be, he is in many respects far more genial than are we. When angry or bored, he can be cruel—more cruel than any one of us. But it takes time for him to bare his fangs. He is easier to please than we are, and laughs readily at jokes at which none of us would smile if we were exposed to them alone.

He is blessed with a poor memory. Luckily for him, but not so luckily for the theatre, he has a talent for discovering novelty in subjects with which we as individuals have long been familiar. What may be twenty years old to us as readers still seems new to him, even as it may to us, when we hear ideas that have grown venerable in books or private conversation uttered for the first time in his presence. Such is his credulity that he is willing to believe grass grows on asphalt streets. Such is his unadventurousness that he is contented to ride in the caboose rather than the engine of his own day's train of thought. He is always just catching up with, and being startled by, the views of Nietzsche and Schopenhauer as restated by Mr. Shaw, of Freud as interpreted by Mr. O'Neill, or of Karl Marx as dramatized by Mr. Odets, seasons after they have become landmarks to each and every one of us.

The truth is, Demos is a reactionary. Intellectually he is a timid soul who resembles Caspar Milquetoast much more than he does Caliban. He is, too, a prude, destined always to be the last Puritan. He can be shocked with the same facility with which he can be amused. His morals and his thinking are not the personal morals or thoughts of those of us who combine to make him what he is. He frowns on innovations, preferring not to have his established convictions altered or assaulted by what he is offered in a theatre but to have them echoed or reaffirmed.

Such is his romanticism and so unashamed is his fondness for fairy stories in which no single one of us retains our faith, that he is suspect of thinking "grim" must always be spelt with a capital G and concluded with two m's. He does not like gossip about Santa Claus and is squeamish on the subject of sex. You and I as individuals may be rapscallions, pickpockets, bankers with shady records, drugstore Casanovas, ladies of easy virtue, smoking-room raconteurs, or the most hardened of cynics, but not so Demos, who is made up of us all. He lives by an ethical code to which none of us can lay claim and insists upon wearing a suit of shining armor which ill becomes us all. Hypocritical cousin to St. George that he is, he is ever ready to have the dragon of wickedness attacked, and is happiest when he sees virtue rewarded and vice punished.

In spite of his shortcomings, it must be admitted Demos has a contagious personality. It is this which makes him dangerous and compels us to be on our guard against him. He is a highly undependable fellow whose tastes and prejudices can be worse than misleading. Fortunately, remaining true to ourselves and our own standards in his presence is not as difficult as some would have us believe. Yet such is his persuasion that, whether we happen to find ourselves in agreement or disagreement with him, we cannot help being interested in him and his reactions.

His laugh is one of the pleasantest of life's experiences. It is such a hearty, thunderous, deep-throated and yet relaxing affair that its volcanic rumble delights us even when we cannot join in it, or are mystified, or sickened, by what may have provoked it. The silences by means of which he shows his attention has been captured are no less compelling. Their giant lack of sound is almost audible. Surely the world knows no music as savage or as terrifying as is the stabbing half-whistle he emits when, in the darkness of an auditorium, he releases his anger in a hiss; and boasts no melody as sweet or as intoxicating as is that cacophony he produces when, to show his approval or surrender, he beats those giant hands of his together in applause.

Do not be misled by Demos's charm. Or deceived by his size.

Deep down in his huge heart he is a coward, subject to such apprehensions as do not overtake us singly. The intervening footlights, which give us new courage and compassion, do not embolden him. The diminished self-interest we experience as individuals in a theatre may have opened our hearts and minds and curiosities wider than they are ever opened in life. But by crowding into a playhouse we have brought Demos with us, and his courage, no less than his intellect, is lower than our own. He is prey to group fears which counter-balance the new-found willingness for adventure each one of us feels in a playhouse.

Dramatists know Demos not only as a friend but as an enemy. He supports them even as he curtails them. The freedom they gain by our release from ourselves in a theatre, they come near to losing because of his presence there. Often they seem to dread him more than they respect us. Sometimes they match his cowardice with their own by fawning on him; by being afraid to take any chances with him; by choosing to be led by him rather than to lead him; by determining upon the lowest instead of the highest common denominator as their goal; by writing as if they felt no audience were stronger than its weakest brain. They suffer when they do so. And so do we, and so does the theatre. Their best work is done when, without forgetting he is present, they remember he is composed of individuals, and are intrepid enough to speak to what is best in each of them, even while in their way of getting it said they contrive to command his attention.

We cannot blame these playwrights for remembering Demos. They would be worse than fools if they forgot him and the enlargements in their writing made necessary by his size. To ignore him completely would be to fail as dramatists and to misuse a medium which flourishes and is healthy only when it has his approval. He may limit the stage intellectually and bully it into innumerable timidities which shame it. But he is the theatre's greatest emotional stimulant, its protector against coteries, its bulwark against preciosity, its readiest weeper, its thousand-throated cheer leader, its final justification and explanation.

Demos could not exist without us any more than the theatre could exist without him. Necessary as we are to him, he is even more necessary to the theatre than we are as individuals. He is the drama's constant; we are its variables. He is the norm established by us all, not on a single night but at performance after performance after performance. This or that one of us may be above or below it. Yet that norm, which reflects his mass anxieties, his group prejudices, his collective morals, his distaste for subtleties that are over-subtle, his need for having a thing repeated, underscored, or overstressed, and his fondness for white that is white and black that is black, is bound to impose certain restraints upon the work of playwrights and, in part at least, condition it.

Stand at the entrance to any theatre when Demos is assembling; look into his multitudinous face; study his varying expressions; attempt to gauge the separate minds which are mere cells in his composite brain; think of the conflicting interests, perceptions, backgrounds, vocabularies, sympathies, standards, convictions, consciences, and levels of sophistication from which his giant body is sprung, and the challenges and difficulties faced by dramatists in presenting such situations, ideas, and characters as will be comprehensible and acceptable to Demos, even while they are satisfactorily meeting our own quite different individual demands, will be made clearer for us than any textbook on dramatic technique has ever been able to make them.

Some of the problems that theatrical reviewers have always presented to themselves as well as to their readers, and a discussion of the functions and challenges of criticism.

[1930]

THE MEN ON THE AISLE

WHEN DICKENS said of Mr. Pecksniff that some people likened him unto a signpost because he was always pointing the way and never going there himself, he touched upon a popular conception of dramatic criticism which, while it may have won the critic a certain warrantable envy, has never granted him an unreserved esteem. To the majority of people, and even to that highly specialized majority of theatre people, the dramatic critic seems, at best, a spiritless person who prefers the indolence of opinions to the trials of action. Because his interest leads him only into judgment and away from performance, the world can never quite forgive him or take him with that final seriousness he undoubtedly desires. It presumes, believing it to be a charitable presumption, that he must have turned dramatic critic because he is either waiting to do some real work in the theatre or because he has failed there. As a matter of course it infers his job to be a stop-gap of a nature somewhere between a nursery and an asylum for would-be playwrights. But of one thing it is certain, and that is its unwillingness to admit that the nightly drudgery of sitting before another person's work constitutes an independent and self-respecting profession.

The inertia that persuades an able-bodied and supposedly able-minded man to take up the prideless task of sitting, sitting, sitting, and then rushing into print instead of action, is not the only reason why the merest mention of a dramatic critic can often be an enjoyable excuse for head-shaking and laughter. The other and far more basic cause is the simple fact that one man assumes the right to pass judgment on his peers, to say nothing of his betters. In itself that offers an impertinence which mankind does not gracefully overlook, and which never fails to irritate the reading public of the critic when it finds itself at variance with his judgment.

By donning the official robes of justice and setting himself up as a self-anointed authority, he lays himself open to an implication of superiority which Americans, in particular, are quicker to resent than they are to forgive. More than that, as a judge without a courtroom, and with no officers to give the weight of actual correction to his verdicts, he does not confine himself to the recognized limits of jurisprudence. The ordinary judge, even when he does not depend upon the jury for his opinions, leaves the praise of good conduct to the pastors, and limits himself to seeing that the long arm of the law reaches out and enfolds only those who have been brought before him for their misdeeds.

Not so the dramatic critic. With one grandiloquent gesture of omniscience he combines the two functions, and digs into the grab-bag of his thesaurus for both awards and penalties. Calling no court to order, and turning to no jury, he delivers himself of a sentence. Though it is couched in all the familiar terms of legal infallibility, though it barks aggressively or may even suggest constructively, it carries with it no promise of action, because its only authority is its print. It is not unnatural, therefore, that the dramatic critic, who dares to speak *ex cathedra,* should invite the derision of all who are expected to submit to his judgment. They know, as he does, that the foundations of his authority are highly contestable. He has attended no special school, won no particular diploma, and passed none of those examinations which are the legal gates to other professions. Nor has he been put in office because of any popular referendum. He does not even hold his scepter by virtue of anything he has done in the theatre. Usually the less he has himself done the more he is entitled to his badge of office.

He is a figure, and often a power, in the larger cities, but his readers share with him the knowledge that the roots of his sway go no farther than an opinion he happens to have formed in a crowded theatre, where everyone else may have been forming radically different opinions. When, therefore, he speaks—as he is sometimes tempted to—too confidently, too arbitrarily, as though he were the one and only chosen representative of the earthly estates of Thalia, his position is somewhat precarious and not a little ludicrous. No one is forced to share his opinions, and no one concerned, either in the audience or on the stage, may be in the slightest degree affected by them. He clears his throat, and presumably his mind, and speaks. And, in his natural moments of despair it must often seem to him that the only minions of enforcement who carry out his word are, on the first day, an army of newsboys, and, on the second, touchingly indifferent but completely efficient delegates from the Department of Street Cleaning.

There is, of course, an ample sufficiency of other reasons which might well cause the dramatic critic to wonder why he should bother to have an opinion at all, and why his particular opinion should be singled out to be caught in the amber of print. He realizes (and if he forgets it all those whom he abuses or who disagree with him are quick to remind him) that the play he is discussing has not been written for his special knowledge. He does not have to be convinced that it is not for him or for his tribe that the theatre exists, any more than that it is not by him or his tribe that it lives. He may sputter and spurt to the limit of his inkstand, but he is a powerless nonentity when the playwright, or the actor and the director, succeeds in reaching beyond the critic's prejudices and touching what is common to the heart of mankind.

The critic cannot help but be aware of this, and is deservedly absurd if he is not glad to admit it. It is one of the bitter realities— and the glories—of his trade that he is only pitting one man's very human reactions against those of many. To a challenger (and the theatre is healthy only when the lists are full) he can only say what he has already said, parade his reasons perhaps more fully, and conclude, with a knowledge of what it is worth, "I think" against "You think." And, in this democratic age, when opinions are supposed to be within everybody's reach, the dramatic critic cannot help but ponder on what he is trying to do, and why he should be asked to do it at all.

He, more than any other kind of critic, must, because of the very nature of his subject, confront challengers at every turn. Certainly more people feel entitled to speak with finality on the theatre than on any other art. The franchise is not more universally enjoyed than is the right to damn or praise a play or a performance. The unpaid critics of the theatre may be stenographers or the most fashionable of hostesses or the most callous of Babbitts, but on the question of the merits or demerits of a play they share an identical readiness to air their views. In summing up their reactions, their mind's total may be, "Gee, but it's rotten," or "God, what a swell show," or "Wasn't it just too beautiful," murmured with eyebrows arched. But in each case the verdict is equally unhesitant, and equally satisfactory in betraying the speaker's attitude and reactions.

In the case of the other arts far fewer people feel equipped to give so cursory a criticism, because the technical difficulties in medium and execution presuppose a technical knowledge on the part of critics which most people are willing to admit is beyond them. But the very men and women who are embarrassed, if not mute, before a painting, who hiss for silence in a concert hall, and never even bother to notice the architectural or engineering feats of which they take advantage every day, require no persuasion to follow in the footsteps of Aristotle. Their readiness is the final indication of the theatre as the most democratic of the arts, and one which makes its most irresistible appeal to the greatest number of people on the grounds of the spectator's identification of himself with what is happening on the stage. Also, the very medium of the theatre is too impure, too mixed and human to set up any academic barriers. It employs human actors to play in human situations that might have engulfed anyone. It necessitates no knowledge of brush-stroke, or modeling, or counterpoint and fugue to share its myster-ies.

Apparently the theatre is a simple and direct touchstone to the sympathies and emotions of its audiences. As a mirror in which they can face their own problems, see their own aspirations, and recognize the virtues and shortcomings of their neighbors, it invites them to judge by that standard of judgment of which no one is will-ing to admit ignorance, namely, their knowledge of life. The aver-age person may not know his Aristotle. He may not know the dif-ference between Inigo, Henry Arthur, and Robert Edmond Jones. He may be completely uninformed as to Hroswitha or a cyclorama, but he feels instinctively that his experience of life is the only spe-cial knowledge that he needs to draw upon in judging the theatre.

Hence it is that the scrubwoman, who may be untouched by the Mona Lisa or a Beethoven symphony, because she recognizes nothing in them that is common to herself, may still be moved by Juliet. In the lyric enchantment of the balcony scene, in which all tremulous young love is caught for a moment on a moonlit night, the scrubwoman sighs with Juliet because Juliet is what she wishes her own youth might have been. Her Romeo may have been a plumber, but beneath his inexpressive courtship there was an emotion which her partial eyes gratefully recognize in Romeo. By her memory of her plumber, that night they went on a picnic, she judges those young lovers of Verona, on that night when one of them scaled the walls of his enemy's garden. If the scrubwoman has had no plumber, she still has seen enough, heard enough, and dreamed enough to know what lies beneath their lyricism, and judge their actions by the standards her hearsay, her intuition, and her hopes have given her. Add to the thin voice of the scrubwoman the many voices of those who have a far wider and more glamorous experience than hers, who can establish a thousand other claims for judgment, and whose instinct and knowledge direct them down the path to many more situations in which they can recognize themselves or identify their acquaintances, and you have a babble of voices that whips the critic into a more final examination as to what and why he is.

In daring to lift his voice above the crowd the critic may feel justified because of his delusion that what he writes so unhesitatingly is an expert opinion, whereas what they feel is only an immediate and unthinking emotional reaction. He may hope against hope that this will endow his words with their due finality. But if he has recourse to his dictionary, he only adds to his confusion. Though he may be comforted by reading that a reaction is a "responsive or reciprocal action," or the "response of an organ, etc., to external stimulus," he is disheartened to learn that an opinion is only a "judgment *based on grounds short of proof*," "*a provisional* conviction," or at best a "formal statement by an expert when consulted of what *he holds to be* the facts or the right course." In other words the dramatic critic is always far short of infallibility, and the sooner he learns it the better it will be for him and his profession. His truth at best is his truth to himself and his own temperament but even in his statement of this one truth that can be absolutely his he is often fallible. His fallibility, however, leaves him once more as only a single voice raised against many.

It is that very fact upon which the unprofessional critics, who constitute the general public, base the oldest of the reproaches brought against the professional critic. He is too like themselves to be important. He is not set aside by the divine gift of the creative faculty. And because he is not a creator he cannot, therefore, speak with authority upon his special subject. This method of attack, which is perennial and often effectively used to destroy the illusion of importance with which the critic is fond of veiling his judgment, goes even further. It contends with a certain logic that, for example, only the man who paints and who knows paints can write of painting, just as only the man who can write poetry is qualified to criticize it in its own terms.

Untrustworthy and specious as this identification of the creative and critical faculties has been proven to be, the argument contains an element of truth which is too frequently forgotten, and which has a special bearing on the multiple arts that confront the dramatic critic. Though it seeks for criticism among the thin ranks of the creative, who have something so much more important to do, it does at least imply a rather wistful quest for authority on the part of the public. It means that they want the critic to do more than translate a canvas into the entirely different world of phrases. They want him to know the tools of the artist's trade, and speak with that knowledge which they feel is the ready property of a true practitioner. In short, it means that they hope he will understand the artist's problem from the artist's point of view even when he is appraising it from the viewpoint of his public.

In dramatic criticism, more than in any other form of appraisal, it is apparent that one man cannot speak with a complete knowledge of the many aspects of a production which combine to make it effective. He is faced with the sorry dilemma of speaking not only intelligently but also authoritatively as a playwright, an actor, a scenic artist, a director, an electrician, a costume mistress, and a member of the audience. More than that, in the course of a single week of professional theatregoing he may meet, not one kind of playwriting, or one kind of scenery, or one kind of direction, or acting, or one historical period and specialized locale, but as many as six, with their corresponding styles in costume, language, and demeanor. Obviously his lot is not a happy one if he attempts to muster facts toward authority. Accordingly what he does is to seek means of escape. And in means of escape his profession abounds.

For one thing, he takes refuge in the highly debatable purposes of his job. He catechizes himself with such questions as the following, and finds asylum in the easiest answers. Is he writing to tell his public what happened and who was there? Is he only an audible member of the audience whose reactions are valuable mainly as they serve as a common denominator to what the town may think? Is he trying to help the actor and the playwright by constructive suggestions, or is he merely to describe them for prospective ticket buyers? Is he a middleman or an autocrat, a press agent or a synopsis manufacturer? Do his readers want to know what he thinks or learn about what they may like? Is he to parade his understanding or his adjectives, his knowledge or his enthusiasms? Is he to treat each production as an isolated unit, or judge it by comparative values? Is he paid to analyze technicalities or to amuse his public? Is he to turn crusader and fight for a play or a production or a group in which he believes, even when they are not ripened enough to warrant his praise, or is he to pass judgment only on the finished product? Is he to measure what he is asked to see by a general theory of the theatre, or come receptive, with his mind and body fresh for new impressions? In short—and this is more important than it may seem—is he to be a reporter, a reviewer, or a critic?

If he is content to be a reporter, and nothing more, his job is a comparatively easy one. He is burdened with no standards and bothered by no misgivings, and the merit of his work depends entirely upon his aptitude for his own profession. He approaches the theatre as any of his fellow journalists might track down an assignment. Working for a newspaper, he has the ideal of his office, "Accuracy, Speed, and Interest." His special gift is that his mind quickly orders what he has seen, just as his real value is that he tries, as far as it is humanly possible, not to thrust himself between the event and the reader. Accordingly his copy flows easily, because it is written without doubts, just as it reads easily, because it raises no questions. It is candidly a voice of the people, speaking for the people, and making no other personal claim to attention than that which it deserves by the facility of its narration.

As reporting, its function is news, not judgment, though as in all good reporting an opinion is tactfully expressed. In this case, however, it is not so much a private opinion as an acute, if unconscious, guess at a general reaction. Its aim is to strike a norm, to represent the majority of its readers, to parallel their minds and their morals, and to reach them by information rather than instruction. Treated frankly as an account of only ephemeral interest, it takes its place beside the other news of the day, to be skimmed for its momentary worth and then discarded.

The reviewer, on the other hand, takes himself and his position more seriously, just as he hopes his readers do. Though he is concerned primarily with journalism, his position on a newspaper is a compromise between the news and editorial departments. He is a reporter with opinions, which are backed up by intuition, learning, or diligent servitude. But the very fact that he is allowed to sign his name shows that he is speaking for himself as well as his paper. He emerges, therefore, as an individual, and, according to his temperament and equipment, as a personality. He is a special correspondent of letters, who even before he is a critic, is a journalist. The past is not his province, nor the future his concern, but the present is his obligatory passion. In the theatre his business is, first and foremost, the particular play he has seen on a particular night. It is his duty to report it, even as the reporter must, but it is his privilege to write of it in the terms of his own undisguised reactions.

Most often, and quite rightly, his market is the daily press, and the rules of the press are, to a great extent, his rules. His editors want him to tell what he has seen and thought in a straightforward and popular way. But they impose upon him the difficulties which are inherent in his job. He has no time to reconsider. His first report must come quickly and he must wait for his Sunday page for deliberation. In his daily work he must do his thinking as rapidly as he does his writing. Often the first pages of his copy are on the press before the last sheets have been finished. Accordingly he must have words and phrases on his keyboard to clothe his impressions that are still warm. The marvel is that his work is as fluent and coherent and satisfactory both as reading and reaction as it almost always is. Its very warmth endows it with the authenticity of a first-hand report and the speed of its composition tends to bring it nearer to the average playgoer's reactions.

Because of the size of his audience, the reviewer's responsibility is immense. He can as everyone knows, including himself, come near to breaking or making a play. Hence it is that, though he may speak personally, he must still bear his readers in mind, for his likes may not necessarily be theirs. He is their guide and they respect him, as a rule, only in so far as his opinion coincides with theirs. As a result they ask him to point out to them what they may think even while he is stating what he thinks. Not unnaturally he prides himself upon not being a professional lily-clasper and glories in the fact that his feet are, as a rule, planted firmly on the asphalt of Broadway. He is content with the event of the moment because it is "copy," and as such he treats it in detail.

His usual method is to begin with a sentence that expresses his own feelings in the color of its adjectives, even while it states the facts in its who, when, where, and what. This is followed with a detailed plot summary, for the benefit of his readers who may not be able to see the play but who still want to talk about it, or who want to know whether it is the kind of play to which they can safely take their husbands and children. Then comes a paragraph on the acting, and, perhaps, a slight sentence on the direction and setting, and, if the reviewer has something of Pepys in him, a final bit of news which says who was there, and what someone behind him said during the intermission. As a rule the reviewer avoids "I" and gets around it by such apologetic phrases as "to this reporter" or— in a more jocose mood—"your old correspondent," by which he frankly admits his own relationship to his readers and his journal, as well as his function in the theatre.

The dramatic critic differs from the reporter and the reviewer in that he is more interested in the idea behind the event than in the event itself. Sharing with them an indebtedness to another man's work, or rather in his case the work of other men, he is, like them, a lean-to in literature and cannot stand alone. He needs an incentive, if not an excuse, for his work, but he does not find it in the date which heads the page of a daily newspaper. Supposedly the reflections he has to make are not confined only to a passing interest because they are based upon eternal principles. His realm is the idea rather than the fact. He sees a play or a performance not in relation to what it may say to a prospective ticket-buyer, but in terms of what it does contribute to the theatre and to life. Even if he makes no mention of the past, its contribution and its sequence are somehow in his mind. To him the past is not dead because it is past any more than the present is alive merely because it is the present. There again he shows that his interests are time-less and transcends a mere date because to him, as Arthur Symons phrased it, "No perfect thing" of any time or period "is too small for eternal recollection," just as "any living insignificance is already dead." To him only the first-rate is important. It is that which is his ceaseless goal, and his constant standard of comparison.

Unlike the reviewer, whose copy is due the next morning and sure to be of a certain presentable length in print regardless of the merits of its subject matter, the critic has a greater latitude in rejecting what is patently beneath his notice. Even when he contemplates mediocrity, which is his tireless foe, he is attracted to it only by its relation to distinction. Because he is an essayist, not a journalist, because he writes—when he writes—for weeklies and monthlies instead of dailies, and has the time for mulling instead of reporting, his measuring rod can be the best instead of the popular. To him news is no end in itself. It is only a demonstration of principles, a moment that is never self-sustaining or isolated but that has come from somewhere and leads somewhere.

The ritual of the opening sentence colored with preferential adjectives and followed by the plot synopsis and an adjectival dismissal of the performance does not satisfy him. In his own way he may cover the same material, but always with a different end in view, because he prefers deductions to appearances and reflections to statements. He is fired by his own curiosity rather than by the desire to satisfy someone else's curiosity. He seeks what is peculiar to and yet universal in the man rather than what is worth reporting in his single play; or in the actor what is peculiar to his style of acting, even while it is universal in it, rather than stringing together a succession of adjectives to describe his current performance. He watches for growth, and traces retrogressions. And in doing this he is not afraid that all knowledge is pedantry, because he writes to appease himself rather than to consider his reader. Accordingly his method is constantly comparative, because to judge one performance, or one play, he feels he must see it in terms of an accumulation of effort, and against the background of its time. He takes all knowledge as his goal, and refuses to limit himself to the provincial confines of any single theatrical rialto. He tracks down forces relentlessly, unsparingly because his preoccupation is with tendencies as well as single instances.

Like the reviewer, the critic is, presumably, a human being, subject to all those physical causes which add to or detract from enjoyment and receptivity. His verdict, however, is not nearly so dependent, as his readers may be inclined to think, upon such prejudicial comforts and inconveniences as a good or bad dinner, an agreeable or uncongenial companion, a headache or a feeling of bodily exuberance. The mysterious register which is largely responsible for his final judgment is what he identifies, for lack of a better name, as his "sense of theatre." He can no more explain what he means by that than the reviewer could, or, for that matter, the playwright, the actor, the designer, or the producer. It is as individual to him as it is to each of them—baffling, intangible, inexplicable, but real. Call it instinct, intuition, a sixth sense, or what you will, but he, like these others, is guided by some voice deep within him which only half articulates his dream of what the theatre at its best should be. Partly conscience, partly impulse, partly editor's blue pencil, partly nebulous memories of glowing moments already experienced in the theatre, partly a romantic notion of plumes and capes, long flights of steps and pursuing trains, partly a knowledge of the possibilities of each element contributing to a production, partly the electricity of imaginative discontent, partly a yearning for a moment drained of its last emotion, and an insatiable craving for Olympus, this inner voice of the critic, which is the basis of his "sense of theatre," guides him unconsciously in his separation of what he is anxious to accept from what he cannot but reject.

Within himself this voice is an echo of perfection, which holds the deed up to the ideal it has invoked. It has much to say to the critic, but the authority of its tone depends largely upon how much he has trained it to a knowledge of the stuff of which perfection, in all its various manifestations, is made, and how skillfully he conjures up its image without being able to create it himself. For him this voice is an important guide to judgment. It speaks to him of style and all that that implies, of fidelity to a certain chosen medium or form, and points out what the style, or form, or medium should be when once the actual creator has selected it. Even while the critic sees what is happening on the stage, something within himself is measuring what he sees by what it might have been or should be. His vision is continually bifocal, because both the subject as written and acted, and the potentialities which it indicates, come simultaneously within its range.

His voice cannot speak in the gruff tones of dogmatism because it has no pitch at all until the playwright or the performers give him a new one each night. It must wait for them, regard the performance as its prompt-book, and take its cue from what the first few lines or scenes indicate as to the performers' choice of material, manner, and style. But when once the performers have established their intention, then the inner voice of the critic must unceasingly inform him of the nature of their chosen goals which the performers have pointed out themselves. These goals may be as manifold as are the number of actors and plays and theatres in the world. They may be a thousand times more inconstant than the moon, and vary entirely from play to play, and production to production. But when once the goal has been selected it takes on a quality of inevitability, and it is for this that the critic must watch and by this, to a certain extent, that he must judge.

A play or a production is, in a way, like a horse taking a jump. There are countless manners in which a horse may approach a fence, and any two horses approaching the same fence do so not only in a manner that is peculiar to each of them but different every time they come to the barrier. When once a horse has left the ground, however, when it has taken its last preparatory step, when the jump itself has begun and the animal's body is arching upward in the air, there is only one inevitable way in which that particular jump can be concluded. It is the duty of the critic to be completely alert during the preparatory moments of a play, those initial seconds in which it is preparing for its take-off. But when it has once got under way, establishing its own style as it does so, indicating its chosen course, and leaving the firm ground of rehearsals and rewriting behind it, there is only one inevitable manner that belongs to perfection in which it can continue to its close. And it is the arc of that inevitable effort which the inner register of the critic must follow even while he is following the mishaps that may have overtaken the play, just as it is the deviation from that course which will unconsciously arouse his inner voice to protest.

When the critic is a figure of any real importance he has a definite conviction of his own, a theory of the theatre, which is the springboard to many of his enthusiasms and detestations. In his littlest examples he may be merely a critic, seeing what he sees only in terms of what he has viewed in the theatre or read at home rather than what he has lived. He may exclude life from his province, and yet perform a valuable service as a technician, a rule-giver, a "professional dramatic critic" and nothing more. But the more he is a lean-to in life as well as in letters the more circumscribed is his value, because side by side with his "sense of the theatre" he must draw upon his knowledge of life to understand and appraise the thing he is asked to judge. How much more he is than a dramatic critic depends entirely upon how much more there is in him, and how thirsty his sympathies and emotions as well as his intellect have been. Like the scrubwoman, he draws upon his fund of personal experience as a guide to what is probable, and a means of recognizing the truth and rejecting the specious. And his verdict on this score is more important than hers only in proportion to how much greater, deeper, more passionate and sensitive is his range of experience and his comment on human nature.

Obviously the separation of the functions of the reporter, the reviewer, and the critic is not as final in current practice as any arbitrary catalogue of their various differences may indicate. There are, of course, many moments when the critic and the reviewer invade the territory of the reporter, or when the critic does not leave the province of the reviewer or the reviewer annexes the realm of the critic. Obviously, too, the critic such as here described exists but rarely, if, indeed, he exists at all. But in principle their functions are as everlastingly separated as are the ideas and special equipment which color their work and determine its character.

Too frequently, however, the general public and even the "profession" itself does not distinguish between them. And it is the theatre which suffers more than the language by this confusion of terms—the theatre because of the inevitable cheapening in standards this confusion entails. Just as every Southern gentleman was once supposed to have been born with a colonelcy attached to his rattle, so, in the loose phrase of the moment, any journalist, regardless of his equipment, who is paid to go to see a performance and report it for a publication is immediately and without question dubbed a dramatic critic. He is allotted space and authority. And if he continues to write long enough over his own signature on the same page of the same metropolitan daily he will, by sheer force of habit, sooner or later develop a personal following.

Apparently the last thing that is expected of him is an academic knowledge of the theatre's background, or any active familiarity with the technical means of the current theatre. He may have been a police reporter, an editorial writer, a sports writer, or an obituary editor, but overnight he is expected to turn into a dramatic critic. If he succeeds in being a journalist when he is functioning as a dramatic critic, he will succeed in being a satisfactory dramatic critic from the standpoint of his readers and his editors. He may, and often does, do extraordinarily well both for himself and his editors by establishing himself as a wit, a wag, or what you will. His perspicacity, his amusing exhibitionism, his infectious enthusiasms and delightful malice may command for him a public of such dimensions that his commercial value to his journal is high.

There may be no limit to his fairness in "covering" a play, and no end to the popularity of his advice to ticket-buyers.

But before he is a dramatic critic, and not a reporter or a reviewer, he must have standards that are born of the theatre itself and not of the press room. He must serve it, and dedicate himself to its interests rather than to his own or those of his editors or his readers. He must be the first to realize that the traditions of hard-boiled journalism which the reviewer and the reporter have held up to the stage as its final standards have less than nothing to do with the theatre and can only harness and imprison the imagination that is its life blood. He must know the theatre's traditions and see behind its mysteries as well as record his personal impressions. He must not limit his concern to the commerce and gossip of the rialto, or to proving that he is shrewder than the managers in guessing at successes or failures. Sitting before an art, he cannot look upon it merely as a trade, nor can he hold it as lightly as his editors are willing to confess they do by leaving it so often to the mercy of cub reporters. When all is said and done, the fact remains that he is not an agent for the manager but a servant of the art which the manager exploits.

Something of a seismograph, something of an echo, something of a teacher, a truant officer, a prophet, a guide, a coxswain, a preacher, a courier, and, particularly, a lover, he must welcome the realization that he alone is responsible for the range to his authority, and that, no matter how far he may extend it, his opinions will always fall far short of infallibility. The knowledge of his own fallibility, however, must not discourage him. To him his very limitations must offer the inviting mirage of possible conquest, and parch his curiosity the more. His curiosity must indeed be as endless as the subject he guards and as all-embracing as the ramifications it includes. Only by its promptings can he add to his fund of knowledge, mellow his sensitivity, and sharpen his intuition. By it alone can he learn to hear all the languages which the theatre speaks. He, more than all the artists for whom he writes, must devote himself to self-training, for, while the artists have only themselves to perfect, the perfection of them all is his one ambition that touches the fringe of greatness.

In the course of his single life he can never hope to know all he needs to know and ought in fairness to know before he can set himself up as a judge. But it is the search for that knowledge which is his life work, and a life work of such a scale that it leaves him no time to dream of being a novelist, a playwright, or a producer. If he takes the time to putter on the side, or looks upon criticism as a convenient and easy meal ticket, a means instead of an end of ineffable complexity, he is only robbing the theatre and himself, and holding his profession as cheaply as he so often gives others reason to hold it. Regardless of what outsiders may think of the sacrifices in time and energy he is forced to make for what may seem to them at best a second-hand job, he must content himself with the knowledge that it may be well for the theatre that he should do so.

Though the critic, like the reviewer or the reporter, is only a signpost when he writes of what other men have done and are doing, it is his special duty to point the way not to one playhouse or one play but to the theatre itself. Unlike the signpost, however, if he is worthy of the title of dramatic critic, he is unwilling to point the way without going there himself. In his negative, passive way he must be something of an artist himself. Denied the divinity of creation, he must at least be blessed with the gifts of re-creation. In his mind's eye rather than in deed he must constantly travel to the goal at which he aims. In fact, it is only by projecting himself in that direction that he can pretend to a knowledge of the distance which was to have been covered, or to describe the citadel which was the artist's dream. And, though he has been pressed against the wall by the journalistic tradition which has swamped our theatre as well as our literature, the dramatic critic is still needed by the theatre's public, both as a standard bearer and a signpost. Perhaps we have never needed him more than we do today. But in any event it is worth while to keep his proper title for him until he does appear, and to snatch it away from those of us who now usurp his seats on the aisle.

*The danger of squandering big words on little things, of
bringing no standards to judgment, and of surrendering to
what Stark Young once called "community swoons."*

[1930]

WE—OF THE AUDIENCE

AS AUDIENCES who assemble in the theatres that the architects
have planned, to watch the work of these playwrights, these actors,
these designers and directors, and as theatregoers who may even
bother to follow the reviews next day, we want to have that confident, exhilarating feeling which informs us that what we are sitting
before each night is the best—the very best that ever was. Well, if
not quite that, at any rate the topnotch; the topnotch of this season's offerings; or at least the best that this week is apt to reveal.
We want it to be the very best because we have no middle register
to our enthusiasms.

We spend superlatives as if they were Confederate money. We
like it when our critics hail, as they do each season, some pretty
young thing as "a second Duse" after she has taken a panting curtain call which is artfully planned to make us believe that because
she has worked hard in her hysterics scene she must also have
worked well. We do not want the word "great" kept in the ice-box
too long. And we are particularly fond of having "the great American drama" in our midst each year, even though there may be, as
there occasionally are, three or four plays in town at one time that
we have crowned with that perennial superlative.

We like to have both our idols and the excitement of serving on
their welcoming committees. We enjoy the sensation of endowing
each moment with importance because from the importance we
give those moments a certain second-hand importance is bound to
come rippling back to our own shores. We prefer to feel that glory
and grandeur did not die with Greece and Rome, and that not only
our lifetimes but our immediate presents are somehow tinged with
glory, because we like the surrender which the "best" entails.

It involves a comforting emotion—and a warming one. And it saves us from thought. It spares us wearisome, hair-splitting refinements, theory that gets nowhere, because we like to believe that, when a thing is once dubbed "great" or "the best," we of the audience are thereupon relieved of the nuisance of having to decide for ourselves about its merits. Any one of the veteran superlatives is such a reassuring word and carries with it such conviction, even such finality. When it is once bestowed—and the sooner it is bestowed the happier we are—the qualities of the thing in question seem somehow to have become unquestionable.

Its merits or its blemishes have passed beyond our control even as they have departed from our sphere of worry. It has arrived. And when it has once "arrived" and we have thus succeeded in making it unassailable—a sort of Cæsar's wife in art—we can dismiss it from our consideration, put away our scales and close our minds to the qualities which may have made it "arrive" with a thankful "That is that." Then, according to the myth, we are ready to enjoy it. And we want to enjoy it. More than that we want our neighbors to enjoy it, because we are prepared for what Stark Young once called "community swoons." We have succumbed to a group emotion, gone back, as Mr. Young pointed out, to the *Chanson de Roland* and selected Charlemagne and his warriors as patterns for modernity.

" 'Christ God,' said King Charlemagne in the *Chanson,* 'in evil case am I,' and tore his beard in a great wrath and wept sore; and with him wept all the horsemen of the Franks. There were twenty thousand in the ranks that fainted on the ground." That, as Mr. Young noted, "was a group emotion indeed, twenty thousand swooning at once, not to speak of the very handsome sympathy of it. And so it is in this town of New York about the theatre very often, though too mildly swooned to work very much towards artistic creation. Great patches of us are blown down together by something or other; and that settles it. The thing is great art, is immense, grand, the height of one's artistic adventures, the thrill of one's life, what else is to be said." Only now, when we faint on the ground, we do it to the tune of hundreds of thousands.

He, she, or it (the actor, the actress, or the play) is then a success. A success is above carping because it carries the double authority of art and the box office. And nothing succeeds like success, because it must be good or it would never have succeeded. It is we of the audience who have made it a success; the critics have merely chosen our adjectives for us or pointed the way.

We want the vote to be unanimous. There is something so comforting, so friendly about a unanimous vote. It bespeaks such harmony and avoids even more discussions than it spares wounded feelings. When once the vote is taken, however, woe to the person who does not run with the pack, to those who may entertain their reservations, to the contrary-minded. They are lacking in graciousness. They are cranks. They are crotchety. They have not the right spirit at all. And who are they, anyway, to get up on such a high horse? For all their talking we bet they could not do half so well themselves. Woe to them because they are thinking as individuals, because they have not bowed to the will of the majority, and have only tried to spoil the fun. But woe, most emphatically woe, to the theatre that such should be the state of things.

Of the fact that it is, there can be but little question. Explain it away by citing mankind's "mysterious preference for the best." Call it a delightful enthusiasm, a charming good will, a healthy optimism in the *genus Americanus,* or what you like. But do not dodge the truth of what it means to the theatre. These "community swoons" lay the ax to all "standards of excellence." They mislead the performers even more than they indicate that we have been misled. They reduce the great battles for merited recognition in an art to petty hand-to-hand skirmishes between seductive personalities or second-rate talents and a public that is ready to cry "Kamerad" before the encounters commence. Not only do they remove those brambles by which Hugo said "the avenues of art should be obstructed" for the near best, but they leave them more thickly clumped than ever before for the true best. They lead manager-producers into thinking—and quite rightly too—that we do not know the false from the genuine, the good from the bad, the best from the not-so-good.

They tempt actors to palm off any applause- or phrase-catching device that is fool-proof; dramatists to turn out stuff that will pass; directors to rely on the mustache-pullings that Arthur Hopkins abhors; and scenic artists to design settings which will "get a hand" when the curtain goes up. But mainly these swoonings and their attendant hyperboles show that we of the audience have failed the theatre as badly, as wretchedly, as the theatre has ever failed us. We have not been audiences at all, but cattle stampeded by some common alarum and rounded up in a pen. We—and the critics —may have made the "he, she, or it" of the production happy for the moment because we have given them money for their bank accounts and phrases for their scrapbooks. But we have given them no real reason for self-respect. We have merely thrown away the rudder which it is our lot to hold. We have palavered in a parlor but not in a friendly way. And they, if they are intelligent, cannot but be the first to realize and resent it.

When as audiences we have succumbed to a group emotion of such a kind, we have cheated ourselves of the truest pleasures the theatre can offer as an art or as a place for adult entertainment. We have robbed ourselves of the delights of individual discovery. Instead of letting the theatre speak to us as individuals, instead of allowing its truth or its beauty, its wisdom or its wit, to reach out to us and conquer us, we have come to it too supine to make a conquest worthy of its best efforts.

In the process, we have reduced appreciation from an experience to a rumor. Like true Americans we have not inhaled the fumes of our liquor but sent it racing down our throats, all at one gulp, muttering a summary though unconvincing "Fine." We have brought no comparative judgment into play, awakened no memories, only released a well-oiled superlative as a résumé to what must have been a complicated process of emotion or thought, if we were at all aware of it or ready for each of its joys as it came along. In being willing to do this, not only have we denied the theatre all the shadows that give it interest and make its highlights stronger, but we have also betrayed how cheaply we hold it. We have shown that to us it is not even an entertainment. It is merely a passage of time that is unworthy of our thought or of the courage that might make us stand apart from the herd to nourish or defend our own discoveries. Nor is it humility before an art which contents us with a final adjective or two. It is merely the indifference we feel to the thing which has conjured them.

What are we to do if we are content, as we generally are, to squander big words on little things, when, once or twice in a lifetime, the truly big things come along? What can we call perfection, if we are ever asked to face it, when we have sunk into the habit of greeting mediocrity by perfection's rightful name? If we refuse to think for ourselves, and if our kindness leads us into wanting an unquestionable success each week, why not—for our own sake, if not out of consideration for the theatre—say so frankly and call things by their proper names? Let us flock with the town if we must, let us swell the receipts of a success so that its success is elevated beyond question. But—and it requires only the slightest thought to do so—let us of the audience leave our adjectives which pretend to criticism at the box office with our dollars if success is all we want, or keep our heads clear as to the differences that exist between what is good, indifferent, worst, good, better, or best. For it is we of the audience who imperil the theatre by our "community swoons," our nightly "wonderfuls," weekly "bests" and monthly "greats"; imperil it by debasing its standards.

That, of course, is not the only way in which we fail the theatre. But from this yearning for the indisputable best that grants the mind a leave of absence come other evils. One of these is the corollary to the swoons, and has again to do with our lack of a middle register. It is our love of wholesale invectives, born as it is of the same blindness to gradations and the identical willingness to reduce all the complexities of the theatre to the unmistakable terms of black and white. It is our readiness to avoid thinking which once again causes us to jump from "swell" or "great" (according to our pretensions) to "rotten" or "the worst." Here, too, we indicate that in our haste to reach some kind of a conclusion that sounds conclusive we have ignored the details of the whole and merely tagged the result with the first adjective or two our thesaurus may have offered, or our neighbors may have uttered. We have forgotten that in the world between these extremes, which we refuse so often to consider, lie all the hopes for growth, the reasons for failures, the seeds of greatness, the human and artistic weakness, and the virtues which give the theatre its mystery and its charm and make its very incalculability inviting.

Worse than our habit of jumping on a headlong express from the basement to the roof is the shortness of our stay when we have reached the top. The view from the summit seems to hold none of the rewards which a more gradual climb might have made apparent. Having gone as far as we can, we do not pause to look down or to enjoy the altitude.

The fact that we wear our best adjectives on our sleeves each night not only means we have kept no Sunday best at home, it also betrays the sorry truth that in our praises we must constantly be Indian-givers. We bestow a superlative on Monday night which by Thursday we have taken back and re-bestowed, without thinking of the infidelity involved—just as if on Monday night it were not already soiled and wrinkled, even mutilated, from ten or twenty or thirty years of hard usage.

This habit of speaking only in terms of stencils of the ultimate makes us as ungenerous in our praise as we are impatient with everything except the unassailable. For that very reason it tends to make us wary of experiment because the whole point of an experiment is not the finished or the unassailable (as though anything really possessed either quality) but the unfinished and the assailable. It is in its willingness to be incomplete that the courage of an experiment lies and that it asks for courage from its audiences. But when we want the swoons and welcome the thumbs-down, we show that the transitional, which is always imperative to the health of any art, and the flux, which is its one recipe for vital and continuous living, are not included in our interests.

Our preferences for the safety of harbors does not imply any permanent partisanship. We wait only for the next one to be sufficiently advertised, and then we come trooping to it, running with the pack. We are—and in our more rational moments we must admit it—as a rule as fickle as we are unthinking. The first crow's foot, the first fattening of the arm, is enough to turn us from the pretty young thing before whom we were prostrate last year—or was it last week?—because we have invested our affections in her person rather than in her talents. We make of our playgoing an endless series of coronations, and coronations are as costly in the theatre as they are out of it. For all our talk about caring for "better drama" and "a better theatre" and "the higher things," we do not let the theatre seep far enough into ourselves to touch our loyalties. Why should we? We would have to bother then to see beyond personalities into principles or at least to see personalities in terms of principles. We would have to make up our minds as to what really was a good play, or why each play could be good in its particular way, or in certain of its portions.

Of course we want the theatre to succeed, and the best to succeed in the theatre, and this to be the best of all possible worlds. But we of the audience have taken a strange manner of making our successes and justifying our superlatives. Our friendly, but apparently somewhat starved, social spirit has led us away from the detachment of impersonal judgment, for a new and exciting and personal element has entered into it all. We have discovered, since actors are no longer rogues and vagabonds, and since some of the "nicest girls" do go to dramatic schools and even on to the stage, that actors and actresses are really human beings. More than that, they are drawing cards if we announce them as guests of honor for our club meetings and our public dinners. Accordingly, instead of troubling to think about the theatre, we of the audience—and particularly the women—have organized ourselves to stand behind the theatre as it was never stood behind before.

We form theatregoing clubs. It makes running with the pack much simpler. And, as we have five hundred or more members, we represent a federated unit which it is not safe for the manager-producers to ignore. We may, once a month, go to their playhouses *en masse,* and they like the business that we bring them. Who can blame them—or us—when we take five hundred or more good tickets off their hands at one time? Though being herded to the theatre like a group of orphans on a picnic may destroy our desire, even our need, for thinking for ourselves, since Madame President or her Playgoing Committee has thought it all out for us, who can be so foolish as to doubt the good we do the theatre?

Nor is this the limit of our good work. We give luncheons and dinners, play luncheons and drama dinners, and we stud the guests-of-honor table with the great of the stage. What we do not see is how unfair it is to ask an actress or an actor to sit down at a table in street clothes, in the disillusioning glare of a dining room, and to be one of us; to be one of us in fact when all five hundred of us are forgetting the glamour that he or she may have had for us in the theatre, and are turning a thousand curious eyes on him as he drinks his soup, chews his hard rolls, and handles his asparagus.

Yet because of some perverse human weakness we do insist upon these dinners, these teas, and these luncheons; draining the actors of their energies, holding the dinners at the very hour when we should be going to the theatre instead of making it come to us.

We do it because it is amusing—to us. We do it no doubt with very good intentions, but what we do not see is that, if the theatre means all the things to us that we say it does at those dinners, our chief duty is to be facing a stage instead of a speaker's table. We must learn, even though it robs us of a certain amount of pleasure and undeniable thrill, that the business of our hands is not hand-shaking with the actor but applause for his performance, and that, for our sakes as well as theirs, actors should be seen but not met.

Learning that and leaving society to society and the theatre to the theatre we might then, *perhaps,* have time enough left in which to permit our adjectives to be the result of our ideas instead of group emotions. We might even outgrow our naïve longings to have the best with us each night, and observe our players and our productions more closely so as to try to discover the stuff of which the best will be made when it does come. Then, as audiences, we may be said to be doing our duty, even—though I hesitate to use the word—our best, and our patronage may mean more than dollars and cents to the theatre.

Some challenges, agreeable and irksome, both of conducting a column and writing in general are touched upon in personal terms.

[1949]

PLEASANT AGONY

FOR SEVERAL years now, mine has been the privilege, hence the pleasant agony, of filling a page each week, or almost every week, in the *Saturday Review of Literature.* I say pleasant agony because I know of no other words with which to describe what writing is to me.

I claim no singularity in this. There may be, there must be, writers to whom writing comes as effortlessly as breathing. There may even be (though I doubt it) writers whose happiness is complete while they are actually writing. But most of us who live by putting words together are not so fortunate. We are tortured while we write and would be tortured were we not allowed to do so. Although when we are done we feel "delivered," as Sainte-Beuve put it, this delirium of delivery is not accomplished without labor pains for which medicine has, as yet, provided no soothing drugs. If all attempts to coerce words into doing what we would have them do are at best painful pleasures, the pains and pleasures of summoning the right words to meet a weekly deadline are of a special kind.

A cook faced with getting dinner when lunch is over knows something of the routine, if not all the anguishes, of a columnist. No mortals, however, have appetites as insatiable as a column's. A column is an omnivorous beast. Its hunger is never appeased. Feed it, and almost at once it demands to be fed again.

Though he used a different image to express this same idea, even Shaw, seemingly the most easeful of writers, knew this. When he abandoned the job of drama critic on London's *Saturday Review*, he protested against the weekly deadlines which had confronted him for nearly four years. He likened himself to a man fighting a windmill. "I have hardly time," wrote he, "to stagger to my feet from the knock-down blow of one sail, when the next strikes me down."

His successor in the same job on that same fortunate magazine shared an identical dislike of deadlines. For twelve years, Max Beerbohm admitted in his valedictory article, Thursdays had been for him the least pleasant day of the week. Why Thursday? Because that was the day, the latest possible one, he set aside each week to get his writing done. On every Wednesday, therefore, he would be engulfed by "a certain sense of oppression, of misgiving, even of dread." It was only on Friday, when once the danger was passed, that the sun would shine again. Then he would move on dancing feet.

I quote my betters to console myself by the reminder that they too knew the pangs of weekly columnizing. Yet the consolation I seek is denied me when I discover, for example, that it took Beerbohm one, and only one, short day of pain to turn out the delectable copy which he could write. Shaw, I am certain, was also a one-day man. I wish I were. I wish even more ardently that I could claim any of the merits which glorify their reviews for what it takes me two, three, or sometimes five days of ceaseless sweating to produce as fodder for my columns.

Beerbohm ascribed his disrelish for the act of writing to "the acute literary conscience" with which he had been cursed. It was this conscience, he maintained, which kept his pen from ever running away with him. I know what he means. Unblessed with any of his gifts, I am nonetheless cursed with something of his conscience. Beerbohm insisted that "to seem to write with ease and delight is one of the duties which a writer owes to his readers." If he worked hard at his sentences, it was because Beerbohm hoped they would read easily. In other words, he was in complete agreement with Sheridan's "easy writing's vile hard reading." One statement of Beerbohm's I could truthfully apply to my own efforts for the *SRL*. It runs, "I may often have failed, in my articles here, to disguise labor. But the effort to disguise it has always been loyally made."

There is a passage in *The Goncourt Journals* which has haunted me since I read it. Envy has kept it green for me, and wonder (or is it disbelief?) has kept it alive. I have in mind Gautier's boast that he never thought about what he was going to write. "I take up my pen," he explained, "and write. I am a man of letters and am presumed to know my job. . . . I throw my sentences into the air and I can be sure that they will come down on their feet, like cats. . . . Look here: here's my script: not a word blotted."

When I think of the one-legged kittens that land on my pages; when I remember the false starts, illegible scribblings, unfinished sentences, discarded drafts, changed constructions, and altered words which mark my beginnings, my continuings, and my endings, I blush with shame and, like the voyagers in Dante's realm, abandon all hope.

In these journalistic days the first word that pops into an author's mind is held to be the acceptable, if not the best, word. We are supposed to smile because Wordsworth, at a day's end, was wearied from his quest for the exact word. But where Wordsworth the man may win a smile, Wordsworth the writer, fatiguing himself by doing what is a writer's duty, is far from laughable. The *mot juste* is not just any word. Even if it eludes its pursuer, the search for it seems to me to remain among the obligations of authorship. Indeed, the true hope of anyone who loves the language and respects it is to stumble upon, not the correct word or phrase, but the word or phrase which is so right that it seems inevitable.

The word and the phrase are not the only hurdles—and joys—of authorship. The sentence and the paragraph, by means of which points are made, thoughts communicated, emotions transferred, pictures painted, personalities caught, rhythms established, and cadences varied, offer other challenges and should supply their own sources of delight and pride. When so much hurried writing is done for hurried reading, I find it comforting to have Shaw, a veritable geyser with words and ideas, admit in his *Sixteen Self Sketches* how depleting he found his labors as a weekly feuilletonist for ten years. Why? Because, says he, of "taking all the pains I was capable of to get to the bottom of every sentence I wrote."

One of the modern world's luckier occurrences was what happened at Harrow when a boy named Winston Churchill was being "menaced with Education." Three times, he tells us in *A Roving Commission,* his backwardness as a classical scholar forced him to remain in the same form and hence repeat the same elementary course in English. "Thus," writes he (and who can question him?), "I got into my bones the essential structure of the ordinary British sentence—which is a noble thing. . . . Naturally I am biased in favor of boys learning English. I would make them all learn English: and then I would let the clever ones learn Latin as an honor, and Greek as a treat. But the only thing I would whip them for would be for not knowing English. I would whip them hard for that." One trembles to think how many of us whose profession is writing would be flogged today if lapses in English, or American, were whippable offenses.

Later on in that same grand book, Churchill has his more precise say on the subtleties, intricacies, and the possibilities of the writer's craft. It is his opinion, and one worth heeding, that, "just as the sentence contains one idea in all its fullness, so the paragraph should embrace a distinct episode; and as sentences should follow one another in harmonious sequence, so the paragraphs must fit on to one another like the automatic couplings of railway carriages."

I quote Churchill and these others belonging to the peerage of prose writers because, for any author with a memory, one of the disheartening and humbling aspects of writing is the recollection, as his own pen moves, of how those whom he admires have faced and solved identical problems. This recollection of what has been done, this sensing of what could and should be done, this awareness of what one hopes to do regardless of whether one can or cannot do it—these are parts of that literary conscience, mentioned by Beerbohm, which keeps a writer's pen from running away with him. I know they are factors in retarding my own pen (meaning my typewriter, pencil, or dictation) even on those happy days when a subject seems to write itself, when sentences come easily, and one paragraph gives way to another.

Style is a strange and mysterious thing. Some contemporary writers appear to get along without it and to want to do so, and most of us rightly disparage it when it shows the effort that has gone into it. Few of us, for example, can read Pater today without being irritated and put off by the labyrinthian intricacies of his sentences. His style, once held to be a model, remains a model, although as we see it it is one to be avoided rather than followed. Pater could not bring himself to say a simple thing simply. His orchestration is so elaborate that the melody of his thought is lost.

Hazlitt comes closer to present-day tastes. More than being the enemy of the gaudy and "Occult" schools of writing, Hazlitt was not only a champion but at his best a matchless practitioner of "The Familiar Style." Although he had the art to make a long sentence seem short, he knew the value of short sentences. "I hate anything," wrote he, "that occupies more space than it is worth. I hate to see a load of band-boxes go along the street, and I hate to see a parcel of big words without any meaning in them."

The perpetual challenge of writing, the challenge presented by each new sentence, is to say exactly what one wants to say exactly as one wants to say it. This is where the anguish of composition mixes with the delights. This is where, too, style, as I see it, comes into the picture. Style is merely the means, chosen or instinctive (doubtless both), by which a writer has his precise and personal say.

Certainly, style is not affectation. Conscious though it may be, when self-conscious it is an obstruction. Its purpose, to my way of thinking, is to give the reader pleasure by sparing him the work which the writer is duty-bound to have done for him. Writers, notwithstanding their hopes or ambitions, may or may not be artists. But there is no excuse for their not being artisans. Although in the final and spiritual sense the style is the man, it is more than that. It is the writing man *in print*. It is, so to speak, his written voice and, if it is truly his voice, even in print it should be his and his alone. The closer it comes to the illusion of speech, perhaps the better. Yet the closeness of the written word to the spoken can, and in fact should, never be more than an illusion. For the point of the written word is planning, as surely as the charm of the spoken word can be its lack of planning.

Without shame I confess that, regardless of how unsatisfactory the results may be, I have labored when writing my weekly pieces to lighten the labor of those who may read them. That I have failed again and again I know to my own chagrin, but I can honestly say I have tried. I not only rewrite; I often rewrite and rewrite again. I do this though I am well aware that the result is sentences and paragraphs which do not bear rereading. I rewrite partly in longhand, partly by dictation, occasionally sitting down, sometimes walking, but most often snaking my way across the floor on my stomach. My desk, a migratory one, is the small piece of beaverboard I push before me. On it are sheets of typewriter paper darkened with hieroglyphics which must be deciphered immediately to be read at all.

Endeavoring to square my writing with my writing conscience, and having to live with the difference between what I would like to have done and am able to do, is one of the reasons why writing is to me an agony, however pleasant.

There are other contributors to the pleasures and the agonies of trying to keep columns fed. Time is one of these; time in the sense that it confronts a writer for a magazine with a special problem.

Newspapermen, accustomed to meeting daily deadlines, must

think it absurd for a fellow on a weekly to mention time at all. Compared to the one frantic hour, or even two or three hours, of enforced fluency at their disposal, the seven long days I have, if need be, in which to do my stint must seem to the daily boys the life span of a Methuselah. No wonder they might be inclined to sneer at me for daring to speak of pressure, or mutter, "How much time does he want? What does he think he's writing, anyway?"

Once I would have shared their astonishment, had anyone told me it could take the better (or is it the worse?) part of a week to get a review done. Once I would have laughed at a schedule so leisurely and a pace so snail-like. But that would have been during those thirteen hard-driven years before the war when, in ways at present mysterious to me, I also managed to meet daily deadlines, first on the *New York Evening Post* and later on the *New York World-Telegram*. Now, however, I know that, as surely as the daily journalist fights against the clock, the weekly journalist must contend with the calendar. Both are the victims of time, the one because of having too little, the other because of having too much (though never enough).

In my newspaper days—and nights—I used to read, and re-read, with envy the sentence with which Matthew Arnold introduced his essay on Amiel and his *Journal*. It ran, "It is somewhat late to speak of Amiel, but I was late in reading him." As a man who was the thrall of what had happened last night; as a person whose job naturally did not permit him to be "somewhat late" in seeing, reading, or writing anything; as someone then laboring furiously under the tyranny of news, this lead by Matthew Arnold seemed to me an expression of the finest and most desirable kind of journalistic freedom. It still does. But I have come to realize such freedom imposes its own responsibilities.

Newspaper reviewing and columnizing, especially when the theatre was the only subject allowed me, was quite different. It was bound to be so. It was at once far more arduous and much simpler and, if I may say so, not nearly so much fun. It had its agreeable aspects, however. One of these was the Western Union messenger boys, oldish men most of them, with a GAR look. Since I worked for evening papers with offices far downtown, these messengers were merciful enough to stop by my apartment every night to pick up the copy. They would jab the front doorbell with an energy at once frightening and insistent, and were always in a hurry. Their coming meant there was no chance to rewrite, to alter, to discard, or to add. What I had written before their arrival was hurriedly marked for the printer and no less speedily folded into an envelope. Off it would go beyond recall—off until the next noon, when I would be confronted with it on the newsstands.

Time after time, this confrontation left me sick of heart, mind, and hope, and feeling slightly ill. My one desire was to stay in hiding all that day. Yet, even while in hiding, I would console myself by saying, "It's not really my fault. It's the messenger's. If only he had come half an hour or an hour later, my stuff might have been what it ought to have been and what I wanted it to be." The truth is I miss those nightly messengers. By appearing no longer they have robbed me of a soothing alibi. Now I have no one to blame for the inadequacies of a week's work except myself. This means my periods of hiding are not as brief as they once were.

There were other consolations in a daily deadline. For instance, there was the mere phrase, "Last night at such-and-such a theatre," which, because of the hocus-pocus of journalistic ritual, had to be incorporated somehow or other in the introductory paragraph of almost every play review I wrote. This used to irritate me mightily. My conviction was that the subhead or the box giving the cast covered such a temporal fact. But the fact, even the phrase, was not without its simplifying advantages.

News interest, as well I know, supplies copy with water wings of undeniable buoyancy. Although a real news story does not write itself, it does not have to be written carefully to possess interest. A daily review, regardless of what else it may be and frequently is, is bound to be news, good or bad. In itself this helps the writer on many a tired night. This I also know well, because in moments of fatigue, inanition, apathy, confusion, or mental paralysis I often used to take advantage of it.

The more a first-night review sticks to the point, the better. Its job is to cover a specific opening, not go beyond it. It is written hot, not cold; written as a reflex to an experience just had rather than from a re-created or treasured emotion. (Count this another aid.) Once a satisfactory lead has been found that will establish the tone and mood of the opinion stated, its outline is almost provided for it by these inevitable topics which in turn must be touched upon—the play, the acting, the direction, the settings, the costumes, and the music, if there is any. The sooner a first-night review has its direct say, and hence proves its serviceability to the reader, the better. Unlike articles appearing in a national magazine such as the *SRL*, newspaper notices are chiefly written for the use of those living in the towns where they are printed. However agreeable they may be as reading, they are meant to do a definite, practical, and immediate service for the reader.

New Yorkers, for example, may or may not be devotees of criticism. But they are prospective ticket buyers. Understandably, they want to know if what has just opened is something which they would be wise to see or avoid. Their first concern (and often their last except, perhaps, on Saturdays or Sundays) is whether the critical light is green or red. Reading quickly and not without self-interest, they are the more apt to forgive the worn-out phrases upon which the writer who writes quickly is sometimes forced to rely.

Poverty might but horses could not drag me back to daily reviewing or newspaper work. Or, for that matter, to writing only about the theatre. My debt to the *SRL* is a genuine one. The *SRL* has relieved me from the constabulary duties which must be done, night after night, for the theatre's sake as well as the public's, and which my confreres perform with incredible patience and skill. It has spared me from having to sit before those dreary ineptitudes, those costly and dispiriting barbiturates, those utter time-wasters and monumental bores which seem bound to form so large a percentage of every season's offerings. It has permitted me to put away the flit-gun which has to be used on so many of Broadway's fly-by-night productions and which once upon a time I enjoyed using myself.

It has allowed me to pick and choose, to write about only the better plays or those which, though failures, were interesting in their faults. Above all, it has not limited me to the theatre. Each week it has left the choice of subject up to me, and given me full latitude in everything I have written.

If it were not that each week the writing of these pieces had to be done, I would have to thank the *SRL* for providing me with the ideal set-up. But the writing must be done, and trying to get it done in a manner that in any way justifies such freedom is where both the pleasure and the agony come in.

There was a time when the theatre as theatre seemed to me all-absorbing. That, however, was before the war. Though I still dote upon it at its best, even at its best it no longer interests me merely as theatre. For me, as for many another, the world has forced open the windows that once seemed securely shut, and it is for drafts from this outer world that I now look even in a playhouse. The point of a weekly article, regardless of its subject, is, as I see it, to keep these windows open.

As impatient readers may have observed to their annoyance, I no longer try or want to write a review which is a notice and only that. If I lack the inclination to do so, I think I also lack the excuse. The cream of the news has been skimmed off long before I come to my desk and even longer before the *SRL* appears. Sometimes, I admit, what emerges is a straight notice. But when this happens, it is contrary to my intentions. Endeavoring, no matter how unsuccessfully, to do something more than that involves an effort, an approach, and a method which are very different from daily reviewing.

My hope each week, even when "covering" a play, a movie, or a book, is to be led by the specific instance from the particular to the general. This means attempting (please note that I say *attempting*) to reflect as well as to react, to apply no less than to report, and to use a topic not as an end in itself but as a springboard to something larger. It means searching for the overtones, parallels, and implications suggested by a subject, and not limiting myself to the subject itself.

The real work of weekly columnizing lies, I find, not in the actual writing, hard as that is for me, but in the getting ready to write. In other words, it lies in the quest for a point of view, hence a point of departure, which is not dependent upon news as news. My deadline being what it is, I do not come to my typewriter hot from the thing seen, though naturally I struggle to retain or recapture something of that first heat. I have the time to live with my reactions for two or three days and nights, to let them simmer in my thoughts, to rummage in my mind and memory for experiences or illustrations which have a bearing on the subject discussed.

If I dare to be discursive, my digressions are deliberate and, to me, relevant. Their aim is to widen the ripple of application, to extend the subject by following up the hints it has given. For what I struggle to write each week is an article which, though it may not manage to become an essay, is in intention at least nearer to the essay-review than to the review.

The *SRL* has made it possible for me to write of what I want to write about and to avoid having to have my say on plays, pictures, or books which have said nothing to me. The fact that I do not swat flies as jubilantly as once I did does not mean I have grown benevolent (or is the word mellow?). It means merely that fly-swatting is no longer one of my chores.

Shaw in his reviewing days once insisted that the artist who accounted for his personal disparagement by alleging personal animosity on his part was quite right. "When people do less than their best, and do that less at once badly and self-complacently," he fumed with that delectable immoderation which can be his, "I hate them, I loathe them, detest them, long to tear them limb from limb and strew them in gobbets about the stage or platform." Shaw's point was that the man with a genuine critical spirit "becomes your personal enemy on the sole provocation of a bad performance, and will only be appeased by a good [one]."

Although I share his fierce point of view fiercely, and trust I remain the implacable foe of the bogus, the pretentious, the empty, and the mediocre, the longer I live the more convinced I am that the most challenging function of criticism is rising to appreciation rather than excelling at denunciation. It is easier by far to hold the attention while damning than when praising. If this were not true, so many conversationalists would not be considered witty whose sole equipment is malice. The bludgeon, the nightstick, the ax, the bazooka, and the flame-thrower are weapons every critic should have in his armory. But criticism of the arts, which as I see it is bound to be a criticism of life, would be a dull and sorry business were it prepared only to stalk, attack, and extinguish.

Although the heat of proper indignation or contempt is a heat both necessary and healthy, it is not by any means the only heat with which I, for one, would choose to have my copy warmed. There are the juices, the joys, the pains, the dilemmas of living, and something of these I wish I could capture. This is why the jargon of the so-called "new critics" repels me. It has no compassion, little humanity, and less gaiety. It is arid, bloodless, and absurdly, cloyingly over-specialized. It does not flow from the heart but trickles from the head, and only a small part of that. It is written from books rather than life; written, and most successfully written, to be unreadable.

I deplore this other approach to writing because I belong to a different, more conciliatory school. Without shame I confess I am a writer who would like to be readable and read. I do not ask or expect to be agreed with. The only truth I can state (and it takes struggling to get it half stated) is a personal one. Accordingly, I have no other choice than to write personally. What a man is is the basis of what he dreams and thinks, accepts and rejects, feels and perceives. It is, too, the stuff from which he writes. If he can speak with any accuracy for himself, he may speak with some accuracy for others. But only if he interests them. It is in the hard, hard rock-pile labor of seeking to win, hold, or deserve a reader's interest that the pleasant agony of writing again comes in.

10. Backgrounds

*A chronicle of some of the major tendencies and develop-
ments which have characterized the modern theatre and
charted its course the world over.*

[1929]

THE MODERN THEATRE IN REVOLT

THE CONCERN of these chapters is not dates, nor history, in
the sense of something that is past and dead, but ideas—the
living, contagious antagonistic ideas of the contrary-minded that
have contributed in their various ways to making the contemporary
theatre what it is. They reveal the modern theatre only at its moments of high tide, when new men, new theories, new experiments
and new movements have appeared, bringing to it the spirit of
protest which is so largely responsible for its magnificent vitality.
They form the annals of change, reappraisal, and rediscovery that
have made of the last fifty years one of the greatest periods of
theatrical renascence the world has seen. It is, in short, the theatre
of these active, exciting years that this book records, caught at its
pivotal moments of ignition.

The approaches to the theatre herein examined have nothing in
common save the deep-throated discontent with the established
order that they all reflect. Each of them, in spite of the familiarity
which may by now have robbed it of the glamour of novelty, first
appeared in its own time as a doctrine of revolt, an ardent attempt
at reform, the ultimatum of a new order or a new prophet. The
Naturalists broke with the Romantic tradition which had gone before them. The so-called New Movement in the theatre—the visual
impetus that Craig, Appia, Reinhardt, and the rest inaugurated—
appeared as an equally positive rebellion from the traditions the
Naturalists had fought to inaugurate. From the general order and
many forms of its protest came the next phase of change, when
the playwright's theatre of the mind which Ibsen had introduced
and that theatre of the eye which the designer and the director had
fought to establish combined to produce that theatre of the mind's

eye known as Expressionism. And finally, as a special manifestation of the constant rebellions these fifty years have seen, Constructivism rears its naked outlines on the stages of Soviet Russia, discarding both realism and the customary decorative details of the New Movement, and converting the theatre itself into a militant instrument, not for any single camp of artistic revolt, but for social rebellion itself. In general that is the order in which the stress and storm of the modern theatre have shown themselves. But only in general, for the annals of any art stubbornly refuse to admit that neat cleavage into "isms" and "ists" which exists only on the pages of the books that record them. In actual practice, they defy these convenient but purely arbitrary separations, because they are so frequently coexistent forms that consciously or unconsciously borrow freely from each other.

Some of the movements described in these pages are already dead, dead as only victorious causes in art can be. Some of them are the dreams of prophets, the visionary men, the theorists the theatre is so fond of exiling to the side lines. Others are special phases, even fads. But all of them, it is worth remembering, came into being as battle cries to be fought for, responsible for new "ists" and "isms," and the founding of those new schools that each lucky generation lives to see established. They are the work of the revolutionists who are always needed to bring flux and experiment to the arts, to save them from the blight of exhaustion, and keep them in that state of transition which is their one condition of health.

THE COMING OF NATURALISM

The red and gold walls of the old Théâtre Français trembled with the clamor of discord on the evening of February 25, 1830. Surely there was more than the scent of battle in the air on that first night among first nights, when the *Hernani* of Victor Hugo— the young man of the bulbous forehead the cartoonists were so fond of enlarging, not the old man of the grizzly beard—was to open and the Romantics were to fight their way into the French theatre. Had not the conservatives, the good Classicists, who believed in an Aristotle of their own imagining, and admired the bloodless abstractions of Corneille, Racine, and Voltaire, listened at the doors while rehearsals were in progress? And had not the eavesdroppers gladly pounced upon single lines from the play, and parodied them with a cruel wit throughout the length and breadth of Paris? Had not the company at the Comédie, with but one exception, taken up their parts with a manifest lack of enthusiasm? Was not the arcade of the Rue de Rivoli splotched with signs that read *"Vive Victor Hugo,"* signs written by those eccentric young men who were already the sworn disciples of this equally young messiah? Of course. Every one knew that, and more. Was not this same Victor Hugo to be threatened? No mild threat, to be sure, but one that involved death "if he did not withdraw his filthy play." All the disciples knew this, then, and the graybeards knew it too, though perhaps they may not have known that Hugo, declining to employ the paid claque custom prescribed, had distributed some three hundred tickets among his friends, young artists of all kinds—painters, poets, sculptors, and musicians—who crowded into the pit, the proud possessors of little slips of red paper, upon which, in a decisive hand, was written *Hierro* (Spanish for iron), the grim watchword Hugo had given them to remind them that they must "put up an iron front."

The scene of the death struggle between Romanticism and Classicism in France forms one of the most familiar and oft-told tales in the annals of the French stage. It involved celebrities even as it changed history. Gautier was there in his famous rose-colored waistcoat, a disciple of the new order, a disciple among a host of others whom Madame Hugo described as "a troop of wild, extraordinary creatures, with beards and long hair, dressed in every fashion except that of the day—in woolen jerseys and Spanish cloaks, Robespierre waistcoats and Henry III caps—displaying themselves in broad daylight at the doors of the theatre with the clothing of all ages and countries on their backs," ready to applaud and to fight. Ready, in fact, to do even more. Because it must not be supposed that partisan feeling or personal devotion such as this stopped here. It soared to higher altitudes, the altitudes, in fact, that Charlet, the painter, achieved in that most amazing of amazing letters which he wrote to Hugo seeking the honor of protecting him during the first nights of this bitter struggle for Romanticism.

"Four of my Janissaries," it ran, "offer me their strong arms. I send them to prostrate themselves at your feet, begging for four places this evening, if it is not too late. I answer for my men; they are fellows who would gladly cut off their heads for the sake of the wigs. I encourage them in this noble spirit, and do not let them go without my fatherly blessing. They kneel. I stretch out my hands and say: God protect you, young men! The cause is a good one; do your duty! They rise and I add: Now, my children, take good care of Victor Hugo. God is good, but He has so much to do that our friend must in the first instance rely upon us. Go, and do not put him you serve to shame— Yours with life and soul, Charlet."

The irrepressible question all this rhetoric about Janissaries and a protecting, though busy, God invites is why—why this feeling, sweeping through Paris, and why this fanatical subservience to Hugo. Granting that Romanticism was forcing its way into the theatre, that this first night of *Hernani* came as the climax to a tempest that had long been brewing, admitting that Dumas père had written his *Henri III et sa Cour,* and that Hugo, too, had turned to the theatre but found no doors open for his *Cromwell,* still the question is a fair one that asks by what special magic did this Victor Hugo, just turned twenty-nine, deserve these "Janissaries," and because of what extraordinary principles was the Paris of 1830 so inflamed?

First of all, and most obviously, because it was Paris, the natural home of the movements in art, and hence of arts that have been kept in constant motion. But more specifically because this same Victor Hugo had written three years earlier a short preface to his unacted *Cromwell* which had become the rallying point of a new school, and the formation of a new school acquires a special significance in Paris. "There is a mysterious magic about the process," writes George Brandes in a fine paragraph which catches something of the exultation these young men must have shared on that memorable first night. "Some one remarkable man, after a long unconscious or half-conscious struggle, finally with full consciousness frees himself from prejudices and attains to clearness of vision; then, everything being ready, the lightning of genius illuminates what he beholds. Such a man gives utterance (as did Hugo in a prose preface of some score of pages) to some thoughts which have never been thought or expressed in the same manner before. They may be only half true, they may be vague, but they have this remarkable quality that, in spite of more or less indefiniteness, they affront all traditional prejudices and wound the vanity of the day where it is most vulnerable, whilst they ring in the ears of the younger generation like a call, like a new, audacious watchword. . . . Seldom, however, in the world's history has the mutual admiration accompanying an artistic awakening been carried to such a pitch as it was by the generation of 1830. It became positive idolatry. All the literary productions of the period show that the youth of the day were intoxicated with the feeling of friendship and brotherhood. Hugo's poems to Lamartine, Louis Boulanger, Sainte-Beuve, and David D'Angers; Gautier's to Hugo, Jehan du Seigneur, and Petrus Borel; De Musset's to Lamartine, Sainte-Beuve, and Nodier; and, very especially, Sainte-Beuve's to all the standard bearers of the school; Madame de Girardin's articles; Balzac's dedications; George Sand's *Lettres d'un Voyageur*— all testify to a sincere, ardent admiration, which entirely precluded the proverbial jealousy of authors."

And why? Because in that epoch-making prose preface of some score of pages Hugo—as spokesman for the school at its moment of insurrection—dared to say "Let us take the hammer to poetic systems. Let us throw down the old plastering that conceals the façade of art. *There are neither rules nor models; or, rather, there are no other rules than the general laws of nature.*"

Move forward forty years or so in that same Paris, dispense with those Henry III caps, those Spanish cloaks and Robespierre waistcoats, and come to a generation which fits more amicably into the prosaic uniform of a triumphant bourgeoisie. Another iconoclast is thundering his ultimatum in the ears of a listening generation, a prophet who has already grown into a myth, a man who has been scurrilously attacked in the press, scored a triumph in the novel, tried his hand at playwriting, and who awaits, without knowing it, the cruelest persecution of his life, the Dreyfus affair, which is to lift him beyond the limits of his natural timidity and gild him with more than a tinge of the heroic. It is, of course, Zola, the Zola of *L'Assommoir*, the arch-Naturalist, the bitter foe of the Romantics, the author of a Naturalist play, *Thérèse Raquin,* and a considerable factor in the successful founding of the *Théâtre Libre.* He too is speaking the hot words of prophecy, the words which "affront all traditional prejudices and wound the vanity of the day where it is most vulnerable." He too is giving an "audacious watchword" to the Goncourts, Flaubert, Becque, and a host of others, a watchword of such a rich contagion that it is to push far beyond the limits of a humiliated France and score a decisive victory under the very chin of Bismarck. He too was a champion, uttering new doctrines, a prophet—come to reform not only the novel but also the theatre. And his words, which were blessed with such a special alchemy, were these, *"There should no longer be any school, no more formulas, no standards of any sort: there is only life itself, an immense field where each may study and create as he likes."*

In other words, within less than fifty years of each other two great French insurrectionists were formulating the doctrines of new schools. Romantic Hugo was breaking with the Classic past, Naturalistic Zola was breaking with Romantic Hugo, and each, at first glance, seems to have turned rebel to the same tune; the *Nature-as-a-model* motif which is such a favorite pattern for rebellion in the arts. When playwrights—or in fact artists of any kind—swear allegiance to "Nature," the oath may mean much or little. But one thing is certain and that is it will never mean the same thing twice. For "Nature" is as different as the men who see it, the times at which they see it, the eyes, the hearts, the minds, and even the racial characteristics through which it is envisaged. Between the "nature" Hugo fought for and that which Zola championed was that chasm which divides two radically different points of view and equally different purposes: the cleavage between the grotesque and the commonplace, the picturesque and the factual, the Gothic revival and the scientific spirit, the cloak and swords of yesteryear and the slums of today. It was, in short, the difference between "Nature" (capitalized, of course) that borrows the enchantment of distance, and human nature observed through the myopic eyes of men and women avid for the detail close at hand.

Hugo was attacking the fatiguing monotony of the "ancients," their fondness for piling "sublime upon sublime," and their stupidity in failing to use the "grotesque," which he held could alone lend contrast to literature. His reasoning took advantage of illustrations that in a moment betray the quality of his realism. In such characteristic phrases as "The salamander gives relief to the water-sprite; the gnome heightens the charm of the sylph," he battled for his points. And with an epic lack of humor he condemned the classic past because—because it could not have produced *Beauty and the Beast*.

"It seems to us that someone has already said that a drama is a mirror wherein nature is reflected," he wrote with a nice forgetfulness for one who was strongly influenced by Shakespeare, and then came to the kernel of his argument. "But if it is an ordinary mirror, a smooth and polished surface, it will give only a dull image of objects, with no relief—faithful but colorless. . . . The drama, therefore, must be a concentrating mirror, which, instead of weakening, concentrates and condenses the colored rays, which makes of a mere gleam a light, and of a light a flame. Then only is the drama acknowledged by art." He pointed out that local color should not "be on the surface of a drama, but in its substance, in the very heart of the work." And his reason was an artist's reason and an artist's pride in his profession. "It is well that the avenues of art should be obstructed by those brambles from which everybody recoils except those of powerful will. Besides, it is this very study, fostered by an ardent inspiration, which will insure the drama against a vice that kills it—the commonplace."

The grotesque, not the commonplace, the grotesque as an aid to artifice, a device for contrast, not an unpleasant actuality, were Hugo's special pleadings. As craftsman, he insisted that the theatre consist of arrangement, and that the drama be inaccessible to all except the willful and the inspired. As artist he wished to be judged by his selections, and have his chosen *métier* insured against the vice of the commonplace. That, and that alone, constituted his submission to the general laws of "Nature."

Hugo's whole contention was, of course, denied by Zola, denied because Zola as the arch-prophet of Naturalism dared to speak against art and its imperative selections. "I am for no schools," he wrote, "because I am for human truth, which excludes all sects and all systems." And then Zola came to the grounds for fundamental disagreement. "The word *art* displeases me: it contains I do not know what ideas of necessary arrangement, of absolute ideal. To make art, is it not to make something which is outside of man and of nature?" And once more, though in different words, he came back to the laws of Nature, though it should be noted that Zola's "Nature" was in both instances "life"—and the difference is more important than it may at first seem. With "life" as his model, even his ambition, he continued, "I wish that you should make *Life:* I wish that you should be alive, that you should create afresh, outside of all things, according to your own eyes and your own temperament. What I seek first of all in a picture is a man, and not the picture."

Zola was impatient with an art that pretended to "arrange" but that "arranged" only to falsify and "pass outside of man and nature." He surveyed the theatre of the Paris of his day—or rather the theatre before his day—and his impatience became as active as only the discontent of new leaders can be. "The historical drama is in its death throes," he wrote, ". . . dying a natural death, of its own extravagances and platitudes. If comedy still maintains its place amid the general disintegration of the stage, it is because comedy clings closer to the actual, and is often true. I defy the last of the Romanticists to put upon the stage a heroic drama; at the sight of all the paraphernalia of armor, secret doors, poisoned wines, and the rest, the audience would only shrug its shoulders. And melodrama, that bourgeois offspring of the romantic drama, is in the hearts of the people more dead than its predecessor; its false sentiment, its complication of stolen children and discovered documents, its impudent gasconnades have finally rendered it despicable so that any attempt to revive it proves abortive." So much for the conditions of the time as Zola saw them. He then proceeded to pay tribute to the change his predecessors in revolt had wrought, at the same time that he declared the independence of the new order. "The great works of 1830 will always remain advance-guard works, landmarks in a literary epoch, superb efforts which laid low the scaffolding of the classics. But, now that everything is torn down, the swords and capes rendered useless, it is time to base our works on truth."

To achieve this Zola hoped to bring the theatre into contact with the times. In particular he wanted to establish a "closer relation with the great movement toward truth and experimental science which has, since the last century, been on the increase in every manifestation of the human intellect. The movement was started by the new methods of science; then, Naturalism revolutionized criticism and history, in submitting man and his works to a system of precise analysis, taking into account all circumstances, environment, and 'organic cases.' Then in turn, art and letters were carried along with the current." The historical canvases, as he pointed out, gave way to realistic paintings, the novel broadened its scope and took in "all the activities of man" and the stage was at last to be awakened by the new impulse. The stage at last, because the theatre, as the most democratic of the arts, is bound to move more slowly, waiting for its audiences to receive their initiation elsewhere; waiting, in fact, as it almost always has, for the new to become the accepted outside the playhouses before offering it as the new inside them.

This nineteenth century that mothered both Hugo and Zola was remarkable for many things far more remarkable than they. It was the most complex century history had known, in which for the first time the full welter of the modern world was sensed with all its baffling wonderment. Intricate, even confused beyond simplification, a mighty panorama without apparent beginning or end, its forces and its men moved with kaleidoscopic swiftness across a crowded scene. Reviewed in retrospect—and without our depending upon those easy and inviting pegs, those key men and key dates, on which history is so often made to hang its trappings, there was not a single placid, uneventful year throughout its entire length. At least not a single year in which at some corner of the globe new ideas, new inventions, new systems of thought or experiments in government were not appearing to disturb the mind and peace of man, to tear down the old structure of human life, or prepare the way for readjustments that would some day be exacted. When Hugo wrote *Hernani* machines were already throbbing in the factories. Eleven years before that memorable first night the steam-driven paddlewheels of the *Savannah* had churned their way across the Atlantic. Steam, too, had already come as a challenge to the stage coach and was sending trains across the landscapes of both continents for brave first "runs." In short, the Industrial and Mechanical Revolutions were well under way. And, side by side with them, the ever-increasing contributions of the scientists were making themselves felt—the result of quiet diligence and painstaking, selfless love. More important than anyone can say, and defying precise evaluation, these contributions from the laboratories were to touch every department of human living and human thinking, and play a larger, though less showy, part in the drama of mankind than was ever played by the glittering personalities who walk away with the spotlight of history. All these forces were burgeoning in that France, that France of tarnished glory, of a dull kingship and constant changes in the social order, which Hugo and his Janissaries stormed. In that same France, too, such painters as Géricault and Delacroix had been fighting the prelude to the battle of Romanticism with such Classicists as David and Ingres for a full decade before *Hernani* opened. But in their dramas the Romantics showed few signs of living in an age subject to other than literary change. Instead they preferred to take refuge in a costumed paradise of their own imagining, a world remote from steam or industrial revolutions and reflecting in no way the early dawning of the scientific spirit.

With Zola and the Naturalists, however, the case was different. Science had made fresh and epochal advances before they appeared. The trans-Atlantic cable was down. The Bessemer and the open-hearth processes had been discovered to aid in the completion of man's conquest of metals, and make the "Machine Age" of our own times possible. The history of the rocks which geology told was challenging the Biblical story of the Creation. Faith and reason were contesting in an open antagonism. Darwin had published his *Origin of the Species* and the *Descent of Man* and all the world engaged in the dispute which they invited, the dispute between the apes and angels, as Disraeli stated it when he announced that as far as he was concerned he was "on the side of the angels." Robert Owen and Karl Marx had spread the doctrine of socialism and challenged the capitalistic order; Schopenhauer had preached the gospel of pessimism. The daguerreotype, which had satisfied the public from the late thirties on, was replaced in 1888 by the Kodak of Eastman, the climax of a long series of camera experiments made in the fifties, sixties, and eighties which came as an important adjunct to Naturalism, if not a symbol of its methods. These and a thousand other developments were prodding the mind of man.

Even in so summary and incomplete a catalogue, however, it is not difficult to see what those crowded forty years or so, between the Romantics and Naturalists, were bound to mean in offering to the dramatist a new mankind for dramatic material, a new manner of treating him, and a different purpose in undertaking to treat him at all. It is slight wonder, therefore, that the swords of the Romantics should have been dulled with rust and their cloaks left to the moths, or that Zola should have invited science to invade the playhouses. And even less wonder that the theatre should have been subject to the contagion of the age and attempted to submit "man and his work to a system of precise analysis, taking into account all circumstances, environment, and 'organic cases.' " With that as the new aim, in a time when the whole desire was to face facts rather than escape them, it was equally to be expected that the new ideal of the theatre should be what Zola stated as "the fragment of life" (*lambeau d'existence*), or what Jean Jullien paraphrased as the *tranche de vie*—the "slice of life" ideal which is still a favorite phrase in critical jargon and the dominant ideal of so many contemporary playwrights and theatres.

With the brevity of a creed, the "slice of life" stated the aims and hopes of the Naturalists at the moment when they fought their way into the French theatre. But it did not come without forebears, in fact without half a century of indirect preparation, which gave the Naturalists a tradition both to expand and to reject. Even when Hugo was depending on the stout arms of Charlet's Janissaries for protection, there had been an amiable precursor named Eugène Scribe who was to exert a far more profound effect on the future of the theatre than that which resulted from all the noisy but short-lived manifestoes of the Romantics. If he did not introduce believable or subtle characters onto the stage, Scribe had, at least, put recognizable types behind the footlights, and the step was an important one. From his over-facile pen came those "everlasting colonels, rich heiresses whose dowries were the object of continual pursuit . . . artists supported by bankers' wives; . . . Legion of Honor crosses obtained in adultery . . . all-powerful millionaires," and "shopgirls who led queens by the nose" against which the younger Dumas railed. Scribe's types, in his vacuous farce-comedies and *vaudevilles,* may have been important milestones along the path to realism. But his contributions to realism were trivial when compared to the contributions he made to the science of play-building. He was the father of the "well-made play," "the most extraordinary improviser we have had in our drama," wrote Dumas fils, "the most expert at manipulating characters that had no life." Messageless, characterless, devoid of ideas as he was, the structural sense of this "shadowless Shakespeare" was borrowed the world over as the much-admired model of what a play should be. It was on the basis of his blueprints that so much of the nineteenth-century drama was built, that Sardou reared his melodramas, that Augier pushed the cause of bourgeois drama to new levels of reality, and that Dumas fils inaugurated the problem play with its inevitable *raisonneur*. And it was the problem play, built more or less according to Scribe's specifications, which, by espousing the cause of moral correction, was to salve the conscience of the younger Dumas by allowing him to feel that he had performed both his "part as a poet" and "his duty as a man."

It was, of course, the contributions these playwrights had made to realism which the Naturalists wished to advance. And with an equal obviousness, it was the sense of theatre they had inherited from Scribe—the water-tight structure of the "well-made play" with its infinite unreality and tawdry artifice—which the Naturalists insisted upon discarding. They wanted more than simple types, more, too, then *raisonneurs,* who while they were not types of the old kind were still points of view rather than people. They wanted life and truth, as they understood them toward the end of this century in which the scientific spirit had steadily been gathering momentum—plays that were true to life instead of the theatre. They wanted what Ibsen had shown them that the theatre might be. Not the earlier Ibsen of the poetic dramas to be sure, but the Ibsen of *A Doll's House, Ghosts, An Enemy of the People, The Wild Duck,* and *Rosmersholm,* all of which were written before the Free Theatre idea spread over Europe; the Ibsen whom Björnson advised as early as 1868 to try "photography by comedy"; the Ibsen who, though he employed the form of the "well-made play" was able to put it to a different and exciting use. In short, the Ibsen who could present problems at the same time that he was unveiling characters of infinite subtlety and bringing the tremendous drive of his intellect to a theatre that stood in sad need of it. And they wanted more.

But before the dreams of preface writers or literary insurrectionists could be realized in the theatres of Paris—and Berlin and London, too—before the "slice of life" could be cut to the taste of the audiences of the day a man of the theatre had to be found, and the theatres themselves prepared for the change. The deadwood of the outmoded traditions had to be cut away. Actors of a new kind had to be developed, settings of a different nature employed. But above all, it was necessary for a director to emerge who could dispense with the old conventions and establish new ones, fitted to the new ideals. Then, and then alone, could a phrase of theory become, in truth, a "slice of life."

FREE THEATRES AND NEW PLAYWRIGHTS

Surely the Naturalists themselves could not have invented a more appropriate legend for the founding of their theatre than the one which fate had in store for them. For the man who was destined to realize their dreams was none other than an obscure clerk in the Paris Gas Company who happened to amuse himself in his spare moments with amateur theatricals. He "had not," at that time, "the slightest idea of becoming a professional actor or director" and would, in his words, have "laughed heartily if any one had predicted then that we were going to revolutionize dramatic art." This man, who was to emerge from the "little world of clerkdom," be transformed "into a sort of meteorite," and "become the leader of forces I did not even dream of" was, of course, André Antoine. When history discovered him, fourteen years after Zola had published *Thérèse Raquin* and five years after Becque had written *Les Corbeaux,* he was adding a few sous to the meager salary of one hundred and fifty francs that the gas company paid him monthly by serving in the upper gallery of the Odéon as an "auxiliary to the chiefs of the *claque.*"

Though he may have had no thought of becoming a professional actor or director in 1887, when his little group of amateurs from the Cercle Gaulois was to win the attention of Paris, it should be pointed out that Antoine had entertained the idea before. As early as 1875 he had for the first time rented his manual strength to the Comédie Française and become a member of its official *claque.* Once he had had the happy privilege of leading the applause at that famous house, even as the great Auguste had led it at the Opéra. But far more important, in the eyes of what the future was to demand of him, was the fact that as a *claqueur* he had the chance of learning "the great tradition" of the Comédie before he undertook to break with it. As *claqueur* and shortly afterward as a supernumerary—for he soon tired of merely directing the applause—he had the invaluable opportunity of watching night after night the greatest actors of the time and determining at close range what was false and glorious in their methods. "For a number of years," he has himself confessed, "I took part in the whole repertory, eyes wide open, ears cocked for everything that happened . . . and I stuck as close to the actors as their shadows." In brief, he was doing what all revolutionists should do, and too few ever do, and that is of course mastering the old rules before attempting to make new ones. In fact, his approach to the theatre was so faithful to the existing conventions that it is difficult to discern in it either a gleam of discontent or a premonition of revolt. At first glance he seems merely a conformist, and an unsuccessful one at that. He studied diction at the Gymnase de la Parole and there began his career as a director with plays written in that very tradition he was later to abandon. He even had his hopeful hour at the Conservatoire, where he suffered the humiliation of being rejected because his recitation was immediately recognized by the judges as only a servile copy of Got's reading of the same speech. Though it was natural enough for Antoine to have imitated Got, since he had heard him read the speech some sixty times, this incident at the Conservatoire can hardly be named as a promising beginning for an important insurrectionist. Five years of military service followed, which gave him a blunt, plainspoken authority, and then, in 1883, those uneventful years at the gas company.

That is the record of the man before he was hurled, without ever quite understanding why, "into the midst of Parisian theatrical life." And an undistinguished, commonplace record it makes, of average hopes not even realized with average success. Ten years of drifting, trying to win a foothold in the old theatre, rejection, military service and the gas company! Ten years without any of that amazing direction or that genius for notoriety which lent such glamor to the Romantics. Here is no general's son who has already won success as a poet, only a clerk who has failed. Here are no Janissaries, no plots against his life, no Robespierre waistcoats and Henry III caps, only an everyday young man, who, though he possesses the courage of his convictions, cannot win the limelight by having the courage of his eccentricities, because he has no eccentricities.

He appears upon the scene with none of those definite, prearranged programs which invite alignments and are designed to win adherents or enemies *before* he invades the theatre. In fact he stumbles upon the men, and even the idea with which he is to "affront all traditional prejudices and wound the vanity of the day where it is most vulnerable." But though he enters, without the benefit of discord, without stinging ultimatums, or protests which fill Paris with dissension, even without apparent foresight or planning, the story of his revolt is no less dramatic than that of the Romantics and *Hernani*. It is, in fact, one of the most moving stories of courage, devotion, and growth the theatre has to tell.

Surveying the situation in Paris at the time of his emergence, Antoine felt, as he long afterward wrote, that "The preceding generation was exhausted but still stanchly upheld its comradeship, and in front of it was a whole generation, disarmed and fretting under restraint. . . . The battle was already won in the literary field by the Naturalists, in painting by the Impressionists, and in music by the Wagnerians. It was about to shift its center of operations"—in its usual tardy manner—"to the theatre." In 1887, however, Antoine did not suspect what was about to happen nor the part he was to play in the change. As a member of the Cercle Gaulois who was "wrapped up in the progress of the Club" he looked with intelligent jealousy upon the doings of the Cercle Pigalle, a rival amateur group. He wanted to have his club do something which would outdistance the Cercle Pigalle. He knew that each year his richer rivals mounted a revue and that the great Sarcey, the dramatic critic all Parisian theatres courted, "did not disdain to attend these affairs and to comment upon them in his *Temps* supplement." But Antoine's plan, formulated at a time when Perrin, the director of the Comédie, is reported to have said, "I need no new authors: Dumas one year, Sardou another, and Augier the next," was far more important than he guessed. It had nothing to do with schools. It simply contended with a nice logic that "if it amused us to play at acting, there must be other young people amusing themselves at playwriting. The only necessary thing was to find them. My project was adopted and each member started on a hunt." And that was the way in which Antoine, who is so constantly tagged as a Naturalist, and only as a Naturalist, undertook his work, and that, it should be added, was the policy he pursued even in his later years.

The first play to be unearthed was by Arthur Byl, "a one-act play without much structure and of rather naïve violence; but, after all, it was something unproduced." Byl brought to Antoine and his friends Jules Vidal, "a big gun of this time, who had already published a volume and was a familiar of the Goncourt Garret at Auteuil." In other words, the simple idea of this little gas clerk was already assailing the seats of the mighty, carrying with it a persuasion that was irresistible. It gathered momentum like a snowball. Vidal introduced Antoine to Paul Alexis, and the chain letter was spreading, even coming near to "the master" himself, because Alexis was a friend of Zola's, and Alexis "let us have an unpublished act (*Mademoiselle Pomme*) discovered in Duranty's papers." To Antoine the program seemed complete, composed as it was of Vidal's *La Cocarde,* Byl's *Un Préfet,* and the *Mademoiselle Pomme* of Edmond Duranty and Paul Alexis. Had it ended there and stayed within Antoine's hopes, the history of the venture might have been different. "But," continues Antoine, "I was absolutely stunned the day Alexis announced that having spoken of our affair to Léon Hennique, another of the Medan group, whose one-act play based on a tale of Emile Zola's had just been refused by the Odéon, Hennique had said that he would be disposed to confide it to us." The manager's eye, with its special sense of values, awoke in Antoine, the gas-clerk amateur. "In a flash I realized that Zola's name on our program would win us Sarcey's attention. Hennique sent me the manuscript of *Jacques Damour* and we set to work." And there, in Antoine's own phrases, is the account of the origin of that famous first bill which was played on May 30, 1887—a matter of the rivalry of amateurs and those happy coincidences that shape events.

' The course was not an easy one, however, even then with Zola's name attached to the program. Other members of his own club, conservatives who wanted to maintain the old traditions, revive such "banalities" as Scribe's *La Chanoinesse,* and keep respectably aloof from sensationalism, feared Antoine's innovation and the notoriety invited by Zola's play. As conservatives they promptly forbade him to use the club's name, though also as conservatives they agreed to accept any rent he might pay them for the use of their hall at 37, Passage de l'Elysée-des-Beaux-Arts. Forced to find a name for their protestant group Antoine and Byl first thought of "The Theatre in Liberty," which was taken from Victor Hugo. But both of them decided with much wisdom that it smacked too much of romanticism, and Byl, stirring his Pernod, as they thrashed the matter out at the Café Delta, exclaimed *"Le Théâtre Libre."* Thus armed with a name, and financed by his own one hundred fifty francs from the gas company and the few additional sous he earned as a *claqueur* at the Odéon, Antoine undertook the venture singlehanded and assumed all its costs.

The record is worth pursuing for its own sake as well as in the light of what it meant for the future. "I was in the greatest perplexity," writes Antoine, "to find furniture and accessories which I could not possibly hire. My mother, to whom I spoke, allowed me to take her dining-room furniture, her tables and her chairs, for the rear of the butcher shop in *Jacques Damour,* and at five o'clock, when the office was closed—I did not want to ask for any leave, as the publicity in the papers had already drawn down on me the attention of the severe subhead of our department—I hired a pushcart and hauled our furniture myself the length of the Boulevard Rochechouart from the rue Delta to the Elysée-des-Beaux-Arts." In the scant free time his clerkdom, acting, and directing left him Antoine visited the papers, hoping to gain a few notices for his "affair." But at one of the final rehearsals fortune smiled upon him, for Zola, "the Master," appeared to see his *Jacques Damour* and encouraged the embarrassed, hopeful Antoine. "It's very good," he said, as Antoine floundered "under his searching gaze," "it's very fine, hey! Hennique, isn't it true that it's very good? We'll come back tomorrow." And back he came to the last rehearsal, bringing Duret, Céard, Chincholle of the *Figaro* and "above all" Alphonse Daudet. Bringing to Antoine, too, the interest of Paris in a theatre where Zola's dreams of naturalism were at last to be realized on the stage.

Up those same narrow stairs came Jules Lemaître the next night and history too. Lemaître, without suspecting just what this little-known theatre was housing, described the scene. "The hall is very small and rather naïvely decorated; it resembles the concert hall of a county seat. One might stretch out one's hands to the actors over the footlights and put one's legs on the prompter's box. The stage is so narrow that only the most elementary scenery can be used on it, and it is so near us that scenic illusion is impossible. If there is an illusion, it is because we ourselves create it, just as in Shakespeare's time the audience saw what a sign commanded it to see, and in Molière's day the action of a play was in no way disturbed by the goings and comings of the candle snuffer."

One other glimpse of Antoine the man is decidedly worth remembering. It paints a final picture of what went on behind the scenes of the Théâtre Libre, before taking into account what the theatre was to contribute to the playwrights of Europe. It comes when the first bill is over, when a second bill has scored a far more decisive victory than was won by its predecessor, and the question of the next program is in the air. Antoine, as shrewd here as he was in sensing the value of Zola's name to his enterprise, is now setting about the task of getting subscribers. He has decided that printed circulars are not enough. Accordingly he sets to work to write personal letters to all his hoped-for subscribers. But Antoine tells the story more simply and effectively than it could possibly be retold. "All my nights were taken up with the letter writing, and however much I was accustomed to hard work, it was an enormous labor, as each letter was four pages long and there had to be thirteen hundred of them. As it was impossible to meet the expense of the stamps for such a quantity, I carried the letters by hand, once they were done, delivering them at night. . . . At last I had finished delivering the thirteen hundred copies of our program. I began these rounds toward six in the evening, and kept at it until five or six in the morning. As I had to be at the office at nine, I slept mostly on my feet. The last letter delivered was the one to Clemenceau, in the Avenue Montaigne; and I was so dizzy with sleep that it took me a good five minutes in the rosy dawn to find the house letterbox under the ivy of the little wrought-iron gate."

It was from a background of such fortitude, even of such chance, that the Théâtre Libre emerged, the first of the Free Theatres which the end of the nineteenth and the dawning of the twentieth centuries were to see. The parent theatre in Paris was never a financial success. From its founding, however, came an idea which quickly spread over Europe, an idea which was to unleash the talents of a new generation of playwrights and indirectly inspire a major theatrical renascence. Antoine's victories over the deep-rooted prejudices of theatrical Paris and his ability to attract new dramatists to his theatre were all that was needed to give a fresh and vital impetus to a European theatre which was everywhere stagnant in its submission to an exhausted tradition. The protest he had stumbled upon became in other countries a matter of definite policy. And rebellion, which had long been fermenting, broke out. Had it stood in need of a borrowed ultimatum it could have found one in that stinging exhortation Strindberg uttered in the eighties when he said, "Let us have a free theatre where there is room for everything but incompetence, hyprocrisy, and stupidity! . . . where we can be shocked by what is horrible, where we can laugh at what is grotesque, where we can see life without shrinking back in terror if what has hitherto lain veiled behind theological or esthetic conceptions is revealed to us."

In the words of Strindberg and the deeds of Antoine the clarion had been sounded. The contagion of Free Theatres swept over Europe and minority playhouses began to dot the map. In 1889 the Freie Bühne, the result of much advance critical pleading by such men as Heinrich and Jules Hart, Michael Conrad and Arno Holz, opened its doors in Berlin at the Lessingtheater, headed by Otto Brahm and a committee of nine that included Maximilian Harden and Gerhart Hauptmann. In 1891 George Moore argued for a Free Theatre in England and by spring J. T. Grein had established the Independent Theatre in Tottenham Court Road with George Meredith, Thomas Hardy, Arthur Wing Pinero, and Henry Arthur Jones on its advisory board.

In both London and Berlin the rebels stormed the barricades of the old order with Ibsen's *Ghosts*. The censor had already frowned on the play in Berlin, but the Freie Bühne, which was to be "free of censorship," boldly chose to give it a second hearing, and circumvented the authorities by means of a subscription audience. In London the tempest *Ghosts* provoked may be taken as a last stand of Victorianism against the modern spirit. It was no picayune struggle, to be sure, but a fierce and bitter battle, in which so doughty a warrior as Clement Scott generaled the conservative forces, and Edmund Gosse, William Archer, and Shaw combined to lead the liberals. A fair conception of its controversial heat may be gained on those vitriol-drenched pages of *The Quintessence of Ibsenism*, where Shaw has republished the most thunderous bolts of the Anti-Ibsenites which William Archer once collected "as a nucleus for a Dictionary of Abuse." They were no halfway indictments, these phrases Clement Scott and the other redoubtables hurled against the play. Their scope is as remarkable as their gusto and their imagery. They range from "an open drain," "a loathsome sore unbandaged," "a dirty act done publicly," "crapulous stuff," and "a lazar-house with all its doors and windows open" to "merely dull dirt drawn out," "lugubrious diagnosis of sordid impropriety," "maunderings of nookshotten Norwegians," "garbage and offal," and "as foul and filthy a concoction as has ever been allowed to disgrace the boards of an English theatre."

But for all their range, these untempered invectives have far more to say about the mind of England in the nineties than they have points to make against Ibsen. They, as much as anything else, indicate what any sincere, uncompromising playwright of the day was forced to combat, and aid in clarifying the kind of work it was necessary for the minority theatres to perform, particularly in England. Nor did the real services of these "free theatres" lie in the importations which initiated their audiences into what was being done abroad and hence outraged their insularity. Instead they were centered in those native playwrights they cradled and the new talents they encouraged. Because of the Freie Bühne Hauptmann started his work for the German stage, and with his *Before Sunrise* gave Berlin an opening of an excitement and significance in many ways comparable to the *bataille d'Hernani*. In its second season, when a first year that included *Ghosts, Thérèse Raquin,* and George Moore's *The Strike at Arlingford* was over, the Independent Theatre had the honor of introducing George Bernard Shaw to the English stage with *Widowers' Houses*. After a sterile century of Bulwer-Lyttons, Charles Reades, Sheridan Knowleses, Dion Boucicaults and Tom Robertsons, the English theatre stood in sad need of an awakening. Some idea of the paralysis which had overtaken it can at least be glimpsed in reading what so distinguished, even so sacrosanct a critic as Matthew Arnold was led to say about that high-flown and absurd melodrama called *The Silver King* which Henry Arthur Jones and Henry Herman had concocted for the delight of London just nine years before the English première of *Ghosts.* "In general throughout the piece the diction and sentiments are natural, they have sobriety and propriety, they are literature. It is an excellent and hopeful sign to find playwrights capable of writing in this style, actors capable of rendering it, a public capable of enjoying," ran the gospel according to St. Matthew. And there is ample reason for finding a text in this gospel of optimism, founded as it was on a play that is beneath despising and springing as it did from the dark despair of those barren years of the early eighties. It is worth noting, too, that it was set down a full decade before Pinero and Jones as reformed by Ibsen were to write *The Second Mrs. Tanqueray* and *Michael and His Lost Angel* and the younger playwrights were to appear.

The Independent Theatre was short-lived from the standpoint of years, but, like so many theatres of its kind, its life was long enough to accomplish its purpose. On its heels came a flood of successors: the Stage Society, the Play Actors, the Oncomers, the Drama Society, the Pioneer Players, and, finally, the formation of repertory companies in Manchester, Glasgow, Liverpool, and Birmingham. In addition to being given an opportunity of sharing the plays of Maeterlinck, Ibsen, and Hauptmann with the mother countries, England was suddenly awakened—due to these adventurous and hospitable theatres—to a new generation of dramatists, dramatists of note, men such as Shaw, Galsworthy, Masefield, Granville-Barker, St. John Hankin, Stanley Houghton, Arnold Bennett. Ireland, too, stirred to the fresh impulse. In 1899 the Irish Literary Theatre was founded, to be followed in 1904 at the rent-free Abbey Theatre, Dublin, which the ever-experimental Miss A. E. F. Horniman provided, by the Irish National Dramatic Society, and Yeats, Lady Gregory, and Synge, writing authoritatively of the Irish folk and folklore, became world-known figures. In Germany the Freie Bühne, after a short two years of purposeful life, had ceased its operations. Meanwhile, such offshoots as the Deutsche Bühne and the Freie Volksbühne had sprung up, and theatres patterned more or less on the same plan and fired by the same idea had put in their appearance in Munich, Leipzig, Breslau, Hamburg, and Vienna.

Even in far-distant Moscow, though stemming from a different root, a new theatre, fitted to the needs of the new day, had appeared. Ever since the 1830s and in spite of the success of the popular imitators of Kotzebue, known as the "Kotzebuists," an independent tradition of realism had been manifesting itself in Russia. Beginning with such plays as Griboyedov's *Intelligence Comes to Grief* and Gogol's *Revizor,* it had been amplified and developed in the dramas of Turgenev and Ostrovski. Now in 1898 it blossomed into a full-blown maturity when, after a soul-searching, principle-hunting conversation that lasted in true Russian fashion for a mere matter of fifteen consecutive hours, Stanislavski and Nemirovitch-Dantchenko, the head of an amateur group and an acting school, pooled their resources and founded the Moscow Art Theatre. After patient years of self-discovery and humble dedication to its initial idea, the Moscow Art Theatre has grown into the most perfect flowering of realism the modern theatre has seen. In the plays of Chekhov—and Chekhov was the greatest discovery of the Art Theatre—and even in such dramas as Gorki's *Night's Lodging,* its directors and the members of its amazing company have managed to go beyond the ordinary limits of realism. They have given it a depth, a beauty and a spiritual and interpretative quality which are conspicuously absent in the work of most of the early naturalists or later realists. Always they have studied documents, and even reality itself, not, however, as an end, but as a means. Following the example of Stanislavski they have tracked down "all that pictures the outer life of men," not because of any preoccupation with its surface detail but because of the way in which it characterizes "the inner life of their spirit."

At the turn of the century in Russia this new theatre appeared as a violent malcontent, a defiant challenge to the conventions of the day. "The founding of our new Moscow Art and Popular Theatre," says Stanislavski in *My Life in Art,* "was in the nature of a revolution. We protested against the customary manner of acting, against theatricality, against pathos, against declamation, against the bad manner of production, against the habitual scenery, against the star system which spoiled the ensemble, against the light and farcical repertoire which was being cultivated on the Russian stage at that time. . . . Like all revolutionists we broke the old and exaggerated the new. . . . Those who think that we sought for naturalism on the stage are mistaken. We never leaned toward such a principle. Always, then as now, we sought for inner truth, for the truth of feeling and experience, but as spiritual technique was only in its embryonic stage among the actors of our company, we, because of necessity and helplessness, and against our desires, fell now and then into an outward and coarse naturalism."

Meanwhile the life of the Théâtre Libre continued, falling into those periods which Antoine has noted as "from 1887 to 1895 against the champions of the theatre at that time; from 1896 to 1906 at the Théâtre Antoine for the conquest of the general public, and from 1906 to 1914 at the Odéon [where Antoine had once been hired as a *claqueur* in the balcony]—the final struggle against official tradition and administrative routine." Meanwhile, too, his idea was spreading like an epidemic across Europe. New playwrights were everywhere appearing, of all schools and all nationalities, thus putting an end to the century-old French domination of the world's theatre. In these same rich years Antoine was ringing up his curtain in parochial Paris on the plays of Björnson, Hauptmann, Heijermans, Strindberg, Tolstoi, Turgenev, and Ibsen, even as he was discovering for France—to choose from a long list—such dramatists as Eugène Brieux, Georges Courteline, François de Curel, and Georges de Porto-Riche.

In short the theatre of the Western World was everywhere shaking off its lethargy. Suddenly it found itself vital and active again, more generally active, in fact, from the standpoint of authorship than at any previous period in its long history. The playwrights who emerged in almost every country were no longer merely playwrights. They were authors who were proudly conscious of being authors, men who had deliberately broken with the fustian of the old theatre, and who had something very definite to say in their own rights. In the main they took the "slice of life" as their ideal, writing realistic, even photographic plays of average people caught in average situations. They forswore the remote world to which the romantics of all periods have had recourse, the imaginative or purely creative flights into a realm of fantasy dominated by prototypes rather than individuals, for the minutely observed details of the close at hand. In their realism they were not content merely to hold the mirror up to nature. They wanted more and, accordingly, tried to do away with anything so indirect as a reflection. Instead they presented—as nearly as they could—the "genuine article." They wrote for a theatre based on the all-important assumption that the curtain was only the "fourth wall" removed, an assumption which was to revolutionize the art of the theatre and dictate most of its conventions. The people revealed by this fourth wall were, of course, presumed to be unaware of the audience out front. They were supposed to be seen as they would be seen if the fourth wall of any living room or bedroom were suddenly removed and an audience permitted to watch unsuspecting, everyday mortals going about their everyday business in an everyday manner. This new theatre gave its greatest pleasure by allowing the audience to recognize the details of the plot, characters, and settings as something that they knew and had lived with outside the playhouses. From recognition came identification, literal and absolute identification of the spectator with the trials of the performers, and the final victory of Naturalism was won, and the second of the two great mainstays of realism introduced. What followed was no longer a theatre in which people looked at an actor as he made his "points" and said, "How well he does this or that," but a theatre in which a delighted audience gasped, "How true that is. It happened to a friend of mine once."

The Naturalists came and went, the Realists were to succeed them, the Realists who took for granted almost all the things for which the Naturalists had had to struggle. Though Naturalism was to prove historically but a small eddy in the mighty current of Realism, the realistic traditions of the modern theatre were fathered by it. For in many ways Naturalism was only Realism when it had to be fought for, when it was a cause to be defended, a rallying point. The theatre that came crowding in its wake was still dedicated to the "slice of life" ideal and the theory of the "fourth wall" removed. Or what has been called by those who have attacked this continual spying on small souls in small conflicts, the "peepshow" theatre of realism.

THE FOURTH WALL

Just as the Naturalistic playwrights had had to fight their way into the theatre, so the actors, directors and designers were forced to fight for the changes in acting and stagecraft demanded by their plays. Obviously the actors who were trained in the "representational" method of the Classic or Romantic tradition had to unlearn most of the frankly unreal devices in which their craft abounded, if they were not to be ridiculous in the "representational" theatre of the Naturalists. Accustomed to verse, expected to play not to each other but for themselves, schooled in all the tricks of taking center stage and holding it, disciplined to thunderous tirades and an audience which found its pleasure in recitation rather than reality, they naturally were forced to make a violent readjustment to the new technique of acting required by the new ideal of playwriting. Obviously, too, they could not act *Widowers' Houses, Before Sunrise,* or *Thérèse Raquin* in the same way they might once have played *The Hunchback, The Robbers,* and *Phèdre.* The acting methods demanded by these plays were leagues apart, as drastically divorced from one another in fact as *Ghosts* is from *Hernani,* or the technical approaches of two such contemporary actresses as Pauline Lord and Cecile Sorel. The older methods, however, were the dominant methods when the naturalists were knocking at the doors of the playhouses throughout the length and breadth of Europe. The conventions, even the state of acting in the eighties, and the changes which had to be made, are revealed in that wistful hope Strindberg—the Strindberg of *Miss Julie* and *The Father*—uttered when he said, "I dare not even dream of beholding the actor's back throughout an important scene, but I wish with all my heart that crucial scenes might not be played in the center of the proscenium like duets meant to bring forth applause."

What was true of acting was no less true of setting and direction. They, too—as integral and indispensable factors in realizing the "slice of life" ideal—had been adapted to fit the new demands. From England and Germany in particular came two traditions of production that prepared the way for what was coming. As an earlier, though different manifestation of the realistic tradition, and a significant, even a pivotal, contribution to the idea of ensemble playing and accurate detail, these two traditions, born of this same crowded century, may be taken as signposts to change. One thing is certain. They did make the transition easier when it came.

It must not be supposed that the Naturalists, though they were the first to demand a faithful transcription of the everyday upon their stages, were by any means the first to espouse fidelity to facts as an ideal in the theatre. There were many others who anticipated them in this. Only—and the distinction is worth noting—these predecessors were faithful not to their own times but to the historical periods they endeavored to re-create. They were archaeologists rather than Naturalists, realists about the past rather than the present, men who had little or no sense of the theatre but a vast devotion to history. Especially in England these archaeologists were to play a decisive part in the theatrical fate of William Shakespeare and the history of the nineteenth-century stagecraft. They were destined, too, to inaugurate a tradition which paved the way, in theory at least, for the Naturalists who were to come after them.

One of them—which it does not matter—apparently strolled one luckless day into the British Museum as even Britishers occasionally are apt to do. But when he left he carried an idea with him, an idea that was to grow into a great tradition. Perhaps he had been the night before to see a performance of Shakespeare at Drury Lane or Covent Garden. Or perhaps, even as late as 1849, he had dropped into Sadler's Wells to see that performance of *Antony and Cleopatra* which the *Illustrated London News* called *vraisemblable*, because of the indication of Egypt on the backdrops. He may have observed that Mr. Phelps, dressing his Antony with a fair accuracy, was evidently undismayed by the prospect of courting Miss Glyn as Cleopatra, wearing, as she did, a costume which might readily have been filched from Victoria's wardrobe at Windsor. Regardless of which theatre he visited the night before, however, it may be taken for granted, especially toward the beginning of the century, that his sense of history was disturbed by the amazing inconsistencies he had seen, characteristic though they were of the carefree and inaccurate English stage of that time. If his interest in the theatre or prints was keen, he may have ruminated on the past and recalled that even the great Garrick, toward the middle of the previous century, had dressed a Danish Hamlet in the fashionable clothes of the Paris of Garrick's day, that this same Garrick had worn the regal robes of the Georges for a Lear of prehistoric England, and thought nothing of stalking through *Macbeth* quite innocent of plaids and kilts. Perhaps, though this is purely guesswork, this stray archaeologist was looking at the cases in the Egyptian room, or wandering through the Roman collection. Or he may have been admiring the Elgin marbles the Seventh Earl of Elgin had brought from Greece (at that time many would have been less charitable in their selection of a verb). As he scrutinized the draperies of a caryatid which had lost its occupation, he may have remembered that the British government had thought enough of antiquity to pay thirty-six thousand pounds for this collection in 1816. But be that as it may—for it really does not matter— the fact remains that an idea, a fine idea came rushing in upon him.

He thought back to the night before. Shakespeare's Cleopatra dressed from Victoria's wardrobe when in the heart of London was a museum which might easily be used as a means of telling actors exactly what they should and should not do! Was not *Julius Caesar* set in Rome? And *Antony and Cleopatra* in . . . ? And? And? He quickly ran over the titles of the plays. And off he rushed with no inconsiderable excitement to seek out his favorite actor-manager. Even if the actor's half of the actor-manager's make-up did not share the archaeologist's passion for the past, the managerial side of his being informed him that his learned friend had had an inspiration. Here was an idea which might save the box office, and the box office needed saving just then when the horses at Astley's had proved more popular than the plays of William Shakespeare. Certainly it meant a new attack in advertising. It was educational, too. And, more than that, it provided English audiences with a spectacle, and spectacles from the time of *The Masque of Queens* to *Chu-Chin-Chow* have always found favor in England.

If it took the actor-manager but a few minutes to realize all the values of the archaeologist's proposition, it did not take him so very much longer to do away with the venerable tradition of acting Shakespeare in modern dress—a tradition, by the way, which Shakespeare must have endorsed and which lasted a good two hundred years after his death. Overnight the actor-manager established for poor Shakespeare, with his little Latin and less Greek, the tradition of historically correct productions. His eye for the period detail—which was in a later day to become an eye for contemporary detail—was the literal eye of the realist. In fact, by the middle of the century, the tradition had gained so strong a hold on actors and audiences alike that it can in many ways be taken as an anticipation of what the Naturalists were to demand when they fought their way into the theatre. Only the archaeologists battled for a literal transcription of museums rather than a literal transcription of life.

How far the matter went is betrayed by the determined historicity of Charles Kean's announcement of a production of *The Winter's Tale*. Shakespeare, Kean explained in one of the most curious of theatre documents, "has left the incidents of the play alternating between Sicily and Bohemia, without assigning any specific date to the time of action. Chronological contradictions abound through the five acts; inasmuch as reference is made to the Delphic oracle, Christian burial, an Emperor of Russia, and an Italian painter of the sixteenth century. It is evident that when an attempt is made to combine truth with history, conflicting epochs cannot all be illustrated; and I have therefore thought it permissible to select a period which, while it accords with the spirit of the play, may be considered the most interesting, as well as the most instructive . . . an opportunity is thus afforded of reproducing a classical era, and placing before the eyes of the spectator *tableaux vivants* of the private and public life of the ancient Greeks at a time when the arts flourished. . . . To connect the country known as 'Bohemia' with an age so remote would be impossible; I have therefore followed the suggestion of Sir Thomas Hammer by the substitution of Bithynia. . . . The architectural portions of the play have, as on many former occasions, been kindly superintended by George Godwin, Esq., F.R.S. . . . and my thanks are peculiarly due to George Scarf, Esq., Jun., F.S.A. (author of the *Handbook to the Greek and Pompeian Courts of the Crystal Palace*) . . . whose pictorial mind has suggested many important details. The vegetation peculiar to Bithynia is adopted from his private drawings, taken on the spot."

This flora and fauna tradition, enlisting as it did the services of F.R.S.'s and F.S.A.'s and authors of *Handbooks to the Greek and Pompeian Courts of the Crystal Palace,* had, of course, less than nothing to do with the theatre. It was on the face of it absurd. But it won ever-increasing adherents even past the turn of the century and trained several generations of English playgoers to expect scenery that was learned, even footnoted. It prided itself first on its accuracy and later, in the days of Irving and Tree, upon its opulence. But it accustomed the eyes of playgoers to truth, literal, detailed, recognizable truth. From the recognition that these picture-postcard backdrops of the past kindled in the minds of cultured audiences, to the identification invited by the endless snapshots of reality of the present-day stage was not as long a step as it may seem. When it was once taken the age of realism was at hand.

Far more important to the stagecraft of Europe as a whole, and especially to the work the Naturalists were to do, were the productions of the Meiningen players. From 1874 to 1890 this troupe that the Herzog George II of Meiningen sponsored proved itself one of the great educational and liberating forces in the Continental theatre. During those eventful years it toured up and down the continent, visiting, as Thomas H. Dickinson states in his *Outline of the Contemporary Drama,* "thirty-eight cities, twenty in Germany, two in Holland, five in Russia, five in Austria, two in Belgium, and one each in Switzerland, England, Denmark, and Sweden. A total of 2591 performances was given in all." Its repertory generally consisted of romantic dramas and excelled in Shakespeare, although in later years it included plays by such "moderns" as Ibsen, Tolstoi, and Björnson. That the Meiningen players borrowed something from the Kean tradition may be surmised from the fact that Bodenstedt saw Kean's productions in London six years before he became director of the troupe in 1865. But they borrowed more from Wagner's famous theory of *Gesammtkunstwerk,* or synthesis and joint production in the arts of the theatre. In 1849 Wagner had written, "The highest conjoint work of art is the drama; it can be at hand in all its possible fullness only when in it each separate branch of art is at hand in its utmost fullness. The true is only conceivable as proceeding from a common urgence of every art toward the most direct appeal to a common public. In this drama, each separate art can bare its utmost secret to a common public only through a mutual parleying with other arts; for the purpose of each separate branch of art can be attained only by the reciprocal agreement and co-operation of all the branches of their common message." In many respects the Meiningen company became a first embodiment of Wagner's theory of synthesis. After the turn of the century and especially after the so-called New Movement in the theatre, this theory of synthesis was to become the axiomatic ideal of modern productions.

The Meiningen stood for three principles which were at that time revolutionary. In the first place, they attached a legitimate importance to the contribution of the director. They did not regard him as a mere stage manager. Nor were they willing to place their confidence in actor-managers who were free, and apt, to cut the text or arrange the groupings so as to place the final emphasis upon themselves and their own importance. The Duke of Meiningen and his company, in a day when the older theatre was a happy paradise for exhibitionism, thought more of the total effect—the production—than of the individual. Accordingly they developed an ensemble which was unique, and which offered to European directors everywhere an ideal of how a mob scene should be treated and a production handled so as to get a collective effect. Breaking all conventions of the day they dispensed with the star system, and drilled into their actors a co-operative, self-effacing quality which enabled them to play a leading part one night and on the next evening lose themselves contentedly in the mob. In costuming their crowds as well as their principals they did not stop at the mere matter of historicity. They went further, and, while they paid strict attention to authentic detail, they were careful not to let their sense of history obliterate their sense of theatre. In their costumes, as in the training of their actors, they sought for the total effect rather than the individual's pleasure or advantage. To do this they took infinite pains, building up their colors in mob scenes, so that they, too, played a contributive part in their general scheming.

In each of these three matters, the Meiningen Players were innovators, and in each they were widely imitated by the leading directors of Europe. Irving, who had been in complete control of the management of the Lyceum only three years, was greatly impressed by them when in 1881 they played *Julius Caesar, Twelfth Night,* and *The Winter's Tale* in London. Stanislavski found both a model and an inspiration in their costuming and their theories of direction when in 1890 they visited Moscow. "I must confess that the Meiningen Players brought but little that was new into the old stagy methods of acting," he writes in *My Life in Art.* But in other matters he learned much from them. "Under the influence of the Meiningen Players," he says of an early production of *Uriel Acosta,* "we put more hope than necessary on the outward side of the production, especially on the costumes, the historical truthfulness to the epoch of the play, and most of all on the mob scenes, which at that time were a great novelty in the theatre and brought success and created a sensation for the production and the Society." In Kronek, a director who came after Bodenstedt, Stanislavski found a model. "The restraint and cold-bloodedness of Kronek were to my taste and I wanted to imitate him. With time I also became a despotic stage director. Very soon the majority of Russian stage directors began to imitate me in my despotism as I imitated Kronek. There was a whole generation of despotic stage directors, who, alas, did not have the talents of Kronek or of the Duke of Meiningen. . . . Only with time as I began to understand the wrongness of the principle of the director's despotism, I valued that good which the Meiningen Players brought to us, that is their director's methods of showing the spiritual contents of the drama. For this they deserve great thanks. My gratitude to them is unbounded and will always live in my soul."

To Antoine, the performance by the Meiningen Players he attended in Brussels came as a revelation. His letter, written to Sarcey and published by him in *Le Temps* at a time when Antoine was planning to produce the Goncourts' *Patrie en Danger,* paints a valuable picture of the French stage in the eighties. "Since I have been going to the theatre," he wrote, "I have been annoyed with what we do with our supernumeraries. If I except *La Haine,* and the circus in *Theodora,* I have never seen anything which has given me the sensation of multitude. Well, I did get that sensation from the Meiningen. They showed us things absolutely new and very instructive. Their crowds are not like ours, composed of elements picked haphazard, working men hired for a dress rehearsal, badly clothed and unaccustomed to wearing strange and uncomfortable costumes, especially when they are exact. Immobility is almost always required of the crowds on our stage, whereas the supernumeraries of the Meiningen must act and mime their characters. Don't understand by that that they force the note and that the attention is distracted from the protagonists. No, the tableau is complete, and in whatever direction you may look, you fix your eyes on a detail in the situation or character. . . . Why should not these new, logical, and not at all costly things eventually replace those unsupportable conventions which everybody endures with us without knowing why? . . . Why shouldn't we appropriate for ourselves the best elements of these interesting innovations? I am going to put a little of what I have seen in Brussels into the Goncourts' *Patrie en Danger* and Hennique's *Mort du duc d'Enghien.*"

Regardless of the indirect forerunners they may have had in the theatre, the Naturalists everywhere were forced to find their own solutions to the problems raised by the new scripts they championed. In a second letter to Sarcey, written some two years later, when such dramas as *La Parisienne, Le Maître,* and *Grand'mère* had failed at the Comédie and other reactionary playhouses, Antoine faced this issue squarely. "The fact is," he wrote, "that this new (or renewed) drama required new interpreters. Works of observation (or so-called works of observation) ought not to be played as other plays of the repertory or as fanciful comedies are presented. To get under the skin of these modern characters, one must throw overboard all the old conventions. A realistic play must be played realistically, just as a classic must be declaimed, since the character is, more often than not, nothing but an abstraction, a synthesis without material life. The characters of *La Parisienne* or of *Grand'mère* are people like ourselves, living, not in immense halls of cathedral-like dimensions, but in interiors like ours, at their firesides, under the lamp, around the table, and not at all, as in the old repertory, in front of the prompter's box. They have voices like ours, their language is that of our daily lives, with its elisions, its familiar terms, and not the rhetorical and noble style of our classics."

The demand thus presented was based so firmly on common sense that its logic carried its own persuasion. And logic, needless to say, became an ever more important factor in determining both the conquest of realism and the form it would take. Antoine solved the problems of actors at the Théâtre Libre by working almost exclusively with amateurs, players who were unschooled in the old tradition, fresher, more untrammeled, and physically equipped to play the parts assigned to them. In those first seasons at the Théâtre Libre when, as Antoine has pointed out, his actors "were a constant source of wonder," his company consisted of the head budget clerk in the government office, a dressmaker, a telegraph clerk, a wine dealer, an architect, and a clerk who sold walking sticks. Little wonder that these people who had nothing to forget and everything to learn, built up a tradition in acting which was glove-fitted to the new playwrights of the nineties. Little wonder that the principle of fidelity to truth should be pushed to further and further extremes, that Stanislavski should ask himself why on the stage "all lovers are handsome and curly-haired?" and let logic answer his own question by asking another, "Can it be that young men who are not handsome have no right to love?" Little wonder, too, that character actors should appear—most frqeuently the offstage prototypes of their onstage selves—and that casting to type should become a reasonable commonplace.

As the inroads of logic spread, there was even less wonder in the fact that, when the voice, the movement, and the dress of the actor were subdued to an everyday pitch, the settings should also be made subject to consistency. If the archaeologists could give verisimilitude to history, the Naturalists could give it to their reproductions of daily life. The step was a natural, even an inevitable one. In that same second letter Antoine wrote to Sarcey about *La Parisienne* he seized upon the essential logic which was to alter the history of scenery everywhere. "And that salon!" he complained. "Did you ever see in the home of a Paris bourgeois a salon like it? Is that the dwelling of a chief clerk? A dwelling without the slightest suggestion of a corner where one may feel as one does in the house of any of us, that there is somewhere a preferred spot for a chat, an armchair where one may loaf, after a day's work is done? I know your objection, the setting is secondary. Yes, perhaps, in the classic play, all right. But why not use a realistic setting, since it can be done with care and moderation and would in no way injure the play? In modern works written in a vein of realism and naturalism, where the theory of environment and the influence of exterior things have become so important, is not the setting the indispensable complement of the work? Should it not assume on the stage the same importance as description in a novel? Is it not a sort of exposition of the subject? We shall certainly never portray absolutely true conditions, since on the stage—no one can deny it

—there are a minimum number of conventions that must be observed. But why not make an effort to reduce that minimum?"

Reason questioned and reason answered. And it was to making "an effort to reduce that minimum" that the theatres of the nineties set themselves definitely to work, and to which the majority of modern theatres are applying themselves. Electricity had come, to make the backstage more pliant and illusionary than ever before. The machinist had arrived to invent revolving, wagon, and sinking stages—devices by which heavy settings could be built with all the detail, even the solidity of truth, and yet be manageable on the stage. Painted woodwork and draperies disappeared for true mahogany and genuine velvet. Antoine carried off from Heidelberg the furnishings of a student's room to insure veracity in his production of *Old Heidelberg*. Max Reinhardt cut down a forest of birches for his *Midsummer Night's Dream* of 1905. David Belasco, America's most important innovator in the realistic tradition and a perfector of infinite patience, reproduced the whole of a Childs restaurant in *The Governor's Lady*. The Moscow Art Theatre raised its curtain on settings in which the chairs and sofas lined the front of the stage to further emphasize the convention of "the fourth wall" removed. Woodwings and flies were cast into the discard. Warfare was waged on footlights. Costumes were supplied by fashionable *couturières*. For the Naturalists had battled and the Realists had won. By conscious design the actual was everywhere replacing the theatrical, because the theories of "the fourth wall" and the "slice of life" were victorious. But to many, even while the conflict was raging, the triumph of these ideas spelt a defeat for the theatre. To the malcontents who were next to appear it seemed that the theatre had turned its back on the theatre, just as Strindberg had once hoped the actor would some day turn his back on the footlights.

THE VISUAL IMPETUS

The Naturalists had scarcely won their first theatrical victories when the prophetic voice of Nietzsche was raised against the principles of their school in general. His words of denunciation gave utterance to ideas which were to be echoed many times in the so-called New Movement that was coming. One year after Antoine opened his Théâtre Libre and one year before Otto Brahm was to follow his example in Berlin, Nietzsche turned the fire of his contempt on the "notebook psychology on a large or small scale" that so characterized the average Naturalist. "Such a man," he thundered, in his *Twilight of the Idols*, "is constantly spying on reality, and every evening he bears home a handful of fresh curios. . . . But look at the result! A mass of daubs, at best a piece of mosaic, in any case something heaped together, restless and garish. . . . From an artistic point of view, nature is no model . . . this lying in the dust before trivial facts is unworthy of the thorough artist. To see *what is* . . . is the function of another order of intellect, the anti-artistic, the matter of fact."

Shortly after Nietzsche had spoken his mind, and even while the throats of the Naturalists were still hoarse with battle cries, a younger generation of malcontents was already preparing an attack upon them. This time, however, it was no literary discontent which spilled over onto the stage. It was a protest born of the theatre and nurtured by men whose concern was not the facts of life but what they unashamedly referred to as the art of the theatre. It was, in brief, the visual impetus that was burgeoning, inspired and headed by Adolphe Appia and Gordon Craig, and a legion of other artists and virtuoso directors of a new type. It was this same visual impetus which, after the turn of the century, was to invade Europe and America under the proud but naïve title of the New Movement. With its coming the theatre everywhere responded to a stimulation comparable only in importance and vitality to the intellectual impetus Ibsen had once brought to it, or the impulse for reality such ringmasters of Naturalism as Zola and Antoine had fostered.

The protest of this New Movement was double-barreled. If it was opposed to the older theatre against which the Naturalists had warred, its opposition to the kind of theatre they had put in its place was even more drastic. For it came as the revolt of artists against both the false aesthetics of the older stages and the non-selection of the Naturalists. It was anti-realistic and anti-scientific because it wanted to treat the theatre as a special world apart, subject to its own laws and its own effects, a place for beauty and exaltation, a shrine for spiritual release and bold imagining. It felt no embarrassment before symbols and no shame before imagination. It sought for a heightening in line and color which was faithful to the content, not the fact. Its hope was the unfettering of a new order of interpretative artists, and a new kind of theatre benefiting by a synthesis of talents and endeavors such as the theatre had never known. Its champions gloried in that very word *art* which had been such a source of discomfort to Zola. They desired the "necessary arrangement" and "absolute ideal" against which he had stormed, and were proudly conscious that in making art they were making "something outside of man and nature," something which was true to its medium of expression rather than the life it oppressed and hence truest to the theatre itself. With Shaw's Louis Dubedat they believed "in the might of design, the mystery of color," and "the redemption of all things by Beauty everlasting."

The objections to the older theatre's scenery of painted back-drops and woodwings were clear to the young protestants at the turn of the century. To their eyes they were tawdry and unlovely, and possessed neither the virtue of being real nor meaningful. They lacked simplicity and were too frequently the work of hacks, who, though they were masters of a fair technical proficiency, had nothing to say and less to contribute on their rights. Furthermore, their perspective painting stubbornly refused to take the actor into consideration, because the nearer his body came to the converging sight lines on the backdrop, the larger he seemed to grow. Then, too, these older settings were cluttered and unreposeful, hindrances rather than aids to the enjoyment of a play.The Naturalists and the designers of the New Movement were not the first to object to the painted scenery of the past. The nineteenth century saw several attempts to do away with it, attempts by such men as Tieck and Immermann, Godwin, and Perfall and Savits at architectural stages intended for Shakespeare which in many ways anticipated the simplification the New Movement was to introduce.

Long before it came, however, in fact in that same prose preface to *Cromwell* which was both a preamble and a creed to the French Romantics, Victor Hugo had stated an idea of scenery that was to become of steadily increasing significance to the scenic artists of a later day. "The speaking or acting characters are not the only ones who engrave on the minds of the spectators a faithful representation of the facts," wrote Hugo, pleading for an entirely different case. "The place where this or that catastrophe took place becomes a terrible and inseparable witness thereof; and the absence of *silent characters* of this sort would make the greatest scenes of history incomplete in the drama." The designers of the twentieth century, who have worked in the experimental forms of the New Movement, certainly have had no concern with history and even less with what Hugo called "exact localization." But they have aimed at making the new scenery a visual participant in the drama, saying to the eyes what the text said to the ear, a reminder of fate, a builder of mood, in brief, a *silent character* of no slight importance. Sensing their settings in this light, they have wanted them to be interpretative so that they might be really contributive. For that reason they have objected to the endless non-selective reproductions of reality demanded by Naturalism and Realism, scorning them as unworthy of an artist. They have mocked, too —as Coleridge pointed out long before them—the blindness of the Realists in failing to see that the nearer the theatre came to the true, the further it went from what conveys the illusion of truth on the stage. With Arthur Hopkins, they began to see that "if a Childs restaurant in all its detail is offered it remains for the audience to recall its memory photograph of a Childs restaurant and check it up with what is shown on the stage. . . . The result of the whole mental comparison process is to impress upon the auditor that he is in the theatre witnessing a very accurate reproduction, *only remarkable because it is not real.*"

Believing, as Hugo had believed, in scenery which was more than an inanimate background, and advancing the idea of settings which were "silent characters" and "terrible and inseparable witnesses" of the "catastrophe," the leaders of the New Movement approached their work in an entirely different manner from that which either the older backdrop painters or the Naturalistic assemblers of reality had employed. The new designer came to the theatre not as a spiritless hack but as an artist entitled to the privileges of interpretation and expecting to be judged as a creator. He was, in short, no longer a scene painter, but a scenic artist, and the difference is enormous. Describing the working method of the new designer, and outlining the ramifications of his task, Gordon Craig named some of the major considerations which differentiate him, and his theatre, from the scene painters who had gone before him.

"Remember," wrote Craig, "he does not merely sit down and draw a pretty or historically accurate design with enough doors and windows in picturesque places, but he first of all chooses certain colours which seem to him to be in harmony with the spirit of the place, rejecting other colours as out of tune. He then weaves into a pattern certain objects—an arch, a fountain, a balcony, a bed —using the chosen object as the center of his design. Then he adds to this all the objects which are mentioned in the play, and which are necessary to be seen. To these he adds, one by one, each character which appears in the play and gradually each movement of each character and each costume. He is as likely as not to make several mistakes in his pattern. If so, he must, as it were, unpick the design, and rectify the blunder even if he has to go right back to the beginning and start the pattern all over again—or he may even have to begin with a new pattern. At any rate, slowly, harmoniously, must the whole design develop, so that the eye of the beholder will be satisfied. While this pattern for the eye is being devised, the designer is being guided as much by the sound of the verse or prose as by the sense or spirit. And shortly all is prepared and the actual work can be commenced."

When Craig mentions the gradual addition of "each movement of each character and each costume" he touches upon that basic element of stage design which distinguishes it from all the other arts and which must ever be one of the designer's major considerations. For, though the scenic artist is, because of the proscenium arch which frames his setting, subject to the same laws of composition and balance that dictate the composition of a painting, the designer's task is not as simple as the painter's. He cannot concentrate as the painter can on a single grouping, caught for eternity at a single moment and place it against a background arranged so as to fit that single grouping perfectly within the space his frame allows him. His setting must house not only the action of the unfolding drama but the endless minor actions of the players: the shifting groupings, the crowded scenes, and the single scenes as well. The fabrics, the colors and the lights which simplify the painter's task by being fixed, are, of course, never static in the theatre. Yet somehow the designer must contrive to maintain his composition throughout that sequence of movement which lies at the heart of the theatre.

It was, in a way, due to a reconsideration of these very demands necessitated by movement that what is appropriately identified as the New Movement in the theatre came into being. To Adolphe Appia and Gordon Craig, those prophets and high priests of the changes it was to bring about, the synthesis between movement and setting was a matter of vital importance. Of the two men, Appia, a Swiss who is little known in this country and difficult to read in German or in French, was the first to appear, and exerted a strong influence on the continental designers. In 1893 a brochure by Appia, written in French and treating the problem that the settings which Wagner's operas presented, was printed. He followed this by sketches to illustrate his theories. In 1899, *Die Musik und die Inscenierung*, as translated into German, was published, which contains the most important statement of his beliefs. Like Craig he was more than a dreamer or a critic, and was, as his marvelous drawings for Wagner's *Ring* amply prove, a designer of the first magnitude. He surveyed the painted scenery of the nineties and found it wanting, because, as Kenneth Macgowan has stated it in *The Theatre of Tomorrow*, "the fundamental error that he saw" was "the conflict of the dead setting and the living actor." His interest in Wagner and the *Ring* led him to aesthetic conclusions which were to prove revolutionary in the theatre. Doing away with the trembling rocks of wood and canvas on which the fleshly gods of Wagner had walked so precariously—the Coney Island, scenic-railway backgrounds for sublimity—he sought a synthesis between actor and setting of which Wagner—radical as he was both in music and actual stage production—had never dreamed. His reasoning, as Sam Hume presents it in *Twentieth Century Stage Decoration* was that "poetry and music develop in time; painting, sculpture and architecture in space. So, since the art of the theatre is addressed to our eyes as well as to our ears, how is it possible to reconcile in a harmonious unity these two opposing elements of time and space: elements which by themselves unfold on apparently different planes? . . . In order that the music may emanate from the actor, filling the stage ensemble, there must be a material point at which the actor and the stage decoration meet. This point will be the 'practicality'—that is to say, the plastic character of the setting and the groundwork on which the actor moves."

Pursuing his theory further Appia contended, "The two primary conditions for the artistic display of the human body on the stage are these: a light which gives it plastic value, and a plastic arrangement of the setting which gives values to its attitudes and movements. The movement of the human body must have obstacles in order to express itself. All artists know that beauty of movement depends on the variety of points of support offered it by the ground and by natural objects. The movement of the actor can be made artistic only through the appropriate shape and arrangement of the surfaces of the setting," a point, by the way, which is admirably illustrated in Appia's widely imitated design for the rock in *Die Walküre*.

To achieve this Appia banished the painter and turned to the electric light as a savior from false perspective and tawdry brush strokes. "An object or an actor," he wrote, "takes on a plastic quality only through the light that strikes it, and ɪe plasticity can be of artistic value only when the light is artistically handled." In making light the theatre's supreme painter, he solved the question of synthesis, and found a means of achieving the "rhythmic spaces" he sought in a plastic setting, while he advanced a theory of epochal importance to modern stagecraft, a stagecraft, incidentally, which is more indebted to Thomas Edison than anyone has ever stated or than Mr. Edison could ever have surmised.

Of far more importance to the spreading of the new theories in the English-speaking countries, and as spokesman of the New Movement the world over, has been Gordon Craig. Craig is one of the most many-sided and arresting geniuses the theatre has known, presenting at almost every turn the challenge of a paradox. As an irritant and a stimulant he knows no equal, combining as he does the attributes of greatness and pettiness. Strange and baffling mixture that he is of prophet and gossip, redeemer and scold, Mahomet and hen, his very vagaries and inconsistencies have lent a ceaseless readability to his writings. Of this, however, there can be no question: he has been the greatest inspiration to which the New Movement has responded.

The son of Ellen Terry, from 1889 to 1896 he acted with Irving and Terry, learning the rudiments of his craft as a practical man of the theatre. It was not until 1902 that he had his first exhibitions and not until 1905 that his theories were first published in connected form. As producer, teacher, author, editor, antiquarian, seer, and designer he has brought to the theatre a wealth of talents equaled only by the theatrical superman of Craig's own imagining. Working but seldom in the actual theatre, and even then with but qualified success, this Englishman who lives in voluntary exile in Italy has, like the best of the Romantics, had the courage of his eccentricities and the gift of wounding the traditional "vanity of the day where it is most vulnerable." In his designs, in the great vertical spaces of his hauntingly beautiful drawings, with their lines that "seem to tower miles into the air" his prophetic gift has reached its highest altitudes. They, too, are prophecies rather than facts, ideals rather than actual settings, magnificent dreams of what the theatre, as he sees it, might be. And there is scarcely a designer working in the newer manner that has not been influenced by them.

In his writings he is no less stimulating. In his magazine, *The Mask,* his hopes, his theories, his hates, his idealism, his egotism, his "purple passages," his scholarship, and his back-fence scoldings are to be found signed by himself or by an "official spokesman" such as Mr. Coolidge preferred. They are at times personal beyond propriety, petty beyond belief, but almost always, and beyond doubt, worthy of attention. In his books, as well as in *The Mask,* he is endlessly provocative. His style is that of a camp-meeting exhortation spoken by the fireside, Biblical and colloquial all at one breath. It is dotted with "I's" and warm with a sense of divine mission. But for all that it has a kind of singing beauty of its own. It is the work of an artist who can write even as he can draw. To try to hold his writings down to consistency is no more fair than it would be to condemn his designs because they are beyond realization. Naturally enough Craig's value as a prophet and an irritant does not lie in his gifts as a logician, which are almost negligible. In the white heat of his epic, truly magnificent discontent, an unproven statement followed by a "therefore" is taken as a point proved, an argument won, and he is ready for the next onslaught. Whether he wins his points or not, however, does not matter, for he always wins that greater victory of prodding his reader to consider them. Irritating as he may be, shrill as he often is, childish as he may make himself seem, he is never dull. And therein lies his great power as a stimulant, because, though working from the sidelines, he has managed to put his stamp, directly or indirectly, on most of the men who have come after him.

It is difficult to find a definite, final creed in Mr. Craig's writings. But throughout them all is an earnest, humble search for the laws of the theatre, and a love for its past and present which is in itself inspiring. "It is because of this," he writes, "because the Laws have not been inscribed, because neither the priests nor the worshipers know the Law, *that all action is useless at present.* The laws must be discovered and recorded. Not what each of us personally takes to be the law, but what it actually is." As a prophet on the mountain he speaks, "And I am here to tell of this, and I claim the Theatre for those born in the Theatre, and we will have it! Today, or tomorrow, or in a hundred years, but we *will have it!* So you see I do not wish to remove the plays from the Stage from any affectations, but first because I hold the plays are spoiled in the theatre; secondly, I hold that the plays and the playwrights are spoiling us, that is to say, are robbing us of our self-reliance and our vitality." It was seeking for the laws of the theatre, for a theatre which is true to itself and pure as an art medium, that made him turn on the actor, and offer the "Uber-Marionette" in his place, an ideal and tentative solution of Craig's which has been widely misunderstood and misquoted. With that special logic he alone commands, Craig advances his argument against the actor. "Acting is not an art. It is therefore incorrect to speak of the actor as an artist. For accident is an enemy of the artist. Art is the exact antithesis of pandemonium, and pandemonium is created by the tumbling together of many accidents. Art arrives only by design. Therefore in order to make any work of art it is clear we may work only in those materials with which we can calculate. Man is not one of these materials. . . . The actions of the actor's body, the expressions of his face, the sounds of his voice, all are at the mercy of the winds of his emotions."

It is the same search for a pure artistic medium in the theatre which causes him to plead for a "Superman," who can write, produce, set and costume, light, and direct the play, and invent what machinery or compose what music that may be needed for it. Looking at the modern theatre he sees it the result of "seven directors instead of one, and nine opinions instead of one," and concludes: "Now, then, it is impossible for a work of art ever to be produced where more than one brain is permitted to direct; and if works of art are not seen in the Theatre this one reason is a sufficient one, though there are plenty more."

A passage which in many ways best shows not only Craig's methods but his standards of work is his famous description of making a design for *Macbeth*. It more than anything else indicates the change which has come over the theatre since the time of Kean's announcement for *The Winter's Tale*. In its feeling both against the realistic and for the selective, it is representative of the whole New Movement. "First and foremost comes the *scene*," writes Craig. "It is idle to talk about the distraction of scenery, because the question here is not how to create some distracting scenery, but rather how to create a place which harmonizes with the thoughts of the poet.

"Come now, we take *Macbeth*. We know the play well. In what kind of a place is the play laid? How does it look, first of all to our mind's eye, secondly to our eye?

"I see two things. I see a lofty and steep rock, and I see the moist cloud which envelops the head of this rock. That is to say, a place for fierce and warlike men to inhabit, a place for phantoms to nest in. Now then, you are quick in your question as to what actually to create for the eye. I answer as swiftly—place there a rock! Let it mount up high. Swiftly I tell you, convey the idea of a mist which hugs the head of this rock. Now, have I departed one-eighth of an inch from the vision which I saw in my mind's eye?

"But you ask me what form this rock shall take and what colour? What are the lines which are the lofty lines, and which are to be seen in any lofty cliff? Go to them, glance but a moment at them; now quickly set them down on your paper; *the lines and their direction,* never mind the cliff. Don't be afraid to let them go high; they cannot go high enough; and remember that on a sheet of paper which is but two inches square you can make a line which seems to tower miles in the air, and you can do the same thing on your stage, for it is all a matter of proportion and has nothing to do with actuality.

"You ask about the colours? What are the colours that Shakespeare has indicated for us? Do not look first at Nature, but look in the play of the poet. Two: one for the rock, the man; one for the mist, the spirit. Now, quickly take and accept this statement from me. Touch not a single other colour, but only these two colours through your whole progress of designing your scene and your costumes, yet forget not that each colour contains many variations. If you are timid for a moment and mistrust yourself of what I tell, when the scene is finished you will not see with your eye the effect you have seen with your mind's eye, when looking at the picture which Shakespeare has indicated.

"It is this lack of courage, lack of faith in the value which lies in limitation and proportion which is the undoing of all good ideas which are born in the minds of scene designers. They wish to make twenty statements at once. They wish to tell us not only of the lofty crag and the mist which clings to it; they wish to tell you of the moss of the Highlands and of the particular rain which descends in the month of August. . . .

"By means of suggestion you may bring to the stage a sense of all things—the rain, the sun, the wind, the snow, the hail, the intense heat—but you will never bring them there by attempting to wrestle and close with Nature, in order so that you may seize some of her treasure and lay it before the eyes of the multitude. By means of suggestion in movement you may translate all the passions and the thoughts of vast numbers of people, or by means of the same you can assist your actors to convey the thoughts and emotions of the particular character he impersonates. Actuality, accuracy of detail, is useless upon the stage."

In the wake of Craig and Appia the visual impetus spread with a hot contagion over Europe, a movement, not a school, hence having prophets and high priests but lacking any single leader or any one panacea. The variety of its manifestations was as great as the number of countries in which it appeared and the number of talents that were attracted to it. From Russia such artists as Bakst, Golovin, Benois, and Roerich came to the theatre as painters who gloried in the huge canvases that backdrops afforded. They were renovators rather than innovators, continuing the old practices of the painter but treating them in a new way, abolishing the false perspective of an unreal realism and putting in its place the vivid sensuous colors of their racial palettes. They, too, were interpreters; artists discovered by the opera and especially the Ballet Russe, and the influence of their color was strong and unfettering. It was this same Ballet Russe, transferred by Diaghilev to France after the Russian Revolution and the war, which brought the talents of a new generation of artists to the theatre, painters like Marie Laurencin, Picasso, and Matisse, who once again reanimated the tradition of stage painting.

Far more in line with the pathfinding of Craig and Appia were the experiments in plastic settings and sculptural and architectural stages which western Europe and America made. A legion of designers appeared—men like Fuchs, Linnebach, Roller, Sievert, Pirchan, and Jouvet—with marked, individual talents, working in the new forms, simplifying, interpreting, intensifying, serving the theatre and not the truth and serving in a hundred different ways, making permanent stages, decorative settings, permanent settings, using color, line, and composition, and planning backgrounds fitted to movement and aiming to evoke a new response to the play. Architects, too—men such as Littmann, Kaufmann, Poelzig, and Strnad—feeling the force of this fresh impulse sought new kinds of theatre buildings, playhouses of all kinds, great and small, circus and intimate, static and revolving, in the hope of establishing a new relationship between audiences and actors. Electricians invented new systems and means of lighting. The Fortuny system which had, with its reflected light, been an important aid to the "artistic" lighting mentioned by Appia was replaced by direct lighting of the Ars System of Schwabe and Hasait. New dimmers, spotlights, borders, balcony strips, and sources of control were perfected. The machines the engineers had devised to move heavy settings were amplified so that not only the whole stage but segments of its surface were capable of independent elevation. And the war on the monotony and limitations of the flat stage floor, which was later to acquire a special form in Revolutionary Russia, was commenced.

In America, too, the New Movement made itself felt, revealing a kind of beauty both the Realists and the older men had shut out of the theatre. It is but a scant fifteen years or so since it first reached New York, but in that time designers of such quality as Joseph Urban, Robert Edmond Jones, Lee Simonson and Norman Bel Geddes have emerged, as much prophets, high priests, and chief practitioners in the scenic renascence America was to see as Craig and Appia were to Europe. They were the advance guard and are still the leaders, having given the contemporary American theatre many of its most exciting and exalting moments. Already, however, a younger generation has followed them, which includes such hopeful and accomplished scenic artists as Jo Mielziner, Boris Aronson, and Donald Oenslager. In Europe and America the new designers have made their great mistakes. They have hurt plays and productions by turning them into scene-makers' holidays, which were as harmful as any of the examples of willful exhibitionism the older actors ever afforded. But at their best they have liberated a kind of beauty and granted an unsuspected meaning to the plays they have set. At their best, too, they have sensed the subsidiary and yet evocative responsibilities of their calling, realizing with Arthur Hopkins that "the stage setting of an artist never seeks to be a complete thing. It is part of something infinite that trails along the ground, but the part that trails opens within the beholders vistas—glorious, grotesque, breathless—vistas that eye has never beheld, and these are the vistas wherein the artist has found the essence, and if the artist and the beholder be blessed, the beholder finds it too."

Meanwhile a director of a new sort had appeared, ready and anxious to work with the designer. He was the practical man of the theatre who could realize the dreams of the scenic artist. No longer content to be a servile figure, secondary to the actor or the playwright, he has seen his function in a new light. He too has claimed the rights of an interpretative artist and pointed out the needs of his complete artistic authority. Maintaining that the actor had no right to treat a play as vehicle, he also contended that the playwright, as a literary man, was not the person to dominate the theatre. It was, as he saw it, a theatre man, who alone could co-ordinate and fuse the whole production into a cogent whole. And it was as such a man that the new director emerged. Spurning the idea of "the play's the thing," he offered in its place the truer theatrical truth, "the production's the thing." This new director was an autocrat, a final interpreter, who orchestrated the entire performance, treating the script as a conductor would treat a score under his baton, and making of each production a statement of the play as seen through his temperament. Naturally he was interested in groupings, in movement, in color and arrangement. Like the designer he sought for plays that gave him the freest expression of his individual talents. And, like the designer, because he found the cupboard of the modern realistic drama empty of opportunities, he was forced to turn to the great romantic dramas of the past, and particularly to the plays of Shakespeare.

Of directors of this new caliber and kind there have been many in Europe, but, up to the present, none has so far made himself felt in America. In many ways the most typical is Max Reinhardt, a superman in energy, with a restless, hungry desire for fresh experiment which has kept him in constant revolt not only from the theatre but also from himself. Having no definite, at least no apparent, artistic creed except that which each new production may present, borrowing freely when he stands in need of borrowing, he has been the master showman, the Barnum of the New Movement. An interesting mixture of genius and opportunist, of artist and administrator, his tireless drive has led him through almost the full rounds of the modern theatre. In realism he had his beginning under Otto Brahm. But he soon broke from Brahm and became—as he apparently must in all that he undertakes—a "super"-realist in his own right. Inspired by Craig (Craig would say more than that) he emerged as the champion of the new ideas. Then the spectacle caught his eye and he aimed at the super-spectacle. He first dedicated himself to the "theatre of the five thousand" when he tried mob productions at the Grosses Schauspielhaus in Berlin, and then rushed off to Vienna to reopen the Redoutensaal, Maria Theresa's baroque ballroom, as a theatre for the "five hundred." And now, in his new theatres in Berlin and Vienna, he has returned, except for his summer spectacles at Salzburg, to what is known as "neo-realism."

There were many other virtuoso directors, of course. Typical of these are Jessner in Berlin, who is associated with his exciting but often obvious use of steps as a physical symbol for the spiritual ascent or descent of a drama's leading character; and Copeau, who on the architectural stage of the Vieux Colombier in Paris did away with the designer and provided a background of Elizabethan simplicity. The list is a long one, however, including Granville-Barker in London, Kvapil and Hilar in Prague, Hevesi in Budapest, Harald Andre at the Royal Opera in Stockholm; Lugné-Poë, Jouvet, Pitoev, and Dullin in Paris; and Stanislavski, Tairov, Vakhtangov, and Meyerhold in Russia—men whose methods of work are as diversified as those which the designers have employed. But all of them have this in common. They are men of the theatre, not scientists or novelists, or poets or actors. They, too, have felt the impact of the visual impetus, and have in most cases worked hand in hand with their designers: Reinhardt with Stern, Jessner with Pirchan, Weichert with Sievert, and Arthur Hopkins with Robert Edmond Jones. Together they have waged war on facts and actualities, fighting for a theatre of the imagination, aiming at a theatre of spiritual release rather than of detailed recognition. And their chiefest weapon of conquest has been the eye of the beholder, awakened from a long rest, granted a vision that sees beyond the everyday, into that special world of meaning and suggestion, of rapture and beauty which lie within the theatre's province to evoke.

PLAYWRIGHTS OF PROTEST

The visual impetus of the New Movement was by no means the only revolt from realism the modern theatre was to see. There were playwrights, too, who soon turned their backs on the "notebook psychology" for which Nietzsche said it stood and shared his contempt for its "constant spying on reality" and its "lying in the dust before trivial facts." They were men who were neither satisfied with the habitual forms of realism nor contented with the basic aims which motivated it, men who rebelled against its preordained concern with appearances and hated the technical clichés through which it spoke. They felt that Zola's complaint against arrangement—which inspired the Naturalists—had had but little influence on the realists who came after him, because they had reverted without a struggle to the "well-made play" in a form that was but slightly altered. They fretted, too, under the confinement of the conventional play of three or four acts, lodging their complaints, however, not against arrangement in general but the particular kind of arrangement it necessitated. Unlike Zola's, their criticism sprang from a conviction that the ordinary realistic play was an art form which as a form was lacking in true selection, real truth, or opportunities above the humdrum.

These playwrights, who for convenience were later to be la-beled "Expressionists," wanted to do more than contemplate the surface of things. They sought for deeper conflicts than those granted by the good old external "situations" of the "well-made plays"—even as treated by the realists. They looked for a freer means of presentation and a wider range of narrative than their restricted formula afforded. They wanted to see not the surface alone, but beneath the surface too. It was Stanislavski who said "realism ends where the superconscious begins," and the supercon-scious was the object of their quest. They hoped to enjoy some-thing of that sense of omniscience which is the usual province of the novelist, to exercise his freedom in selecting one character through which to see events, and to write with a point of view which was impossible when "the fourth wall" was removed and a mere "slice of life" revealed. They wanted to look within their characters, treat them subjectively, tap their streams of conscious-ness if need be, penetrate into their innermost beings, and lay bare their dreams, their inhibitions, and the hidden workings of their minds—reactions and mental states which could not be in-cluded in the external observation of the camera. In short, they sought the eye of the X-ray instead of the camera.

In pursuing their aims, they did not want to concentrate on one event, but on a series of events—pivotal, revelatory moments which were free of claptrap and innocent of padding, moments which marched bravely into the essence of the event, which deter-mined character or registered growth or retrogression, crucial mo-ments of crisis rather than half hours of preparation. They sought biographies, or at least partial biographies, rather than single in-stances. Like the designers, they were not afraid of symbols, and, like the designers, they too employed suggestion rather than repre-sentation. Frequently they forswore particularized characters tagged with definite names. In their place they chose, as the old morality plays had chosen, a man, a woman, any man, any woman, everyman, everywoman, and set them against the background of their time, types not individuals, freighted with a full charge of symbolism. Occasionally they even dispensed with types, replac-ing them by groups, sections of the community, choruses caught at moments of revolt, or seen as victims of the machine age which surrounded them. If, however, they pursued individualized characters they did so with an interest which was centered in a series of events rather than a single and arbitrary quandary.

As their concern frequently was not the outer world at all but the inner life of the mind and spirit, they availed themselves of the discoveries and the language of the newer psychologists, and particularly the psychoanalysts and psychiatrists who had appeared since the turn of the century. Just as Darwin and the budding scientific spirit had anticipated in the world of thought a tendency which was to enter the playhouses some twenty years later under the name of Naturalism, so Freud and Jung were the trail-breakers of the Expressionistic playwrights—dramatists, by the way, who first became marked enough in their tendencies to win a label some twenty years after Freud had made his earliest explorations in dreams, hysteria, and the subconscious.

In the purely technical matters of playmaking these insurgent dramatists found much to condemn in the customary form of the realistic play that pretended to realism. They felt, with a warrantable conviction, that its regulation acts of a certain fixed and inviolable length were external divisions which had less than nothing to do with the treatment required by the subject at hand. To them these acts of traditional length were the epitome of the anti-realistic because, for one thing, it was necessary to place them in rooms in which all the characters might logically assemble at a logical hour; and, for another, because the length of the act was usually much more than its main situation needed or could stand. Accordingly they objected to the manner in which the "well-made plays" were padded to fill, given subplots, minor characters, comic relief, and a lesser love interest which were as artificial as they were unimportant and distracting. The Expressionists looked with disfavor upon the patient preparation of such plays. To them this habit of devoting one act to exposition, another one or two acts to realizing the complication, and a final one to extrication was as wasteful as it was false. Usually built around one "big scene" or "situation," these plays had none of the sweep of life—its pace, its confusion, its mad, unfaltering onrush—and gave, to their thinking, none of the kaleidoscopic sequence of events or the true complexities of character. As the Expressionists saw them they took into account only what men said, never what they left unsaid, and were, accordingly, eternally preoccupied with surfaces and appearances. They included too many characters to let any one of them be fully revealed or honestly observed. The very dialogue they employed was a matter of superficial epigrams or trivial small talk, artificially manufactured and polished by stylists, thrust down the throats of characters rather than springing naturally to their lips. It was neither self-searching, nor completely unveiling, because it was used to show not the dual nature of the inner man, but that single aspect of the outer man which the other characters and the audience were allowed to hear. It was, moreover, unfitted to the needs of that new center of conflict these insurgent playwrights had found. For they were not satisfied with the old sources of action. They, like their times, had stumbled upon new ones. They did not want to present mankind grappling with outside forces. Rather they sought to dramatize his struggle with himself. And for this the old dialogue was patently inadequate.

In their search for freedom the Expressionists turned, consciously or unconsciously, to the models the Elizabethans afforded. Shakespeare and his contemporaries had felt no need for lengthy scenes that outstayed their dramatic necessity. They had spun their dramas on a stage bare of details but rich in suggestion, and told them by means of a quickly unfolding series of scenes caught only at their moments of fullest need and most vigorous meaning. Their plays had been active, wasting no time on such indirections as "cover scenes" or concealed exposition which are tricks that modern dramatists have brought to a laborious perfection. Instead they had marched to their points and their conclusions with a superb freedom. No Unities had stood in their way, nor had they bowed to any of the academic niceties which sapped the vitality of the French Classicists. Their stage was the world and their scripts were nomads traveling at will to its farthest corners, jumping from Rome to Alexandria or England to France with no other consideration in view than an adamant desire for dramatic effectiveness. Accordingly in the breathless pace of a *Dr. Faustus* or an *Antony and Cleopatra,* the Expressionists found a form suited to their needs. They did not borrow it wholesale, however, but put it to a new use. For where the Elizabethans had developed a technique which was hospitable to their vital, sprawling yarns, the Expressionists looked for one which would give them psychological freedom of a similar kind.

Undoubtedly the Expressionists were as much influenced by the motion pictures as they were by the novelists, the psychoanalysts, or, for that matter, the Elizabethans. The camera's eye was a roving eye, able to look at its characters only when they were doing something, and then turn with a prompt impatience to the next event as soon as the first was over. It was never stationary. More than that, it was constantly switching to fresh and arresting points of vantage. Steadily trained as it was, on moments of realized conflict, it possessed a ubiquity of which even the Elizabethans had never dreamed. But ubiquity was not its only claim to envy because it was also prepared to change its focus at will, shifting from "long shots" to "close-ups" with a suppleness which, to say the least, must have offered an inviting model to dramatists who had for several generations been subjected to the unvarying form of the three- or four-act play.

Be that as it may, the Expressionist appeared, prepared, as Rosamond Gilder has said, to "let off his Gatling gun of experiences—a volley of scenes in rapid succession, each one complete, climactic, independent, connected only by the thread of life itself—the life of the human being whose individual and typical experience it unfolded." He was ready and anxious to use both the aside and the soliloquy, for, having cast the ordinary tenets of realism to the wind, he sought both of these once despised devices as the simplest means of reaching the inner processes of his principal characters. As a literary form, the plays he wrote were drama stripped to its most basic essence, just as the settings of the New Movement were scenery stripped to its most basic essence. Certainly, as a dramatic form, this came nearest to the ideals of the directors and designers who, faced with the endless living rooms and kitchens of photographic realism, had been forced to seek opportunities equal to their aims in the romantic drama of the past. In the stream of this Expressionistic protest, the leaders of the New Movement and the modern playwrights, who had been pursuing simultaneous but separate courses, approached the closest union the contemporary theatre has seen, because in it the theatre of the mind the playwright had inaugurated joined hands with the theatre of the eye the New

Movement had inspired, and the result was that theatre of the mind's eye which was to be known as Expressionism.

Though the playwrights using its technique have won a common title they have but rarely been consolidated into a group or school. In spite of certain similarities in "methods of attack" and, above all, in the common desire for experimentation which has characterized their work the world over, the protest of the Expressionists has been largely individual. Frequently, in fact, the tag of Expressionism has been loosely and incorrectly used as a synonym for any kind of definite experiment in playwriting or any kind of anti-realistic stunt in production. At its best it has resulted not half so much from a studious or self-conscious preoccupation with external modes as from a spontaneous and internal relationship between form and content. In Europe and America it has been the weapon of men who were discontented with the clichés of everyday playwriting and the salvation of those who have had something to say which could not be said in the traditional way. At its worst it has been the refuge of imitators who have had nothing to say and who have had the bad judgment to turn to a form which demands, above all others, not only something to say, but "beneath it," as Ludwig Lewisohn has pointed out, "a fundamental brain-work, thinking as resilient as steel and as clear-cut as agate."

To find a first manifestation of Expressionism is difficult beyond possibility, because Expressionism, like all artistic developments, is so inseparably linked with what preceded it both in and out of the theatre, in the arts and in living, in the sciences and in thought, that there is no single moment, nor any single instance, which marks its birth. In an abstract way and as an origin outside the playhouses, Nietzsche may be taken as its courier, the Nietzsche of *Thus Spake Zarathustra,* that magnificent soliloquy of protestant self-probing which in its thinking, its questioning, and its prophetic note has so much in common with what the so-called Expressionists were to do later. Inside the theatre the first foreshadowing may possibly be seen in the symbolism of Ibsen's later plays, in *Little Eyolf, When We Dead Awaken* and *The Master Builder,* though Ibsen's own reaction to such a statement raises an interesting conjecture. In any case it was of the speech of Hilda and Solness in *The Master Builder* that Maeterlinck said, "it resembles nothing we have ever heard," blending as it does in "one expression both the inner and the outer dialogue." Strindberg was, however, the first practitioner of the newer aims to cast the unmistakable shadow of his influence over those who were to follow him. It was a different Strindberg from the author of *Miss Julie* and *The Stronger*, a Strindberg who had put Naturalism behind him, and suffered the partial insanity of those dark years recorded in the agonizing, introspective pages of *The Inferno*. It was, oddly enough, as Donald Clive Stuart has indicated in *The Development of Dramatic Art*, a Strindberg who after the "Inferno years" (1896-1899) had awakened, as he himself said, to "find Maeterlinck again, and then he seemed like a new land and a new era." It was Maeterlinck, the mystic and the symbolist, who captured his imagination, the Maeterlinck who had stated his famous theory of inactive drama, his conviction that a motionless old man, who gives an "unconscious ear to all the eternal laws that reign about his house" lives, "motionless as he is . . . in reality a deeper, more human, and more universal life than the lover who strangles his mistress, the captain who conquers in battle, or the husband who avenges his honor." It was, in short, the Maeterlinck who had spurned the machine-made patterns of the drama and formulated a new conception of the dramatic to whom Strindberg turned, finding a kinship in his mysticism, admiring his flights from the factual, his mood-dramas, his unreality.

Just when Europe was witnessing a rebirth of romanticism in the plays of Rostand, D'Annunzio, Benelli, Stephen Phillips, and Von Hofmannsthal, the beginnings of the Expressionistic tendency were making themselves felt. Strindberg, who had been a symbolist in *Lucky Peer*, was, in *The Dream Play, The Spook Sonata*, the two parts of *The Dance of Life* and the three parts of *Towards Damascus* blazing new dramatic trails and abandoning Naturalism. Furthermore—and this was particularly important in the light of what followed—he was turning to the dream as a theatrical device suited to his new aims. It was not, of course, the hoary old dream trick which so many plays had made familiar. No longer did a leading character, who was sipping a whisky and soda before a roaring fire in a wainscoted room, doze off, at the end of the first act, into a sleep which found him a knight at the Round Table in the second, and awake in the third. The dream was now to be used not as means for such *Connecticut Yankee* charades, but as a legitimate springboard to the unedited, uninhibited wanderings of the mind. It was now to become a psychological instead of a fairy-tale device.

Strindberg and Wedekind, the Wedekind of *Erdgeist, Pandora's Box,* and *The Awakening of Spring,* with his Earth Spirit, his impatience with an over-literary world, and his frank delineation of passion and sex, were the precursors. In Russia Andreyev and Evreinov followed, Andreyev with such a symbolic fable of the cycle of existence as *The Life of Man,* or, much later, such reachings for philosophical truth as *He Who Gets Slapped* or *The Waltz of the Dogs;* Evreinov with the idea of "Mono-drama" and such plays as *The Theatre of the Soul,* or such a masked comedy of appearances and illusion as *The Chief Thing.*

It was in Germany, however, and particularly in the Germany of war and postwar days that Expressionism assumed the staccato scene sequence which is usually associated with its name. The works of Kaiser, Toller, and Hasenclever offered new examples of construction, more marked in their tendencies and aggressive in their individuality than the first steps of the forerunners had been, definite enough in fact to warrant the tag which their common characteristics won for them. They came as dramas of disillusionment, of social unrest and tormented mortals. Depending as a rule on only a few indicative properties and cut-outs picked out by sharp shafts of light which stabbed the darkness of stages surrounded by black curtains, their simple production demands were, no doubt, conveniently adapted to the financial capacities of an impoverished Germany. But it must not be supposed that they were only the children of poverty. Instead they were the offspring of human and artistic discontent, born of a rich zest for adventure, children of the spirit and not of the purse. And in such a swift, concentrated biography as Kaiser's *From Morn to Midnight;* such dramas of rebellion as Toller's *Man and the Masses* and *The Machine Wreckers*—so different as they are from the external approaches to class conflicts of an earlier day like Hauptmann's *The Weavers* or Galsworthy's *Strife;* such a saga of industrialism as Kaiser's *Gas;* or such a tragedy of secret yearnings as Hasenclever's *Beyond,* where a man and a woman speak freely to each other from the hidden language of the mind, the way was pointed to some of the uses to which Expressionism was later to be put.

Postwar France also felt the tidal wave of protest, the reaction against the old clichés. To a theatre that was as dead and sterile as that to which Antoine had once brought the breath of life, came a new generation of playwrights, men like Pellerin, Gantillon, and Lenormand: Pellerin, who wrote *Têtes de Rechanges* in which a man leaves for dinner as one individual only to find on reaching his destination that he has separated into six different and distinct persons; Gantillon, who in *Maya* found a symbol for illusion in the person of a Marseilles prostitute because she was a different woman to each man who sought her out, fashioned in the image of his particular need or desire; and Lenormand who in *The Failures* told with an unswerving directness the poignant story of the misfortunes which overtake a tenth-rate actress and her author-husband who follows her on the road. Such instances picked at random from a crowded list are typical, nothing more. Nor were France and Germany the only countries to react to the new tendencies.

From Czechoslovakia came Frantizek Langer with *Peripherie*; from Russia Ossip Dymow with *Nju*; from England has recently come Velona Pilcher with *The Searcher*. Italy, too, made its contributions in Pirandello and Rosso de San Secondo, who, though they used the traditional forms of the regulation play, belonged by every philosophical and spiritual right to the new order, and proved their kinship to it by their endless search for truth and their continual tracking down of illusion and the multiplicity of fact and appearance. From Hungary came Molnar's *Liliom,* only another indication of the change, illustrating the new viewpoint particularly in its heaven scene, where Paradise is shown not as a place of pearly gates or celestial dignity but as a petty police court, because the dramatist is allowing his audience to see it through the mind's eye of his principal character, a bum, whose earthly experiences have given him no other idea of divine justice.

America, too, the America of the skyscraper and the jazz age, the land of machinery, of standardization and vaudeville, the saxophone and the blues, with a thousand native rhythms and a tempo of life peculiarly suited to such acceleration and distortion, responded to the new impulse. So far the most notable results have been seen in the vivid, simultaneous, omniscient flashes of biography which John Howard Lawson's *Roger Bloomer* revealed, and in the strident, vaudeville insistency of that same Mr. Lawson's *Processional*; in the sordid tragedy of a "Guy" and a "Jane" that Francis Edwards Faragoh set against the pushing, impersonal background of New York in *Pinwheel*; in some of the fine, singing moments of John Dos Passos' *The Moon Is a Gong*; in the earlier half of Elmer Rice's stingingly satirical *The Adding Machine*; and in such familiar examples as Eugene O'Neill's *The Emperor Jones* and *The Hairy Ape*.

Regardless of the slim merits of many of the plays built in the image of Expressionism, and even of the faults of monotony and obscurity which often mar the best of them, these dramas come as tokens of revolt. They too are attempts to "throw down the old plastering that," as Hugo said, "conceals the façade of art," and must always conceal it for each new generation until it has found a medium of expression true to itself and native to its own time. They are attempts to break from the "well-made play" Scribe established; sallies against the Naturalism for which Antoine fought. They speak from the mind of a new day, using its idiom, catching something of its rhythm, answering some of its needs, and following the pace it sets for them. These authors feel with Velona Pilcher that "a show on the stage should not be an imitation, but an expansion of experience," that "walls should not be built about a vision of life to keep in illusion if they keep out illumination," that "dramatic speech should not be daily dialogue, but something wonderfully different," that "a miracle of mimicry is not worth an ounce of imagination" . . . and, finally, that, "theatre life of the twentieth century cannot . . . be confined behind a conventional fourth wall while the rest of the world is exploring the fourth dimension."

The plays of these dramatists are not only tokens of protest but also symbols of vitality. For they at least show that the modern playwright, who has lagged behind his theatrical co-workers in pliancy and courage, has awakened to experiment and shown a willingness to try to plant his flag on new dominions of his own discovery. And as such they are hopeful symbols, encouraging portents that are not to be despised. Because, in its last analysis, the theatre of each age is forever at the mercy of its playwrights. Only when their courage is high, their imagination unfettered, and the hot blood of protest is running through their veins can its other artists be granted those opportunities which call forth their best talents and give the theatre that quality of being theatre, and being proud of the fact, which is its one condition of glory.

RUSSIA'S THEATRE OF SOCIAL REVOLT

Unique among all recent forms of theatre protest, and different in a thousand basic ways from such revolts in aesthetic theory as the Romantics, the Naturalists, the New Movement, and the Expressionists represented, is that crudely vital theatre which has invaded and conquered the playhouses of Moscow and Leningrad during the first eleven years of the Soviet rule in Russia. Here is a very special kind of theatre, the reflection of a very definite kind of social protest, that knows no parallel in the world today. It is, of course, the Theatre of the Revolution, belonging to the proletarians, nurtured by the protecults, and indigenous to the emotions and the moment in Moscow. In these respects, as in many others, it is different even among its many distinguished Russian predecessors. The Moscow Art Theatre, in which spiritual realism rose to unequaled heights of perfection; the Musical Studio, with its tingling stylizations of *Lysistrata* and *Carmencita*; the Habima, in which the religious ecstasy of a Hebrew company gave a strange and stirring quality to its performances; and Balieff, with the rippling gaiety of his *Chauve-Souris* that was so reminiscent of the old régime, have crossed the Atlantic and been understood. But the vivid propagandist theatre of the Revolution, unlike the theatre forms which have originated in artistic protest alone, can never survive transplanting. To be understood it must be seen in its native setting. It needs the shadows of the Kremlin and the flaming banners of Moscow's Comintern, or Leningrad's bleeding memories of October, before its voice can roar with the thunder of complete authority.

The productions of the new theatre of Communist Russia which are recorded in the State Bakhrushin Theatre Museum and which are actually to be seen in Moscow at Meyerhold's Theatre, the Theatre of the Revolution, the Satiric Theatre, the playhouses in the parks, the workingmen's club, and which have even forced their way in a modified form to the stages of the Moscow Art

Theatre, the Musical Studio, and Tairov's Kamerny Theatre, are phenomena isolated in aim and method from all other productions the contemporary theatre offers. All of them bear in some degree the stamp of Vsevolod Meyerhold's personality, for he is the "People's Artist" who plays in the revolutionary theatre the role Stanislavski played in the bourgeois theatre. As a daring and violent innovator, and a tireless agitator, he has led his compatriots in dedicating the revolutionary theatre to the masses in those dirty, milling streets of Red Russia. It is so much a part of them, and they are so much a part of it, that it is almost impossible to tell where the drama of the street leaves off and the drama of the playhouses begins.

It is the drama of the streets, however, and particularly of the streets of Moscow, which is an essential background to the shrill turbulence of the Soviet theatres. It is Moscow, moldering, Asiatic, and mud-splashed, with its glittering star-spangled onion domes, the blues and reds and faded yellow of its old buildings, and the dull gray masses or fresh white horizontal planes of the recent structures of the machine age, that is the scenery which is always present in the minds of the men and women who meet in the playhouses to look at the bare brick walls of the stages which scowl at them from behind the zigzag outlines of Constructivist settings. It is Moscow, awakened from a slumbering past, half conscious of an uncomfortable present, and dreamily idealizing a difficult future, that is the heart and head of all that is happening throughout the vast stretches of the U.S.S.R.—a city quivering with a mysterious and exciting vitality that somehow surges upward through all its dreary ugliness—stern, relentless, and triumphant.

For melodramatic contrasts Moscow is without an equal. The most flagrant of these is, of course, the ever-present paradox of a crumbling, malodorous Oriental capital, at least, two hundred years behind the rest of the world when judged by all the usual tokens of enlightenment, boldly striking out to realize a Marxian Utopia by methods no other nation would dare to try even if it wanted to. Other contrasts are to be found at every step—in the Royal Riding School, now used as a public garage; in the famous inscription, "Religion is an opiate for the people," which looks down on the little Iberian chapel ignored by the peasants, who continue to prostrate themselves before its ancient icon; and even in the coronation

square of the Kremlin itself, which now resounds to the lusty choruses of passing squads of a Citizens' Army. These are but a few
physical symbols, and minor ones at that, of the silent conflict the
new Moscow is daily waging with its past. Even a revolution has
not been able to readjust the solid stones of architecture to the
needs of a new and totally different government. Accordingly, the
Revolution seems still to be fought in the streets, waged now with
a melancholy irony instead of shrapnel, between the old buildings
and the new purposes they serve and the new people they house.

That it is a new people is affirmed by every minute spent in the
streets, the stores, the hotels, restaurants, trams, and stations—a
new people in command, as new to Moscow as they are to the rest
of the world. It is when this drab proletarian army is seen, and then
alone, that the propagandist theatre which feeds it becomes expli-
cable. Surely Moscow affords no greater shock to the foreigner than
his initial impact with its citizenry. For the first time the wholesale social change, and the sacrifices, following in the wake of the
Revolution, of all those minor manifestations of comfort and luxury which we take for granted without ever stopping to consider
how much they contribute to the dignity of everyday life, are made
brutally clear. These men and women, though assembled from
all corners of the Union, present, when first seen, fewer contrasts
than the people of any other metropolis. In fact, in a city which is
alive with every shading of variety, they alone are robbed of it.
The color of individuality seems to have faded from them. The
men, with their gray blouses, black trousers, and boots or burlap
shoes, and the women, with their shawls and shapeless calicoes,
fuse into a mighty, unified host of workers, almost as strictly uni-
formed as soldiers, and apparently as forced as they are to submerge their personalities beneath the clothing that is common to
them all. It is only after several days of being one of them, when
the eye is adjusted and the mind relaxed and the heart quickened
to an imminent sense of something terrible and great in the air,
that the foreigner is able to see the individuals hidden in the mobs.

They are the army of the down-trodden, now in command. Today Moscow is their city, Russia their country, and the world their
dream. They swarm over the city's full length, penetrate the chan-
deliered dining rooms of the best hotels, sit in the imperial boxes

at the theatre, inhabit the houses of the fallen bourgeoisie, and spend their vacations in rest camps made from the estates of the old nobility. If they are not equally rich, they are all equally poor. Their sad past has given most of them the patience and the courage to put up with the discomforts brought on by the Revolution, and enabled them to consider the present only an unavoidable period of transition and experiment. More backward than the laborers of any other country, held down through long centuries of serfdom and illiteracy, accustomed to few conveniences and no comforts, these new people have been able to bring but few of the requisites of living to their new liberty. They are a simple, grim, robust, and slightly bewildered horde, whose men are without vanity and whose women are without coquetry. They crowd the markets, the Soviet stores, and every inch of ancient Moscow, and their strong, bronzed peasant bodies gleam naked in the summer's sun on the bathing beaches by the brown water of the city's canals. The elegances and refinements which the former ruling classes demanded and enjoyed have slipped into oblivion. With the triumph of this particular proletariat style and beauty in a thousand minor forms, individual taste and all the by-products of sophistication have, temporarily at least, been blotted out.

For the most part, however, these new people seem happy and contented. Having once realized that the Revolution did not mean the end of all work, they are slowly waking to the new privileges within their reach. They have gone back to their daily chores with a new sense of the importance of their labors. They haggle in the markets, wait patiently for the clerks in stores and banks alike to do their sums on the wooden balls of Chinese counting boards, and push forward good-naturedly in their crowded but efficient street cars. Their jawbones rotate with an almost American tempo as they chew sunflower seeds and spit out the shells wherever they happen to be. They can be seen clustering in front of the innumerable little booths on the sidewalks, or standing knee-deep in the forest of uncut grass which fringes the streets. Often they bounce over the cobblestones of the tortuous thoroughfares in their springless wagons—dead drunk, with their eyes glazed and their legs seeming to walk on air as they dangle over the sides. The luckier and more impetuous ones loll back on the filthy seats of droshkies that have not been cleaned since the war, their legs sprawled over the potato sacks they are carrying, or their arms clutched tightly around big-horn gramophones of a prehistoric vintage.

What their life lacks in those incidentals that are imperative to our happiness is apparently small cause of complaint to them. In spite of the woeful overcrowding of their living conditions, their poverty, or their dirt, they feel they suffer in a good cause. Because when all is said and done is not Karl Marx in his heaven and all right with the world? And they can seek a welcome forgetfulness in the rationed quota of vodka they are allowed each day. They do not miss what they have never had, nor are they far enough along in education or prosperity to have been fully tested by their dearth of comforts. Even their lack of liberty under the iron dictatorship of the new régime must seem to the toilers of Moscow an advance on what is in the background of their experience. It is, at any rate, a government that proudly proclaims it is of and for the working classes, and shows its good intentions in a thousand ways. Its rigid supervision, which to the world at large may seem only another form of Fascist coercion, cannot surprise a people who have been brought up on the old secret service, and to whom *lettres de cachet,* mysterious executions, and Siberia have been familiar as far back as they can remember. This government speaks as the people's organ, faces cruelly difficult times, and has the perpetual alibi of continuing what is virtually a period of martial law until it is strong enough to encourage or tolerate an opposition.

The real victims of the new regime have, of course, been wiped out by death or exile or forced into a voiceless retirement. The majority of those who remain and crowd the streets of Moscow cannot have suffered by the adoption of Communism. Having for so long been property themselves, they were peculiarly susceptible to the idea of eradicating everything for which it stood. Even its perquisites have come to symbolize for them all the vices of the bourgeoisie and capitalism. This new citizenry, ignored and despised by the old government, has suddenly found itself courted by the new one, and taught to believe, in theory at least, that it is itself the government. And it is in that other side of the picture, and the side which deals not with the people but with what is being done to them, that the second explanation of the revolutionary theatre lies.

No authority could have been quicker to utilize every means at their command to win support and keep their constituents inflamed than the Soviets. They have watched and edited the public press with a jealous, all-seeing eye. They have sent out special exhibition trains to teach the peasants, opened a Museum of the Revolution in every major city and a Red Corner or a Lenin Room in almost every public building. Under them has been sponsored and organized a network of clubs and unions, which are an informal and invaluable means of instructing the people as well as feeling their pulse. Inspired by what amounts to genius, they have left the worst relics of Czarism—the ugliest statues and the most hideously furnished palaces—intact as a visual plea against the bad taste of kings. In many of Moscow's largest squares they have set up radios to bark out the news of the day to illiterates in the voices and phrases of the government. They have suppressed all forms of opposition, and watched the frontiers for dangerous literature which might mislead their people. Nor have they forgotten the youth of the country, because they are wise enough to see that the real test of Sovietism will come with the next generation and prosperity. Accordingly they have organized the children as militantly as Mussolini has in Italy, and taken every precaution to train them in the new order. By fostering a particularly telling form of the poster art, and instigating innumerable pageants to celebrate the triumphs of October, they have, in short, fed the people on all conceivable forms of propaganda ever since the fall of Kerenski's provisional government. It was inevitable that a government which is in advance of every other government in its scientific mastery of the art of propaganda should sooner or later realize the importance of the motion pictures and the stage as instruments of propaganda. That the Soviet Union perceived their extraordinary value from the beginning is both a credit to its perspicacity and an explanation of what the last twelve years have meant to the Russian Theatre.

Faced, first of all, with the paramount problem of winning the public, then of unifying and controlling it, and finally of keeping it stirred to a constant pitch of dedication and excitement, the government has found the theatre a meeting place ideally suited to its needs. Here was a forum where all the usual rigmarole of a political meeting—the facts, statistics, and appeals to the reason of a backward people—could be dispensed with, a rostrum from which the authorities could reach out with the utmost directness and touch the emotions of their voters.

The government knew, as all theatre people know, that an audience does not meet to exercise its logic, to heckle, or to interrupt. It assembles not to tell but to be told, not to debate but to hear a story. The more unsophisticated it is as an audience, the more it wants its thinking done for it, and the more it craves its villains painted in bold, broad, unmistakable strokes. It is not concerned with whether the cards are stacked or not. In fact, when they are stacked against a common enemy,—whether Punch in the *guignols* of the Parisian boulevards, or the "Huns" in an American war play—the audience enjoys itself all the more, because it then feels that its secret emotions of cruelty and hatred not only can be released but are being publicly condoned and justified. If an audience is at all times at the mercy of its theatre, asking only to be amused or moved or interested, it is in any time of public upheaval particularly easy prey. When the bands are playing, the flags waving, and common foes are introduced upon the stage, and playwrights and managers turn the theatres into but ill-disguised recruiting stations, then an audience is receptivity itself.

In Russia there has been, and is, so much drama being acted outside of the playhouses, and drama in which the public plays a prominent and heroic part, that the audience is half conquered from the theatre point of view even before it enters the auditorium. Particularly in Moscow and Leningrad, where the spirit of revolt fermented into decisive action, audiences bring an emotion to the plays they are given which is already strong enough to put flesh and blood upon the skeleton of any drama they may be asked to see. Their theatre is not a world apart, where they can forget themselves. They have not as yet been granted any productions devised purely for the recreation of tired revolutionists. During the eleven years of the Soviet régime they have been asked to remember themselves and hate their enemies, to be aware of this present which is theirs and prepared for the future to which it may lead. Such, in fact, is their momentary fervor that the merest mention of Lenin's name by a captured American soldier in such a play as *The Armored Car* can arouse an audience to a pitch of enthusiasm that a big scene, built up to by a whole act of steady preparation, could not equal in the theatre of other countries. Hence it is that the foreigner, unless he has some personal inkling of what these last eleven years have meant to the workers of Russia, and has actually seen them in the grip of their new ideas and fresh surroundings, is often both puzzled and unmoved by what is obviously most affecting in their productions. The emotions of the Soviets are fired not half so much by the technique of their dramatists as by the preparation of their politics. For theirs is a uniquely local and topical theatre, which belongs to and exists for the new people of the new Russia. Without them it would fall on deaf ears, for they are its only consideration. As a result, it is the details of their daily life, the events of proletarian history which they have shaped, the wickedness of those who have oppressed them or who are now opposing them, that are the incessant subjects of their plays.

The Soviet government, and the more radical theatre agitators, have not stopped here. Nor have their instructions ended with the strains of the "Internationale" or with splashing the old régime with mud. They have had positive theories to spread and new ideals to preach. And these are linked up heart and soul with the focusing of the new order and the character of the new theatre. Holding the individual in but slight esteem, and trying to persuade him that the "mass soul" should be substituted for religions which hope to save the individual soul, the authorities have devoted their stages to spreading the doctrines of the "superpersonal" and the idea of "collective man." Even Meyerhold, the greatest of the modern Russian theatrical insurgents, is quoted by René Fülöp-Miller in the *Mind and Face of Bolshevism* as saying that the purpose of the stage is to organize the mass collectively, and that the principles of the propagandist theatre are "in entire conformity with those of Marxism, because they try to emphasize the elements which make prominent what is common to all men, the *unindividual!*" With such an ideal, it is not strange that phrases like "little rickety ego," "worthless soul junk," and "cracking the old nuts of psychological riddles" should be freely used against the realistic theatre to which we, and the world at large, are accustomed. Nor is it odd that, in the place of our dramas which revolve around the particularized love of one Jack for his Jill, and which are acted in one drawing room or kitchen, a new type of play should evolve, set in a new manner.

Certainly it is not odd when the social background of this propagandist theatre is remembered. And it seems almost inescapable when that background is coupled with the managerial problems faced by the insurgent directors. Theirs has been a task which not only involved persuasion, but which also had to find means of persuasion that would appeal to their new public. Their public was, to a large extent, as new to the theatre as it was unaccustomed to holding the reins of power, as Stanislavski has recounted in a fine chapter in *My Life in Art*. Since the Soviet authorities were inciting the people to a deep detestation of everything for which the bourgeoisie had stood, all the bourgeois interiors that had been an integral part of the old realistic theatres were denied them. The old methods could only arouse either a sentimental or a jealous curiosity concerning the comforts of the old régime. Moreover, on those who had not lived in bourgeois interiors, the labor of reproducing them meticulously in the theatre would have been wasted, as their details would have lost their claims to recognition and hence to realism. This new public had the same right that the old public had exercised, of seeing their plays set in a setting which had its roots in their everyday experience.

Accordingly, as a final burning of all bridges that might possibly connect the present with the past, and as a bold glorification of the machines of the industrial age which was at hand, the so-called Constructivist settings of the revolutionary theatre came into being. They had, as things most generally do have that are the product of necessity, both logic and meaning behind them. The Constructivists waged a rebellious war on beauty, as the Western theatre understands it, and dedicated themselves to the gaunt ribs and bare platforms of functionalism. On their stages, at any rate, as they could not possibly hope to do with the old buildings of Moscow and Leningrad, the Soviets were able to raise structures which caught the spirit of the present and the mood of labor. Instead of aiming to use the stage as a camera by which elaborate interiors could be photographed and the "fourth wall" removed for the delectation of this public that knew nothing about the other three walls, the radical designers sought the laths and beams and whirring wheels of machinery which was the ideal of the new proletarian state. Looking westward to New York as the supreme achievement of mechanization, they found in the red steel ribs of its unfinished skyscrapers a basis for the physical aspect of their workingmen's theatre. Paint and canvas and all the pretty knick-knacks of realism were relegated to the dustbin, and the decorative was left "to the secessionists and the Vienna and Munich restaurants." The cry of the industrial present, which was to prove to the workingman the dignity of being one of many, working at machines for the good of all, was for the sternly practical. The ornamental was despised for its past, and hated as the flowering of a decadent and acquisitive idleness. In its place, the crude, sweaty tools and outlines of the factories were reared upon the propagandist stages, symbolizing the present, and encouraging backward Russia to take its place among the industrial nations of the earth.

With their levels and platforms, elevators and whirling circles within circles, and their vehement avoidance of reality, these new settings—whether they were Constructivist in the most literal meaning of the word, or whether they were influenced only by its spirit—quite naturally revolutionized all the arts of the theatre they served. The old conception of the representational theatre was banished as a relic of the past, or permitted to continue, as in the case of the Moscow Art Theatre, out of reverence and love, in an eddy apart from, and generally untouched by, the mad current of reform. In its place a new ideal was introduced, the ideal of the "theatre theatrical." In their special usage of the phrases Meyerhold and his disciples meant simply a theatre which was proud to confess at all times and in all ways that it was a theatre, which never devoted itself to being a slavish imitation of life, and which withheld no secrets from its audiences. When the Russian radicals broke with realism and put their theories into practice, instead of turning to the wagon, sinking, or revolving stages of the Germans, or any of the other contraptions devised to create illusion, they cleared their stages of machines, because the new Constructivist settings were in themselves machines which had the additional merit of functioning in full view of the spectators. Nor did the revolutionists, when their theatre was performing such a definite social service, seek the abstract forms of beauty sought by the Expressionists of postwar Europe and America. Though the new directors shared with the Expressionists the conviction that realism had had its day, they had a different substitute in mind, intended for a different audience. As proletarians these *regisseurs* wanted to share their backstages collectively with proletarian audiences.

Accordingly, Meyerhold and his followers came to regard the front curtain of their theatres as a symbol of the old-fashioned "peep-show" theatre, and allowed their audiences to take their seats facing a stage already set in the image of their own factory life. Nor did they allow the curtain to be lowered between the acts, or make any such concessions to a habit of the past that was foreign to their present purpose. If there were changes of scene to make, the directors sent their scene-shifters on in overalls to rearrange the setting and show that workingmen were assisting in the performance. And, as directors of a propagandist theatre that worshiped all that was practical, they left the brick walls of the back stage bare and undecorated behind their settings as a final tribute to functionalism. Believing as they did, and do, in the glorification of the practical, they were proud to grant the naked bricks of the back stage a dignity which the realistic theatre had consistently denied them.

On such a stage and in such a theatre, it was inevitable that the actor should have to make violent readjustments. Certainly a theatre dedicated to the "unindividual" must have cost the old-time performers untold difficulties, to say nothing of humiliations. In the theatre the world over, the actor, whether he is encouraged to believe it or not, considers his task the supreme expression of his individuality. His justification is a more than logical one, because he, of all artists, has only himself and his own body to use as a medium of expression. In the Soviet theatre he was asked to forget almost everything he knew and lived by and try to become merely a member of the masses, acting very often in overalls. His ears, not to mention his pride, must have been considerably stunned by such a phrase as that of Meyerhold's in which the actor was told that he was no longer a star, acting for his own aggrandizement, but "an instrument for social manifestoes." Furthermore, he was informed that to survive he must feel himself a vital part of the new society and the new stage. If he was accustomed to the easy chairs and ash trays of the old methods, Constructivism must have come as an unwelcome innovation. Its perilous levels not only violated all the old rules of "center stage," and controlling a scene, but demanded an entirely new style of acting. Often he was told that to catch the new rhythms he must forget himself and become an acrobat among acrobats. He, too, must serve the machines and perfect himself in the dynamic movements that are known in Russia as "bio-mechanics." The cultivation of his body was what he owed to society, and the subjugation of his individuality was what he owed to the stage. He could no longer indulge even in the pleasant details of veraciously observed character acting, in which Russian actors had always excelled with particular distinction. For the dizzy structure behind him, he must find a new, broad, unreal, exaggerated, posteresque enlargement adapted to it. He must excel at "grotesques," caricature, horseplay, and violent, stirring movement, and, as a member of the masses, devote himself to serving them.

As a theatre without contemporary precedent, its form has been restricted by none of those inhibitions which are commonly known as conventions. Its playwrights, as well as its directors, have felt free in blazing a trail to choose any materials or combinations of material so long as they have their proper effect upon a proletarian audience. The playwrights, like the actors, found their profession reoriented. Everything they remembered in the dramatic practice of their own or other literature they were asked to forget. Speaking to a new audience, they had to aim at an untried and different denominator of the intellect as well as of the emotion. Their chambermaids and butlers and all the worn devices they had relied on to oil the genteel drama of the past, were proscribed. In a world where every one was of one class, where titles were done away with and officials hailed waiters as comrades, there was no longer any justification for presenting menials on the stage who had nothing better to do than to talk conveniently about their master's business.

That favorite pastime of "bourgeois" playwrights of using a microscope to study the sufferings of small and great souls, was also listed as the supercargo of the past. "Soul junk" and "rickety ego" hurt the dramatists' inherited subject matter as much as it wounded the actor's pride, because with the glorification of the "unindividual," the playwrights were suddenly forced to forget particularized characters for bluntly outlined types. All their painfully learned tricks of creating illusion, their "cover scenes," delayed climaxes, and the rest, were swept aside with one decisive gesture by the lightning tempo and physical differences of the new methods. What must have been most difficult of all, however, was that these propagandist playwrights found they could no longer flirt with the theories of futility which had been the mainstay of Russian dramatists for several generations. In the place of the "Russian soul," the unhappy Annas and Fedyas whose despairing inertia had sent them slowly to a suicide's grave, they were asked to put the "mass soul" of victorious workers and sing the joys of collective man. Their audiences were not any more concerned with refinements inside the theatre than outside, and did not want their problems or their emotions obscured by any of the ambushes so sacred to gentility. They wanted them raw and tingling, outspoken and obvious.

Outside of the playhouses, the workingman found that his old religion and all its glamorous superstitions were being discouraged. He was being told that the faith in which he had been reared was his enemy, an opiate for his mind and a foe to the government of which he was a part. He had even seen several of his most holy cathedrals closed as houses of God and reopened as people's museums. He could observe, too, in the hundreds of churches the government did not close, the empty frames from which sacred icons that contained stones or metals of any value had been taken by the authorities as a means of saving Soviet Russia in the darkest hours of her public credit. Though he knew his government stood in theory for religious toleration, he was given to understand that an age of reason was at hand. He was encouraged— as an act of reason—to worship the machines, which would bring him immediate well-being, rather than the holy images, which could offer him no practical benefits. But whether the churches or the machines were to be an outlet of his ecstasy and superstition had but little to do with the fact that he was both superstitious and ecstatic by temperament. No legislative act could rob him of that part of his being he had known as his "soul." No one was more aware of this than the authorities, or more aware that a people trained to being onlookers at processions of a visual splendor the modern world has rarely equaled could not suddenly be deprived of their ceremonies and their ritual and remain contented. With uncanny wisdom, the authorities did not try to change the spirit of the worker's heart, but to divert it into a new outlet. They opened the doors to the playhouses at the lowest possible cost a generous official subsidy would permit, and allowed the workingman to carry into the theatre something of the fervor he had brought to his churches. They designed the new productions to satisfy this among other needs, and in Karl Marx and Lenin they provided him with the real gods of the moment of emancipation, even though by doing so they seemed to contradict their theory of the "unindividual." In short, in an age turbulently alive to the excitements of liberty, they gave the people a theatre which was, in its last analysis, only a High Mass sung to the spirit of revolution.

To satisfy this new need, the playwrights sought constantly to keep the fervor of victory alive and achieve an ecstasy worthy of a paradise that was being realized for the first time. They forgot style and all the usual embellishments of language and took the heart of the common people as their target. In words as simple and unornamented as Lenin's own, they reached out for the new public before them, employing catchwords of the moment to excellent advantage, and drumming in their points by effective repetition. The themes of their plays became journalistic and topical. They wrote government editorials in the form of headlines and told them with the relentless visualization of the tabloids. Where they were afraid a point might pass unnoticed, they set up a silver screen above their stages and ran ringing shibboleths upon it to accompany the action. The present was, quite naturally, their province, the present of the proletariat, as *The Wheels Are Turning, Mandate, Soufflé,* and any number of their dramas prove. They were allowed to make excursions into the past, but they looked backward only to fortify and justify the present. If they revived a classic, such as in *The Inspector General,* or *Intelligence Comes to Grief,* in their most revolutionary theatres, they felt at liberty to alter its text and meaning to suit their aims. To them history was, and is, a mine rich in the ores of czarist villainies or glorious with the misfortunes of early revolutionists, as is indicated by *1881, The Decembrists,* and *The Plot of the Empress* (the last Czarina, of course, and Rasputin).

When not concerned with history, or Soviet uprisings, or the wonders of Communism, or the need of sports, the playwrights have been permitted to graze elsewhere to find illustrations of the downtrodden whom Soviet Russia may save. American and English capitalists were villains ready-made to fit their needs, and they were introduced upon the stage as drooling fools whose hearts were as black as the records of their past, as *D. E.* (*The Destruction of Europe*) and *Roar China!* testify. Even in the old Imperial Opera House in Moscow, now owned and operated by the state, the voice of the Soviet raises itself above the clamor of the orchestra, and a new opera, like *The Red Poppy,* shows a Russian crew come to the defense of some oppressed coolies and ends with the waving of the red flag. And often, too, when the playwrights invite the proletarians to wander from their local problems, they show them the proletarians of other countries shaking off the shackles of capitalistic bondage. The hope of a world uprising of the masses is kept steadily before them, because the radical directors have realized with Lenin that "one must have something to dream of."

Outside of the regular propagandist theatres, such as Meyerhold's or the Theatre of the Revolution, the work of flag waving and propagandizing goes on with the same insistency. Though Tairov and Stanislavski may hold back from its most violent forms of expression, its methods spill over into a thousand different outlets. Especially in the workingmen's clubs and unions, which operate even in farthest Siberia, the theatre is the servant of the new state. In the Blue Blouse performances of the clubs it takes the pleasant form of amateur vaudeville, and includes sports numbers, timely songs, playlets, humorous speeches, and unavoidable jingles at the expense of Chamberlain—who, by the way, is not only a favorite joke of the Russians, but is also the symbol of European capitalism, shot in the shooting galleries and burned in effigy in the streets. Or propaganda lifts its head in the thin disguise of *Living Newspapers,* those pointed charades that the government has found so effective in relaying to illiterate groups its own version of the day's news.

It is slight wonder, therefore, that this propagandist theatre should be linked inseparably with the present in Russia, and particularly with all that Moscow stands for as its capital. By its own intention it is not an artist's theatre, and admits no art that exists by and of itself. Its directors have willfully snatched the theatre out of the hazy limbo of the impractical and the purely entertaining, and forced it into the harshness of public service. They have made a "house organ" of it, and as such it can no more make a serious claim of being art, in our sense of the word or in its usual aesthetic implication, than can a government pamphlet on horse breeding. It is to the theatre, as we understand it, what a Chautauqua is to Shakespeare, what sky writing is to poetry, or what a poster is to a painting. Like the poster, it does not pretend that its beauty is its reason for being. Speaking to the majority, it proscribes all the subtleties that might appeal to the minority. Accordingly it puts a ban on genius and a premium on ingenuity. It is the paradise of the opportunist, of the man who is one step ahead of the streets today and two steps behind the theatre of next month. It has no time to think of posterity, and hardly enough time to keep up with the present. It is the loudspeaker of the masses, and is therefore bound to be more conscious of its public than any New York manager has ever been of his box office. It produces what the government wants the people to want in such a way that they are forced to want it.

Crude, infantile, noisy, obstreperous, cheap, confused, and formless as it is, it has, however, a thrilling quality of life that has made it magnificently successful in being what it set out to be—a propagandist theatre. Already rumors are abroad in Moscow that the proletarians are weary of propaganda and tired of having to consider the waving of a red flag the highest emotional climax a drama can reach. The fact that they were not tired of its shouting and any number of its rasping puerilities nine years ago shows how shrewd this propagandist theatre has been in its attack, and how much it was needed both by the government and by the people. It indicates, too, how skillful the radical producers have been in changing their needles each time so as not to wear out the same old record they have been forced to play over and over again.

Even to its leaders, however, this theatre has not seemed a final form. They know just how precariously topical it is, and how close it is to the need that has mothered it. But to them, imbued as they are with strident and irrepressible social theories, this new theatre does not seem the prostitution of an art that it does to us. They are proud of their success in prostituting an art which they have made their own. Certainly when one measures them by their intentions, or judges them by some of their liberating experiments in technique they have stumbled onto, one must admit that they have reason to be proud. Because both as a herald and as an echo to the sufferings and hopes of a sorely tried and yet ecstatic Russia, this propagandist theatre has performed a superb function as the first step toward the true people's theatre which may some day take its place.

EPILOGUE: ALBEE, THE ABSURD, AND AFFIRMATION

TIME IS always being foreshortened in the theatre. Take the matter of generations. In life about thirty-three years are usually assumed to divide one generation from another. Not so in the arts, including the theatre. In them fresh voices become familiar more rapidly and successors rush forward on swifter feet. A decade is enough to produce a new generation. Within the last ten years such a generation has appeared, writing in a different manner, with a different purpose, from a different view of man in a melodramatically altered world. This new generation has by no means taken over the whole of the theatre. It is as yet a force mainly on the fringes. How long its vogue will last and how abiding its influence prove, no one can say. But its coming was needed and its impact has been healthy.

The theatre had become middle-aged. It lacked daring. For the most part it was repeating, however adeptly, what it had said before and breaking no new paths. It was saying what older people still hoped rather than what younger people felt. It was out of touch with the times and appeared unwilling, if not unable, to tangle with the problems of a new day. In spite of the power and skill of many of the plays produced, Broadway had relied too long on the playwrights who had established themselves in the exuberant twenties or the angry thirties. Since Pearl Harbor only three outstanding career dramatists had appeared in America—Arthur Miller, Tennessee Williams, and William Inge. Even in 1956 the play that was biggest in every way was Eugene O'Neill's autobiographical *Long Day's Journey into Night,* produced three years after his death.

Then suddenly it all happened, not to everyone's satisfaction, not to anyone's satisfaction all the time, and often to the angry befuddlement of those who could not adjust themselves to the unaccustomed forms or understand the old words that were being used in new ways. It happened almost as in Stephen Leacock's story about the solitary horseman who flung himself upon his horse and went riding off in all directions. Only in this case he was not alone. With him was a band of solitary horsemen riding off in all directions. From different nations Samuel Beckett, Eugene Ionesco, Arthur Adamov, Jean Genet, Edward Albee, Fernando Arrabal, Jack Gelber, Harold Pinter, Arthur Kopit, and others came charging on the field, each going his own way though seeming to head in more or less the same direction.

They were individuals living in private worlds, whose plays in the public mind were soon to be grouped together under the title of the Theatre of the Absurd, a name given to them by their able chronicler and expositor, Martin Esslin. Unlike the Romantics, the Naturalists, or the Expressionists before them, these dramatists have not, as Mr. Esslin stressed in *The Theatre of the Absurd*,* formed part of a self-conscious school or movement, and each of them has thought of himself as a lone outsider.

When he used the word "absurd," Mr. Esslin did not have "ridiculous" in mind, though that is what all their plays have seemed to some and what some of their plays have unquestionably been. Mr. Esslin pointed out that "absurd" originally was a musical term meaning "out of harmony," hence its extension to "out of harmony with reason or propriety; incongruous, unreasonable, illogical." It was in this sense, he noted, that Camus used "absurdity" when trying "to diagnose the human situation in a world of shattered beliefs," and that Ionesco employed "absurd" when he defined it as "that which is devoid of purpose," adding, "Cut off from his religious, metaphysical, and transcendental roots, man is lost; all his actions become senseless, absurd, useless."

"Senseless, absurd, useless" are key words to any comprehension of the different approach which the dramatists of the Theatre of the Absurd have to life and, therefore, to the theatre. The two go together. Writers of any significance have always played an oddly dual role. They have been voices and echoes at one and the same time. They have spoken for others while speak-

---

* *The Theatre of the Absurd,* by Martin Esslin. Doubleday Anchor Original, 1961.

ing for themselves. Although their voices have been theirs uniquely, in them they have expressed the unphrased needs of others. They have been spokesmen for their eras too. And an aspect of our times has found expression in the work of the dramatists of the Theatre of the Absurd, giving it at its best its weird validity and making it an echo of some of the doubts and fears which gnaw at playgoers.

Literature is co-authored by events, taking its tone and color from the stress and character of the times in which it is written. To speak for a world that seemed well-made, there was once the "well-made" play. That was before the threats and confusions of the present. To reflect a world that to more and more people has seemed ill-made, the "unmade" play came into being, the play which by intention was as untidy as an unmade bed. It was, in the jargon of the avant-garde, "anti-play" and "anti-theatre" and as different from a conventional play as in painting the work of to-day's abstract expressionist is from yesterday's realist. Its lack of logic was its sole claim to logic, because authors employing its form did not believe logic could be superimposed on an illogical world.

These playwrights may not always have known what they were doing or let audiences know it, but they have known what they were *not* doing. They have not written as their predecessors and contemporaries have. They have turned their backs on all the neat devices by means of which life has been funneled into plots, meticulously advanced in terms of exposition, foreshadowing, "big scenes," and effective "curtains." The familiar voices heard in the plays of the modern theatre have been those of Ibsen, Chekhov, Strindberg, Shaw, Freud, and Marx. In the work of the dramatists of the Theatre of the Absurd there have been echoes of Brecht, Joyce, Kafka, Camus, and Sartre.

The recognition of the senselessness of life has not come as a discovery even to the moderns. Giraudoux stated it in the daffy sanity of *The Madwoman of Chaillot* and Sartre in the trapped agony of his three characters condemned to a windowless room that is the hell in *No Exit*. But, where these dramatists argued for this senselessness in conventionally lucid terms, the playwrights of the Theatre of the Absurd, as Mr. Esslin shrewdly observed, have renounced arguing about the absurdity of the human condition and merely presented it as they see it. Ultimately, he has maintained, the Theatre of the Absurd "does not reflect despair or a return to irrational forces but expresses modern man's endeavor to come to terms with the world in which he lives. It attempts to make him face up to the human condition as it really is, to free him from illusions that are bound to cause constant maladjustments and disappointment. . . . For the dignity of man lies in his ability to face reality in all its senselessness; to accept it freely, without fear, without illusions—and to laugh at it."

To this Edward Albee, the most gifted of the younger, emerging Americans, has publicly said "Amen," adding that, as he sees it, the Theatre of the Absurd is "an absorption-in-art of certain existentialist and post-existentialist philosophical concepts having to do, in the main, with man's attempts to make sense for himself out of his senseless position in a world which makes no sense— which makes no sense because the moral, religious, political and social structures man has erected to 'illusion' himself have collapsed."

The characters who have served as spokesmen for "reality in all its senselessness" in the Theatre of the Absurd have been a strange lot. For the most part they have been derelicts (Beckett's *Waiting for Godot*), spongers (Pinter's *The Caretaker*), drug addicts (Gelber's *The Connection*), illusion-seekers in a brothel (Genet's *The Balcony*), and conversationalists trapped in sand or emerging from ashcans (Beckett's *Happy Days* and *Endgame*). The recurrent themes of the Theatre of the Absurd have been the impossibility of communication between people, the falsity of most human values, man's aloneness, the living who without knowing it are dead, old people who in their senility have become children again, and the parallels between animals and humans who live in a zoo of their own.

As George Oppenheimer of *Newsday* has observed, if the playwrights of the Absurd "have been blazing trails, the trails have inevitably led to a charred wilderness. If they have been breaking molds, all that has been left in their place has been breakage. Most of them have specialized in displaying the wounds of our world and then, having painfully and, I suspect, gaily ripped off the bandages, they have walked away without a thought of administering a poultice or a stitch." Some of their plays have been no more than foolish freaks and dull enough to test endurance. Some have so defied comprehension that they have called to mind Robert Frost's saying to a poet whose poems he could not understand, "If this is your secret, keep it." But the better of their plays have been strong with a strange, new, nudging strength, and by their unconventionality of style and attitude have brought to the theatre, on Broadway as well as off, a freshness and a challenge that have been invigorating.

Outstanding among these plays, newly molded and newly felt, has been *Waiting for Godot* which, however imprecise in meaning, reached out unforgettably to include audiences in the lonely despair of its tramps waiting for the coming of someone, possibly God, to collect them. And *The Caretaker,* which, though it never explained why two brothers should have taken a physically filthy but proud ingrate into their flat, was made memorable by the abrasive power with which Pinter laid his characters bare. And *Rhinoceros,* in which Ionesco, in spite of extending a one-act idea into three acts, wrote a witty and frightening fantasy about people being such conformists that they turned into a herd of rhinoceroses. And *Oh Dad, Poor Dad, Mamma's Hung You in the Closet and I'm Feeling So Sad,* Kopit's concisely titled and hilarious spoof of a spoof on momism, described as "A Pseudo-Classical Farce in a Bastard French Tradition." And, most assuredly, the plays of Albee—*The American Dream, The Death of Bessie Smith, The Zoo Story,* and, above all, notwithstanding the falsity of its dream-child premise and the weakness of its last act, such an overlong but stunning and utterly absorbing study of drunks, frustration, and sterility as *Who's Afraid of Virginia Woolf?*

In the arts the new becomes old with merciless speed, and these new playwrights already seem in need of something new to say. At their best, however, they have given theatrical expression to the spiritual fallout which has been as much a reality as the physical fallout in their imperiled times. They have written from and for a world which has long since lost its optimism, in which faith in the inevitable forward sweep of progress has vanished, and few would contend, as John Steinbeck did in Stockholm, that "a writer who does not passionately believe in the perfectibility of man has no dedication nor any membership in literature." To believe in man is one thing, to believe in his perfectibility another. These playwrights of the Absurd have believed in neither, and this has been one of their limitations. Nonetheless, they have already served their purpose. Like the various innovators working in various forms described in *The Modern Theatre in Revolt,* they have brought "flux and experiment" to the stage, saved it from "the blight of exhaustion," and kept it in "that state of transition which is its one condition of health."

They have been the dramatists of man's littleness, and they have not been alone. Too many playwrights, employing conventional techniques and in no way connected with the Theatre of the Absurd, have of recent years taken the same small view. They have not been wanting in skill; they have only been lacking in dimension. Fortunately, there have been exceptions, playwrights such as Jean Anouilh, Archibald MacLeish, and Robert Bolt, who even in a darkening world have not been embarrassed by a larger vision. They have seen man and seen him plain, and therefore seen him whole, recognizing the strengths that exist within him side by side with the weaknesses and the good that go with the evil. They have not been blind to what Dostoevski called "the fury and the mire of human veins." But, in the interest of the total rather than the fractional truth, they have acknowledged what it is that man can rise to in spite of his mortal frailties.

Prudery, piety, and copybook morality have nothing to do with their attitude toward life, as *Becket, J.B.,* and *A Man for All Seasons* have proved. Anouilh, MacLeish, and Bolt have been as unafraid of evil as they have been prepared to admit virtue. They have sensed that people are what they prove to be in the moments of being most cruelly tested. With Gide they would have agreed that "man's finest works bear the persistent marks of pain," and with him they would have asked themselves, "What would there be in a story of happiness? Only what prepares it, only what destroys it can be told." Their characters have risen to the testing and sought for the reasons which have caused it rather than submitted to the sheer senselessness of things.

Anouilh's Becket, frivolous, worldly, and seemingly incapable of love, a man with icicles in his heart, rose to genuine love of God at the moment when he defied his King to invite martyrdom. Bolt, in our age of organization men and grayed personalities, was attracted to Sir Thomas More because he was an individual blessed with "an adamantine sense of self." He had every capacity for life in its greatest variety and "almost greedy quantities." Yet, in spite of this, he "found something in himself without which life was valueless and when that was denied him he was able to grasp his death." He was a man at home with compromise but man enough to be incapable of the final compromise which Henry VIII demanded of him when he asked him to approve of his marriage to Anne Boleyn.

In *J.B.* MacLeish was more ambitious in his reach. His J.B. was a modern Job, a happily married American businessman plagued with present-day trials. The comforters of his Biblical predecessor tried to solace Job by assuring him that he was punished because he was guilty. J.B.'s comforters offered him no such solace. They told him that he was punished in spite of being innocent. MacLeish saw his trials in terms of "the enormous nameless disasters that have befallen whole cities, entire peoples, in two great wars and many small ones" and "destroyed the innocent together with the guilty with no 'cause' our minds can grasp." Instead of reconstructing the Bible story, he built "a modern play inside the ancient majesty of the Book of Job." When J.B.'s fortune had been wiped out, his children killed, and his wife had deserted him, his cry from the heart was

> *The hand of God has touched me. Look at me!*
> *Every hope I ever had,*
> *Every task I put my mind to,*
> *Every work I've ever done*
> *Annulled as though I had not done it.*
> *My trace extinguished in the land,*
> *My children dead, my father's name*
> *Obliterated in the sunlight everywhere. . . .*
> *Love too has left me. . . .*
>   *My*
> *Sin! Teach me my sin! My wickedness!*
> *Surely iniquity that suffers*
> *Judgment like mine cannot be secret.*

As dramatists, MacLeish, Bolt, and Anouilh have shown themselves possessed of gifts as sizable as their themes. To a theatre that has sadly lacked them, these three plays of theirs have restored largeness, strength, beauty, and importance. They have made the theatre during the years of their successes "the dwelling place of wonder" which it was to Robert Emmet Sherwood. I trust it is clear in these pages that this is what the theatre always has been at its best. This is what it is now, though all too intermittently, and this is what it must be in the years ahead if it is to survive. And, in spite of its present dangers, survive it will. Of that I am confident.

Index

543